Hearts for Him Through Time:

Missions to Modern Marvels

A Learning Program for Ages 12-14

(with extensions for 9th – 10th graders)

Written by Carrie Austin, M.Ed.

Editor:	Cover Designer:
Julie Grosz	Merlin DeBoer

Heart of Dakota Publishing
www.heartofdakota.com

Special Thanks to:

Our Lord and Savior, Jesus Christ, for giving us the desire to train up our children in the Lord. May He be glorified through this work.

My parents, Ken and Marlene Mellema, for their faithful example of living for Christ and their steadfast commitment to family that has lasted a lifetime. I am so blessed by their unwavering support. They have lovingly encouraged me to pursue the Lord's will for my life and have watched over my children as I've written this book. I can only hope to live up to their example one day.

Julie Grosz for her countless hours of editing, her teaching expertise and knowledge, her listening ear, and her eye for detail. I am so thankful for her steadfast support and encouragement and her enthusiasm for using our programs with her own children. God blessed me with Julie.

Dave and Cindy Madden for forging a new path by homeschooling their seven precious children. We are so thankful that they have gone before us and are a living example of how to live our lives for Christ. I am blessed to call Cindy my sister and my friend.

Mike Austin for his unending support and love, his patient encouragement, and consistent hard work without complaint. I am blessed by his faithful commitment to prayer. He is the love of my life and a cherished father to our four boys. Without him, there would be no Heart of Dakota Publishing.

Cole, Shaw, Greyson, and Beau Austin, my sons, who are the motivation for my writing and my teaching. They are truly an inspiration to me and are wonderful blessings from our Father in heaven.

Copyright 2012 by Carrie Austin
Heart of Dakota Publishing, Inc.
1004 Westview Drive
Dell Rapids, SD 57022

Website: www.heartofdakota.com
Phone (605) 428-4068

ISBN 978-1-4675-4490-0

Table of Contents

Introduction

Complete Plans

Hearts for Him Through Time: Missions to Modern Marvels features 35 units with complete daily plans for ages 12-14 with extensions for ages 15-16. Each unit lasts 4 days, which gives you the 5th day of each week to use as you wish. The 4-day plan can be stretched to cover 5 days if needed. This guide is meant to save you time, so instead of planning, you can spend your time guiding and facilitating your student's learning as you watch your child grow both academically and spiritually. Activities are rotated daily, so you can cover many areas that might often be neglected, without lengthening your school day. These plans are designed to provide an academic, well-balanced approach to learning, but more importantly to help you reach your children's hearts and minds.

Easy to Use

Straightforward daily plans are provided on each two-page spread. The subjects can be done in any order. Each day of plans is divided into the following 2 parts: "Learning Through History" and "Learning the Basics". Each segment of plans is further designated as "Teacher Directed = T", "Semi-Independent = S", or "Independent = I". Dividing the plans in this manner is meant to help you move your students toward more independent work, as the guide becomes **their** planner, which you borrow to teach the "T" boxes. Easy to follow daily plans are divided into 10-11 boxes, which can be spaced throughout the day as time allows.

Learning Through History

The "Learning Through History" part of the program provides a deeper look at the time period from the 1890s through the present day. This year of study is meant to provide students with a Christ-centered overview of the time when modern missions began, and the world was forever changed by inventions, industries, discoveries, and modern marvels. *Missions to Modern Marvels* is meant to provide students with a narrative look at American history set within a worldwide context. Students will be immersed in the setting and events of the modern time period as they read about statesmen, scientists, artists, musicians, writers, inventors, revolutionaries, and leaders of this time. This narrative approach does not overlook the sins of a fallen world, yet it also shows how God is sovereign in history and how He moves both men and nations toward their destiny in Jesus Christ. Church history, modern missions, and the lives of Christian heroes are woven in and out of the narrative at the proper places in history, leading students to see that all of history belongs to God and is actually "His" story.

The following areas are linked with the history readings: creative history projects, research entries on the presidents of the United States, Socratic discussions of primary source documents, oral and written narrations, images of period memorabilia, history read-alouds, atlas connections, full-color mapping exercises, an audio overview of history, timeline sketches, *Draw and Write Through History* sketches, copywork of excerpts of famous speeches, full-color student notebook pages, log of economic principles, and history connections through photographs, newspaper headlines, captions, notes, outlines, quotes, as well as audio and video clips. A study of your individual state is also a recommended option in *Missions to Modern Marvels*.

Learning the Basics

The "Learning the Basics" part of the program focuses on language arts, math, Bible, nature journal, and science. The language arts area includes dictation practice and passages, a scheduled grammar text, formal literature study, and an expository, informative, and persuasive writing program. "Learning the Basics" also includes a choice of math texts. The science area includes living book readings about 20th Century scientists, chemistry topics, and creation vs. evolution, as well as science experiments with written lab sheets emphasizing the scientific process. Oral narration, written narration, notebooking, vocabulary study, comprehension questions, hands-on experiment kits, and a nature journal with nature-themed poetry further enhance the science study. An in-depth Bible study of Romans, Galatians, and James, Bible passage memory work, and a discussion-based Bible study focused on developing a Biblical worldview of self-image complete the Bible study area.

Quick Activities

Missions to Modern Marvels was written with the busy homeschool teacher in mind. It provides a way to do enriching activities without all of the usual planning and preparation. Quick and easy activities require little or no preparation and use materials you're likely to have on hand.

Fun Ideas

Engaging daily lessons take approximately 4½-5 hours to complete. More time will be needed if you linger on activities or draw out discussions. The activities are filled with ideas that get students thinking, exploring, and learning in a meaningful way.

Balanced

Each day's lessons are carefully planned to provide a balance of oral, written, and hands-on work. In this way, oral narrations are practiced each week, but in a variety of subject areas. Written work is required daily, but care is taken to balance it with other forms of assessment. Hands-on experiences are provided in each day's plans, but they do not require overwhelming amounts of time.

Flexible

Lesson plans are written to allow you to customize the program to suit your child's needs. A choice of resources is provided. An Extension Pack Schedule in the Appendix extends the area of history to include more advanced reading material. This allows your older students to learn along with your younger students.

Resources

All of the resources noted in *Missions to Modern Marvels* are available from Heart of Dakota Publishing. Resources may be ordered online at www.heartofdakota.com, by mail using the printable online order form, or by telephone at (605) 428-4068. Resource titles are listed below.

History Resources (Required)

Rescue and Redeem: Chronicles of the Modern Church by Mindy and Brandon Withrow (Christian Focus Publications Ltd., 2009)

The Story of the World Volume 4: The Modern Age by Susan Wise Bauer (Peace Hill Press, 2005)

All American History Volume II: The Civil War to the 21st Century by Celeste W. Rakes (Bright Ideas Press, 2008)

Hero Tales Volume II by Dave and Neta Jackson (Bethany House Publishers, 1997)

* *Hero Tales Volume III* by Dave and Neta Jackson (Bethany House Publishers, 1998)

Great Events in American History by Rebecca Price Janney (God and Country Press, 2009)

Great American Speeches for Young People by Suzannne McIntire (Jossey-Bass, 2001)

Who Am I? And What Am I Doing Here? by John Hay and David Webb (Apologia Press, 2010)

Draw and Write Through History: Invention, Exploration, and War – The 20th Century by Carylee Gressman and illustrated by Peggy Dick (CPR Publishing, 2011)

Map Trek: Missions to Modern Marvels by Terri Johnson (Knowledge Quest, Inc. 2012) Note: This printable CD of *Map Trek* is especially made for Heart of Dakota.

Mission to Modern Marvels Student Notebook designed by Merlin DeBoer (Heart of Dakota Publishing, 2012) Note: These pages are in full-color and are not reproducible. A copy is required for each student.

Faith at Work: Romans, Galatians & James Student book and Answer Key by Marni Shideler McKenzie and Nancy S. Bridges (Explorer's Bible Study, 2004) Note: This book is consumable. A copy is needed for each student.

Common Sense Business for Kids by Kathryn Daniels (Bluestocking Press, 2006)

Whatever Happened to Penny Candy? by Richard J. Maybury (Bluestocking Press, 2010)

Hymns for a Kid's Heart: Volume Two by Bobbie Wolgemuth and Joni Eareckson Tada (Heart of Dakota Publishing, Inc., 2012)

Nature Drawing & Journaling by Barry Stebbing (How Great Thou Art Publications, 2011)

What in the World? Vol. 3: World Empires, World Missions, World Wars by Diana Waring (Answers in Genesis, 2008) Note: This audio CD set is available in several different versions, but only the 2008 Answers in Genesis version matches with the track numbers in this guide and includes the audio material needed for this study. Heart of Dakota carries this version. If you previously used *Revival to Revolution,* you will already own this audio set.

United States History Atlas (Maps.com, 2012) Note: If you previously used *Revival to Revolution,* you will already own this atlas.

The Presidents: The Lives and Legacies of the 43 Leaders of the United States DVD Set by the History Channel (A&E Television Networks, 2005)

*_Our Presidents: Their Lives and Stories_ by Nancy J. Skarmeas (Ideals Publications, 2008)

*_President Student Notebook_ designed by Merlin DeBoer (Heart of Dakota Publishing, 2012) Note: These pages are in full-color and are not reproducible. A copy is required for each student.

*_State History from a Christian Perspective_ by Joy Dean (A Helping Hand, 2005) Note: We recommend that your student complete a study of his/her individual state during _Missions to Modern Marvels_. You may use any state study that you choose, however we recommend and schedule _State History from a Christian Perspective_. It is available for purchase at http://www.statehistory.net.

History Read-Alouds: Basic Package (Highly Recommended – Listed in Appendix)

Self-Study Extension Package (Required for Older Students – Listed in Appendix)

Science Resources (Required, unless you have your own science)

*_Exploring the World of Chemistry_ by John Hudson Tiner (Master Books, 2001)

*_Marie Curie and the Discovery of Radium_ by Ann E. Steinke (Barron's Educational Series, Inc. 1987)

*_Chemistry C500 Experiment Kit_ by Thames & Kosmos (Thames & Kosmos, 2012) Note: There is a previous version of this kit. The 2012 version coordinates with our plans and is carried by Heart of Dakota.

*_Genetics & DNA Experiment Kit_ by Thames & Kosmos (Thames & Kosmos, 2012) Note: There is a previous version of this kit. The 2012 version coordinates with our plans and is carried by Heart of Dakota.

*_The Elements: Ingredients of the Universe_ by Ellen Johnston McHenry (Basement Workshop, 2009)

*_Atoms in the Family_ by Laura Fermi (University of Chicago Press, 1954)

*_Albert Einstein and the Theory of Relativity_ by Robert Cwiklik (Barron's Educational Series, Inc., 1987)

*_Evolution: The Grand Experiment_ – Student Text by Dr. Carl Werner (New Leaf Press, 2007)

*_Evolution: The Grand Experiment_ – Teacher's Manual by Dr. Carl Werner (New Leaf Press, 2008)

*_Evolution: The Grand Experiment_ – Episode One: The Quest for an Answer DVD by Dr. Carl Werner (New Leaf Press, 2009)

Resource Choices (Considered to be necessary choices)

*Choose one of the following reading options to use with this program:

1. _Drawn into the Heart of Reading: Level 6/7/8_ by Carrie Austin (Heart of Dakota Publishing, 2000)
2. Your own program

*Choose one of the following English options to use with this program:

1. _Progressing With Courage: English 6_ by Rod and Staff Publishers (Rod and Staff Publishers, Inc., 1994)
2. Your own program

*Choose one of the following writing options to use with this program:

1. _Write with the Best: Volume 2_ by Jill J. Dixon (Diagnostic Prescriptive

Services, 2003)
    2. Your own program
*Choose one of the following math options to use with this program:
    1. *Singapore Primary Mathematics 6A/6B: U.S. Edition*
       by Singapore Ministry of Education (Times New Media, 2003)
    2. *Singapore Discovering Mathematics Common Core 7A/7B* by Singapore
       Math Inc. (Star Publishing Pte. Ltd, 2007, 2012)
    3. *Singapore Discovering Mathematics Common Core 8A/8B* by Singapore
       Math Inc. (Star Publishing Pte. Ltd, 2007, 2012)
    4. *No-Nonsense Algebra* by Richard Fisher (Math Essentials, 2011)
    5. *VideoText Algebra* by Tom Clark (VideoText Interactive, 2006)
    6. Your own program

Note: Since resources sometimes go out of print or undergo changes, you may check the "Updates" portion of our website at www.heartofdakota.com for any needed replacement texts and schedules pertaining to our products. Since *Missions to Modern Marvels* is focused upon modern times, quite a few Internet addresses of audio and visual resources are included throughout the curriculum. As the Internet is always changing, these addresses may change or become unavailable. Whenever possible, multiple options of Internet addresses have been included. If an address is no longer valid, and another option is not provided, check the "Updates" portion of our website for a replacement.

"Learning Through History" Components

Reading about History

The "Learning Through History" part of the program is told in narrative form and provides a deeper look at the time period from the late 1800s through the present day. This year of study is meant to give students an exciting look at American history set within the worldwide context of the industrial revolution, social reform, immigration, world wars, the rise of Communism, the Space Race, and the spread of the Gospel through modern missions.

History stories are scheduled for the students to read independently each day using the following resources: *Rescue and Redeem* by Mindy and Brandon Withrow, *The Story of the World Volume 4* by Susan Wise Bauer, *All American History Volume II* by Celeste W. Rakes, *Hero Tales Volume II* and *III* by Dave and Neta Jackson, and *Great Events in American History* by Rebecca Price Janney. These resources provide the focus for this part of the plans. Each of the areas that follow are linked to the daily stories once each unit:

*Give an oral narration by retelling the history reading using some of the key words provided in the guide. Oral narration tips can be found in the Appendix for help as needed.
*Study images of period memorabilia in the *Missions to Modern Marvels Student Notebook*. Commentary and questions are provided in the guide to link the memorabilia to the history reading and place them in their proper historical context.
*Connect a photograph or a newspaper article provided in the *Missions to Modern Marvels Student Notebook* to the history reading through captions, bulleted notes, outlines, headlines, quotes, and excerpts.
*Write a written narration to reflect upon the history reading. The *Student Notebook* provides a place for recording written narrations. Written narration tips are provided in the Appendix of *Missions to Modern Marvels* for help as needed.

The *Student Notebook* has been especially created for *Missions to Modern Marvels* to provide a timeless keepsake of what was learned throughout the year. Full-color pages complete with period memorabilia, areas to record written narrations, a timeline to update in each unit, project helps, excerpts from primary source documents, history-related photographs and articles, and places to record copywork of famous speeches grace the pages of this lovely resource. The *Student Notebook* pages can be stored in a 3-ring binder with a place to insert a cover page.

Timeline

To understand the flow of history, students keep a timeline in their *Student Notebook* of some of the major events and people studied throughout the year. Planning how to illustrate the timeline entry along with drawing the entry itself, forces students to call upon what they have learned and apply it. What students take time to create they retain, because it has become their own.

"Learning Through History" Components
(continued)

The timeline created by the students specifically matches the *Missions to Modern Marvels* history readings. Additional entries in the *Student Notebook* provide a fuller picture of the time period and better help students place the timeline entries within their historical context.

<u>Note</u>: Beginning with the *Student Notebook* in *Creation to Christ*, students add a section to their timeline with each consecutive guide for four years. The section in *Missions to Modern Marvels* completes the *Book of Time*.

Geography

One day in each unit includes mapping activities that directly relate to the historical time period using the *United States History Atlas* and *Map Trek: Missions to Modern Marvels*. Studying geography in this manner helps students recognize how geography has impacted history. The purpose of the mapping activities is to teach students to use a variety of maps, to cross-reference maps and assimilate that information, and to create and label their own historically accurate maps.

Step-by-step mapping activities connect history with geography by directing students to find various locations on historical maps. Here is a list of maps that are included on the special printable CD of *Map Trek* produced for Heart of Dakota by the publisher.

USA (Jim Crow Laws/Right to Vote)
USA (Major Centers of Immigration)
World Empires 1900
The Balkan Wars
World War I (map 1)
World War I (map 2)
The Russian Revolution
The Division of Ireland
Europe, Post WWI
Iberian Peninsula
Famous Early Flights (Lindbergh/Earhart)
The Great Depression
Totalitarianism
China and Japan at War
World War II (map 1 - Europe)
The Bombing of Pearl Harbor
World War II (map 2 - S. Pacific)
The Growth of Communism
Independence for India
The Middle East
The Nation of Israel
The Cold War
The Korean War

The Vietnam War
The Wars in Asia
Cuba
The Gulf War
9/11 - Attack on the U.S.
Conflict in Iraq

Maps needed for the "Geography" part of the *Missions to Modern Marvels* plans must be printed from the provided *Map Trek* CD. Teacher Answer Maps are in full-color and may either be viewed on your computer screen or printed in color using the CD. Student Maps may be printed in black and white or in color from the CD.

Worthy Words

One day in each unit includes reading Worthy Words from a primary source that directly relates to the history study for that day. A primary source is something that originates in the historical time period being studied. Letters and the text of speeches written during the time period are primary sources. The *Missions to Modern Marvels Student Notebook* and *Book of Great American Speeches for Young People* contain all the primary sources needed for this study.

Within the Worthy Words activity, students read, analyze, and evaluate the primary source document by answering provided questions on an index card to prepare for a Socratic dialogue. A Socratic dialogue is one in which the participants come prepared to share their thoughts, feelings, and opinions about the spoken and written word. Before beginning the dialogue, a parent reads the provided primary source document out loud. Next, participants discuss the questions in the guide. All participants should use life experiences, and/or the text to support their responses. Students are expected to refer to their notes throughout the dialogue.

Studying the speeches and letters of famous men and women through history in this manner helps students begin to recognize various points of view, learn how words can stir emotions and impact history, and gain a glimpse into the mind of the speaker. Speeches have been chosen for their narrative quality and their ability to paint a diverse picture of American and world history, as well as their capability to give a glimpse into the speaker's wit, deep-rooted beliefs, emotions, and passions. You will need 35 index cards and a place to store them for this activity.

Economics

One day in each unit requires students to read a chapter from either *Whatever Happened to Penny Candy?* by Richard J. Maybury or *Common Sense Business for Kids* by Kathryn Daniels. After reading each chapter, students are asked to summarize one or more economic principle(s) gained from the reading. Economic Principles are recorded in the *Missions to Modern Marvels Student Notebook*.

In *Whatever Happened to Penny Candy?*, "Uncle Eric's" clever letters are sure to help you make some real sense of economics. Historical events like the stock market crash will have you counting your pennies as you learn about recession, inflation, the demand for money, government spending, investment cycles, velocity, and more. Using sound judgment and real world examples in *Common Sense Business for Kids*, Richard Maybury shares realities behind basic business principles like salesmanship, market potential, fixed and variable cost, price strategies, and more... and proves that even though business success seems complicated, it's really just 'common sense'!

History Project

Three days in each unit are devoted to a meaningful, hands-on project that is designed to bring the history stories to life. Each project is scheduled to be easily completed by the student semi-independently. Projects require little or no preparation and use materials you are likely to have on hand. Unique art supplies for the projects scheduled within this guide include oil pastels and index cards. Several recipes are included as projects. You may wish to look ahead in your guide to be sure that you have the needed ingredients. Otherwise, general art supplies should be sufficient. Projects correlate closely with the history stories and provide an important creative outlet for students to express what they've learned.

Projects range from creating a Chinese character wall hanging, to designing a Barnum & Bailey Circus ride; from making a salt painting, to baking Czechoslovakian cookies; from role playing life under a dictator's control, to copying Matthew 7:21 in Korean writing; from having an ice cream social, to drawing and coloring an Olympic stamp; from praying for Christians in Uganda, to making homemade peanut butter; from creating a Japanese family crest, to folding a paper airplane; from baking Tollhouse cookies, to watching Edison's first feature-length movie "The Great Train Robbery"; from comparing Christianity, Hinduism, Islam, and Judaism, to baking and icing a war cake, and much more!

Note: As a way to help the modern time period come to life, some projects do include Internet addresses to audio and visual media. Since the Internet is always changing, these addresses may change or become unavailable. Whenever possible, multiple options of Internet addresses have been included. If an address is no longer valid, and another option is not provided, check the "Updates" portion of our website for a replacement.

It is also important to note that the use of the Internet is not intended to become a frustration in your school day. So, in most instances, if you have tried the listed addresses and cannot access the intended content, it is fine to move on without going to great lengths to locate the content. As always, parental supervision is recommended when students use the Internet.

President Study

Two days in each unit require students to research the lives of the presidents of the United States. This study of the presidents focuses on true-life stories of the remarkable men who have presided over the Oval Office. The History Channel introduces you to each president, from George Washington to George Bush, through *The Presidents: The Lives and Legacies of the 43 Leaders of the United States* DVD. Snapshots of each of these Commanders-in-Chief, rare and unseen photographs, and footage sharing their personalities, weaknesses, major achievements, and historical significance are shared in this engaging DVD.

While you might not always agree with the political slant in this DVD series, the images and footage alone make this a valuable resource in bringing the U.S. presidents to life. We encourage you to watch and discuss this DVD along with your students this year as they use it as one resource for researching the presidents. It brought up many good discussions at our house as to what my husband and I remembered about the later presidents, from our own childhood and adulthood, and how that compared to what was portrayed within the DVD series. Be warned that the series does not gloss over some of the past presidents' indiscretions or scandals, so it is for a 7th grade on up viewing audience only.

A second resource in book format further enhances this chance to "meet" the presidents! *Our Presidents: Their Lives and Stories* is rich with history of the White House and our nation. This fascinating look at the lives of the presidents of the United States includes interesting details about their backgrounds, political careers, the changes they saw, and the causes they championed. Famous photographs or historical images of each president add depth to this resource. While all resources about the presidents include some political bias, this resource is more neutral and factual than many others, making it a solid choice for research. You are welcome to choose your own resource for research on the presidents instead, however you may find as we did that it is difficult to find resources that are free from political bias!

A full-color *President Notebook* was specially made to accompany the "President Study" in *Missions to Modern Marvels*. The notebook pages come 3-hole punched on heavy paper with a cover page for easy insertion into a ½" binder. This notebook will help students delve into the lives of the presidents and their greatest accomplishments. Each student needs his or her own *President Notebook*.

The purpose of this research activity is to train students to read to find information, to make brief notes, to sift and sort information, and to create a written entry from the information they've gathered. At the close of the year students will have a beautiful *President Notebook* to remember their research by, as well as an appreciation for the men who have guided America through its history.

"Learning Through History" Components
(continued)

Independent History Study

Daily independent history assignments that correspond with the historical time period are scheduled using these resources: *What in the World? Vol. 3* by Diana Waring, *Draw and Write Through History: Invention, Exploration, and War – The 20th Century* by Carylee Gressman and illustrated by Peggy Dick, and *Missions to Modern Marvels Student Notebook* designed by Merlin DeBoer. Audio presentations, copywork of speeches, notebook entries, guided drawing lessons, primary source documents, and additional mapping activities are all included in the independent history study part of the plans.

The books in the "Reading about History" part of the plans and the resources listed in the "Independent History Study" part of the plans are included in the **Economy Package**, sold as a set or individually at www.heartofdakota.com.

State Study

We recommend that your student complete a study of his/her individual state during this year. Time is allotted once weekly for this purpose. While you may use any state study you choose, we recommend and schedule *State History from a Christian Perspective* by Joy Dean in *Missions to Modern Marvels*. To complete the study, you will need your individual state's *Student Booklet* (one for each student), the *Master Lesson Plan Book* (one copy), and your choice of creating a binder or using *My State Notebook* in conjunction with the study. These resources are available for purchase at http://www.statehistory.net.

The *Student Booklet* provides you with text, maps, and full-color state symbols for your state. The text covers history, geography, map skills, weather, industry, agriculture, major cities, citizenship, and state and local government. Students use this material to create their own personalized state history notebook. Quizzes, tests, and answer keys are included in the *Student Booklet*. Some assignments also require either tourist brochures for your state or pictures printed from the Internet of places to visit in your state. You may wish to order tourist information for your state at http://www.50states.com.

Storytime

Daily storytime sessions are linked to the "Reading about History" box of the plans by historical time period. These books provide the historical backdrop, or a panoramic view of history, while the "Reading about History" readings provide a more factual view.

These scheduled read-alouds are highly recommended, unless you need to economize. Complete listings and book descriptions for these books can be found in the Appendix. These books are sold as a set as a **Basic Package**, or sold individually, at www.heartofdakota.com.

"Learning Through History" Components
(continued)

The "Storytime" box of plans includes bookmark prompts that target higher-level responses. Students select lines to quote and comment upon, use quick sketches to provide visual commentary, ask clarifying and probing questions, make written connections, and share observations, reflections, and musings.

Leading students to think in this manner goes beyond finding one right answer. Rather, students are encouraged to analyze, synthesize, and evaluate what they've read to reach their own conclusions. Bookmarks must be copied from the Appendix of *Missions to Modern Marvels* once every 6 units as directed in the guide.

Note: If you are already doing a Storytime package with a different Heart of Dakota program, you may choose to have 7th-8th grade students read the books in this package on their own by following the plans in the "Storytime" box.

Independent History Study for Older Students

An Extension Package Schedule in the Appendix extends the area of history to include more advanced independent reading material. This allows your older students to learn along with your younger students. This Extension Package is best suited for ninth and tenth graders who are independent readers.

Adding this package to the Economy Package extends the study of history for students in grades 9 - 10. The books in this package are not intended to fulfill your student's high school literature credit, as students need to be reading separate higher-level literature to fulfill that need. Instead, the books in this package were chosen to help students experience various historical time periods, bringing the past to life through the pages of these books. A reading schedule for these books is provided in the Appendix of the Teacher's Guide. Due to some mature content and themes contained in this time period (i.e. famine, war, disease, martyrdom, mentions of suicide, persecution, revolution, discrimination, segregation, terrorism, poverty, communism, etc.), students younger than grades 9-10 should use the Basic Package instead.

A schedule of daily independent readings for these books is provided in the Appendix of *Missions to Modern Marvels*. General suggestions for follow-up assignments are also included at the beginning of the Extension Package Schedule. Complete listings and book descriptions for these books can be found in the Appendix. These books are sold as a set in the **Extension Package**, or individually, at www.heartofdakota.com. This package is an optional part of *Missions to Modern Marvels*.

Note: As students are entering their high school years and are reading higher-level literature, there can be more language to be aware of within the readings. For this reason, it will be very important to carefully read the warnings provided in the Extension Schedule.

"Learning The Basics" Components

Grammar, Mechanics, and Usage

English 6 is scheduled at two different speeds in *Missions to Modern Marvels* to allow you to customize the pacing to suit your student. Schedules include a choice of either the last half of English 6, for those who completed the first half in the previous guide, or all of English 6. Both schedules assign English daily. In order to keep the area of language arts in balance within our guides, while still using a rigorous English program, our goal is for students to complete English 6 by the end of grade 8. This will prepare students well for high school level English requirements. Students in grade 7, who have had little grammar instruction, should use English 5 instead (since it is considered to be a foundational level of the text).

9th and 10th graders, who have had significant grammar by completing all of English 6, or its equivalent, may use English 7 instead. *Building Securely: English 7* is not scheduled within *Missions to Modern Marvels,* but the lessons are divided in the Rod and Staff text for ease of use. For high school students, we recommend completing half of English 7 in grade 9 and the other half in grade 10. The scope and sequence of English 7 is worthy of high school credit.

Within the English text, systematic lessons focus on one rule or concept per lesson. In order to keep the lessons short, you may want to do most of the lesson orally or on a white board, requiring only one set of practice exercises to be written by the student each day. The Teacher's Manual is considered to be necessary at this level. See the "Table of Contents" in *Progressing With Courage: English 6* for a scope and sequence. Students need a lined composition book or notebook for their written work.

Since Rod and Staff is a complete English program, which teaches not only grammar but also a full range of English and writing skills, replacing Rod and Staff with another "grammar only" program will not suffice. Within our Heart of Dakota plans, we are expecting that you are teaching the full range of English skills that are introduced and practiced within Rod and Staff.

Writing

Writing lessons are scheduled twice in each unit using *Write with the Best: Vol. II.* Literary passages from respected and well-loved authors are used to teach students how to write. Creative activities break the writing into manageable chunks and help students identify what makes a literary work "great". Students are encouraged to make writing more vivid and ultimately produce writing that models the genre of the literary passage. Guidelines for evaluating and grading writing and student proofreading and writing guides are valuable parts of the program. Each daily lesson takes only 25-30 minutes, is addressed to the student, and includes step-by-step guidance. The program includes all needed excerpts from the literature that it models so that teachers are not required to purchase additional material.

"Learning The Basics" Components
(continued)

This writing program is a genuine, incremental (step-by-step) program that requires minimal teacher involvement towards the goal of mastery of higher-level forms of writing. *Missions to Modern Marvels* schedules lessons from this guide twice weekly. For grades 6 -12 (but best suited for grades 7 on up in our opinion).

Topics covered include:
Taking Notes
Writing Outlines
Writing Summaries
Persuasive Essays
Expository Essays
Literary Critiques
Book Reviews
Newspaper Articles
Speeches

Note: We omit units 1 and 2 (free verse poetry and business letter) due to these topics being well covered in Rod and Staff English. We also omit unit 8 (dramatic monologue) to keep the area of writing in balance, as a full level of Rod and Staff English is scheduled too, which also includes instruction in writing. Students need a lined composition book or notebook for their written work.

Dictation
Studied dictation to practice spelling skills is scheduled three days in each unit. Levels 6, 7, and 8 of dictation are provided in the Appendix. Dictation Levels 7 and 8 have fewer passages than the preceding levels of dictation. This is intentional, as the passages grow in length and difficulty.

Students should continue to do studied dictation three days a week in each unit no matter what level of dictation they are doing. Whenever students complete the final dictation passage in Level 8, they are finished with dictation. Dictation passage levels do not necessarily correspond to grade levels, so students may be continuing dictation during their high school years.

Special instructions for the dictation passages are included in the Appendix. It is important to read and follow these instructions carefully in order to correctly implement the method of studied dictation.

The Charlotte Mason method of studied dictation is used. In this method, students study the passage prior to having it dictated. This is an important step in learning to visualize the correct spelling of words. All items in the passage must be written correctly, including punctuation marks, before going on to the next passage. Studied dictation focuses on the goal of using correct spelling within the context of writing. Permission is granted for you to make copies of the "Dictation Passages Key" to log your children's progress in dictation. A lined composition book is needed for dictation.

Copywork

Copywork is scheduled from a variety of sources such as Scriptures, quotes, and excerpts from speeches. By copying from a correctly written model, students gain practice in handwriting, spelling, grammar, capitalization, punctuation, and vocabulary. Work should be required to be done neatly and correctly. It is important for students to produce careful, quality work, rather than to produce a large quantity of work that is carelessly done.

At this age, students may choose whether to complete copywork assignments in cursive or in manuscript. All copywork is either written in the *Common Place Book,* the *Student Notebook,* or the *Nature Journal,* as directed within the *Missions to Modern Marvels* lesson plans.

A *Common Place Book* is often a bound composition book with lined pages. It provides a common place to copy anything that is timeless, memorable, or worthy of rereading. It is for copying text and not for original writing. Throughout the year, as students memorize Romans 12 and James 4 for their Bible quiet time, they will copy the verses from these chapters in their *Common Place Book.*

Reading

Three days in each unit recommend using *Drawn into the Heart of Reading* for literature study. This reading program is multi-level and is designed to use with any books you choose. It is available for students in levels 2-8. It is divided into nine literature units, which can be used in any order.

Drawn into the Heart of Reading is based on instructions and activities that work with any literature. It can be used with one or more students of multiple ages at the same time because it is structured around daily plans that are divided into three levels of instruction. *Drawn into the Heart of Reading* is intended for use year after year as you move students through the various levels of instruction. It is designed to teach students to evaluate characters using a Christian standard that is based on Godly traits.

In order to use *Drawn into the Heart of Reading* with your independent reader, you need the *Drawn into the Heart of Reading* Teacher's Guide and the *Level 6/7/8 Student Book.* You may also choose whether to purchase these optional resources: *Level 6/7 Book Pack, Level 7/8 Girl Interest Book Pack, Level 7/8 Boy Interest Book Pack,* or the *Sample Book Ideas List.* Packages for *Drawn into the Heart of Reading* are available at www.heartofdakota.com. Descriptions of books within each pack can be viewed online.

"Learning The Basics" Components
(continued)

Bible Quiet Time

Each daily Bible quiet time includes independent Bible lessons from *Explorer's Bible Study: Quest - Faith at Work.* This in-depth Bible study of Romans, Galatians, and James helps 7th through 12th graders develop their own Bible quiet time to study what their Bible says, what it means, and how to apply it. Heartfelt lessons help students learn to think, evaluate, understand, and apply what God is communicating in His Word! As this is consumable, each student needs a copy of *Quest – Faith at Work.*

Each quiet time also includes a prayer focus and Scripture memory work. The prayer focus includes the 4 parts of prayer: adoration, confession, thanksgiving, and supplication. Students keep a daily prayer journal in *Quest – Faith at Work*, using the "Preparing Your Heart for Prayer" questions as a starting place. Students memorize all of Romans 12 and James 4 through recitation and repetition and also copy these passages in their *Common Place Books.* Instilling the habit of a daily Bible Quiet Time from an early age is one of the most important ways to encourage a lifelong desire to meet with the Lord each day.

Music is another heartfelt way to praise the Lord. For this purpose, *Hymns for Kid's Heart: Volume Two* is part of each day's quiet time as well. Students learn 12 of the greatest hymns ever composed with richly orchestrated music, hymn writers' stories, heartfelt prayers, Scripture verses, and printed sheet music. This beautiful full-color book and fully orchestrated CD set is sure to feed the mind and stir the soul.

Biblical Worldview Study

Two days in each unit are focused on the Biblical worldview study *Who Am I? And What Am I Doing Here?* The plans in *Missions to Modern Marvels* intend for the pages within *Who Am I? And What Am I Doing Here?* to be read either silently, by both parent and child, or read aloud to the child by the parent. Either method of reading lends itself to deeper thinking about the topics and questions presented in the text. This study also has much to be gained by discussion, as it provides an excellent opportunity to share what **you** believe.

Each lesson in the book features an introduction to the main topic, learning objectives, a narrative story, thought-provoking questions, important vocabulary words, two Bible memory verses, interesting interdisciplinary topics, Godly character traits for students to demonstrate, a prayer, and a worldview portion. The worldview sections provide a youth's perspective on being a Muslim, a New Age spiritualist, a Hindu, a Buddhist, a Communist, etc., allowing students to see the difference between these belief systems and Christianity. Probing questions help students think through how various religions compare to what God tells us in His Word, and give parents the chance to keep dialogue flowing during these middle school and high school years on topics that matter for eternity!

This Bible study gives you the tools to teach your children a Christian worldview and pairs beautifully with the *Explorer's Bible Study: Quest - Faith at Work*. The partnership of a parent-led Biblical worldview study with a student-led Bible quiet time works together with Scripture memorization and hymn singing to help students draw nearer to the Lord each day through time spent in His Word. *Who Am I? And What Am I Doing Here?* will help students begin to see everything as God sees it by using Scripture as the lens through which to view themselves. It gives a much needed way to teach a Biblical self image and a sense of God-given purpose that, hopefully, will last a lifetime.

Poetry

Different classic nature-themed poems written by William Wordsworth, Walt Whitman, and Henry Wadsworth Longfellow are studied throughout the year. Each poem was chosen for its enduring quality, its ability to withstand the test of time, and its capacity to describe nature in vivid ways. These poems complement assignments from *Nature Drawing and Journaling* once in each unit. As poems are read aloud and discussed with a parent, they add a new dimension to the nature study by helping students appreciate the world around them.

Nature Journal

Two days in each unit focus on nature journaling using lessons from *Nature Drawing and Journaling*. In this book, award-winning artist Barry Stebbing shares 40 years' worth of insights on studying nature and keeping a nature journal. Full-color illustrations, inspirational quotes, journal entries, and copies of Stebbing's own journal will have you making your own Charlotte-Mason style nature journal in no time.

Clear instructions, poignant reflections, and space for your work are provided in this spiral-bound softcover book. Also included are over 47 nature-related art lessons to guide your student in learning to sketch and appreciate the outdoors. Art lessons and nature journal sessions are scheduled twice weekly for the student to enjoy in *Missions to Modern Marvels*. The nature-themed poetry of Wordsworth, Longfellow, and Whitman is scheduled once weekly to enhance the nature journal sessions.

Materials for Journaling:

Hardbound, unlined journal (ideally with a strap to hold pages in place)
Set of 12 soft lead, good quality, rich-colored pencils
2 extra fine or very fine black drawing pens
2 black writing pens (experiment to find your favorite kind)
Acid-free tape
Inexpensive set of fine-tipped washable markers
Inexpensive set of broad-tipped washable markers
#6 round paintbrush
Semi-gloss paper (several sheets)

Glue stick
Optional: legal pad
Optional: large rubber band (only needed if your journal has no strap)

Math Exploration

A math instruction reminder is listed in the plans daily. *Missions to Modern Marvels* offers a choice of *Singapore Primary Mathematics 6A, 6B; Discovering Mathematics Common Core 7A, 7B, 8A, 8B; No-Nonsense Algebra,* or *VideoText Algebra.*

Singapore Primary Mathematics 6A, 6B and *Discovering Mathematics 7A, 7B, 8A, 8B, each* cover one semester of instruction; so, both an "A" and a "B" set are needed for a full year of math instruction. *Primary Mathematics* sets include both a textbook and a workbook. A daily schedule for *Singapore Primary Mathematics 6A, 6B* is included in the Appendix of *Missions to Modern Marvels.*

The *Discovering Mathematics Common Core Series* requires *Textbook 7A, Teaching Notes and Solutions 7A, Textbook 7B,* and *Teaching Notes and Solutions 7B.* The *Discovering Mathematics Common Core Teaching Notes and Solutions* contain notes for the lesson, and an answer key with fully worked solutions. An **optional** *Discovering Mathematics Common Core 7A Workbook* and *7A Workbook Solutions,* and an **optional** *Discovering Mathematics Common Core 7B Workbook* and *7B Workbook Solutions,* provide extra practice at the end of each chapter. An answer key is included in the back of each textbook and workbook; however, if you desire fully worked solutions, you will need to purchase the corresponding *Solutions Manual.*

The *Discovering Mathematics Common Core Series* approaches math in an integrated manner. This means that Pre-Algebra, Algebra I, Geometry, and Algebra II are integrated throughout the series. *Discovering Mathematics 7A, 7B* includes pre-algebra, some Algebra I, and some geometry. It is equivalent to pre-algebra, especially when combined with *Singapore Primary Mathematics 5A, 5B, 6A, 6B.* *Discovering Mathematics 8A, 8B* includes Algebra I and some geometry. It is equivalent to Algebra I when combined with *Discovering Mathematics 7A, 7B.*

Since *Discovering Mathematics* is being revised, the schedules for *Discovering Mathematics 7A, 7B, 8A, 8B* will be available for purchase upon their completion from Heart of Dakota along with the accompanying math books.

For further help with Singapore math placement, go to www.singaporemath.com and click "PARENTS". Then, scroll down to "Step 3" and click on the blue "assessment tests" link for a free math placement test. Choose the U.S. version of the *Singapore Primary Mathematics* test.

"Learning The Basics" Components
(continued)

To ensure accurate placement, parents should not help students with the test. It is common for students who are switching to Singapore math to place lower than their grade level. However, it is important to start students where they place according to the test. Placement tests are also available for *Discovering Mathematics* at the bottom of the "assessment tests" page described in the paragraph above.

Both *No-Nonsense Algebra* and *Videotext Algebra* are alternatives to *Discovering Mathematics*. Both incorporate some pre-algebra, a video component, and follow-up workbook assignments. *No-Nonsense Algebra* uses short, concise lessons to explain each topic in Algebra I in a way that is easy to understand. Multiple examples with fully explained step-by-step solutions, ample reviews built into each of the lessons, and chapter tests help students measure their progress and improve their test scores. Each lesson in the book has a corresponding online video lesson taught by award-winning math teacher and author Richard W. Fisher. To view a clickable description and Table of Contents, click on the "Packages" page of *Missions to Modern Marvels* at www.heartofdakota.com and scroll down to *No-Nonsense Algebra*. You may purchase *No-Nonsense Algebra* directly from Heart of Dakota.

VideoText Algebra is an interactive, video-based program that teaches Pre-Algebra, Algebra I, and Algebra II in an integrated manner. Due to the integrated manner in which *VideoText* teaches algebra, once you begin *VideoText* it is best to complete the course because all modules work together to teach Pre-Algebra, Algebra I, and Algebra II. Therefore, to claim credit for both Algebra I and Algebra II all modules must be completed. All students must begin *VideoText Algebra* with Module A, regardless of previous math experience with Algebra.

The main components of *VideoText* are the video lessons and the worktext. However, unlike textbooks that may use a video supplement, in this case the video lessons "are" the textbook. With each module of the course, you receive the video lessons (each 5-10 minutes in length, either on DVD or online), course notes, worktext, solutions manual, progress tests, and an instructor's guide with detailed solutions to all quizzes and test problems. Students will love the brief lessons and the clear explanations of concepts in *VideoText Algebra*. To view samples and purchase *VideoText Algebra* visit http://www.videotext.com.

If you have a different math program that you are already comfortable using, feel free to substitute it for the math portion of the plans.

Independent Science Exploration

Three days in each unit, science readings are scheduled using books contained in the Science Package. This living book approach focuses on an introduction to chemistry, 20th Century scientists, and a study on evolution vs. creation. It is considered necessary, unless you have your own science.

"Learning The Basics" Components
(continued)

Reading material is meant for students to read independently. These resources are sold as a set in the **Economy Package: Science Add-On**, or individually, at www.heartofdakota.com. This package includes these 9 engaging resources:

Exploring the World of Chemistry by John Hudson Tiner
Marie Curie and the Discovery of Radium by Ann E. Steinke
Chemistry C500 Experiment Kit by Thames & Kosmos (2012 version)
Genetics & DNA Experiment Kit by Thames & Kosmos (2012 version)
The Elements: Ingredients of the Universe by Ellen Johnston McHenry
Atoms in the Family by Laura Fermi
Albert Einstein and the Theory of Relativity by Robert Cwiklik
Evolution: The Grand Experiment – Student Text and Teacher's Manual by
  Dr. Carl Werner
Evolution: The Grand Experiment – Episode One: The Quest for an Answer
  DVD by Dr. Carl Werner

Experiments use tiered lab forms emphasizing the scientific method, while notebooking entries about the scientists, oral narrations, questions, vocabulary, and written narrations encourage students to apply what they've learned. This balance of living books, hands-on experiments, and scientific methods provides an enjoyable way to learn science.

A "Science Lab Form" is provided in the Appendix of *Missions to Modern Marvels* and may be reproduced for students to log their science experiment results. Loose-leaf notebook paper will be used for all remaining science work. The students need a place to store their notebook entries, answers to questions, written narrations, and science experiment forms. Use a one-inch 3-ring binder with one tab labeled "Science Work" and another tab labeled "Science Lab Forms" for this purpose. Another one-inch 3-ring binder with a place to insert a cover page is needed for *The Elements: Ingredients of the Universe*.

Additional Unusual Supplies Needed:
For all units: safety glasses (included in kit), smock, and smooth gloves

Unit 1 – Day 4:   about 2 tsp. white vinegar

Unit 2 – Day 4:   matches, about 4 tsp. white vinegar, 1 tealight candle, 1 small fireproof plate (ceramic will work)

Unit 3 – Day 4:   a very small can of denatured alcohol or methylated spirits, highly flammable (available at Walmart, Lowes, paint supply stores, and hardware stores)

Unit 4 – Day 4:   1 drop of white vinegar, 1 lemon (optional), small plastic container

"Learning The Basics" Components
(continued)

Unit 5 – Day 4:   10 drops of white vinegar, bar of soap

Unit 8 – Day 4:   3 tsp. sparkling mineral water, 3 tsp. stale, flat sparkling mineral water (let it sit out for a day), 3 tsp. plain bottled water

Unit 12 – Day 4:   white or very light pillowcase (optional), fabric markers (optional), GITD glow-in-the-dark paint (optional)

Unit 13 – Day 4:   about ¼ cup liquid bleach (with adult supervision), small amount of red food coloring

Unit 14 – Day 1:   a magnifying glass; choice of small marshmallows, grapes, clay balls, tinker toys, or K'nex; 2 tsp. of Epsom salt (optional), 1 tsp. of liquid cleaning ammonia (optional)

Unit 15 – Day 1:   1 onion or garlic clove (optional), horticultural charcoal from a gardening shop (optional)

Unit 15 – Day 2:   1 bag of small colored marshmallows, 1 box of toothpicks

Unit 16 – Day 1:   5 pieces of steel wool (optional), 1 bottle of white vinegar (optional), thermometer (optional), large clear container with lid (optional), 4 small clear containers with lids (optional)

Unit 17 – Day 4:   1 bar of soap, 6 tsp. distilled water, 4 tsp. flat mineral water (let it sit out for a day)

Unit 18 – Day 4:   3 drops liquid soap or shower gel, a little mineral water

Unit 19 – Day 4:   2 drops liquid soap or shower gel

Unit 21 – Day 4:   1 sheet parchment colored writing paper to write a secret message on, blotting paper (or a white coffee filter), either a calligraphy pen with a metal nib or a fine-tipped paintbrush

Unit 22 – Day 4:   1 shiny iron nail

Unit 23 – Day 4:   1 nine-volt square battery, 8 T. of table salt

Unit 24 – Day 4:   1 nine-volt square battery (the same one can be used that was used before), 8 T. of table salt, either a white coffee filter or blotting paper, 1 copper penny

Unit 25 – Day 4:   1 nine-volt square battery (the same one can be used that was used before), 2 T. of table salt, 1 drop of white vinegar

"Learning The Basics" Components
(continued)

Unit 27 – Day 4:   a very small can of denatured alcohol or methylated spirits, highly flammable (available at Walmart, Lowes, paint supply stores, and hardware stores), 10 tsp. liquid dishsoap, 1 tsp. salt, 1 tomato, 2 large empty yogurt containers (or other disposable plastic containers)

Unit 29 – Day 4:   1 red felt-tipped pen (or red marker)

Unit 35 – Day 4:   1 well-rinsed, used jelly jar

Lesson Plans

Reading about History [I]

Read about history in the following resource:

⭐ *The Story of the World: Vol. 4* p. 123 – top of p. 127

After today's reading, orally narrate or retell to an adult the portion of text that you read today. Use the *Narration Tips* in the Appendix for help as needed. Some possible key words to include in your narration might be *Great Britain, Ireland, Protestant, Catholic, Parliament, rotting potatoes, blight, starving, landlords, Corn Laws, Robert Peel, William Gladstone,* and *Home Rule Bill.*

Key Idea: After King Henry VIII of England claimed Ireland in 1541, a quarrel began between the two countries that lasted hundreds of years. Much of the quarrel had to do with religion. The famine in 1845 magnified the quarrel.

History Project [S]

In this unit, you will do an activity to glimpse life under the rule of a dictator. A dictator is one who rules with absolute power. Get 6 index cards. Number the cards from '1'-'6'. Copy the following numbered freedoms on the matching numbered card: 1) Select music for listening, 2) Pick which clothes to wear for the day, 3) Select which book to read for free reading, 4) Choose how to comb your hair, 5) Decide what to do for a profession, 6) Plan how to use your free time. Save the cards.

Key Idea: By the time of the famine, Ireland had merged with Great Britain and was ruled in London. Many in Ireland wanted to be free.

President Study [I]

⭐ Read p. 4-5 in *Our Presidents...* Then, open your *President Notebook* to George Washington. Use today's reading to help you complete the information about Washington.

Key Idea: Research George Washington.

Storytime [T/I]

Read the following assigned pages:

⭐ *Under the Hawthorn Tree* p. 1-15

After today's reading, photocopy the **two** "Bookmark" pages from the Appendix. Place the copied pages back-to-back and staple them together at the 4 corners. Then, tri-fold the stapled page into thirds to make a bookmark. Save the bookmark in your book until Day 2.

Key Idea: Relate to the text in various ways.

Timeline [I]

You will be adding to the timeline in your *Student Notebook* today. In Unit 1 – Box 1, draw and color a potato. Label it, *Great Irish Potato Famine (1845-1852 A.D.).*

In Box 2, draw and color an iron fist. Label it, *Dom Pedro II Rules in Brazil (1841-1889 A.D.).*

In Box 3, draw and color a regal crown as shown on the banknote in Box 5. Label it, *Alexander II Assassinated – Alexander III Becomes Czar (1881 A.D.).*

Key Idea: As Irish immigrants fled from the famine in Ireland, Dom Pedro was ruling in Brazil. Alexander II's father, Nicholas I, was ruling in Russia at that time.

Independent History Study [I]

On p. 33 of the *United States History Atlas,* find the states with the highest foreign-born population (immigrants). During the years of famine in Ireland, nearly 1,000,000 Irish immigrants came to the U.S. These immigrants settled mainly in Boston and New York at first. By 1850, 43% of the foreign-born population in the U.S. was Irish.

Key Idea: Most Irish immigrants were Catholic, which caused Catholicism to rise in the U.S. This triggered some of the same problems between Protestants and Catholics in the U.S. that there had been in Ireland.

Learning the Basics
Focus: Language Arts, Math, Bible, Nature Journal, and Science

Nature Journal [I]

Read the assigned pages in the resource below.

⭐ *Nature Drawing & Journaling* p. V "Introduction" – p. 5

After reading, make a list of any needed supplies from p. 4-5. Discuss the list with your parent. It is important to note that there are blank pages in the back of *Nature Drawing & Journaling* that can be used for lessons.

Key Idea: Introduce nature journaling.

Language Arts [S]

Help students complete one lesson from the following reading program:

⭐ *Drawn into the Heart of Reading*

Help students complete **one** English option.

⭐ *Progressing With Courage:* Lesson 1

⭐ *Progressing With Courage:* Lesson 67 (Save Written Exercises 'B' for Day 2.)

⭐ Your own grammar program

Work with the students to complete **one** of the writing options listed below:

⭐ *Write with the Best: Vol. 2* Unit 3 – Day 1 p. 25 (A newspaper or magazine article is needed.) Note: Units 1 and 2 are omitted.

⭐ Your own writing program

Key Idea: Practice language arts skills.

Bible Quiet Time [I]

Bible Study: Read and complete the assigned pages in the following resource:

⭐ *Faith at Work: Lesson 1 – Day One* p. 1

Prayer Focus: Photocopy "Preparing Your Heart for Prayer" from the Appendix. Refer to the questions for praying with **adoration**. Then, pray a prayer of adoration to worship and honor God. After your prayer, write 'adoration' at the bottom of today's lesson in *Faith at Work* above *Day Two*. Next to 'adoration', either list key phrases or write a sentence to summarize your prayer. This will be your prayer log. Last, place the copy of "Preparing Your Heart for Prayer" inside your Bible.

Scripture Memory: Read aloud Romans 12:1 three times from your Bible.

Music: Read p. 15-16 in *Hymns for a Kid's Heart*. Refer to p. 18 as you sing with Track 1 "*Praise to the Lord, the Almighty*" (verse 1).

Key Idea: Introduce the study of Romans.

Math Exploration [S]

Choose **one** of the math options listed below (see Appendix for details).

⭐ *Singapore Primary Mathematics 6A/6B, Discovering Mathematics 7A/7B, 8A/8B, No-Nonsense Algebra* or *Videotext Algebra*

⭐ Your own math program

Key Idea: Use a step-by-step math program.

Science Exploration [I]

⭐ Read *Exploring the World of Chemistry* p. 4-10. After reading the chapter, turn to p. 11 of *Exploring the World of Chemistry*. Write the answer to each numbered question from p. 11 on lined paper. You do not need to copy the question.

Key Idea: Iron, tin, and lead are metals that have been used for centuries. Cast iron, steel, and wrought iron have differing amounts of carbon. Bronze and pewter are alloys that use tin. Lead is a heavy ancient metal.

Learning Through History

Focus: Irish Famine, Ottoman and Russian Oppression, & Ethiopian Freedom

Unit 1 - Day 2

Reading about History [I]

Read about history in the following resource:

 ★ *The Story of the World: Vol. 4* p. 134-144
After today's reading, open your *Student Notebook* to Unit 1. Use colored pencils to color the postcard in Box 7 of Abdulhamid II and his home in Salonika. Abdulhamid was held under house arrest in this home, after being deposed by the Young Turks in 1909. He was the last dictator-type Ottoman sultan. Write your own caption under the postcard to convey the significance of the card's image.

Key Idea: While Pedro II was ruling in Brazil, Abdulhamid II was ruling the Ottoman Empire. He ruled with an "iron fist" from 1876-1909, crushing rebellion and earning the nickname "Abdulhamid the Red".

History Project [S]

Get the cards that you copied on Day 1. You need cards '1', '2', and '3' today. Enlist the help and oversight of a parent. Then, go to the shortest person in your home (excluding an infant). This person is the dictator with absolute power for today's cards. Have the "dictator" read card '1' and select the music you must listen to today. You may only listen to music that the dictator selects. Next, read card '2'. The dictator will select an outfit for you to wear from **your** closet. You must wear it today. Then, read card '3'. The dictator will select the book you **must** read for free reading.

Key Idea: Abdulhamid II was a dictator.

President Study [I]

★ On *The Presidents* DVD Volume 1, select the Chapter "Washington to Monroe" and watch **only** Program 1: George Washington. Then, open your *President Notebook* to George Washington. Use today's viewing to add further information about George Washington.

Key Idea: Research George Washington.

Storytime [T/I]

Read the following assigned pages:

★ *Under the Hawthorn Tree* p. 17-38

Get the bookmark you made on Day 1. Find the section of the bookmark that has only **two** options at the bottom. At the top of this section of the bookmark, write the book title and the page numbers you read today. Select **one** of the two options at the bottom and place a checkmark next to it. In the blank space under today's pages, respond in writing using your checked option. Keep the bookmark in your book.

Key Idea: Relate to the text in various ways.

Worthy Words [T]

Open your *Student Notebook* to Unit 1 – Box 8. You will read, analyze, and evaluate this speech. After reading the speech, answer the following questions on an index card: *What are some of the main topics in the speech? Can you elaborate on the reason why Borden compared Canada and Brazil? How has your knowledge and understanding of Brazil changed after reading the speech? What is your opinion of Dom Pedro I and II?* Next, meet with a parent to have a Socratic dialogue about the speech. A Socratic dialogue is one in which the participants come prepared to share their thoughts, feelings, and opinions about the spoken/written word. Before beginning the dialogue, the parent reads Box 8 out loud. Next, discuss the questions using your notes. All participants should use life experiences and/or the text to support their responses.

Key Idea: Dom Pedro II ruled Brazil 48 years.

Independent History Study [I]

Open your *Student Notebook* to Unit 1. Choose an important part of the speech from Box 8 to copy in quotation marks in Box 6. Write the name of the speaker at the bottom of Box 6.

Key Idea: Brazil is a South American country.

Learning the Basics

Focus: Language Arts, Math, Bible, Nature Journal, and Science

Biblical Self-Image T

The *Biblical Worldview of Self-Image* Study listed below is scheduled twice weekly for you and your child to do together. Our plans intend for the listed pages in *Who Am I? And What Am I Doing Here?* to be read either silently by both you and your child, or read aloud to the child by you. This study also has much to be gained by discussion, as it provides an excellent opportunity to share what **you** believe. Read and discuss with the students the following pages in the resource below.

 Who Am I? And What Am I Doing Here? p. 15-16

Key Idea: Introduce the worldview study.

Language Arts S

Have students complete one studied dictation exercise (see Appendix for directions and passages).

Help students complete one lesson from the following reading program:

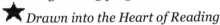 *Drawn into the Heart of Reading*

Help students complete **one** English option.

★ *Progressing With Courage:* Lesson 2

★ *Progressing With Courage:* Lesson 67 (Written Exercises 'B' only)

★ Your own grammar program

Key Idea: Practice language arts skills.

Bible Quiet Time I

Bible Study: Read and complete the assigned pages in the following resource:

★ *Faith at Work: Lesson 1 – Day Two* p. 1-2

Prayer Focus: Get your copy of "Preparing Your Heart for Prayer" that you placed in your Bible on Day 1. Refer to the questions for **confession.** Then, pray a prayer of confession to admit or acknowledge your sins to God. After your prayer, write 'confession' at the bottom of today's lesson in *Faith at Work* above *Day Three.* Next to 'confession', either list key phrases or write a sentence to summarize your prayer. Last, place the copy of "Preparing Your Heart for Prayer" inside your Bible.

Scripture Memory: Memorize Romans 12:1 from your Bible and recite it.

Music: Refer to p. 18 in *Hymns for a Kid's Heart* as you sing with Track 1: *"Praise to the Lord, the Almighty"* (verse 1).

Key Idea: Introduce the study of Romans.

Math Exploration S

Choose **one** of the math options listed below (see Appendix for details).

★ *Singapore Primary Mathematics 6A/6B, Discovering Mathematics 7A/7B, 8A/8B, No-Nonsense Algebra* or *Videotext Algebra*

★ Your own math program

Key Idea: Use a step-by-step math program.

Science Exploration I

★ Read *Exploring the World of Chemistry* p. 12-16. After reading the chapter, turn to p. 17 of *Exploring the World of Chemistry.* Write the answer to each numbered question from p. 17 on lined paper. You do not need to copy the question.

Key Idea: The ancient metals silver, gold, and copper are used in money. They are often known as money or coinage metals. Silver and gold are soft metals, so they are often mixed with copper to strengthen them. Mercury is another ancient metal. Like lead, it is poisonous.

Learning Through History

Focus: Irish Famine, Ottoman and Russian Oppression, & Ethiopian Freedom

Unit 1 - Day 3

Reading about History | I

Read about history in the following resource:

★ *The Story of the World: Vol. 4* p. 146 – middle of p. 150

After today's reading, open your *Student Notebook* to Unit 1. Look at the image of the banknote from 1909 in Box 5. Notice the picture of Alexander III on the note. This banknote was worth 25 rubles. The ruble is still the currency in Russia today. What signs of royalty do you notice on the note? How is Alexander III made to look regal and powerful? According to today's reading, where else would you find portraits of Alexander III during his rule? Why?

Key Idea: After the death of Alexander II, his son Alexander III became the czar in Russia.

History Project | S

Get the cards that you copied on Day 1. You need cards '4', '5', and '6' today. Enlist the help and oversight of a parent. Then, go to the tallest person in your home. This person is the dictator with absolute power for today's cards. Have the "dictator" read card '4' and choose a way for you to comb your hair for today. You **must** comb your hair in the way in which the dictator selects. Next, read card '5'. The dictator will decide a profession for you and tell you his decision. Then, read card '6'. The dictator will plan your free time today. You **must** do as the dictator says. At the end of the day, share with a parent what you learned about dictators and life under a dictatorship.

Key Idea: Alexander III ruled as a dictator.

State Study | T

★ This is an **optional** part of the plans. If you have chosen to study your state using *State History from a Christian Perspective*, do Lesson 1 from the *Master Lesson Plan Book*.

Key Idea: Study your individual state.

Storytime | T/I

Read the following assigned pages:

★ *Under the Hawthorn Tree* p. 39-56

After today's reading, orally narrate or retell the portion of the story that was read today. See *Narration Tips* in the Appendix as needed.

Key Idea: Practice orally narrating, or retelling, a portion of a story.

Geography | I

For today's activities, use the map listed below.

★ *Map Trek CD: Missions to Modern Marvels* p. 36-37

Print the "World Empires 1900" Student Map found on p. 37 of the *Map Trek* CD. Refer to or print the *Map Trek* Teacher's Answer Map on p. 36 to guide you as you label and color the Russian Empire and the Ottoman Empire on your Student Map. Then, use a globe and the map on p. 134 of *The Story of the World* to help you outline, label, and lightly color Brazil in brown on your Student Map. File the map in your *Student Notebook*. You will add to your map in the next few units.

Key Idea: When Emperor Pedro II of Brazil ended his rule in 1889, Abdulhamid II was ruling as sultan of the Ottoman Empire, and Alexander III was ruling as czar of the Russian Empire. Alexander III was a member of the royal Romanov family. He ruled Russia as an autocracy with absolute power.

Independent History Study | I

Listen to *What in the World? Vol. 3* Disc 2, Track 8: "The Turn of the Century & Russia".

Key Idea: The Russian Empire covered 1/6 of the globe at the turn of the century. More than 80% of Jews in the world lived in Russia at this time. The nobility, the peasants, and the factory workers were the 3 classes in Russia.

Nature Journal & Poetry | S

The poetry of Longfellow, Wordsworth, and Whitman is scheduled on Day 3 in each unit to complement the nature journaling sessions. Read aloud and discuss today's poem *"Becalmed"* (see Appendix) with a parent. Then, follow the directions in the resource below to begin your Nature Journal.

⭐ *Nature Drawing & Journaling: Lesson I* p. 6 (paragraphs 1 and 2 only)

Note: The "Journal Primer" is located in *Nature Drawing & Journaling* on p. 127.

<u>Key Idea</u>: Appreciate nature as God's creation.

Language Arts | S

Have students complete one studied dictation exercise (see Appendix for passages).

Help students complete **one** English option.

⭐ *Progressing With Courage:* Lesson 3

⭐ *Progressing With Courage:* Lesson 68 (first half only)

⭐ Your own grammar program

Work with the students to complete **one** of the writing options listed below:

⭐ *Write with the Best: Vol. 2* Unit 3 – Day 2 p. 25-26 (The same newspaper or magazine article used on Day 1 is needed.)

⭐ Your own writing program

<u>Key Idea</u>: Practice language arts skills.

Bible Quiet Time | I

Bible Study: Read and complete the assigned pages in the following resource:

⭐ *Faith at Work: Lesson 1 – Day Three* p. 2

Prayer Focus: Get your copy of "Preparing Your Heart for Prayer" that you placed in your Bible. Before praying today, refer to the questions for **thanksgiving**. Then, pray a prayer of thanksgiving to express gratitude to God for His divine goodness. After your prayer, write 'thanksgiving' at the bottom of today's lesson in *Faith at Work* above *Day Four*. Next to 'thanksgiving', either list key phrases or write a sentence to summarize your prayer. Place the copy of "Preparing Your Heart for Prayer" back inside your Bible.

Scripture Memory: Copy Romans 12:1 in your Common Place Book.

Music: Refer to p. 18 in *Hymns for a Kid's Heart* as you sing with Track 1: *"Praise to the Lord, the Almighty"* (verse 1).

<u>Key Idea</u>: Introduce the study of Romans.

Math Exploration | S

Choose **one** of the math options listed below (see Appendix for details).

⭐ *Singapore Primary Mathematics 6A/6B, Discovering Mathematics 7A/7B, 8A/8B, No-Nonsense Algebra* or *Videotext Algebra*

⭐ Your own math program

<u>Key Idea</u>: Use a step-by-step math program.

Science Exploration | I

⭐ Read *Exploring the World of Chemistry* p. 18-26. After reading the chapter, turn to p. 27 of *Exploring the World of Chemistry*. Write the answer to each numbered question from p. 27 on lined paper. You do not need to copy the question.

<u>Key Idea</u>: The seven ancient metals were gold, silver, brass (copper), tin, lead, mercury, and iron. Sulfur and carbon were two nonmetallic elements used by ancient chemists. Sulfuric acid is the most important compound of sulfur. Charcoal, coal, graphite, and diamonds are forms of carbon.

Learning Through History

Focus: Irish Famine, Ottoman and Russian Oppression, & Ethiopian Freedom

Reading about History | I |

Read about history in the following resource:

 The Story of the World: Vol. 4 middle of p. 150 – p. 155

You will be writing a narration about the chapter *Ethiopia and Italy*. To prepare for writing your narration, look back over p. 150-155 in *The Story of the World: Vol. 4*. Think about the main idea and the most important moments in this part of the reading.

After you have thought about what you will write and how you will begin your narration, turn to Unit 1 in your *Student Notebook*. For more guidance on writing a narration, see *Written Narration Tips* in the Appendix.

In Box 4, write a 12-16 sentence narration about the reading. When you have finished writing, read your sentences out loud to catch any mistakes. Check for the following things: *Did you include **who** or **what topic** the reading was mainly about? Did you include **descriptors** of the important thing(s) that happened? Did you include a **closing sentence**? If not, add those things.* Use the *Written Narration Skills* in the Appendix as a guide for editing the narration.

Key Idea: By 1900, all but two countries in Africa were ruled by European countries. Liberia governed itself, as a protectorate of the United States; and Ethiopia remained free. Both Yohannes IV and Menelik II claimed to be the sole emperor of Ethiopia, yet they agreed on a sort of truce and an alliance against any European invasion. After Yohannes IV was killed in battle, Menelik ruled Ethiopia alone. Menelik signed a treaty with Italy that tricked him into making Ethiopia a protectorate of Italy. Menelik decided to fight the Italians for Ethiopia's freedom and won.

Storytime | T/I |

Read the following assigned pages:

 Under the Hawthorn Tree p. 57-71
Note: p. 63 contains a graphic description.

Get the bookmark that you placed in your book on Day 2. Locate the same section of the bookmark that you used on Day 2. Beneath Day 2's entry, write the book title and the page numbers you read today. Select the one remaining response option at the bottom of the bookmark, and place a checkmark next to it. In the blank space under today's pages, respond in writing using your checked option. Keep the bookmark in your book.

Key Idea: Relate to the text in various ways.

Economics | I |

Read about economics in the following resource:

 Whatever Happened to Penny Candy? p. 18-21 (Note: You will need one of each type of coin and a one dollar bill.)

After the reading, open your *Student Notebook* to the "Economic Principles" section at the front of your notebook. Under "Economic Principle", write one line or one sentence that summarizes the economic principle you learned from today's reading.

Key Idea: Coins and paper money have changed through the years, affecting recession and inflation.

Independent History Study | I |

Get the "World Empires 1900" Student Map that you filed in your *Student Notebook* on Day 3. Refer to the *Map Trek* Teacher's Answer Map p. 36 to guide you as you label and color the French holdings and the British Empire **in Africa** on your Student Map. You will add to your map in the next few units.

Key Idea: In Africa, Ethiopia remained free.

President Study | I |

Read p. 6-7 in *Our Presidents…* Then, open your *President Notebook* to John Adams. Use today's reading to help you complete the information about John Adams.

Key Idea: Research John Adams.

Biblical Self-Image ☐ T

Read and discuss with the students the following pages in the resource below.

★ *Who Am I? And What Am I Doing Here?*
p. 17-25

Note: For "Make a Note of It" on p. 25 either discuss the responses, being sure to share examples from your own life, or have each person respond in writing in his/her journal instead.

Key Idea: God created each of us in His image.

Language Arts ☐ S

Have students complete one studied dictation exercise (see Appendix for directions and passages).

Help students complete one lesson from the following reading program:

★ *Drawn into the Heart of Reading*

Help students complete **one** English option.

★ *Progressing With Courage:* Lesson 4

★ *Progressing With Courage:* Lesson 68 (last half only)

★ Your own grammar program

Key Idea: Practice language arts skills.

Bible Quiet Time ☐ I

Bible Study: Complete the assignment below.

★ *Faith at Work: Lesson 1 – Day Four*
p. 2-3

Prayer Focus: Refer to **supplication** on "Preparing Your Heart for Prayer". Then, pray a prayer of supplication to make a humble and earnest request of God. Write 'supplication' at the bottom of today's lesson in *Faith at Work* above *Day Five*. Next to it, either list several key phrases or write a sentence to summarize your prayer. Keep "Preparing Your Heart for Prayer" inside your Bible.

Scripture Memory: Recite Romans 12:1.

Music: Refer to p. 18 in *Hymns for a Kid's Heart* as you sing with Track 1: *"Praise to the Lord, the Almighty"* (verse 1).

Key Idea: Introduce the study of Romans.

Math Exploration ☐ S

Choose **one** of the math options listed below (see Appendix for details).

★ *Singapore Primary Mathematics 6A/6B, Discovering Mathematics 7A/7B, 8A/8B, No-Nonsense Algebra* or *Videotext Algebra*

★ Your own math program

Key Idea: Use a step-by-step math program.

Science Exploration ☐ I

★ Copy the Science Lab Form from the Appendix of this guide. Read *Chemistry C500 Experiment Manual* p. 1-2 and p. 4-8. Then, put on your safety glasses from the Experiment Kit and the smooth gloves and smock recommended on p. 6 of the Experiment Manual. Reread Basic Rule 10 on p. 6. Next, follow the directions to perform "Experiment 1" from p. 10 of the *Chemistry C500 Experiment Manual*. After completing Experiment 1, in the top box of the Science Lab Form write: *Will tartaric acid form carbon dioxide when combined with sodium carbonate?* In the second box of the form, write your hypothesis. Follow the directions for "Experiment 2" on p. 11 of the Chemistry *C500 Experiment Manual* and complete the box "Perform an Experiment" on your lab form. Then, have a parent help you follow the arrows to complete the rest of the Science Lab Form. To clean up, refer to "How to Dispose of Waste" on p. 7 and Basic Rules 5, 6, 7, and 11 on p. 6.

Key Idea: Sodium carbonate and tartaric acid react and give off carbon dioxide when water is added.

Learning Through History

Focus: Missions Through Hudson Taylor in China and Niijima Jo in Japan

Reading about History | S

Read about history in the following resource:

⭐ *Rescue and Redeem* p. 11-16
After today's reading, orally narrate or retell to an adult the portion of text that you read today. As you retell, the adult will write or type your narration. Some possible key words to include in your narration might be *modern church, the Enlightenment, democracy, agriculture, overpopulate, labor unions, inventions, global Christianity, rescue,* and *redeem*. When the narration is complete, tri-fold the typed or written narration to fit in Unit 2 – Box 10 of the *Student Notebook*. Glue the folded narration in Box 10, so it can be opened and read.

Key Idea: The spread of Christianity around the globe is a goal of the modern church.

Storytime | T/I

Read the following assigned pages:

⭐ *Under the Hawthorn Tree* p. 73-88
Note: p. 75 uses God's name in a less than worshipful way.

Get the bookmark that you placed in your book last unit. Choose a new section of the bookmark with **three** options at the bottom. At the top of this section of the bookmark, write the book title and the page numbers you read today. Select **one** of the three options at the bottom and place a checkmark next to it. In the blank space under today's pages, respond in writing using your checked option. Keep the bookmark in your book.

Key Idea: Relate to the text in various ways.

History Project | S

Today you will age paper for a Chinese scroll. Cut a 4½" x 9¾" piece of white paper. Then, have an adult **either** make a very strong cup of black coffee with 5 times the strength usually used, **or** make tea and steep the tea bag in hot water. **If you made coffee**, pour it in a cake pan and allow the paper to float on top of the coffee. Then, spoon the coffee over top of the paper. Last, remove the paper, letting it drip and blot it with a paper towel. **If you made tea,** place your paper on a paper towel and smear the wet teabag across the paper. Dip your teabag in the tea as needed to keep it wet. Then, **for either method**, bake the paper on a cookie sheet in the oven at 200 degrees for 3-7 min. until the paper is dry. Do not get your paper too hot, or it can catch on fire!

Key Idea: Modern missions spread to China.

Timeline | I

You will be adding to the timeline in your *Student Notebook* today. In Unit 2 – Box 1, draw and color the outline of Japan. Label it, *Nicholas of Japan – Russian Orthodox Priest to Japan (1861 -1912 A.D.).*

In Box 2, draw and color a samurai sword. Label it, *Niijima Jo – Missionary to Japan (1875-1890 A.D.).*

In Box 3, draw and color the outline of China. Label it, *Hudson Taylor – Missionary to China (1865-1902 A.D.).*

Key Idea: Nicholas of Japan was a Russian Orthodox priest who aided Niijima Jo's conversion to Christianity. About this same time, Hudson Taylor was ministering in China.

Independent History Study | I

⭐ Use p. 248-249 of *Rescue and Redeem* to find China, Korea, Japan, and India. Then, use p. 250 to find the United States, Hawaiian Islands, and Mexico. Last, use p. 251 to find the United Kingdom, Germany, and Uganda (in Africa). These are all places you will read about in *Rescue and Redeem*.

Key Idea: As technology and travel improved, missions to new places around the world increased.

Learning the Basics
Focus: Language Arts, Math, Bible, Nature Journal, and Science

Unit 2 - Day 1

Nature Journal ⬛ I

Read and follow the directions in the resource below to draw in your Nature Journal.

★ *Nature Drawing & Journaling: Lesson I* p. 6 (beginning with paragraph 3) – p. 10

Note: The "Journal Primer" is located in *Nature Drawing & Journaling* on p. 127.

Key Idea: A nature journal is artwork in progress.

Language Arts ⬛ S

Help students complete one lesson from the following reading program:

★ *Drawn into the Heart of Reading*

Help students complete **one** English option.

★ *Progressing With Courage:* Lesson 5

★ *Progressing With Courage:* Lesson 69 (Save Written Exercises for Day 2.)

★ Your own grammar program

Work with the students to complete **one** of the writing options listed below:

★ *Write with the Best: Vol. 2* Unit 3 – Day 3 p. 26 (The same newspaper or magazine article used previously is needed.)

★ Your own writing program

Key Idea: Practice language arts skills.

Bible Quiet Time ⬛ I

Bible Study: Read and complete the assigned pages in the following resource:

★ *Faith at Work: Lesson 1 – Day Five* and *Notes* p. 3-6

Prayer Focus: Get your copy of "Preparing Your Heart for Prayer" that you placed in your Bible. Refer to the questions for **adoration.** Then, pray a prayer of adoration to worship and honor God. After your prayer, write 'adoration' at the bottom of today's lesson on p. 3 in *Faith at Work*. Next to 'adoration', either list key phrases or write a sentence to summarize your prayer. Keep "Preparing Your Heart for Prayer" inside your Bible.

Scripture Memory: Read aloud Romans 12:2 three times from your Bible.

Music: Read p. 17 in *Hymns for a Kid's Heart*. Refer to p. 18-19 as you sing with Track 1 *"Praise to the Lord, the Almighty"* (vs. 1-3).

Key Idea: Introduce the study of Romans.

Math Exploration ⬛ S

Choose **one** of the math options listed below (see Appendix for details).

★ *Singapore Primary Mathematics 6A/6B, Discovering Mathematics 7A/7B, 8A/8B, No-Nonsense Algebra* or *Videotext Algebra*

★ Your own math program

Key Idea: Use a step-by-step math program.

Science Exploration ⬛ I

★ Read *Exploring the World of Chemistry* p. 28-34. After reading the chapter, turn to p. 35 of *Exploring the World of Chemistry*. Write the answer to each numbered question from p. 35 on lined paper. You do not need to copy the question.

Key Idea: Henry Cavendish discovered a new gas that became known as hydrogen. It is found in petroleum and water and is an abundant element. Hydrogen is also the lightest element. Joseph Priestley studied carbon dioxide and discovered oxygen, and Daniel Rutherford discovered nitrogen gas. By the late 1700s, over 25 elements had been discovered. Berzelius suggested using letters as symbols for elements.

Learning Through History

Focus: Missions Through Hudson Taylor in China and Niijima Jo in Japan

Reading about History | I

Read about history in the following resource:

⭐ *Rescue and Redeem* p. 17-37
After today's reading, open your *Student Notebook* to Unit 2. Label the image in Box 7, *Niijima Jo*. Label the image in Box 8, *Takuma Sawabe*. In the blank space connecting Box 7 and 8, list bulleted notes to explain how the two men are similar and how they are connected. Hint: Takuma Sawabe is mentioned on p. 37 of *Rescue and Redeem*.

Key Idea: Niijima Jo was a Japanese samurai who chose to serve and obey God. He was helped by the Russian Orthodox priest Nicholai at Hakodate. Niijima traveled to America for Bible training and returned to Japan as a missionary. Takuma Sawabe was a Shinto priest converted by Nicholai in Hakodate.

Storytime | T/I

Read the following assigned pages:

⭐ *Under the Hawthorn Tree* p. 89-105
Note: p. 90 uses God's name in a less than worshipful way, and p. 97 needs discussing as to why Michael may think there is no God (when he had previously believed in God) or why he may think of God as a monster now. Discuss how sorrows can bring us closer to God. Get the bookmark that you placed in your book. Locate the same section of the bookmark that you used on Day 1. Beneath Day 1's entry, write the book title and the page numbers you read today. Select one of the **two** remaining response options at the bottom of the bookmark, and place a checkmark next to it. In the blank space under today's pages, respond in writing using your checked option.

Key Idea: Relate to the text in various ways.

History Project | S

Get the 4½" x 9¾" paper that you aged on Day 1. Lay the paper vertically. Use a pencil to make light marks to divide the paper into horizontal thirds, with each section being 3¼" tall. Open your *Student Notebook* to Unit 2. You will be painting the 3 Chinese characters in the order shown in Box 9 down your aged paper, placing one character in each section. On scratch paper, practice using black watercolor paint and a paintbrush to paint each character. Then, paint the Chinese character on your aged paper.

Key Idea: The characters mean "Christ's Disciple" or "Christ's Apprentice" and can be read by Chinese and Japanese Christians.

Economics | I

Read about economics in the resource below.

⭐ *Whatever Happened to Penny Candy?* p. 22-27

After the reading, open your *Student Notebook* to the "Economic Principles" section at the front of your notebook. Under "Economic Principle", write a one line or one sentence summary for each of the **two** economic principles you learned from today's reading.

Key Idea: The principle of TANSTAAFL means "there ain't no such thing as a free lunch". Gresham's Law says, "bad money drives good money out of circulation".

President Study | I

⭐ On *The Presidents* DVD Volume 1, select the Chapter "Washington to Monroe" and watch **only** Program 2: John Adams. Then, open your *President Notebook* to John Adams. Use today's viewing to add further information about John Adams.

Key Idea: Research John Adams.

Independent History Study | I

On p. 8 of *Rescue and Redeem,* read through the entries from 1860-1874 on the "Modern Church Timeline". What interesting facts do you notice?

Key Idea: Niijimo returned to Japan in 1874.

Learning the Basics
Focus: Language Arts, Math, Bible, Nature Journal, and Science

Unit 2 - Day 2

Biblical Self-Image [T]

Our plans intend for the listed pages in *Who Am I? And What Am I Doing Here?* to be read either silently by both you and your student, or read aloud to the student by you. With this in mind, read and discuss the following pages in the resource below.

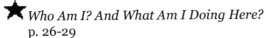★ *Who Am I? And What Am I Doing Here?* p. 26-29
Note: For "Make a Note of It" on p. 29 either discuss the responses, being sure to share examples from your own life, or have each person respond in writing in his/her journal.

Key Idea: God designed you and has plans for you. You are a child of God.

Language Arts [S]

Have students complete one studied dictation exercise (see Appendix for directions and passages).

Help students complete one lesson from the following reading program:

★ *Drawn into the Heart of Reading*

Help students complete **one** English option.

★ *Progressing With Courage:* Lesson 6

★ *Progressing With Courage:* Lesson 69 ("Written Exercises" only)

★ Your own grammar program

Key Idea: Practice language arts skills.

Bible Quiet Time [I]

Bible Study: Read and complete the assigned pages in the following resource:

★ *Faith at Work: Lesson 2 – Day One* p. 7
Note: Refer to p. 4-6 to complete the lesson.

Prayer Focus: Get your copy of "Preparing Your Heart for Prayer" that you placed in your Bible. Refer to the questions for **confession.** Then, pray a prayer of confession to admit or acknowledge your sins to God. After your prayer, write 'confession' at the bottom of today's lesson in *Faith at Work* above *Day Two*. Next to 'confession', either list key phrases or write a sentence to summarize your prayer. This will be your prayer log. Keep "Preparing Your Heart for Prayer" inside your Bible.

Scripture Memory: Memorize Romans 12:2 from your Bible and recite it.

Music: Refer to p. 18-19 as you sing with Track 1 *"Praise to the Lord, the Almighty"* (vs. 1-3).

Key Idea: Study Paul's missionary journeys.

Math Exploration [S]

Choose **one** of the math options listed below (see Appendix for details).

★ *Singapore Primary Mathematics 6A/6B, Discovering Mathematics 7A/7B, 8A/8B, No-Nonsense Algebra* or *Videotext Algebra*

★ Your own math program

Key Idea: Use a step-by-step math program.

Science Exploration [I]

★ Read *Exploring the World of Chemistry* p. 36-42. After reading the chapter, turn to p. 43 of *Exploring the World of Chemistry.* Write the answer to each numbered question from p. 43 on lined paper. You do not need to copy the question.

Key Idea: In 1800, Alessandro Volta made the first electric battery. Humphry Davy experimented with Volta's battery by using its electric current to separate elements from oxygen. This resulted in Davy's quick discovery of potassium, sodium, barium, strontium, calcium, and magnesium.

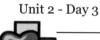

Reading about History | I

Read about history in the following resource:

 Rescue and Redeem p. 39-43

After today's reading, open your *Student Notebook* to Unit 2. Look at the image of the map of the nine unreached provinces of China in 1865 shown in black in Box 5. Read aloud the names of the nine provinces unreached by the message of the Gospel in 1865. These provinces were the goal of the China Inland Missions founded by Hudson and Maria Taylor, and missionaries were eventually sent to each of the 9 provinces.

Key Idea: In the decades following William Carey's call to international missions, missionary societies began organizing and sending missionaries around the world.

History Project | S

Choose a red, green, or brown colored piece of paper for the background of your Chinese scroll. Cut the colored paper to 6" x 11". Then, glue your aged paper with its black Chinese characters onto the colored paper, leaving an edging of colored paper showing around the aged paper. If you wish to roll up your scroll, you may glue a dowel, chopstick, or popsicle stick to the back of your scroll at both the top and bottom. If you prefer to leave your scroll as a wall hanging instead, then glue a yarn or ribbon loop at the top of the scroll, which you can use to hang your scroll on a bulletin board or wall.

Key Idea: The Taylors worked in China to spread the Good News of Christ inland.

State Study | T

 This is an **optional** part of the plans. If you have chosen to study your state using *State History from a Christian Perspective,* do Lesson 2 from the *Master Lesson Plan Book.*

Key Idea: Study your individual state.

Storytime | T/I

Read the following assigned pages:

 Under the Hawthorn Tree p. 107-123

After today's reading, orally narrate or retell the portion of the story that was read today. See *Narration Tips* in the Appendix as needed.

Key Idea: Practice orally narrating, or retelling, a portion of a story.

Worthy Words | T

Open your *Student Notebook* to Unit 2 – Box 11. You will read, analyze, and evaluate this letter. After reading the letter, answer the following questions on an index card: *How does the letter begin? What significance does the beginning of the letter have? Why was Hudson Taylor's soul in agony? What caused the change in Taylor's feelings? How can you relate your Christian walk to the feelings Hudson Taylor shared in his letter?* Next, meet with a parent to have a Socratic dialogue about the letter. A Socratic dialogue is one in which the participants come prepared to share their thoughts, feelings, and opinions about the spoken/written word. Before beginning the dialogue, the parent reads Box 11 out loud. Next, discuss the questions using your notes. All participants should use life experiences and/or the text to support their responses.

Key Idea: Hudson and Maria Taylor founded the China Inland Mission Society. Maria died of cholera in 1870 while in China.

Independent History Study | I

Open your *Student Notebook* to Unit 2. Choose an important part of the letter from Box 11 to copy in quotation marks in Box 6. Write "Hudson Taylor" at the bottom of Box 6.

Key Idea: Hudson Taylor married Maria in 1858. In 1869, at the time of the letter, the Taylors were in Yangzhou in the Kiang-su province.

Learning the Basics
Focus: Language Arts, Math, Bible, Nature Journal, Poetry, and Science

Nature Journal & Poetry S

The poetry of Longfellow, Wordsworth, and Whitman is scheduled on Day 3 in each unit to complement the nature journaling sessions. Read aloud and discuss today's poem *"The Tables Turned"* (see Appendix) with a parent. Then, follow the directions in the resource below to begin your Nature Journal.

★ *Nature Drawing & Journaling: Lesson II* p. 11-15

Note: The lessons assume that you have also purchased a hardback sketchbook for a journal.

<u>Key Idea</u>: Personalize your journal's cover.

Language Arts S

Have students complete one studied dictation exercise (see Appendix for passages).

Help students complete **one** English option.

★ *Progressing With Courage:* Lesson 7

★ *Progressing With Courage:* Lesson 70 (first half only)

★ Your own grammar program

Work with the students to complete **one** of the writing options listed below:

★ *Write with the Best: Vol. 2* Unit 3 – Day 4 p. 26 (The same newspaper or magazine article used previously is needed.)

★ Your own writing program

<u>Key Idea</u>: Practice language arts skills.

Bible Quiet Time I

Bible Study: Read and complete the assigned pages in the following resource:

★ *Faith at Work: Lesson 2 – Day Two* p. 7-8

Prayer Focus: Get your copy of "Preparing Your Heart for Prayer" that you placed in your Bible. Refer to the questions for **thanksgiving**. Then, pray a prayer of thanksgiving to express gratitude to God for His divine goodness. After your prayer, write 'thanksgiving' at the bottom of today's lesson on p. 8 in *Faith at Work*. Next to 'thanksgiving', either list key phrases or write a sentence to summarize your prayer. This will be your prayer log. Keep "Preparing Your Heart for Prayer" inside your Bible.

Scripture Memory: Copy Romans 12:2 in your Common Place Book.

Music: Refer to p. 18-19 as you sing with Track 1 *"Praise to the Lord, the Almighty"* (vs. 1-3).

<u>Key Idea</u>: Study Paul's missionary journeys.

Math Exploration S

Choose **one** of the math options listed below (see Appendix for details).

★ *Singapore Primary Mathematics 6A/6B, Discovering Mathematics 7A/7B, 8A/8B, No-Nonsense Algebra* or *Videotext Algebra*

★ Your own math program

<u>Key Idea</u>: Use a step-by-step math program.

Science Exploration I

★ Read *Exploring the World of Chemistry* p. 44-50. After reading the chapter, turn to p. 51 of *Exploring the World of Chemistry*. Write the answer to each numbered question from p. 51 on lined paper. You do not need to copy the question.

<u>Key Idea</u>: By the 1830s, 60 elements had been discovered. These elements are the building blocks of millions of compounds. In the 1860s, Dimitri Mendeleyev used each element's atomic weight, valence, and chemical properties to make an organized table of elements. This is called the Periodic Table.

Reading about History | I

Read about history in the following resource:

 Rescue and Redeem p. 45-62

You will be writing a narration about the chapter *Hudson and Maria Taylor: To China's Perishing Millions*. To prepare for writing your narration, look back over p. 45-62 in *Rescue and Redeem*. Think about the main idea and the most important moments in this part of the reading.

After you have thought about what you will write and how you will begin your narration, turn to Unit 2 in your *Student Notebook*. For more guidance on writing a narration, see *Written Narration Tips* in the Appendix.

In Box 4, write a 12-16 sentence narration about the reading. When you have finished writing, read your sentences out loud to catch any mistakes. Check for the following things: *Did you include **who** or **what topic** the reading was mainly about? Did you include **descriptors** of the important thing(s) that happened? Did you include a **closing sentence**? If not, add those things.* Use the *Written Narration Skills* in the Appendix as a guide for editing the narration.

Key Idea: After completing his medical training, Hudson Taylor sailed with his wife, Maria, and 16 other missionaries to China on the *Lammermuir*. Their goal was to spread the gospel to the interior, or inland provinces, of China. The China Inland Mission was formed as an inter-denominational mission, pledging to work together to spread the gospel. The missionaries adopted Chinese dress and ways of doing things, as long as these ways did not conflict with the gospel.

Storytime | T/I

Read the following assigned pages:

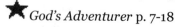 *God's Adventurer* p. 7-18

Get the bookmark that you placed in your book. Locate the same section of the bookmark that you used on Day 2. Beneath Day 2's entry, write the book title and the page numbers you read today. Select the one remaining response option at the bottom of the bookmark, and place a checkmark next to it. In the blank space under today's pages, respond in writing using your checked option. Keep the bookmark in your book.

Key Idea: Relate to the text in various ways.

Geography | I

For today's activities, use the map listed below.

 Map Trek CD: Missions to Modern Marvels p. 36-37

Get the "World Empires 1900" Student Map that you filed in your *Student Notebook* in Unit 1. Refer to the *Map Trek* Teacher's Answer Map p. 36 to guide you as you label and color the Chinese Empire in red on your Student Map. You will continue to add to your map in the next few units.

Key Idea: The Chinese Empire had been evangelized along the coast of China in the mid-1800s, but the interior of China remained an area where millions perished without ever hearing the gospel. The Taylors vowed to change this fact and fulfilled their mission at great personal cost.

President Study | I

 Read p. 8-9 in *Our Presidents...* Then, open your *President Notebook* to Thomas Jefferson. Use today's reading to help you complete the information about Thomas Jefferson.

Key Idea: Research Thomas Jefferson.

Independent History Study | I

Listen to *What in the World? Vol. 3* Disc 2, Track 6: "China and Hudson Taylor".

Key Idea: The ancient nation of China was home to the longest enduring civilization and 400 million people.

Learning the Basics
Focus: Language Arts, Math, Bible, Nature Journal, and Science

Biblical Self-Image | T |

This study has much to be gained by discussion, as it provides an excellent opportunity to share what **you** believe. Read and discuss with the students the following pages in the resource below.

★ *Who Am I? And What Am I Doing Here?* p. 30 – middle of p. 33

Key Idea: God is eternal, immutable, and omnipresent.

Language Arts | S |

Have students complete one studied dictation exercise (see Appendix for directions and passages).

Help students complete one lesson from the following reading program:

★ *Drawn into the Heart of Reading*

Help students complete **one** English option.

★ *Progressing With Courage:* Lesson 8

★ *Progressing With Courage:* Lesson 70 (last half only)

★ Your own grammar program

Key Idea: Practice language arts skills.

Bible Quiet Time | I |

Bible Study: Complete the assignment below.

★ *Faith at Work: Lesson 2 – Day Three* p. 9

Prayer Focus: Refer to **supplication** on "Preparing Your Heart for Prayer". Then, pray a prayer of supplication to make a humble and earnest request of God. Write 'supplication' at the bottom of today's lesson in *Faith at Work* above *Day Four*. Next to it, either list several key phrases or write a sentence to summarize your prayer. Keep "Preparing Your Heart for Prayer" inside your Bible.

Scripture Memory: Recite Romans 12:1-2.

Music: Refer to p. 18-19 as you sing with Track 1 *"Praise to the Lord, the Almighty"* (vs. 1-3).

Key Idea: Study Paul's missionary journeys.

Math Exploration | S |

Choose **one** of the math options listed below (see Appendix for details).

★ *Singapore Primary Mathematics 6A/6B, Discovering Mathematics 7A/7B, 8A/8B, No-Nonsense Algebra* or *Videotext Algebra*

★ Your own math program

Key Idea: Use a step-by-step math program.

Science Exploration | I |

★ Copy the Science Lab Form from the Appendix of this guide. Then, put on your safety glasses, smooth gloves, and smock as recommended on p. 6 of the *Chemistry C500 Experiment Manual*. Next, follow the directions to perform "Experiment 3" from p. 12 of the Experiment Manual. After completing Experiment 3, refer to "How to Dispose of Waste" on p. 7. Then, in the top box of the Science Lab Form write: *What will happen to a flame when it is exposed to carbon dioxide?* In the second box of the form, write your hypothesis. Reread Basic Rule 12 on p. 6 of the Experiment Manual. Follow the directions for "Experiment 4" on p. 13 of the Experiment Manual and complete the box "Perform an Experiment" on your lab form. Then, follow the arrows to complete the rest of the Science Lab Form. Next, read p. 14. To clean up, refer to "How to Dispose of Waste" on p. 7 and Basic Rules 5, 6, 7, and 11 on p. 6.

Key Idea: Oxygen is necessary for burning, or combustion. Carbon dioxide is heavier than air, so it pushes oxygen out. Carbon dioxide does not support combustion, which makes it good for extinguishing fires.

Learning Through History

Focus: Korean Bible Smuggler, Sino-Japanese War, Missions to Child Widows in India

Unit 3 - Day 1

Reading about History · I

Read about history in the following resource:

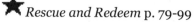 *Rescue and Redeem* p. 79-99

After today's reading, orally narrate or retell to an adult the portion of text that you read today. Some possible key words to include in your narration might be *Mukden, Samuel Moffett, John Ross, Bible translation, Korea, Robert Thomas, Captain Page, Mr. Preston, ship called 'General Sherman', Chinese Bibles, Manchuria, Han Suk-Chin,* and *decorated walls.*

Key Idea: John Ross worked on translating the Bible into the Korean language. Before Moffett began ministering in Korea, Ross told Samuel Moffett the story of Robert Thomas and his attempts to smuggle Bibles into Korea.

History Project · S

In this unit, you will write Matthew 7:12 as it appears in the Korean Common Translation. Open your *Student Notebook* to Unit 3. In Box 9, copy the portion of Matthew 7:12 shown below in Korean. You will finish the rest of Matthew 7:12 tomorrow.

너희는 남에게서 바라는 대로 남에게 해주어라.

Key Idea: There are Christians in Korea today.

President Study · I

 On *The Presidents* DVD Volume 1, select the Chapter "Washington to Monroe" and watch **only** Program 3: Thomas Jefferson. Then, open your *President Notebook* to Thomas Jefferson. Use today's viewing to add further information about Thomas Jefferson.

Key Idea: Research Thomas Jefferson.

Storytime · T/I

Read the following assigned pages:

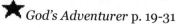 *God's Adventurer* p. 19-31

Get the bookmark that you placed in your book last unit. Choose a new section of the bookmark with **three** options at the bottom. At the top of this section of the bookmark, write the book title and the page numbers you read today. Select **one** of the three options at the bottom and place a checkmark next to it. In the blank space under today's pages, respond in writing using your checked option. Keep the bookmark in your book.

Key Idea: Relate to the text in various ways.

Timeline · I

You will be adding to the timeline in your *Student Notebook* today. In Unit 3 – Box 1, draw and color a Bible. Label it, *Robert Thomas – Korean Bible Smuggler (1865-1866 A.D.).*

In Box 2, outline and color Korea. Use the map on p. 156 of *The Story of the World: Vol. 4* to help you draw the outline of Korea. Label it, *Sino-Japanese War (1894-1895 A.D.).*

In Box 3, outline and color India. Label it, *Pandita Ramabai – Missionary to India (1881-1922 A.D.).*

Key Idea: As Korea was opening to Christians under Queen Min, Pandita Ramabai was returning to India to minister to widows.

Independent History Study · I

On p. 249 of *Rescue and Redeem,* find Mukden in China and Pyongyang in Korea. Mukden is where Samuel Moffett met John Ross. Pyongyang is where Robert Thomas was killed and Moffett eventually became a missionary.

Key Idea: Being a Christian in Korea was dangerous.

Nature Journal | I |

Read and follow the directions in the resource below to draw in your Nature Journal.

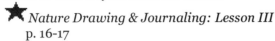 *Nature Drawing & Journaling: Lesson III* p. 16-17

Note: The lessons assume that you have also purchased a hardback sketchbook for a journal.

Key Idea: Format the inside cover of the journal.

Language Arts | S |

Help students complete one lesson from the following reading program:

★ *Drawn into the Heart of Reading*

Help students complete **one** English option.

★ *Progressing With Courage:* Lesson 9

★ *Progressing With Courage:* Lesson 71 (Save Written Exercises for Day 2.)

★ Your own grammar program

Work with the students to complete **one** of the writing options listed below:

★ *Write with the Best: Vol. 2* Unit 3 – Day 5 p. 26 (The same newspaper or magazine article used previously is needed.)

★ Your own writing program

Key Idea: Practice language arts skills.

Bible Quiet Time | I |

Bible Study: Read and complete the assigned pages in the following resource:

★ *Faith at Work: Lesson 2 – Day Four* p. 9

Prayer Focus: Get your copy of "Preparing Your Heart for Prayer" that you placed in your Bible. Refer to the questions for **adoration.** Then, pray a prayer of adoration to worship and honor God. After your prayer, write 'adoration' at the bottom of today's lesson on p. 9 in *Faith at Work*. Next to 'adoration', either list key phrases or write a sentence to summarize your prayer. Keep "Preparing Your Heart for Prayer" inside your Bible.

Scripture Memory: Read aloud Romans 12:3 three times from your Bible.

Music: Read the verse and pray the prayer from p. 19 in *Hymns for a Kid's Heart*. Refer to p. 18-19 as you sing with Track 1 *"Praise to the Lord, the Almighty"* (vs. 1-5).

Key Idea: Study Paul's missionary journeys.

Math Exploration | S |

Choose **one** of the math options listed below (see Appendix for details).

★ *Singapore Primary Mathematics 6A/6B, Discovering Mathematics 7A/7B, 8A/8B, No-Nonsense Algebra* or *Videotext Algebra*

★ Your own math program

Key Idea: Use a step-by-step math program.

Science Exploration | I |

★ Read *Exploring the World of Chemistry* p. 52-60. After reading the chapter, turn to p. 61 of *Exploring the World of Chemistry*. Write the answer to each numbered question from p. 61 on lined paper. You do not need to copy the question.

Key Idea: Because each element emits identifying bands of light, a spectroscope can use light to reveal the elements in a substance. Hidden elements like cesium, rubidium, helium, neon, argon, krypton, xenon, and radon were all revealed through the spectroscope. This helped chemists fill in the periodic table.

Learning Through History

Focus: Korean Bible Smuggler, Sino-Japanese War, Missions to Child Widows in India

Unit 3 - Day 2

Reading about History | I

Read about history in the following resource:

★ *The Story of the World: Vol. 4* p. 156 – middle of p. 161

After today's reading, open your *Student Notebook* to Unit 3. Look at the cover image in Box 7 of the French journal from August 13, 1894. This cover shows the Korean capital on the eve of the outbreak of the Sino-Japanese War. Next to the journal cover, at the top of Box 8, write your own bolded headline for the cover. Beneath your headline, write a catchy opening sentence to begin an article describing what is happening in Korea at this time. Continue the article with 3-5 more sentences.

<u>Key Idea</u>: Queen Min and King Kojong ruled Korea at the time of the outbreak of the Sino-Japanese War on Korean soil.

History Project | S

Today you will finish copying Matthew 7:12 as it appears in the Korean Common Translation. Open your *Student Notebook* to Unit 3. In Box 9, copy the last portion of Matthew 7:12 as shown below in Korean.

이것이 율법과 예언서의 정신이다.

<u>Key Idea</u>: Korea's Queen Min allowed and welcomed Christian missionaries into Korea. She showed religious tolerance to Christianity.

President Study | I

★ Read p. 10-12 in *Our Presidents*... Then, open your *President Notebook* to James Madison. Use today's reading to help you complete the information about James Madison.

<u>Key Idea</u>: Research James Madison.

Storytime | T/I

Read the following assigned pages:

★ *God's Adventurer* p. 32-47

Get the bookmark that you placed in your book. Locate the same section of the bookmark that you used on Day 1. Beneath Day 1's entry, write the book title and the page numbers you read today. Select one of the **two** remaining response options at the bottom of the bookmark, and place a checkmark next to it. In the blank space under today's pages, respond in writing using your checked option.

<u>Key Idea</u>: Relate to the text in various ways.

Geography | I

For today's activities, use the map listed below.

★ *Map Trek CD: Missions to Modern Marvels* p. 37

Get the "World Empires 1900" Student Map that you filed in your *Student Notebook* in Unit 1. Refer to the map on p. 156 in *The Story of the World: Vol. 4* to guide you as you label Korea and Japan on your Student Map. You will continue to add to your map in the next unit.

<u>Key Idea</u>: After the Sino-Japanese War ended, Queen Min tried to get Russia to be Korea's ally against Japan and China. This resulted in Queen Min's assassination on October 1895. Fifteen years later, Japan took over Korea.

Independent History Study | I

On the map on p. 156 of *The Story of the World: Vol. 4*, find Korea. Notice where China and Japan are located in relation to Korea. Find the Chinese province of Manchuria.

<u>Key Idea</u>: China and Japan fought each other in Korea during the Sino-Japanese War. After the war, China lost its control over Korea and also lost some of its large territories to Japan.

Learning the Basics
Focus: Language Arts, Math, Bible, Nature Journal, and Science

Biblical Self-Image T

Read and discuss with the students the following pages in the resource below.

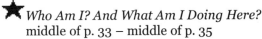 *Who Am I? And What Am I Doing Here?* middle of p. 33 – middle of p. 35

Note: This includes locating and reading the Scriptures for the first 3 bulleted traits under "God Is a Person" on p. 35.

Key Idea: God is omnipotent, omniscient, and holy. He is a personal being with creativity, thoughts, and feelings. We are created in God's image.

Language Arts S

Have students complete one studied dictation exercise (see Appendix for directions and passages).

Help students complete one lesson from the following reading program:

★ *Drawn into the Heart of Reading*

Help students complete **one** English option.

★ *Progressing With Courage:* Lesson 10

★ *Progressing With Courage:* Lesson 71 (Written Exercises only)

★ Your own grammar program

Key Idea: Practice language arts skills.

Bible Quiet Time I

Bible Study: Read and complete the assigned pages in the following resource:

★ *Faith at Work: Lesson 2 – Day Five* and *Notes* p. 10-16

Prayer Focus: Get your copy of "Preparing Your Heart for Prayer" that you placed in your Bible. Refer to the questions for **confession.** Then, pray a prayer of confession to admit or acknowledge your sins to God. After your prayer, write 'confession' at the bottom of today's lesson on p. 10 in *Faith at Work*. Next to 'confession', either list key phrases or write a sentence to summarize your prayer. This will be your prayer log. Keep "Preparing Your Heart for Prayer" inside your Bible.

Scripture Memory: Memorize Romans 12:3 from your Bible and recite it.

Music: Refer to p. 18-19 in *Hymns for a Kid's Heart* as you sing with Track 1: *"Praise to the Lord, the Almighty"* (vs. 1-5).

Key Idea: Study Paul's missionary journeys.

Math Exploration S

Choose **one** of the math options listed below (see Appendix for details).

★ *Singapore Primary Mathematics 6A/6B, Discovering Mathematics 7A/7B, 8A/8B, No-Nonsense Algebra* or *Videotext Algebra*

★ Your own math program

Key Idea: Use a step-by-step math program.

Science Exploration I

★ Read *Exploring the World of Chemistry* p. 62-68. After reading the chapter, turn to p. 69 of *Exploring the World of Chemistry*. Write the answer to each numbered question from p. 69 on lined paper. You do not need to copy the question.

Key Idea: All elements are made up of atoms. Atoms contain protons, electrons, and neutrons. Electrons are negatively charged, protons are positively charged, and neutrons have no electric charge.

Learning Through History

Focus: Korean Bible Smuggler, Sino-Japanese War, Missions to Child Widows in India

Unit 3 - Day 3

Reading about History | I

Read about history in the following resource:

 The Rescue and Redeem p. 101-105

After today's reading, open your *Student Notebook* to Unit 3 – Box 5. This is an image of the ten 20th Century Christian martyrs that are buried at Westminster Abbey in London, England. Janini Luwum is one of the ten martyrs buried there. Luwum was an Anglican Archbishop who was assassinated during Idi Amin's rule in Uganda. If you remember, Uganda was one of Africa's countries that was part of the British Empire until 1962. Luwum died in 1977.

Key Idea: Human rights and civil rights should be governed by the *Golden Rule* laid forth by Christ in God's Word in Matthew 7:12.

History Project | S

Confucius was a Chinese philosopher and teacher who influenced religion in China and Korea. As a religion, Confucianism does not show belief in a personal God. Yet, some parts of Confucianism sound like Christianity. One of the tenets of Confucianism is "What you do not wish for yourselves, do not do to others." Compare this to the words of Jesus in Matthew 7:12. What similarities and differences do you notice? Since Confucius lived over 500 years before Christ, how could Confucius' ideas sound like Christ's words? Read Matthew 22:34-40 to see where Christ's teachings on the "Golden Rule" originate. Notice that the Ten Commandments predate Confucius.

Key Idea: God's Word endures through time.

State Study | T

 This is an **optional** part of the plans. If you have chosen to study your state using *State History from a Christian Perspective,* do Lesson 3 from the *Master Lesson Plan Book.*

Key Idea: Study your individual state.

Storytime | T/I

Read the following assigned pages:

 God's Adventurer p. 48-54

After today's reading, orally narrate or retell the portion of the story that was read today. See *Narration Tips* in the Appendix as needed.

Key Idea: Practice orally narrating, or retelling, a portion of a story.

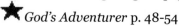

Economics | I

Read about economics in the following resource:

 Whatever Happened to Penny Candy? p. 28-30

After the reading, open your *Student Notebook* to the "Economic Principles" section at the front of your notebook. Under "Economic Principle", write one line or one sentence that summarizes the economic principle you learned from today's reading.

Key Idea: The law of supply and demand says that when the supply goes up, the price goes down. This is true for the supply of money, as well as for the supply of anything else. Inflation is an increase in the supply of money, which causes the value of the money to go down. As the value goes down, prices rise because it takes more money to buy what you need. Inflation is happening in countries all over the world, not just in America.

Independent History Study | I

Read Matthew 7:12 in your Bible. Why might this be called the *Golden Rule?* How can this verse help us know how to live our lives in a way that is pleasing to our Lord?

Key Idea: Jesus' words are written for us to live by and should help govern the way we think and act toward others.

Learning the Basics

Focus: Language Arts, Math, Bible, Nature Journal, Poetry, and Science

Unit 3 - Day 3

Nature Journal & Poetry | S |

The poetry of Longfellow, Wordsworth, and Whitman is scheduled on Day 3 in each unit to complement the nature journaling sessions. Read aloud and discuss today's poem *"A Day of Sunshine"* (see Appendix) with a parent. Then, follow the directions in the resource below.

★ *Nature Drawing & Journaling: Lesson IV* p. 18-19

Note: The lessons assume that you have also purchased a hardback sketchbook for a journal.

Key Idea: Practice using portrait and landscape figure boxes to format your page.

Language Arts | S |

Have students complete one studied dictation exercise (see Appendix for passages).

Help students complete **one** English option.

★ *Progressing With Courage:* Lesson 11

★ *Progressing With Courage:* Lesson 72 (p. 316-317 Class Practice 'A' – 'G' only)

★ Your own grammar program

Work with the students to complete **one** of the writing options listed below:

★ *Write with the Best: Vol. 2* Unit 3 – Day 6 p. 26-27 (The same newspaper or magazine article used previously is needed.)

★ Your own writing program

Key Idea: Practice language arts skills.

Bible Quiet Time | I |

Bible Study: Read and complete the assigned pages in the following resource:

★ *Faith at Work: Lesson 3 – Day One* p. 17
Note: Refer to p. 12-16 for help with the lesson.

Prayer Focus: Get your copy of "Preparing Your Heart for Prayer" that you placed in your Bible. Refer to the questions for **thanksgiving**. Then, pray a prayer of thanksgiving to express gratitude to God for His divine goodness. After your prayer, write 'thanksgiving' at the bottom of today's lesson on p. 17 in *Faith at Work*. Next to 'thanksgiving', either list key phrases or write a sentence to summarize your prayer. This will be your prayer log. Keep "Preparing Your Heart for Prayer" inside your Bible.

Scripture Memory: Copy Romans 12:3 in your Common Place Book.

Music: Refer to p. 18-19 in *Hymns for a Kid's Heart* as you sing with Track 1: *"Praise to the Lord, the Almighty"* (vs. 1-5).

Key Idea: Study Paul's missionary journeys.

Math Exploration | S |

Choose **one** of the math options listed below (see Appendix for details).

★ *Singapore Primary Mathematics 6A/6B, Discovering Mathematics 7A/7B, 8A/8B, No-Nonsense Algebra* or *Videotext Algebra*

★ Your own math program

Key Idea: Use a step-by-step math program.

Science Exploration | I |

★ Read *Exploring the World of Chemistry* p. 70-76. After reading the chapter, turn to p. 77 of *Exploring the World of Chemistry*. Write the answer to each numbered question from p. 77 on lined paper. You do not need to copy the question.

Key Idea: Atoms have a central nucleus surrounded by negatively charged electrons. A chemical reaction takes place when atoms gain, lose, or share electrons. Atoms form compounds as unlike charges attract.

Reading about History I

Read about history in the following resource:

 Rescue and Redeem p. 107-126
Note: p. 109-110 contain violent descriptions.

You will be writing a narration about the chapter *Pandita Ramabai: Miseries Into Sweetnesses*. To prepare for writing your narration, look back over p. 107-126 in *Rescue and Redeem*. Think about the main idea and the most important moments in this part of the reading.

After you have thought about what you will write and how you will begin your narration, turn to Unit 3 in your *Student Notebook*. For more guidance on writing a narration, see *Written Narration Tips* in the Appendix.

In Box 4, write a 12-16 sentence narration about the reading. When you have finished writing, read your sentences out loud to catch any mistakes. Check for the following things: *Did you include* **who** *or* **what topic** *the reading was mainly about? Did you include* **descriptors** *of the important thing(s) that happened? Did you include a* **closing sentence**? *If not, add those things.* Use the *Written Narration Skills* in the Appendix as a guide for editing the narration.

Key Idea: Pandita Ramabai helped Brahmin Hindu child-widows by founding Sharada Sadan, House of Wisdom. In founding the school, Pandita had to agree not to teach the Bible or stop her students from worshipping Hindu gods, but she did leave her door open during prayer time and did not hide her love of Jesus. Pandita originally suffered for sharing Jesus with her students, but over time her school grew and she opened Mukti, "Salvation".

President Study I

 On *The Presidents* DVD Volume 1, select the Chapter "Washington to Monroe" and watch **only** Program 4: James Madison. Then, open your *President Notebook* to James Madison. Use today's viewing to add further information about James Madison.

Key Idea: Research James Madison.

Storytime T/I

Read the following assigned pages:

 God's Adventurer p. 55-63

Get the bookmark that you placed in your book. Locate the same section of the bookmark that you used on Day 2. Beneath Day 2's entry, write the book title and the page numbers you read today. Select the one remaining response option at the bottom of the bookmark, and place a checkmark next to it. In the blank space under today's pages, respond in writing using your checked option.

Key Idea: Relate to the text in various ways.

Worthy Words T

Open your *Student Notebook* to Unit 3. Read the excerpt in Box 10. After reading the excerpt, answer the following questions on an index card: *What is Pandita's past prior to learning about the Bible? How does her past give her the desire to know more about Christianity? When does she realize that Hinduism and Christianity are very different? What can you learn from Pandita's thoughts on the difference between 'finding the Christian religion' and 'finding Christ'?* Next, meet with a parent to have a Socratic dialogue about the speech. A Socratic dialogue is one in which the participants come prepared to share their thoughts, feelings, and opinions about the spoken/written word. Before beginning the dialogue, the parent reads Box 10 out loud. Next, discuss the questions using your notes. All participants should use life experiences and/or the text to support their responses.

Key Idea: Pandita read her Bible to find Christ.

Independent History Study I

Open your *Student Notebook* to Unit 3. Choose an important part of the excerpt from Box 10 to copy in quotation marks in Box 6 and write "Pandita Ramabai" at the bottom.

Key Idea: Pandita was a widow in India.

Learning the Basics
Focus: Language Arts, Math, Bible, Nature Journal, and Science

Biblical Self-Image [T]

Read and discuss with the students the following pages in the resource below.

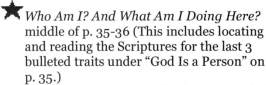 *Who Am I? And What Am I Doing Here?* middle of p. 35-36 (This includes locating and reading the Scriptures for the last 3 bulleted traits under "God Is a Person" on p. 35.)

Note: Discuss responses to "Make a Note of It" on p. 36 rather than writing them.

Key Idea: God is without sin or imperfection.

Language Arts [S]

Have students complete one studied dictation exercise (see Appendix for directions and passages).

Help students complete one lesson from the following reading program:

⭐ *Drawn into the Heart of Reading*

Help students complete **one** English option.

⭐ *Progressing With Courage:* Lesson 12

⭐ *Progressing With Courage:* Lesson 72 (p. 317-318 Written Exercises 'A' – 'D' only)

⭐ Your own grammar program

Key Idea: Practice language arts skills.

Bible Quiet Time [I]

Bible Study: Complete the assignment below.

⭐ *Faith at Work: Lesson 3 – Day Two* p. 18

Prayer Focus: Refer to **supplication** on "Preparing Your Heart for Prayer". Then, pray a prayer of supplication to make a humble and earnest request of God. Write 'supplication' at the bottom of today's lesson in *Faith at Work* above *Day Three*. Next to it, either list several key phrases or write a sentence to summarize your prayer. Keep "Preparing Your Heart for Prayer" inside your Bible.

Scripture Memory: Recite Romans 12:1-3.

Music: Refer to p. 18-19 in *Hymns for a Kid's Heart* as you sing with Track 1: *"Praise to the Lord, the Almighty"* (vs. 1-5).

Key Idea: Study Romans 1:1-17.

Math Exploration [S]

Choose **one** of the math options listed below (see Appendix for details).

⭐ *Singapore Primary Mathematics 6A/6B, Discovering Mathematics 7A/7B, 8A/8B, No-Nonsense Algebra* or *Videotext Algebra*

⭐ Your own math program

Key Idea: Use a step-by-step math program.

Science Exploration [I]

⭐ Put on your safety glasses, smooth gloves, and smock as recommended on p. 6 of the *Chemistry C500 Experiment Manual*. Next, reread p. 4-5. Then, read the directions to perform "Experiment 5" from p. 16 of the Experiment Manual. Follow only **steps 1-2** today. Allow the sealed test tube to sit overnight before doing steps 3 and 4. **Note:** You will need denatured alcohol, or methylated spirits, for steps 3-4 of the experiment.

After the sealed test tube has been allowed to sit overnight, proceed with steps 3-4 on p. 16 of the Experiment Manual. **You will need a parent's help** for these steps. After completing Experiment 5, refer to "How to Dispose of Waste" on p. 7. To clean up, refer to Basic Rules 5, 6, 7, and 11 on p. 6. You will use the litmus solution that you made in Experiment 5 in future experiments.

Key Idea: Litmus is a type of dye made up of plant-derived materials. The dye causes acid to produce characteristic colors. Adding a small amount of denatured alcohol extends the shelf life of litmus solution.

Learning Through History

Focus: The Fight for Land in the U.S. and for Independence in Hawaii and Cuba

Unit 4 - Day 1

Reading about History | S

Read about history in the following resource:

★ *Rescue and Redeem* p. 127-147

After today's reading, orally narrate or retell to an adult the portion of text that you read today. As you retell, the adult will write or type your narration. Some possible key words to include in your narration might be *Uncle Kalakaua, monarch, Hawaii, Aunt Lili'uokalani, Four Sacred Ones, Princess Ka'iulani, England, Christian, American businessmen, landowners, vote, Annexation Treaty, Grover Cleveland, President McKinley, grand dinner, aloha*. When the narration is complete, fold the typed or written narration to fit in Unit 4 – Box 9 of the *Student Notebook*. Glue the folded narration in Box 9, so it can be opened and read.

Key Idea: Ka'iulani was a Hawaiian princess.

History Project | S

Today you will begin making a lei, or a Hawaiian flower necklace. On an index card, draw the outline of a flower that is about 3½" in diameter with scalloped edges. This will be your pattern. Cut the flower pattern out. Then, lay the pattern on top of a piece of black paper, trace around it, and cut the traced black flower out. Next, trace around the pattern and cut out 13 more black flowers so that you have 14 flowers in all. After that lay the flowers flat on a paper towel, and use oil pastels to color around the outside edge of each flower. Last, use oil pastels to draw lines radiating out from the center of each flower. Do this to both sides.

Key Idea: A lei is a symbol of affection or love.

Storytime | T/I

Read the following assigned pages:

★ *God's Adventurer* p. 64-79

Get the bookmark that you placed in your book last unit. Choose a new section of the bookmark with **three** options at the bottom. At the top of this section of the bookmark, write the book title and the page numbers you read today. Select **one** of the three options at the bottom and place a checkmark next to it. In the blank space under today's pages, respond in writing using your checked option. Keep the bookmark in your book.

Key Idea: Relate to the text in various ways.

Timeline | I

You will be adding to the timeline in your *Student Notebook* today. In Unit 4 – Box 1, draw and color the head of a longhorn cow. Label it, *Era of Long Cattle Drives (1865-1885 A.D.)*.

In Box 2, draw and color a flowered lei. Label it, *Hawaii Is Annexed to the United States (July 7, 1898 A.D.)*.

In Box 3, draw and color an exploding ship with 'The Maine' on it. Label it, *Spanish-American War (1898 A.D.)*.

Key Idea: Soon after the long Texas cattle drives ended, and the west was becoming more settled, Hawaii was annexed to the United States. The same year of Hawaii's annexation, the U.S. went to war with Spain over Cuba.

Independent History Study | I

★ On p. 8 of *Rescue and Redeem,* read through the entries from 1883-1893 on the "Modern Church Timeline". What interesting facts do you notice?

Key Idea: Princess Ka'iulani was educated in England. In 1893, when she was 17, Ka'iulani visited the United States to address the American people. She did not return to Hawaii until November 9, 1897.

Learning the Basics

Focus: Language Arts, Math, Bible, Nature Journal, and Science

Nature Journal [I]

Read and follow the directions in the resource below to draw in your Nature Journal.

⭐ *Nature Drawing & Journaling: Lesson V*
p. 20-21

Note: Today you will only do the illustration to frame your page. On Unit 4 – Day 3 you will add the composition, or writing to the page.

Key Idea: Practice framing a journal page with an illustration.

Language Arts [S]

Help students complete one lesson from the following reading program:

⭐ *Drawn into the Heart of Reading*

Help students complete **one** English option.

⭐ *Progressing With Courage:* Lesson 13

⭐ *Progressing With Courage:* Lesson 72
   (p. 318-319 Written Exercises 'E' – 'H only)

⭐ Your own grammar program

Work with the students to complete **one** of the writing options listed below:

⭐ *Write with the Best: Vol. 2* Unit 3 – Day 7
   p. 27 (Your notes, outline, and topic
   sentence from previous days are needed.)

⭐ Your own writing program

Key Idea: Practice language arts skills.

Bible Quiet Time [I]

Bible Study: Read and complete the assigned pages in the following resource:

⭐ *Faith at Work: Lesson 3 – Day Three*
p. 18

Prayer Focus: Refer to **adoration** on "Preparing Your Heart for Prayer". Then, pray a prayer of adoration to worship and honor God. After your prayer, write 'adoration' at the bottom of today's lesson in *Faith at Work* above *Day Four*. Next to 'adoration', either list key phrases or write a sentence to summarize your prayer. Keep "Preparing Your Heart for Prayer" inside your Bible.

Scripture Memory: Read aloud Romans 12:4-5 three times from your Bible.

Music: Read p. 21-22 in *Hymns for a Kid's Heart.* Refer to p. 24 as you sing with Track 2 "*Fairest Lord Jesus*" (verse 1).

Key Idea: Read and study Romans 1:1-17.

Math Exploration [S]

Choose **one** of the math options listed below (see Appendix for details).

⭐ *Singapore Primary Mathematics 6A/6B,
   Discovering Mathematics 7A/7B, 8A/8B,
   No-Nonsense Algebra* or *Videotext Algebra*

⭐ Your own math program

Key Idea: Use a step-by-step math program.

Science Exploration [I]

⭐ Read *Exploring the World of Chemistry* p. 78-84. After reading the chapter, turn to p. 85 of *Exploring the World of Chemistry*. Write the answer to each numbered question from p. 85 on lined paper. You do not need to copy the question.

Key Idea: The uneven electric charge around the water molecule attracts molecules from other substances. Bentley's photographs of snowflakes showed that water molecules attract to each other. Water molecules also absorb heat energy from the electrical attraction between molecules.

Reading about History | I |

Read about history in the following resources:

 *The Story of the World: Vol. 4* bottom of p. 161-167

★ *Great Events in American History* p. 59-61

After today's reading, open your *Student Notebook* to Unit 4 – Box 7. Read the headlines of the front page of the *New York Journal* shown in Box 7. William Hearst owned the *New York Journal*. In Box 8, copy Hearst's quote from the bottom of p. 164 of *The Story of the World*. Write 'William Randolph Hearst' beneath the quote. How does this quote better explain the headlines in Box 7? What perspective of the war does p. 59-61 of *Great Events in American History* provide?

<u>Key Idea</u>. During the "Cuban crisis", as Cubans fought for independence from Spain, American newspapers often inflated stories to sell papers.

History Project | S |

Today you will make paper beads for your lei. Look at your lei and choose two different paper colors that will go well with the colors of your lei. Cut out six 2"x 6" strips of one color paper and six 2"x 6" strips of the other color paper. Roll one strip of paper tightly around a pencil. Then, slide the paper bead off the pencil and use clear tape or a gluestick to secure the paper's edge to form a tube-shaped bead. You will make 12 beads in all. Save them for Day 3.

<u>Key Idea</u>: Leis are a Polynesian island tradition. Hawaii is a U.S. state made up of islands. Cuba and the Philippines are islands too.

President Study | I |

★ Read p. 13 in *Our Presidents...* Then, open your *President Notebook* to James Monroe. Use today's reading to help you complete the information about James Monroe.

<u>Key Idea</u>: Research James Monroe.

Storytime | T/I |

Read the following assigned pages:

★ *God's Adventurer* p. 80-94

Get the bookmark that you placed in your book. Locate the same section of the bookmark that you used on Day 1. Beneath Day 1's entry, write the book title and the page numbers you read today. Select one of the **two** remaining response options at the bottom of the bookmark, and place a checkmark next to it. In the blank space under today's pages, respond in writing using your checked option. Place your bookmark in your book.

<u>Key Idea</u>: Relate to the text in various ways.

Geography | I |

For today's activities, use the map listed below.

★ *Map Trek CD: Missions to Modern Marvels* p. 37

Get the "World Empires 1900" Student Map that you filed in your *Student Notebook* in Unit 1. Refer to *The Story of the World: Vol. 4* p. 162 to guide you as you label Cuba, Puerto Rico, and the Philippine Islands on your Student Map. Color these places pink to show the U.S. ruled them after the war. Then, find these same places (including Guam) on p. 35 of the *United States History Atlas*.

<u>Key Idea</u>: Due to Spain's actions in Cuba, the U.S. declared war on Spain on April 19, 1898. U.S. ships attacked the Spanish navy in Cuba, Puerto Rico, and the Philippines. Spain surrendered, and the Treaty of Paris was signed on December 10, 1898.

Independent History Study | I |

Listen to *What in the World? Vol. 3* Disc 2, Track 7: "Japan, Salvation Army, & Spanish-American War".

<u>Key Idea</u>: The sinking of the *Maine* led to war.

Learning the Basics
Focus: Language Arts, Math, Bible, Nature Journal, and Science

Biblical Self-Image [T]

Our plans intend for the listed pages in *Who Am I? And What Am I Doing Here?* to be read either silently by both you and your student, or read aloud to the student by you. With this in mind, read and discuss the following pages in the resource below.

 Who Am I? And What Am I Doing Here? p. 37-43

Key Idea: All people are valuable to God because God created us in His image. The biblical Christian view of God differs from the Muslim view of Allah.

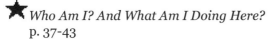

Language Arts [S]

Have students complete one studied dictation exercise (see Appendix for directions and passages).

Help students complete one lesson from the following reading program:

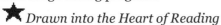 *Drawn into the Heart of Reading*

Help students complete **one** English option.

★ *Progressing With Courage:* Lesson 14

★ *Progressing With Courage:* Lesson 73 (first half only)

★ Your own grammar program

Key Idea: Practice language arts skills.

Bible Quiet Time [I]

Bible Study: Read and complete the assigned pages in the following resource:

★ *Faith at Work: Lesson 3 – Day Four* p. 18-19

Prayer Focus: Refer to **confession** on "Preparing Your Heart for Prayer". Then, pray a prayer of confession to admit or acknowledge your sins to God. After your prayer, write 'confession' at the bottom of today's lesson in *Faith at Work* above *Day Five*. Next to 'confession', either list key phrases or write a sentence to summarize your prayer. This will be your prayer log. Keep "Preparing Your Heart for Prayer" inside your Bible.

Scripture Memory: Memorize Romans 12:4-5 from your Bible and recite it.

Music: Refer to p. 24 in *Hymns for a Kid's Heart* as you sing with Track 2: *"Fairest Lord Jesus"* (verse 1).

Key Idea: Read and study Romans 1:1-17.

Math Exploration [S]

Choose **one** of the math options listed below (see Appendix for details).

★ *Singapore Primary Mathematics 6A/6B, Discovering Mathematics 7A/7B, 8A/8B, No-Nonsense Algebra* or *Videotext Algebra*

★ Your own math program

Key Idea: Use a step-by-step math program.

Science Exploration [I]

★ Read *Exploring the World of Chemistry* p. 86-94. After reading the chapter, turn to p. 95 of *Exploring the World of Chemistry*. Write the answer to each numbered question from p. 95 on lined paper. You do not need to copy the question.

Key Idea: Carbon forms more compounds than any other element because carbon atoms readily share electrons with other elements in many different ways.

Learning Through History
Focus: The Fight for Land in the U.S. and for Independence in Hawaii and Cuba
Unit 4 - Day 3

Reading about History | I

Read about history in the following resource:

★ *All American History: Vol. II* p. 155 – middle of p. 161
After today's reading, open your *Student Notebook* to Unit 4 – Box 5. Look at the poster for Pawnee Bill's Wild West Show from 1903. This poster advertises seats available for 10,000 people to see a group of over 1000 people and horses; including an army of Indians, scouts, cowboys, and early pioneers. How does this poster help you glimpse the things for which the Wild West was known?

Key Idea: The American central plains were referred to as the "Great American Desert", before this area was settled by early pioneers. As pioneers traveled west and cultivated the land, this area's rich soil made it one of the best agricultural areas in the world! Farming, mining, and cattle ranching were all occupations in the western frontier.

History Project | S

Today, you will assemble your lei. Cut a 30" piece of string or yarn. Use clear tape to tape one end of the string/yarn, so you can thread it through your flowers and your beads. Then, tie a large knot on the other end of the string/yarn. Use a scissors to poke a hole in the center of each flower. Then, thread the yarn through one flower and slide the flower down to the knot. Next, thread the yarn through one colored bead and slide the bead down to the flower. Continue alternating flowers and beads until they are all threaded. Then, tie the two ends of the string/yarn together and try it on.

Key Idea: A lei can be a gesture of goodwill.

State Study | T

★ This is an **optional** part of the plans. If you have chosen to study your state using *State History from a Christian Perspective*, do Lesson 4 from the *Master Lesson Plan Book*.
Key Idea: Study your individual state.

Storytime | T/I

Read the following assigned pages:

★ *God's Adventurer* p. 95-112

After today's reading, orally narrate or retell the portion of the story that was read today. See *Narration Tips* in the Appendix as needed.

Key Idea: Practice orally narrating, or retelling, a portion of a story.

Worthy Words | T

Read, analyze, and evaluate the speech below.

★ *Book of Great American Speeches for Young People* p. 99-100
After reading the speech, answer the following questions on an index card: *Summarize the history of the Chiricahua Apaches that Cochise gives at the beginning of this speech. Which 3 groups of people came to settle in New Mexico and fought with the Apaches? Why does Cochise wish to end the war with the white man? Do you think that Cochise was being honest in this speech? Explain. What are your thoughts about Native American Indian reservations?* Next, meet with a parent to have a Socratic dialogue about the speech. Before beginning the dialogue, the parent reads the speech out loud. Next, discuss the questions using your notes. All participants should use life experiences and/or the text to support their responses.

Key Idea: As settlers moved west, the battle for land waged. Over time, the Native Americans lost land and were moved to reservations.

Independent History Study | I

Open your *Student Notebook* to Unit 4. Choose an important part of the speech from p. 99-100 of *Book of Great American Speeches...* to copy in quotation marks in Box 6. Write "Cochise" at the bottom of Box 6.

Key Idea: Cochise was an Apache chief.

Learning the Basics
Focus: Language Arts, Math, Bible, Nature Journal, Poetry, and Science

Nature Journal & Poetry 〔S〕

The poetry of Longfellow, Wordsworth, and Whitman is scheduled on Day 3 in each unit to complement the nature journaling sessions. Read aloud and discuss today's poem *"Lines Written in Early Spring"* (see Appendix) with a parent. Then, read the journal entry in the resource below.

★ *Nature Drawing & Journaling* p. 24
Note: Today, you will add writing to the journal page that you framed on Unit 4 – Day 1. If you are not sure what to write, you may wish to copy the poem that you studied today.

<u>Key Idea</u>: Add composition to a journal entry.

Language Arts 〔S〕

Have students complete one studied dictation exercise (see Appendix for passages).

Help students complete **one** English option.

★ *Progressing With Courage:* Lesson 15

★ *Progressing With Courage:* Lesson 73 (last half only)

★ Your own grammar program

Work with the students to complete **one** of the writing options listed below:

★ *Write with the Best: Vol. 2* Unit 3 – Day 8 p. 27 (The "How to Write a Summary" guide is on p. 90-91.)

★ Your own writing program

<u>Key Idea</u>: Practice language arts skills.

Bible Quiet Time 〔I〕

Bible Study: Read and complete the assigned pages in the following resource:

★ *Faith at Work: Lesson 3 – Day Five, Bible Skill Builder,* and *Notes* p. 19-24

Prayer Focus: Refer to the questions for **thanksgiving** on "Preparing Your Heart for Prayer". Then, pray a prayer of thanksgiving to express gratitude to God for His divine goodness. After your prayer, write 'thanksgiving' at the bottom of today's lesson on p. 19 in *Faith at Work*. Next to 'thanksgiving', either list key phrases or write a sentence to summarize your prayer. This will be your prayer log. Keep "Preparing Your Heart for Prayer" inside your Bible.

Scripture Memory: Copy Romans 12:4-5 in your Common Place Book.

Music: Refer to p. 24 in *Hymns for a Kid's Heart* as you sing with Track 2: *"Fairest Lord Jesus"* (verse 1).

<u>Key Idea</u>: Read and study Romans 1:1-17.

Math Exploration 〔S〕

Choose **one** of the math options listed below (see Appendix for details).

★ *Singapore Primary Mathematics 6A/6B, Discovering Mathematics 7A/7B, 8A/8B, No-Nonsense Algebra* or *Videotext Algebra*

★ Your own math program

<u>Key Idea</u>: Use a step-by-step math program.

Science Exploration 〔I〕

★ Read *Exploring the World of Chemistry* p. 96-102. After reading the chapter, turn to p. 103 of *Exploring the World of Chemistry*. Write the answer to each numbered question from p. 103 on lined paper. You do not need to copy the question.

<u>Key Idea</u>: Compounds that came from living organisms, or plants and animals, were called organic compounds. Eventually, chemists could make organic compounds in the lab. Since these compounds all contained carbon, organic chemistry then became the study of carbon compounds.

Reading about History | I

Read about history in the following resource:

 *All American History: Vol. II* middle of p. 161-167

★ **Optional:** *The Story of the World: Vol. 4* p. 168 – middle of p. 173

You will be writing a narration about **either** the cowboys **or** the Native Americans you read about today. To prepare for writing your narration, look back over p. 161-165 in *All American History: Vol. II.* Think about the main idea and the most important moments in this part of the reading.

After you have thought about what you will write and how you will begin your narration, turn to Unit 4 in your *Student Notebook.* For more guidance on writing a narration, see *Written Narration Tips* in the Appendix.

In Box 4, write a 12-16 sentence narration about the reading. When you have finished writing, read your sentences out loud to catch any mistakes. Check for the following things: *Did you include* **who** *or* **what topic** *the reading was mainly about? Did you include* **descriptors** *of the important thing(s) that happened? Did you include a* **closing sentence**? *If not, add those things.* Use the *Written Narration Skills* in the Appendix as a guide for editing the narration.

Key Idea: 1865-1885 was the era of the longhorn cattle drive. The Santa Fe Trail, Goodnight-Loving Trail, and Chisholm Trail were the most important cow trails. With the arrival of the railroad, the open range came to a close. During this same time, the slaughter of the buffalo and the seizing of land eventually forced Native Americans onto reservations.

Storytime | T/I

Read the following assigned pages:

★ *Factory Girl* p. 5-23

Get the bookmark that you placed in your book. Locate the same section of the bookmark that you used on Day 2. Beneath Day 2's entry, write the book title and the page numbers you read today. Select the one remaining response option at the bottom of the bookmark, and place a checkmark next to it. In the blank space under today's pages, respond in writing using your checked option. Keep the bookmark in your book.

Key Idea: Relate to the text in various ways.

Economics | I

Read about economics in the resource below.

★ *Whatever Happened to Penny Candy?* p. 31-38

After the reading, open your *Student Notebook* to the "Economic Principles" section at the front of your notebook. Under "Economic Principle", write a one line or one sentence summary for the economic principle you learned from today's reading.

Key Idea: A dollar represents one ounce of silver. Up until 1960, a dollar was an IOU or a banknote for one ounce of silver that was on deposit at the U.S. Treasury. Today, the dollar is a Federal Reserve Note, instead of a Silver Certificate. Law backs the legal tender statement on the note, because unless people will trade for it it's not considered money.

President Study | I

★ On *The Presidents* DVD Volume 1, select the Chapter "Washington to Monroe" and watch **only** Program 5: James Monroe. Then, open your *President Notebook* to James Monroe. Use today's viewing to add further information about James Monroe.

Key Idea: Research James Monroe.

Independent History Study | I

On p. 30 of the *United States History Atlas,* notice the land lost by Native Americans between 1850-1890. Then, find where the reservations are located. Next, compare the trails in the *United States History Atlas* p. 32 to the trails on p. 157 of *All American History.*

Key Idea: The open range diminished quickly.

Learning the Basics
Focus: Language Arts, Math, Bible, Nature Journal, and Science

Biblical Self-Image   T

Read and discuss with the students the following pages in the resource below.

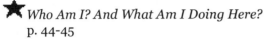 *Who Am I? And What Am I Doing Here?* p. 44-45

Key Idea: God gives us truths within His Word, the Bible, upon which our lives should be based. When we believe in Jesus as God's only Son, we will work to become more like Him.

Language Arts   S

Have students complete one studied dictation exercise (see Appendix for directions and passages).

Help students complete one lesson from the following reading program:

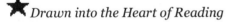 *Drawn into the Heart of Reading*

Help students complete **one** English option.

★ *Progressing With Courage:* Lesson 16

★ *Progressing With Courage:* Lesson 74 (first half only)

★ Your own grammar program

Key Idea: Practice language arts skills.

Bible Quiet Time   I

Bible Study: Complete the assignment below.

★ *Faith at Work: Lesson 4 – Day One* p. 25
Note: Refer to p. 20-24 to complete the lesson.

Prayer Focus: Refer to **supplication** on "Preparing Your Heart for Prayer". Then, pray a prayer of supplication to make a humble and earnest request of God. Write 'supplication' at the bottom of today's lesson in *Faith at Work* above *Day Two*. Next to it, either list several key phrases or write a sentence to summarize your prayer. Keep "Preparing Your Heart for Prayer" inside your Bible.

Scripture Memory: Recite Romans 12:1-5.

Music: Refer to p. 24 in *Hymns for a Kid's Heart* as you sing with Track 2: *"Fairest Lord Jesus"* (verse 1).

Key Idea: Read and study Romans 1:1-17.

Math Exploration   S

Choose **one** of the math options listed below (see Appendix for details).

★ *Singapore Primary Mathematics 6A/6B, Discovering Mathematics 7A/7B, 8A/8B, No-Nonsense Algebra* or *Videotext Algebra*

★ Your own math program

Key Idea: Use a step-by-step math program.

Science Exploration   I

★ Copy the Science Lab Form from the Appendix of this guide. Then, put on your safety glasses, smooth gloves, and smock as recommended on p. 6 of the *Chemistry C500 Experiment Manual*. Next, follow the directions to perform "Experiment 6" from p. 17 of the Experiment Manual. After completing Experiment 6, in the top box of the Science Lab Form write: *What will happen to the blue litmus solution when tartaric acid is added?* In the second box of the form, write your hypothesis. Follow the directions for "Experiment 7" on p. 18 of the Experiment Manual and complete the box "Perform an Experiment" on your lab form. If you do not have a lemon, you can skip step 2 on p. 18. Then, follow the arrows to complete the rest of the Science Lab Form. To clean up, refer to "How to Dispose of Waste" on p. 7 and Basic Rules 5, 6, 7, and 11 on p. 6.

Key Idea: Litmus is a type of dye made up of plant-derived materials. The litmus dye causes acids, like tartaric acid and citric acid, to produce characteristic color changes.

Learning Through History
Focus: Industrialization and Immigration in the Gilded Age

Unit 5 - Day 1

Reading about History | I |

Read about history in the following resources:

★ *All American History: Vol. II* p. 169 – top of p. 174

★ *Great Events in American History* p. 71-73
Note: p. 72-73 contain graphic descriptions.

After today's reading, orally narrate or retell to an adult the portion of text that you read today from *All American History*. Some possible key words to include in your narration might be *Gilded Age, industrialization, factories, cities, immigration, Chicago Fire 1871, San Francisco Earthquake 1906, fortunes, John Rockefeller, Andrew Carnegie, Cornelius Vanderbilt, "muckraker" journalists, Pilgrim's Progress, labor unions,* and *AFL.*

Key Idea: As families moved to the cities for factory jobs, industrialization shaped American life during the Gilded Age. Urbanization led to new problems and new advancements.

History Project | S |

In this unit, you will learn about Andrew Carnegie, the richest man in the world in 1901. To read about Carnegie's life, use **one** of the following Internet addresses:
http://www.pbs.org/wgbh/amex/carnegie/sfeature/meet.html

http://www.americaslibrary.gov/aa/carnegie/aa_carnegie_parents_1.html

http://www.ushistory.org/us/36c.asp

Key Idea: Andrew Carnegie owned Carnegie Steel and was a prominent industrialist in the U.S. during the Gilded Age.

President Study | I |

★ Read p. 14-15 in *Our Presidents…* Then, open your *President Notebook* to John Quincy Adams. Use today's reading to help you complete the information about him.
Key Idea: Research John Quincy Adams.

Storytime | T/I |

Read the following assigned pages:

★ *Factory Girl* p. 24-39
Get the bookmark that you placed in your book. Choose a new section of the bookmark with **three** options at the bottom. At the top of this section of the bookmark, write the book title and the page numbers you read today. Select **one** of the three options at the bottom and place a checkmark next to it. In the blank space under today's pages, respond in writing using your checked option.

Key Idea: Relate to the text in various ways.

Worthy Words | T |

Read, analyze, and evaluate the speech below.

★ *Book of Great American Speeches for Young People* p. 127-128
After reading the speech, answer the following questions on an index card: *Why did Rose Schneiderman give this speech? Why do you think the factory doors were locked and the fire escape was barred? If the conditions were so bad, why didn't the girls work somewhere else? How would the perspective of the speech change if the Triangle Shirtwaist Co. was giving the speech? Why was the charity gift not appreciated or accepted?* Next, meet with a parent to have a Socratic dialogue about the speech. Before beginning the dialogue, the parent reads the speech out loud. Next, discuss the questions using your notes. All participants should use life experiences and/or the text to support their responses.

Key Idea: Unions fought for child labor laws.

Independent History Study | I |

Choose an important part of the speech from p. 116 of *Book of Great American Speeches…* to copy in quotation marks in your *Student Notebook* Unit 5 – Box 6. Write "Harry Gladstone" at the bottom of Box 6.

Key Idea: Children worked just like adults did.

Learning the Basics
Focus: Language Arts, Math, Bible, Nature Journal, and Science

Nature Journal | I

Read and follow the directions in the resource below to draw in your Nature Journal.

 *Nature Drawing & Journaling: Lesson VI* p. 22-23

Note: Make sure to cut the legal-sized paper to fit the page in your journal before beginning to work. You do not have to fill the page but rather just make a beginning today.

Key Idea: Format the left side of the journal.

Language Arts | S

Help students complete one lesson from the following reading program:

 *Drawn into the Heart of Reading*

Help students complete **one** English option.

★ *Progressing With Courage:* Lesson 17

★ *Progressing With Courage:* Lesson 74 (last half only)

★ Your own grammar program

Work with the students to complete **one** of the writing options listed below:

★ *Write with the Best: Vol. 2* Unit 3 – Day 9 p. 28 (Note: You are proofreading the summary that you wrote of the article.)

★ Your own writing program

Key Idea: Practice language arts skills.

Bible Quiet Time | I

Bible Study: Read and complete the assigned pages in the following resource:

★ *Faith at Work: Lesson 4 – Day Two* p. 25-26

Prayer Focus: Refer to **adoration** on "Preparing Your Heart for Prayer". Then, pray a prayer of adoration to worship and honor God. After your prayer, write 'adoration' at the bottom of today's lesson in *Faith at Work* above *Day Three*. Next to 'adoration', either list key phrases or write a sentence to summarize your prayer. Keep "Preparing Your Heart for Prayer" inside your Bible.

Scripture Memory: Read aloud Romans 12:6 three times from your Bible.

Music: Read p. 23 in *Hymns for a Kid's Heart*. Refer to p. 24-25 in *Hymns for a Kid's Heart* as you sing with Track 2: *"Fairest Lord Jesus"* (vs. 1-2).

Key Idea: Read and study Romans 1:18-32.

Math Exploration | S

Choose **one** of the math options listed below (see Appendix for details).

★ *Singapore Primary Mathematics 6A/6B, Discovering Mathematics 7A/7B, 8A/8B, No-Nonsense Algebra* or *Videotext Algebra*

★ Your own math program

Key Idea: Use a step-by-step math program.

Science Exploration | I

★ Read *Exploring the World of Chemistry* p. 104-110. After reading the chapter, turn to p. 111 of *Exploring the World of Chemistry*. Write the answer to each numbered question from p. 111 on lined paper. You do not need to copy the question.

Key Idea: Explosives contain carbon, but their essential element is nitrogen. Nitrogen does not form compounds easily and must be forced near other atoms to share its electrons. This makes nitrogen compounds unstable. Nitroglycerin was discovered when glycerin was added to nitric acid and sulfuric acid. Alfred Nobel worked to make nitroglycerin safe to transport and use. He invented dynamite.

Learning Through History
Focus: Industrialization and Immigration in the Gilded Age

Unit 5 - Day 2

Reading about History | I |

Read about history in the following resource:

 The Story of the World: Vol. 4 bottom of p. 173-177

After today's reading, open your *Student Notebook* to Unit 5 - Box 7, which shows Frank Leslie's *Illustrated Weekly* from July 14, 1892. The headline highlights the Homestead Lockout that took place at Carnegie Steel in Homestead, PA. The fight was between Pinkerton detectives and AA Labor Union workers. Read the first paragraph at the top of p. 174 in *All American History* to better understand the importance of this strike. Then, choose an important portion of this paragraph to copy in Box 8.

Key Idea: Andrew Carnegie became a rich man through Carnegie Steel. He was a philanthropist, but he also had labor issues with his steel workers.

History Project | S |

Today you will read about Carnegie's work ethic and his steel business. Use **one** of the following Internet addresses to research this:
http://www.pbs.org/wgbh/amex/carnegie/sfeature/mf_flames.html

http://www.americaslibrary.gov/aa/carnegie/aa_carnegie_work_3.html

http://www.clpgh.org/exhibit/neighborhoods/oakland/oak_n751.html

Key Idea: Carnegie Steel was very profitable.

President Study | I |

On *The Presidents* DVD Volume 1, select the Chapter "John Q. Adams to Polk" and watch **only** Program 1: John Quincy Adams. Then, open your *President Notebook* to John Quincy Adams. Use today's viewing to add further information about John Quincy Adams.

Key Idea: Research John Quincy Adams.

Storytime | T/I |

Read the following assigned pages:

Factory Girl p. 40 – middle of p. 53

Get the bookmark that you placed in your book. Locate the same section of the bookmark that you used on Day 1. Beneath Day 1's entry, write the book title and the page numbers you read today. Select one of the **two** remaining response options at the bottom of the bookmark, and place a checkmark next to it. In the blank space under today's pages, respond in writing using your checked option.

Key Idea: Relate to the text in various ways.

Timeline | I |

You will be adding to the timeline in your *Student Notebook* today. In Unit 5 – Box 1, draw and color a skyscraper. Label it, *The Gilded Age (1865-1896 A.D.)*.

In Box 2, draw and color a factory labeled *"Carnegie Steel"* with smokestacks pouring smoke into the air. Label it, *The Homestead Strike (June 30, 1892 – July 6, 1892 A.D.)*.

In Box 3, draw and color a ship in a harbor with the Statue of Liberty in the distance. Label it, *Immigration in the Gilded Age (1865-1900 A.D.)*.

Key Idea: The Gilded Age included violent labor strikes, an influx of immigrants, huge growth in industry, movement to the cities, and advances in railway and communications.

Independent History Study | I |

Choose someone to whom you can explain what a "stockholder" is and also explain why people began to buy "stock" in a company. Hint: These are explained on p. 176 of *The Story of the World: Vol. 4*.

Key Idea: Investors invest money in a company in return for a share of the profit, or stock. This is called being a stockholder.

Learning the Basics
Focus: Language Arts, Math, Bible, Nature Journal, and Science

Biblical Self-Image [T]

Read and discuss with the students the following pages in the resource below.

 ★ *Who Am I? And What Am I Doing Here?* p. 46 – middle of p. 48

Note: This includes locating and reading the Scriptures noted in parentheses on p. 46-48.

Key Idea: God created all things to glorify Him. We can glorify Him through music, art, poetry, work, and other ways in which we worship our Creator.

Language Arts [S]

Have students complete one studied dictation exercise (see Appendix for directions and passages).

Help students complete one lesson from the following reading program:

★ *Drawn into the Heart of Reading*

Help students complete **one** English option.

★ *Progressing With Courage:* Lesson 18 (p. 85-88 Class Practice 'A' – 'K' only)

★ *Progressing With Courage:* Lesson 75 (Save Written Exercises for Day 3.)

★ Your own grammar program

Key Idea: Practice language arts skills.

Bible Quiet Time [I]

Bible Study: Read and complete the assigned pages in the following resource:

★ *Faith at Work: Lesson 4 – Day Three* p. 26

Prayer Focus: Refer to **confession** on "Preparing Your Heart for Prayer". Then, pray a prayer of confession to admit or acknowledge your sins to God. After your prayer, write 'confession' at the bottom of today's lesson in *Faith at Work* above *Day Four*. Next to 'confession', either list key phrases or write a sentence to summarize your prayer. This will be your prayer log. Keep "Preparing Your Heart for Prayer" inside your Bible.

Scripture Memory: Memorize Romans 12:6 from your Bible and recite it.

Music: Refer to p. 24-25 in *Hymns for a Kid's Heart* as you sing with Track 2: *"Fairest Lord Jesus"* (vs. 1-2).

Key Idea: Read and study Romans 1:18-32.

Math Exploration [S]

Choose **one** of the math options listed below (see Appendix for details).

★ *Singapore Primary Mathematics 6A/6B, Discovering Mathematics 7A/7B, 8A/8B, No-Nonsense Algebra* or *Videotext Algebra*

★ Your own math program

Key Idea: Use a step-by-step math program.

Science Exploration [I]

★ Read *Exploring the World of Chemistry* p. 112-118. After reading the chapter, turn to p. 119 of *Exploring the World of Chemistry*. Write the answer to each numbered question from p. 119 on lined paper. You do not need to copy the question.

Key Idea: Silicon is the second most abundant element in the earth's crust. It has properties similar to carbon. The simplest compound of silicon and oxygen is silica. Quartz and precious gems contain silica. Silicone is silicon made in a laboratory. Silicone can take the form of a lubricant, an oily liquid, or a putty.

Reading about History | I

Read about history in the following resource:

 *All American History: Vol. II* p. 174-180
After today's reading, open your *Student Notebook* to Unit 5. Look at the picture of the Statue of Liberty in Box 5. Notice the image in the top left corner of the French sculptor, Bartholdi, who designed the statue. The statue was presented as a gift from France to the U.S. in 1886 and stands on Bedloe's Island in the New York Harbor. The Statue of Liberty became a symbol of welcome to the immigrants who passed through the inspection station at Ellis Island.

Key Idea: During the Gilded Age, approximately 26 million immigrants poured into the United States.

History Project | S

Today, you will read about Carnegie's role as a philanthropist. Choose **one** of the following websites to research this part of Carnegie's life:
http://www.americaslibrary.gov/aa/carnegie/aa_carnegie_phil_1.html

http://www.mtc.gov.on.ca/en/libraries/carnegie_bio.shtml

http://www.pbs.org/wgbh/amex/carnegie/sfeature/philantrophy101.html

Next, open your *Student Notebook* to Unit 5. In Box 9, write a paragraph to share your opinion of Andrew Carnegie based on your research from Days 1-3.

Key Idea: Carnegie was a Scottish immigrant.

State Study | T

 This is an **optional** part of the plans. If you have chosen to study your state using *State History from a Christian Perspective*, do Lesson 5 **number 1 only** from the *Master Lesson Plan Book*. Note: Do only **Quiz 1**.

Key Idea: Study your individual state.

Storytime | T/I

Read the following assigned pages:

 *Factory Girl* p. 53-69

After today's reading, orally narrate or retell the portion of the story that was read today. See *Narration Tips* in the Appendix as needed.

Key Idea: Practice orally narrating, or retelling, a portion of a story.

Geography | I

For today's activities, use the map listed below.

 *Map Trek CD: Missions to Modern Marvels* p. 34-35
Print the "Major Centers of Immigration" Student Map found on p. 35 of the *Map Trek* CD. Refer to or print the *Map Trek* Teacher's Answer Map on p. 34 to guide you as you label each state and the major centers of immigration on your Student Map. Then, use the map on p. 33 of the *United States History Atlas* to guide you as you lightly shade in red those states that had 30% or more of their population that were immigrants (or foreign-born) in 1890. Add a key at the bottom of your Student Map to explain what the red color represents on your map. File the map in your *Student Notebook*.

Key Idea: Between 1865 and 1900, immigrants usually came to the U.S. for jobs, land, religious freedom, or to flee from compulsory military service.

Independent History Study | I

Reread the second and third paragraphs on p. 177 of *All American History*. Then, read p. 109-111 in the *Book of Great American Speeches...* Choose an important part of the speech to copy in quotation marks in Unit 5 – Box 10 of your *Student Notebook* and write "William Jennings Bryan" at the bottom.

Key Idea: Bryan ran for President in 1896.

Nature Journal & Poetry　S

The poetry of Longfellow, Wordsworth, and Whitman is scheduled on Day 3 in each unit to complement the nature journaling sessions. Read aloud and discuss today's poem *"Eliot's Oak"* (see Appendix) with a parent. Then, follow the directions in the resource below.

★ *Nature Drawing & Journaling: Lesson VII* p. 25 – part of p. 27

Note: Stop after completing the first tree from p. 24. Then, cut out the tree sketch you drew based on p. 24 and tape or glue it onto your journal page.

Key Idea: Practice shading with lines.

Language Arts　S

Have students complete one studied dictation exercise (see Appendix for passages).

Help students complete **one** English option.

★ *Progressing With Courage:* Lesson 18 (p. 88-91 Written Exercises only)

★ *Progressing With Courage:* Lesson 75 (Written and Review Exercises only)

★ Your own grammar program

Work with the students to complete **one** of the writing options listed below:

★ *Write with the Best: Vol. 2* Unit 3 – Day 10 p. 28

★ Your own writing program

Key Idea: Practice language arts skills.

Bible Quiet Time　I

Bible Study: Read and complete the assigned pages in the following resource:

★ *Faith at Work: Lesson 4 – Day Four* p. 26-27 (Note: Today's lesson discusses homosexuality in light of God's Word. On p. 27, question 3 refers to Jude 1:7. Questions 4-6, refer to 1 Corinthians 6:9-11, 13. Question 7, refers to 1 Corinthians 6:18 and 7:2-3.)

Prayer Focus: Refer to **thanksgiving** on "Preparing Your Heart for Prayer". Then, pray a prayer of thanksgiving to express gratitude to God for His divine goodness. After your prayer, write 'thanksgiving' at the bottom of today's lesson in *Faith at Work* above *Day Five*. Next to 'thanksgiving', either list key phrases or write a sentence to summarize your prayer. Keep "Preparing Your Heart for Prayer" inside your Bible.

Scripture Memory: Copy Romans 12:6 in your Common Place Book.

Music: Refer to p. 24-25 in *Hymns for a Kid's Heart* as you sing with Track 2: *"Fairest Lord Jesus"* (vs. 1-2).

Key Idea: Read and study Romans 1:18-32.

Math Exploration　S

Choose **one** of the math options listed below (see Appendix for details).

★ *Singapore Primary Mathematics 6A/6B, Discovering Mathematics 7A/7B, 8A/8B, No-Nonsense Algebra* or *Videotext Algebra*

★ Your own math program

Key Idea: Use a step-by-step math program.

Science Exploration　I

★ Read *Exploring the World of Chemistry* p. 120-126. After reading the chapter, turn to p. 127 of *Exploring the World of Chemistry*. Write the answer to each numbered question from p. 127 on lined paper. You do not need to copy the question.

Key Idea: Hall and Heroult passed electric current through molten cryolite to extract aluminum from bauxite. Becquerel discovered uranium's radiation. The Curies discovered polonium and radium.

Reading about History | I |

Read about history in the following resources:

 All American History: Vol. II p. 183-187

 Book of Great American Speeches... p. 125-126

You will be writing a narration about Teddy Roosevelt. To prepare for writing your narration, look back over p. 184-187 in *All American History: Vol. II.* Think about the main idea and the most important moments in this part of the reading.

After you have thought about what you will write and how you will begin your narration, turn to Unit 5 in your *Student Notebook.* For more guidance on writing a narration, see *Written Narration Tips* in the Appendix.

In Box 4, write a 12-16 sentence narration about the reading. When you have finished writing, read your sentences out loud to catch any mistakes. Check for the following things: *Did you include* **who** *or* **what topic** *the reading was mainly about? Did you include* **descriptors** *of the important thing(s) that happened? Did you include a* **closing sentence**? *If not, add those things.* Use the *Written Narration Skills* in the Appendix as a guide for editing the narration.

Key Idea: Progressivism was a political reform movement that gained power in the early part of the twentieth century. When Teddy Roosevelt became president after the assassination of McKinley, he often spoke about Progressive values. Roosevelt focused on a "square deal" for all Americans. He also earned a reputation as a "trustbuster". During his presidency, Roosevelt pushed for legislation that doubled the number of national parks. In foreign policy, he advocated the need to "speak softly, and carry a big stick".

President Study | I |

 Read p. 16-17 in *Our Presidents...* Then, open your *President Notebook* to Andrew Jackson. Use today's reading to help you complete the information about Jackson.

Key Idea: Research Andrew Jackson.

Storytime | T/I |

Read the following assigned pages:

 Factory Girl p. 70-86
Get the bookmark that you placed in your book on Day 2. Locate the same section of the bookmark that you used on Day 2. Beneath Day 2's entry, write the book title and the page numbers you read today. Select the one remaining response option at the bottom of the bookmark, and place a checkmark next to it. In the blank space under today's pages, respond in writing using your checked option. Keep the bookmark in your book.

Key Idea: Relate to the text in various ways.

Economics | I |

Read about economics in the resource below.

 Whatever Happened to Penny Candy? p. 39-42
After the reading, open your *Student Notebook* to the "Economic Principles" section at the front of your notebook. Under "Economic Principle", write a one line or one sentence summary for the economic principle you learned from today's reading.

Key Idea: Inflation can occur under a dictator or a democracy. Dictators fear revolution, so they print money rather than raising taxes too high. In a democracy, there is also inflation as elected officials need to come up with a way to pay for what they have promised the voters without raising taxes too high. So, large governments tend to cause inflation to occur.

Independent History Study | I |

Read p. 117-119 in the *Book of Great American Speeches...* Choose an important part of the speech to copy in quotation marks in Unit 5 – Box 11 of your *Student Notebook* and write "Mother Jones" at the bottom of Box 11.

Key Idea: Mary Harris Jones, or "Mother" Jones, advocated for better pay and working conditions for miners and working children.

Learning the Basics
Focus: Language Arts, Math, Bible, Nature Journal, and Science

Biblical Self-Image [T]

Our plans intend for the listed pages in *Who Am I? And What Am I Doing Here?* to be read either silently by both you and your student, or read aloud to the student by you. With this in mind, read and discuss the following pages in the resource below.

★ *Who Am I? And What Am I Doing Here?* middle of p. 48 – middle of p. 57

Key Idea: People were created to worship God, fellowship with Him, and enjoy His presence.

Language Arts [S]

Have students complete one studied dictation exercise (see Appendix for directions and passages).

Help students complete one lesson from the following reading program:

★ *Drawn into the Heart of Reading*

Help students complete **one** English option.

★ *Progressing With Courage:* Lesson 19

★ *Progressing With Courage:* Lesson 76 (first half only)

★ Your own grammar program

Key Idea: Practice language arts skills.

Bible Quiet Time [I]

Bible Study: Complete the assignment below.

★ *Faith at Work: Lesson 4 – Day Five* and *Notes* p. 27-31 (Note: p. 31 discusses sexual perversion in light of Romans 1.)

Prayer Focus: Refer to **supplication** on "Preparing Your Heart for Prayer". Then, pray a prayer of supplication to make a humble and earnest request of God. Write 'supplication' at the bottom of today's lesson on p. 27 in *Faith at Work*. Next to it, either list several key phrases or write a sentence to summarize your prayer.

Scripture Memory: Recite Romans 12:1-6.

Music: Refer to p. 24-25 in *Hymns for a Kid's Heart* as you sing with Track 2: *"Fairest Lord Jesus"* (vs. 1-2).

Key Idea: Read and study Romans 1:18-32.

Math Exploration [S]

Choose **one** of the math options listed below (see Appendix for details).

★ *Singapore Primary Mathematics 6A/6B, Discovering Mathematics 7A/7B, 8A/8B, No-Nonsense Algebra* or *Videotext Algebra*

★ Your own math program

Key Idea: Use a step-by-step math program.

Science Exploration [I]

★ Copy the Science Lab Form from the Appendix of this guide. Then, put on your safety glasses, smooth gloves, and smock as recommended on p. 6 of the *Chemistry C500 Experiment Manual*. Next, follow the directions to perform "Experiment 8" from p. 19 of the Experiment Manual. After completing Experiment 8, in the top box of the Science Lab Form write: *What will happen to the litmus solution mixed with vinegar when soapy water is added?* In the second box of the form, write your hypothesis. Follow the directions for "Experiment 9" on p. 20 of the Experiment Manual and complete the box "Perform an Experiment" on your lab form. Then, follow the arrows to complete the rest of the Science Lab Form. To clean up, refer to "How to Dispose of Waste" on p. 7 and Basic Rules 5, 6, 7, and 11 on p. 6.

Key Idea: Litmus is a dye that acts as an indicator to detect whether there is more acid or more alkali in a solution. Litmus causes acid to produce a light red color and alkali to produce a blue color. Vinegar is an acid. Sodium carbonate and sodium hydroxide (or soda lye) are alkalis. Alkalis and acids are opposites.

Learning Through History
Focus: Progressivism, Prohibition, *Plessy v. Ferguson,* and Mass Production

Unit 6 - Day 1

Reading about History | S |

Read about history in the following resources:

⭐ *All American History: Vol. II* p. 188-193

⭐ *Great Events in American History* p. 75-77

After today's reading, orally narrate or retell to an adult the portion of text that you read today about **either** William Taft, **or** Woodrow Wilson, **or** Evangelist John Harper. As you retell, the adult will write or type your narration. Some possible key words to include in your narration about William Taft might be *president, Progressive reform, antitrust suits, federal budget,* and *chief justice.* Key words for a narration about Woodrow Wilson might be *speaker, president, "New Freedom", prohibition, women's vote.* Key words for a narration about John Harper might be *Titanic, iceberg, North Atlantic, forgiveness of sins, passengers.* When the narration is complete, tri-fold the typed or written narration to fit in Unit 6 – Box 8 of the *Student Notebook.* Glue the folded narration in Box 8, so it can be opened and read.

Key Idea: The *Titanic* sank on April 15, 1912.

History Project | S |

Today you will draw and color the *RMS Titanic.* Open your *Student Notebook* to Unit 6 – Box 10. Follow the directions from *Draw and Write Through History* p. 8-10 (steps 1-6). You will finish coloring your sketch on Day 3.

Key Idea: After hitting an iceberg in the North Atlantic, the *Titanic* sank in just over 2½ hours. More than 1500 passengers drowned, or froze to death in the frigid waters, and just over 700 passengers survived.

Storytime | T/I |

Read the following assigned pages:

⭐ *Factory Girl* p. 87-103
Get the bookmark that you placed in your book last unit. Choose a new section of the bookmark with **three** options at the bottom. At the top of this section of the bookmark, write the book title and the page numbers you read today. Select **one** of the three options at the bottom and place a checkmark next to it. In the blank space under today's pages, respond in writing using your checked option.

Key Idea: Relate to the text in various ways.

Worthy Words | T |

Read, analyze, and evaluate the speech below.

⭐ *Book of Great American Speeches for Young People* p. 135-136

After reading the speech, answer the following questions on an index card: *What does Woodrow Wilson say makes the United States different from other countries? To whom does he say the citizens owe allegiance? According to Wilson, how does a person know when he/she has become an "American"? Do you agree? What does being an American, or a citizen of your country, mean to you?* Next, meet with a parent to have a Socratic dialogue about the speech. Before beginning the dialogue, the parent reads the speech out loud. Next, discuss the questions using your notes. All participants should use life experiences and/or the text to support their responses.

Key Idea: Woodrow Wilson was President of the United States from 1913-1921.

Independent History Study | I |

⭐ Eugene V. Debs ran for president as a Socialist candidate against Taft and Roosevelt in the 1912 election. Read about socialism in Deb's speech on p. 146-148 in the *Book of Great American Speeches.* What are your thoughts about Deb's views?

Key Idea: Eugene V. Debs was defeated by Republican Party candidate William Taft in the 1912 election.

Learning the Basics
Focus: Language Arts, Math, Bible, Nature Journal, and Science

Nature Journal | I |

Read and follow the directions in the resource below to draw in your Nature Journal.

★ *Nature Drawing & Journaling: Lesson VII* last part of p. 27

Note: Begin with the directions that tell you to go outside to draw a portion of another tree.

Key Idea: Practice shading with lines.

Language Arts | S |

Help students complete one lesson from the following reading program:

★ *Drawn into the Heart of Reading*

Help students complete **one** English option.

★ *Progressing With Courage:* Lesson 20

★ *Progressing With Courage:* Lesson 76 (last half only)

★ Your own grammar program

Work with the students to complete **one** of the writing options listed below:

★ *Write with the Best: Vol. 2* Unit 4 – Day 1 p. 29-33 (Note: For the brief research on Thomas Paine you need an encyclopedia. With parental oversight, you could use http://en.wikipedia.org/wiki/Thomas_Paine)

★ Your own writing program

Key Idea: Practice language arts skills.

Bible Quiet Time | I |

Bible Study: Read and complete the assigned pages in the following resource:

★ *Faith at Work: Lesson 5 – Day One* p. 32
Note: Refer to p. 28-31 to complete the lesson.

Prayer Focus: Refer to **adoration** on "Preparing Your Heart for Prayer". Then, pray a prayer of adoration to worship and honor God. After your prayer, write 'adoration' at the bottom of today's lesson in *Faith at Work* above *Day Two*. Next to 'adoration', either list key phrases or write a sentence to summarize your prayer. Keep "Preparing Your Heart for Prayer" inside your Bible.

Scripture Memory: Read aloud Romans 12:7 three times from your Bible.

Music: Read the verse and pray the prayer from p. 25 in *Hymns for a Kid's Heart*. Refer to p. 24-25 as you sing with Track 2 *"Fairest Lord Jesus"* (vs. 1-4).

Key Idea: Read and study Romans 1:18-32.

Math Exploration | S |

Choose **one** of the math options listed below (see Appendix for details).

★ *Singapore Primary Mathematics 6A/6B, Discovering Mathematics 7A/7B, 8A/8B, No-Nonsense Algebra* or *Videotext Algebra*

★ Your own math program

Key Idea: Use a step-by-step math program.

Science Exploration | I |

★ Read *Exploring the World of Chemistry* p. 128-134. After reading the chapter, turn to p. 135 of *Exploring the World of Chemistry*. Write the answer to each numbered question from p. 135 on lined paper. You do not need to copy the question.

Key Idea: Robert Boyle, Henry Cavendish, Antoine Laurent Lavoisier, John Dalton, Humphry Davy, Jons Jakob Berzelius, Michael Faraday, Louis Pasteur, Dmitri Ivanovich Mendeleev, and William Ramsay are ten great chemists that you have studied.

Reading about History | I |

Read about history in the following resources:

⭐ *All American History: Vol. II* p. 195 – middle of p. 201

⭐ *Book of Great American Speeches* p. 120-121

After today's reading, open your *Student Notebook* to Unit 6. Look at the picture of the Sears catalog in Box 5. Notice the year on the catalog. Sears, Roebuck and Co. competed with Montgomery Ward for mail-order business in rural areas. What types of things do you see advertised on the cover of the catalog in Box 5? According to Florence Kelley's speech on p. 120-121 of the *Book of Great American Speeches*, what role did children play in the making of clothing?

Key Idea: During the Gilded Age, mail order catalog companies and department stores were established.

History Project | S |

In the early 1900s, clothing in the U.S. was manufactured mainly in the U.S. To discover where the clothes your family wears are manufactured, find at least 10 articles of clothing with a label declaring their country of manufacture. List on an index card or a sticky note the country of origin for each of the 10 articles of clothing. Try to survey a mix of both women's and men's clothing. Include items like shoes, pants/shorts, tops, and skirts. What conclusions can you draw from your survey?

Key Idea: Textile manufacturing has changed.

President Study | I |

⭐ On *The Presidents* DVD Volume 1, select the Chapter "John Q. Adams to Polk" and watch **only** Program 2: Andrew Jackson. Then, open your *President Notebook* to Andrew Jackson. Use today's viewing to add further information about Andrew Jackson.

Key Idea: Research Andrew Jackson.

Storytime | T/I |

Read the following assigned pages:

⭐ *Factory Girl* p. 104 – bottom of p. 120

Get the bookmark that you placed in your book. Locate the same section of the bookmark that you used on Day 1. Beneath Day 1's entry, write the book title and the page numbers you read today. Select one of the **two** remaining response options at the bottom of the bookmark, and place a checkmark next to it. In the blank space under today's pages, respond in writing using your checked option. Place your bookmark in your book.

Key Idea: Relate to the text in various ways.

Timeline | I |

You will be adding to the timeline in your *Student Notebook* today. In Unit 6 – Box 1, draw and color a worn hat labeled *"Jim Crow"*. Label the box, *Plessy v. Ferguson Upheld by Supreme Court (1896 A.D.)*.

In Box 2, draw and color a sinking ship by an iceberg. Label it, *RMS Titanic Sinks (April 15, 1912 A.D.)*.

In Box 3, draw and color a sign that says, *"VOTE"*. Label it, *The 19th Amendment Gives Women the Right to Vote (August 18, 1920 A.D.)*.

Key Idea: Prejudice, prohibition, and women's suffrage were a part of the Gilded Age.

Independent History Study | I |

Read **either** p. 101-103 **or** p. 106-108 in the *Book of Great American Speeches*. Choose an important part of the speech you read to copy in quotation marks in Unit 6 – Box 6 of your *Student Notebook*. Write the name of the speaker at the bottom of the box (either Susan B. Anthony **or** Elizabeth Cady Stanton).

Key Idea: Women fought for the right to vote.

Learning the Basics

Focus: Language Arts, Math, Bible, Nature Journal, and Science

Biblical Self-Image [T]

Read and discuss with the students the following pages in the resource below.

 Who Am I? And What Am I Doing Here? middle of p. 57-60

After reading, discuss ways that both you and your students can work "with all your heart, as working for the Lord..." in your daily life.

Key Idea: God has a special purpose for each believer's life. He will gift you and equip you to fulfill His purpose.

Language Arts [S]

Have students complete one studied dictation exercise (see Appendix for directions and passages).

Help students complete one lesson from the following reading program:

 Drawn into the Heart of Reading

Help students complete **one** English option.

 Progressing With Courage: Lesson 21

 Progressing With Courage: Lesson 77 (first half only)

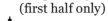 Your own grammar program

Key Idea: Practice language arts skills.

Bible Quiet Time [I]

Bible Study: Read and complete the assigned pages in the following resource:

 Faith at Work: Lesson 5 – Day Two p. 32-33

Prayer Focus: Refer to **confession** on "Preparing Your Heart for Prayer". Then, pray a prayer of confession to admit or acknowledge your sins to God. After your prayer, write 'confession' at the bottom of today's lesson in *Faith at Work* above *Day Three*. Next to 'confession', either list key phrases or write a sentence to summarize your prayer. This will be your prayer log. Keep "Preparing Your Heart for Prayer" inside your Bible.

Scripture Memory: Memorize Romans 12:7 from your Bible and recite it.

Music: Refer to p. 24-25 as you sing with Track 2 *"Fairest Lord Jesus"* (vs. 1-4).

Key Idea: Read and study Romans 2.

Math Exploration [S]

Choose **one** of the math options listed below (see Appendix for details).

 Singapore Primary Mathematics 6A/6B, Discovering Mathematics 7A/7B, 8A/8B, No-Nonsense Algebra or *Videotext Algebra*

 Your own math program

Key Idea: Use a step-by-step math program.

Science Exploration [I]

 Read *Marie Curie and the Discovery of Radium* p. 1-15. After reading the chapters, read the definition for *Csar* on p. 119, *Manya* on p. 120, *physics* on p. 121, and *typhus* on p. 122. Then, either discuss question 7 on p. 116 with a parent or write an answer to the question on paper.

Key Idea: Marya Salomee Sklodowska was born on November 7, 1867, in Warsaw, Poland. Poland was ruled by Russia, Germany, and Austria during this time. Marya's mother was a principal, and her father was a physics professor. Her mother died of tuberculosis on May 9, 1878.

Learning Through History

Focus: Progressivism, Prohibition, *Plessy v. Ferguson,* and Mass Production

Unit 6 - Day 3

Reading about History | I |

Read about history in the following resource:

 All American History: Vol. II p. 201-205

After today's reading, open your *Student Notebook* to Unit 6 - Box 7, which shows the *New York Times* headlines after the *Titanic* sunk. The headline highlights Ismay, who was the chairman of the White Star Line of steamships that built the *Titanic*. It also highlights Mrs. Astor, wife of John Jacob Astor IV, whose great-grandfather was the first American millionaire. You will read about John Astor's mother on Day 4. Why would the headlines mention Ismay and Astor? In looking at the numbers reported of those rescued and those who perished, we now know the numbers are not correct. Why would this be? What can you learn about journalism and its accuracy from the headlines in Box 7?

Key Idea: As America grew and prospered, American magazines and newspapers shared news about those who were wealthy.

History Project | S |

In 1877, Quaker Oats created a cereal made from oats, and oatmeal became popular. Around that same time, the Kellogg brothers created wheat flakes and then corn flakes. Several versions of granola were also produced during this time. Check your kitchen cupboard to see whether you have any Quaker or Kellogg cereals. Does your family eat cold cereal, granola, or oatmeal? Did you know these have been American breakfast foods for 130+ years?

Key Idea: Foods began to be mass-produced.

State Study | T |

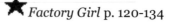 This is an **optional** part of the plans. If you have chosen to study your state using *State History from a Christian Perspective,* do the **last** part of Lesson 5 (numbers 2-3) from the *Master Lesson Plan Book.*

Key Idea: Study your individual state.

Storytime | T/I |

Read the following assigned pages:

Factory Girl p. 120-134

After today's reading, orally narrate or retell the portion of the story that was read today. See *Narration Tips* in the Appendix as needed.

Key Idea: Practice orally narrating, or retelling, a portion of a story.

Economics | I |

Read about economics in the resource below.

Whatever Happened to Penny Candy? p. 43-50 and p. 133

After the reading, open your *Student Notebook* to the "Economic Principles" section at the front of your notebook. Under "Economic Principle", write a one or two sentence summary for the economic principle you learned from today's reading.

Key Idea: Decreases or increases in the supply of money affect wages and prices similarly. The wage/price spiral is a result of inflation. When the government uses wage/price controls, shortages and illegal or "black" market selling can develop.

Independent History Study | I |

Open your *Student Notebook* to Unit 6 – Box 10. Follow the directions from *Draw and Write Through History* p. 11 (step 7) to finish coloring the *Titanic.* Then, in Box 9 of your *Student Notebook,* copy the **first paragraph** of text in cursive from *Draw and Write Through History* p. 12.

Key Idea: John Jacob Astor IV was the richest passenger on the *Titanic.* As the ship began to sink, women and children were placed in the lifeboats first. After putting his pregnant wife in a lifeboat, Astor went down with the ship.

Learning the Basics
Focus: Language Arts, Math, Bible, Nature Journal, Poetry, and Science

Nature Journal & Poetry | S |

The poetry of Longfellow, Wordsworth, and Whitman is scheduled on Day 3 in each unit to complement the nature journaling sessions. Read aloud and discuss today's poem *"Petals"* (see Appendix) with a parent. Then, follow the directions in the resource below.

 Nature Drawing & Journaling: Lesson VIII p. 28 – half of p. 29 (Note: Do only the first half of p. 29, stopping after the first paragraph.)

<u>Key Idea</u>: Practice drawing bricks and flowers that have overlapping patterns.

Language Arts | S |

Have students complete one studied dictation exercise (see Appendix for passages).

Help students complete **one** English option.

 Progressing With Courage: Lesson 22

 Progressing With Courage: Lesson 77 (last half only)

 Your own grammar program

Work with the students to complete **one** of the writing options listed below:

 Write with the Best: Vol. 2 Unit 4 – Day 2 p. 33 – top of p. 34

 Your own writing program

<u>Key Idea</u>: Practice language arts skills.

Bible Quiet Time | I |

Bible Study: Read and complete the assigned pages in the following resource:

★ *Faith at Work: Lesson 5 – Day Three* p. 33

Prayer Focus: Refer to **thanksgiving** on "Preparing Your Heart for Prayer". Then, pray a prayer of thanksgiving to express gratitude to God for His divine goodness. After your prayer, write 'thanksgiving' at the bottom of today's lesson in *Faith at Work* above *Day Four*. Next to 'thanksgiving', either list key phrases or write a sentence to summarize your prayer. Keep "Preparing Your Heart for Prayer" inside your Bible.

Scripture Memory: Copy Romans 12:7 in your Common Place Book.

Music: Refer to p. 24-25 in *Hymns for a Kid's Heart* as you sing with Track 2: *"Fairest Lord Jesus"* (vs. 1-4).

<u>Key Idea</u>: Read and study Romans 2.

Math Exploration | S |

Choose **one** of the math options listed below (see Appendix for details).

 Singapore Primary Mathematics 6A/6B, Discovering Mathematics 7A/7B, 8A/8B, No-Nonsense Algebra or *Videotext Algebra*

 Your own math program

<u>Key Idea</u>: Use a step-by-step math program.

Science Exploration | I |

★ Read *Marie Curie and the Discovery of Radium* p. 16-28. After reading the chapters, read the definition for *Sorbonne* on p. 122. Then, write a written narration about p. 16-28. Refer to *Written Narration Tips* in the Appendix for help as needed. Read your written narration out loud after you have finished writing it to catch any mistakes that need fixing. Refer to *Written Narration Skills* for help in editing.

<u>Key Idea</u>: Manya attended a Russian high school. Upon graduation, she won a gold medal for her academic excellence. She then spent almost a year in the country recovering from the strain of studying. Then, she became a governess to support her sister Bronya's education at the Sorbonne in Paris.

Reading about History | I |

Read about history in the following resource:

 All American History: Vol. II p. 207 – middle of p. 212

You will be writing a narration about **one** of the sections that you read about today (either "Mrs. Astor's Four Hundred", "Gilded Age Social Reform", or "Jim Crow"). To prepare for writing your narration, look back over p. 207-212 in *All American History: Vol. II.* Think about the main idea and the most important moments in this part of the reading.

After you have thought about what you will write and how you will begin your narration, turn to Unit 6 in your *Student Notebook.* For more guidance on writing a narration, see *Written Narration Tips* in the Appendix.

In Box 4, write a 12-16 sentence narration about the reading. When you have finished writing, read your sentences out loud to catch any mistakes. Check for the following things: *Did you include **who** or **what topic** the reading was mainly about? Did you include **descriptors** of the important thing(s) that happened? Did you include a **closing sentence**? If not, add those things.* Use the *Written Narration Skills* in the Appendix as a guide for editing the narration.

Key Idea: Caroline Astor was a wealthy New York heiress who sought to exclude America's *nouveau riche* from society. Her list of 400 "socially prominent New Yorkers" became legendary. During this same time, reformer Jane Addams founded Hull House in Chicago to help the city's poor. Other social reformers, like The Women's Christian Temperance Union, advocated prohibition of alcohol. During the Gilded Age, segregation of whites and African Americans was enforced through Jim Crow laws that remained nearly 60 years.

President Study | I |

 Read p. 18-19 in *Our Presidents...* Then, open your *President Notebook* to Martin Van Buren. Use today's reading to help you complete the information about Van Buren.

Key Idea: Research Martin Van Buren.

Storytime | T/I |

Read the following assigned pages:

 Mama's Bank Account p. 3-17

Get the bookmark that you placed in your book. Locate the same section of the bookmark that you used on Day 2. Beneath Day 2's entry, write the book title and the page numbers you read today. Select the one remaining response option at the bottom of the bookmark, and place a checkmark next to it. In the blank space under today's pages, respond in writing using your checked option.

Key Idea: Relate to the text in various ways.

Geography | I |

For today's activities, use the map listed below.

 Map Trek CD: Missions to Modern Marvels p. 32-33

Print the "States with the Harshest Jim Crow Laws..." Student Map found on p. 33 of the *Map Trek CD.* Refer to or print the *Map Trek* Teacher's Answer Map on p. 32 to guide you as you label each state shown in red and the number of laws on your Student Map. Next, label each remaining state with its abbreviation and copy the corresponding year that women were granted the right to vote in each blue star on your Student Map. Which states allowed women to vote the earliest? File the map in your *Student Notebook.*

Key Idea: Virginia, North Carolina, South Carolina, Georgia, Alabama, and Mississippi had the harshest Jim Crow Laws.

Independent History Study | I |

Refer to p. 36 of the *United States History Atlas* to see which states allowed women to vote prior to the 19th Amendment, which granted all women this right. What pattern do you notice?

Key Idea: Women had more rights in the West.

Biblical Self-Image   T

Our plans intend for the listed pages in *Who Am I? And What Am I Doing Here?* to be read either silently by both you and your student, or read aloud to the student by you. With this in mind, read and discuss the following pages in the resource below.

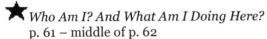 *Who Am I? And What Am I Doing Here?* p. 61 – middle of p. 62

Key Idea: God gives us skills and abilities and fills us with His Spirit.

Language Arts   S

Have students complete one studied dictation exercise (see Appendix for directions and passages).

Help students complete one lesson from the following reading program:

⭐ *Drawn into the Heart of Reading*

Help students complete **one** English option.

⭐ *Progressing With Courage:* Lesson 23

⭐ *Progressing With Courage:* Lesson 78 (first half only)

⭐ Your own grammar program

Key Idea: Practice language arts skills.

Bible Quiet Time   I

Bible Study: Complete the assignment below.

⭐ *Faith at Work: Lesson 5 – Day Four* p. 33-34

Prayer Focus: Refer to **supplication** on "Preparing Your Heart for Prayer". Then, pray a prayer of supplication to make a humble and earnest request of God. Write 'supplication' at the bottom of today's lesson in *Faith at Work* above *Day Five*. Next to it, either list several key phrases or write a sentence to summarize your prayer. Keep "Preparing Your Heart for Prayer" inside your Bible.

Scripture Memory: Recite Romans 12:1-7.

Music: Refer to p. 24-25 in *Hymns for a Kid's Heart* as you sing with Track 2: *"Fairest Lord Jesus"* (vs. 1-4).

Key Idea: Read and study Romans 2.

Math Exploration   S

Choose **one** of the math options listed below (see Appendix for details).

⭐ *Singapore Primary Mathematics 6A/6B, Discovering Mathematics 7A/7B, 8A/8B, No-Nonsense Algebra* or *Videotext Algebra*

⭐ Your own math program

Key Idea: Use a step-by-step math program.

Science Exploration   I

⭐ Put on your safety glasses, smooth gloves, and smock as recommended on p. 6 of the *Chemistry C500 Experiment Manual*. Next, follow the directions to perform "Experiment 10" from p. 21 of the Experiment Manual for an audience. Rather than using Experiment 10 as a "magic trick", refer to it as a scientific demonstration. Omit the "magic spell", and instead explain the demonstration to your audience scientifically. After completing Experiment 10, clean up carefully referring to "How to Dispose of Waste" on p. 7 and Basic Rules 5, 6, 7, and 11 on p. 6.

Key Idea: Litmus is a dye that acts as an indicator to detect whether there is more acid or more alkali in a solution. Acids, like sodium carbonate, turn blue litmus solution red. Alkalis turn red litmus solutions back to a blue color. The litmus solution is not destroyed in the back-and-forth process of indicating acids and alkalis.

Learning Through History

Focus: The Prince of Preachers, Barnum & Bailey, and the Great Chicago Fire

Unit 7 - Day 1

Reading about History — I

Read about history in the following resource:

★ *Hero Tales: Vol. II* p. 141-151

After today's reading, orally narrate or retell to an adult **one** portion of text that you read today. Some possible key words to introduce your narration might be *Maryland, slavery, Underground Railroad, Pennsylvania, Civil War, washing, and ironing*. For "Going to the Fair", some possible words to include might be *fair, Charlie, salvation*. For "Two Dollars for India", some possible words to include might be *two dollars, India, Maizie's shoes, Brother Brummel, dinner plates*. For "The Best Way to Fight", some possible words to include might be *Charles Brown, Will Darcy, harsh words, forgiveness*.

Key Idea: Amanda Smith tried to live life in obedience to God's call. She trusted in Him.

History Project — S

During the Gilded Age, as machines made tasks easier and quicker to complete, recreational pastimes like fairs, amusement parks, and the circus began to emerge. Open your *Student Notebook* to Unit 7. Look at the poster for Barnum & Bailey's circus ride in Box 9. In this unit, you will be designing your own type of ride and sketching it on the poster in Box 10. Today, **on scratch paper**, make a few very quick sketches of some possible rides.

Key Idea: Amanda Smith was an evangelist who shared the message of salvation and hope. She once attended a fair at the Lord's urging.

President Study — I

★ On *The Presidents* DVD Volume 1, select the Chapter "John Q. Adams to Polk" and watch **only** Program 3: Martin Van Buren. Then, open your *President Notebook* to Martin Van Buren. Use today's viewing to add further information about Van Buren.

Key Idea: Research Martin Van Buren.

Storytime — T/I

Read the following assigned pages:

★ *Mama's Bank Account* p. 18-34

After today's reading, photocopy the **two** "Bookmark" pages from the Appendix. Place the copied pages back-to-back and staple them together at the 4 corners. Then, tri-fold the stapled page into thirds to make a bookmark. Save the bookmark in your book until Day 2.

Key Idea: Relate to the text in various ways.

Worthy Words — T

Open your *Student Notebook* to Unit 7 – Box 8. You will read, analyze, and evaluate the preface from Amanda's book. After reading the preface, answer the following questions on an index card: *What barriers held Amanda back from writing her book? Why did she finally decide to write a book? What can you learn about Amanda's faith by reading the preface to her book? Where did Amanda go to seek answers? How could you follow Amanda's example when you have a decision that needs to be made? Why did she mention her education? Does she see lack of education as an excuse for not doing God's will? What are your thoughts about this?* Next, meet with a parent to have a Socratic dialogue about the excerpt. A Socratic dialogue is one in which the participants share their thoughts, feelings, and opinions about the written word. Before beginning the dialogue, the parent reads Box 8 out loud. Next, discuss the questions using your notes. All participants should use life experiences or text to support their responses.

Key Idea: Amanda wrote an autobiography.

Independent History Study — I

Open your *Student Notebook* to Unit 7. Choose an important part of the preface from Box 8 to copy in quotation marks in Box 6. Write "Amanda Smith" at the bottom of Box 6.

Key Idea: Amanda had very little education.

Learning the Basics

Focus: Language Arts, Math, Bible, Nature Journal, and Science

Nature Journal [I]

Read and follow the directions in the resource below to draw in your Nature Journal.

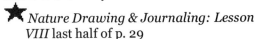 *Nature Drawing & Journaling: Lesson VIII* last half of p. 29

Note: Follow the directions in only the last two paragraphs of p. 29.

Key Idea: Practice drawing flowers with overlapping patterns.

Language Arts [S]

Help students complete one lesson from the following reading program:

 *Drawn into the Heart of Reading*

Help students complete **one** English option.

★ *Progressing With Courage:* Lesson 24

★ *Progressing With Courage:* Lesson 78 (last half only)

★ Your own grammar program

Work with the students to complete **one** of the writing options listed below:

★ *Write with the Best: Vol. 2* Unit 4 – Day 3 p. 34

★ Your own writing program

Key Idea: Practice language arts skills.

Bible Quiet Time [I]

Bible Study: Read and complete the assigned pages in the following resource:

★ *Faith at Work: Lesson 5 – Day Five* and *Notes* p. 34-39

Prayer Focus: Refer to **adoration** on "Preparing Your Heart for Prayer". Then, pray a prayer of adoration to worship and honor God. After your prayer, write 'adoration' at the bottom of today's lesson on p. 34 in *Faith at Work*. Next to 'adoration', either list key phrases or write a sentence to summarize your prayer. Keep "Preparing Your Heart for Prayer" inside your Bible.

Scripture Memory: Read aloud Romans 12:8 three times from your Bible.

Music: Read p. 27-28 in *Hymns for a Kid's Heart*. Refer to p. 30 as you sing with Track 3 *"To God Be the Glory"* (verse 1).

Key Idea: Read and study Romans 2.

Math Exploration [S]

Choose **one** of the math options listed below (see Appendix for details).

★ *Singapore Primary Mathematics 6A/6B, Discovering Mathematics 7A/7B, 8A/8B, No-Nonsense Algebra* or *Videotext Algebra*

★ Your own math program

Key Idea: Use a step-by-step math program.

Science Exploration [I]

★ Read *Marie Curie and the Discovery of Radium* p. 29-40. After reading the chapters, read the definition for *laboratory* and *Latin Quarter* on p. 119. Then, on a piece of paper, make a list of traits that you discovered about Marie from today's reading.

Key Idea: In the summer of 1889, Marie moved back to Warsaw. Her new governess job allowed her to return to the "Floating University", where she began reproducing experiments from chemistry and physics texts. In the fall of 1891, she began school at the Sorbonne in Paris. She worked long, hard hours to learn French and to get a double degree in physics and mathematics. The studying took a toll on her health.

Reading about History | I

Read about history in the following resource:

★ *Hero Tales: Vol. III* p. 177-187

After today's reading, open your *Student Notebook* to Unit 7. In Box 7, you will outline p. 177-178 to tell about Charles Albert Tindley. Each Roman numeral in Box 7 stands for one paragraph. So, 'I' means the first paragraph on p. 177. Next to 'I' in Box 7, write one sentence to tell who or what the first paragraph was about and the main thing that person did. This is not a summary, but rather just the main topic. Next to 'II' in Box 7, write the main topic of the second paragraph on p. 177. Continue this pattern for the 6 paragraphs on p. 177-178.

Key Idea: Charles Tindley was born into a slave family. In 1863, the Emancipation Proclamation freed him. Tindley taught himself to read from the Bible and pursued an education while working as a brick carrier and later as a church janitor. Tindley was ordained as a pastor in 1885.

History Project | S

Open your *Student Notebook* to Unit 7. In Box 9, what slogan (or catchy phrase), do you see on the Barnum & Bailey poster? Today, you will choose one of your quick sketches from Day 1 to develop into a ride you can draw on the poster in Box 10. Complete the drawing of your ride today in Box 10 so that you can color it on Day 3. Add your own catchy description in the bottom right corner of Box 10.

Key Idea: During the Gilded Age, while some families were looking for new amusements, other families were hungry and without work.

President Study | I

★ Read p. 20 in *Our Presidents...* Then, open your *President Notebook* to William Henry Harrison. Use today's reading to help you complete the information about Harrison.

Key Idea: Research William Henry Harrison.

Storytime | T/I

Read the following assigned pages:

★ *Mama's Bank Account* p. 35-56
Note: p. 38 contains hurtful prejudice.
Get the bookmark you made on Day 1. Find the section of the bookmark that has only **two** options at the bottom. At the top of this section of the bookmark, write the book title and the page numbers you read today. Select **one** of the two options at the bottom and place a checkmark next to it. In the blank space under today's pages, respond in writing using your checked option. Keep the bookmark in your book.

Key Idea: Relate to the text in various ways.

Geography | I

For today's activities, use the map listed below.

★ *United States History Atlas* p. 25 and 31
Charles Tindley was born in 1856 in Maryland, prior to the outbreak of the Civil War. Find Maryland on p. 25 of the *United States History Atlas*. The map on p. 25 shows the states that seceded in 1861. What do you notice about the location of Maryland? What effect might being a "border state" have on those who lived there? After the Civil War, Tindley moved with his wife, Daisy, to Philadelphia in Pennsylvania. Find Pennsylvania on p. 31 of the *United States History Atlas*. Why do you think Tindley heard there were better opportunities for blacks in Philadelphia than in Maryland at that time?

Key Idea: Tindley's church in Philadelphia eventually had 7,000 members.

Independent History Study | I

Choose at least one of Tindley's hymns to listen to while you read the hymn's lyrics at the following Internet site:
http://www.hymntime.com/tch/bio/t/i/n/tindley_ca.htm

Key Idea: Charles Tindley wrote 47 hymns, several of which became very famous.

Learning the Basics
Focus: Language Arts, Math, Bible, Nature Journal, and Science

Biblical Self-Image [T]

Read and discuss with the students the following pages in the resource below.

★ *Who Am I? And What Am I Doing Here?* middle of p. 62-65

For "Make a Note of It" on p. 65, discuss real-life examples rather than having students write a poem, a song, or a short story.

Key Idea: Our gifts come from the Lord and should be used to glorify Him. He promises to bless the work of our hands if we obey Him and keep His commands.

Language Arts [S]

Have students complete one studied dictation exercise (see Appendix for directions and passages).

Help students complete one lesson from the following reading program:

★ *Drawn into the Heart of Reading*

Help students complete **one** English option.

★ *Progressing With Courage:* Lesson 25

★ *Progressing With Courage:* Lesson 79 (first half only)

★ Your own grammar program

Key Idea: Practice language arts skills.

Bible Quiet Time [I]

Bible Study: Read and complete the assigned pages in the following resource:

★ *Faith at Work: Lesson 6 – Day One* p. 40
Note: Refer to p. 35-39 to complete this lesson.

Prayer Focus: Refer to **confession** on "Preparing Your Heart for Prayer". Then, pray a prayer of confession to admit or acknowledge your sins to God. After your prayer, write 'confession' at the bottom of today's lesson on p. 40 in *Faith at Work*. Next to 'confession', either list key phrases or write a sentence to summarize your prayer. This will be your prayer log. Keep "Preparing Your Heart for Prayer" inside your Bible.

Scripture Memory: Memorize Romans 12:8 from your Bible and recite it.

Music: Refer to p. 30 as you sing with Track 3 *"To God Be the Glory"* (verse 1).

Key Idea: Read and study Romans 3.

Math Exploration [S]

Choose **one** of the math options listed below (see Appendix for details).

★ *Singapore Primary Mathematics 6A/6B, Discovering Mathematics 7A/7B, 8A/8B, No-Nonsense Algebra* or *Videotext Algebra*

★ Your own math program

Key Idea: Use a step-by-step math program.

Science Exploration [I]

★ Read *Marie Curie and the Discovery of Radium* p. 41-54. After reading the chapters, read the definition for *pitchblende* and *radiation* on p. 121 and *uranium* and *X-ray* on p. 122. Then, give a summary oral narration to an adult about p. 41-54. The oral narration should be no longer than 6-8 sentences and should summarize the reading. As you narrate, hold up one finger for each sentence shared. The focus of the narration should be on the big ideas, rather than on the details. See *Narration Tips* in the Appendix.

Key Idea: Marie married Pierre Curie in 1895. While working on her thesis, Marie discovered radiation.

Learning Through History

Focus: The Prince of Preachers, Barnum & Bailey, and the Great Chicago Fire

Reading about History | I

Read about history in the following resource:

⭐ *All American History: Vol. II* p. 212-217

After today's reading, open your *Student Notebook* to Unit 7. Look at the poster shown in Box 5 of P.T. Barnum's Circus. Notice its slogan the "Greatest Show on Earth". Phineas T. Barnum started the circus in 1871. When he joined with Bailey in 1887, they developed the Big Top-3-ring circus with a Big Top tent that could seat 20,000 people at one time! Jumbo the elephant was the star of the circus.

Key Idea: During the Gilded Age, people had more time for recreation. Amusement parks, country clubs, bicycling, croquet, board games, and the circus were favorite pastimes.

History Project | S

Open your *Student Notebook* to Unit 7. Use colored pencils to color your drawing of the ride that you designed in Box 10. Make sure to use bright colors so that your drawing looks like an advertisement for your ride.

Key Idea: In the United States, the years 1870-1920 were considered to be the golden age of the circus. The Ringling Brothers founded their circus in 1884. They bought the Barnum and Bailey Circus in 1907. The two circuses were separate for over 10 years after that, but they eventually merged to become the Ringling Brothers and Barnum & Bailey Circus.

State Study | T

⭐ This is an **optional** part of the plans. If you have chosen to study your state using *State History from a Christian Perspective,* do Lesson 6 from the *Master Lesson Plan Book.* Tourist pictures from brochures or printed from the Internet will be needed next lesson.

Key Idea: Study your individual state.

Storytime | T/I

Read the following assigned pages:

⭐ *Mama's Bank Account* p. 57-71

After today's reading, orally narrate or retell the portion of the story that was read today. See *Narration Tips* in the Appendix as needed.

Key Idea: Practice orally narrating, or retelling, a portion of a story.

Timeline | I

You will be adding to the timeline in your *Student Notebook* today.

In Unit 7 – Box 1, draw and color a stained glass window. Label it, *Dwight Moody - Evangelist (1837-1899 A.D.).*

In Box 2, draw and color a raging fire. Label it, *Great Chicago Fire (October 8-10, 1871 A.D.).*

In Box 3, draw and color music notes. Label them, *Charles Albert Tindley – Prince of Preachers (1851-1933 A.D.).*

Key Idea: During the Gilded Age, Dwight Moody and Charles Tindley were both sharing the Good News of Jesus through their preaching. Tindley worked to help the hungry and homeless in Philadelphia, and Moody found many opportunities to minister in Chicago after the Great Chicago Fire. During this same time, Fanny Crosby was writing hymns. She wrote over 8,000 hymns during her lifetime.

Independent History Study | I

Listen to Fanny Crosby's *"Blessed Assurance"* while you read the hymn's lyrics at the Internet site below. Notice the comments by Ira Sankey, who was Dwight Moody's vocalist. http://www.hymntime.com/tch/htm/b/l/e/blesseda.htm

Key Idea: Fanny Crosby wrote 8,000 hymns.

Nature Journal & Poetry | S |

The poetry of Longfellow, Wordsworth, and Whitman is scheduled on Day 3 in each unit to complement the nature journaling sessions. Read aloud and discuss today's poem *"The Day Is Done"* (see Appendix) with a parent. Then, follow the directions in the resource below.

★ *Nature Drawing & Journaling: Lesson VIX* p. 30-31

If you are not sure what to write, you could consider copying a portion of today's poem in your journal.

Key Idea: Practice seeing God's poetic nature.

Language Arts | S |

Have students complete one studied dictation exercise (see Appendix for passages).

Help students complete **one** English option.

★ *Progressing With Courage:* Lesson 26

★ *Progressing With Courage:* Lesson 79 (last half only)

★ Your own grammar program

Work with the students to complete **one** of the writing options listed below:

★ *Write with the Best: Vol. 2* Unit 4 – Day 4 p. 34 (Note: Some possible history topics might be Prohibition, *Plessy v. Ferguson*, women's suffrage, immigration laws, unions, or child labor laws.)

★ Your own writing program

Key Idea: Practice language arts skills.

Bible Quiet Time | I |

Bible Study: Read and complete the assigned pages in the following resource:

★ *Faith at Work: Lesson 6 – Day Two* p. 41

Prayer Focus: Refer to **thanksgiving** on "Preparing Your Heart for Prayer". Then, pray a prayer of thanksgiving to express gratitude to God for His divine goodness. After your prayer, write 'thanksgiving' at the bottom of today's lesson in *Faith at Work* above *Day Three*. Next to 'thanksgiving', either list key phrases or write a sentence to summarize your prayer. Keep "Preparing Your Heart for Prayer" inside your Bible.

Scripture Memory: Copy Romans 12:8 in your Common Place Book.

Music: Refer to p. 30 as you sing with Track 3 *"To God Be the Glory"* (verse 1).

Key Idea: Read and study Romans 3.

Math Exploration | S |

Choose **one** of the math options listed below (see Appendix for details).

★ *Singapore Primary Mathematics 6A/6B, Discovering Mathematics 7A/7B, 8A/8B, No-Nonsense Algebra* or *Videotext Algebra*

★ Your own math program

Key Idea: Use a step-by-step math program.

Science Exploration | I |

★ Read *Marie Curie and the Discovery of Radium* p. 55-69. Next, read the definitions for *radiation sickness* and *polonium* on p. 121 and *radioactivity* and *radium* on p. 122. Then, write a written narration about p. 55-69. Refer to *Written Narration Tips* in the Appendix for help as needed. Read your written narration out loud after you have finished writing. Refer to *Written Narration Skills* for help in editing.

Key Idea: Marie and Pierre Curie discovered two new elements. They named them *polonium* and *radium*.

Reading about History | I

Read about history in the following resource:

 Rescue and Redeem p. 63-78

You will be writing a narration about the chapter *Dwight Moody and Ira Sankey: What Will You Do with Christ?* To prepare for writing your narration, look back over p. 63-78 in *Rescue and Redeem*. Think about the main idea and the most important moments in this part of the reading.

After you have thought about what you will write and how you will begin your narration, turn to Unit 7 in your *Student Notebook*. For more guidance on writing a narration, see *Written Narration Tips* in the Appendix.

In Box 4, write a 12-16 sentence narration about the reading. When you have finished writing, read your sentences out loud to catch any mistakes. Check for the following things: *Did you include **who** or **what topic** the reading was mainly about? Did you include **descriptors** of the important thing(s) that happened? Did you include a **closing sentence**? If not, add those things.* Use the *Written Narration Skills* in the Appendix as a guide for editing the narration.

Key Idea: Dwight Moody was a well-known evangelist when he asked Ira Sankey to join his gospel ministry. Moody needed someone to lead the music at his meetings. Moody and Sankey were in Chicago preaching on October 8, 1871, when the Great Chicago Fire began. By the time it was done burning, it had consumed 18,000 buildings and left 90,000 - 100,000 people homeless. Moody and Sankey escaped with their lives and with new purpose.

Storytime | T/I

Read the following assigned pages:

 Mama's Bank Account p. 72-85
Note: p. 80 contains one word of profanity.

Get the bookmark that you placed in your book on Day 2. Locate the same section of the bookmark that you used on Day 2. Beneath Day 2's entry, write the book title and the page numbers you read today. Select the one remaining response option at the bottom of the bookmark, and place a checkmark next to it. In the blank space under today's pages, respond in writing using your checked option. Keep the bookmark in your book.

Key Idea: Relate to the text in various ways.

Economics | I

Read about economics in the following resource:

 Whatever Happened to Penny Candy? p. 51-57

After the reading, open your *Student Notebook* to the "Economic Principles" section at the front of your notebook. Under "Economic Principle", write one line or one sentence that summarizes the economic principle you learned from today's reading.

Key Idea: The business cycle is the cycle of inflation followed by a correction period of recession or depression. The recession or depression then leads to further inflation.

President Study | I

 On *The Presidents* DVD Volume 1, select the Chapter "John Q. Adams to Polk" and watch **only** Program 4: William Henry Harrison. Then, open your *President Notebook* to William Henry Harrison. Use today's viewing to add further information about Harrison.

Key Idea: Research William Henry Harrison.

Independent History Study | I

On p. 8 of *Rescue and Redeem*, read over the entries from 1860-1893 on the "Modern Church Timeline". Even though you have read these entries before, pay special attention to what was going on about the same time as the Great Chicago Fire and Moody's ministry.

Key Idea: Moody urged people to accept Jesus' gift of salvation before it was too late.

Learning the Basics
Focus: Language Arts, Math, Bible, Nature Journal, and Science

Biblical Self-Image `T`

Read and discuss with the students the following page in the resource below.

 Who Am I? And What Am I Doing Here? p. 66

For "Make a Note of It" on p. 66, first read the Scripture written under each heading on p. 31-35 for the attributes of God. For those attributes that have a Psalm, read **only** the Psalm. For "God Is a Person", read only the list of attributes, not the Scriptures. Then, have students write a brief Psalm.

Key Idea: Our time, talent, and love are God's.

Language Arts `S`

Have students complete one dictation exercise (see Appendix for directions and passages).

Help students complete one lesson from the following reading program:

 Drawn into the Heart of Reading

Help students complete **one** English option.

 Progressing With Courage: Lesson 27

Progressing With Courage: Lesson 80 (first half only)

Key Idea: Practice language arts skills.

Bible Quiet Time `I`

Bible Study: Complete the assignment below.

 Faith at Work: Lesson 6 – Day Three p. 41-42

Prayer Focus: Refer to **supplication** on "Preparing Your Heart for Prayer". Then, pray a prayer of supplication to make a humble and earnest request of God. Write 'supplication' at the bottom of today's lesson in *Faith at Work* above *Day Four*. Next to it, either list several key phrases or write a sentence to summarize your prayer. Keep "Preparing Your Heart for Prayer" inside your Bible.

Scripture Memory: Recite Romans 12:1-8.

Music: Refer to p. 30 as you sing with Track 3 *"To God Be the Glory"* (verse 1).

Key Idea: Read and study Romans 3.

Math Exploration `S`

Choose **one** of the math options listed below (see Appendix for details).

Singapore Primary Mathematics 6A/6B, Discovering Mathematics 7A/7B, 8A/8B, No-Nonsense Algebra or *Videotext Algebra*

Your own math program

Key Idea: Use a step-by-step math program.

Science Exploration `I`

Put on your safety glasses, smooth gloves, and smock as recommended on p. 6 of the *Chemistry C500 Experiment Manual*. Next, read p. 23 and follow the directions to perform "Experiment 11" from p. 24 of the Experiment Manual. For step 2 on p. 24, you will need to refer to Experiment 3 on p. 12. As you perform Experiment 3, you will **omit** the part with the burning match and instead place a stopper in the test tube that contains the mixture of sodium carbonate, tartaric acid, and water. Then, you will return to Experiment 11 on p. 24 to "pour" the gas-like carbon dioxide from your stoppered tube into a third test tube, making sure **not** to pour in any of the liquid. Place a stopper in test tube 3 to capture the gas. Now, you are ready to perform step 4 on p. 24 for an audience as a scientific demonstration. After the demonstration, clean up referring to "How to Dispose of Waste" on p. 7 and Basic Rules 5, 6, 7, and 11 on p. 6.

Key Idea: Carbonic acid is created when carbon dioxide dissolves in water. The blue litmus solution turns red as the acid causes the blue color to disappear.

Reading about History [S]

Read about history in the following resource:

Storytime [T/I]

Read the following assigned pages:

★ *All American History: Vol. II* p. 219 – middle of p. 225

After today's reading, choose **two** sections from p. 219-225 to orally narrate or retell to an adult. As you retell, the adult will write or type your narration. When the narration is complete, fold the typed or written narration to fit in Unit 8 – Box 9 of the *Student Notebook*. Glue the folded narration in Box 9, so it can be opened and read.

Key Idea: The Centennial Exposition in Philadelphia and the World's Columbian Exposition in Chicago were both world fairs that took place during the Gilded Age. Fair exhibits reflected advancements in machinery, technology, and horticulture. Entertainment reflected period music, food, drama, and art.

★ *Mama's Bank Account* p. 86-103
Get the bookmark that you placed in your book last unit. Choose a new section of the bookmark with **three** options at the bottom. At the top of this section of the bookmark, write the book title and the page numbers you read today. Select **one** of the three options at the bottom and place a checkmark next to it. In the blank space under today's pages, respond in writing using your checked option.

Key Idea: Relate to the text in various ways.

Worthy Words [T]

Read, analyze, and evaluate the speech below.

History Project [S]

Read about Edison's work with animation and motion pictures at one of the websites below.
http://www.americaslibrary.gov/jb/gilded/jb_gilded_kinetscp_1.html

http://www.exeter.ac.uk/bdc/young_bdc/movingpics/movingpics1.htm

Next, plan your own animation. On paper, sketch a quick plan of an animation you could do in a flipbook-style of a historical event from this period, such as the sinking of the *Titanic*, the Great Chicago Fire, or the Ferris wheel. Keep the images simple with slight changes from frame to frame. Plan for 25-50 frames.

Key Idea: Thomas Edison made many advancements in the motion picture industry.

★ *Book of Great American Speeches for Young People* p. 122-124
After reading the speech, answer the following questions on an index card: *To what audience is Mark Twain speaking? What is the Associated Press? How does Twain flatter the press in his opening paragraph? What does Twain say is his motive in promoting simplified spelling? How does Twain use humor to make his point? Do you think that Twain really was in favor of the simplified spelling movement? In what instances do people use simplified spelling today?* Next, meet with a parent to have a Socratic dialogue about the speech. Before beginning the dialogue, the parent reads the speech out loud. Next, discuss the questions using your notes. All participants should use life experiences and/or the text to support their responses.

Key Idea: Twain wrote with humor and satire.

Independent History Study [I]

★ Choose an important part of the speech from p. 122-124 of *Book of Great American Speeches* to copy in quotation marks in your *Student Notebook* Unit 8 – Box 6. Write "Mark Twain" at the bottom of Box 6.

Key Idea: Mark Twain coined the phrase "Gilded Age" through his writing. He remains famous today.

Learning the Basics

Focus: Language Arts, Math, Bible, Nature Journal, and Science

Nature Journal [I]

Read and follow the directions in the resource below to draw in your Nature Journal.

 Nature Drawing & Journaling: Lesson X p. 32-33 and first two paragraphs p. 34

Note: Save paragraph 3 on p. 34 to do on Unit 8 – Day 3.

Key Idea: Practice creating tones of green.

Language Arts [S]

Help students complete one lesson from the following reading program:

★ *Drawn into the Heart of Reading*

Help students complete **one** English option.

★ *Progressing With Courage:* Lesson 28

★ *Progressing With Courage:* Lesson 80 (last half only)

★ Your own grammar program

Work with the students to complete **one** of the writing options listed below:

★ *Write with the Best: Vol. 2* Unit 4 – Day 5 p. 35 (Note: For the research you will need a parent's help, guidance, and supervision. Follow p. 87-90 to write your information in outline form. You will write one paragraph for **each** argument or topic in your outline on Unit 9 – Day 1.)

★ Your own writing program

Key Idea: Practice language arts skills.

Bible Quiet Time [I]

Bible Study: Read and complete the assigned pages in the following resource:

★ *Faith at Work: Lesson 6 – Day Four* p. 42-43

Prayer Focus: Refer to **adoration** on "Preparing Your Heart for Prayer". Then, pray a prayer of adoration to worship and honor God. After your prayer, write 'adoration' at the bottom of today's lesson in *Faith at Work* above *Day Five*. Next to 'adoration', either list key phrases or write a sentence to summarize your prayer. Keep "Preparing Your Heart for Prayer" inside your Bible.

Scripture Memory: Read aloud Romans 12:9 three times from your Bible.

Music: Read p. 29 in *Hymns for a Kid's Heart*. Refer to p. 30-31 as you sing with Track 3 *"To God Be the Glory"* (vs. 1-2).

Key Idea: Read and study Romans 3.

Math Exploration [S]

Choose **one** of the math options listed below (see Appendix for details).

★ *Singapore Primary Mathematics 6A/6B, Discovering Mathematics 7A/7B, 8A/8B, No-Nonsense Algebra* or *Videotext Algebra*

★ Your own math program

Key Idea: Use a step-by-step math program.

Science Exploration [I]

★ Read *Marie Curie and the Discovery of Radium* p. 70-87. After reading the chapters, read the definition for *Nobel Prize* on p. 120 and *treatise* on p. 122. Then, either discuss questions 8, 10, and 11 on p. 116-117 with a parent or write answers to the questions on paper.

Key Idea: After proving the existence of radium, the Curies were awarded the Nobel Prize in physics. The fame that came with winning the prize made it difficult for the Curies to continue their work. In 1905, they began work in a new lab. On April 19, 1906, Pierre was killed by a horse-drawn wagon. Marie continued their work and was given Pierre's job at the Sorbonne.

Reading about History | I

Read about history in the following resources:

 All American History: Vol. II p. 225-230

After today's reading, open your *Student Notebook* to Unit 8. Look at the picture of the Vaudeville-style poster in Box 5. What type of act is the poster advertising? Vaudeville shows often had multiple acts and performers with a variety of talents. Acts included things like comedy, card tricks, daring feats, pantomime, dramatic monologues, singing, dancing, and acrobatic feats. Vaudeville was a theatrical type of entertainment that was popular from the 1880s-1920s.

Key Idea: During the Gilded Age, vaudeville replaced minstrel shows as the most popular type of entertainment in America. During this same era, ragtime was a new kind of music, and realism and naturalism emerged as new focuses in literature.

History Project | S

Animation is a series of images or frames flipped quickly so that the images merge, creating the sensation of motion. To make your own animation, you need 25-50 small index cards, or small sheets of paper, measuring 3" x 4" or 3" x 5". Follow the plan for your animation that you drew on Day 1. Draw the first frame on one paper or card and the last frame on another paper or card. Then, draw the frames in between. Draw the images close to the bottom and toward the right side, because you will bind your cards on the left side. Use simple images with small changes.

Key Idea: Edison's Vitascope was an early film projector that produced animation.

President Study | I

 Read p. 21 in *Our Presidents...* Then, open your *President Notebook* to John Tyler. Use today's reading to help you complete the information about Tyler.

Key Idea: Research John Tyler.

Storytime | T/I

Read the following assigned pages:

 Mama's Bank Account p. 104-121

Get the bookmark that you placed in your book. Locate the same section of the bookmark that you used on Day 1. Beneath Day 1's entry, write the book title and the page numbers you read today. Select one of the **two** remaining response options at the bottom of the bookmark, and place a checkmark next to it. In the blank space under today's pages, respond in writing using your checked option. Place your bookmark in your book.

Key Idea: Relate to the text in various ways.

Timeline | I

Student Notebook today. In Unit 8 – Box 1, draw a theater curtain. Label the box, *Vaudeville Entertainment (1880-1920 A.D.)*.

In Box 2, draw and color a skyscraper. Label it, *1st U.S. Skyscraper - Chicago (1885 A.D.)*.

In Box 3, use p. 178 of *The Story of the World* to help you draw the outline of China and color it in. Label it, *Boxer Rebellion (1900 A.D.)*.

Key Idea: While the United States was growing and changing, the "Society of Righteous and Harmonious Fists" was fighting to keep Western ideals out of China. This resulted in the Boxer Rebellion and the eventual end to the Qing Dynasty.

Independent History Study | I

Listen to *"The Maple Leaf Rag"* at one of the sites below.
http://archive.org/details/MapleLeafRag

http://cantorion.org/music/500/Maple-Leaf-Rag-Original-version

Key Idea: *"The Maple Leaf Rag"* was the most famous ragtime piece written by Scott Joplin.

Learning the Basics
Focus: Language Arts, Math, Bible, Nature Journal, and Science

Biblical Self-Image |T|

Read and discuss with the students the following pages in the resource below.

★ *Who Am I? And What Am I Doing Here?* p. 67-68

After reading, discuss ways that both you and your students can show humility in areas where God has gifted you with talent.

Key Idea: Your value or worth comes from being made in God's image and being called His child. Worth does not come from the things of the world such as beauty, fashion, fame, wealth, or achievements.

Language Arts |S|

Have students complete one studied dictation exercise (see Appendix for directions and passages).

Help students complete one lesson from the following reading program:

★ *Drawn into the Heart of Reading*

Help students complete **one** English option.

★ *Progressing With Courage:* Lesson 29

★ *Progressing With Courage:* Lesson 81 (first half only)

★ Your own grammar program

Key Idea: Practice language arts skills.

Bible Quiet Time |I|

Bible Study: Read and complete the assigned pages in the following resource:

★ *Faith at Work: Lesson 6 – Day Five* and *Notes* p. 43-47

Prayer Focus: Refer to **confession** on "Preparing Your Heart for Prayer". Then, pray a prayer of confession to admit or acknowledge your sins to God. After your prayer, write 'confession' at the bottom of today's lesson on p. 43 in *Faith at Work*. Next to 'confession', either list key phrases or write a sentence to summarize your prayer. This will be your prayer log. Keep "Preparing Your Heart for Prayer" inside your Bible.

Scripture Memory: Memorize Romans 12:9 from your Bible and recite it.

Music: Refer to p. 30-31 as you sing with Track 3 *"To God Be the Glory"* (vs. 1-2).

Key Idea: Read and study Romans 3.

Math Exploration |S|

Choose **one** of the math options listed below (see Appendix for details).

★ *Singapore Primary Mathematics 6A/6B, Discovering Mathematics 7A/7B, 8A/8B, No-Nonsense Algebra* or *Videotext Algebra*

★ Your own math program

Key Idea: Use a step-by-step math program.

Science Exploration |I|

★ Read *Marie Curie and the Discovery of Radium* p. 88-98. After reading the chapters, read the definition for *Albert Einstein* on p. 119. Then, either discuss questions 1, 4, and 9 on p. 116 with a parent or write answers to the questions on paper.

Key Idea: In 1914, the Sorbonne and the Pasteur Institute completed the Radium Institute of Paris on a street named after Pierre Curie, the Rue Pierre Curie. Marie was the director of the laboratory for radioactivity. Professor Claude Renard was in charge of the biological research lab and Curietherapy.

Learning Through History

Focus: Entertainment in the Gilded Age and Rebellion and Missions in China

Unit 8 - Day 3

Reading about History [I]

Read about history in the following resource:

★ *The Story of the World: Vol. 4 p.* 178-183
After today's reading, open your *Student Notebook* to Unit 8. Look at the French political cartoon from 1898 shown in Box 7. Notice from left to right across the front of the cartoon: Queen Victoria of the United Kingdom, William II of Germany, Nicholas II of Russia, and the Meiji Emperor of Japan. In the back, notice the Qing Chinese official unable to stop the division of "Chine", or "China", throwing up his hands. Next to him notice Marianne of France (the national emblem of France), who is looking over Nicholas II of Russia's shoulder. In Box 8, explain in your own words what you think is being represented in the political cartoon. This cartoon was in the French newspaper in 1898, and the Boxer Rebellion occurred in 1900.

Key Idea: To fight "invasion" by the West, Chinese rebels formed a secret society. The Westerners called this society "Boxers".

History Project [S]

Get your flipbook that you began on Day 2. Place the frames of your flipbook in a stack in order, and loop a rubber band around the stack on the left side. Then, hold the rubber-banded stack with your left hand and flip the pages quickly with your right hand. In places where you notice the action jumps too much as you flip, add an additional page or two of frames in between to make the transition smoother.

Key Idea: Edison was experimenting with motion pictures in 1888.

State Study [T]

★ This is an **optional** part of the plans. If you have chosen to study your state using *State History from a Christian Perspective,* do **part** of Lesson 7 (numbers 1-4 only) from the *Master Lesson Plan Book.*

Key Idea: Study your individual state.

Storytime [T/I]

Read the following assigned pages:

★ *Mama's Bank Account* p. 122-132

After today's reading, orally narrate or retell the portion of the story that was read today. See *Narration Tips* in the Appendix as needed.

Key Idea: Practice orally narrating, or retelling, a portion of a story.

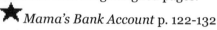

Geography [I]

For today's activities, use the map listed below.

★ *The Story of the World: Vol. 4 p.* 178

Compare the map on p. 178 of *The Story of the World,* showing China at the end of the Qing Dynasty, with the borders of China as shown on a modern-day map or globe. Notice the countries that bordered China on p. 178 compared to those that border China now. Next, on your globe or world map, find the United Kingdom, Germany, Russia, Japan, and France. Notice the distance from China for each of these countries. These countries each had a presence and an interest in China at the time of the Qing dynasty.

Key Idea: When the Boxer Rebellion ended, Cixi returned to Beijing to rule as the Empress Dowager. Western ideas were taught, and some traditional Chinese practices were outlawed. After Cixi's death, Puyi became China's last Qing emperor.

Independent History Study [I]

On Day 4, you will read about the Boxer Rebellion from the perspective of a missionary who was working in China during the time of the rebellion. How do you think that the missionary's perspective will differ from the perspective of the story that you read in *The Story of the World* today?

Key Idea: Each part of history has many facets.

Learning the Basics
Focus: Language Arts, Math, Bible, Nature Journal, Poetry, and Science

Nature Journal & Poetry $\boxed{S}$

The poetry of Longfellow, Wordsworth, and Whitman is scheduled on Day 3 in each unit to complement the nature journaling sessions. Read aloud and discuss today's poem *"A Whirl-Blast from Behind the Hill"* (see Appendix) with a parent. Notice the mentions of the green trees and bowers in the poem. Then, follow the directions in the resource below.

★ *Nature Drawing & Journaling: Lesson X* p. 34 (Note: Do paragraph 3 only.)

<u>Key Idea</u>: Practice using many different greens in your nature study.

Language Arts $\boxed{S}$

Have students complete one studied dictation exercise (see Appendix for passages).

Help students complete **one** English option.

★ *Progressing With Courage:* Lesson 30

★ *Progressing With Courage:* Lesson 81 (last half only)

★ Your own grammar program

Work with the students to complete **one** of the writing options listed below:

★ *Write with the Best: Vol. 2* Unit 4 – Day 6 p. 35

★ Your own writing program

<u>Key Idea</u>: Practice language arts skills.

Bible Quiet Time $\boxed{I}$

Bible Study: Read and complete the assigned pages in the following resource:

★ *Faith at Work: Lesson 7 – Day One* p. 48
Note: Refer to p. 44-47 to complete the lesson.

Prayer Focus: Refer to **thanksgiving** on "Preparing Your Heart for Prayer". Then, pray a prayer of thanksgiving to express gratitude to God for His divine goodness. After your prayer, write 'thanksgiving' at the bottom of today's lesson in *Faith at Work* above *Day Two*. Next to 'thanksgiving', either list key phrases or write a sentence to summarize your prayer. Keep "Preparing Your Heart for Prayer" inside your Bible.

Scripture Memory: Copy Romans 12:9 in your Common Place Book.

Music: Refer to p. 30-31 as you sing with Track 3 *"To God Be the Glory"* (vs. 1-2).

<u>Key Idea</u>: Read and study Romans 3.

Math Exploration $\boxed{S}$

Choose **one** of the math options listed below (see Appendix for details).

★ *Singapore Primary Mathematics 6A/6B, Discovering Mathematics 7A/7B, 8A/8B, No-Nonsense Algebra* or *Videotext Algebra*

★ Your own math program

<u>Key Idea</u>: Use a step-by-step math program.

Science Exploration $\boxed{I}$

★ Read *Marie Curie and the Discovery of Radium* p. 99-115. After reading the chapters, read the definition for *artificial radioactivity, atoms, cataracts,* and *ion* on p. 119. Then, read the definitions for *League of Nations, molecule,* and *nuclear* on p. 120. Next, read the definition for *pernicious anemia* on p. 121 and *tuberculosis* on p. 122. Last, **either** write a written narration about p. 99-115 **or** meet with a parent to answer questions 1, 2, 3, and 5 on p. 116. If you chose to write a written narration, refer to *Written Narration Tips* and *Written Narration Skills* in the Appendix as needed.

<u>Key Idea</u>: After WWI ended, Poland gained its freedom. Marie returned to teaching, and her daughter Irene joined her in the study of radium. Marie helped raise funding for a radiation institute in Poland.

Learning Through History
Focus: Entertainment in the Gilded Age and Rebellion and Missions in China

Unit 8 - Day 4

Reading about History | I

Read about history in the following resource:

 Hero Tales: Vol. III p. 117-127

You will be writing a narration about **one** of the sections that you read about today (either "From Southern Belle to Chinese Missionary", "The Heavenly Foot Society", "On the Road with Jesus", or "Taking a Beating for Jesus"). To prepare for writing your narration, look back over your chosen section in *Hero Tales: Vol. III*. Think about the main idea and the most important moments in this part.

After you have thought about what you will write and how you will begin your narration, turn to Unit 8 in your *Student Notebook*. For more guidance on writing a narration, see *Written Narration Tips* in the Appendix.

In Box 4, write a 12-16 sentence narration about the reading. When you have finished writing, read your sentences out loud to catch any mistakes. Check for the following things: *Did you include* **who** *or* **what topic** *the reading was mainly about? Did you include* **descriptors** *of the important thing(s) that happened? Did you include a* **closing sentence**? *If not, add those things.* Use the *Written Narration Skills* in the Appendix as a guide for editing the narration.

Key Idea: Lottie Moon was born in Virginia in 1840. She sailed to China to become a missionary in the province of Shantung, eventually settling in P'ingtu. She fought against the Chinese custom of foot-binding and spent time in the country visiting villages and spreading the gospel. During the Boxer Rebellion, Lottie fled from China to Japan. Today, she is remembered as "The patron saint of Southern Baptist Missions".

Storytime | T/I

Read the following assigned pages:

 Mama's Bank Account p. 133-147

Get the bookmark that you placed in your book. Locate the same section of the bookmark that you used on Day 2. Beneath Day 2's entry, write the book title and the page numbers you read today. Select the one remaining response option at the bottom of the bookmark, and place a checkmark next to it. In the blank space under today's pages, respond in writing using your checked option. Keep the bookmark in your book.

Key Idea: Relate to the text in various ways.

Economics | I

Read about economics in the resource below.

 Whatever Happened to Penny Candy? p. 58-66

After the reading, open your *Student Notebook* to the "Economic Principles" section at the front of your notebook. Under "Economic Principle", write a one line or one sentence summary for the economic principle you learned from today's reading.

Key Idea: Money responds to supply and demand. When demand is high, then velocity (or the speed at which money changes hands) is low. The opposite is also true. Inflation goes through three stages that are caused by the changing demand for money.

President Study | I

 On *The Presidents* DVD Volume 1, select the Chapter "John Q. Adams to Polk" and watch **only** Program 5: John Tyler. Then, open your *President Notebook* to John Tyler. Use today's viewing to add further information about Tyler.

Key Idea: Research John Tyler.

Independent History Study | I

Choose **one** of the sets of questions from the sections of *Hero Tales* that you read today to answer orally with an adult. The questions are found on p. 121, 124, and 127.

Key Idea: Lottie Moon trusted Jesus for her safety and her salvation. She spent almost 40 years working as a missionary in China.

Biblical Self-Image [T]

Our plans intend for the listed pages in *Who Am I? And What Am I Doing Here?* to be read either silently by both you and your student, or read aloud to the student by you. With this in mind, read and discuss the following pages in the resource below.

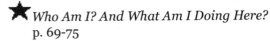 *Who Am I? And What Am I Doing Here?* p. 69-75

Key Idea: Since we are made in God's image, we are the most important part of creation.

Language Arts [S]

Have students complete one studied dictation exercise (see Appendix for directions and passages).

Help students complete one lesson from the following reading program:

★ *Drawn into the Heart of Reading*

Help students complete **one** English option.

★ *Progressing With Courage:* Lesson 31

★ *Progressing With Courage:* Lesson 82 (first half only)

★ Your own grammar program

Key Idea: Practice language arts skills.

Bible Quiet Time [I]

Bible Study: Complete the assignment below.

★ *Faith at Work: Lesson 7 – Day Two* p. 48-49 (Note: for 1b on p. 48, list what you read in today's Scripture and facts from your memory.)

Prayer Focus: Refer to **supplication** on "Preparing Your Heart for Prayer". Then, pray a prayer of supplication to make a humble and earnest request of God. Write 'supplication' at the bottom of today's lesson in *Faith at Work* above *Day Three*. Next to it, either list several key phrases or write a sentence to summarize your prayer. Keep "Preparing Your Heart for Prayer" inside your Bible.

Scripture Memory: Recite Romans 12:1-9.

Music: Refer to p. 30-31 as you sing with Track 3 *"To God Be the Glory"* (vs. 1-2).

Key Idea: Read and study Romans 4.

Math Exploration [S]

Choose **one** of the math options listed below.

★ *Singapore Primary Mathematics 6A/6B, Discovering Mathematics 7A/7B, 8A/8B, No-Nonsense Algebra* or *Videotext Algebra*

★ Your own math program

Key Idea: Use a step-by-step math program.

Science Exploration [I]

★ Copy the Science Lab Form from the Appendix of this guide. Then, put on your safety glasses, smooth gloves, and smock as recommended on p. 6 of the *Chemistry C500 Experiment Manual.* In the top box of the Science Lab Form write: *How can you estimate the carbon dioxide content in water?* In the second box of the form, write your hypothesis. Follow the directions for "Experiment 12" on p. 25 of the Experiment Manual and complete the box "Perform an Experiment" on your lab form. Then, follow the arrows to complete the rest of the Science Lab Form. Read p. 26 to help with your conclusion. To clean up, refer to "How to Dispose of Waste" on p. 7 and Basic Rules 5, 6, 7, and 11 on p. 6.

Key Idea: Mineral water contains carbonic acid, and this acid turns blue litmus red. Since the standard solution is a base, or an alkali, when the amount of alkali added to the water is exactly equal to the amount of acid contained in the water, the solution becomes neutral. Once the acid is cancelled by the alkali, then a surplus of sodium carbonate, or alkali, creates a stable blue color.

Reading about History | I

Read about history in the following resource:

 Hero Tales: Vol. III p. 57-67

After today's reading, orally narrate or retell to an adult **one** portion of text that you read today. Some possible key words to introduce your narration might be *Jonathan Goforth, China, missionary, Rosalind Bell Smith, England, "flaming preacher", Boxer Rebellion.* For "God Must Come First", some possible words to include might be *typhoid fever, Changte, Wallace, baby Constance, trusting God.* For "A Tent for Seven Hundred People", some possible words to include might be *tent, public meetings, "Christian Alley", Mr. Su.* For "The Impossible Letter", some possible words to include might be *offended, Holy Spirit, letter, Pilgrim's Progress, apology.*

Key Idea: Jonathan and Rosalind Goforth worked in China as missionaries for 46 years.

History Project | S

Rosalind Goforth was deeply hurt and offended by another missionary, and she carried the hurt feelings and anger inside of her for years. She felt the Holy Spirit urge her to write a simple apology for her unforgiveness toward the missionary. After writing the apology, relief and joy flooded her soul. Either think of someone who has hurt or offended you, or think of something that you need to confess to the Lord. Write a simple apology or confession. Then, either mail or hand-deliver the apology, or ask the Lord for forgiveness for the sin that you confessed. Last, read Matthew 6:14-15.

Key Idea: Rosalind learned to forgive others.

President Study | I

 Read p. 22-23 in *Our Presidents...* Then, open your *President Notebook* to James K. Polk. Use today's reading to help you complete the information about Polk.

Key Idea: Research James K. Polk.

Storytime | T/I

Read the following assigned pages:

 Angel on the Square p. 1-22

Get the bookmark that you placed in your book last unit. Choose a new section of the bookmark with **three** options at the bottom. At the top of this section of the bookmark, write the book title and the page numbers you read today. Select **one** of the three options at the bottom and place a checkmark next to it. In the blank space under today's pages, respond in writing using your checked option.

Key Idea: Relate to the text in various ways.

Worthy Words | T

Open your *Student Notebook* to Unit 9 – Box 10. You will read, analyze, and evaluate an excerpt from Jonathan's book. After reading the excerpt, answer the following questions on an index card: *Who was Wang Ee? How did the Boxer Rebellion affect missionaries and Chinese Christians? In the years after the Boxer Rebellion, what reason did Wang Ee give for his work not prospering in Takwanchwang? Why do you think Jonathan Goforth asked Wang Ee to come to the meetings in Changteh? Why did Wang Ee send his son instead? How had the Boxer Indemnity affected Wang Ee's ministry? What can you learn about sin and confession from this excerpt?* Next, meet with a parent to have a Socratic dialogue about the excerpt. Before beginning the dialogue, the parent reads Box 10 out loud. Next, discuss the questions using your notes. All participants should use life experiences or text to support their responses.

Key Idea: Jonathan preached in Changteh.

Independent History Study | I

Open your *Student Notebook* to Unit 9. Choose an important part of the excerpt from Box 10 to copy in quotation marks in Box 6 and write "Jonathan Goforth" at the bottom.

Key Idea: God blessed the Goforths' ministry.

Learning the Basics
Focus: Language Arts, Math, Bible, Nature Journal, and Science

Nature Journal ⬛ I

Read and follow the directions in the resource below to draw in your Nature Journal.

★ *Nature Drawing & Journaling: Lesson XI* p. 35 - first paragraph on p. 36

Note: Wait to do paragraph 2 on p. 36 until Unit 9 – Day 3.

Key Idea: Practice mixing various earth tones.

Language Arts ⬛ S

Help students complete one lesson from the following reading program:

★ *Drawn into the Heart of Reading*

Help students complete **one** English option.

★ *Progressing With Courage:* Lesson 32

★ *Progressing With Courage:* Lesson 82 (last half only)

★ Your own grammar program

Work with the students to complete **one** of the writing options listed below:

★ *Write with the Best: Vol. 2* Unit 4 – Day 7 p. 35-36 (Note: You will need the outline with information about your topic that you created on Unit 8 – Day 1.)

★ Your own writing program

Key Idea: Practice language arts skills.

Bible Quiet Time ⬛ I

Bible Study: Read and complete the assigned pages in the following resource:

★ *Faith at Work: Lesson 7 – Day Three* p. 49 (Note: Refer to Romans 4:5-12 to answer questions 1-6 on *Day Three* of p. 49.)

Prayer Focus: Refer to **adoration** on "Preparing Your Heart for Prayer". Then, pray a prayer of adoration to worship and honor God. After your prayer, write 'adoration' at the bottom of today's lesson in *Faith at Work* above *Day Four*. Next to 'adoration', either list key phrases or write a sentence to summarize your prayer.

Scripture Memory: Read aloud Romans 12:10 three times from your Bible.

Music: Read the verse and pray the prayer from p. 31 in *Hymns for a Kid's Heart*. Refer to p. 30-31 as you sing with Track 3 *"To God Be the Glory"* (vs. 1-3).

Key Idea: Read and study Romans 4.

Math Exploration ⬛ S

Choose **one** of the math options listed below (see Appendix for details).

★ *Singapore Primary Mathematics 6A/6B, Discovering Mathematics 7A/7B, 8A/8B, No-Nonsense Algebra* or *Videotext Algebra*

★ Your own math program

Key Idea: Use a step-by-step math program.

Science Exploration ⬛ I

★ Read and follow the directions to complete *The Elements: Ingredients of the Universe* p. 1 – middle of p. 4. As part of today's assignment, you will complete Activity #1, #2, and #3.

Key Idea: Chemical elements are the basic ingredients by which everything else is made. Hydrogen, carbon, nitrogen, oxygen, and silicon are common elements that account for most of the matter in our universe.

Learning Through History

Focus: The Boxer Rebellion, the Russo-Japanese War, and the Balkan Wars

Unit 9 - Day 2

Reading about History [I]

Read about history in the following resource:

★ *The Story of the World: Vol. 4* p. 184-189

After today's reading, open your *Student Notebook* to Unit 9. Look at the 1905 cartoon in Box 7 showing Admiral Togo being elevated by the "world" to a place of honor between Admiral Dewey and Lord Nelson. Dewey gained fame with his victory at Manila Bay in the Spanish-American War and was promoted to Admiral of the U.S. Navy in 1903. Lord Nelson was a flag officer of the British Royal Navy known for his leadership during the Napoleonic Wars. In Box 8, choose a portion of text to copy from *The Story of the World* p. 187-189, which conveys the significance of Japanese Admiral Togo's actions.

<u>Key Idea</u>: After the Boxer Rebellion, Czar Nicholas II began building a railroad in China to transport Russian troops and supplies. To halt the Russians' progress, Japan attacked Russian troops in Port Arthur.

History Project [S]

After Russia lost the Russo-Japanese War, and with it Port Arthur, Russia began looking for a new port city to conquer. Persia, located on Russia's southern border, became the target. On white paper, either photocopy or trace the map from p. 190 of *The Story of the World: Vol. 4.* Then, use colored pencils to lightly color each empire or country a different color. Save your map for Day 3.

<u>Key Idea</u>: Russia needed an ice-free port city.

President Study [I]

★ On *The Presidents* DVD Volume 1, select the Chapter "John Q. Adams to Polk" and watch **only** Program 6: James K. Polk. Then, open your *President Notebook* to James K. Polk. Use today's viewing to add further information about Polk.

<u>Key Idea</u>: Research James K. Polk.

Storytime [T/I]

Read the following assigned pages:

★ *Angel on the Square* p. 23-43

Get the bookmark that you placed in your book. Locate the same section of the bookmark that you used on Day 1. Beneath Day 1's entry, write the book title and the page numbers you read today. Select one of the **two** remaining response options at the bottom of the bookmark, and place a checkmark next to it. In the blank space under today's pages, respond in writing using your checked option.

<u>Key Idea</u>: Relate to the text in various ways.

Timeline [I]

You will be adding to the timeline in your *Student Notebook* today. In Unit 9 – Box 1, draw and color a large tent. Label it, *Jonathan and Rosalind Goforth – Missionaries to China (1888-1930 A.D.).*

In Box 2, draw and color the Japanese flag used by the navy in 1904-1905 with a white rectangular background and a red circle or sun-disk in the center. Label it, *Russo-Japanese War (1904-1905 A.D.).*

In Box 3, draw an outline of the Balkan Penin-sula and color the Mediterranean Sea. Use the description on p. 196 and the map on p. 198 of *The Story of the World* as a guide. Label the box, *The Balkan Wars (1912-1913 A.D.).*

<u>Key Idea</u>: The Goforths were missionaries in China and Manchuria. They had to flee during the Boxer Rebellion of 1900. Later, the Russo-Japanese War and the Balkan Wars took place.

Independent History Study [I]

Listen to *What in the World? Vol. 3* Disc 3, Track 1: "Russia's Repressive Autocracy".

<u>Key Idea</u>: At the turn of the century, millions of Russian peasants were dissatisfied with Czar Nicholas II's rule. The czar was even less popular after losing the Russo-Japanese War.

Biblical Self-Image [T]

Read and discuss with the students the following pages in the resource below.

⭐ *Who Am I? And What Am I Doing Here?* p. 76-78

If time allows consider making blini, or Russian pancakes, following the recipe on p. 77.

<u>Key Idea</u>: It is important to love God with our whole heart, soul, and mind. God's Word shows us what the Lord expects of us.

Language Arts [S]

Have students complete one studied dictation exercise (see Appendix for directions and passages).

Help students complete one lesson from the following reading program:

⭐ *Drawn into the Heart of Reading*

Help students complete **one** English option.

⭐ *Progressing With Courage:* Lesson 33

⭐ *Progressing With Courage:* Lesson 83 (first half only)

⭐ Your own grammar program

<u>Key Idea</u>: Practice language arts skills.

Bible Quiet Time [I]

Bible Study: Read and complete the assigned pages in the following resource:

⭐ *Faith at Work: Lesson 7 – Day Four* p. 49-50 (Note: Refer to Romans 4:13-17 for questions 1, 3, and 4. Refer to Galatians 3:16-18 for question 2.)

Prayer Focus: Refer to **confession** on "Preparing Your Heart for Prayer". Then, pray a prayer of confession to admit or acknowledge your sins to God. After your prayer, write 'confession' at the bottom of today's lesson in *Faith at Work* above *Day Five*. Next to 'confession', either list key phrases or write a sentence to summarize your prayer. This will be your prayer log. Keep "Preparing Your Heart for Prayer" inside your Bible.

Scripture Memory: Memorize Romans 12:10 from your Bible and recite it.

Music: Refer to p. 30-31 as you sing with Track 3 *"To God Be the Glory"* (vs. 1-3).

<u>Key Idea</u>: Read and study Romans 4.

Math Exploration [S]

Choose **one** of the math options listed below (see Appendix for details).

⭐ *Singapore Primary Mathematics 6A/6B, Discovering Mathematics 7A/7B, 8A/8B, No-Nonsense Algebra* or *Videotext Algebra*

⭐ Your own math program

<u>Key Idea</u>: Use a step-by-step math program.

Science Exploration [I]

⭐ Read and follow the directions to complete *The Elements: Ingredients of the Universe* middle of p. 4 – bottom of p. 6. As part of today's assignment, you will complete Activity #4 and Activity #5.

<u>Key Idea</u>: Chemical compounds are made up of a combination of elements. Each compound has its own "recipe" of ingredients from the 109 elements. Each compound's recipe is written using abbreviations, or symbols, for the elements and numbers indicating the number of each type of atom contained in the compound.

Learning Through History

Focus: The Boxer Rebellion, the Russo-Japanese War, and the Balkan Wars

Unit 9 - Day 3

Reading about History | I

Read about history in the following resource:

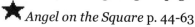 ★ *The Story of the World: Vol. 4* p. 190 – top of p. 196

After today's reading, open your *Student Notebook* to Unit 9 - Box 5, which shows the men who were a part of the first National Consultative Assembly, or *Majles*, in Persia. The center image shows the first chairman of the Majles. Mohammad Ali Shah disbanded the Majles in 1908. Later, the former chairman of the Majles was assassinated in Tehran on February 6, 1911. Under the picture in Box 5, write "*Members of the First Majles: Oct. 7, 1906 – June 23, 1908*".

Key Idea: After much pressure from the Persian people, Mozaffar od-Din Shah agreed to give Persia a constitution and an assembly. After Mozaffar's death, Mohammad Ali became Shah. Both Great Britain and Russia wanted control of Persia. Russia wanted Persia's port city, and Great Britain wanted Persia's oil.

History Project | S

Get the map of "The Fight for Persia" that you traced or copied on Day 2. Cut apart the map so that you have the following pieces: Ottoman Empire, Persia, Indian Ocean, Afghanistan, India, China, and Russian Empire. Then, use the pieces to assemble the map of Persia and her neighbors from memory. Check your work by referring to p. 190 of *The Story of the World*. Save the map pieces in a Ziploc bag or an envelope and file in the *Student Notebook*.

Key Idea: Russia gained control of Persia.

State Study | T

★ This is an **optional** part of the plans. If you have chosen to study your state using *State History from a Christian Perspective*, do the **last** part of Lesson 7 (number 5 only) from the *Master Lesson Plan Book*.

Key Idea: Study your individual state.

Storytime | T/I

Read the following assigned pages:

★ *Angel on the Square* p. 44-63

After today's reading, orally narrate or retell the portion of the story that was read today. See *Narration Tips* in the Appendix as needed.

Key Idea: Practice orally narrating, or retelling, a portion of a story.

Economics | I

Read about economics in the resource below.

★ *Whatever Happened to Penny Candy?* p. 67-74

After the reading, open your *Student Notebook* to the "Economic Principles" section at the front of your notebook. Under "Economic Principle", write a one or two sentence summary for the economic principle you learned from today's reading.

Key Idea: Inflation often causes people to look for investments for their extra money. The more people that invest in something, the higher the price rises. When the government stops creating new money, or inflating, prices stop rising and eventually fall. Investors often then either lose money or sell their investment.

Independent History Study | I

Open your *Student Notebook* to Unit 9. On the map in Box 9, locate the gray area that shows the "Russian Sphere of Influence" in Persia in 1907. Then, locate the pink area that shows the "British Sphere of Influence" in Persia. Last, locate the yellow area which shows Persia's "Neutral Sphere". Notice the location of Afghanistan and the Persian Gulf.

Key Idea: After Mozaffar od-Din Shah's death, Mohammad Ali became Shah of Persia. About this same time, both Russia and Great Britain claimed influence in Persia.

Learning the Basics
Focus: Language Arts, Math, Bible, Nature Journal, Poetry, and Science

Unit 9 - Day 3

Nature Journal & Poetry | S |

The poetry of Longfellow, Wordsworth, and Whitman is scheduled on Day 3 in each unit to complement the nature journaling sessions. Read aloud and discuss today's poem *"Hiawatha's Sailing"* (see Appendix) with a parent. Notice all of the various trees mentioned in the poem. Then, follow the directions in the resource below.

★ *Nature Drawing & Journaling: Lesson XI* p. 36 (Note: Do paragraph 2 only.)

<u>Key Idea</u>: Practice using many different browns for the trees in your nature study.

Language Arts | S |

Have students complete one studied dictation exercise (see Appendix for passages).

Help students complete **one** English option.

★ *Progressing With Courage:* Lesson 34

★ *Progressing With Courage:* Lesson 83 (last half only)

★ Your own grammar program

Work with the students to complete **one** of the writing options listed below:

★ *Write with the Best: Vol. 2* Unit 4 – Day 8 p. 36 (Note: Ideas for attention grabbers are found in #6 on p. 93.)

★ Your own writing program

<u>Key Idea</u>: Practice language arts skills.

Bible Quiet Time | I |

Bible Study: Read and complete the assigned pages in the following resource:

★ *Faith at Work: Lesson 7 – Day Five* and *Notes* p. 50-55

Prayer Focus: Refer to **thanksgiving** on "Preparing Your Heart for Prayer". Then, pray a prayer of thanksgiving to express gratitude to God for His divine goodness. After your prayer, write 'thanksgiving' at the bottom of today's lesson on p. 50 in *Faith at Work*. Next to 'thanksgiving', either list key phrases or write a sentence to summarize your prayer. Keep "Preparing Your Heart for Prayer" inside your Bible.

Scripture Memory: Copy Romans 12:10 in your Common Place Book.

Music: Refer to p. 30-31 as you sing with Track 3 *"To God Be the Glory"* (vs. 1-3).

<u>Key Idea</u>: Read and study Romans 4.

Math Exploration | S |

Choose **one** of the math options listed below (see Appendix for details).

★ *Singapore Primary Mathematics 6A/6B, Discovering Mathematics 7A/7B, 8A/8B, No-Nonsense Algebra* or *Videotext Algebra*

★ Your own math program

<u>Key Idea</u>: Use a step-by-step math program.

Science Exploration | I |

★ Read and follow the directions to complete *The Elements: Ingredients of the Universe* p. 7-10. As part of today's assignment, you will complete Activity #6 and Activity #7. For Activity #7, you will need to listen to the "The Chemical Compounds Song" on the CD that came with *The Elements: Ingredients of the Universe*. Check the back inside cover of *The Elements* as a possible location for the CD.

<u>Key Idea</u>: Elements are often named by the scientist who discovered the element.

Reading about History | I |

Read about history in the following resource:

★ *The Story of the World: Vol. 4* p. 196-201

You will be writing a narration about **part** of the chapter that you read today. Focus your narration on Abdulhamid, the Young Turks, the First Balkan War, and the Second Balkan War. To prepare for writing your narration, look back over p. 200-201 in *The Story of the World: Vol. 4*. Think about the main idea and the most important moments in this part of the reading.

After you have thought about what you will write and how you will begin your narration, turn to Unit 9 in your *Student Notebook*. For more guidance on writing a narration, see *Written Narration Tips* in the Appendix.

In Box 4, write a 12-16 sentence narration about the reading. When you have finished writing, read your sentences out loud to catch any mistakes. Check for the following things: *Did you include **who** or **what topic** the reading was mainly about? Did you include **descriptors** of the important thing(s) that happened? Did you include a **closing sentence**? If not, add those things.* Use the *Written Narration Skills* in the Appendix as a guide for editing the narration.

Key Idea: Until 1878, a large part of the Balkan Peninsula belonged to the Ottoman Empire. Through war in 1818, Russia gained Romania and Anatolia, and Bulgaria gained self-rule. Later, Russia had to give Anatolia back to the Ottomans. The Young Turks forced Ottoman Sultan Abdulhamid out after his violent reaction to an uprising in Macedonia. Desiring independence, the Balkan countries fought against the Young Turks in the First Balkan War. During the Second Balkan War, Greece, Serbia, and Bulgaria fought over Macedonia.

Storytime | T/I |

Read the following assigned pages:

★ *Angel on the Square* p. 64-86

Get the bookmark that you placed in your book. Locate the same section of the bookmark that you used on Day 2. Beneath Day 2's entry, write the book title and the page numbers you read today. Select the one remaining response option at the bottom of the bookmark, and place a checkmark next to it. In the blank space under today's pages, respond in writing using your checked option.

Key Idea: Relate to the text in various ways.

Geography | I |

For today's activities, use the map listed below.

★ *Map Trek CD: Missions to Modern Marvels* p. 38-39

Print the "The Balkan Wars" Student Map found on p. 39 of the *Map Trek* CD. Refer to or print the *Map Trek* Teacher's Answer Map on p. 38 to guide you as you label each country and body of water on your Student Map. Next, notice the countries on the Teacher's Answer Map that have a year listed in parentheses. Add the years to your Student Map to show when the countries achieved independence from the Ottoman Empire. Which country gained independence first? Which 3 countries achieved independence through the treaty of 1878? File the map in your *Student Notebook*.

Key Idea: The quest for independence in the Balkans led to uprisings, conflicts, and wars.

President Study | I |

★ Read p. 24 in *Our Presidents...* Then, open your *President Notebook* to Zachary Taylor. Use today's reading to help you complete the information about Taylor.

Key Idea: Research Zachary Taylor.

Independent History Study | I |

Listen to *What in the World? Vol. 3* Disc 2, Track 9: "The Balkan Wars" and Disc 3, Track 2: "Revival & Balkan Conflict".

Key Idea: The Treaty of Berlin redrew the boundary lines in the Balkans after the Russo-Turkish War. This led to the Balkan Wars.

Learning the Basics

Focus: Language Arts, Math, Bible, Nature Journal, and Science

Biblical Self-Image   T

Our plans intend for the listed pages in *Who Am I? And What Am I Doing Here?* to be read either silently by both you and your student, or read aloud to the student by you. With this in mind, read and discuss the following pages in the resource below.

 Who Am I? And What Am I Doing Here? p. 79 – middle of p. 88

Key Idea: God can transform our sinful hearts and fill them with peace, joy, and love.

Language Arts   S

Have students complete one studied dictation exercise (see Appendix for directions and passages).

Help students complete one lesson from the following reading program:

 Drawn into the Heart of Reading

Help students complete **one** English option.

⭐ *Progressing With Courage:* Lesson 35

⭐ *Progressing With Courage:* Lesson 84 (first half only)

⭐ Your own grammar program

Key Idea: Practice language arts skills.

Bible Quiet Time   I

Bible Study: Complete the assignment below.

⭐ *Faith at Work: Lesson 8 – Day One* p. 56
Note: Refer to p. 51-55 to complete the lesson.

Prayer Focus: Refer to **supplication** on "Preparing Your Heart for Prayer". Then, pray a prayer of supplication to make a humble and earnest request of God. Write 'supplication' at the bottom of today's lesson in *Faith at Work* above *Day Two*. Next to it, either list several key phrases or write a sentence to summarize your prayer. Keep "Preparing Your Heart for Prayer" inside your Bible.

Scripture Memory: Recite Romans 12:1-10.

Music: Refer to p. 30-31 as you sing with Track 3 *"To God Be the Glory"* (vs. 1-3).

Key Idea: Read and study Romans 4.

Math Exploration   S

Choose **one** of the math options listed below (see Appendix for details).

⭐ *Singapore Primary Mathematics 6A/6B, Discovering Mathematics 7A/7B, 8A/8B, No-Nonsense Algebra* or *Videotext Algebra*

⭐ Your own math program

Key Idea: Use a step-by-step math program.

Science Exploration   I

⭐ Read and follow the directions to play "Make Five" on p. 79-83 of *The Elements: Ingredients of the Universe.* If you do not have cardstock, you can make the game on regular white paper instead. Just know that it will not be as sturdy. You will need a partner to play this game about mineral recipes.

Key Idea: Each mineral has a definite chemical composition or recipe. The mineral recipes studied in this game are barite, zircon, hematite, cinnabar, cuprite, fluorite, quartz, galena, pyrite, corundum, talc, calcite, gypsum, chalcopyrite, epsom salt, and diamond/graphite.

Learning Through History
Focus: The Qing Dynasty Ends and Revolution in French Indochina and Mexico Begins

Unit 10 - Day 1

Reading about History [S]

Read about history in the following resource:

⭐ *The Story of the World: Vol. 4* p. 202-205
After today's reading, orally narrate or retell to an adult the portion of text that you read today. As you retell, the adult will write or type your narration. Some possible key words to include in your narration might be *Empress Cixi, Puyi, Forbidden City, foreign control, Sun Yixian, Sichuan revolt, abdicate, Nationalist Party, end of Qing dynasty*. When the narration is complete, tri-fold the typed or written narration to fit in Unit 10 – Box 7 of the *Student Notebook*. Glue the folded narration in Box 7, so it can be opened and read.

Key Idea: After empress Cixi died, Qing prince Puyi became emperor of China. Since Puyi was so young, Qing noblemen acted as regents in his place. In 1911, Sun Yixian led a rebellion in the Sichuan province of China against foreign control. This was the end of the Qing dynasty.

History Project [S]

Choose to make **at least** one of the recipes in the History Project box for this unit. Steamed corn cake was one of Empress Cixi's favorite pastries. Today you will make an oven version of this sweet corn cake. In a bowl, stir together 1 cup cornmeal, 3 cups flour, 1 1/3 cups white sugar, 2 Tbsp. baking powder, and 1 tsp. salt. Add 2/3 cup vegetable oil, 1/3 cup melted butter, 4 beaten eggs, 2 ½ cups whole milk, and 2 Tbsp. honey. Stir to moisten, but do not overmix. Pour batter in a greased 9x13 inch dish. Bake in a preheated oven at 350 degrees for 45 min. The cake is done when it is lightly browned and begins to crack on top.

Key Idea: Cixi was the last Qing empress.

Storytime [T/I]

Read the following assigned pages:

⭐ *Angel on the Square* p. 87-109

Get the bookmark that you placed in your book last unit. Choose a new section of the bookmark with **three** options at the bottom. At the top of this section of the bookmark, write the book title and the page numbers you read today. Select **one** of the three options at the bottom and place a checkmark next to it. In the blank space under today's pages, respond in writing using your checked option. Keep the bookmark in your book.

Key Idea: Relate to the text in various ways.

Timeline [I]

You will be adding to the timeline in your *Student Notebook* today. In Unit 10 – Box 1, draw and color a blue dragon. Label it, *Qing Dynasty in China (1644-1911 A.D.)*.

In Box 2, draw and color a Mexican sombrero. Label it, *Mexican Revolution Begins (1910 A.D.)*.

In Box 3, draw and color a sign that says 'SIL', meaning Summer Institute of Linguistics. Label the box, *Cameron Townsend – Founder Wycliffe Bible Translation (1896-1982 A.D.)*.

Key Idea: As the Qing dynasty was ending in China after over 250 years in power, the Mexican Revolution was taking place across Mexico. About this same time, Cameron Townsend was growing up in California. He would one day found Wycliffe Bible Translation to reach people around the world.

Independent History Study [I]

⭐ On p. 202 of *The Story of the World*, find the province of Sichuan in China. This is where the revolt began in 1911. Then, find Beijing, where the Forbidden City was located. Why do you think Sun Yixian and the Nationalist Party wanted to move the capital from Beijing south to a new location in Nanjing?

Key Idea: Sun Yixian wanted people to live by the principles of democracy, livelihood, and nationalism.

Learning the Basics
Focus: Language Arts, Math, Bible, Nature Journal, and Science

Nature Journal [S]

Read and follow the directions in the resource below.

 Nature Drawing & Journaling: Lesson XII p. 37-38

Note: Only sketch and color one flower today. If you do not have any cut flowers, you may go outside to draw a flower outdoors instead. If flowers are not blooming where you live, then draw a flower from www.enature.com instead. Click on "Wildflowers" under the "Field Guide" heading. Then, click on "Advanced Search" under "Search Field Guide" to specify the flower you wish to sketch.

<u>Key Idea</u>: Practice drawing flowers.

Language Arts [S]

Help students complete one lesson from the following reading program:

★ *Drawn into the Heart of Reading*

Help students complete **one** English option.

★ *Progressing With Courage:* Lesson 36

★ *Progressing With Courage:* Lesson 84 (last half only)

Work with the students to complete **one** of the writing options listed below:

★ *Write with the Best: Vol. 2* Unit 4 – Day 9 p. 36

★ Your own writing program

<u>Key Idea</u>: Practice language arts skills.

Bible Quiet Time [I]

Bible Study: Read and complete the assigned pages in the following resource:

★ *Faith at Work: Lesson 8 – Day Two* p. 56-57

Prayer Focus: Refer to **adoration** on "Preparing Your Heart for Prayer". Then, pray a prayer of adoration to worship and honor God. After your prayer, write 'adoration' at the bottom of today's lesson in *Faith at Work* above *Day Three*. Next to 'adoration', either list key phrases or write a sentence to summarize your prayer. Keep "Preparing Your Heart for Prayer" inside your Bible.

Scripture Memory: Read aloud Romans 12:11 three times from your Bible.

Music: Read p. 35-36 in *Hymns for a Kid's Heart*. Refer to p. 38-39 as you sing with Track 4 *"Trust and Obey"* (vs. 1-2).

<u>Key Idea</u>: Read and study Romans 5.

Math Exploration [S]

Choose **one** of the math options listed below (see Appendix for details).

★ *Singapore Primary Mathematics 6A/6B, Discovering Mathematics 7A/7B, 8A/8B, No-Nonsense Algebra* or *Videotext Algebra*

★ Your own math program

<u>Key Idea</u>: Use a step-by-step math program.

Science Exploration [I]

★ Read and follow the directions to complete *The Elements: Ingredients of the Universe* p. 11-15. The Internet address in Activity #1 does not work, so just read Activity #1 instead. For Activity #2, after typing in the address, click on "interactive flash version". Choose 5-10 elements to click on and then also click "find out more about..." on each of your selected elements to see samples that contain the element. Last, photocopy the cards on p. 85-90 and then cut them out. You will need these cards for Unit 10 – Day 2.

<u>Key Idea</u>: Dmitri Mendeleyev organized the elements into the Periodic Table.

Learning Through History

Focus: The Qing Dynasty Ends and Revolution in French Indochina and Mexico Begins

Unit 10 - Day 2

Reading about History [I]

Read about history in the following resource:

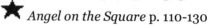 *The Story of the World: Vol. 4* p. 206-209
After today's reading, open your *Student Notebook* to Unit 10. In Box 5, you will see a French Indochina 20 piastre note issued in 1917 in Haiphong, Vietnam. The name 'piastre' comes from the Spanish pieces of eight or peso. Notice the image of Marianne on the left side on the note. Marianne was a French national emblem for liberty and reason dating back to the time of the French revolution. She is wearing a Phrygian cap and holding a spear. Next, notice the Vietnamese man and woman pictured in native dress on the right side of the note. This 20-piastre note was meant to pay homage to both of these cultures.

Key Idea: In Vietnam, Phan Boi Chau revolted against French rule. The rebellion failed.

History Project [S]

Today you will make Vietnamese Iced Coffee. Have an adult help you make one cup of coffee for each person who will be trying this drink. Next, set out a glass for each person. Add ice cubes to fill each glass. Then, pour part of the cup of coffee into each glass. After that pour 2 Tbsp. of sweetened condensed milk over the iced coffee in the glass. Allow the milk to filter down toward the bottom of the glass. Add a splash of milk or half-n-half if desired. Try sipping the coffee with a straw. If it isn't sweet enough, add up to 1 Tbsp. more sweetened condensed milk. If it is too sweet, add more coffee.

Key Idea: Vietnam has its own culture.

President Study [I]

 On *The Presidents* DVD Volume 1, select the Chapter "Taylor to Lincoln" and watch **only** Program 1: Zachary Taylor. Then, open your *President Notebook* to Zachary Taylor and use today's viewing to add further information.

Key Idea: Research Zachary Taylor.

Storytime [T/I]

Read the following assigned pages:

Angel on the Square p. 110-130

Get the bookmark that you placed in your book. Locate the same section of the bookmark that you used on Day 1. Beneath Day 1's entry, write the book title and the page numbers you read today. Select one of the **two** remaining response options at the bottom of the bookmark, and place a checkmark next to it. In the blank space under today's pages, respond in writing using your checked option.

Key Idea: Relate to the text in various ways.

Geography [I]

For today's activities, use the map listed below.

The Story of the World: Vol. 4 p. 206-207

Reread the first paragraph on p. 207 of *The Story of the World* as you use your finger to trace the travel paths described in the paragraph on a globe.

Next, find Siam (or Thailand) on both p. 206 and the globe. Both France and Great Britain claimed Siam. Then, find Vietnam, Laos, and Cambodia on both p. 206 and the globe. France claimed these countries. In the early 1900s, France divided Vietnam into the colonies of Tonkin, Annam, and Cochin China.

Key Idea: France claimed much of Indochina.

Independent History Study [I]

Read the timeline entries from 1902-1916 on p. 482 of *The Story of the World: Vol. 4*. Which names and interesting facts do you notice on the timeline? What major war began in 1914?

Key Idea: Phan Boi Chau was arrested in Shanghai and sentenced to house arrest in Vietnam until his death.

Learning the Basics

Focus: Language Arts, Math, Bible, Nature Journal, and Science

Biblical Self-Image [T]

Our plans intend for the listed pages in *Who Am I? And What Am I Doing Here?* to be read either silently by both you and your child, or read aloud to the child by you. This study also has much to be gained by discussion, as it provides an excellent opportunity to share what **you** believe. Read and discuss with the students the following pages in the resource below.

 Who Am I? And What Am I Doing Here? middle of p. 88 – top of p. 91

Key Idea: Our thoughts determine our actions, and our actions affect others. God cares about our thoughts and actions.

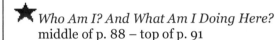

Language Arts [S]

Have students complete one studied dictation exercise (see Appendix for directions and passages).

Help students complete one lesson from the following reading program:

★ *Drawn into the Heart of Reading*

Help students complete **one** English option.

★ *Progressing With Courage:* Lesson 37

★ *Progressing With Courage:* Lesson 85 (first half only)

★ Your own grammar program

Key Idea: Practice language arts skills.

Bible Quiet Time [I]

Bible Study: Read and complete the assigned pages in the following resource:

★ *Faith at Work: Lesson 8 – Day Three* p. 57

Prayer Focus: Refer to **confession** on "Preparing Your Heart for Prayer". Then, pray a prayer of confession to admit or acknowledge your sins to God. After your prayer, write 'confession' at the bottom of today's lesson in *Faith at Work* above *Day Four*. Next to 'confession', either list key phrases or write a sentence to summarize your prayer. This will be your prayer log. Keep "Preparing Your Heart for Prayer" inside your Bible.

Scripture Memory: Memorize Romans 12:11 from your Bible and recite it.

Music: Refer to p. 38-39 as you sing with Track 4 *"Trust and Obey"* (vs. 1-2).

Key Idea: Read and study Romans 5.

Math Exploration [S]

Choose **one** of the math options listed below (see Appendix for details).

★ *Singapore Primary Mathematics 6A/6B, Discovering Mathematics 7A/7B, 8A/8B, No-Nonsense Algebra* or *Videotext Algebra*

★ Your own math program

Key Idea: Use a step-by-step math program.

Science Exploration [I]

★ Get the element cards that you photocopied from p. 85-90 of *The Elements: Ingredients of the Universe* and cut out on Unit 10 – Day 1. Use the element cards to help you complete Activity #3 in *The Elements: Ingredients of the Universe* p. 16. Then, save the cards to use again in Unit 16 – Day 2.

Key Idea: Each element was arranged in Mendeleyev's table by weight and then by chemical properties. This method of arranging the elements resulted in patterns that repeated periodically. So, the table became known as the Periodic Table.

Learning Through History

Focus: The Qing Dynasty Ends and Revolution in French Indochina and Mexico Begins

Unit 10 - Day 3

Reading about History | I

Read about history in the following resource:

★ *The Story of the World: Vol. 4* p. 210 – top of p. 216

Next, read John 12:12-19. What are the parallels between the passage in John and the last paragraph on p. 214 of *The Story of the World*? Why might the American diplomat's wife who was quoted on p. 214 have drawn this parallel? In John 11, Jesus had just raised Lazarus from the dead. Would Madero have had this kind of power to heal? Explain. Who is the one true Messiah? How do we know?

Key Idea: Madero replaced Diaz as president.

History Project | S

Today, you will make Mexican sopapillas. In a bowl, mix together 2 cups all-purpose flour, 1 tsp. baking powder, ½ tsp. salt, and 2 Tbsp. shortening. Stir in ¾ cup warm water and mix dough until smooth. Cover the bowl and let the dough stand 15 min. Then, roll the dough out on a floured surface so the dough is very thin. Cut the dough into 3" squares. **Ask an adult to help with this next part:** Pour oil into a frying pan so the oil is at least an inch deep. Heat the oil to 360-375 degrees. Drop 3 dough squares into the fry pan. Watch out for spattering hot oil! Fry 2 min. on each side until lightly golden. Place fried sopapillas on a paper towel covered cooling rack. Then, fry the next set of sopapillas. Coat sopapillas with cinnamon and sugar and drizzle with honey.

Key Idea: Mexico revolted against Diaz in 1911.

State Study | T

★ This is an **optional** part of the plans. If you have chosen to study your state using *State History from a Christian Perspective,* do Lesson 8 from the *Master Lesson Plan Book.* Note: The directions for step 1 contain a misprint. Instead of step **5**, it should be step **2**.

Key Idea: Study your individual state.

Storytime | T/I

Read the following assigned pages:

★ *Angel on the Square* p. 131-152

After today's reading, orally narrate or retell the portion of the story that was read today. See *Narration Tips* in the Appendix as needed.

Key Idea: Practice orally narrating, or retelling, a portion of a story.

Worthy Words | T

Open your *Student Notebook* to Unit 10 – Box 9. You will read, analyze, and evaluate an excerpt from a 1908 interview with Porfirio Diaz. After reading the excerpt, answer the following questions on an index card: *In the opening paragraphs, how does Diaz describe his government? Which phrases or words hint that Diaz's government is actually more of an autocracy (with power concentrated in one man's hands)? What reasons does Diaz give for having no opposition party? Based on your reading from* The Story of the World *p. 211-214, did Diaz welcome an opposition party as he said he would in this interview? Why do you think Diaz changed his mind not long after this interview? What impression do you get of Diaz from this interview? What can you learn about trusting or accepting everything said in an interview as truth?* Next, meet with a parent to have a Socratic dialogue about the excerpt. Before beginning the dialogue, the parent reads Box 9 out loud. Next, discuss the questions using your notes. All participants should use life experiences or text to support their responses.

Key Idea: Porfirio Diaz ruled Mexico 35 years.

Independent History Study | I

Open your *Student Notebook* to Unit 10. Choose an important part of the excerpt from Box 9 to copy in quotation marks in Box 6. Write "Porfirio Diaz" at the bottom of Box 6.

Key Idea: Diaz was a controversial leader.

Learning the Basics
Focus: Language Arts, Math, Bible, Nature Journal, Poetry, and Science

Nature Journal & Poetry | S |

The poetry of Longfellow, Wordsworth, and Whitman is scheduled to complement the journaling sessions. Read aloud and discuss *"To the Small Celandine"* (see Appendix) with a parent. Then, follow the directions below.

⭐ *Nature Drawing & Journaling: Lesson XII* p. 38

Note: Draw the second flower today. Refer to Unit 10 – Day 1 for directions. Then, copy part of today's poem on your journal page.

Key Idea: Practice sketching flowers.

Language Arts | S |

Have students complete one studied dictation exercise (see Appendix for passages).

Help students complete **one** English option.

⭐ *Progressing With Courage:* Lesson 38

⭐ *Progressing With Courage:* Lesson 85 (last half only)

⭐ Your own grammar program

Work with the students to complete **one** of the writing options listed below:

⭐ *Write with the Best: Vol. 2* Unit 4 – Day 10 p. 36

⭐ Your own writing program

Key Idea: Practice language arts skills.

Bible Quiet Time | I |

Bible Study: Read and complete the assigned pages in the following resource:

⭐ *Faith at Work: Lesson 8 – Day Four* p. 57

Prayer Focus: Refer to **thanksgiving** on "Preparing Your Heart for Prayer". Then, pray a prayer of thanksgiving to express gratitude to God for His divine goodness. After your prayer, write 'thanksgiving' at the bottom of today's lesson on p. 57 in *Faith at Work*. Next to 'thanksgiving', either list key phrases or write a sentence to summarize your prayer. Keep "Preparing Your Heart for Prayer" inside your Bible.

Scripture Memory: Copy Romans 12:11 in your Common Place Book.

Music: Refer to p. 38-39 as you sing with Track 4 *"Trust and Obey"* (vs. 1-2).

Key Idea: Read and study Romans 5.

Math Exploration | S |

Choose **one** of the math options listed below (see Appendix for details).

⭐ *Singapore Primary Mathematics 6A/6B, Discovering Mathematics 7A/7B, 8A/8B, No-Nonsense Algebra* or *Videotext Algebra*

⭐ Your own math program

Key Idea: Use a step-by-step math program.

Science Exploration | I |

⭐ Read and follow the directions to complete *The Elements: Ingredients of the Universe* p. 17-20. To complete Activity #4, you need a copy of the Periodic Table. You may print the Periodic Table at one of the Internet sites that follow: http://chemistry.about.com/library/PeriodicTableallcolor.pdf
http://chemistry.about.com/library/PeriodicTableall.pdf
http://printable.my3gb.com/images/1-periodic-table-printable.jpg
http://profmokeur.ca/chemistry/printable_periodic_tablecol.pdf
For Activity #5, listen to the "The Periodic Jump Rope Rhyme" on the CD that came with *The Elements: Ingredients of the Universe*. Choose whether to just chant the rhyme or to try to jump rope with it.

Key Idea: Each element has a symbol or letter abbreviation that stands for the element.

Learning Through History

Focus: The Qing Dynasty Ends and Revolution in French Indochina and Mexico Begins

Reading about History | I

Read about history in the following resource:

 Hero Tales: Vol. II p. 165-175

You will be writing a narration about **one** of the sections that you read about today (either "Founder of Wycliffe Bible Translators", "Do You Know Senor Jesus?", "The Gospel in the Beer Garden", or "First Check with the Head Honcho"). To prepare for writing your narration, look back over your chosen section in *Hero Tales: Vol. II*. Think about the main idea and the most important moments in this part of the reading.

After you have thought about what you will write and how you will begin your narration, turn to Unit 10 in your *Student Notebook*. For more guidance on writing a narration, see *Written Narration Tips* in the Appendix.

In Box 4, write a 12-16 sentence narration about the reading. When you have finished writing, read your sentences out loud to catch any mistakes. Check for the following things: *Did you include **who** or **what topic** the reading was mainly about? Did you include **descriptors** of the important thing(s) that happened? Did you include a **closing sentence**? If not, add those things.* Use the *Written Narration Skills* in the Appendix as a guide for editing the narration.

Key Idea: While selling Bibles in Guatemala, Cam Townsend discovered that many people could not read the Spanish Bibles that he sold. So, he and his wife, Elvira, moved to a Cakchiquel village and worked to translate the Bible into the Cakchiquel language. He also founded Wycliffe Bible Translators to raise money and promote the Summer Institute of Linguistics, which trained Bible translators. Cam's focus was to "translate the Scriptures into every language".

Storytime | T/I

Read the following assigned pages:

 Angel on the Square p. 153-172
Note: p. 164 mentions Rasputin's advances, and p. 171 includes a violent death.

Get the bookmark that you placed in your book. Locate the same section of the bookmark that you used on Day 2. Beneath Day 2's entry, write the book title and the page numbers you read today. Select the one remaining response option at the bottom of the bookmark, and place a checkmark next to it. In the blank space under today's pages, respond in writing using your checked option. Keep the bookmark in your book.

Key Idea: Relate to the text in various ways.

Economics | I

Read about economics in the resource below.

 Whatever Happened to Penny Candy? p. 75-76 and p. 134-135

After the reading, open your *Student Notebook* to the "Economic Principles" section at the front of your notebook. Under "Economic Principle", write a one line or one sentence summary for the economic principle you learned from today's reading.

Key Idea: In 1971, gold and silver were removed from our money, making it difficult to define what constituted money. It also led to large increases in the circulating money supply.

Independent History Study | I

Open your *Student Notebook* to Unit 10 – Box 8. Follow the directions from *Draw and Write Through History* p. 21-22 (steps 1-5 only) to draw a World War I soldier. You will color your drawing on **Unit 11 – Day 3**.

Key Idea: In 1916, as America entered World War I, Cam Townsend enlisted in the National Guard. His captain released him from a year of guard duty to sell Bibles in Guatemala.

President Study | I

Read p. 25 in *Our Presidents...* Then, open your *President Notebook* to Millard Fillmore. Use today's reading to help you complete the information about Fillmore.

Key Idea: Research Millard Fillmore.

Learning the Basics
Focus: Language Arts, Math, Bible, Nature Journal, and Science

Unit 10 - Day 4

Biblical Self-Image [T]

Read and discuss the following pages in the resource below.

★ *Who Am I? And What Am I Doing Here?* top of p. 91-92

Discuss the questions for "Make a Note of It" on p. 92, rather than having students write their responses. Be sure to share examples from your own experiences as well.

Key Idea: What we choose to watch, read, and listen to influences how we think and act.

Language Arts [S]

Have students complete one studied dictation exercise (see Appendix for directions and passages).

Help students complete one lesson from the following reading program:

★ *Drawn into the Heart of Reading*

Help students complete **one** English option.

★ *Progressing With Courage:* Lesson 39

★ *Progressing With Courage:* Lesson 86 (first half only)

★ Your own grammar program

Key Idea: Practice language arts skills.

Bible Quiet Time [I]

Bible Study: Complete the assignment below.

★ *Faith at Work: Lesson 8 – Day Five* and *Notes* p. 58-62

Prayer Focus: Refer to **supplication** on "Preparing Your Heart for Prayer". Then, pray a prayer of supplication to make a humble and earnest request of God. Write 'supplication' at the bottom of today's lesson on p. 58 in *Faith at Work*. Next to it, either list several key phrases or write a sentence to summarize your prayer. Keep "Preparing Your Heart for Prayer" inside your Bible.

Scripture Memory: Recite Romans 12:1-11.

Music: Refer to p. 38-39 as you sing with Track 4 *"Trust and Obey"* (vs. 1-2).

Key Idea: Read and study Romans 5.

Math Exploration [S]

Choose **one** of the math options listed below.

★ *Singapore Primary Mathematics 6A/6B, Discovering Mathematics 7A/7B, 8A/8B, No-Nonsense Algebra* or *Videotext Algebra*

★ Your own math program

Key Idea: Use a step-by-step math program.

Science Exploration [I]

★ Read and follow the directions to complete *The Elements: Ingredients of the Universe* p. 21 – middle of p. 25. **Omit** Activity #1. For Activity #2, parental supervision is needed as you search for pictures of electron clouds on the Internet.

Key Idea: A single particle is called an atom. An atom is composed of protons and neutrons in its nucleus and electrons traveling in orbits around its nucleus. Protons have a positive electrical charge. Electrons have a negative electrical charge, and neutrons have no charge at all. Electrons are so small and move so quickly that scientists only see cloudy areas for the electrons, rather than seeing the actual electrons.

Learning Through History
Focus: World War I, Revolution in Russia, and the Division of Ireland

Unit 11 - Day 1

Reading about History | I

Read about history in the following resources:

★ *All American History: Vol. II* p. 233-244

★ *Great Events in American History* p. 79-81

After today's reading, orally narrate or retell to an adult the portion of text that you read today from *All American History*. Some possible key words to include in your narration might be *European powers, strongest army, strongest navy, race to gain colonies, Triple Alliance, Triple Entente, Serbian revolutionary, assassination of Archduke Ferdinand, declaration of war in 1914, Central Powers (made up of Germany, Austria-Hungary, Ottoman Empire, Bulgaria), Allies (originally made up of Great Britain, France, Russia), Western Front, trenches, "no man's land", Eastern front, Russian economy near collapse.*

Key Idea: The assassination of Archduke Ferdinand by Serbian revolutionary Gavrilo Princip sparked a world war.

History Project | S

Print the "World War I (map 1)" Student Map from p. 41 of the *Map Trek* CD. To help you label each country on your Student Map, refer to or print the *Map Trek* Teacher's Answer Map p. 40. Then, choose a different color to represent each of the three codes in the "Key", and color the "Key" and the map to match. Use the *United States History Atlas* p. 37 for help.

Key Idea: During World War I, some countries remained neutral.

President Study | I

★ On *The Presidents* DVD Volume 1, select the Chapter "Taylor to Lincoln" and watch **only** Program 2: Millard Fillmore. Then, open your *President Notebook* to Millard Fillmore and use today's viewing to add further information about Fillmore.

Key Idea: Research Millard Fillmore.

Storytime | T/I

Read the following assigned pages:

★ *Angel on the Square* p. 173-197
Get the bookmark that you placed in your book last unit. Choose a new section of the bookmark with **three** options at the bottom. At the top of this section of the bookmark, write the book title and the page numbers you read today. Select **one** of the three options at the bottom and place a checkmark next to it. In the blank space under today's pages, respond in writing using your checked option.

Key Idea: Relate to the text in various ways.

Worthy Words | T

Read, analyze, and evaluate the speech below.

★ *Book of Great American Speeches for Young People* p. 143-145
After reading the speech, answer the following questions on an index card: *How is Goldman described on p. 143? What is an anarchist? Why was Goldman jailed/arrested? Based on her comments in this speech, why do you think Goldman chose not to become a U.S. citizen? What are Goldman's views on American democracy? Why is she against the war and "conscription", or the "draft"? What are your thoughts on the U.S. entering WWI and on the military draft? What if you were drafted? Why is it difficult to determine the boundaries of "free speech"?* Next, meet with a parent to have a Socratic dialogue about the speech. Before beginning the dialogue, the parent reads the speech out loud. Then, discuss the questions. All participants should use life experiences/text to support their responses.

Key Idea: Americans were divided over WWI.

Independent History Study | I

Listen to *What in the World? Vol. 3* Disc 3, Tracks 3-4: "Prologue to War" and "The Spark".

Key Idea: A race for land and arms led to war.

Learning the Basics

Focus: Language Arts, Math, Bible, Nature Journal, and Science

Nature Journal   I

Read and follow the directions in the resource below to begin your Nature Journal.

 *Nature Drawing & Journaling: Lesson XIII* p. 39-40

Note: Only sketch and color one blossom today. If you do not have any blossoms to refer to outside, you may instead sketch the blossom shown on the bottom of p. 39.

Key Idea: Practice drawing blossoms.

Language Arts   S

Help students complete one lesson from the following reading program:

★ *Drawn into the Heart of Reading*

Help students complete **one** English option.

★ *Progressing With Courage:* Lesson 40

★ *Progressing With Courage:* Lesson 86 (last half only)

★ Your own grammar program

Work with the students to complete **one** of the writing options listed below:

★ *Write with the Best: Vol. 2* Unit 4 – Day 11 p. 37 – middle of p. 39 (Note: Refer to "How to Take Notes" at the top of p. 87 to review how to take notes.)

★ Your own writing program

Key Idea: Practice language arts skills.

Bible Quiet Time   I

Bible Study: Read and complete the assigned pages in the following resource:

★ *Faith at Work: Lesson 9 – Day One* p. 63
Note: Refer to p. 59-62 to complete the lesson.

Prayer Focus: Refer to **adoration** on "Preparing Your Heart for Prayer". Then, pray a prayer of adoration to worship and honor God. After your prayer, write 'adoration' at the bottom of today's lesson in *Faith at Work* above *Day Two*. Next to 'adoration', either list key phrases or write a sentence to summarize your prayer. Keep "Preparing Your Heart for Prayer" inside your Bible.

Scripture Memory: Read aloud Romans 12:12 three times from your Bible.

Music: Read p. 37 in *Hymns for a Kid's Heart*. Refer to p. 38-39 as you sing with Track 4 *"Trust and Obey"* (vs. 1-3).

Key Idea: Read and study Romans 5.

Math Exploration   S

Choose **one** of the math options listed below (see Appendix for details).

★ *Singapore Primary Mathematics 6A/6B, Discovering Mathematics 7A/7B, 8A/8B, No-Nonsense Algebra* or *Videotext Algebra*

★ Your own math program

Key Idea: Use a step-by-step math program.

Science Exploration   I

★ Read and follow the directions to complete *The Elements: Ingredients of the Universe* bottom of p. 25-27. To complete Activity #3, you need tokens and the copy of the Periodic Table from Unit 10 – Day 3.

Key Idea: Electron clouds come in four basic arrangements. The 's' orbital is spherical. The 'p' orbital is balloon-like. The 'd' orbital looks like a barbell, and the 'f' orbital looks like an 'X'. The "solar system" method of drawing atoms is less complicated than drawing atoms using the electron cloud method.

Learning Through History
Focus: World War I, Revolution in Russia, and the Division of Ireland

Unit 11 - Day 2

Reading about History | I |

Read about history in the following resources:

★ *All American History: Vol. II* bottom of p. 244 – top of p. 249

★ **Optional:** *The Story of the World: Vol. 4* middle of p. 216-221

After today's reading, open your *Student Notebook* to Unit 11. In Box 5, view the U.S. navy recruitment poster from 1917 showing Lady Liberty with her sword drawn. Notice the writing on the scroll and the battleship setting sail. Then, read Wilson's speech on p. 140-142 of the *Book of Great American Speeches*. Next, choose an important part of the speech to copy in quotation marks in Box 6. Write "Woodrow Wilson" at the bottom of Box 6.

Key Idea: President Wilson was not eager for the U.S. to enter World War I. After instances of aggression by Germany toward the U.S., culminating with German U-boats sinking American ships, Wilson finally called for the U.S. to enter the war in 1917.

History Project ✓ | S |

Today you will draw and color a German U-boat. Open your *Student Notebook* to Unit 11 – Box 9. Follow the directions from *Draw and Write Through History* p. 24-25 to draw and color a German U-boat in Box 9.

Key Idea: German submarines, or U-boats, were used to sink British ships. After a German U-boat sank the British passenger ship *Lusitania*, many Americans wanted to enter the war against Germany. The U.S. joined the war shortly after Germany announced plans to resume unrestricted submarine warfare.

President Study | I |

★ Read p. 26-27 in *Our Presidents...* Then, open your *President Notebook* to Franklin Pierce. Use today's reading to help you complete the information about Pierce.

Key Idea: Research Franklin Pierce.

Storytime ✓ | T/I |

Read the following assigned pages:

★ *Angel on the Square* p. 198-222

Get the bookmark that you placed in your book. Locate the same section of the bookmark that you used on Day 1. Beneath Day 1's entry, write the book title and the page numbers you read today. Select one of the **two** remaining response options at the bottom of the bookmark, and place a checkmark next to it. In the blank space under today's pages, respond in writing using your checked option.

Key Idea: Relate to the text in various ways.

Timeline ✓ | I |

You will be adding to the timeline in your *Student Notebook* today. In Unit 11 – Box 1, draw and color a WWI soldier's helmet. Label it, *World War I (1914-1918 A.D.)*.

In Box 2, draw and color a solid red rectangular flag. This flag was used by the Bolsheviks. Label it, *Russian Revolution (1917 A.D.)*.

In Box 3, draw and color a shamrock. Label the box, *The Division of Ireland (1922 A.D.)*.

Key Idea: As World War I raged, it triggered a revolution in Russia that led to the end of the Romanov reign. Communism rose out of the revolution, as Lenin took power. About this same time, Ireland was warring internally over freedom from Great Britain. Ireland was divided in 1922, with the southern half gaining freedom. The north remained part of Britain.

Independent History Study | I |

Listen to *What in the World? Vol. 3* Disc 3, Track 5: "Trenches & Blockades".

Key Idea: During the beginning of WWI, the Germans planned for a quick victory in Belgium and France, so they wouldn't have to fight a war on two fronts. The Germans did not gain the victory they desired, so the war ended up divided between a Western Front and an Eastern Front.

Biblical Self-Image ✓ [T]

Read and discuss with the students the following pages in the resource below.

★ *Who Am I? And What Am I Doing Here?* p. 93-94

As you read the final paragraph on p. 94, take time to look up each Scripture. Discuss how the first Scripture shows us God's Word is true. Then, discuss what each of the remaining Scriptures listed on p. 94 teach us.

Key Idea: It is important to think about everything that we see, say, or do in light of God's truth revealed in His Word.

Language Arts [S]

Have students complete one studied dictation exercise (see Appendix for directions and passages).

Help students complete one lesson from the following reading program:

★ *Drawn into the Heart of Reading*

Help students complete **one** English option.

★ *Progressing With Courage:* Lesson 41

★ *Progressing With Courage:* Lesson 87 (first half only)

★ Your own grammar program

Key Idea: Practice language arts skills.

Bible Quiet Time ✓ [I]

Bible Study: Read and complete the assigned pages in the following resource:

★ *Faith at Work: Lesson 9 – Day Two* p. 63-64

Prayer Focus: Refer to **confession** on "Preparing Your Heart for Prayer". Then, pray a prayer of confession to admit or acknowledge your sins to God. After your prayer, write 'confession' at the bottom of today's lesson in *Faith at Work* above *Day Three*. Next to 'confession', either list key phrases or write a sentence to summarize your prayer.

Scripture Memory: Memorize Romans 12:12 from your Bible and recite it.

Music: Refer to p. 38-39 as you sing with Track 4 *"Trust and Obey"* (vs. 1-3).

Key Idea: Read and study Romans 6.

Math Exploration [S]

Choose **one** of the math options listed below (see Appendix for details).

★ *Singapore Primary Mathematics 6A/6B, Discovering Mathematics 7A/7B, 8A/8B, No-Nonsense Algebra* or *Videotext Algebra*

★ Your own math program

Key Idea: Use a step-by-step math program.

Science Exploration [I]

★ Read and follow the directions to complete *The Elements: Ingredients of the Universe* p. 28-29. As part of today's assignment, you will complete Activity #4, #5, and #6. To complete Activity #4, refer to p. 26 and to the copy of the Periodic Table from Unit 10 – Day 3. For each element in the Periodic Table, the number in the top left corner is the atomic number, which is equal to the number of protons that element has in a single atom's nucleus. The number of electrons is the same as the number of protons. So, nitrogen has an atomic number of 7 and has 7 electrons. For Activity #5, also refer to the Periodic Table.

Key Idea: Chemists use strings of letters and numbers to show how many electrons each orbital of an atom contains.

Learning Through History

Focus: World War I, Revolution in Russia, and the Division of Ireland

Unit 11 - Day 3

Reading about History

Read about history in the following resource:

 The Story of the World: Vol. 4 p. 222-227

After today's reading, open your *Student Notebook* to Unit 11. Look at the image of Lenin shown in Box 7. Next to the image of Lenin, in Box 8, list bulleted notes with facts about Lenin from p. 226-227 of *The Story of the World: Vol. 4.*

Key Idea: In 1917, the peasants in Russia began to demand that Nicholas II give up the throne of Russia. The revolt against the Romanov royal family was in response to poverty and the deaths of millions of unprepared Russian soldiers dying in WWI. Nicholas II did resign. The Bolsheviks, led by Lenin, eventually seized control of Russia from the Provisional Government. Lenin renamed the Bolshevik party the Communist party.

History Project

Today you will color the World War I soldier that you sketched on Unit 10 – Day 4. Open your *Student Notebook* to **Unit 10** – Box 8. Follow the directions from *Draw and Write Through History* p. 23 to color your World War I soldier in Box 8.

Key Idea: Not long after Czar Nicholas II gave up his throne, two million Russian soldiers left the front and headed home. Even though the Provisional Government in Russia planned to continue the war, when Lenin seized power, he signed a peace treaty with Germany. This took Russia out of World War I.

State Study

⭐ This is an **optional** part of the plans. If you have chosen to study your state using *State History from a Christian Perspective,* do Lesson 9 from the *Master Lesson Plan Book.*

Key Idea: Study your individual state.

Storytime

 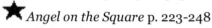

Read the following assigned pages:

⭐ *Angel on the Square* p. 223-248

After today's reading, orally narrate or retell the portion of the story that was read today. See *Narration Tips* in the Appendix as needed.

Key Idea: Practice orally narrating, or retelling, a portion of a story.

Geography

For today's activities, use the map listed below.

⭐ *Map Trek CD: Missions to Modern Marvels* p. 44-45

Print the "The Russian Revolution" Student Map found on p. 45 of the *Map Trek* CD. Refer to or print the *Map Trek* Teacher's Answer Map on p. 44 to guide you as you label each country and body of water on your Student Map. Next, on your Student Map, trace with your finger the line showing the Russian Empire at the start of WWI in 1914. Then, trace with your finger the "German Occupation Line", which shows how far Germany had advanced into Russia by 1918. Last, trace with your finger the outline of Russia "Under Bolshevik Control" in 1919. As you look at your Student Map, by 1922 how much had Russia's boundaries changed? File the map in your *Student Notebook.*

Key Idea: The Russian Revolution stemmed from the division between peasants and nobility. WWI magnified the problems.

Independent History Study

Listen to *What in the World? Vol. 3* Disc 3, Track 6: "Fall of the Central Powers".

Key Idea: In March of 1917, the peasants went on strike in St. Petersburg. This led to the end of the Russian czar and widespread revolution.

Learning the Basics
Focus: Language Arts, Math, Bible, Nature Journal, Poetry, and Science

Nature Journal & Poetry | S |

The poetry of Longfellow, Wordsworth, and Whitman is scheduled on Day 3 in each unit to complement the nature journaling sessions. Read aloud and discuss today's poem *"Flowers"* (see Appendix) with a parent. Then, follow the directions in the resource below.

★ *Nature Drawing & Journaling: Lesson XIII* p. 40

Note: Follow paragraph 2 to draw your second blossom. You may draw the blossom from p. 40 if you do not have access to a blossom outdoors. Then, copy a portion of the poem that you studied today on the page with your blossoms.

Key Idea: Practice drawing flower blossoms.

Language Arts | S |

Have students complete one studied dictation exercise (see Appendix for passages).

Help students complete **one** English option.

★ *Progressing With Courage:* Lesson 42

★ *Progressing With Courage:* Lesson 87 (last half only)

★ Your own grammar program

Work with the students to complete **one** of the writing options listed below:

★ *Write with the Best: Vol. 2* Unit 4 – Day 12 p. 39

★ Your own writing program

Key Idea: Practice language arts skills.

Bible Quiet Time | I |

Bible Study: Read and complete the assigned pages in the following resource:

★ *Faith at Work: Lesson 9 – Day Three* p. 64

Prayer Focus: Refer to **thanksgiving** on "Preparing Your Heart for Prayer". Then, pray a prayer of thanksgiving to express gratitude to God for His divine goodness. After your prayer, write 'thanksgiving' at the bottom of today's lesson on p. 64 in *Faith at Work*. Next to 'thanksgiving', either list key phrases or write a sentence to summarize your prayer. Keep "Preparing Your Heart for Prayer" inside your Bible.

Scripture Memory: Copy Romans 12:12 in your Common Place Book.

Music: Refer to p. 38-39 as you sing with Track 4 *"Trust and Obey"* (vs. 1-3).

Key Idea: Read and study Romans 6.

Math Exploration | S |

Choose **one** of the math options listed below (see Appendix for details).

★ *Singapore Primary Mathematics 6A/6B, Discovering Mathematics 7A/7B, 8A/8B, No-Nonsense Algebra* or *Videotext Algebra*

★ Your own math program

Key Idea: Use a step-by-step math program.

Science Exploration | I |

★ Read and follow the directions to complete *The Elements: Ingredients of the Universe* p. 30-32. As part of today's assignment, you will complete Activity #7. To complete Activity #7, you may refer to the copy of the Periodic Table from Unit 10 – Day 3.

Key Idea: Each element has a symbol that stands for the element. These symbols shorten the name of the element to an abbreviated form.

Learning Through History
Focus: World War I, Revolution in Russia, and the Division of Ireland

Unit 11 - Day 4

Reading about History

Read about history in the following resource:

 *The Story of the World: Vol. 4* p. 233 – middle of p. 237

You will be writing a narration about the chapter *The Easter Uprising*. To prepare for writing your narration, look back over p. 233-237 in *The Story of the World: Vol. 4*. Think about the main idea and the most important moments in this part of the reading.

After you have thought about what you will write and how you will begin your narration, turn to Unit 11 in your *Student Notebook*. For more guidance on writing a narration, see *Written Narration Tips* in the Appendix.

In Box 4, write a 12-16 sentence narration about the reading. When you have finished writing, read your sentences out loud to catch any mistakes. Check for the following things: *Did you include **who** or **what topic** the reading was mainly about? Did you include **descriptors** of the important thing(s) that happened? Did you include a **closing sentence**? If not, add those things.* Use the *Written Narration Skills* in the Appendix as a guide for editing the narration.

Key Idea: As the prime minister of Ireland, William Gladstone worked in Parliament to restore rights to Irish peasants. A resistance group known as Sinn Fein, or "Us Alone" wanted Ireland to have self-rule again. But, the Ulster Volunteer Force was prepared to fight if Britain did give Ireland home-rule. On April 24, 1916, an uprising in Dublin, known as the "Easter Uprising", was forcibly put down by British troops. This resulted in even more Irish people calling for Home Rule.

President Study

 I

On *The Presidents* DVD Volume 1, select the Chapter "Taylor to Lincoln" and watch **only** Program 3: Franklin Pierce. Then, open your *President Notebook* to Franklin Pierce and use today's viewing to add further information about Pierce.

Key Idea: Research Franklin Pierce.

Storytime

 T/I

Read the following assigned pages:

Angel on the Square p. 249-265

Get the bookmark that you placed in your book. Locate the same section of the bookmark that you used on Day 2. Beneath Day 2's entry, write the book title and the page numbers you read today. Select the one remaining response option at the bottom of the bookmark, and place a checkmark next to it. In the blank space under today's pages, respond in writing using your checked option. Keep the bookmark in your book.

Key Idea: Relate to the text in various ways.

Economics

 I

Read about economics in the resource below.

Whatever Happened to Penny Candy? p. 77-81

After the reading, open your *Student Notebook* to the "Economic Principles" section at the front of your notebook. Under "Economic Principle", write a one line or one sentence summary for the economic principle you learned from today's reading.

Key Idea: A deficit is the shortfall between government income and government spending. The federal debt, or national debt, is the total of all federal deficits. To pay its federal debt, the government uses taxes.

Independent History Study

Print "The Division of Ireland" Student Map found on p. 47 of the *Map Trek* CD. Refer to the *Map Trek* Teacher's Answer Map on p. 46 as you label the Student Map. File your map in your *Student Notebook*.

Key Idea: After WWI, Britain gave part of Ireland independence. It became the "Irish Free State". However, Ulster, in Northern Ireland, remained part of Great Britain.

Learning the Basics
Focus: Language Arts, Math, Bible, Nature Journal, and Science

Biblical Self-Image

Our plans intend for the listed pages in *Who Am I? And What Am I Doing Here?* to be read either silently by both you and your student, or read aloud to the student by you. With this in mind, read and discuss the following pages in the resource below.

 Who Am I? And What Am I Doing Here? p. 95 – top of p. 97

Key Idea: God tells us to think about what is noble, right, and pure.

Language Arts [S]

Have students complete one studied dictation exercise (see Appendix for directions and passages).

Help students complete one lesson from the following reading program:

 Drawn into the Heart of Reading

Help students complete **one** English option.

 Progressing With Courage: Lesson 43

 Progressing With Courage: Lesson 88 (Class Practice 'A' – 'J' only)

 Your own grammar program

Key Idea: Practice language arts skills.

Bible Quiet Time

Bible Study: Complete the assignment below.

 Faith at Work: Lesson 9 – Day Four p. 65

Prayer Focus: Refer to **supplication** on "Preparing Your Heart for Prayer". Then, pray a prayer of supplication to make a humble and earnest request of God. Write 'supplication' at the bottom of today's lesson in *Faith at Work* above *Day Five*. Next to it, either list several key phrases or write a sentence to summarize your prayer. Keep "Preparing Your Heart for Prayer" inside your Bible.

Scripture Memory: Recite Romans 12:1-12.

Music: Refer to p. 38-39 as you sing with Track 4 *"Trust and Obey"* (vs. 1-3).

Key Idea: Read and study Romans 6.

Math Exploration [S]

Choose **one** of the math options listed below.

 Singapore Primary Mathematics 6A/6B, Discovering Mathematics 7A/7B, 8A/8B, No-Nonsense Algebra or *Videotext Algebra*

 Your own math program

Key Idea: Use a step-by-step math program.

Science Exploration [I]

 Read and follow the directions to make "The Periodic Table Game" described on p. 94-95 of *The Elements: Ingredients of the Universe*. The copies of the four pattern pages needed to make the game are included in full-color behind the black and white patterns found after the directions on p. 96. Today, you will assemble the gameboard and play the game. To play, you will move your tokens from left to right across the game board moving in chronological order by each element's atomic number (located in the top left corner of each square). So, you will move your token from hydrogen to helium to lithium and so on. You will need a partner to play the game.

Key Idea: In the Periodic Table, the number in the top right corner of each square is the valence number. This is the number of electrons the element wants to either give away or receive. Elements can have more than one valence number, and many elements do. The valencies are one of the repeating patterns in the Periodic Table.

Learning Through History
Focus: The End of WWI, Gandhi in India, and the Roaring Twenties

Reading about History

Read about history in the following resources:

★ *All American History: Vol. II* middle of p. 249 – top of p. 253

★ *The Story of the World: Vol. 4* bottom of p. 227-231

After today's reading, orally narrate or retell to an adult either the text from *All American History* or the text from *The Story of the World* that you read today. As you retell, the adult will write or type your narration. Some possible key words to include in your narration might be *World War I, Russia, U.S., Allies, Woodrow Wilson, Second Battle of Marne, armistice, Great War, peace, debt.* When the narration is complete, tri-fold the typed or written narration to fit in Unit 12 – Box 10 of the *Student Notebook.* Glue the folded narration in Box 10, so it can be opened and read.

Key Idea: World War I ended in 1918 after Kaiser Wilhelm II abdicated and Germany accepted terms for an armistice.

History Project

In this unit you will make a salt painting. Today you will paint your background. Use a wide paintbrush to lightly dampen a sheet of watercolor paper with water. Next, choose two bright paint colors for your background (i.e. blue/purple, red/yellow, green/blue). Do not dilute the paint with water, but instead brush the first color undiluted across the entire background. Then, rinse the brush and use the second color to paint a few broad streaks.

Key Idea: After WWI, salt became a target of boycott in India as a part of the revolt against British rule.

Storytime

Read the following assigned pages:

★ *Angel on the Square* p. 266-288
Get the bookmark that you placed in your book last unit. Choose a new section of the bookmark with **three** options at the bottom. At the top of this section of the bookmark, write the book title and the page numbers you read today. Select **one** of the three options at the bottom and place a checkmark next to it. In the blank space under today's pages, respond in writing using your checked option.

Key Idea: Relate to the text in various ways.

Worthy Words

Read, analyze, and evaluate the speech below.

★ *Book of Great American Speeches for Young People* p. 137-139
After reading the speech, answer the following questions on an index card: *What definition does Shaw give for a 'Republic'? Why does she think that America is not a Republic? By the end of WWI, monarchies fell in Russia, Austria-Hungary, Germany, and the Ottoman Empire. What reference does Shaw make to this divine right of kings in her speech? What other divine right does she say is falling? What is your opinion of the right of women to vote? How would campaigning and elections be different if women could not vote?* Next, meet with a parent to have a Socratic dialogue about the speech. Before beginning the dialogue, the parent reads the speech out loud. Next, discuss the questions using your notes. All participants should use life experiences and/or the text to support their responses.

Key Idea: As the war ended, women gained the right to vote in Great Britain and in the U.S.

Independent History Study

Print the "World War I (map 2)" Student Map p. 43 from the *Map Trek* CD. Label the Student Map as you refer to *Map Trek* Teacher's Answer Map p. 42. Compare your map to *United States History Atlas* p. 38.

Key Idea: In the summer of 1918, U.S. and Allied forces won several important battles. The turning point of the war was the Second Battle of Marne, after which the Allies steadily advanced against the Germans.

Learning the Basics
Focus: Language Arts, Math, Bible, Nature Journal, and Science

Nature Journal

Read and follow the directions in the resource below.

★ *Nature Drawing & Journaling: Lesson XIV* p. 43-45

Note: Draw **one to three** images. Don't forget to write a little something about your day and your sketching experiences outdoors.

Key Idea: Practice sketching little treasures in nature.

Language Arts

Help students complete one lesson from the following reading program:

★ *Drawn into the Heart of Reading*

Help students complete **one** English option.

★ *Progressing With Courage:* Lesson 44

★ *Progressing With Courage:* Lesson 88 (Written Exercises 'A' – 'D' only)

★ Your own grammar program

Work with the students to complete **one** of the writing options listed below:

★ *Write with the Best: Vol. 2* Unit 4 – Day 13 p. 40 (For guidance on writing a **topical** outline, refer to "How To Write an Outline" and "Steps to Writing an Outline" p. 87-90.)

★ Your own writing program

Key Idea: Practice language arts skills.

Bible Quiet Time

Bible Study: Read and complete the assigned pages in the following resource:

★ *Faith at Work: Lesson 9 – Day Five* and *Notes* p. 65-69

Prayer Focus: Refer to **adoration** on "Preparing Your Heart for Prayer". Then, pray a prayer of adoration to worship and honor God. After your prayer, write 'adoration' at the bottom of today's lesson on p. 65 in *Faith at Work*. Next to 'adoration', either list key phrases or write a sentence to summarize your prayer. Keep "Preparing Your Heart for Prayer" inside your Bible.

Scripture Memory: Read aloud Romans 12:13 three times from your Bible.

Music: Read the verse and pray the prayer from p. 39 in *Hymns for a Kid's Heart*. Refer to p. 38-39 as you sing with Track 4 "*Trust and Obey*" (vs. 1-5).

Key Idea: Read and study Romans 6.

Math Exploration

Choose **one** of the math options listed below (see Appendix for details).

★ *Singapore Primary Mathematics 6A/6B, Discovering Mathematics 7A/7B, 8A/8B, No-Nonsense Algebra* or *Videotext Algebra*

★ Your own math program

Key Idea: Use a step-by-step math program.

Science Exploration

★ Read and follow the directions to complete *The Elements: Ingredients of the Universe* p. 33 – top of p. 36. As part of today's assignment, you will complete Activity #1 and Activity #2.

Key Idea: The valence is the number of electrons an atom wants to gain or give away in order to have a full outer shell. A Lewis Dot diagram is a shortcut for showing valence electrons.

Reading about History [I]

Read about history in the following resource:

 The Story of the World: Vol. 4 bottom of p. 237-242

After today's reading, open your *Student Notebook* to Unit 12. Look at the image in Box 7 of Gandhi picking up salt on the Salt March that began on March 12, 1930. This was an act of civil disobedience against the British salt tax and was part of Gandhi's campaign to free India from British rule. Gandhi used salt from the sea to avoid paying the salt tax. Reread the description of the Salt March on p. 242 of *The Story of the World*. Then, in Box 8, write 'civil disobedience' and look up its definition in a dictionary. Copy the definition in Box 8. Under the definition, explain your thoughts on Gandhi's nonviolent tactics to free India.

Key Idea: Gandhi grew up in India in a Hindu family. He went to England to study law and then worked in South Africa before returning home to India. Gandhi led the Congress Party working for independence from Britain.

History Project [S]

Get the background that you painted on Day 1. Place it vertically in front of you. Next, use a pencil to very lightly outline 3-4 flowers with petals in various places on the page. Add a long stem for each flower and outline a leaf or two on each stem. Then, use a squeezable bottle of white glue to carefully trace over the outlines with a thick bead of glue. Last, sprinkle the glue generously with table salt and shake off the excess salt in the garbage. Allow the glue with salt to dry until Day 3.

Key Idea: A salt tax led to protest in India.

President Study [I]

 Read p. 28-29 in *Our Presidents...* Then, open your *President Notebook* to James Buchanan. Use today's reading to help you complete the information about Buchanan.

Key Idea: Research James Buchanan.

Storytime [T/I]

Read the following assigned pages:

 *War Horse* p. 1-16

Get the bookmark that you placed in your book. Locate the same section of the bookmark that you used on Day 1. Beneath Day 1's entry, write the book title and the page numbers you read today. Select one of the **two** remaining response options at the bottom of the bookmark, and place a checkmark next to it. In the blank space under today's pages, respond in writing using your checked option.

Key Idea: Relate to the text in various ways.

Timeline [✓]

You will be adding to the timeline in your *Student Notebook* today. In Unit 12 – Box 1, draw and color a white flag. Label it, *WWI – Peace Treaty at Versailles (June 28, 1919 A.D.)*.

In Box 2, draw and color a sea with a white salty beach. Label it, *Gandhi Resists British Rule in India (1915-1947 A.D.)*.

In Box 3, draw and color a pile of money. Label it, *The Roaring Twenties (1920-1929 A.D.)*.

Key Idea: Gandhi's fight for India's independence lasted more than 3 decades.

Independent History Study [I]

The Sikhs believed Amritsar was a sacred city because of its Golden Temple. Its pool of water was thought to give eternal life. According to John 3:14-18, who is the giver of eternal life? Gandhi was a Hindu. He wrote: *"What then, does Jesus mean to me? To me, he was one of the greatest teachers humanity has ever had. To his believers, he was God's only begotten Son. Could the fact that I do or do not accept this belief make Jesus have any more or any less influence in my life?"* After reading John 3:14-18, how would you answer this question?

Key Idea: Hinduism is tolerant of all religions, seeking to embrace and live at peace with all.

Learning the Basics

Focus: Language Arts, Math, Bible, Nature Journal, and Science

Biblical Self-Image | T |

Our plans intend for the listed pages in *Who Am I? And What Am I Doing Here?* to be read either silently by both you and your child, or read aloud to the child by you. This study also has much to be gained by discussion, as it provides an excellent opportunity to share what **you** believe. Read and discuss with the students the following pages in the resource below.

 Who Am I? And What Am I Doing Here? top of p. 97 – bottom of p. 98

Key Idea: God desires for us to think about whatever is lovely and admirable, rather than dwelling on negative thoughts.

Language Arts | S |

Have students complete one studied dictation exercise (see Appendix for directions and passages).

Help students complete one lesson from the following reading program:

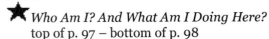 *Drawn into the Heart of Reading*

Help students complete **one** English option.

★ *Progressing With Courage:* Lesson 45

★ *Progressing With Courage:* Lesson 88 (Written Exercises 'E' – 'J' only)

★ Your own grammar program

Key Idea: Practice language arts skills.

Bible Quiet Time | I |

Bible Study: Read and complete the assigned pages in the following resource:

★ *Faith at Work: Lesson 10 – Day One* p. 70 Note: Refer to p. 66-69 to complete the lesson.

Prayer Focus: Refer to **confession** on "Preparing Your Heart for Prayer". Then, pray a prayer of confession to admit or acknowledge your sins to God. After your prayer, write 'confession' at the bottom of today's lesson in *Faith at Work* above *Day Two*. Next to 'confession', either list key phrases or write a sentence to summarize your prayer. This will be your prayer log. Keep "Preparing Your Heart for Prayer" inside your Bible.

Scripture Memory: Memorize Romans 12:13 from your Bible and recite it.

Music: Refer to p. 38-39 as you sing with Track 4 *"Trust and Obey"* (vs. 1-5).

Key Idea: Read and study Romans 6.

Math Exploration | S |

Choose **one** of the math options listed below (see Appendix for details).

★ *Singapore Primary Mathematics 6A/6B, Discovering Mathematics 7A/7B, 8A/8B, No-Nonsense Algebra* or *Videotext Algebra*

★ Your own math program

Key Idea: Use a step-by-step math program.

Science Exploration | I |

★ Read and follow the directions to complete Activity #3 on p. 36 of *The Elements: Ingredients of the Universe*. To complete the activity, you will need the Periodic Table that you printed in a previous lesson. To help you better understand how the riddles work, we will use question 1 as an example. The answer to question 1 is "Boron" which sounds like "boring". Now, solve the remaining riddles in a similar way. This activity is meant to be fun, so if needed you may have a parent help you by checking the answer key.

Key Idea: Learning the names and symbols for the elements is helpful in understanding chemistry.

Learning Through History

Focus: The End of WWI, Gandhi in India, and the Roaring Twenties

Reading about History

Read about history in the following resources:

 The Story of the World: Vol. 4 p. 245-249

 All American History: Vol. II p. 253-255
After today's reading, open your *Student Notebook* to Unit 12 – Box 5. Look at the cover of the Treaty of Peace signed at Versailles. The treaty refers to both "The Treaty of Peace between the Allied and Associated Powers and Germany" and the "Treaty between France and Great Britain respecting Assistance to France in the event of unprovoked aggression by Germany". What do these two titles mean?

<u>Key Idea</u>: In 1919, the leaders of the countries who were victorious in WWI met at Versailles to determine the terms of the Peace Treaty.

History Project

Today you will color the salt on your painting. First, make sure that the salt is dry. If not, wait another day or two until the salt is completely dry. Then, choose several different bright colors of paint for the flowers and leaves, making sure to choose different colors than those used to paint the background. Next, dip the tip of your paintbrush in the paint, and touch the tip of the brush to the salt. Do not drag your brush along the salt. The watercolor paint will spread along the salt path. Repeat the process until all of the salt is "painted" in various colors. Let the painting dry overnight. Note: The salt painting will crumble over time, so you may wish to take a picture of it to keep.

<u>Key Idea</u>: The British salt tax was opposed in India from 1885 until its repeal in 1946.

State Study

 This is an **optional** part of the plans. If you have chosen to study your state using *State History from a Christian Perspective*, do part of Lesson 10 (numbers 1-2 only) from the *Master Lesson Plan Book*.

<u>Key Idea</u>: Study your individual state.

Storytime

Read the following assigned pages:

 War Horse p. 17-30

After today's reading, orally narrate or retell the portion of the story that was read today. See *Narration Tips* in the Appendix as needed.

<u>Key Idea</u>: Practice orally narrating, or retelling, a portion of a story.

Geography

For today's activities, use the map listed below.

 Map Trek CD: Missions to Modern Marvels p. 48-49

Print the "Europe, Post WWI" Student Map found on p. 49 of the *Map Trek* CD. Refer to or print the *Map Trek* Teacher's Answer Map on p. 48 to guide you as you label each country on your Student Map. Next, compare your Student Map with the map of Europe prior to WWI on p. 218 of *The Story of the World*. As you compare the two maps, use colored pencils to lightly color on your Student Map any countries whose borders were changed after WWI. File the map in your *Student Notebook*.

<u>Key Idea</u>: The Treaty of Versailles blamed WWI on Germany and the Central Powers, and forced them to pay for the war's damages. The treaty also redrew the boundary lines of much of Europe and formed a League of Nations. The treaty led to much bitterness and hardship for the Central Powers, especially Germany.

Independent History Study

Listen to *What in the World? Vol. 3* Disc 3, Track 7: "Economic Chaos & Great Depression". Then, in Unit 12 – Box 6 of your *Student Notebook*, copy the text from p. 29 of *Draw and Write Through History*.

<u>Key Idea</u>: The landscape of Europe changed significantly after World War I.

Learning the Basics

Focus: Language Arts, Math, Bible, Nature Journal, Poetry, and Science

Nature Journal & Poetry

The poetry of Longfellow, Wordsworth, and Whitman is scheduled on Day 3 to complement the nature journaling sessions. Read aloud and discuss today's poem *"The Harvest Moon"* (see Appendix) with a parent. Then, follow the directions in the resource below.

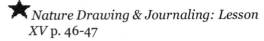

★ *Nature Drawing & Journaling: Lesson XV* p. 46-47

Note: If there are no autumn leaves where you live right now, then go to www.yahoo.com and type "images autumn leaves" in the search bar. Click on pictures until you find a leaf you'd like to draw. Draw **one to three** leaves. Then, either copy part of today's poem or write about your day.

Key Idea: Practice sketching autumn leaves.

Language Arts

Have students complete one studied dictation exercise (see Appendix for passages).

Help students complete **one** English option.

★ *Progressing With Courage:* Lesson 46

★ *Progressing With Courage:* Lesson 89 (first half only)

Work with the students to complete **one** of the writing options listed below:

★ *Write with the Best: Vol. 2* Unit 4 – Day 14 p. 40 (Note: Meet with a parent to discuss possible essay ideas based on p. 94.)

★ Your own writing program

Key Idea: Practice language arts skills.

Bible Quiet Time

Bible Study: Read and complete the assigned pages in the following resource:

★ *Faith at Work: Lesson 10 – Day Two* p. 70-71

Prayer Focus: Refer to **thanksgiving** on "Preparing Your Heart for Prayer". Then, pray a prayer of thanksgiving to express gratitude to God for His divine goodness. After your prayer, write 'thanksgiving' at the bottom of today's lesson in *Faith at Work* above *Day Three*. Next to 'thanksgiving', either list key phrases or write a sentence to summarize your prayer. Keep "Preparing Your Heart for Prayer" inside your Bible.

Scripture Memory: Copy Romans 12:13 in your Common Place Book.

Music: Refer to p. 38-39 as you sing with Track 4 *"Trust and Obey"* (vs. 1-5).

Key Idea: Read and study Romans 7.

Math Exploration

Choose **one** of the math options listed below (see Appendix for details).

★ *Singapore Primary Mathematics 6A/6B, Discovering Mathematics 7A/7B, 8A/8B, No-Nonsense Algebra* or *Videotext Algebra*

★ Your own math program

Key Idea: Use a step-by-step math program.

Science Exploration

★ Read and follow the directions to complete *The Elements: Ingredients of the Universe* p. 37-40. You will complete Activity #4 as part of today's lesson.

Key Idea: Similarities between elements led chemists to divide the elements into groups or families.

Learning Through History
Focus: The End of WWI, Gandhi in India, and the Roaring Twenties

Unit 12 - Day 4

Reading about History

Read about history in the following resource:

★ *All American History: Vol. II* p. 257-262

You will be writing a narration about **one** of the sections that you read about today (either "A Decade of Prosperity", "Warren G. Harding", "Calvin Coolidge", or "Changes in Industry, Business, and Immigration"). To prepare for writing your narration, look back over p. 257-262 in *All American History: Vol. II*. Think about the main idea and the most important moments in this part of the reading.

After you have thought about what you will write and how you will begin your narration, turn to Unit 12 in your *Student Notebook*. For more guidance on writing a narration, see *Written Narration Tips* in the Appendix.

In Box 4, write a 12-16 sentence narration about the reading. When you have finished writing, read your sentences out loud to catch any mistakes. Check for the following things: *Did you include **who** or **what topic** the reading was mainly about? Did you include **descriptors** of the important thing(s) that happened? Did you include a **closing sentence**? If not, add those things.* Use the *Written Narration Skills* in the Appendix as a guide for editing the narration.

Key Idea: After the postwar recession of 1921, the U.S. enjoyed a decade of prosperity and recovery known as the "Roaring Twenties". While millions of Americans invested in the stock market, others still struggled with debt. Warren Harding replaced Woodrow Wilson as president. Harding died while in office, and his vice president Calvin Coolidge became the next president. Coolidge was also elected in 1924.

President Study I

★ On *The Presidents* DVD Volume 1, select the Chapter "Taylor to Lincoln" and watch **only** Program 4: James Buchanan. Then, open your *President Notebook* to James Buchanan and use today's viewing to add further information about Buchanan.

Key Idea: Research James Buchanan.

Storytime

Read the following assigned pages:

★ *War Horse* p. 31-48
Note: p. 34 contains an expletive.

Get the bookmark that you placed in your book. Locate the same section of the bookmark that you used on Day 2. Beneath Day 2's entry, write the book title and the page numbers you read today. Select the one remaining response option at the bottom of the bookmark, and place a checkmark next to it. In the blank space under today's pages, respond in writing using your checked option. Keep the bookmark in your book.

Key Idea: Relate to the text in various ways.

Economics

Read about economics in the resource below.

★ *Whatever Happened to Penny Candy?* p. 82-86

After the reading, open your *Student Notebook* to the "Economic Principles" section at the front of your notebook. Under "Economic Principle", write a one line or one sentence summary for the economic principle you learned from today's reading.

Key Idea: When the government's spending is greater than its income, it borrows money and takes money away from businesses. This results in fewer high-paying jobs being available and both spouses needing to work.

Independent History Study

Open your *Student Notebook* to Unit 12 – Box 9. Follow the directions from *Draw and Write Through History* p. 6-7 to draw and color a Model T.

Key Idea: The Model T was mass-produced beginning in 1908. It came in multiple colors at first, but by 1914, it was only available in black. In 1927, the Model A replaced the Model T.

Learning the Basics

Focus: Language Arts, Math, Bible, Nature Journal, and Science

Biblical Self-Image

Read and discuss the following pages in the resource below.

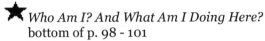 *Who Am I? And What Am I Doing Here?* bottom of p. 98 - 101

Then, prayer the prayer on the bottom of p. 101 together.

Key Idea: What we choose to meditate upon and fill our minds with affects how we think and act.

Language Arts

Have students complete one studied dictation exercise (see Appendix for directions and passages).

Help students complete one lesson from the following reading program:

★ *Drawn into the Heart of Reading*

Help students complete **one** English option.

★ *Progressing With Courage:* Lesson 47

★ *Progressing With Courage:* Lesson 89 (last half only)

★ Your own grammar program

Key Idea: Practice language arts skills.

Bible Quiet Time

Bible Study: Complete the assignment below.

★ *Faith at Work: Lesson 10 – Day Three* p. 71

Prayer Focus: Refer to **supplication** on "Preparing Your Heart for Prayer". Then, pray a prayer of supplication to make a humble and earnest request of God. Write 'supplication' at the bottom of today's lesson in *Faith at Work* above *Day Four*. Next to it, either list several key phrases or write a sentence to summarize your prayer. Keep "Preparing Your Heart for Prayer" inside your Bible.

Scripture Memory: Recite Romans 12:1-13.

Music: Refer to p. 38-39 as you sing with Track 4 *"Trust and Obey"* (vs. 1-5).

Key Idea: Read and study Romans 7.

Math Exploration

Choose **one** of the math options listed below.

★ *Singapore Primary Mathematics 6A/6B, Discovering Mathematics 7A/7B, 8A/8B, No-Nonsense Algebra* or *Videotext Algebra*

★ Your own math program

Key Idea: Use a step-by-step math program.

Science Exploration

★ Choose **either** to play "The Periodic Table Game" described on p. 94-96 **or** to "Make a Periodic Table Pillowcase" as described on p. 109. You already have "The Periodic Table Game" made from Unit 11 – Day 4. To play the game, you move your tokens from left to right across the game board moving in chronological order by each element's atomic number (located in the top left corner of each square). So, you move your token from hydrogen to helium to lithium and so on. You will need a partner to play the game. If you choose to "Make a Periodic Table Pillowcase" instead, you will need a parent's help and the supplies noted on p. 109.

Key Idea: The Periodic Table is an important organizational tool for chemists.

Reading about History

Read about history in the following resources:

★ *All American History: Vol. II* p. 263-268

★ *Great Events in American History* p. 67-69

After today's reading, orally narrate or retell to an adult the portion of text that you read today from *All American History*. Some possible key words to include in your narration might be *1900-1920, golden age of agriculture, George Washington Carver, horse, railroad, automobile, airplane, Henry Ford, Model T, Orville and Wilbur Wright, Kitty Hawk, Charles Lindbergh, Lone Eagle, Amelia Earhart, newspaper, cartoons, Associated Press, tabloid, magazines, advertising, telephone, Alexander Graham Bell, AT&T.*

<u>Key Idea</u>: By the Roaring Twenties, there had been major advancements in agriculture, transportation, and communication.

History Project

Open your *Student Notebook* to Unit 13. In Box 6, copy the **first** paragraph from p. 37 of *Draw and Write Through History*. Then, use **one** of the Internet addresses below to choose a paper airplane pattern to fold and fly. To locate the first address, in a search engine type "smithsonian how things fly paper airplane". Then, click on http://howthingsfly.si.edu/activities/paper-airplane

http://www.amazingpaperairplanes.com/

http://www.funpaperairplanes.com/

<u>Key Idea</u>: Airplanes changed transportation.

President Study

★ Read p. 30-31 in *Our Presidents...* Then, open your *President Notebook* to Abraham Lincoln. Use today's reading to help you complete the information about Lincoln.

<u>Key Idea</u>: Research Abraham Lincoln.

Storytime

Read the following assigned pages:

★ *War Horse* p. 49-62
Note: p. 58 uses God's name in a less than worshipful way.

After today's reading, photocopy the **two** "Bookmark" pages from the Appendix. Place the copied pages back-to-back and staple them together at the 4 corners. Then, tri-fold the stapled page into thirds to make a bookmark. Save the bookmark in your book until Day 2.

<u>Key Idea</u>: Relate to the text in various ways.

Geography

For today's activities, use the map listed below.

★ *Map Trek CD: Missions to Modern Marvels* p. 52-53

Print the "Famous Early Flights" Student Map found on p. 53 of the *Map Trek* CD. Refer to or print the *Map Trek* Teacher's Answer Map on p. 52 to guide you as you label the places and bodies of water on your Student Map. Then, trace with your finger Charles Lindbergh's route and Amelia Earhart's route. File the map in your *Student Notebook*.

<u>Key Idea</u>: Lindbergh's nonstop flight from New York to Paris and Earhart's solo flight across the Atlantic gained worldwide attention.

Independent History Study [I]

Open your *Student Notebook* to Unit 13 – Box 8. Follow the directions from *Draw and Write Through History* p. 26-28 to draw and color the Red Baron's airplane.

<u>Key Idea</u>: Wilbur and Orville Wright's successful flights at Kitty Hawk in 1903 led to military use of airplanes 15 years later in WWI. Manfred von Richthofen, or the Red Baron, was a famous WWI German fighter pilot. He was the top flying ace of the war.

Learning the Basics
Focus: Language Arts, Math, Bible, Nature Journal, and Science

Nature Journal

Read and follow the directions in the resource below to begin your Nature Journal.

⭐ *Nature Drawing & Journaling: Lesson XVI* p. 48-49

Note: If you do not have onions at home, you may instead sketch two of the onions shown on the bottom of p. 49. Don't forget to write a little something about your day.

Key Idea: Practice drawing onions.

Language Arts

Help students complete one lesson from the following reading program:

⭐ *Drawn into the Heart of Reading*

Help students complete **one** English option.

⭐ *Progressing With Courage:* Lesson 48

⭐ *Progressing With Courage:* Lesson 90 (first half only)

⭐ Your own grammar program

Work with the students to complete **one** of the writing options listed below:

⭐ *Write with the Best: Vol. 2* Unit 4 – Day 15 p. 40 (Note: Refer to "How to Write an Outline" and "Steps to Writing an Outline" p. 87-90)

⭐ Your own writing program

Key Idea: Practice language arts skills.

Bible Quiet Time

Bible Study: Read and complete the assigned pages in the following resource:

⭐ *Faith at Work:* Lesson 10 – Day Four p. 71

Prayer Focus: Refer to **adoration** on "Preparing Your Heart for Prayer". Then, pray a prayer of adoration to worship and honor God. After your prayer, write 'adoration' at the bottom of today's lesson on p. 71 in *Faith at Work*. Next to 'adoration', either list key phrases or write a sentence to summarize your prayer. Keep "Preparing Your Heart for Prayer" inside your Bible.

Scripture Memory: Read aloud Romans 12:14-15 three times from your Bible.

Music: Read p. 41-42 in *Hymns for a Kid's Heart*. Refer to p. 44 as you sing with Track 5 "*Wonderful Words of Life*" (verse 1).

Key Idea: Read and study Romans 7.

Math Exploration

Choose **one** of the math options listed below (see Appendix for details).

⭐ *Singapore Primary Mathematics 6A/6B, Discovering Mathematics 7A/7B, 8A/8B, No-Nonsense Algebra* or *Videotext Algebra*

⭐ Your own math program

Key Idea: Use a step-by-step math program.

Science Exploration

⭐ Read and follow the directions to complete *The Elements: Ingredients of the Universe* p. 41 – part of p. 42. Stop just below Activity #2. Make sure that you have adult permission and supervision before using the Internet sites mentioned in Activity #1 and Activity #2.

Key Idea: Alkali metals only look like metal in their pure form. Lithium and sodium are alkali metals.

Reading about History

Read about history in the following resource:

 Hero Tales: Vol. III p. 45-55

After today's reading, open your *Student Notebook* to Unit 13. In Box 7, you will outline p. 45-46 to tell about George Washington Carver. Each Roman numeral in Box 7 stands for one paragraph. So, 'I' means the first paragraph on p. 45. Next to 'I' in Box 7, write one sentence to tell who or what the first paragraph was about and the main thing that person did. This is not a summary, but rather just the main topic. Next to 'II' in Box 7, write the main topic of the second paragraph on p. 45. Continue this pattern for the 6 paragraphs on p. 45-46.

Key Idea: The Carver family raised George Washington Carver after bushwhackers kidnapped his mother. His determination to learn led him to earn a master's degree and two honorary doctorates.

History Project

Scientist George Washington Carver developed over 200 ways to use the peanut. Peanut butter remains a favorite use of peanuts today. To make peanut butter, place 1 cup shelled, salted peanuts and ½ Tbsp. honey in a blender or a food processor and mix. Then, add 1 Tbsp. peanut or vegetable oil to the mixture a little at a time, covering and blending in between, until smooth. For sweeter peanut butter add a bit more honey. For smoother peanut butter add a bit more oil. Store it in the refrigerator.

Key Idea: Carver experimented with peanuts.

President Study I

 On *The Presidents* DVD Volume 1, select the Chapter "Taylor to Lincoln" and watch **only** Program 5: Abraham Lincoln. Then, open your *President Notebook* to Abraham Lincoln and use today's viewing to add further information about Lincoln.

Key Idea: Research Abraham Lincoln.

Storytime

Read the following assigned pages:

 War Horse p. 63-78
Note: p. 76 and 78 make mention of a "horse" god.
Get the bookmark you made on Day 1. Find the section of the bookmark that has only **two** options at the bottom. At the top of this section of the bookmark, write the book title and the page numbers you read today. Select **one** of the two options at the bottom and place a checkmark next to it. In the blank space under today's pages, respond in writing using your checked option. Keep the bookmark in your book.

Key Idea: Relate to the text in various ways.

Timeline

You will be adding to the timeline in your *Student Notebook* today. In Unit 13 – Box 1, draw and color a nurse's hat with a red cross on it. Label the box, *Spanish Flu Epidemic (1918 A.D.)*.

In Box 2, draw and color a peanut in its shell. Label it, *George Washington Carver (1861-1943 A.D.)*.

In Box 3, draw and color a red airplane to represent Earhart's Lockheed Vega propeller plane. Label it, *Amelia Earhart (1897-1937 A.D.)*.

Key Idea: As WWI ended, a severe influenza epidemic called the Spanish Flu raged across the world. Both George Washington Carver and Amelia Earhart were alive at this time.

Independent History Study

Discuss the "Let's Talk About It" section of **either** p. 49, **or** p. 52, **or** p. 55 of *Hero Tales: Vol. III* with an adult.

Key Idea: After an invitation from Booker T. Washington, Carver arrived at Tuskegee Institute in Alabama. He spent his life helping farmers learn to rotate crops in order to renew the land for planting cotton.

Learning the Basics
Focus: Language Arts, Math, Bible, Nature Journal, and Science

Biblical Self-Image

Our plans intend for the listed pages in *Who Am I? And What Am I Doing Here?* to be read either silently by both you and your child, or read aloud to the child by you. With this in mind, read and discuss with the students the following pages in the resource below.

 Who Am I? And What Am I Doing Here? p. 102-108

Key Idea: The Buddhist religion differs from the Christian religion in many ways. Buddhist meditation, belief in reincarnation and earning one's way to heaven, and prayers before a statue of Buddha are some of the differences.

Language Arts [S]

Have students complete one studied dictation exercise (see Appendix for directions and passages).

Help students complete one lesson from the following reading program:

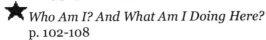 *Drawn into the Heart of Reading*

Help students complete **one** English option.

Progressing With Courage: Lesson 49

Progressing With Courage: Lesson 90 (last half only)

Your own grammar program

Key Idea: Practice language arts skills.

Bible Quiet Time [I]

Bible Study: Read and complete the assigned pages in the following resource:

Faith at Work: Lesson 10 – Day Five and *Notes* p. 72-76

Prayer Focus: Refer to **confession** on "Preparing Your Heart for Prayer". Then, pray a prayer of confession to admit or acknowledge your sins to God. After your prayer, write 'confession' at the bottom of today's lesson on p. 72 in *Faith at Work*. Next to 'confession', either list key phrases or write a sentence to summarize your prayer.

Scripture Memory: Memorize Romans 12:14-15 from your Bible and recite it.

Music: Refer to p. 44 as you sing with Track 5 *"Wonderful Words of Life"* (verse 1).

Key Idea: Read and study Romans 7.

Math Exploration [S]

Choose **one** of the math options listed below (see Appendix for details).

Singapore Primary Mathematics 6A/6B, Discovering Mathematics 7A/7B, 8A/8B, No-Nonsense Algebra or *Videotext Algebra*

Your own math program

Key Idea: Use a step-by-step math program.

Science Exploration [I]

Read and follow the directions to complete *The Elements: Ingredients of the Universe* p. 42-44. As part of today's assignment, you will complete the experiment in Activity #3.

Key Idea: An 'ion' is an atom with an unequal number of protons and electrons. When a halogen connects to an alkali metal through ionic bonding, salt is formed.

Reading about History

Read about history in the following resource:

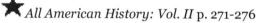 *All American History: Vol. II* p. 271-276

After today's reading, open your *Student Notebook* to Unit 13. In Box 5, look at the 1920s advertisement for a Chevrolet Sedan. Notice that the ad shows two women dressed in fashionable 1920s styles, and one of the women is driving the sedan. How does the fact that this ad targets women show that women were gaining new rights and influence in the 1920s?

Key Idea: In 1920, women gained the right to vote. During the next decade, more and more women began working outside the home.

History Project

Amelia Earhart was one of the most famous women in America in the 1920s and 1930s. Read about the mystery of her disappearance using at least one of the Internet sites below. Then, open your *Student Notebook* to Unit 13. Based on what you read, write a paragraph in Box 9 that explains your opinion of what you think happened to Amelia Earhart.

http://www.historywiz.com/historymakers/earhart.htm

http://ameliaearhart.com/news/2009/11/what-happened-to-amelia-earhart/

http://tighar.org/Projects/Earhart/AEdescr2.html

Key Idea: Amelia Earhart disappeared in 1937.

State Study

 This is an **optional** part of the plans. If you have chosen to study your state using *State History from a Christian Perspective,* do the **last** part of Lesson 10 (steps 3-6) from the *Master Lesson Plan Book.*

Key Idea: Study your individual state.

Storytime

Read the following assigned pages:

 War Horse p. 79-93
After today's reading, orally narrate or retell the portion of the story that was read today. See *Narration Tips* in the Appendix as needed.

Key Idea: Practice orally narrating, or retelling, a portion of a story.

Worthy Words

Read, analyze, and evaluate the speech below.

 Book of Great American Speeches for Young People p. 149-152
After reading the speech, answer the following questions on an index card: *Compare the date of Darrow's speech on p. 149 to the date of the Scopes' trial mentioned on p. 275-276 of All American History. Which trial came first? In the speech, what reasons does Darrow give for life being so cheaply valued? Why would crimes rise after a war? Reread the preface to the speech on p. 149. What is the meaning of a "perfect crime"? On whom does Darrow place the responsibility for this crime? Prior to the trial, Leopold and Loeb confessed to the murder saying they did it for a pure love of excitement and thrills. What do you think is a "just decision" in this case? What does the Bible say?* Next, meet with a parent to have a Socratic dialogue about the speech. Before beginning the dialogue, the parent reads the speech out loud. Next, discuss the questions using your notes. All participants should use life experiences or text to support responses.

Key Idea: Darrow opposed the death penalty.

Independent History Study

Open your *Student Notebook* to Unit 13 – Box 10. Follow the directions from *Draw and Write Through History* p. 31-32 (steps 1-5) to draw Amelia Earhart and her Electra airplane. You will color the drawing on Unit 13 – Day 4.

Key Idea: Earhart began flying in 1921.

Learning the Basics

Focus: Language Arts, Math, Bible, Nature Journal, Poetry, and Science

Nature Journal & Poetry [S]

The poetry of Longfellow, Wordsworth, and Whitman is scheduled on Day 3 in each unit to complement the nature journal sessions. Read aloud and discuss today's poem *"The Rainy Day"* (see Appendix) with a parent. Then, follow the directions in the resource below.

★ *Nature Drawing & Journaling: Lesson XVII* p. 50-51

Note: If you do not have vines anywhere nearby, you may wish to draw one from a photograph. If so, go to www.yahoo.com and type in the Search "images climbing vines". Then, click through the images of vines to find one that you would like to draw.

Key Idea: Practice drawing flower blossoms.

Language Arts [S]

Have students complete one studied dictation exercise (see Appendix for passages).

Help students complete **one** English option.

★ *Progressing With Courage:* Lesson 50

★ *Progressing With Courage:* Lesson 91 (first half only)

Work with the students to complete **one** of the writing options listed below:

★ *Write with the Best: Vol. 2* Unit 4 – Day 16 p. 41 (Note: Refer to #6 on p. 93 for ideas for an attention grabber)

★ Your own writing program

Key Idea: Practice language arts skills.

Bible Quiet Time [I]

Bible Study: Read and complete the assigned pages in the following resource:

★ *Faith at Work: Lesson 11 – Day One* p. 77
Note: Refer to p. 72-76 to complete the lesson.

Prayer Focus: Refer to **thanksgiving** on "Preparing Your Heart for Prayer". Then, pray a prayer of thanksgiving to express gratitude to God for His divine goodness. After your prayer, write 'thanksgiving' at the bottom of today's lesson in *Faith at Work* above *Day Two*. Next to 'thanksgiving', either list key phrases or write a sentence to summarize your prayer. Keep "Preparing Your Heart for Prayer" inside your Bible.

Scripture Memory: Copy Romans 12:14-15 in your Common Place Book.

Music: Refer to p. 44 as you sing with Track 5 *"Wonderful Words of Life"* (verse 1).

Key Idea: Read and study Romans 7.

Math Exploration [S]

Choose **one** of the math options listed below (see Appendix for details).

★ *Singapore Primary Mathematics 6A/6B, Discovering Mathematics 7A/7B, 8A/8B, No-Nonsense Algebra* or *Videotext Algebra*

★ Your own math program

Key Idea: Use a step-by-step math program.

Science Exploration

★ Read and follow the directions to complete *The Elements: Ingredients of the Universe* p. 45-48. As part of today's assignment, you will complete Activity #1, #2, and #3. To complete these activities, you will need parental permission and supervision.

Key Idea: Magnesium and calcium are alkali earth metals. Our bodies need both magnesium and calcium. Alkali earth elements also make the colors you see in fireworks.

Reading about History

Read about history in the following resource:

 All American History: Vol. II p. 277-282

You will be writing a narration about **one** of the sections that you read about today (either "Clothing During the Roaring Twenties", "Health and Hygiene During the Roaring Twenties", or "Nutrition, Eating, and Cooking Habits During the Roaring Twenties"). To prepare for writing your narration, look back over p. 277-282 in *All American History: Vol. II*. Think about the main idea and the most important moments in your chosen section.

After you have thought about what you will write and how you will begin your narration, turn to Unit 13 in your *Student Notebook*. For more guidance on writing a narration, see *Written Narration Tips* in the Appendix.

In Box 4, write a 12-16 sentence narration about the reading. When you have finished writing, read your sentences out loud to catch any mistakes. Check for the following things: *Did you include **who** or **what topic** the reading was mainly about? Did you include **descriptors** of the important thing(s) that happened? Did you include a **closing sentence**? If not, add those things.* Use the *Written Narration Skills* in the Appendix as a guide for editing the narration.

Key Idea: During the 1920s, factories began to mass-produce clothing. Men's styles varied from dark and conservative to open-collared shirts with V-neck sweaters. Women's dresses became shorter and styles became simpler and looser. Americans also began buying cars. This led to growth of roadside diners and of food chains like A&P and Piggly Wiggly. Stricter food regulations followed. Poor sanitation and hygiene remained problematic, and antibiotics hadn't been invented yet.

President Study

 Read p. 32-33 in *Our Presidents...* Then, open your *President Notebook* to Andrew Johnson. Use today's reading to help you complete the information about Johnson.
Key Idea: Research Andrew Johnson.

Storytime

Read the following assigned pages:

 War Horse p. 94-104
Note: p. 104 contains a description of death.

Get the bookmark that you placed in your book. Locate the same section of the bookmark that you used on Day 2. Beneath Day 2's entry, write the book title and the page numbers you read today. Select the one remaining response option at the bottom of the bookmark, and place a checkmark next to it. In the blank space under today's pages, respond in writing using your checked option. Keep the bookmark in your book.

Key Idea: Relate to the text in various ways.

Economics

Read about economics in the resource below.

 Whatever Happened to Penny Candy? p. 87-93
After the reading, open your *Student Notebook* to the "Economic Principles" section at the front of your notebook. Read through your list of principles and compare them to numbers 1-6 on p. 87-88. Under "Economic Principle", add a one line or one sentence summary for an economic principle from the list on p. 87-88 that you do not currently have in your *Student Notebook*.

Key Idea: Inflation affects the economy.

Independent History Study

Open your *Student Notebook* to Unit 13 – Box 10. Follow the directions from *Draw and Write Through History* p. 33 to color your sketch of Amelia Earhart and her Electra.

Key Idea: After Charles Linbergh's 1927 transatlantic flight, Amelia Earhart was selected as part of a transatlantic flight team in 1928. Upon her return, Earhart was a celebrity. She set trends in fashion, designed her own luggage line, and endorsed products.

Learning the Basics
Focus: Language Arts, Math, Bible, Nature Journal, and Science

Biblical Self-Image

Our plans intend for the listed pages in *Who Am I? And What Am I Doing Here?* to be read either silently by both you and your student, or read aloud to the student by you. With this in mind, read and discuss the following pages in the resource below.

★ *Who Am I? And What Am I Doing Here?* p. 109-111

Key Idea: Jesus is our example for how to express our emotions and act in wisdom.

Language Arts

Have students complete one studied dictation exercise (see Appendix for directions and passages).

Help students complete one lesson from the following reading program:

★ *Drawn into the Heart of Reading*

Help students complete **one** English option.

★ *Progressing With Courage:* Lesson 51

★ *Progressing With Courage:* Lesson 91 (last half only)

★ Your own grammar program

Key Idea: Practice language arts skills.

Bible Quiet Time I

Bible Study: Complete the assignment below.

★ *Faith at Work: Lesson 11 – Day Two* p. 77-78

Prayer Focus: Refer to **supplication** on "Preparing Your Heart for Prayer". Then, pray a prayer of supplication to make a humble and earnest request of God. Write 'supplication' at the bottom of today's lesson in *Faith at Work* above *Day Three*. Next to it, either list several key phrases or write a sentence to summarize your prayer. Keep "Preparing Your Heart for Prayer" inside your Bible.

Scripture Memory: Recite Romans 12:1-15.

Music: Refer to p. 44 as you sing with Track 5 *"Wonderful Words of Life"* (verse 1).

Key Idea: Read and study Romans 8:1-17.

Math Exploration S

Choose **one** of the math options listed below.

★ *Singapore Primary Mathematics 6A/6B, Discovering Mathematics 7A/7B, 8A/8B, No-Nonsense Algebra* or *Videotext Algebra*

★ Your own math program

Key Idea: Use a step-by-step math program.

Science Exploration

★ Read the two skits on p. 123-126 in *The Elements: Ingredients of the Universe.* **Optional:** If desired, you could choose to perform one of the skits with other family members or choose to assign parts and read the skit as a "Reader's Theatre" as a family with no props or rehearsals.

Next, perform the lab experiment "A disappearing trick using liquid bleach: NaClO" found at the top of p. 127. You **must have adult supervision**, while using the liquid bleach for the experiment. Make sure to wear your safety glasses, so you **do not get bleach in your eyes.**

Key Idea: In NaClO, the oxygen atom comes unattached easily and combines with the food coloring molecule. Without the oxygen, only NaCl remains. When oxygen combines with food coloring, the food coloring loses its ability to reflect the colors of light. The color seems to disappear, even though the food coloring molecules are still there.

Learning Through History

Focus: Education, Recreation, and Prohibition in the U.S. As Stalin Forms the U.S.S.R.

Unit 14 - Day 1

 ## Reading about History

Read about history in the following resource:

 Hero Tales: Vol. III p. 9-19

After today's reading, orally narrate or retell to an adult **one** portion of text that you read today. Some possible key words to introduce your narration might be *South Carolina, Scotia Seminary, Moody Bible Institute, Africa Daytona, Bethune-Cookman College, advisor President Roosevelt.* For "But...Where's the School?", some possible words to include might be *Daytona Beach, "victory through faith", Mr. Gamble.* For "No Such Thing as a Menial Task", some possible words to include might be *educate head, hands, heart.* For "Whosoever Means You", some possible words to include might be *education, dignity, insult, gracious, Mrs. Bethune.*

<u>Key Idea</u>: Mary McLeod Bethune spent her life serving Christ through educating others.

 ## History Project

Mary McLeod Bethune believed that there was 'no such thing as a menial task'. Today, choose a household task that requires hard work to complete. It should be a task that is not your favorite and that you have to work at doing. Discuss the task with a parent and complete it to his/her satisfaction. Make sure not to take 'a shortcut to thoroughness'. A few possible tasks include sweeping the garage, mopping the floors, cleaning the bathrooms, vacuuming the carpets, scrubbing inside the refrigerator, and cleaning your drawers or closet.

<u>Key Idea</u>: Mrs. Bethune believed in hard work.

 ## President Study

 On *The Presidents* DVD Volume 2, select the Chapter "Andrew Johnson to Arthur" and watch **only** Program 1: Andrew Johnson. Then, open your *President Notebook* to Andrew Johnson. Use today's viewing to add further information about Johnson.

<u>Key Idea</u>: Research Andrew Johnson.

Storytime

Read the following assigned pages:

 War Horse p. 105-120

Note: p. 116 contains two expletives.

Choose a new section of the bookmark with **three** options at the bottom. At the top of this section of the bookmark, write the book title and the page numbers you read today. Select **one** of the three options at the bottom of your chosen section. Under today's page numbers, respond in writing using your checked option.

<u>Key Idea</u>: Relate to the text in various ways.

 ## Worthy Words

Open your *Student Notebook* to Unit 14 – Box 8. You will read, analyze, and evaluate Mary McLeod Bethune's 1939 speech. After reading the speech, answer the following questions on an index card: *What is the main topic or theme of the speech? Explain the 'rich harvest' to which she alludes. What problems does she mention? Why does she refer to 'life, liberty, and the pursuit of happiness' and 'one nation, conceived in liberty and dedicated to the proposition that all men are created equal'? Where do these words come from, and what do they mean to you? Why does she quote 'a government of the people, for the people and by the people shall not perish from the earth'? Where do these words come from? What effect does this speech have upon you?* Next, meet with a parent to have a Socratic dialogue about the excerpt. Before beginning the dialogue, the parent reads Box 8 out loud. Next, discuss the questions with a parent using your notes.

<u>Key Idea</u>: Mary Bethune was director of the Office of Minority Affairs for President F.D.R.

 ## Independent History Study

Open your *Student Notebook* to Unit 14. Choose an important part of the speech from Box 8 to copy in quotation marks in Box 6. Write "Mary McLeod Bethune" at the bottom.

<u>Key Idea</u>: Mary Bethune opened a school.

Nature Journal

Read and follow the directions in the resource below.

★ *Nature Drawing & Journaling: Lesson XVIII* p. 52-53

Note: If it is not the season for thistles or withered flowers where you live, choose a thistle to sketch from www.enature.com instead. Click on "Wildflowers" under the "Field Guide" heading. Then, under "Search Field Guides" type in "thistles". Click on the images of the thistles until you find one you would like to sketch.

Key Idea: Practice sketching thistles.

Language Arts

Help students complete one lesson from the following reading program:

★ *Drawn into the Heart of Reading*

Help students complete **one** English option.

★ *Progressing With Courage:* Lesson 52

★ *Progressing With Courage:* Lesson 92 (first half only)

★ Your own grammar program

Work with the students to complete **one** of the writing options listed below:

★ *Write with the Best: Vol. 2* Unit 4 – Day 17 p. 41

★ Your own writing program

Key Idea: Practice language arts skills.

Bible Quiet Time

Bible Study: Read and complete the assigned pages in the following resource:

★ *Faith at Work: Lesson 11 – Day Three* p. 78-79

Prayer Focus: Refer to **adoration** on "Preparing Your Heart for Prayer". Then, pray a prayer of adoration to worship and honor God. After your prayer, write 'adoration' at the bottom of today's lesson in *Faith at Work* above *Day Four*. Next to 'adoration', either list key phrases or write a sentence to summarize your prayer. Keep "Preparing Your Heart for Prayer" inside your Bible.

Scripture Memory: Read aloud Romans 12:16 three times from your Bible.

Music: Read p. 43 in *Hymns for a Kid's Heart*. Refer to p. 44-45 as you sing with Track 5 *"Wonderful Words of Life"* (vs. 1-2).

Key Idea: Read and study Romans 8:1-17.

Math Exploration

Choose **one** of the math options listed below (see Appendix for details).

★ *Singapore Primary Mathematics 6A/6B, Discovering Mathematics 7A/7B, 8A/8B, No-Nonsense Algebra* or *Videotext Algebra*

★ Your own math program

Key Idea: Use a step-by-step math program.

Science Exploration

★ Read and follow the directions to complete the craft in #6 "Make a Model of an Ionic Compound" on p. 128 of *The Elements: Ingredients of the Universe*. Another option for the model might be tinker toys or K'nex building pieces. **Optional:** You may choose to do p. 128 Lab Experiment #5 "Using Magnesium".

Key Idea: Ionic compounds often form a rectangular lattice shape. For table salt, the lattice is cubic.

Learning Through History
Focus: Education, Recreation, and Prohibition in the U.S. As Stalin Forms the U.S.S.R.
Unit 14 - Day 2

Reading about History

Read about history in the following resource:

 All American History: Vol. II p. 285 – top of p. 291

After today's reading, open your *Student Notebook* to Unit 14. Look at the French poster in Box 7 from 1910 warning of the dangers of absinthe and other forms of alcohol. Absinthe was a popular alcoholic drink in France and was a target of prohibition. By 1915, absinthe was banned in the U.S. and much of Europe. Write your own caption under the poster to convey the significance of the poster's images.

Key Idea: Prohibition refers to prohibiting the manufacture, transport, and sale of alcohol. Periods of prohibition have been enforced in various countries at different times in history. In the United States, prohibition was enforced as law between 1919 and 1933. The 1900s were a time of prohibition in several countries.

History Project

The Great Train Robbery was America's first box office hit movie. Watch *The Great Train Robbery* (12 min.) at one of the following sites: http://prettycleverfilms.com/2012/04/21/the-great-train-robbery-1903/

http://cinewiki.wikispaces.com/The+Great+Train+Robbery (Scroll down to the bottom.)

If these sites are not available, **have a parent help you** search for a site on which to watch Edison's *The Great Train Robbery*.

Key Idea: Movies were a new form of entertainment in the early part of the twentieth century.

President Study

 Read p. 34-35 in *Our Presidents...* Then, open your *President Notebook* to Ulysses S. Grant. Use today's reading to help you complete the information about Grant.

Key Idea: Research Ulysses S. Grant.

Storytime

Read the following assigned pages:

 *War Horse* p. 121-141

Get the bookmark that you placed in your book. Locate the same section of the bookmark that you used on Day 1. Beneath Day 1's entry, write the book title and the page numbers you read today. Select one of the **two** remaining response options at the bottom of the bookmark, and place a checkmark next to it. In the blank space under today's pages, respond in writing using your checked option.

Key Idea: Relate to the text in various ways.

Timeline

You will be adding to the timeline in your *Student Notebook* today. In Unit 14 – Box 1, draw and color symbols for 'head', 'hands', and 'heart'. Label the box, *Mary McLeod Bethune (1875-1955 A.D.)*.

In Box 2, draw and color a bottle of alcohol with a big red 'X' over it. Label it, *Prohibition in the U.S. (1919-1933 A.D.)*.

In Box 3, outline a rectangular flag. In the upper left corner of the flag, color a gold hammer crossed with a gold sickle. Next, color a small gold star above them. Then, color the flag red. Label it, *Russia Becomes the U.S.S.R. Under Stalin (1922 A.D.)*.

Key Idea: The end of World War I led to changes around the world.

Independent History Study

Reread p. 286-287 in *All American History* to discover the problems that led to the repeal of prohibition in 1933. Why was the 18th Amendment repealed in the United States?

Key Idea: In 1933, the 21st Amendment repealed the 18th Amendment. Prohibition had added to the growing problem of gangsters and racketeers.

Learning the Basics

Focus: Language Arts, Math, Bible, Nature Journal, and Science

Biblical Self-Image

Read and discuss the following pages in the resource below.

 Who Am I? And What Am I Doing Here? p. 112 and bottom of p. 121

Key Idea: *The Last Supper* by da Vinci is a famous mural whose theme comes from Jesus' Passover meal with His disciples described in John 13. In giving His life for us, Jesus is our Passover Lamb.

Language Arts

Have students complete one studied dictation exercise (see Appendix for directions and passages).

Help students complete one lesson from the following reading program:

 Drawn into the Heart of Reading

Help students complete **one** English option.

 Progressing With Courage: Lesson 53

 Progressing With Courage: Lesson 92 (last half only)

 Your own grammar program

Key Idea: Practice language arts skills.

Bible Quiet Time

Bible Study: Read and complete the assigned pages in the following resource:

 Faith at Work: Lesson 11 – Day Four p. 79

Prayer Focus: Refer to **confession** on "Preparing Your Heart for Prayer". Then, pray a prayer of confession to admit or acknowledge your sins to God. After your prayer, write 'confession' at the bottom of today's lesson in *Faith at Work* above *Day Five*. Next to 'confession', either list key phrases or write a sentence to summarize your prayer. This will be your prayer log. Keep "Preparing Your Heart for Prayer" inside your Bible.

Scripture Memory: Memorize Romans 12:16 from your Bible and recite it.

Music: Refer to p. 44-45 as you sing with Track 5 *"Wonderful Words of Life"* (vs. 1-2).

Key Idea: Read and study Romans 8:1-17.

Math Exploration

Choose **one** of the math options listed below (see Appendix for details).

 Singapore Primary Mathematics 6A/6B, Discovering Mathematics 7A/7B, 8A/8B, No-Nonsense Algebra or *Videotext Algebra*

 Your own math program

Key Idea: Use a step-by-step math program.

Science Exploration

 You will need to choose **one** of the two projects below from *The Elements: Ingredients of the Universe* to work on for the three days remaining in Unit 14. You may **either** complete Art Project #7 "Element Trading Cards" on p. 129-132 **or** Report #8 "On an Element" on the top of p. 133 and on p. 134. If you choose to do Art Project #7, plan to make 1-2 cards on each of the three days remaining in Unit 14. Begin by making one or two cards today. If you choose to do Report #8, plan to complete 1/3 of the report on p. 134 each of the three remaining days in Unit 14. Begin by doing 1/3 of the report today.

Key Idea: Studying the elements helps you gain a better understanding of the universe's ingredients.

Learning Through History

Focus: Education, Recreation, and Prohibition in the U.S. As Stalin Forms the U.S.S.R.

Unit 14 - Day 3

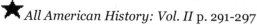

Reading about History ☐ I

Read about history in the following resource:

 All American History: Vol. II p. 291-297

After today's reading, open your *Student Notebook* to Unit 14 - Box 5, which shows a baseball card of George Herman Ruth (or Babe Ruth). This baseball card is from 1933, during Babe Ruth's time with the New York Yankees. Babe Ruth played Major League Baseball from 1914-1935. Compare the baseball card image in Box 5 to the photograph of Babe Ruth shown on p. 289 of *All American History*. What similarities do you notice?

Key Idea: Baseball, the Radio Age, Broadway musicals, ballroom dancing, dance marathons, and jazz were all important parts of the Roaring Twenties.

History Project ☐ S

Ice cream socials were a type of amusement during the Roaring Twenties. Plan an ice cream social for your family. This can be as simple as having sundaes with various toppings. Toppings can be anything from fresh fruit (like strawberries, peaches, or bananas) to various syrups (like chocolate, hot fudge, caramel, or strawberry) to whipped cream, nuts, or sprinkles. Have your ice cream social on a picnic blanket in your backyard, on your deck, in your living room, or in your kitchen. As you eat your ice cream, socialize or visit with those around you.

Key Idea: In the Roaring Twenties, Americans enjoyed picnics, ice cream socials, and amusement parks.

State Study ☐ T

 This is an **optional** part of the plans. If you have chosen to study your state using *State History from a Christian Perspective,* do Lesson 11 from the *Master Lesson Plan Book*.

Key Idea: Study your individual state.

Storytime ☐ T/I

Read the following assigned pages:

 War Horse p. 142-165

After today's reading, orally narrate or retell the portion of the story that was read today. See *Narration Tips* in the Appendix as needed.

Key Idea: Practice orally narrating, or retelling, a portion of a story.

Economics ☐ ✓

Read about economics in the resource below.

 Whatever Happened to Penny Candy? p. 94-99

After the reading, open your *Student Notebook* to the "Economic Principles" section at the front of your notebook. Under "Economic Principle", write a one or two sentence summary for the economic principle you learned from today's reading.

Key Idea: Recessions that proceed unhindered by government interference are likely to self-correct more quickly.

Independent History Study ☐ ✓

Listen and watch a brief video clip of Louis Armstrong in concert at the following Internet site (Click on " Watch Preview" to view): http://www.jazzicons.com/ji_armstrong.html

Also, watch Armstrong perform "Oh When the Saints Go Marching In" at the following link: http://www.edsullivan.com/artists/louis-armstrong

Note: **With a parent's help and permission**, you may also wish to search the Internet for "Louis Armstrong 'Hello Dolly' (live)".

Key Idea: The Roaring Twenties were also known as the Jazz Age. Louis Armstrong was a famous jazz musician in New Orleans.

Nature Journal & Poetry `S`

The poetry of Longfellow, Wordsworth, and Whitman is scheduled on Day 3 to complement the nature journaling sessions. Read aloud and discuss today's poem *"The Reaper and the Flowers"* (see Appendix) with a parent. Then, follow the directions in the resource below.

★ *Nature Drawing & Journaling: Lesson XIX* p. 54-55

Note: Do only one nature study sketch today. You may choose to do something from nature up close or to do a scene from nature such as the garden scene on p. 55. If weather permits, go outside to do the nature study sketch. If not, then do your sketch from your window.

<u>Key Idea</u>: Practice sketching a nature scene.

Language Arts `S`

Have students complete one studied dictation exercise (see Appendix for passages).

Help students complete **one** English option.

★ *Progressing With Courage:* Lesson 54

★ *Progressing With Courage:* Lesson 93 (first half only)

★ Your own grammar program

Work with the students to complete **one** of the writing options listed below:

★ *Write with the Best: Vol. 2* Unit 4 – Day 18 p. 41-42

★ Your own writing program

<u>Key Idea</u>: Practice language arts skills.

Bible Quiet Time `I`

Bible Study: Read and complete the assigned pages in the following resource:

★ *Faith at Work: Lesson 11 – Day Five* and *Notes* p. 79-85

Prayer Focus: Refer to **thanksgiving** on "Preparing Your Heart for Prayer". Then, pray a prayer of thanksgiving to express gratitude to God for His divine goodness. After your prayer, write 'thanksgiving' at the bottom of today's lesson on p. 80 in *Faith at Work*. Next to 'thanksgiving', either list key phrases or write a sentence to summarize your prayer. Keep "Preparing Your Heart for Prayer" inside your Bible.

Scripture Memory: Copy Romans 12:16 in your Common Place Book.

Music: Refer to p. 44-45 as you sing with Track 5 *"Wonderful Words of Life"* (vs. 1-2).

<u>Key Idea</u>: Read and study Romans 8:1-17.

Math Exploration `S`

Choose **one** of the math options listed below (see Appendix for details).

★ *Singapore Primary Mathematics 6A/6B, Discovering Mathematics 7A/7B, 8A/8B, No-Nonsense Algebra* or *Videotext Algebra*

★ Your own math program

<u>Key Idea</u>: Use a step-by-step math program.

Science Exploration `I`

★ Continue **either** Art Project #7 **or** Report #8 that you began on Unit 14 – Day 2. If you chose to do Art Project #7, make 1-2 cards today. If you chose to do Report #8, complete 1/3 of the report today.

<u>Key Idea</u>: Studying the elements helps you gain a better understanding of the universe's ingredients.

Learning Through History

Focus: Education, Recreation, and Prohibition in the U.S. As Stalin Forms the U.S.S.R.

Unit 14 - Day 4

Reading about History

Read about history in the following resource:

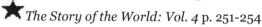 *The Story of the World: Vol. 4* p. 251-254

You will be writing a narration about the chapter *The Rise of Joseph Stalin.* To prepare for writing your narration, look back over p. 251-254 in *The Story of the World: Vol. 4.* Think about the main idea and the most important moments in this part of the reading.

After you have thought about what you will write and how you will begin your narration, turn to Unit 14 in your *Student Notebook.* For more guidance on writing a narration, see *Written Narration Tips* in the Appendix.

In Box 4, write a 12-16 sentence narration about the reading. When you have finished writing, read your sentences out loud to catch any mistakes. Check for the following things: *Did you include* **who** *or* **what topic** *the reading was mainly about? Did you include* **descriptors** *of the important thing(s) that happened? Did you include a* **closing sentence***? If not, add those things.* Use the *Written Narration Skills* in the Appendix as a guide for editing the narration.

<u>Key Idea</u>: After the death of Czar Nicholas II, an army of avengers called the White Army fought against the communist Red Army. When the Red Army was victorious in 1922, supporters of the White Army were forced to leave Russia. This made Russia a totalitarian state, because it had only one political party. Lenin ruled Russia first, followed by Stalin. Under Stalin's rule, countries on the western border of Russia became part of the Union of Soviet Socialist Republics, or U.S.S.R.

Storytime  | T/I |

Read the following assigned pages:

 Gladys Alyward p. 13-17

Get the bookmark that you placed in your book on Day 2. Locate the same section of the bookmark that you used on Day 2. Beneath Day 2's entry, write the book title and the page numbers you read today. Select the one remaining response option at the bottom of the bookmark, and place a checkmark next to it. In the blank space under today's pages, respond in writing using your checked option. Keep the bookmark in your book.

<u>Key Idea</u>: Relate to the text in various ways.

Geography

For today's activities, use the map listed below.

 United States History Atlas p. 39

On the map on p. 39, find the countries of Estonia, Latvia, and Lithuania. These countries were given their freedom from Russia through the Peace Treaty of Versailles at the end of WWI. Later, Russia forced these countries to become a part of the U.S.S.R. Next, find St. Petersburg, or Petrograd, which Stalin named Leningrad after the death of Lenin. Last, find Moscow, where Lenin's body is on display in a glass coffin in Red Square.

<u>Key Idea</u>: With Lenin, and later Stalin, Russia became a communist country under the rule of one man. Collective farming, work camps, starvation, arrest, and execution were part of Stalin's Communist Russia.

President Study | I |

 On *The Presidents* DVD Volume 2, select the Chapter "Andrew Johnson to Arthur" and watch **only** Program 2: Ulysses S. Grant. Then, open your *President Notebook* to Ulysses S. Grant. Use today's viewing to add further information about Grant.

<u>Key Idea</u>: Research Ulysses S. Grant.

Independent History Study

Refer to p. 250 of *The Story of the World* to see the area of famine in the U.S.S.R. Then, find Siberia, which was the location of the 'Gulag' or work camps.

<u>Key Idea</u>: Life in Communist Russia was hard.

Learning the Basics

Focus: Language Arts, Math, Bible, Nature Journal, and Science

Biblical Self-Image [T]

Our plans intend for the listed pages in *Who Am I? And What Am I Doing Here?* to be read either silently by both you and your child, or read aloud to the child by you. With this in mind, read and discuss with the students the following pages in the resource below.

★ *Who Am I? And What Am I Doing Here?* p. 113 – middle of p. 121

Key Idea: Jesus laid down His life for us to set us free from our sins.

Language Arts [S]

Have students complete one studied dictation exercise (see Appendix for directions and passages).

Help students complete one lesson from the following reading program:

★ *Drawn into the Heart of Reading*

Help students complete **one** English option.

★ *Progressing With Courage:* Lesson 55

★ *Progressing With Courage:* Lesson 93 (last half only)

★ Your own grammar program

Key Idea: Practice language arts skills.

Bible Quiet Time [I]

Bible Study: Complete the assignment below.

★ *Faith at Work: Lesson 12 – Day One* p. 86 Note: Refer to p. 81-85 to complete the lesson.

Prayer Focus: Refer to **supplication** on "Preparing Your Heart for Prayer". Then, pray a prayer of supplication to make a humble and earnest request of God. Write 'supplication' at the bottom of today's lesson in *Faith at Work* above *Day Two*. Next to it, either list several key phrases or write a sentence to summarize your prayer. Keep "Preparing Your Heart for Prayer" inside your Bible.

Scripture Memory: Recite Romans 12:1-16.

Music: Refer to p. 44-45 as you sing with Track 5 *"Wonderful Words of Life"* (vs. 1-2).

Key Idea: Read and study Romans 8:1-17.

Math Exploration [S]

Choose **one** of the math options listed below.

★ *Singapore Primary Mathematics 6A/6B, Discovering Mathematics 7A/7B, 8A/8B, No-Nonsense Algebra* or *Videotext Algebra*

★ Your own math program

Key Idea: Use a step-by-step math program.

Science Exploration [I]

★ Complete **either** Art Project #7 **or** Report #8 that you began on Unit 14 – Day 2. If you chose to do Art Project #7, make the final 1-2 cards today. Then, photocopy p. 130 from *The Elements: Ingredients of the Universe* and make the holder for your cards. If you chose to do Report #8, complete the final 1/3 of the report on p. 134 today. Hand in either your cards or your report to be checked by a parent.

Key Idea: Studying the elements helps you gain a better understanding of the universe's ingredients.

Reading about History ✓

Read about history in the following resource:

 The Story of the World: Vol. 4 p. 256 – middle of p. 260

After today's reading, orally narrate or retell to an adult the portion of text that you read today from *The Story of the World*. Some possible key words to include in your narration might be *Abbas II, khedive, Egypt, WWI, martial law, forfeit throne, protectorate Great Britain, sultan Ahmad Fu'ad, Wafd, boycotting, fighting, 1922 freedom for Egypt, King Fu'ad I,* and *Suez Canal*.

<u>Key Idea</u>: Abbas II was the khedive of Egypt under the British consul general. During WWI, Great Britain placed Egypt under martial law and removed Abbas II from his throne. Then, Egypt became a protectorate of Great Britain, and Ahmad Fu'ad became the sultan. In 1922, Egypt won its independence from Britain.

History Project S

In this unit, you will make Japanese Fortune Cookies with Proverbs, rather than fortunes placed inside. Cut 10 slips of paper that each measure 3" x ½". Copy the **first** 5 Proverbs listed below today, writing a different Proverb on each slip of paper. Copy the remaining 5 Proverbs on Day 2. Save the papers for Day 3.

Proverbs 1:7, Proverbs 1:8, Proverbs 3:7, Proverbs 12:15, Proverbs 12:24, Proverbs 16:28 Proverbs 16:33, Proverbs 21:2, Proverbs 27:1, Proverbs 31:30

<u>Key Idea</u>: Four years after Fu'ad became King of Egypt, Hirohito became emperor of Japan.

President Study I

 Read p. 36-37 in *Our Presidents...* Then, open your *President Notebook* to Rutherford B. Hayes. Use today's reading to help you complete the information about Hayes.

<u>Key Idea</u>: Research Rutherford B. Hayes.

Storytime ✓ T/I

Read the following assigned pages:

 Gladys Alyward p. 19-30
Get the bookmark that you placed in your book last unit. Choose a new section of the bookmark with **three** options at the bottom. At the top of this section of the bookmark, write the book title and the page numbers you read today. Select **one** of the three options at the bottom and place a checkmark next to it. In the blank space under today's pages, respond in writing using your checked option.

<u>Key Idea</u>: Relate to the text in various ways.

Worthy Words T

Open your *Student Notebook* to Unit 15 – Box 9. You will read, analyze, and evaluate an article about King Fu'ad. After reading the article, answer the following questions on an index card: *What change in title did Ahmed Fu'ad Pasha have? Why is it significant that the British High Commissioner addressed Fu'ad as "Your Majesty"? What was the focus of King Fu'ad's letter to his "noble nation"? Egypt is 90% Muslim, yet Fu'ad mentions God three times in his letter. How can you explain that? Based on what you read today in <u>The Story of the World</u>, why did Britain abandon the protectorate of Egypt? What possible effects might Egypt's new independence have had on relations with foreign governments and on peace in the Middle East?* Next, meet with a parent to have a Socratic dialogue about the article. Before beginning the dialogue, the parent reads Box 9 out loud. Next, discuss the questions using your notes.

<u>Key Idea</u>: Fu'ad became King of Egypt in 1922.

Independent History Study I

Open your *Student Notebook* to Unit 15. Choose an important part of the letter from Box 9 to copy in quotation marks in Box 6. Write "King Fu'ad I of Egypt" at the bottom.

<u>Key Idea</u>: Egypt gained its independence.

Learning the Basics
Focus: Language Arts, Math, Bible, Nature Journal, and Science

Nature Journal

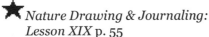

Read and follow the directions in the resource below.

★ *Nature Drawing & Journaling: Lesson XIX* p. 55

Note: Choose one up close floral sketch to do today. Leave it unfinished but labeled with colors as on p. 55. If it is not the season for blooming flowers where you live, then choose a flower to sketch from www.enature.com instead. Click on "Wildflowers" under the "Field Guide" heading. Then, click on "Advanced Search" under "Search Field Guide" to specify the flower you wish to sketch.

Key Idea: Practice sketching from nature.

Language Arts

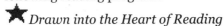

Help students complete one lesson from the following reading program:

★ *Drawn into the Heart of Reading*

Help students complete **one** English option.

★ *Progressing With Courage:* Lesson 56

★ *Progressing With Courage:* Lesson 94 (first only)

Work with the students to complete **one** of the writing options listed below:

★ *Write with the Best: Vol. 2* Unit 4 – Day 19 p. 42

★ Your own writing program

Key Idea: Practice language arts skills.

Bible Quiet Time [I]

Bible Study: Read and complete the assigned pages in the following resource:

★ *Faith at Work: Lesson 12 – Day Two* p. 86-87

Prayer Focus: Refer to **adoration** on "Preparing Your Heart for Prayer". Then, pray a prayer of adoration to worship and honor God. After your prayer, write 'adoration' at the bottom of today's lesson in *Faith at Work* above *Day Three*. Next to 'adoration', either list key phrases or write a sentence to summarize your prayer. Keep "Preparing Your Heart for Prayer" inside your Bible.

Scripture Memory: Read aloud Romans 12:17-18 three times from your Bible.

Music: Read the verse and pray the prayer from p. 45 in *Hymns for a Kid's Heart*. Refer to p. 44-45 as you sing with Track 5 *"Wonderful Words of Life"* (vs. 1-3).

Key Idea: Read and study Romans 8:18-39.

Math Exploration [S]

Choose **one** of the math options listed below (see Appendix for details).

★ *Singapore Primary Mathematics 6A/6B, Discovering Mathematics 7A/7B, 8A/8B, No-Nonsense Algebra* or *Videotext Algebra*

★ Your own math program

Key Idea: Use a step-by-step math program.

Science Exploration [I]

★ Read and follow the directions to complete *The Elements: Ingredients of the Universe* p. 49-53. To complete Activity #1 and Activity #2, you will need parent supervision. Note: On Unit 15 – Day 2, you will need a bag of colored marshmallows and a box of toothpicks. **Optional:** You may also choose to perform Lab Experiment #5 as described on p. 138.

Key Idea: Noble gases are inert because their outer shells of valence electrons are full.

Reading about History

Read about history in the following resource:

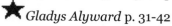 *The Story of the World: Vol. 4* p. 260-266
After today's reading, open your *Student Notebook* to Unit 15 – Box 5 to view the emblem of Mussolini's National Fascist Party. Notice the 'P', 'N', and 'F', which stand for *Partito Nazionale Fascista*. The tri-color part of the emblem remains part of Italy's flag today. Reread the top of p. 265 about the 'fasces', or bundle of sticks, in the emblem.

Key Idea: Mussolini was Italy's prime minister.

History Project

Finish copying the Proverbs listed on Day 1. Then, **wait until Day 3** to bake cookies using the following directions: Spray two cookie sheets with cooking spray and wipe off the excess with a paper towel. In a bowl, mix 2 egg whites, ¼ tsp. vanilla extract, 1 tsp. almond extract, and 2 Tbsp. water. Whip the mixture until it is foamy and frothy but not stiff. Stir into the egg mixture ½ cup all-purpose flour, 4 Tbsp. white sugar, and a pinch of salt. Pour one level tablespoon of batter onto the cookie sheet and evenly spread it into a 3" circle using the back of a metal spoon. The batter should be spread very thin, so you can see through it. Keep cookies 4" apart, as the batter will spread when baking. Make 2 cookies at a time by baking them in a preheated oven at 375 degrees for 5-7 min. Cookies are done when the outer ½" edge is golden and the center is still light colored. Directions are continued on Day 3.

Key Idea: Japan and Italy had military rule.

President Study I

 On *The Presidents* DVD Volume 2, select the Chapter "Andrew Johnson to Arthur" and watch **only** Program 3: Rutherford B. Hayes. Then, open your *President Notebook* to Rutherford B. Hayes. Use today's viewing to add further information about Hayes.

Key Idea: Research Rutherford B. Hayes.

Storytime

Read the following assigned pages:

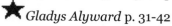 *Gladys Alyward* p. 31-42

Get the bookmark that you placed in your book. Locate the same section of the bookmark that you used on Day 1. Beneath Day 1's entry, write the book title and the page numbers you read today. Select one of the **two** remaining response options at the bottom of the bookmark, and place a checkmark next to it. In the blank space under today's pages, respond in writing using your checked option.

Key Idea: Relate to the text in various ways.

Geography

For today's activities, use the map listed below.

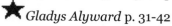 *Map Trek CD: Missions to Modern Marvels* p. 56-57
Print the "Totalitarianism" Student Map found on p. 57 of the *Map Trek* CD. Refer to or print the *Map Trek* Teacher's Answer Map on p. 56 to guide you as you label each country on your Student Map. Then, refer to *The Story of the World* p. 262 to label the bodies of water on your Student Map. Next, notice the countries shown on the map that had dictatorships during the years leading up to WWII. Which countries did not have dictatorships but were surrounded by countries who did? Why might these countries become battlegrounds in a war? File the map in your *Student Notebook*.

Key Idea: After Vittorio Orlando resigned as prime minister, Victor Emmanuel III eventually made Mussolini Italy's prime minister. By 1923, Italy had become a fascist country ruled by the military dictator Mussolini.

Independent History Study

Listen to *What in the World? Vol. 3* Disc 3, Track 8: "Fascist Italy & Militant Japan".

Key Idea: Both Italy and Japan were mainly ruled by military dictators prior to WWII.

Learning the Basics
Focus: Language Arts, Math, Bible, Nature Journal, and Science

Unit 15 - Day 2

Biblical Self-Image [T]

Our plans intend for the listed pages in *Who Am I? And What Am I Doing Here?* to be read either silently by both you and your child, or read aloud to the child by you. This study also has much to be gained by discussion, as it provides an excellent opportunity to share what **you** believe. Read and discuss with the students the following pages in the resource below.

 Who Am I? And What Am I Doing Here? p. 122 – top of p. 124 (Note: Making your own fishing pole as suggested on p. 122 is optional.)

Key Idea: God has emotions and we do too.

Bible Quiet Time [I]

Bible Study: Read and complete the assigned pages in the following resource:

 Faith at Work: Lesson 12 – Day Three p. 87-88

Prayer Focus: Refer to **confession** on "Preparing Your Heart for Prayer". Then, pray a prayer of confession to admit or acknowledge your sins to God. After your prayer, write 'confession' at the bottom of today's lesson in *Faith at Work* above *Day Four*. Next to 'confession', either list key phrases or write a sentence to summarize your prayer. This will be your prayer log. Keep "Preparing Your Heart for Prayer" inside your Bible.

Scripture Memory: Memorize Romans 12:17-18 from your Bible and recite it.

Music: Refer to p. 44-45 as you sing with Track 5 *"Wonderful Words of Life"* (vs. 1-3).

Key Idea: Read and study Romans 8:18-39.

Language Arts [S]

Have students complete one studied dictation exercise (see Appendix for directions and passages).

Help students complete one lesson from the following reading program:

 Drawn into the Heart of Reading

Help students complete **one** English option.

 Progressing With Courage: Lesson 57

 Progressing With Courage: Lesson 94 (last half only)

 Your own grammar program

Key Idea: Practice language arts skills.

Math Exploration [S]

Choose **one** of the math options listed below (see Appendix for details).

 Singapore Primary Mathematics 6A/6B, Discovering Mathematics 7A/7B, 8A/8B, No-Nonsense Algebra or *Videotext Algebra*

 Your own math program

Key Idea: Use a step-by-step math program.

Science Exploration [I]

 Read *The Elements: Ingredients of the Universe* p. 55-56 and p. 136-137. Then, follow the directions on p. 138 to complete Craft #4 "Make Some Delicious Covalent Molecules". The group game described under Craft #4 on p. 138 is optional. Next, with parent supervision, follow the directions to complete as much of Activity #3 on p. 54 as desired. It is **not** necessary to do all of the suggestions.

Key Idea: Non-metal atoms form covalent bonds. In this type of bonding, pairs of electrons are shared between atoms.

Reading about History

Read about history in the following resource:

 The Story of the World: Vol. 4 p. 268-272
After today's reading, open your *Student Notebook* to Unit 15 – Box 7. Look at the photograph of Emperor Hirohito from his 1928 enthronement ceremony. The emperor is wearing a *sokutai*, holding a *shaku* (or scepter), and wearing a hat called a *kanmuri*. In Box 8, list bulleted notes about Hirohito from p. 270-271 of *The Story of the World*.

<u>Key Idea</u>: Hirohito was Japan's 124th emperor.

History Project [S]

Today, you will make Japanese Fortune Cookies. Begin by following the directions in the History Project box for **Day 2**. After you remove the cookies from the oven, you have 20 seconds to complete the following steps, or the cookies will harden and crack. So, work quickly! Use a spatula to remove the hot cookies and flip them face down on a wooden board. Place one paper Proverb in the middle of each cookie and fold each cookie like a taco. Place the folded edge of the cookie across the rim of a glass or a measuring cup and pull the pointed edges of the cookie down to form a fortune cookie shape. To hold the shape, place the folded cookie inside a cup of a muffin pan. Then, fold the next cookie. Using your cool cookie sheet, bake two more cookies. Don't forget to spray the sheet with cooking spray and wipe off the excess between each batch. When all cookies are made, bake them in the muffin pan for 3-5 more min. to crisp them.

<u>Key Idea</u>: Hirohito ruled Japan 63 years.

State Study [T]

 This is an **optional** part of the plans. If you have chosen to study your state using *State History from a Christian Perspective,* do Lesson 12 from the *Master Lesson Plan Book*.

<u>Key Idea</u>: Study your individual state.

Storytime

Read the following assigned pages:

 Gladys Alyward p. 43-56

After today's reading, orally narrate or retell the portion of the story that was read today. See *Narration Tips* in the Appendix as needed.

<u>Key Idea</u>: Practice orally narrating, or retelling, a portion of a story.

Timeline

You will be adding to the timeline in your *Student Notebook* today.

In Unit 15 – Box 1, draw and color a crown. Label it, *Independence for Egypt (1922 A.D.)*.

In Box 2, draw and color a black flag with a golden 'fasces' in the center. Label it, *Mussolini – Prime Minister of Italy (1923-1944 A.D.)*.

In Box 3, outline a white rectangular flag and color a red circle in the center. Label it, *Hirohito – Emperor of Japan (1926-1989 A.D.)*.

<u>Key Idea</u>: As Egypt was gaining independence from Great Britain, Mussolini and the Fascist Party were rising in Italy, and Hirohito was preparing to become emperor of Japan after his father.

Independent History Study

Read over the timeline entries from 1917-1926 on p. 482-484 of *The Story of the World*. Notice how many important world events occur in less than 10 years on this timeline! Based on the events on the timeline, which countries were in chaos over who was in power? What types of governments do you see rising out of this chaos?

<u>Key Idea</u>: The years after WWI led to upheaval in the governments of many countries.

Nature Journal & Poetry | S |

The poetry of Longfellow, Wordsworth, and Whitman is scheduled on Day 3 to complement the nature journaling sessions. Read aloud and discuss today's poem *"September 1815"* (see Appendix) with a parent. Then, follow the directions in the resource below.

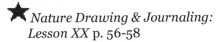
★ *Nature Drawing & Journaling: Lesson XX* p. 56-58

Note: Only draw the branch described in paragraph 1 and the entire tree in its figure box today. Wait to color the tree and to sketch the distant trees described on p. 58 until Unit 16 – Day 1.

Key Idea: Practice sketching trees from a variety of perspectives.

Language Arts | S |

Have students complete one studied dictation exercise (see Appendix for passages).

Help students complete **one** English option.

★ *Progressing With Courage:* Lesson 58

★ *Progressing With Courage:* Lesson 95 (first half only)

Work with the students to complete **one** of the writing options listed below:

★ *Write with the Best: Vol. 2* Unit 4 – Day 20 p. 42

★ Your own writing program

Key Idea: Practice language arts skills.

Bible Quiet Time | I |

Bible Study: Read and complete the assigned pages in the following resource:

★ *Faith at Work: Lesson 12 – Day Four* p. 88

Prayer Focus: Refer to **thanksgiving** on "Preparing Your Heart for Prayer". Then, pray a prayer of thanksgiving to express gratitude to God for His divine goodness. After your prayer, write 'thanksgiving' at the bottom of today's lesson on p. 88 in *Faith at Work*. Next to 'thanksgiving', either list key phrases or write a sentence to summarize your prayer. Keep "Preparing Your Heart for Prayer" inside your Bible.

Scripture Memory: Copy Romans 12:17-18 in your Common Place Book.

Music: Refer to p. 44-45 as you sing with Track 5 *"Wonderful Words of Life"* (vs. 1-3).

Key Idea: Read and study Romans 8:18-39.

Math Exploration | S |

Choose **one** of the math options listed below (see Appendix for details).

★ *Singapore Primary Mathematics 6A/6B, Discovering Mathematics 7A/7B, 8A/8B, No-Nonsense Algebra* or *Videotext Algebra*

★ Your own math program

Key Idea: Use a step-by-step math program.

Science Exploration | I |

★ Read *The Elements: Ingredients of the Universe* p. 57-58 and p. 60-61. Omit Activity #1 on p. 59. To complete Activity #2, you will need the CD that came with *The Elements: Ingredients of the Universe.*

Key Idea: Semi-metals are also called metalloids. They are found on the Periodic Table between the metals and the non-metals. Not all chemists agree on the dividing line for semi-metals. Silicon is a metalloid that can act like a metal or a non-metal. It is used for electronic parts in high-tech equipment.

Learning Through History

Focus: Independence for Egypt, Fascism in Italy, and War Between China and Japan

Unit 15 - Day 4

Reading about History | I |

Read about history in the following resource:

★ *The Story of the World: Vol. 4* p. 273-278

You will be writing a narration about the chapter *The Long March*. To prepare for writing your narration, look back over p. 273-278 in *The Story of the World: Vol. 4*. Think about the main idea and the most important moments in this part of the reading.

After you have thought about what you will write and how you will begin your narration, turn to Unit 15 in your *Student Notebook*. For more guidance on writing a narration, see *Written Narration Tips* in the Appendix.

In Box 4, write a 12-16 sentence narration about the reading. When you have finished writing, read your sentences out loud to catch any mistakes. Check for the following things. *Did you include **who** or **what topic** the reading was mainly about? Did you include **descriptors** of the important thing(s) that happened? Did you include a **closing sentence**? If not, add those things.* Use the *Written Narration Skills* in the Appendix as a guide for editing the narration.

Key Idea: After the last Qing emperor fled, the Kuomintang (or National Party), the warlords, and Chiang Kai-shek's National Revolutionary Army all fought for control of China. During this time of upheaval, Mao Zedong began teaching the Chinese people about communism based on the Russian Communist Party. In China, this came to be known as the Chinese Communist Party, or CCP. Chiang Kai-shek systematically fought the warloads to seize power in China. Meanwhile, Zedong retreated to the mountains and formed the Chinese Soviet Republic. Kai-shek attacked Mao Zedong, until Zedong and his followers fled on the Long March.

President Study | I |

★ Read p. 38-39 in *Our Presidents...* Then, open your *President Notebook* to James A. Garfield. Use today's reading to help you complete the information about Garfield.

Key Idea: Research James A. Garfield.

Storytime | T/I |

Read the following assigned pages:

★ *Gladys Alyward* p. 57-68

Note: p. 67 contains a graphic description. Get the bookmark that you placed in your book. Locate the same section of the bookmark that you used on Day 2. Beneath Day 2's entry, write the book title and the page numbers you read today. Select the one remaining response option at the bottom of the bookmark, and place a checkmark next to it. In the blank space under today's pages, respond in writing using your checked option. Keep the bookmark in your book.

Key Idea: Relate to the text in various ways.

Economics | I |

Read about economics in the resource below.

★ *Whatever Happened to Penny Candy?* p. 100-108

After the reading, open your *Student Notebook* to the "Economic Principles" section at the front of your notebook. Under "Economic Principle", write a one or two sentence summary for the economic principle you learned from today's reading.

Key Idea: The economic prosperity of a country is related directly to its legal system. The two types of law, or legal systems, are natural law and civil law.

Independent History Study | I |

Print the "China and Japan at War" Student Map found on p. 59 of the *Map Trek* CD. Refer to the *Map Trek* Teacher's Answer Map on p. 58 as you label and color the Student Map. With your finger, trace the Long March. Notice the growing area occupied by Japan in just nine years' time! File your map in your *Student Notebook*.

Key Idea: After WWI, China was in turmoil, and Japan began fighting to control more land.

Learning the Basics
Focus: Language Arts, Math, Bible, Nature Journal, and Science

Biblical Self-Image ⟨T⟩

Our plans intend for the listed pages in *Who Am I? And What Am I Doing Here?* to be read either silently by both you and your child, or read aloud to the child by you. Read and discuss the following pages listed below.

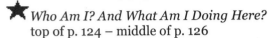 *Who Am I? And What Am I Doing Here?* top of p. 124 – middle of p. 126

Key Idea: We need to make decisions based on God's Word and its truth, not on our feelings.

Language Arts ⟨S⟩

Have students complete one studied dictation exercise (see Appendix for passages).

Help students complete one lesson from the following reading program:

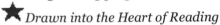 *Drawn into the Heart of Reading*

Help students complete **one** English option.

⭐ *Progressing With Courage:* Lesson 59 (first half only)

⭐ *Progressing With Courage:* Lesson 95 (last half only)

⭐ Your own grammar program

Key Idea: Practice language arts skills.

Bible Quiet Time ⟨I⟩

Bible Study: Complete the assignment below.

⭐ *Faith at Work: Lesson 12 – Day Five* and *Notes* p. 89-93 (Note: This lesson mentions the Millennial Kingdom on p. 90 and predestination on p. 92. You may wish to discuss these sections with your parent to discover your family's views on these areas.)

Prayer Focus: Refer to **supplication** on "Preparing Your Heart for Prayer". Then, pray a prayer of supplication. Write 'supplication' at the bottom of today's lesson on p. 89 in *Faith at Work*. Next to it, list several key phrases or write a sentence to summarize your prayer.

Scripture Memory: Recite Romans 12:1-18.

Music: Refer to p. 44-45 as you sing with Track 5 *"Wonderful Words of Life"* (vs. 1-3).

Key Idea: Read and study Romans 8:18-39.

Math Exploration ⟨S⟩

Choose **one** of the math options listed below.

⭐ *Singapore Primary Mathematics 6A/6B, Discovering Mathematics 7A/7B, 8A/8B, No-Nonsense Algebra* or *Videotext Algebra*

⭐ Your own math program

Key Idea: Use a step-by-step math program.

Science Exploration ⟨I⟩

⭐ Read p. 63-64 in *The Elements: Ingredients of the Universe*. Then, do Activity #4 on p. 62. The 7 parts in the video of Marie Curie are listed below. Once you find part 1 of the video online, you can often find the next part to click and play on the right. If not, try the address below. The set takes 29 minutes.
Part 1 (3 min. 14 sec.): http://www.youtube.com/watch?v=BF3FfngPgmM&feature=relmfu
Part 2 (4 min. 22 sec.): http://www.youtube.com/watch?v=neVu2QXryfU&feature=relmfu
Part 3 (5 min. 4 sec.): http://www.youtube.com/watch?v=sF45ZzsFTwM&feature=relmfu
Part 4 (2 min. 55 sec.): To locate this part, in the youtube search, type "marie curie part 4 belfer0691".
Part 5 (1 min. 10 sec.): http://www.youtube.com/watch?v=CmeGM6wK_pM&feature=relmfu
Part 6 (6 min. 50 sec.): http://www.youtube.com/watch?v=6lpscOUeXIo&feature=relmfu
Part 7 (4 min. 22 sec.): http://www.youtube.com/watch?v=5i9BvNvtg1U&feature=relmfu
Optional: You may choose to complete Activity #3 and Activity #5 in place of Activity #4.

Key Idea: The three types of bonding are covalent bonding, ionic bonding, and metallic bonding.

Reading about History   S

Read about history in the following resources:

 All American History: Vol. II p. 299 – middle of p. 306

⭐ *Great Events in American History* p. 83-86

After today's reading, orally narrate or retell to an adult the portion of text that you read today in *All American History*. As you retell, the adult will write or type your narration. Some possible key words to include in your narration might be *Big Bull Market, stocks, Black Thursday, President Hoover, Stock Market Crash, unemployment, Depression, Bonus Expeditionary Force, Hoovervilles, Franklin Delano Roosevelt, polio,* and *New Deal*. When the narration is complete, tri-fold the typed or written narration to fit in Unit 16 – Box 9 of the *Student Notebook*. Glue the folded narration in Box 9, so it can be opened and read.

Key Idea: The stock market crashed in 1929, and America was plunged into a depression.

History Project   S

Just prior to the Great Depression, the United States enjoyed great prosperity. However, by 1933 one-fourth of Americans were out of work. On paper, list things that you have that are examples of prosperity. Some suggestions might include a home, a car, toys, enough food to eat, a bed, books, clothes, shoes, coats, a TV, telephones, a computer, heat, air conditioning, clean water to drink, water for bathing, etc. In looking at the pictures on p. 303-304 and p. 306-307 of *All American History,* which of the things on your list were many Americans living without during the Depression?

Key Idea: The Depression lasted eleven years.

Storytime   T/I

Read the following assigned pages:

 Gladys Alyward p. 69-80

Get the bookmark that you placed in your book last unit. Choose a new section of the bookmark with **three** options at the bottom. At the top of this section of the bookmark, write the book title and the page numbers you read today. Select **one** of the three options at the bottom and place a checkmark next to it. In the blank space under today's pages, respond in writing using your checked option. Keep the bookmark in your book.

Key Idea: Relate to the text in various ways.

Timeline   I

You will be adding to the timeline in your *Student Notebook* today. In Unit 16 – Box 1, draw and color dollar bills in the air falling. Label the box, *Black Tuesday - Stock Market Crash (October 29, 1929 A.D.).*

In Box 2, draw and color a bank with a sign that says 'Closed'. Label it, *The Great Depression (1929-1940 A.D.).*

In Box 3, draw and color a sign that says 'FDR'. Label the box, *Franklin D. Roosevelt – 32nd U.S. President (1933-1945 A.D.).*

Key Idea: Herbert Hoover was president of the U.S. when the stock market crashed in 1929. Midway through the Great Depression that followed the crash, Franklin D. Roosevelt became president. He was elected 4 times to the presidency and died during his fourth term in office in 1945.

Independent History Study   I

⭐ Alfred E. Smith ran for president against Herbert Hoover in the 1928 election. Smith talks about prejudice in his speech on p. 153-154 in the *Book of Great American Speeches*. What examples of prejudice does he share?

Key Idea: In the 1928 election, Republican Party candidate Herbert Hoover defeated Alfred Smith.

Learning the Basics
Focus: Language Arts, Math, Bible, Nature Journal, and Science

Nature Journal $\boxed{I}$

Read and follow the directions in the resource below.

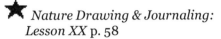 *Nature Drawing & Journaling: Lesson XX* p. 58

Note: Color the tree that you drew on Unit 15 – Day 3, and then sketch the distant trees described on p. 58. After that, select one of the quotes about trees from the tops of p. 57-63 to copy in your Nature Journal.

Key Idea: Practice sketching trees.

Language Arts $\boxed{S}$

Help students complete one lesson from the following reading program:

 *Drawn into the Heart of Reading*

Help students complete **one** English option.

★ *Progressing With Courage:* Lesson 59 (last half only)

★ *Progressing With Courage:* Lesson 96 (first half only)

★ Your own grammar program

Work with the students to complete **one** of the writing options listed below:

★ *Write with the Best: Vol. 2* Unit 5 – Day 1 p. 43 – top of p. 46

★ Your own writing program

Key Idea: Practice language arts skills.

Bible Quiet Time $\boxed{I}$

Bible Study: Read and complete the assigned pages in the following resource:

★ *Faith at Work: Lesson 13 – Day One* p. 94
Note: Refer to p. 90-93 to complete the lesson. This lesson mentions predestination on p. 92. You may wish to discuss this with your parent to discover your family's views on this area.

Prayer Focus: Refer to **adoration** on "Preparing Your Heart for Prayer". Then, pray a prayer of adoration to worship and honor God. After your prayer, write 'adoration' at the bottom of today's lesson in *Faith at Work* above *Day Two*. Next to 'adoration', either list key phrases or write a sentence to summarize your prayer. Keep "Preparing Your Heart for Prayer" inside your Bible.

Scripture Memory: Read aloud Romans 12:19 three times from your Bible.

Music: Read p. 47-48 in *Hymns for a Kid's Heart*. Refer to p. 50-51 as you sing with Track 6 *"Onward, Christian Soldiers"* (vs. 1-2).

Key Idea: Read and study Romans 8:18-39.

Math Exploration $\boxed{S}$

Choose **one** of the math options listed below (see Appendix for details).

★ *Singapore Primary Mathematics 6A/6B, Discovering Mathematics 7A/7B, 8A/8B, No-Nonsense Algebra* or *Videotext Algebra*

★ Your own math program

Key Idea: Use a step-by-step math program.

Science Exploration $\boxed{I}$

★ Read and follow the directions to complete *The Elements: Ingredients of the Universe* p. 65-67. As part of today's assignment, you will scroll through the website listed in Activity #1. The "elephant" mentioned in Activity #1 is no longer at the end of the website. Instead, it is shown closer to the beginning.
Optional: You may choose to complete Lab Experiment #3 on p. 139-140 "What happens when iron combines with oxygen?"

Key Idea: Lanthanides and actinides are part of the transition metal group, or semi-metals.

Learning Through History

Focus: The Stock Market Crash, the Great Depression, and the New Deal

Unit 16 - Day 2

Reading about History | I

Read about history in the following resource:

★ *All American History: Vol. II* middle of p. 306-312

After today's reading, open your *Student Notebook* to Unit 16. In Box 7, you will see the front page of *The World* Editorial Section from Sunday, Nov. 8, 1929. Notice the reference to "Castles in the Air". The other headlines read, "Behind the Exciting Show Window of Frenzied Wall Street Is an Endless Pageant of Obscure Tragedies". Another headline reads, "Plans Go Glimmering in Thousands of Homes as Margins Melt and Savings of Lifetime are Swept Away". Choose a section of text from "Impact" on p. 310-312 of *All American History* to copy in Box 8 that reflects the headlines shown in Box 7.

Key Idea: The economic collapse of the Great Depression was made worse by the dust storms and floods that occurred during this same time.

History Project | S

At the Internet site below, read about the Dust Bowl. Listen as survivors share memories from those years.
http://www.livinghistoryfarm.org/farminginthe30s/water_02.html

If the link above doesn't work, go to www.livinghistoryfarm.org. Click on "Farming in the 1930s". Scroll down and click on "Water" at the bottom of the page. Next, click on "Dust Bowl" on the left side of the page.

Key Idea: Dust storms covered the Great Plains from Canada to Texas.

President Study | I

★ On *The Presidents* DVD Volume 2, select the Chapter "Andrew Johnson to Arthur" and watch **only** Program 4: James A. Garfield. Then, open your *President Notebook* to James A. Garfield and add further information.

Key Idea: Research James A. Garfield.

Storytime | T/I

Read the following assigned pages:

★ *Gladys Alyward* p. 81-93
Note: p. 85-86 contains an execution.
Get the bookmark that you placed in your book. Locate the same section of the bookmark that you used on Day 1. Beneath Day 1's entry, write the book title and the page numbers you read today. Select one of the **two** remaining response options at the bottom of the bookmark, and place a checkmark next to it. In the blank space under today's pages, respond in writing using your checked option.

Key Idea: Relate to the text in various ways.

Geography | I

For today's activities, use the map listed below.

★ *Map Trek CD: Missions to Modern Marvels* p. 54-55
Print the "The Great Depression" Student Map found on p. 55 of the *Map Trek* CD. On your Student Map, color all of the states numbered '1' yellow. Color all of the states numbered '2' brown. Color all of the states numbered '3' orange. Color all of the states numbered '4' red. Then, color the map key to match your map. Which states had the highest unemployment during 1934? Look on the map on p. 40 of the *United States History Atlas* to see which states were part of the Dust Bowl. Compare the map on p. 40 to your Student Map. File the map in your *Student Notebook*.

Key Idea: The Dust Bowl occurred during the Depression. It affected farm families.

Independent History Study | I

Open your *Student Notebook* to Unit 16 – Box 12. Follow the directions from *Draw and Write Through History* p. 34-36 to draw and color the Golden Gate Bridge.

Key Idea: The Golden Gate Bridge was built during the Great Depression, with construction beginning in 1933 and finishing in 1937.

Learning the Basics

Focus: Language Arts, Math, Bible, Nature Journal, and Science

Biblical Self-Image [T]

Our plans intend for the listed pages in *Who Am I? And What Am I Doing Here?* to be read either silently by both you and your child, or read aloud to the child by you. Read and discuss the following pages listed below.

 Who Am I? And What Am I Doing Here? middle of p. 126 – middle of p. 128

Orally read and discuss "Make a Note of It" on p. 128, rather than having students write their responses.

Key Idea: Jesus is our example for how to obey our heavenly Father rather than our emotions.

Language Arts [S]

Have students complete one studied dictation exercise (see Appendix for directions and passages).

Help students complete one lesson from the following reading program:

★ *Drawn into the Heart of Reading*

Help students complete **one** English option.

★ *Progressing With Courage:* Lesson 60

★ *Progressing With Courage:* Lesson 96 (last half only)

★ Your own grammar program

Key Idea: Practice language arts skills.

Bible Quiet Time [I]

Bible Study: Read and complete the assigned pages in the following resource:

★ *Faith at Work: Lesson 13 – Day Two* p. 94-95

Prayer Focus: Refer to **confession** on "Preparing Your Heart for Prayer". Then, pray a prayer of confession to admit or acknowledge your sins to God. After your prayer, write 'confession' at the bottom of today's lesson in *Faith at Work* above *Day Three*. Next to 'confession', either list key phrases or write a sentence to summarize your prayer. This will be your prayer log. Keep "Preparing Your Heart for Prayer" inside your Bible.

Scripture Memory: Memorize Romans 12:19 from your Bible and recite it.

Music: Refer to p. 50-51 as you sing with Track 6 *"Onward, Christian Soldiers"* (vs. 1-2).

Key Idea: Read and study Romans 9.

Math Exploration [S]

Choose **one** of the math options listed below (see Appendix for details).

★ *Singapore Primary Mathematics 6A/6B, Discovering Mathematics 7A/7B, 8A/8B, No-Nonsense Algebra* or *Videotext Algebra*

★ Your own math program

Key Idea: Use a step-by-step math program.

Science Exploration [I]

★ Read p. 69-70 in *The Elements: Ingredients of the Universe*. Then, read and follow the directions in Activity #2 and Activity #3 on p. 68. You will need a parent's permission to access the websites mentioned in the activities. Then, read Activity #4.

Next, photocopy the cards on p. 116-121 and cut them out. Add them to the cards that you photocopied and cut out from p. 85-90 on Unit 10 – Day 2. You will need both sets of cards for Unit 16 – Day 3.

Key Idea: Lanthanides are rare earth metals, and actinides are radioactive elements.

Learning Through History

Focus: The Stock Market Crash, the Great Depression, and the New Deal

Unit 16 - Day 3

Reading about History — I

Read about history in the following resource:

⭐ *All American History: Vol. II* p. 315 – middle of p. 319

After today's reading, open your *Student Notebook* to Unit 16. Look at the ad in Box 5 for Spam, which was a new canned meat that appeared during the 1930s when fresh meat was a luxury. Why would canned meat be a needed product during the Depression? What references to the military do you notice in this ad? In Box 11, copy **paragraph 2** from p. 37 of *Draw and Write Through History*.

Key Idea: During the years of the Depression, families had a hard time feeding and clothing their children. Jobs were scarce, and schools were often closed. Poverty affected health too.

History Project — S

In 1930, Ruth Wakefield invented chocolate chip cookies at the Toll House Inn. Today, you'll make the original Toll House® recipe. Combine 2¼ cups flour, 1 tsp. baking soda, and 1 tsp. salt in a small bowl. In a large mixing bowl, beat 1 cup (2 sticks) softened butter, ¾ cup white sugar, ¾ cup packed brown sugar, and 1 tsp. vanilla until creamy. Add 1 egg and beat well. Then, add a second egg and beat well. Gradually beat in the flour mixture. Stir in 2 cups semi-sweet chocolate chips. If desired, add 1 cup chopped nuts. Drop dough by rounded tablespoons onto an ungreased baking sheet. Bake 9-11 minutes at 375 degrees until golden brown. Cool cookies on the baking sheet for 2 minutes and remove to wire racks to cool further.

Key Idea: Wakefield sold her recipe to Nestle.

State Study — T

⭐ This is an **optional** part of the plans. If you have chosen to study your state using *State History from a Christian Perspective*, do Lesson 13 from the *Master Lesson Plan Book*.

Key Idea: Study your individual state.

Storytime — T/I

Read the following assigned pages:

⭐ *Gladys Alyward* p. 95-105

After today's reading, orally narrate or retell the portion of the story that was read today. See *Narration Tips* in the Appendix as needed.

Key Idea: Practice orally narrating, or retelling, a portion of a story.

Worthy Words — T

Read, analyze, and evaluate the speech below.

⭐ *Book of Great American Speeches for Young People* p. 155-157

After reading the speech, answer the following questions on an index card: *Franklin D. Roosevelt is known for the line "... the only thing we have to fear is fear itself...". Based on the third paragraph of his speech on p. 155, what does that mean? In his speech, what material problems does Roosevelt mention? What solutions does Roosevelt propose? Do you see any potential benefits or problems in Roosevelt's solution? Refer to p. 309-310 of All American History. Discuss the issue of states' rights versus the rights of the federal government. What issues remain today as remnants of the New Deal?* Next, meet with a parent to have a Socratic dialogue about the speech. Before beginning the dialogue, the parent reads the speech out loud. Next, discuss the questions using your notes. All participants should use experiences or text to support their responses.

Key Idea: FDR was elected President 4 times.

Independent History Study — I

Choose an important part of the speech from p. 155-157 of *Book of Great American Speeches* to copy in quotation marks in your *Student Notebook* Unit 16 – Box 6. Write "Franklin D. Roosevelt" at the bottom of Box 6.

Key Idea: Roosevelt's radio broadcasted "Fireside Chats" were inspirational.

Learning the Basics
Focus: Language Arts, Math, Bible, Nature Journal, Poetry, and Science

Nature Journal & Poetry [S]

The poetry of Longfellow, Wordsworth, and Whitman is scheduled on Day 3 to complement the nature journaling sessions. Read aloud and discuss today's poem *"Simon Lee: The Old Huntsman"* (see Appendix) with a parent. Then, follow the directions below.

⭐ *Nature Drawing & Journaling: Lesson XXI* p. 59-60

Note: After completing your sketch, choose a quote about trees from the tops of p. 57-63 to copy in your Nature Journal.

Key Idea: Practice sketching a tree stump.

Language Arts [S]

Have students complete one studied dictation exercise (see Appendix for passages).

Help students complete **one** English option.

⭐ *Progressing With Courage:* Lesson 61

⭐ *Progressing With Courage:* Lesson 97 (first half only)

⭐ Your own grammar program

Work with the students to complete **one** of the writing options listed below:

⭐ *Write with the Best: Vol. 2* Unit 5 – Day 2 p. 46

⭐ Your own writing program

Key Idea: Practice language arts skills.

Bible Quiet Time [I]

Bible Study: Read and complete the assigned pages in the following resource:

⭐ *Faith at Work: Lesson 13 – Day Three* and *Day Four* p. 95-96

Prayer Focus: Refer to **thanksgiving** on "Preparing Your Heart for Prayer". Then, pray a prayer of thanksgiving to express gratitude to God for His divine goodness. After your prayer, write 'thanksgiving' at the bottom of today's lesson in *Faith at Work* above *Day Five*. Next to 'thanksgiving', either list key phrases or write a sentence to summarize your prayer. Keep "Preparing Your Heart for Prayer" inside your Bible.

Scripture Memory: Copy Romans 12:19 in your Common Place Book.

Music: Refer to p. 50-51 as you sing with Track 6 *"Onward, Christian Soldiers"* (vs. 1-2).

Key Idea: Read and study Romans 9.

Math Exploration [S]

Choose **one** of the math options listed below (see Appendix for details).

⭐ *Singapore Primary Mathematics 6A/6B, Discovering Mathematics 7A/7B, 8A/8B, No-Nonsense Algebra* or *Videotext Algebra*

⭐ Your own math program

Key Idea: Use a step-by-step math program.

Science Exploration [I]

⭐ Get the deck of cards that you photocopied and cut out on Unit 16 – Day 2. This deck of cards should include the cards from p. 85-90 and p. 116-121. Read and follow the directions for Group Game #1 "One of my elements is missing!" on p. 149 of *The Elements: Ingredients of the Universe*. First, lay the cards out in the formation of the Periodic Table. To do this, refer to the Periodic Table that you printed on Unit 10 – Day 3. As you play the game described in Group Game #1 on p. 149, you may refer to your copy of the Periodic Table to help you locate and say the name of the missing element.

Key Idea: The Periodic Table grew and changed through the years as new elements were discovered.

Reading about History | I |

Read about history in the following resources:

 All American History: Vol. II p. 319-327

Book of Great American Speeches for Young People p. 158-159

You will be writing a narration about the pages that you read today. To prepare for writing your narration, look back over p. 319-327 in *All American History: Vol. II*. Think about the main idea and the most important moments in this part of the reading. Plan to write 2-3 sentences for each bolded section in the reading.

After you have thought about what you will write and how you will begin your narration, turn to Unit 16 in your *Student Notebook*. For more guidance on writing a narration, see *Written Narration Tips* in the Appendix.

In Box 4, write a 12-16 sentence narration about the reading. When you have finished writing, read your sentences out loud to catch any mistakes. Check for the following things: *Did you include **who** or **what topic** the reading was mainly about? Did you include **descriptors** of the important thing(s) that happened? Did you include a **closing sentence**?* If not, add those things. Use the *Written Narration Skills* in the Appendix as a guide for editing the narration.

Key Idea: During the Depression years, movies and radio were the main forms of entertainment. Professional sports and Broadway musicals were also popular. Swing and big band music were new on the music scene, and Penguin Books launched the first paperback books. During this time, art deco style architecture was dominant. The Empire State Building is a reflection of this style.

President Study | I |

Read p. 40-41 in *Our Presidents...* Then, open your *President Notebook* to Chester A. Arthur. Use today's reading to help you complete the information about Arthur.

Key Idea: Research Chester A. Arthur.

Storytime | T/I |

Read the following assigned pages:

 Gladys Alyward p. 107-118

Get the bookmark that you placed in your book. Locate the same section of the bookmark that you used on Day 2. Beneath Day 2's entry, write the book title and the page numbers you read today. Select the one remaining response option at the bottom of the bookmark, and place a checkmark next to it. In the blank space under today's pages, respond in writing using your checked option. Keep the bookmark in your book.

Key Idea: Relate to the text in various ways.

Economics | I |

Read about economics in the resource below.

Whatever Happened to Penny Candy? p. 109 and p. 125
After the reading, refer to the bottom of p. 107, and then glance through p. 110-121. According to p. 107, which nations have a low rating? Which nations have a high rating? Open your *Student Notebook* to the "Economic Principles" section at the front of your notebook. Under "Economic Principle", write a one line or one sentence summary for the economic principle you learned from today's reading.

Key Idea: The stability of a country's legal system affects the country's economics.

Independent History Study | I |

Open your *Student Notebook* to Unit 16 – Box 10. Follow the directions from *Draw and Write Through History* p. 44-45 to draw and color Mount Rushmore.

Key Idea: Mount Rushmore was completed in 1941. The project took Borglum and his team 14 years to complete and was funded by the federal government during the Great Depression. Many tourists visit the site of this national monument each year.

Biblical Self-Image | T |

Read and discuss with the students the following pages in the resource below.

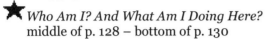 *Who Am I? And What Am I Doing Here?* middle of p. 128 – bottom of p. 130

Orally read and discuss "Make a Note of It" on p. 130 imagining a fight with a friend or a sibling. Rather than having students write their responses, instead be the scribe for your students and write for them. You do not have to organize your notes like a menu.

<u>Key Idea</u>: We should not be controlled by our emotions. Instead, we should choose how to express our emotions in a healthy way.

Language Arts | S |

Have students complete one studied dictation exercise (see Appendix for directions and passages).

Help students complete one lesson from the following reading program:

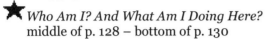 *Drawn into the Heart of Reading*

Help students complete **one** English option.

★ *Progressing With Courage:* Lesson 62

★ *Progressing With Courage:* Lesson 97 (last half only)

★ Your own grammar program

<u>Key Idea</u>: Practice language arts skills.

Bible Quiet Time | I |

Bible Study: Complete the assignment below.

★ *Faith at Work: Lesson 13 – Day Five* and *Notes* p. 96-101

Prayer Focus: Refer to **supplication** on "Preparing Your Heart for Prayer". Then, pray a prayer of supplication to make a humble and earnest request of God. Write 'supplication' at the bottom of today's lesson on p. 96 in *Faith at Work.* Next to it, either list several key phrases or write a sentence to summarize your prayer. Keep "Preparing Your Heart for Prayer" inside your Bible.

Scripture Memory: Recite Romans 12:1-19.

Music: Refer to p. 50-51 as you sing with Track 6 *"Onward, Christian Soldiers"* (vs. 1-2).

<u>Key Idea</u>: Read and study Romans 9.

Math Exploration | S |

Choose **one** of the math options listed below.

★ *Singapore Primary Mathematics 6A/6B, Discovering Mathematics 7A/7B, 8A/8B, No-Nonsense Algebra* or *Videotext Algebra*

★ Your own math program

<u>Key Idea</u>: Use a step-by-step math program.

Science Exploration | I |

★ Photocopy "Test Your Knowledge" p. 151-152 from *The Elements: Ingredients of the Universe.* These pages will be used as a review activity. **Do not look at the "Answer Key" on p. 153, as this would be cheating.** You should refer to your copy of the Periodic Table and look back at Chapters 1-8 on p. 1-67 as needed to help you complete the review. When you have finished "Test Your Knowledge", you may eat **one** of the radioactive snacks described in #4 on p. 149.

<u>Key Idea</u>: Our bodies deal with the tiny amount of naturally-occurring radiation that we eat and drink each day.

Learning Through History
Focus: Hitler, Mussolini, Hirohito, and Churchill

Reading about History | I

Read about history in the following resource:

⭐ *The Story of the World: Vol. 4* p. 286-290
After today's reading, orally narrate to an adult. Some words to include in your narration might be *Depression, reparations, Adolf Hitler, Germany, anti-Semitism, National Socialists, fuhrer, Nazis,* and *German chancellor.*

Key Idea: The Great Depression affected countries in Europe and the rest of the world. As Germany struggled to pay its debts and reparations from WWI, the National Socialist political party gained momentum in Germany. Adolf Hitler became the fuhrer, or leader, of the National Socialist party.

Storytime | T/I

Read the following assigned pages:

⭐ *Gladys Alyward* p. 119-128
Note: p. 123 includes a violent scene.

Get the bookmark that you placed in your book last unit. Choose a new section of the bookmark with **three** options at the bottom. At the top of this section of the bookmark, write the book title and the page numbers you read today. Select **one** of the three options at the bottom and place a checkmark next to it. In the blank space under today's pages, respond in writing using your checked option. Keep the bookmark in your book.

Key Idea: Relate to the text in various ways.

History Project | S

Read the following list of persecutions of Jews in Germany during the first years of Nazi rule.
March 9, 1933: First anti-Jewish riots in Berlin
March 13, 1933: Jewish lawyers and judges expelled from the law courts in Breslau
April 1, 1933: Jewish shops boycotted in Berlin
May 10, 1933: Public burning of Jewish books
October 1933: Berlin hospitals declared "free" of Jewish doctors
1933: "Jews Not Wanted" signs posted throughout Germany on buildings and roads
1935: One hundred thousand German children swear "eternal enmity" to the Jews
September 15, 1935: Nuremberg Laws make Jews second-class citizens
November 9, 1938: Fire set to 191 synagogues
November 15, 1938: Schools closed to Jews

Key Idea: The Nazis were anti-Semitic. Hitler believed Aryans were the chosen race.

Timeline | I

You will be adding to the timeline in your *Student Notebook* today. In Unit 17 – Box 1, draw and color a red swastika. Label it, *Adolf Hitler - German Chancellor (1932 A.D.).*

In Box 2, draw a Spanish flag with a wide horizontal yellow stripe in the center and a narrow red stripe above and below the yellow stripe. Label it, *Francisco Franco – Spanish Head of State (1936-1975 A.D.).*

In Box 3, outline and color a 'V' symbol for victory. Label it, *Winston Churchill – British Prime Minister (1940-1945, 1951-1955 A.D.).*

Key Idea: As Hitler was rising to power in Germany, Francisco Franco was warring for power in Spain, and Winston Churchill was serving under Neville Chamberlain in Britain.

President Study | I

⭐ On *The Presidents* DVD Volume 2, select the Chapter "Andrew Johnson to Arthur" and watch **only** Program 5: Chester A. Arthur. Then, open your *President Notebook* to Chester A. Arthur and add further information.

Key Idea: Research Chester A. Arthur.

Independent History Study | I

Listen to *What in the World? Vol. 3* Disc 3, Track 9: "Hitler's Germany & Revivals".

Key Idea: With discontent, unemployment, and poverty raging in Germany, Adolf Hitler was elected chancellor of Germany in 1932. Hitler was a gifted orator and a strong leader.

Learning the Basics
Focus: Language Arts, Math, Bible, Nature Journal, and Science

Nature Journal [I]

Read and follow the directions in the resource below.

 Nature Drawing & Journaling: Lesson XXII p. 61-63

Key Idea: Practice sketching a barren tree.

Language Arts [S]

Help students complete one lesson from the following reading program:

 Drawn into the Heart of Reading

Help students complete **one** English option.

 Progressing With Courage: Lesson 63

 Progressing With Courage: Lesson 98 (first half only)

 Your own grammar program

Work with the students to complete **one** of the writing options listed below:

 Write with the Best: Vol. 2 Unit 5 – Day 3 p. 46 (Read only 1-5 and 7-9 on p. 96-98.)

★ Your own writing program

Key Idea: Practice language arts skills.

Bible Quiet Time [I]

Bible Study: Read and complete the assigned pages in the following resource:

★ *Faith at Work: Lesson 14 – Day One* p. 102 (Note: Refer to p. 97-101 to complete the lesson.)

Prayer Focus: Refer to **adoration** on "Preparing Your Heart for Prayer". Then, pray a prayer of adoration to worship and honor God. After your prayer, write 'adoration' at the bottom of today's lesson in *Faith at Work* above *Day Two*. Next to 'adoration', either list key phrases or write a sentence to summarize your prayer. Keep "Preparing Your Heart for Prayer" inside your Bible.

Scripture Memory: Read aloud Romans 12:20 three times from your Bible.

Music: Read p. 49 in *Hymns for a Kid's Heart*. Refer to p. 50-51 as you sing with Track 6 *"Onward, Christian Soldiers"* (vs. 1-3).

Key Idea: Read and study Romans 9.

Math Exploration [S]

Choose **one** of the math options listed below (see Appendix for details).

★ *Singapore Primary Mathematics 6A/6B, Discovering Mathematics 7A/7B, 8A/8B, No-Nonsense Algebra* or *Videotext Algebra*

★ Your own math program

Key Idea: Use a step-by-step math program.

Science Exploration [I]

★ Read *Atoms in the Family* p. 3-21. Note: p. 9 mentions "pantheistic worship". After reading the chapters, on paper make a list of characteristics that you have learned about Enrico Fermi from today's reading. Save the list to add to in future units. Then, explain the meaning of the quote on p. 17, "There had been no need for others because the two completed each other to form a molecule. They had no free valency to hook onto others."

Key Idea: Enrico Fermi's family came from the countryside around Piacenza, Italy, in the Po River valley.

Learning Through History
Focus: Hitler, Mussolini, Hirohito, and Churchill

Reading about History [I]

Read about history in the following resource:

★ *The Story of the World: Vol. 4* p. 292-297

After today's reading, open your *Student Notebook* to Unit 17. In Box 5, view the bulletin written by Franco dated April 1, 1939. Translated, it reads, "Today, the Red Army has been captured and disarmed. The national troops have achieved their final military objective. The war is over." Spain was now in Nationalist hands.

Key Idea: Even though Spain remained neutral during WWI, it was troubled when the war ended. After Alfonso XIII was crowned king of Spain, revolutionaries known as "Red Spain", tried to get rid of him. Those who wanted Spain to remain a monarchy were known as "Black Spain". In 1931, Alfonso left Spain. In 1936, war erupted in Spain among its varying political groups. The Spanish Army rebelled against the government, and Francisco Franco emerged as head of the "Nationalist" party.

History Project [S]

Open your *Student Notebook* to Unit 17. Look at the caricature in Box 10 of Hitler, Franco, and Mussolini with a sickly child symbolizing the first anniversary of the Spanish military's rebellion against Alfonso XIII and the government of the Second Spanish Republic. Why would Spain be like a sickly child, and why would Hitler and Mussolini be wondering what to do about it along with Francisco Franco? Color the caricature using colored pencils.

Key Idea: Spain had civil war for three years.

President Study [I]

★ Read p. 42-43 in *Our Presidents...* Then, open your *President Notebook* to Grover Cleveland. Use today's reading to help you complete the information about Cleveland.

Key Idea: Research Grover Cleveland.

Storytime [T/I]

Read the following assigned pages:

★ *Gladys Alyward* p. 129-140
Note: p. 139 includes a scene after a bombing.

Get the bookmark that you placed in your book. Locate the same section of the bookmark that you used on Day 1. Beneath Day 1's entry, write the book title and the page numbers you read today. Select one of the **two** remaining response options at the bottom of the bookmark, and place a checkmark next to it. In the blank space under today's pages, respond in writing using your checked option.

Key Idea: Relate to the text in various ways.

Geography [I]

For today's activities, use the map listed below.

★ *Map Trek CD: Missions to Modern Marvels* p. 50-51
Print the "Iberian Peninsula" Student Map found on p. 51 of the *Map Trek* CD. Refer to the *Map Trek* Teacher's Answer Map on p. 50 to guide you as you label the countries, peninsulas, islands, cities, mountain ranges, rivers, and bodies of water on your Student Map. Find the cities of Barcelona and Madrid, where the final fighting took place between the fascist Nationalist party and the Communist Popular party. Place a star on these two cities. File the map in your *Student Notebook*.

Key Idea: In 1939, the Nationalist Party was victorious over the Popular Party in Spain.

Independent History Study [I]

Refer to the "Totalitarianism" Student Map p. 57 that you filed in your *Student Notebook* in Unit 15. Find Spain on the map. Notice that in today's reading in *The Story of the World* that Spain had become a dictatorship under the rule of Franco and the Nationalist Party.

Key Idea: Franco ruled Spain for almost 40 years as an authoritarian head of state.

Learning the Basics
Focus: Language Arts, Math, Bible, Nature Journal, and Science

Biblical Self-Image [T]

Our plans intend for the listed pages in *Who Am I? And What Am I Doing Here?* to be read either silently by both you and your child, or read aloud to the child by you. Read and discuss the following pages listed below.

 Who Am I? And What Am I Doing Here? bottom of p. 130 – bottom of p. 132

Then, pray the prayer together at the bottom of p. 132.

Key Idea: God is our refuge and strength. He hears our prayers and will help us control our fears, our sadness, and our grief.

Language Arts [S]

Have students complete one studied dictation exercise (see Appendix for directions and passages).

Help students complete one lesson from the following reading program:

★ *Drawn into the Heart of Reading*

Help students complete **one** English option.

★ *Progressing With Courage:* Lesson 64

★ *Progressing With Courage:* Lesson 98 (last half only)

★ Your own grammar program

Key Idea: Practice language arts skills.

Bible Quiet Time [I]

Bible Study: Read and complete the assigned pages in the following resource:

★ *Faith at Work: Lesson 14 – Day Two* p. 102-103

Prayer Focus: Refer to **confession** on "Preparing Your Heart for Prayer". Then, pray a prayer of confession to admit or acknowledge your sins to God. After your prayer, write 'confession' at the bottom of today's lesson in *Faith at Work* above *Day Three*. Next to 'confession', either list key phrases or write a sentence to summarize your prayer. This will be your prayer log. Keep "Preparing Your Heart for Prayer" inside your Bible.

Scripture Memory: Memorize Romans 12:20 from your Bible and recite it.

Music: Refer to p. 50-51 as you sing with Track 6 *"Onward, Christian Soldiers"* (vs. 1-3).

Key Idea: Read and study Romans 10.

Math Exploration [S]

Choose **one** of the math options listed below (see Appendix for details).

★ *Singapore Primary Mathematics 6A/6B, Discovering Mathematics 7A/7B, 8A/8B, No-Nonsense Algebra* or *Videotext Algebra*

★ Your own math program

Key Idea: Use a step-by-step math program.

Science Exploration [I]

★ Read *Atoms in the Family* p. 22-32. Then, give a descriptive oral narration to an adult about p. 22-32. A detailed, descriptive narration is the goal. See *Narration Tips* in the Appendix for help as needed.

Key Idea: Enrico Fermi left Rome for Pisa in 1918 when he was only 17 years old. World War I was just ending, and Italy's enemies Germany and Austria had been defeated. Fermi went to Pisa to attend the university as a physics student. After Fermi completed his education at Pisa, he returned to Rome to discover that Mussolini's Fascist Party had begun to seize control in Italy.

Learning Through History
Focus: Hitler, Mussolini, Hirohito, and Churchill

Unit 17 - Day 3

Reading about History ☑

Read about history in the following resources:

 All American History: Vol. II p. 329-332

★ *The Story of the World: Vol. 4* p. 298-302

After today's reading, open your *Student Notebook* to Unit 17. The image in Box 7 shows 3 young ladies (one Italian, one Japanese, and one German) holding Japanese *hagoita's,* or paddles, bearing the images of Hitler, Mussolini, and Prince Konoe. Hitler was the German chancellor, Mussolini was the Italian prime minister, and Prince Konoe was Japan's prime minister under Emperor Hirohito. Use p. 330-331 of *All American History* to list in Box 8 of your *Student Notebook* what Hitler, Mussolini, and Hirohito had in common.

Key Idea: Germany, Italy, and Japan were each ruled by dictatorships prior to WWII.

History Project ☑

Open your *Student Notebook* to Unit 17 – Box 9. Follow the directions on p. 42-43 (steps 1-4) of *Draw and Write Through History* to draw Winston Churchill in Box 9. You will color your drawing on Day 4. Then, in Box 6 of your *Student Notebook*, copy the **first paragraph** of p. 46 of *Draw and Write Through History*.

Key Idea: Winston Churchill became prime minister of Great Britain after Neville Chamberlain resigned in 1940. Churchill would not give in to Hitler or consider an armistice with Germany. In 1940, Great Britain alone fought against the Axis powers in Europe. Churchill's goal was victory.

State Study ☐ T

 ★ This is an **optional** part of the plans. If you have chosen to study your state using *State History from a Christian Perspective,* do Lesson 14 from the *Master Lesson Plan Book*.

Key Idea: Study your individual state.

Storytime ☑

Read the following assigned pages:

★ *Gladys Alyward* p. 141-153

After today's reading, orally narrate or retell the portion of the story that was read today. See *Narration Tips* in the Appendix as needed.

Key Idea: Practice orally narrating, or retelling, a portion of a story.

Economics ☑

Read about economics in the resource below.

★ *Whatever Happened to Penny Candy?* p. 123 and p. 129

After the reading, open your *Student Notebook* to the "Economic Principles" section at the front of your notebook. Under "Economic Principle", write a one or two sentence summary for the economic principle you learned from today's reading.

Key Idea: Taxes are the way that governments get money, and taxes are often used to pay the government's debt.

Independent History Study ☑

Listen to *What in the World? Vol. 3* Disc 4, Tracks 1-2: "Jewish Palestine & German Conquest" and "Miracle at Dunkirk".

Key Idea: The Jews of western Europe had tried to assimilate into the cultures of the countries where they had settled with limited success. The idea of Zionism, or a homeland for the Jews, in Palestine grew. Hitler's Anti-Semitism drove many Jews to Palestine. As Hitler waged war across Europe, he temporarily halted his German tanks. This allowed a miraculous evacuation of British and French soldiers to occur at Dunkirk.

Learning the Basics
Focus: Language Arts, Math, Bible, Nature Journal, Poetry, and Science

Nature Journal & Poetry

The poetry of Longfellow, Wordsworth, and Whitman is scheduled on Day 3 to complement the nature journaling sessions. Read aloud and discuss today's poem *"Changed"* (see Appendix) with a parent. Then, follow the directions in the resource below.

★ *Nature Drawing & Journaling: Lesson XXIII* p. 64-66

Note: Do only the first sketch described in paragraphs one and two on p. 65 today. The assignment in the third paragraph is **optional.**

Key Idea: Practice sketching a woodland.

Language Arts [S]

Have students complete one studied dictation exercise (see Appendix for passages).

Help students complete **one** English option.

★ *Progressing With Courage:* Lesson 65

★ *Progressing With Courage:* Lesson 99 (Class Practice 'A' – 'E' only)

★ Your own grammar program

Work with the students to complete **one** of the writing options listed below:

★ *Write with the Best: Vol. 2* Unit 5 – Day 4 p. 46 – top of 47 (Note: Types of attention grabbers are listed in #6 on p. 93.)

★ Your own writing program

Key Idea: Practice language arts skills.

Bible Quiet Time [I]

Bible Study: Read and complete the assigned pages in the following resource:

★ *Faith at Work: Lesson 14 – Day Three* p. 103

Prayer Focus: Refer to **thanksgiving** on "Preparing Your Heart for Prayer". Then, pray a prayer of thanksgiving to express gratitude to God for His divine goodness. After your prayer, write 'thanksgiving' at the bottom of today's lesson on p. 103 in *Faith at Work*. Next to 'thanksgiving', either list key phrases or write a sentence to summarize your prayer. Keep "Preparing Your Heart for Prayer" inside your Bible.

Scripture Memory: Copy Romans 12:20 in your Common Place Book.

Music: Refer to p. 50-51 as you sing with Track 6 *"Onward, Christian Soldiers"* (vs. 1-3).

Key Idea: Read and study Romans 10.

Math Exploration [S]

Choose **one** of the math options listed below (see Appendix for details).

★ *Singapore Primary Mathematics 6A/6B, Discovering Mathematics 7A/7B, 8A/8B, No-Nonsense Algebra* or *Videotext Algebra*

★ Your own math program

Key Idea: Use a step-by-step math program.

Science Exploration [I]

★ Read *Atoms in the Family* p. 33-48. Then, write a written narration about p. 33-48. Refer to *Written Narration Tips* in the Appendix for help as needed. Read your written narration out loud after you have finished writing. Refer to *Written Narration Skills* for help in editing.

Key Idea: By 1926, Fermi was a full professor of physics at the University of Rome. He was interested in the way that molecules, atoms, and electrons behave. He was also interested in statistical questions and in the distribution of energy in radiation emission. It was a time of new theories in atomic physics.

Learning Through History
Focus: Hitler, Mussolini, Hirohito, and Churchill

Unit 17 - Day 4

 Reading about History ✓

Read about history in the following resource:

 All American History: Vol. II p. 333 – middle of p. 336

You will be writing a narration about the pages that you read today. To prepare for writing your narration, look back over p. 333-336 in *All American History: Vol. II*. Think about the main idea and the most important moments in this part of the reading. Plan to write 2-3 sentences for each bolded section in the reading.

After you have thought about what you will write and how you will begin your narration, turn to Unit 17 in your *Student Notebook*. For more guidance on writing a narration, see *Written Narration Tips* in the Appendix.

In Box 4, write a 12-16 sentence narration about the reading. When you have finished writing, read your sentences out loud to catch any mistakes. Check for the following things: *Did you include* **who** *or* **what topic** *the reading was mainly about? Did you include* **descriptors** *of the important thing(s) that happened? Did you include a* **closing sentence**? *If not, add those things.* Use the *Written Narration Skills* in the Appendix as a guide for editing the narration.

Key Idea: Hitler conquered the Rhineland, Austria, and Sudetenland in quick succession between 1936 and 1938. Stalin and Hitler signed a nonaggression pact in 1939, and then Hitler invaded Poland. Italy entered the war in 1940 on the side of the Axis powers. France surrendered that same year, leaving Britain to fight the Axis powers in Europe alone. Hitler invaded the Soviet Union in 1941, forcing Stalin to side with the Allies instead.

 President Study I

 On *The Presidents* DVD Volume 2, select the Chapter "Cleveland to Taft" and watch **only** Programs 1 **and** 3: Grover Cleveland. Then, open your *President Notebook* to Grover Cleveland. Use today's viewing to add further information about Cleveland.

Key Idea: Research Grover Cleveland.

 Storytime ✓/I

Read the following assigned pages:

 Gladys Alyward p. 155-165
Note: p.156-158 and p. 160-161 include disturbing scenes.
Get the bookmark that you placed in your book. Locate the same section of the bookmark that you used on Day 2. Select the one remaining response option at the bottom of the bookmark, and respond beneath Day 2's entry.

Key Idea: Relate to the text in various ways.

 Worthy Words T

Read, analyze, and evaluate the speech below.

 Book of Great American Speeches for Young People p. 160-161
After reading the speech, answer the following questions on an index card: *How does Ickes define an American? He refers to the second sentence of the Declaration of Independence, which reads, "We hold these truths to be self-evident, that all men are created equal, that they are endowed by their Creator with certain unalienable rights, that among these are Life, Liberty, and the pursuit of Happiness." What does this have to do with aiding Britain? What things does Ickes say that dictators practice? What might have happened if the U.S. hadn't entered the war on the side of the Allies?* Next, meet with a parent to have a Socratic dialogue about the speech.

Key Idea: Before Pearl Harbor, Americans were divided over whether to enter the war.

Independent History Study I

Open your *Student Notebook* to Unit 17 – Box 9. Follow the directions from *Draw and Write Through History* p. 43 to color the sketch of Winton Churchill. Then, listen to *What in the World? Vol. 3* Disc 4, Track 3: "Battle of Britain".

Key Idea: Hitler did not succeed in destroying the Royal Air Force in the Battle of Britain.

Learning the Basics
Focus: Language Arts, Math, Bible, Nature Journal, and Science

Biblical Self-Image ☑

Read and discuss with the students the following pages in the resource below.

 Who Am I? And What Am I Doing Here? p. 133-139

Key Idea: Mormons study the *Book of Mormon,* which is the most important book in the Mormon Church. They also have three other sacred books, one of which is the Bible.

Language Arts ⬚ S

Have students complete one studied dictation exercise (see Appendix for directions and passages).

Help students complete one lesson from the following reading program:

 *Drawn into the Heart of Reading*

Help students complete **one** English option.

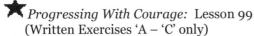*Progressing With Courage:* Lesson 66

Progressing With Courage: Lesson 99 (Written Exercises 'A – 'C' only)

Your own grammar program

Key Idea: Practice language arts skills.

Bible Quiet Time ☑

Bible Study: Complete the assignment below.

Faith at Work: Lesson 14 – Day Four p. 104

Prayer Focus: Refer to **supplication** on "Preparing Your Heart for Prayer". Then, pray a prayer of supplication to make a humble and earnest request of God. Write 'supplication' at the bottom of today's lesson in *Faith at Work* above *Day Five.* Next to it, either list several key phrases or write a sentence to summarize your prayer. Keep "Preparing Your Heart for Prayer" inside your Bible.

Scripture Memory: Recite Romans 12:1-20.

Music: Refer to p. 50-51 as you sing with Track 6 *"Onward, Christian Soldiers"* (vs. 1-3).

Key Idea: Read and study Romans 10.

Math Exploration ⬚ S

Choose **one** of the math options listed below.

Singapore Primary Mathematics 6A/6B, Discovering Mathematics 7A/7B, 8A/8B, No-Nonsense Algebra or *Videotext Algebra*

Your own math program

Key Idea: Use a step-by-step math program.

Science Exploration ⬚ I

 Copy the Science Lab Form from the Appendix of this guide. Next, follow the directions to perform "Experiment 13" from p. 28 of the *Chemistry C500 Experiment Manual.* **Save the soap solution for future experiments.** After completing Experiment 13, in the top box of the Science Lab Form write: *What effect will mineral water have on the foam in the soap solution?* In the second box of the form, write your hypothesis. Then, **let the mineral water sit open for a while** to allow the carbon dioxide to escape and the minerals to be left behind. Follow the directions for "Experiment 14" on p. 29 of the Experiment Manual and complete the box "Perform an Experiment" on your lab form. Then, follow the arrows to complete the rest of the Science Lab Form. To clean up, refer to Basic Rules 5, 6, and 7 on p. 6.

Key Idea: Mineral water is hard water. It causes the soap foam to collapse and leaves a soap scum.

Learning Through History
Focus: Pearl Harbor, the Flying Scotsman, and Watchman Nee

Reading about History

Read about history in the following resources:

★ *The Story of the World: Vol. 4* p. 304 – middle of p. 309

★ *Great Events in American History* p. 87-89

After today's reading, orally narrate or retell to an adult the text from *The Story of the World* that you read today. As you retell, the adult will write or type your narration. Some possible key words to include in your narration might be *World War II, Allies, Axis, Kuomintang, Japanese army, Beijing, Second Sino-Japanese War, Nanjing, General Hideki Tojo, Hirohito, attack U.S., Pearl Harbor, battleship "Arizona", Hong Kong, Philippine Islands, Malaya, Battle of Midway,* and *War in the Pacific.* When the narration is complete, tri-fold the typed or written narration to fit in Unit 18 – Box 11 of the *Student Notebook*. Glue the folded narration in Box 11, so it can be opened and read.

<u>Key Idea</u>: The Second Sino-Japanese War took place between the Kuomintang and the Japanese Army. As WWII continued, the war in the Pacific mingled with the war in China.

History Project

Print "The Bombing of Pearl Harbor" Student Map from p. 65 of the *Map Trek* CD. To help you label your Student Map, refer to or print the *Map Trek* Teacher's Answer Map p. 64. Then, refer to the map on p. 35 of the *United States History Atlas* to see where the Hawaiian Islands (and Pearl Harbor) are located in comparison to Japan and the U.S.

<u>Key Idea</u>: The U.S. joined the Allies in WWII after Japan bombed Pearl Harbor.

Storytime

Read the following assigned pages:

★ *Gladys Alyward* p. 167-179
Get the bookmark that you placed in your book last unit. Choose a new section of the bookmark with **three** options at the bottom. At the top of this section of the bookmark, write the book title and the page numbers you read today. Select **one** of the three options at the bottom and place a checkmark next to it. In the blank space under today's pages, respond in writing using your checked option.

<u>Key Idea</u>: Relate to the text in various ways.

Worthy Words

Read, analyze, and evaluate the speech below.

★ *Book of Great American Speeches for Young People* p. 162-164
After reading the speech, answer the following questions on an index card: *What does Roosevelt mean when he says, "...a date which will live in infamy..."? What is the irony of the situation described in paragraphs two and three of the speech? List the attacks made by Japanese forces mentioned in the speech. Why does Roosevelt list them? Why do you think Roosevelt refers to the will of Congress and the will of the people? What words are used in the last paragraphs that convey strong emotion? How does this speech impact you?* Next, meet with a parent to have a Socratic dialogue about the speech. Before beginning the dialogue, the parent reads the speech out loud. Next, discuss the questions using your notes. All participants should use life experiences and/or the text to support their responses.

<u>Key Idea</u>: On December 8, 1941, Roosevelt called for Congress to declare war on Japan.

Independent History Study

Listen to *What in the World? Vol. 3* Disc 4, Track 4: "Pearl Harbor, Midway, El Alamein". Find Pearl Harbor and Midway on p. 42 of the *United States History Atlas*. Find El Alamein and Stalingrad on p. 41.

<u>Key Idea</u>: The U.S. had cracked the Japanese code, so the U.S. knew when and where attacks were coming.

Learning the Basics

Focus: Language Arts, Math, Bible, Nature Journal, and Science

Nature Journal

Read and follow the directions in the resource below.

 Nature Drawing & Journaling: Lesson XXIV p. 67-69

Note: Do only the sketch described in the **first** paragraph on p. 69 today. Wait to follow the instructions in the remaining paragraphs until Unit 18 – Day 3.

<u>Key Idea</u>: Practice using a viewfinder.

Language Arts S

Help students complete one lesson from the following reading program:

 Drawn into the Heart of Reading

Help students complete **one** English option.

Progressing With Courage: Lesson 67

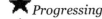*Progressing With Courage:* Lesson 99 (Written Exercises 'D' – 'F' only)

Your own grammar program

Work with the students to complete **one** of the writing options listed below:

★*Write with the Best: Vol. 2* Unit 5 – Day 5 p. 47

★Your own writing program

<u>Key Idea</u>: Practice language arts skills.

Bible Quiet Time

Bible Study: Read and complete the assigned pages in the following resource:

★*Faith at Work: Lesson 14 – Day Five* and *Notes* p. 104-108

Prayer Focus: Refer to **adoration** on "Preparing Your Heart for Prayer". Then, pray a prayer of adoration to worship and honor God. After your prayer, write 'adoration' at the bottom of today's lesson on p. 104 in *Faith at Work*. Next to 'adoration', either list key phrases or write a sentence to summarize your prayer. Keep "Preparing Your Heart for Prayer" inside your Bible.

Scripture Memory: Read aloud Romans 12:21 three times from your Bible.

Music: Read the verse and pray the prayer from p. 51 in *Hymns for a Kid's Heart*. Refer to p. 50-51 as you sing with Track 6 *"Onward, Christian Soldiers"* (vs. 1-5).

<u>Key Idea</u>: Read and study Romans 10.

Math Exploration S

Choose **one** of the math options listed below (see Appendix for details).

★*Singapore Primary Mathematics 6A/6B, Discovering Mathematics 7A/7B, 8A/8B, No-Nonsense Algebra* or *Videotext Algebra*

★Your own math program

<u>Key Idea</u>: Use a step-by-step math program.

Science Exploration I

★Read *Atoms in the Family* p. 49-68. Note: p. 52 mentions Fermi's agnostic attitude, and p. 58 uses a descriptive word meaning 'mule'. After today's reading, add to the list of characteristics about Enrico Fermi that you began in Unit 17 – Day 1. Save the list to add to in the next unit.

<u>Key Idea</u>: Enrico Fermi married Laura Capon on July 19, 1928, in Rome, Italy. They met while Laura was a student at the University of Rome. After marriage, Fermi continued as a professor of physics at the University of Rome.

Reading about History ☑

Read about history in the following resource:

 Hero Tales: Vol. II p. 81-91

Open your *Student Notebook* to Unit 18 – Box 7 that contains a picture of Eric Liddell's 1934 wedding to Florence Mackenzie in Tianjin. Liddell died in China in confinement in 1945 and was buried at the internment camp where he was confined. In Box 8, copy Isaiah 40:31, which is inscribed on Liddell's memorial headstone.

Key Idea: Eric Liddell was born in China to missionary parents. He attended school in London, England, and then in Edinburgh, Scotland. He was known as the "Flying Scotsman" for his skill as a sprinter.

History Project ☑

On December 26, 1941, after Japan's bombing of Pearl Harbor, Winston Churchill addressed a joint session of the U.S. Congress. At the time, Churchill was prime minister of Great Britain. Watch and listen to Churchill's famous speech at **one** of the following Internet sites: http://watchlaterapp.com/3uoG

http://www.timetape.com/ (Type "Winston Churchill" in Search and click on "Now We Are Masters of Our Fate" speech.)

Or, in a search engine, type "Winston Churchill Now We Are Masters of Our Fate".

Key Idea: At the time that Winston Churchill gave his famous speech in the U.S., Eric Liddell was serving in China as a missionary. Liddell served in China from 1925-1945 and died in a Japanese internment camp.

President Study ☐ I

 Read p. 44-45 in *Our Presidents*... Then, open your *President Notebook* to Benjamin Harrison. Use today's reading to help you complete the information about Harrison.

Key Idea: Research Benjamin Harrison.

Storytime ☐ T/I

Read the following assigned pages:

 Gladys Alyward p. 181-189

Get the bookmark that you placed in your book. Locate the same section of the bookmark that you used on Day 1. Beneath Day 1's entry, write the book title and the page numbers you read today. Select one of the **two** remaining response options at the bottom of the bookmark, and place a checkmark next to it. In the blank space under today's pages, respond in writing using your checked option.

Key Idea: Relate to the text in various ways.

Timeline ☑

You will be adding to the timeline in your *Student Notebook* today. In Unit 18 – Box 1, draw and color smoke, fire, and explosions in the water. Label it, *Japan Bombs Pearl Harbor (December 7, 1941 A.D.)*.

In Box 2, draw and color an Olympic gold medal. Label it, *Eric Liddell – Olympic Medalist & Chinese Missionary (1902-1945 A.D.)*.

In Box 3, draw the outline of a Chinese house. Label it, *Watchman Nee – Chinese House Church Movement (1903-1972 A.D.)*.

Key Idea: At the time of the Japanese bombing of Pearl Harbor, Eric Liddell was serving at a mission station in Shaochang, China. Invading Japanese forces soon took over the mission station. During this same time, Watchman Nee was working to found churches throughout China.

Independent History Study ☑ I

A fellow missionary said that upon his death Liddell's final words were *"It's complete surrender."* Eric Liddell had surrendered his life completely to God.

Key Idea: Eric Liddell died of a brain tumor in 1945, while in confinement at the Weihsien Internment Camp.

Learning the Basics
Focus: Language Arts, Math, Bible, Nature Journal, and Science

Biblical Self-Image

Our plans intend for the listed pages in *Who Am I? And What Am I Doing Here?* to be read either silently by both you and your child, or read aloud to the child by you. Read and discuss the following pages listed below.

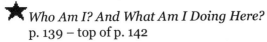 *Who Am I? And What Am I Doing Here?* p. 139 – top of p. 142

Key Idea: The Bible is our guide for how to conduct ourselves and make good choices. Jesus is our example, and the Holy Spirit is our Counselor. We should avoid hasty decisions that are based on emotions and feelings alone.

Language Arts [S]

Have students complete one studied dictation exercise (see Appendix for directions and passages).

Help students complete one lesson from the following reading program:

 *Drawn into the Heart of Reading*

Help students complete **one** English option.

★ *Progressing With Courage:* Lesson 68

★ *Progressing With Courage:* Lesson 100 (first half only)

★ Your own grammar program

Key Idea: Practice language arts skills.

Bible Quiet Time

Bible Study: Read and complete the assigned pages in the following resource:

★ *Faith at Work: Lesson 15 – Day One* p. 109 (Note: Refer to p. 105-108 to complete the lesson.)

Prayer Focus: Refer to **confession** on "Preparing Your Heart for Prayer". Then, pray a prayer of confession to admit or acknowledge your sins to God. After your prayer, write 'confession' at the bottom of today's lesson in *Faith at Work* above *Day Two*. Next to 'confession', either list key phrases or write a sentence to summarize your prayer. Keep "Preparing Your Heart for Prayer" inside your Bible.

Scripture Memory: Memorize Romans 12:21 from your Bible and recite it.

Music: Refer to p. 50-51 as you sing with Track 6 *"Onward, Christian Soldiers"* (vs. 1-5).

Key Idea: Read and study Romans 10.

Math Exploration [S]

Choose **one** of the math options listed below (see Appendix for details).

★ *Singapore Primary Mathematics 6A/6B, Discovering Mathematics 7A/7B, 8A/8B, No-Nonsense Algebra* or *Videotext Algebra*

★ Your own math program

Key Idea: Use a step-by-step math program.

Science Exploration [I]

★ Read *Atoms in the Family* p. 69-82. Then, give a summary oral narration to an adult about p. 69-82. The oral narration should be no longer than 6-8 sentences and should summarize the reading. As you narrate, hold up one finger for each sentence shared. The focus of the narration should be on the big ideas, rather than on the details. See *Narration Tips* in the Appendix.

Key Idea: After being appointed to the newly established chair of theoretical physics at the University of Rome, Fermi's next accomplishment was being named to the Royal Academy of Italy in 1929.

Learning Through History
Focus: Pearl Harbor, the Flying Scotsman, and Watchman Nee

Unit 18 - Day 3

 Reading about History | I |

Read about history in the following resource:

 Hero Tales: Vol. II p. 93-103

Open your *Student Notebook* to Unit 18 – Box 5 to see a WWII Chinese propaganda poster for the Kuomintang, or Chinese Nationalist Party.

Key Idea: Watchman Nee founded many local Christian house churches in China. He was arrested by Chinese Communists in 1956 and imprisoned until his death in 1972.

 History Project | ✓ |

Open your *Student Notebook* to Unit 18. Look at the *kamons,* or Japanese family crests in Box 9. Notice the crest of the Togo warlord clan. Togo was a famous Japanese fleet admiral that was also responsible for the education of the future emperor Hirohito. The other crests in Box 9 are of famous Christian warlords Konishi Yukinaga, Otomo, Otani, Arima, and the samurai clan Ito. Samurai used these crests for family identification and on their battle armor. Later, merchants and artisans put crests on business items too. Today, you will design your own Christian family crest. In Box 10, use a pencil to lightly trace around a small circular object like a milk jug lid or the bottom of a small circular jar or bottle. Typical crests were .8" – 1.8". Then, lightly draw a pattern inside the circle's outline for your crest. Next, erase the outside circle if it is not part of the crest. Last, used colored pencils to color the crest in Box 10 in black and white. Write your family name under the crest.

Key Idea: Watchman Nee encouraged believers that even in times of war, Chinese and Japanese Christians were united in Christ.

 State Study | T |

 This is an **optional** part of the plans. If you have chosen to study your state using *State History from a Christian Perspective,* do Lesson 15 from the *Master Lesson Plan Book.*
Key Idea: Study your individual state.

 Storytime | T/I |

Read the following assigned pages:

 Gladys Alyward p. 191-203
Note: p. 198 includes executions.
After today's reading, orally narrate or retell the portion of the story that was read today. See *Narration Tips* in the Appendix as needed.

Key Idea: Practice orally narrating, or retelling, a portion of a story.

 Geography | I |

For today's activities, use the map listed below.

 United States History Atlas p. 42
Locate China on the map on p. 42 of the *United States History Atlas.* Then, find the area along the coast of China, between Hong Kong and Shanghai. This is where Watchman Nee joined the Church of Heavenly Peace in 1920. Watchman Nee went on to start hundreds of local churches on China's mainland. Due to his ministry, local churches were also started in the Philippines, in Singapore (in Malaya), in Thailand, and in Indonesia (which is Sumatra, Borneo, and the Dutch East Indies on the map). Find these locations on the map on p. 42.

Key Idea: Before his arrest in 1956, Watchman Nee helped start more than 600 local churches in China.

 Independent History Study | ✓ |

Open your *Student Notebook* to Unit 18. In Box 6, copy the following quote by Nee, which was found on a scrap of paper under Nee's pillow upon his death in confinement in 1972:

"Christ is the Son of God Who died for the redemption of sinners and was resurrected after three days. This is the greatest truth in the universe. I die because of my belief in Christ." Watchman Nee

Key Idea: Watchman Nee was a believer in Christ until his death in 1972.

Learning the Basics
Focus: Language Arts, Math, Bible, Nature Journal, Poetry, and Science

Nature Journal & Poetry | S

The poetry of Longfellow, Wordsworth, and Whitman is scheduled to complement the journaling sessions. Read aloud and discuss today's poem *"Sunrise on the Hills"* (see Appendix) with a parent. Then, follow the directions below.

★ *Nature Drawing & Journaling: Lesson XXIV* p. 69

Note: Do only the sketch described in paragraphs two and three on p. 69 today. A gallery of Monet's paintings can be found at http://www.claudemonetgallery.org/

Key Idea: Practice capturing an impression.

Language Arts | S

Have students complete one studied dictation exercise (see Appendix for passages).

Help students complete **one** English option.

★ *Progressing With Courage:* Lesson 69

★ *Progressing With Courage:* Lesson 100 (last half only)

★ Your own grammar program

Work with the students to complete **one** of the writing options listed below:

★ *Write with the Best: Vol. 2* Unit 5 – Day 6 p. 47 (Note: Refer to the "Steps to Writing an Outline" on p. 88-90)

★ Your own writing program

Key Idea: Practice language arts skills.

Bible Quiet Time | I

Bible Study: Read and complete the assigned pages in the following resource:

★ *Faith at Work: Lesson 15 – Day Two* and *Day Three* p. 109-110

Prayer Focus: Refer to **thanksgiving** on "Preparing Your Heart for Prayer". Then, pray a prayer of thanksgiving to express gratitude to God for His divine goodness. After your prayer, write 'thanksgiving' at the bottom of today's lesson in *Faith at Work* above *Day Four*. Next to 'thanksgiving', either list key phrases or write a sentence to summarize your prayer. Keep "Preparing Your Heart for Prayer" inside your Bible.

Scripture Memory: Copy Romans 12:21 in your Common Place Book.

Music: Refer to p. 50-51 as you sing with Track 6 *"Onward, Christian Soldiers"* (vs. 1-5).

Key Idea: Read and study Romans 11.

Math Exploration | S

Choose **one** of the math options listed below (see Appendix for details).

★ *Singapore Primary Mathematics 6A/6B, Discovering Mathematics 7A/7B, 8A/8B, No-Nonsense Algebra* or *Videotext Algebra*

★ Your own math program

Key Idea: Use a step-by-step math program.

Science Exploration | I

★ Read *Atoms in the Family* p. 83-96. Then, write a written narration about p. 83-96. Refer to *Written Narration Tips* in the Appendix for help as needed. Read your written narration out loud after you have finished writing. Refer to *Written Narration Skills* for help in editing.

Key Idea: French physicist Frederic Joliet and his wife Irene Curie, daughter of Marie Curie, discovered artificial radioactivity in 1930. They bombarded aluminum with fast alpha particles, which are positively charged helium nuclei. This led Fermi to try to produce artificial radioactivity with neutrons.

Reading about History | I

Read about history in the following resource:

 Hero Tales: Vol. II p. 9-19

You will be writing a narration about **one** of the sections that you read about today (either "He Dared to Stand Up to Hitler", "A German in Harlem", "Church, Remain a Church!", or "Double Agent...and Pastor"). To prepare for writing your narration, look back over your chosen section in *Hero Tales: Vol. II*. Think about the main idea and the most important moments in this part.

After you have thought about what you will write and how you will begin your narration, turn to Unit 18 in your *Student Notebook*. For more guidance on writing a narration, see *Written Narration Tips* in the Appendix.

In Box 4, write a 12-16 sentence narration about the reading. When you have finished writing, read your sentences out loud to catch any mistakes. Check for the following things: *Did you include **who** or **what topic** the reading was mainly about? Did you include **descriptors** of the important thing(s) that happened? Did you include a **closing sentence**? If not, add those things.* Use the *Written Narration Skills* in the Appendix as a guide for editing the narration.

Key Idea: Dietrich Bonhoeffer was born in Breslau, Germany, to a well-known German family. He studied theology in Berlin and then in New York. His time in New York led him to better understand racism. Upon his return to Germany, he formed the "Confessing Church", which proclaimed allegiance to Christ alone as Lord. Dietrich refused to discriminate against Jews and became involved in a resistance movement to overthrow Hitler.

Storytime | VI

Read the following assigned pages:

 Shadow of His Hand p. 9-22

Get the bookmark that you placed in your book. Locate the same section of the bookmark that you used on Day 2. Beneath Day 2's entry, write the book title and the page numbers you read today. Select the one remaining response option at the bottom of the bookmark, and place a checkmark next to it. In the blank space under today's pages, respond in writing using your checked option. Keep the bookmark in your book.

Key Idea: Relate to the text in various ways.

Economics | √

Read about economics in the resource below.

 Whatever Happened to Penny Candy? p. 131-133

After the reading, open your *Student Notebook* to the "Economic Principles" section at the front of your notebook. Under "Economic Principle", write a one or two sentence summary that either defines a new economic term or describes a new economic principle learned from today's reading.

Key Idea: The Consumer Price Index, or CPI, measures the monthly average price of items bought by consumers. This information is used to measure inflation in the U.S. The CPI does not include stocks or taxes.

President Study | I

 On *The Presidents* DVD Volume 2, select the Chapter "Cleveland to Taft" and watch **only** Program 2: Benjamin Harrison. Then, open your *President Notebook* to Benjamin Harrison. Use today's viewing to add further information about Harrison.

Key Idea: Research Benjamin Harrison.

Independent History Study | √

Choose **one** of the sets of questions from the sections of *Hero Tales: Vol. II* that you read today to answer orally with an adult. The questions are found on p. 13, 16, and 19.

Key Idea: Dietrich Bonhoeffer was arrested by the Gestapo in 1943 and killed in 1945, shortly before Germany surrendered to Allied forces.

Learning the Basics
Focus: Language Arts, Math, Bible, Nature Journal, and Science

Biblical Self-Image

Read and discuss with the students the following pages in the resource below.

★ *Who Am I? And What Am I Doing Here?* middle of p. 142 and middle of p. 150 – top of p. 151

Key Idea: During the Middle Ages, knights were expected to live with honor, fight for justice, uphold righteousness, remain loyal, and protect those who could not defend themselves.

Language Arts   S

Have students complete one studied dictation exercise (see Appendix for directions and passages).

Help students complete one lesson from the following reading program:

★ *Drawn into the Heart of Reading*

Help students complete **one** English option.

★ *Progressing With Courage:* Lesson 70

★ *Progressing With Courage:* Lesson 101 (first half only)

★ Your own grammar program

Key Idea: Practice language arts skills.

Bible Quiet Time   I

Bible Study: Complete the assignment below.

★ *Faith at Work: Lesson 15 – Day Four* p. 110-111

Prayer Focus: Refer to **supplication** on "Preparing Your Heart for Prayer". Then, pray a prayer of supplication to make a humble and earnest request of God. Write 'supplication' at the bottom of today's lesson in *Faith at Work* above *Day Five*. Next to it, either list several key phrases or write a sentence to summarize your prayer. Keep "Preparing Your Heart for Prayer" inside your Bible.

Scripture Memory: Recite Romans 12:1-21.

Music: Refer to p. 50-51 as you sing with Track 6 *"Onward, Christian Soldiers"* (vs. 1-5).

Key Idea: Read and study Romans 11.

Math Exploration   S

Choose **one** of the math options listed below.

★ *Singapore Primary Mathematics 6A/6B, Discovering Mathematics 7A/7B, 8A/8B, No-Nonsense Algebra* or *Videotext Algebra*

★ Your own math program

Key Idea: Use a step-by-step math program.

Science Exploration   I

★ Copy the Science Lab Form from the Appendix of this guide. Put on your safety glasses, smooth gloves, and smock as recommended on p. 6 of the *Chemistry C500 Experiment Manual*. Next, follow the directions to perform "Experiment 15" from p. 30 of the Experiment Manual. After completing Experiment 15, in the top box of the Science Lab Form write: *What effect will liquid soap have on litmus solution mixed with tartaric acid?* In the second box of the form, write your hypothesis. Follow the directions for "Experiment 16" on p. 31 of the Experiment Manual and complete the box "Perform an Experiment" on your lab form. Then, follow the arrows to complete the rest of the Science Lab Form. To clean up, refer to "How to Dispose of Waste" on p. 7 and Basic Rules 5, 6, 7, and 11 on p. 6.

Key Idea: Liquid soap contains strong alkalis balanced by strong acids, so it does not turn the litmus solution back to blue. Conventional soap is made with strong lye, so it has an alkaline effect instead.

Reading about History | I

Read about history in the following resource:

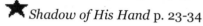 *The Story of the World: Vol. 4* p. 309-314
Note: p. 312 includes disturbing content about the Holocaust.

After today's reading, orally narrate or retell to an adult the portion of text that you read today from *The Story of the World*. Some possible key words to include in your narration might be *Hitler, Germans, Aryan, inferior people, Jews, Olympics, Jesse Owens, Lutz Long, Kristallnacht, Star of David, ghettos, concentration camps, final solution, genocide, Holocaust, Denmark, ten Booms*, and *War Refugee Board*.

Key Idea: Hitler believed that anyone who did not fit his definition of "Aryan" was inferior. He targeted Jews especially and moved them into ghettos first and later into concentration camps. Before WWII ended, millions of Jews and others labeled as "inferior" died in the Holocaust.

History Project | S

At the 1936 Olympics in Berlin, Hitler wished to prove to the world that his "Aryan" race was superior. Jesse Owens was an African American athlete who competed from the United States. As an African American, Owens was a non-Aryan in Hitler's Germany. Watch and listen as Owens wins four gold medals:

http://www.timetape.com/ (Type "Jesse Owens" in Search and click on "Jesse Owens – 1936 Olympics" which shows a picture of Owens and Lutz Long.)

Key Idea: Hitler did not acknowledge Owens.

President Study | I

 Read p. 46-47 in *Our Presidents...* Then, open your *President Notebook* to William McKinley. Use today's reading to help you complete the information about McKinley.

Key Idea: Research William McKinley.

Storytime | T/I

Read the following assigned pages:

 Shadow of His Hand p. 23-34

After today's reading, photocopy the **two** "Bookmark" pages from the Appendix. Place the copied pages back-to-back and staple them together at the 4 corners. Then, tri-fold the stapled page into thirds to make a bookmark. Save the bookmark in your book until Day 2.

Key Idea: Relate to the text in various ways.

Timeline | I

You will be adding to the timeline in your *Student Notebook* today. In Unit 19 – Box 1, outline and color a beach with bombs blowing up on it. Label it, *D-Day Invasion - Normandy (June 6, 1944 A.D.)*.

In Box 2, draw a yellow six-pointed "Star of David" by drawing one triangle with its tip pointing up and another triangle laid over it with its tip pointing down. Label it, *Dietrich Bonhoeffer (1906-1945 A.D.)*.

In Box 3, draw and color a Dutch windmill. Label it, *Corrie ten Boom (1892-1983 A.D.)*.

Key Idea: Shortly before the Allied forces liberated Germany, German pastor Dietrich Bonhoeffer was hung in a concentration camp. Dutch Christian Corrie ten Boom survived the concentration camp and preached forgiveness.

Independent History Study | I

The "Star of David" contains two triangles intertwined with one pointing up to God and the other pointing down to man. The Jews first in 17th century Prague and later in the 1897 Zionist movement adopted this symbol. It is also on the national flag of Israel today.

Key Idea: Hitler used the Star of David as a symbol to mark Jews.

Learning the Basics

Focus: Language Arts, Math, Bible, Nature Journal, and Science

Nature Journal [I]

Read and follow the directions in the resource below.

 Nature Drawing & Journaling: Lesson XXV p. 70-71

Note: Do **only** the colored pencil and black pen landscapes described on p. 71 today.

Key Idea: Practice drawing using foreground, middle ground, and background.

Language Arts [S]

Help students complete one lesson from the following reading program:

 Drawn into the Heart of Reading

Help students complete **one** English option.

 Progressing With Courage: Lesson 71

 Progressing With Courage: Lesson 101 (last half only)

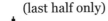 Your own grammar program

Work with the students to complete **one** of the writing options listed below:

 Write with the Best: Vol. 2 Unit 5 – Day 7 p. 48 (Note: Another example of today's assignment is given in #5 on p. 97.)

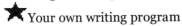 Your own writing program

Key Idea: Practice language arts skills.

Bible Quiet Time [I]

Bible Study: Read and complete the assigned pages in the following resource:

 Faith at Work: Lesson 15 – Day Five and *Notes* p. 111-117

Prayer Focus: Refer to **adoration** on "Preparing Your Heart for Prayer". Then, pray a prayer of adoration to worship and honor God. After your prayer, write 'adoration' at the bottom of today's lesson on p. 111 in *Faith at Work*. Next to 'adoration', either list key phrases or write a sentence to summarize your prayer. Keep "Preparing Your Heart for Prayer" inside your Bible.

Scripture Memory: Read aloud James 4:1 three times from your Bible.

Music: Read p. 55-56 in *Hymns for a Kid's Heart*. Refer to p. 58-59 as you sing with Track 7 *"When We All Get to Heaven"* (vs. 1-2).

Key Idea: Read and study Romans 11.

Math Exploration [S]

Choose **one** of the math options listed below (see Appendix for details).

 Singapore Primary Mathematics 6A/6B, Discovering Mathematics 7A/7B, 8A/8B, No-Nonsense Algebra or *Videotext Algebra*

 Your own math program

Key Idea: Use a step-by-step math program.

Science Exploration [I]

 Read *Atoms in the Family* p. 97-114. Note: p. 103 describes a terrible crime and a missing person, and p. 108 mentions Laura Fermi's thoughts that Jesus is not God's Son and Enrico's questions about God's existence. After today's reading, add to the list of characteristics about Enrico Fermi that you began in Unit 17 – Day 1. Save the list to add to in the next unit.

Key Idea: In 1934 Fermi, Rasetti, Amaldi, D'Agostino, Pontecorvo, Trabacchi, and Segre applied for a patent for the process of producing artificial radioactivity through slow neutron bombardment.

Learning Through History
Focus: The Holocaust, Dietrich Bonhoeffer, D-Day, and the End of WWII

Unit 19 - Day 2

Reading about History | I

Read about history in the following resource:

 Rescue and Redeem p. 171-191

After today's reading, open your *Student Notebook* to Unit 19. Box 5 shows a 1942 Nazi propaganda poster with Hitler's portrait. The poster reads, "Hitler the Liberator". In 1937, Hitler's Minister for Church Affairs spoke to an audience of Protestant pastors, delivering the following message: *"Positive Christianity Is National Socialism... National Socialism is the doing of God's will. Dr. Zoellner... has tried to tell me that Christianity consists in faith in Christ as the Son of God. That makes me laugh... Christianity is not dependent upon the Apostle's Creed... (but) is represented by the Party... the German people are called... by the Fuhrer to a real Christianity... The Fuhrer is the herald of a new revelation.* 'Liberator' means to set free from oppression, foreign control, or confinement. According to the quote above, was Hitler really a liberator? Read 1 John 5:1-12. According to verse 5, how is Christ our liberator? What do verses 9-12 say about those who do not believe in Christ as the Son of God?

Key Idea: The Confessing Church believed in Jesus as Lord and objected to Hitler's control.

History Project | S

Open your *Student Notebook* to Unit 19 – Box 9. Follow the directions from *Draw and Write Through History* p. 39-40 to draw a Sherman Tank. You will color your drawing on Day 3.

Key Idea: Bonhoeffer did not survive the war.

President Study | I

 On *The Presidents* DVD Volume 2, select the Chapter "Cleveland to Taft" and watch **only** Program 4: William McKinley. Then, open your *President Notebook* to William McKinley and add further information.

Key Idea: Research William McKinley.

Storytime | T/I

Read the following assigned pages:

Shadow of His Hand p. 35-43
Get the bookmark you made on Day 1. Find the section of the bookmark that has only **two** options at the bottom. At the top of this section of the bookmark, write the book title and the page numbers you read today. Select **one** of the two options at the bottom of the bookmark and respond to that option in writing in the blank space under today's pages.

Key Idea: Relate to the text in various ways.

Worthy Words | T

Read, analyze, and evaluate the speech below.

Book of Great American Speeches for Young People p. 261-262
After reading the speech, answer the following questions on an index card: *From what were Esther and her family liberated? Why were she and her family persecuted? Explain the meaning of what Esther's father said to her. What resemblance does this have to John 15:1-8? Summarize what liberation meant to Esther. What does freedom, or liberation, mean to you? How do you have freedom in Christ?* Next, meet with a parent to have a Socratic dialogue about the speech. Before beginning the dialogue, the parent reads the speech out loud. Next, discuss the questions using your notes. All participants should use life experiences and/or the text to support their responses.

Key Idea: Liberation meant a gradual sense of safety, security, and freedom for holocaust survivor Esther Cohen.

Independent History Study | I

Open your *Student Notebook* to Unit 19. Copy an important part of p. 261-262 from the *Book of Great American Speeches...* in Box 6. Write "Esther Cohen" at the bottom of Box 6.

Key Idea: 'Holocaust' means sacrifice by fire.

Learning the Basics

Focus: Language Arts, Math, Bible, Nature Journal, and Science

Unit 19 - Day 2

Biblical Self-Image [T]

Our plans intend for the listed pages in *Who Am I? And What Am I Doing Here?* to be read either silently by both you and your child, or read aloud to the child by you. Read and discuss the following pages listed below.

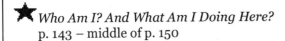 *Who Am I? And What Am I Doing Here?* p. 143 – middle of p. 150

Key Idea: As a child of the one true God and King of creation, you are special in God's eyes. When you believe that the Lord Jesus Christ is God's Son and that He died for your sins, you are given the right to be called a child of God.

Language Arts [S]

Have students complete one studied dictation exercise (see Appendix for directions and passages).

Help students complete one lesson from the following reading program:

⭐ *Drawn into the Heart of Reading*

Help students complete **one** English option.

⭐ *Progressing With Courage:* Lesson 72 (first half only)

⭐ *Progressing With Courage:* Lesson 102 (first half only)

⭐ Your own grammar program

Key Idea: Practice language arts skills.

Bible Quiet Time [I]

Bible Study: Read and complete the assigned pages in the following resource:

⭐ *Faith at Work: Lesson 16 – Day One* p. 118 (Note: Refer to p. 112-117 to complete the lesson.)

Prayer Focus: Refer to **confession** on "Preparing Your Heart for Prayer". Then, pray a prayer of confession to admit or acknowledge your sins to God. After your prayer, write 'confession' at the bottom of today's lesson in *Faith at Work* above *Day Two*. Next to 'confession', either list key phrases or write a sentence to summarize your prayer. Keep "Preparing Your Heart for Prayer" inside your Bible.

Scripture Memory: Memorize James 4:1 from your Bible and recite it.

Music: Refer to p. 58-59 as you sing with Track 7 *"When We All Get to Heaven"* (vs. 1-2).

Key Idea: Read and study Romans 11.

Math Exploration [S]

Choose **one** of the math options listed below (see Appendix for details).

⭐ *Singapore Primary Mathematics 6A/6B, Discovering Mathematics 7A/7B, 8A/8B, No-Nonsense Algebra* or *Videotext Algebra*

⭐ Your own math program

Key Idea: Use a step-by-step math program.

Science Exploration [I]

⭐ Read *Atoms in the Family* p. 115-124. Then, give a descriptive oral narration to an adult about p. 115-124. A detailed, descriptive narration is the goal. See *Narration Tips* in the Appendix for help as needed.

Key Idea: In 1938, Enrico Fermi was nominated for the Nobel Prize in physics. By this time, Fascist Italy had formed an alliance with Nazi Germany. In 1938, Hitler occupied Austria. In that same year, Mussolini launched a campaign against Jews in Italy saying they did not belong to the Italian race.

Reading about History | I

Read about history in the following resources:

★ *The Story of the World: Vol. 4* p. 316-322

★ *Great Events in American History* p. 91-93

★ **Optional:** *All American History: Vol. II* p. 336-342

After today's reading, open your *Student Notebook* to Unit 19. The image in Box 7 shows the newspaper headlines on May 2, 1945. In Box 8, copy a portion from *The Story of the World* p. 322 that more fully explains the newspaper headlines and the end of the war.

Key Idea: On D-Day, the Allied forces landed on the beaches in Normandy, France, to attack German troops in France. After liberating France, Allied forces marched into Germany. Meanwhile, the Soviet forces marched toward Berlin from the east. The last German offensive was at the Battle of the Bulge in Belgium. In April 1945, the Soviet troops entered Berlin. Hitler shot himself on April 30.

History Project | S

Open your *Student Notebook* to Unit 19 – Box 9. Follow the directions on p. 41 of *Draw and Write Through History* to color your Sherman Tank.

Key Idea: The D-Day landing included ships, airplanes, and tanks. It was a full-scale invasion by the Allied troops on the Normandy beaches to free France from German rule.

State Study | T

★ This is an **optional** part of the plans. If you have chosen to study your state using *State History from a Christian Perspective,* do Lesson 16 from the *Master Lesson Plan Book*.

Key Idea: Study your individual state.

Storytime | T/I

Read the following assigned pages:

★ *Shadow of His Hand* p. 45-53

After today's reading, orally narrate or retell the portion of the story that was read today. See *Narration Tips* in the Appendix as needed.

Key Idea: Practice orally narrating, or retelling, a portion of a story.

Economics | I

Read about economics in the resource below.

★ *Common Sense Business for Kids* p. 7-11

After the reading, open your *Student Notebook* to the "Economic Principles" section at the front of your notebook. Under "Economic Principle", write a one or two sentence summary for the economic principle you learned from today's reading.

Key Idea: In business, common sense means being observant and thinking things through before making a decision. This helps you see what people's needs are and how you could fill those needs. Business is mainly about people.

Independent History Study | I

Listen to *What in the World? Vol. 3* Disc 4, Tracks 5: "D-Day & the Atom Bomb". Read Dwight Eisenhower's D-Day speech on p. 167-168 of *Book of Great American Speeches for Young People*.

Key Idea: The D-Day attack included 5,000 ships and 10,000 airplanes and resulted in the death of over 5,000 Allied soldiers on "Omaha Beach" alone. General Dwight D. Eisenhower commanded the Allied forces that managed to capture the beach. The main troops were from the United Kingdom, America, and Canada. Units from free France, Poland, Norway, Australia, New Zealand, Czechoslovakia, Greece, the Netherlands, and Belgium also contributed to the Allied forces.

Learning the Basics
Focus: Language Arts, Math, Bible, Nature Journal, Poetry, and Science

Nature Journal & Poetry | S |

The poetry of Longfellow, Wordsworth, and Whitman is scheduled to complement the journaling sessions. Read aloud and discuss today's poem *"Nature"* (see Appendix) with a parent. Then, follow the directions below.

★ *Nature Drawing & Journaling: Lesson XXV* p. 71

Note: Do **only** the colored marker landscape described on p. 71 today. Do the landscape based on one of Monet's paintings found at http://www.claudemonetgallery.org/

Key Idea: Practice capturing an impression.

Language Arts | S |

Have students complete one studied dictation exercise (see Appendix for passages).

Help students complete **one** English option.

★ *Progressing With Courage:* Lesson 72 (last half only)

★ *Progressing With Courage:* Lesson 102 (last half only)

★ Your own grammar program

Work with the students to complete **one** of the writing options listed below:

★ *Write with the Best: Vol. 2* Unit 5 – Day 8 p. 48 (Note: Additional details are given in #7 on p. 98.)

★ Your own writing program

Key Idea: Practice language arts skills.

Bible Quiet Time | I |

Bible Study: Read and complete the assigned pages in the following resource:

★ *Faith at Work: Lesson 16 – Day Two* p. 118

Prayer Focus: Refer to **thanksgiving** on "Preparing Your Heart for Prayer". Then, pray a prayer of thanksgiving to express gratitude to God for His divine goodness. After your prayer, write 'thanksgiving' at the bottom of today's lesson on p. 118 in *Faith at Work*. Next to 'thanksgiving', either list key phrases or write a sentence to summarize your prayer. Keep "Preparing Your Heart for Prayer" inside your Bible.

Scripture Memory: Copy James 4:1 in your Common Place Book.

Music: Refer to p. 58-59 as you sing with Track 7 *"When We All Get to Heaven"* (vs. 1-2).

Key Idea: Read and study Romans 12.

Math Exploration | S |

Choose **one** of the math options listed below (see Appendix for details).

★ *Singapore Primary Mathematics 6A/6B, Discovering Mathematics 7A/7B, 8A/8B, No-Nonsense Algebra* or *Videotext Algebra*

★ Your own math program

Key Idea: Use a step-by-step math program.

Science Exploration | I |

★ Read *Atoms in the Family* p. 125-135. Then, write a written narration about p. 125-135. Refer to *Written Narration Tips* in the Appendix for help as needed. Read your written narration out loud after you have finished writing. Refer to *Written Narration Skills* for help in editing.

Key Idea: The Fermi's left Rome on December 6, 1938, for the Nobel Prize ceremony in Stockholm. From there, they immigrated to America to escape Fascism and persecution due to Laura's Jewish ancestry.

Reading about History | I |

Read about history in the following resource:

 Hero Tales: Vol. II p. 153-163

You will be writing a narration about the section "The Watchmaker's Daughter" that you read today on p. 153-154 of *Hero Tales: Vol. II*. To prepare for writing your narration, look back over the chosen section in *Hero Tales: Vol. II*. Think about the main idea and the most important moments in this part.

After you have thought about what you will write and how you will begin your narration, turn to Unit 19 in your *Student Notebook*. For more guidance on writing a narration, see *Written Narration Tips* in the Appendix.

In Box 4, write a 12-16 sentence narration about the reading. When you have finished writing, read your sentences out loud to catch any mistakes. Check for the following things: *Did you include* **who** *or* **what topic** *the reading was mainly about? Did you include* **descriptors** *of the important thing(s) that happened? Did you include a* **closing sentence**? *If not, add those things.* Use the *Written Narration Skills* in the Appendix as a guide for editing the narration.

Key Idea: Corrie ten Boom was born in Holland in 1892. Her father owned a watch repair shop, and her family lived above the shop in the "Beje". Corrie and her sister Betsie never married, but instead worked with their father and remained at the "Beje". As Dutch Christians, they hid their Jewish friends until the Ten Booms were betrayed and sent to a Nazi concentration camp. All of Corrie's family died, except for her brother Willem, yet Corrie spent the rest of her life sharing God's love and His message of forgiveness all over the world.

Storytime | T/I |

Read the following assigned pages:

 Shadow of His Hand p. 55-65
Get the bookmark that you placed in your book on Day 2. Locate the same section of the bookmark that you used on Day 2. Beneath Day 2's entry, write the book title and the page numbers you read today. Select the one remaining response option at the bottom of the bookmark, and place a checkmark next to it. In the blank space under today's pages, respond in writing using your checked option.

Key Idea: Relate to the text in various ways.

Geography | I |

For today's activities, use the map listed below.

 Map Trek CD: Missions to Modern Marvels p. 62
Print the "World War II (map 1 – Europe)" **Teacher's Map** found on p. 62 of the *Map Trek CD*. Beneath the map "Key", use a colored pencil to write "Jewish death toll by country of origin for WWII". Use the same color to write the following numbers on the listed countries on the map: Norway = 762; Denmark = 60; Finland = 7; Soviet Union (U.S.S.R.) = 1,000,000; Estonia = 1500; Latvia = 70,000; Lithuania = 140,000; Poland = 2,900,000; Germany = 134,500; Holland = 100,000; Belgium = 28,900; France = 77,320; Luxembourg = 1,950; Czechoslovakia 146,150; Austria = 50,000; Italy = 7,680; Hungary = 550,000; Romania 271,000; Yugoslavia = 56,200; Bulgaria = 0; Greece = 60,000.

Key Idea: Over 5 million Jews died in WWII.

President Study | I |

 Read p. 48-49 in *Our Presidents...* Then, open your *President Notebook* to Theodore Roosevelt. Use today's reading to help you complete the information about Theodore Roosevelt.

Key Idea: Research Theodore Roosevelt.

Independent History Study | I |

Choose **one** of the sets of questions from the sections of *Hero Tales: Vol. II* that you read today to answer orally with an adult. The questions are found on p. 157, 160, and 163.

Key Idea: Corrie and Betsie ten Boom lived for Christ, even when in the concentration camps.

Learning the Basics
Focus: Language Arts, Math, Bible, Nature Journal, and Science

Biblical Self-Image [T]

Read and discuss with the students the following pages in the resource below.

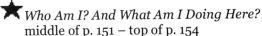 *Who Am I? And What Am I Doing Here?* middle of p. 151 – top of p. 154

For "Make a Note of It" on p. 154, work with the students as their scribe to make a combined list of 5 decisions that either of you made today. Then, briefly jot down under each decision why you chose the decision that you did and the consequences of the decision.

Key Idea: God desires us to choose wisely.

Language Arts [S]

Have students complete one studied dictation exercise (see Appendix for directions and passages).

Help students complete one lesson from the following reading program:

★ *Drawn into the Heart of Reading*

Help students complete **one** English option.

★ *Progressing With Courage:* Lesson 73

★ *Progressing With Courage:* Lesson 103 (first half only)

★ Your own grammar program

Key Idea: Practice language arts skills.

Bible Quiet Time [I]

Bible Study: Complete the assignment below.

★ *Faith at Work: Lesson 16 – Day Three* p. 119-120

Prayer Focus: Refer to **supplication** on "Preparing Your Heart for Prayer". Then, pray a prayer of supplication to make a humble and earnest request of God. Write 'supplication' at the bottom of today's lesson in *Faith at Work* above *Day Four.* Next to it, either list several key phrases or write a sentence to summarize your prayer. Keep "Preparing Your Heart for Prayer" inside your Bible.

Scripture Memory: Recite James 4:1.

Music: Refer to p. 58-59 as you sing with Track 7 *"When We All Get to Heaven"* (vs. 1-2).

Key Idea: Read and study Romans 12.

Math Exploration [S]

Choose **one** of the math options listed below.

★ *Singapore Primary Mathematics 6A/6B, Discovering Mathematics 7A/7B, 8A/8B, No-Nonsense Algebra* or *Videotext Algebra*

★ Your own math program

Key Idea: Use a step-by-step math program.

Science Exploration [I]

★ Copy the Science Lab Form from the Appendix of this guide. Put on your safety glasses, smooth gloves, and smock as recommended on p. 6 of the *Chemistry C500 Experiment Manual.* You will also need the soap solution from "Experiment 13" on p. 28. Next, follow the directions to perform "Experiment 17" from p. 32 of the Experiment Manual. After completing Experiment 17, in the top box of the Science Lab Form write: *What happens when tartaric acid solution is added to liquid soap solution?* In the second box of the form, write your hypothesis. Follow the directions for "Experiment 18" on p. 33 of the Experiment Manual and complete the box "Perform an Experiment" on your lab form. Read p. 34 in the Experiment Manual. Then, follow the arrows to complete the rest of the Science Lab Form. To clean up, refer to "How to Dispose of Waste" on p. 7 and Basic Rules 5, 6, 7, and 11 on p. 6.

Key Idea: The acids in liquid soaps dissolve in water, so they do not separate out when acid is added.

Learning Through History

Focus: The Big Three, the End of World War II, and Bible Translation in Mexico

Reading about History [S]

Read about history in the following resources:

★ *All American History: Vol. II* p. 343-349

★ *The Story of the World: Vol. 4* p. 323-327

After today's reading, orally narrate or retell to an adult the text from *All American History*. As you retell, the adult will write or type your narration. Some possible key words to include in your narration might be *General Douglas MacArthur, Admiral Chester Nimitz, Battle of Midway, leapfrog approach, liberate the Philippines, Japanese navy, fight to the death, Marines, Iwo Jima, Okinawa, Albert Einstein, superbomb, Manhatten Project, Truman, Enola Gay, "Little Boy", Hiroshima, "Fat Man", Nagasaki, Emperor Hirohito, surrender, V-J Day, peace conference, United States, Soviet Union, division East and West Germany*. When the narration is complete, tri-fold the typed or written narration to fit in Unit 20 – Box 9 of the *Student Notebook*. Glue the folded narration in Box 9, so it can be opened.

Key Idea: World War II ended in 1945 after atomic bombs were dropped on Hiroshima and Nagasaki.

History Project [S]

To see how God works in even the most difficult circumstances, read *Great Events in American History* p. 95-97. Then, read more about Jacob DeShazer in the following article: http://en.wikipedia.org/wiki/Jacob_DeShazer

Last, listen as DeShazer tells his own story by playing the video at the following link: http://jacobdeshazer.com/

Key Idea: Jacob DeShazer was a Japanese prisoner of war who returned to Japan as a missionary after World War II.

Storytime [T/I]

Read the following assigned pages:

★ *Shadow of His Hand* p. 67-80
Get the bookmark that you placed in your book last unit. Choose a new section of the bookmark with **three** options at the bottom. At the top of this section of the bookmark, write the book title and the page numbers you read today. Select **one** of the three options at the bottom and place a checkmark next to it. In the blank space under today's pages, respond in writing using your checked option.

Key Idea: Relate to the text in various ways.

Geography [I]

For today's activities, use the map listed below.

★ *Map Trek CD: Missions to Modern Marvels* p. 66

Print the "World War II (map 2 – South Pacific)" **Teacher's Answer Map** found on p. 66 of the *Map Trek CD*. Refer to p. 42 of the *United States History Atlas* to guide you as you color in green on your Teacher's Answer Map all the areas under Japanese control. Next, refer to p. 42 of the *United States History Atlas* to help you draw red arrows and red stars on your Teacher's Answer Map to show the movement of Allied forces and the major battles. Label the red arrows and battles to match p. 42. Last, draw blue stars to mark Nagasaki and Hiroshima on your Student Map, along with the dates that the atomic bombs were dropped in those locations. Make a "Key" on your Teacher's Answer Map to match the key shown on p. 42 of the *United States History Atlas*. File your Teacher's Answer Map in your *Student Notebook*.

Key Idea: Approximately 20 million soldiers and 40 million civilians died in WWII.

Independent History Study [I]

Open your *Student Notebook* to Unit 20. In Box 6, copy the **second** paragraph from p. 47 of *Draw and Write Through History*.

Key Idea: German forces surrendered in Italy on April 29. Japan formally surrendered August 15, 1945.

Learning the Basics

Focus: Language Arts, Math, Bible, Nature Journal, and Science

Nature Journal   I

Read and follow the directions in the resource below.

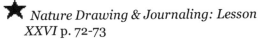 *Nature Drawing & Journaling: Lesson XXVI* p. 72-73

Note: You will need to take a bit of water, a small paintbrush, and a set of markers outside for the marker study part of today's lesson. Make sure to leave plenty of time to return indoors and complete the colored pencil landscape for today's lesson.

Key Idea: Practice sketching landscapes.

Language Arts   S

Help students complete one lesson from the following reading program:

 *Drawn into the Heart of Reading*

Help students complete **one** English option.

★ *Progressing With Courage:* Lesson 74

★ *Progressing With Courage:* Lesson 103 (last half only)

★ Your own grammar program

Work with the students to complete **one** of the writing options listed below:

★ *Write with the Best: Vol. 2* Unit 5 – Day 9 p. 48-49

★ Your own writing program

Key Idea: Practice language arts skills.

Bible Quiet Time   I

Bible Study: Read and complete the assigned pages in the following resource:

★ *Faith at Work: Lesson 16 – Day Four* p. 120-121

Prayer Focus: Refer to **adoration** on "Preparing Your Heart for Prayer". Then, pray a prayer of adoration to worship and honor God. After your prayer, write 'adoration' at the bottom of today's lesson in *Faith at Work* above *Day Five*. Next to 'adoration', either list key phrases or write a sentence to summarize your prayer. Keep "Preparing Your Heart for Prayer" inside your Bible.

Scripture Memory: Read aloud James 4:2 three times from your Bible.

Music: Read p. 57 in *Hymns for a Kid's Heart*. Refer to p. 58-59 as you sing with Track 7 *"When We All Get to Heaven"* (vs. 1-3).

Key Idea: Read and study Romans 12.

Math Exploration   S

Choose **one** of the math options listed below (see Appendix for details).

★ *Singapore Primary Mathematics 6A/6B, Discovering Mathematics 7A/7B, 8A/8B, No-Nonsense Algebra* or *Videotext Algebra*

★ Your own math program

Key Idea: Use a step-by-step math program.

Science Exploration   I

★ Read *Atoms in the Family* p. 139-153. After today's reading, add to the list of characteristics about Enrico Fermi that you began in Unit 17 – Day 1. Save the list to add to in the next unit.

Key Idea: On January 2, 1939, the Fermi family arrived in America on the ship *Franconia*. At first they lived in New York City near Columbia University where Enrico was a professor. After 6 months, the family moved to Leonia, New Jersey, due to encouragement from chemist and 1934 Nobel Prize winner Harold Urey, who also lived in Leonia.

Reading about History | I

Read about history in the following resource:

★ *All American History: Vol. II* p. 351 – top of p. 356

After today's reading, open your *Student Notebook* to Unit 20. Look at the poster in Box 7 that was meant to encourage U.S. workers to increase production of wartime weapons. Notice Hitler, Mussolini, and Hirohito running from the big foot labeled "Production". How could wartime production be keeping those three men on the run? To what promise do you think the headlines refer? Write several sentences under the poster to explain the poster's images and sayings.

Key Idea: As the U.S. entered WWII, wartime production in the U.S. jumped from 8.4 billion to 30 billion dollars in one year's time! Meanwhile, Churchill, Roosevelt, and Stalin met to plan the Allied strategy. These three leaders became known as the Big Three.

History Project | S

Even famous actors like Jimmy Stewart from *It's a Wonderful Life* took part in WWII. Stewart flew 20 combat missions as a bomber pilot, won 3 silver stars, and was promoted to Brigadier General. On his missions, Stewart carried a copy of Psalm 91 given to him by his father. Jimmy said, "What a promise for an airman. I placed in His Hands the squadron I would be leading. And, as the psalmist promised, I felt myself borne up." Read Psalm 91 and choose a portion to copy in Box 8.

Key Idea: The war affected people everywhere.

President Study | I

★ On *The Presidents* DVD Volume 2, select the Chapter "Cleveland to Taft" and watch **only** Program 5: Theodore Roosevelt. Then, open your *President Notebook* to Theodore Roosevelt and add information about him.

Key Idea: Research Theodore Roosevelt.

Storytime | T/I

Read the following assigned pages:

★ *Shadow of His Hand* p. 81-90

Get the bookmark that you placed in your book. Locate the same section of the bookmark that you used on Day 1. Beneath Day 1's entry, write the book title and the page numbers you read today. Select one of the **two** remaining response options at the bottom of the bookmark, and place a checkmark next to it. In the blank space under today's pages, respond in writing using your checked option.

Key Idea: Relate to the text in various ways.

Timeline | I

You will be adding to the timeline in your *Student Notebook* today. In Unit 20 – Box 1, outline a rectangular flag divided into three vertical sections. From left to right, color the sections green, white, and red like the Mexican flag. Label it, *Marianna Slocum Bible Translation - Mexico (1940 A.D.)*.

In Box 2, draw and color a bomb. Label it, *Atom Bomb - Hiroshima (August 6) Nagasaki (August 9, 1945 A.D.)*

In Box 3, draw a line down the middle of the box. On the left side of the line, write 'West Germany'. On the right side, write 'East Germany'. Label the box, *Occupied Germany Becomes East and West Germany (1949 A.D.)*.

Key Idea: World War II led to devastation, death, and political change around the world.

Independent History Study | I

Look at the map on p. 41 of the *United States History Atlas* to see the Axis nations and the countries occupied by the Axis forces during WWII. Name the few nations that managed to remain neutral and the Allied nations. Can you imagine what the world would be like today had the Axis forces not been stopped?

Key Idea: The war's end led to division and occupation of Austria, Germany, and Korea.

Learning the Basics
Focus: Language Arts, Math, Bible, Nature Journal, and Science

Biblical Self-Image [T]

Read and discuss with the students the following pages in the resource below.

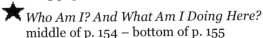 *Who Am I? And What Am I Doing Here?* middle of p. 154 – bottom of p. 155

For "Make a Note of It" on p. 155, first learn how to read nutrition labels by going to http://www.kelloggs.com/en_US/home.html. Then, click on "Nutrition" in the top row. Next, under "The Benefits of Cereal" click on "How to Read a Nutrition Label". After reading about labels, click and read **each** category on the left side under "The Benefits of Cereal".

Key Idea: God desires us to make wise choices.

Language Arts [S]

Have students complete one studied dictation exercise (see Appendix for directions and passages).

Help students complete one lesson from the following reading program:

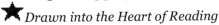 *Drawn into the Heart of Reading*

Help students complete **one** English option.

⭐ *Progressing With Courage:* Lesson 75

⭐ *Progressing With Courage:* Lesson 104 (first half only)

⭐ Your own grammar program

Key Idea: Practice language arts skills.

Bible Quiet Time [I]

Bible Study: Read and complete the assigned pages in the following resource:

⭐ *Faith at Work: Lesson 16 – Day Five* and *Notes* p. 121-127

Prayer Focus: Refer to **confession** on "Preparing Your Heart for Prayer". Then, pray a prayer of confession to admit or acknowledge your sins to God. After your prayer, write 'confession' at the bottom of today's lesson on p. 121 in *Faith at Work*. Next to 'confession', either list key phrases or write a sentence to summarize your prayer. Keep "Preparing Your Heart for Prayer" inside your Bible.

Scripture Memory: Memorize James 4:2 from your Bible and recite it.

Music: Refer to p. 58-59 as you sing with Track 7 *"When We All Get to Heaven"* (vs. 1-3).

Key Idea: Read and study Romans 12.

Math Exploration [S]

Choose **one** of the math options listed below (see Appendix for details).

⭐ *Singapore Primary Mathematics 6A/6B, Discovering Mathematics 7A/7B, 8A/8B, No-Nonsense Algebra* or *Videotext Algebra*

⭐ Your own math program

Key Idea: Use a step-by-step math program.

Science Exploration [I]

⭐ Read *Atoms in the Family* p. 154-161. Then, give a summary oral narration to an adult about p. 154-161. The oral narration should be no longer than 6-8 sentences and should summarize the reading. As you narrate, hold up one finger for each sentence shared. The focus of the narration should be on the big ideas, rather than on the details. See *Narration Tips* in the Appendix.

Key Idea: In 1939 Hahn, Strassman, and Meitner discovered uranium fission. The fission, or splitting, occurred as uranium atoms were bombarded with slow neutrons.

Reading about History | I

Read about history in the following resource:

 All American History: Vol. II p. 356-363

After today's reading, open your *Student Notebook* to Unit 20. Look at the poster in Box 5 by J. Howard Miller done for Westinghouse in 1942. The poster shows Geraldine (Hoff) Doyle at age 17. It was meant to boost morale among women working in Westinghouse factories in the U.S. during WWII. A 1942 song titled "Rosie the Riveter" was likely the inspiration for this poster.

Key Idea: In the U.S., millions of women joined the workforce to help with war production efforts because so many men were away serving in the armed forces. The war was funded in the U.S. through a federal income tax and through the selling of war bonds and stamps. Ration coupons were used to purchase items that were in short supply.

History Project | S

Today, you will pray the words of Scripture for those who protect our country with their lives by serving in the military. First, read Psalm 46:1 in your Bible. Then, pray for our men and women in the military to feel God's presence, strength, and help in times of trouble. Second, read Deuteronomy 31:6. Then, pray for those in the military to be strong and courageous in the Lord. Third, read Psalm 31:15. Then, pray for those in the military to know that they are in God's hands. Pray for them to be delivered from their enemies. Fourth, read 1 Peter 5:7. Pray for those in the military to cast their cares on the Lord, because He cares for them.

Key Idea: Remember to pray for our military.

State Study | T

 This is an **optional** part of the plans. If you have chosen to study your state using *State History from a Christian Perspective,* do Lesson 17 from the *Master Lesson Plan Book.*

Key Idea: Study your individual state.

Storytime | T/I

Read the following assigned pages:

 Shadow of His Hand p. 91-100
After today's reading, orally narrate or retell the portion of the story that was read today. See *Narration Tips* in the Appendix as needed.

Key Idea: Practice retelling the story.

Worthy Words | T

Read, analyze, and evaluate the speech below.

 Book of Great American Speeches for Young People p. 276-278
After reading the speech, answer the following questions on an index card: *What was the purpose of Executive Order 9066? After Executive Order 9066 was issued, why did Daniel Inouye and so many other Japanese Americans petition to serve their country in combat? What made the Battle of the Lost Battalion so significant to the 442nd Infantry Regimental Combat Team? How did that battle remove the stigma of "enemy alien" from the Japanese Americans of the 442nd Infantry? What reasons did Daniel Inouye give for volunteering for combat? What is the meaning of "...Americanism is a matter of mind and heart; Americanism is not, and never was, a matter of race or ancestry." Do you agree?* Next, meet with a parent to have a Socratic dialogue about the speech. Before beginning the dialogue, the parent reads the speech out loud. Next, discuss the questions with your parent using your notes.

Key Idea: Japanese Americans fought in WWII.

Independent History Study | I

Listen to *What in the World? Vol. 3* Disc 4, Track 6: "Cold War & the Iron Curtain". Read Albert Einstein's speech on p. 176-178 of *Book of Great American Speeches for Young People.*

Key Idea: After the war, only the U.S. escaped devastation. This left the United States and the Soviet Union as the two major world powers.

Learning the Basics
Focus: Language Arts, Math, Bible, Nature Journal, Poetry, and Science

Nature Journal & Poetry $\boxed{\text{S}}$

The poetry of Longfellow, Wordsworth, and Whitman is scheduled to complement the journaling sessions. Read aloud and discuss today's poem *"Sundown"* (see Appendix) with a parent. Then, follow the directions below.

★ *Nature Drawing & Journaling: Lesson XXVII* p. 74-75

Then, place the picture you drew in your nature journal and copy one stanza of the poem that you studied today on the page.

<u>Key Idea</u>: Practice softening the edges or using "spumato" in your sketches.

Language Arts $\boxed{\text{S}}$

Have students complete one studied dictation exercise (see Appendix for passages).

Help students complete **one** English option.

★ *Progressing With Courage:* Lesson 76

★ *Progressing With Courage:* Lesson 104 (last half only)

★ Your own grammar program

Work with the students to complete **one** of the writing options listed below:

★ *Write with the Best: Vol. 2* Unit 5 – Day 10 p. 49

★ Your own writing program

<u>Key Idea</u>: Practice language arts skills.

Bible Quiet Time $\boxed{\text{I}}$

Bible Study: Read and complete the assigned pages in the following resource:

★ *Faith at Work: Lesson 17 – Day One* p. 128 (Note: Refer to p. 122-127 to complete the lesson.)

Prayer Focus: Refer to **thanksgiving** on "Preparing Your Heart for Prayer". Then, pray a prayer of thanksgiving to express gratitude to God for His divine goodness. After your prayer, write 'thanksgiving' at the bottom of today's lesson in *Faith at Work* above *Day Two*. Next to 'thanksgiving', either list key phrases or write a sentence to summarize your prayer. Keep "Preparing Your Heart for Prayer" inside your Bible.

Scripture Memory: Copy James 4:2 in your Common Place Book.

Music: Refer to p. 58-59 as you sing with Track 7 *"When We All Get to Heaven"* (vs. 1-3).

<u>Key Idea</u>: Read and study Romans 12.

Math Exploration $\boxed{\text{S}}$

Choose **one** of the math options listed below (see Appendix for details).

★ *Singapore Primary Mathematics 6A/6B, Discovering Mathematics 7A/7B, 8A/8B, No-Nonsense Algebra* or *Videotext Algebra*

★ Your own math program

<u>Key Idea</u>: Use a step-by-step math program.

Science Exploration $\boxed{\text{I}}$

★ Read *Atoms in the Family* p. 162-175. Then, write a written narration about p. 162-175. Refer to *Written Narration Tips* in the Appendix for help as needed. Read your written narration out loud after you have finished writing. Refer to *Written Narration Skills* for help in editing.

<u>Key Idea</u>: In 1939, Albert Einstein sent a cover letter to President Roosevelt along with a letter by several other physicists. The letter was about Fermi's and Szilard's research in atomic energy. Roosevelt immediately appointed an "Advisory Committee on Uranium". Fermi's nuclear research had become war work.

Reading about History | I

Read about history in the following resource:

⭐ *Rescue and Redeem* p. 149-169
Note: p. 157 contains a violent image.

You will be writing a narration about the chapter "Marianna Slocum: Plant the Good Seed in Your Heart" that you read about today. To prepare for writing your narration, look back over p. 151-169 in *Rescue and Redeem*. Think about the main idea and the most important moments in this part.

After you have thought about what you will write and how you will begin your narration, turn to Unit 20 in your *Student Notebook*. For more guidance on writing a narration, see *Written Narration Tips* in the Appendix.

In Box 4, write a 12-16 sentence narration about the reading. When you have finished writing, read your sentences out loud to catch any mistakes. Check for the following things: *Did you include **who** or **what topic** the reading was mainly about? Did you include **descriptors** of the important thing(s) that happened? Did you include a **closing sentence**? If not, add those things.* Use the *Written Narration Skills* in the Appendix as a guide for editing the narration.

Key Idea: Marianna Slocum worked among the Tzeltal people in Chiapas, Mexico, as a missionary and a Bible translator. Her fiancé, Bill Bentley, had been a missionary among the Tzetals before her. The Tzeltals were descendents of the Mayans, who worshiped the sun as god and believed that shaman were holy men who could curse or heal others. Martin was Marianna's first convert. He helped her begin to translate the New Testament into the Tzetal language.

President Study | I

⭐ Read p. 50-51 in *Our Presidents...* Then, open your *President Notebook* to William Howard Taft. Use today's reading to help you complete the information about William Howard Taft.

Key Idea: Research William Howard Taft.

Storytime | T/I

Read the following assigned pages:

⭐ *Shadow of His Hand* p. 101-110

Get the bookmark that you placed in your book. Locate the same section of the bookmark that you used on Day 2. Beneath Day 2's entry, write the book title and the page numbers you read today. Select the one remaining response option at the bottom of the bookmark, and place a checkmark next to it. In the blank space under today's pages, respond in writing using your checked option. Keep the bookmark in your book.

Key Idea: Relate to the text in various ways.

Economics | I

Read about economics in the resource below.

⭐ *Common Sense Business for Kids* p. 12-14

After the reading, open your *Student Notebook* to the "Economic Principles" section at the front of your notebook. Under "Economic Principle", write a one or two sentence summary that either defines a new economic term or describes a new economic principle learned from today's reading.

Key Idea: Under-capitalization, or lack of money or capital needed to run a business, is the biggest cause of business failure. Having six months capital in reserve before beginning a business is a good guideline.

Independent History Study | I

Read through the timeline entries from 1901 – 1945 on p. 8-9 of *Rescue and Redeem*. Which names do you recognize in the timeline entries? Which entries leave you wondering about their meaning?

Key Idea: Marianna Slocum was working as a missionary and a Bible translator in Chiapas, Mexico, during WWII.

Learning the Basics

Focus: Language Arts, Math, Bible, Nature Journal, and Science

Biblical Self-Image [T]

Read and discuss with the students the following pages in the resource below.

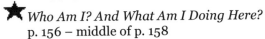 *Who Am I? And What Am I Doing Here?* p. 156 – middle of p. 158

Note: Stop **prior** to reading about the 1962 Cuban Missile Crisis.

Key Idea: When making a decision, it is wise to ask God first. Then, it is important to listen to the Holy Spirit and to seek wise counsel.

Language Arts [S]

Have students complete one studied dictation exercise (see Appendix for passages).

Help students complete one lesson from the following reading program:

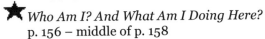 *Drawn into the Heart of Reading*

Help students complete **one** English option.

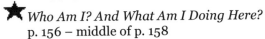 *Progressing With Courage:* Lesson 77

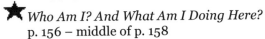 *Progressing With Courage:* Lesson 105 (first half only)

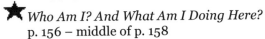 Your own grammar program

Key Idea: Practice language arts skills.

Bible Quiet Time [I]

Bible Study: Complete the assignment below.

 Faith at Work: Lesson 17 – Day Two p. 128-129

Prayer Focus: Refer to **supplication** on "Preparing Your Heart for Prayer". Then, pray a prayer of supplication to make a humble and earnest request of God. Write 'supplication' at the bottom of today's lesson in *Faith at Work* above *Day Three*. Next to it, either list several key phrases or write a sentence to summarize your prayer. Keep "Preparing Your Heart for Prayer" inside your Bible.

Scripture Memory: Recite James 4:1-2.

Music: Refer to p. 58-59 as you sing with Track 7 *"When We All Get to Heaven"* (vs. 1-3).

Key Idea: Read and study Romans 13.

Math Exploration [S]

Choose **one** of the math options listed below.

 Singapore Primary Mathematics 6A/6B, Discovering Mathematics 7A/7B, 8A/8B, No-Nonsense Algebra or *Videotext Algebra*

 Your own math program

Key Idea: Use a step-by-step math program.

Science Exploration [I]

 Copy the Science Lab Form from the Appendix of this guide. Put on your safety glasses, smooth gloves, and smock as recommended on p. 6 of the *Chemistry C500 Experiment Manual*. Then, read the warnings for ammonium iron sulfate and potassium hexacyanoferrate on p. 7. Next, follow the directions to perform "Experiment 19" from p. 36 of the Experiment Manual. **A parent's help is suggested for Experiment 19.** After completing Experiment 19, in the top box of the Science Lab Form write: *What effect will sodium carbonate solution have on Prussian blue?* In the second box of the form, write your hypothesis. Follow the directions for "Experiment 20" on p. 37 of the Experiment Manual and complete the box "Perform an Experiment" on your lab form. Then, follow the arrows to complete the rest of the Science Lab Form. To clean up, refer to "How to Dispose of Waste" on p. 7 and the Basic Rules on p. 6.

Key Idea: Potassium hexacyanoferrate(II) is an indicator, or reagent, for iron. When it's mixed with ammonium iron (III) sulfate, it forms Prussian blue. If allowed to undergo an alkaline reaction, Prussian blue is unstable. Both potassium hexacyanoferrate(II) and ammonium iron(III) sulfate contain iron.

Reading about History | I |

Read about history in the following resource:

★ *Hero Tales: Vol. III* p. 153-163

After today's reading, orally narrate or retell to an adult the **first** portion of text that you read on p. 153-154 of *Hero Tales*. Some possible key words to introduce your narration might be *British rule of India, Hmar, Welsh missionary, Watkin Roberts, Chawnga, Rochunga, mission school, translate, Bible Institute in Scotland, Pioneer Mission, Mawii, Bibles for the World.*

Key Idea: Chawnga Pudaite was converted to Christianity when Watkin Roberts shared the Gospel in Chawnga's Hmar village. Chawnga's vision for his son, Rochunga, was to translate God's Word into his own people's language. Rochunga completed the translation of the New Testament in 1958. He also started the organization Bibles of the World.

History Project | S |

In this unit, you will read about Christians, Hindus, Muslims, and Jews. You will do some research to compare their religions. Open your *Student Notebook* to Unit 21 – Box 7. Today, you will complete the column, "Christianity". Next to the question in each row, list a brief answer under the column "Christianity". To help with your answers, use the following Scriptures for each question topic listed in parentheses: (God) Isaiah 46:5-9; (Christ) Matthew 16:13-17; (Holy book) 2 Timothy 3:16-17; (sin) Romans 3:23; (salvation or life after death) John 3:16.

Key Idea: Rochunga lived in India, which is mainly Hindu, yet he was a Christian.

President Study | I |

★ On *The Presidents* DVD Volume 2, select the Chapter "Cleveland to Taft" and watch **only** Program 6: William Howard Taft. Then, open your *President Notebook* to William Howard Taft and add further information.

Key Idea: Research William Howard Taft.

Storytime | T/I |

Read the following assigned pages:

★ *Shadow of His Hand* p. 111-118
Choose a new section of the bookmark with **three** options at the bottom. At the top of this section of the bookmark, write the book title and the page numbers you read today. Select **one** of the three options at the bottom and place a checkmark next to it. In the blank space under today's pages, respond in writing using your checked option.

Key Idea: Relate to the text in various ways.

Timeline | I |

You will add to the timeline in your *Student Notebook* today. In Unit 21 – Box 1, draw the outline of India and East and West Pakistan, as shown on p. 328 of *The Story of the World*. Label it, *India Is Independent, Pakistan Is Born (August 1947 A.D.).*

In Box 2, draw a white rectangular flag. Color a horizontal blue stripe near the top and bottom of the flag. Then, draw and color a blue star in the center of the flag. Label it, *Israel Declares Independence (May 14, 1948 A.D.).*

In Box 3, outline a canal of water running between two large banks. Label it, *Suez Canal Crisis (1956 A.D.).*

Key Idea: As India gained independence, Pakistan was born, and the United Nations advised that Palestine be partitioned. Soon after this, Israel declared its independence. As Rochunga Pudaite was completing his New Testament in the Hmar language, Egypt was heading for the Suez Crisis.

Independent History Study | I |

Choose **one** of the sets of questions from the sections of *Hero Tales: Vol. III* that you read today to answer orally with an adult. The questions are found on p. 157, 160, and 163.

Key Idea: Rochunga Pudaite was faithful to answer God's call in his life to translate the Bible into the language of the Hmar people.

Learning the Basics

Focus: Language Arts, Math, Bible, Nature Journal, and Science

Nature Journal   I

Read and follow the directions in the resource below.

 Nature Drawing & Journaling: Lesson XXVIII p. 76-77

Note: Do **only** the outdoor sketch described in the first part of p. 77 today. Wait to copy one of Turner's pictures until Unit 21 – Day 3.

<u>Key Idea</u>: Practice creating atmospheric perspective in your drawings.

Language Arts   S

Help students complete one lesson from the following reading program:

 Drawn into the Heart of Reading

Help students complete **one** English option.

 Progressing With Courage: Lesson 78

 Progressing With Courage: Lesson 105 (last half only)

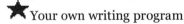 Your own grammar program

Work with the students to complete **one** of the writing options listed below:

★ *Write with the Best: Vol. 2* Unit 5 – Day 11 p. 50 – middle of p. 53

★ Your own writing program

<u>Key Idea</u>: Practice language arts skills.

Bible Quiet Time   I

Bible Study: Read and complete the assigned pages in the following resource:

★ *Faith at Work: Lesson 17 – Day Three* and *Day Four* p. 129-130

Prayer Focus: Refer to **adoration** on "Preparing Your Heart for Prayer". Then, pray a prayer of adoration to worship and honor God. After your prayer, write 'adoration' at the bottom of today's lesson in *Faith at Work* above *Day Five*. Next to 'adoration', either list key phrases or write a sentence to summarize your prayer. Keep "Preparing Your Heart for Prayer" inside your Bible.

Scripture Memory: Read aloud James 4:3 three times from your Bible.

Music: Read the verse and pray the prayer from p. 59 in *Hymns for a Kid's Heart*. Refer to p. 58-59 as you sing with Track 7 *"When We All Get to Heaven"* (vs. 1-4).

<u>Key Idea</u>: Read and study Romans 13.

Math Exploration   S

Choose **one** of the math options listed below (see Appendix for details).

★ *Singapore Primary Mathematics 6A/6B, Discovering Mathematics 7A/7B, 8A/8B, No-Nonsense Algebra* or *Videotext Algebra*

★ Your own math program

<u>Key Idea</u>: Use a step-by-step math program.

Science Exploration   I

★ Read *Atoms in the Family* p. 176-189. After today's reading, add to the list of characteristics about Enrico Fermi that you began in Unit 17 – Day 1. Save the list for the next unit.

<u>Key Idea</u>: In December of 1942, under Enrico Fermi's direction, the first chain reaction and first atomic pile operated successfully. To accomplish the chain reaction, neutrons had to be slowed down to cause uranium fission, and the loss of neutrons into the air or matter had to be reduced. This led to carbon being tried as a moderator and to alternating highly pure graphic and metallic uranium to make an atomic pile.

Learning Through History

Focus: Bible Translation in India, India and Palestine Are Partitioned, and Egypt Rebels

Unit 21 - Day 2

Reading about History | I

Read about history in the following resource:

⭐ *The Story of the World: Vol. 4* p. 328-332

After today's reading, open your *Student Notebook* to Unit 21 – Box 5. Look at the cover of *The New York Times* from January 30, 1948. The headline reads "Gandhi Is Killed by a Hindu; India Shaken, World Mourns; 15 Die in Rioting in Bombay". You will read this article online as part of "Worthy Words" today. Why was it so shocking that a Hindu killed Gandhi?

<u>Key Idea:</u> When India gained independence in 1947, it was partitioned to create the Islamic Republics of East and West Pakistan.

History Project | S

Open your *Student Notebook* to Unit 21 – Box 7. Today, you will do some research to complete the columns, "Hinduism" and "Islam". Use the Internet sites below to help you briefly answer each question in Box 7. You may ask a parent for assistance if needed. Remember, this is meant as an introduction to these religions, not an exhaustive study.
Hinduism: http://www.himalayanacademy.com/basics/nineb/

http://www.thatreligiousstudieswebsite.com/Religious_Studies/World_Faith/Hinduism/hinduism.php

Islam: http://btw.imb.org/beliefs.asp

http://www.islamicwisdom.net/ (On left side, under "Religion", click "Summary of Islamic Principles")

<u>Key Idea:</u> Hindus and Muslims were divided.

President Study | I

⭐ Read p. 52-53 in *Our Presidents...* Then, open your *President Notebook* to Woodrow Wilson. Use today's reading to help you complete the information about Wilson.

<u>Key Idea:</u> Research Woodrow Wilson.

Storytime | T/I

Read the following assigned pages:

⭐ *Shadow of His Hand* p. 119-132

Locate the same section of the bookmark that you used on Day 1. Beneath Day 1's entry, write the book title and the page numbers you read today. Select one of the **two** remaining response options at the bottom of the bookmark, and place a checkmark next to it. In the blank space under today's pages, respond in writing using your checked option.

<u>Key Idea:</u> Relate to the text in various ways.

Worthy Words | T

Find today's article at www.nytimes.com. In the "Search" type "Gandhi Is Killed by a Hindu". Read, analyze, and evaluate the online article about Gandhi's death. Then, answer the following questions on an index card: *According to the article, why did Gandhi's death bring India to a crossroads? What appeal did Prime Minister Nehru make in his radio address after Gandhi's death? Why was India in turmoil even before Gandhi's death?* (Note: Refer to p. 329-332 in *Story of the World*.) *Of what religion was Gandhi a member? What can you learn about Hinduism from the article? How does it differ from Christianity?* Next, meet with a parent to have a Socratic dialogue about the article. Before beginning the dialogue, the parent reads the article out loud. Next, discuss the questions using your notes. All participants should use life experiences/text to support responses.

<u>Key Idea:</u> Partitioning did not bring peace.

Independent History Study | I

Print the "India for Independence" **Teacher's Answer Map** on p. 72 of the *Map Trek* CD. On the map, color E. Pakistan and Pakistan. Place a star on Kashmir, which was divided. File your map in your *Student Notebook*.

<u>Key Idea:</u> Gandhi's death was a blow to peace.

Learning the Basics

Focus: Language Arts, Math, Bible, Nature Journal, and Science

Biblical Self-Image [T]

Our plans intend for the listed pages in *Who Am I? And What Am I Doing Here?* to be read either silently by both you and your child, or read aloud to the child by you. Read and discuss the following pages listed below.

 Who Am I? And What Am I Doing Here? middle of p. 158 – top of p. 160

Key Idea: During the Cuban Missile Crisis in 1962, President Kennedy called and asked President Hoover, President Truman, and President Eisenhower for advice. Even Solomon, the wisest man in the world, sought wise counsel from trusted advisors.

Language Arts [S]

Have students complete one studied dictation exercise (see Appendix for passages).

Help students complete one lesson from the following reading program:

★ *Drawn into the Heart of Reading*

Help students complete **one** English option.

★ *Progressing With Courage:* Lesson 79

★ *Progressing With Courage:* Lesson 106 (first half only)

★ Your own grammar program

Key Idea: Practice language arts skills.

Bible Quiet Time [I]

Bible Study: Read and complete the assigned pages in the following resource:

★ *Faith at Work: Lesson 17 – Day Five* and *Notes* p. 130-133

Prayer Focus: Refer to **confession** on "Preparing Your Heart for Prayer". Then, pray a prayer of confession to admit or acknowledge your sins to God. After your prayer, write 'confession' at the bottom of today's lesson on p. 130 in *Faith at Work*. Next to 'confession', either list key phrases or write a sentence to summarize your prayer. Keep "Preparing Your Heart for Prayer" inside your Bible.

Scripture Memory: Memorize James 4:3 from your Bible and recite it.

Music: Refer to p. 58-59 as you sing with Track 7 *"When We All Get to Heaven"* (vs. 1-4).

Key Idea: Read and study Romans 13.

Math Exploration [S]

Choose **one** of the math options listed below (see Appendix for details).

★ *Singapore Primary Mathematics 6A/6B, Discovering Mathematics 7A/7B, 8A/8B, No-Nonsense Algebra* or *Videotext Algebra*

★ Your own math program

Key Idea: Use a step-by-step math program.

Science Exploration [I]

★ Read *Atoms in the Family* p. 190-199. Note: p. 190 contains an expletive. Then, give a descriptive oral narration to an adult about p. 190-199. A detailed, descriptive narration is the goal. See *Narration Tips* in the Appendix for help as needed.

Key Idea: The first effective atomic pile was built in the Squash Court under the West Stands of the University of Chicago stadium. The pile took the shape of a 26 foot sphere of chunks of uranium imbedded in graphic bricks supported by a square frame. Cadmium rods were inserted in the pile to absorb neutrons and prevent a chain reaction. Then, the rods were all pulled out except one, which was carefully pulled up one foot at a time until the expected chain reaction occurred.

Reading about History | I

Read about history in the following resource:

⭐ *The Story of the World: Vol. 4* p. 332-336

After today's reading, open your *Student Notebook* to Unit 21 – Box 6. Look at the 1946 poster for Keren Hayesod (the Palestine Foundation Fund). This fund was a way for Zionists and non-Zionists to make contributions toward "building" the land of Israel. Zionism means Jewish nationalism, or support for the Jewish country. The poster reads, "Help Him Build Palestine – The Plough Breaks Through". What do you think the captions and pictures on the poster mean?

Key Idea: In 1948, Palestine was partitioned into an Arab country and a Jewish country.

History Project | S

Open your *Student Notebook* to Unit 21 – Box 7. Today, you will do some research to complete the column, "Judaism". This refers to the religion of the Jews. Use the Internet sites below to help you briefly answer each question in Box 7. You may ask a parent for assistance if needed. Remember, this is an introduction to this religion, not an exhaustive study.
Judaism: http://www.jewfaq.org/beliefs.htm

http://www.gotquestions.org/Judaism.html

All religions: (The /0/ below is a zero.)
http://www.vancouver.anglican.ca/Portals/0/
Downloads/Program/EMU-WorldReligions.
pdf

Key Idea: The nation state of Israel is located on the site of part of the twelve tribes of Israel.

State Study | T

⭐ This is an **optional** part of the plans. If you have chosen to study your state using *State History from a Christian Perspective,* do Lesson 18 from the *Master Lesson Plan Book.*

Key Idea: Study your individual state.

Storytime | T/I

Read the following assigned pages:

⭐ *Shadow of His Hand* p. 133-148
Note: p. 137 contains a violent description.

After today's reading, orally narrate or retell the portion of the story that was read today. See *Narration Tips* in the Appendix as needed.

Key Idea: Practice orally narrating, or retelling, a portion of a story.

Geography | I

For today's activities, use the map listed below.

⭐ *Map Trek CD: Missions to Modern Marvels* p. 74-75

Print "The Middle East" Student Map found on p. 75 of the *Map Trek* CD. Refer to or print the *Map Trek* Teacher's Answer Map on p. 74 to guide you as you label each country, mountain, river, and body of water on your Student Map.

Next, use colored pencils to lightly color the Arab countries of Lebanon, Syria, Jordan, Iraq, and Egypt on your Student Map. What do you notice about the location of these countries? These countries attacked Israel on the day that Israel declared independence. File the map in your *Student Notebook.*

Key Idea: Israel declared independence on May 14, 1948. It was attacked by the five surrounding Arab nations on that same day. Yet, Israel was able to win the war, and peace agreements were signed in 1949 (with the exception of Iraq).

Independent History Study | I

Listen to *What in the World? Vol. 3* Disc 4, Track 9: "Decolonization & Israel".

Key Idea: Between 1945-1949, there was a struggle between the Jews, the Arabs, and Great Britain in the Middle East. The United Nations voted for partitioning Palestine, and the British government granted a Jewish state in Palestine. This nation state became Israel.

Learning the Basics
Focus: Language Arts, Math, Bible, Nature Journal, Poetry, and Science

Nature Journal & Poetry | S

The poetry of Longfellow, Wordsworth, and Whitman is scheduled to complement the journaling sessions. Read aloud and discuss today's poem *"The Sun Has Long Been Set"* (see Appendix) with a parent. Then, follow the directions below.

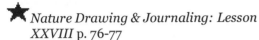 *Nature Drawing & Journaling: Lesson XXVIII* p. 76-77

Note: Today, follow the directions on p. 77 to copy one of Turner's pictures from p. 76.

Key Idea: Practice showing depth in your pictures by merging the landscape with the sky.

Language Arts | S

Have students complete one studied dictation exercise (see Appendix for passages).

Help students complete **one** English option.

⭐ *Progressing With Courage:* Lesson 80

⭐ *Progressing With Courage:* Lesson 106 (last half only)

⭐ Your own grammar program

Work with the students to complete **one** of the writing options listed below:

⭐ *Write with the Best: Vol. 2* Unit 5 – Day 12 p. 53

⭐ Your own writing program

Key Idea: Practice language arts skills.

Bible Quiet Time | I

Bible Study: Read and complete the assigned pages in the following resource:

⭐ *Faith at Work: Lesson 18 – Day One* and *Day Two* p. 134-135 (Note: Refer to p. 131-133 to complete the lesson for *Day One*.)

Prayer Focus: Refer to **thanksgiving** on "Preparing Your Heart for Prayer". Then, pray a prayer of thanksgiving to express gratitude to God for His divine goodness. After your prayer, write 'thanksgiving' at the bottom of today's lesson in *Faith at Work* above *Day Three*. Next to 'thanksgiving', either list key phrases or write a sentence to summarize your prayer. Keep "Preparing Your Heart for Prayer" inside your Bible.

Scripture Memory: Copy James 4:3 in your Common Place Book.

Music: Refer to p. 58-59 as you sing with Track 7 *"When We All Get to Heaven"* (vs. 1-4).

Key Idea: Read and study Romans 13-14.

Math Exploration | S

Choose **one** of the math options listed below (see Appendix for details).

⭐ *Singapore Primary Mathematics 6A/6B, Discovering Mathematics 7A/7B, 8A/8B, No-Nonsense Algebra* or *Videotext Algebra*

⭐ Your own math program

Key Idea: Use a step-by-step math program.

Science Exploration | I

⭐ Read *Atoms in the Family* p. 200-211. Then, write a written narration about p. 200-211. Refer to *Written Narration Tips* in the Appendix for help as needed. Read your written narration out loud after you have finished writing. Refer to *Written Narration Skills* for help in editing.

Key Idea: After the successful chain reaction in nuclear fission at the University of Chicago, the duPont company planned to erect big piles to produce plutonium in Washington. Meanwhile, in Tennessee separation of very fissionable and less fissionable uranium was to take place. Last, the study of problems related to the design and construction of an atomic bomb were to take place in Los Alamos, New Mexico.

Reading about History I

Read about history in the following resource:

⭐ *The Story of the World: Vol. 4* p. 339-343

You will be writing a narration about the chapter *The Suez Crisis.* To prepare for writing your narration, look back over p. 339-343 in *The Story of the World: Vol. 4.* Think about the main idea and the most important moments in this part of the reading.

After you have thought about what you will write and how you will begin your narration, turn to Unit 21 in your *Student Notebook.* For more guidance on writing a narration, see *Written Narration Tips* in the Appendix.

In Box 4, write a 12-16 sentence narration about the reading. When you have finished writing, read your sentences out loud to catch any mistakes. Check for the following things: *Did you include* **who** *or* **what topic** *the reading was mainly about? Did you include* **descriptors** *of the important thing(s) that happened? Did you include a* **closing sentence***? If not, add those things.* Use the *Written Narration Skills* in the Appendix as a guide for editing the narration.

<u>Key Idea</u>: In 1948, Egypt was one of the five Arab countries that invaded newly formed Israel. At that time, King Fu'ad's son, Faruk, was ruling in Egypt. Four years after losing the war, King Faruk was deposed by Gamal Abdel Nasser. When U.S. President Eisenhower refused to give Nasser a loan to build a dam across the Nile River, Nasser closed the Suez Canal. In retaliation, Israel, France, and Britain met to plan an invasion of Egypt. Soon after, the United Nations got involved and ordered France and Britain out of Egypt.

President Study I

⭐ On *The Presidents* DVD Volume 2, select the Chapter "Wilson to Franklin D. Roosevelt" and watch **only** Program 1: Woodrow Wilson. Then, open your *President Notebook* to Woodrow Wilson. Use today's viewing to add further information about Wilson.

<u>Key Idea</u>: Research Woodrow Wilson.

Storytime T/I

Read the following assigned pages:

⭐ *Coming In on a Wing and a Prayer* p. 3-17

Get the bookmark that you placed in your book on Day 2. Locate the same section of the bookmark that you used on Day 2. Beneath Day 2's entry, write the book title and the page numbers you read today. Select the one remaining response option at the bottom of the bookmark, and place a checkmark next to it. In the blank space under today's pages, respond in writing using your checked option. Keep the bookmark in your book.

<u>Key Idea</u>: Relate to the text in various ways.

Economics I

Read about economics in the following resource:

⭐ *Common Sense Business for Kids* p. 15-16

After the reading, open your *Student Notebook* to the "Economic Principles" section at the front of your notebook. Under "Economic Principle", write one line or one sentence that summarizes the economic principle you learned from today's reading.

<u>Key Idea</u>: When considering a business, it is important to weigh start-up costs and operating costs. This is because "there is more to business than what you pay for the product".

Independent History Study I

Open your *Student Notebook* to Unit 21 – Box 7. Read the questions in Box 7 one at a time, and then read the responses to that question for each religion. From a Christian perspective, what significant differences do you notice among the religions that you researched in this unit?

<u>Key Idea</u>: Egypt's state religion is Islam.

Learning the Basics

Focus: Language Arts, Math, Bible, Nature Journal, and Science

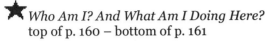

Biblical Self-Image 　 T

Read and discuss with the students the following pages in the resource below.

 ★ *Who Am I? And What Am I Doing Here?* top of p. 160 – bottom of p. 161

Note: Pray "A Prayer" together with the students at the end of today's lesson.

Key Idea: It is important to choose to put Jesus first in our lives through our thoughts, words, actions, and deeds.

Language Arts 　 S

Have students complete one studied dictation exercise (see Appendix for directions and passages).

Help students complete one lesson from the following reading program:

★ *Drawn into the Heart of Reading*

Help students complete **one** English option.

★ *Progressing With Courage:* Lesson 81

★ *Progressing With Courage:* Lesson 107 (first half only)

★ Your own grammar program

Key Idea: Practice language arts skills.

Bible Quiet Time 　 I

Bible Study: Complete the assignment below.

★ *Faith at Work: Lesson 18 – Day Three* p. 135

Prayer Focus: Refer to **supplication** on "Preparing Your Heart for Prayer". Then, pray a prayer of supplication to make a humble and earnest request of God. Write 'supplication' at the bottom of today's lesson in *Faith at Work* above *Day Four*. Next to it, either list several key phrases or write a sentence to summarize your prayer. Keep "Preparing Your Heart for Prayer" inside your Bible.

Scripture Memory: Recite James 4:1-3.

Music: Refer to p. 58-59 as you sing with Track 7 *"When We All Get to Heaven"* (vs. 1-4).

Key Idea: Read and study Romans 14.

Math Exploration 　 S

Choose **one** of the math options listed below.

★ *Singapore Primary Mathematics 6A/6B, Discovering Mathematics 7A/7B, 8A/8B, No-Nonsense Algebra* or *Videotext Algebra*

★ Your own math program

Key Idea: Use a step-by-step math program.

Science Exploration 　 I

★ Copy the Science Lab Form from the Appendix of this guide. Put on your safety glasses, protective gloves, and smock as recommended on p. 6 of the *Chemistry C500 Experiment Manual*. Next, in the top box of the Science Lab Form write: *What will happen to a message written in ammonium iron(III) sulfate solution when it comes into contact with potassium hexacyanoferrate(II) solution?* In the second box of the form, write your hypothesis. Follow the directions for "Experiment 21" on p. 38 of the Experiment Manual and complete the box "Perform an Experiment" on your lab form. **Be sure to wear gloves in step 3 when touching the blotting paper soaked with chemical solution!** Then, follow the arrows to complete the rest of the Science Lab Form. To clean up, refer to "How to Dispose of Waste" on p. 7 and Basic Rules 5, 6, 7, and 11 on p. 6.

Key Idea: Ammonium iron(III) sulfate and potassium hexacyanoferrate(II) react to form Prussian blue.

Learning Through History

Focus: The Marshall Plan, the Berlin Wall, South African Apartheid, and Chairman Mao

Unit 22 - Day 1

Reading about History | S |

Read about history in the following resource:

★ *The Story of the World: Vol. 4* p. 344-349

After today's reading, orally narrate or retell to an adult the text from *The Story of the World* that you read today. As you retell, the adult will write or type your narration. Some possible key words to include in your narration might be *England, Hitler, ration book, bombing, children leave London, 1945 war ends, repairs, Secretary of State Marshall, help Europe recover, twenty billion dollars, Marshall Plan, Stalin, East and West Germany, Berlin Wall.* When the narration is complete, tri-fold the typed or written narration to fit in Unit 22 – Box 7 of the *Student Notebook.* Glue the folded narration in Box 7, so it can be opened and read.

Key Idea: The Marshall Plan gave 20 billion dollars to help European countries rebuild.

History Project | S |

Today, you will begin making war cake. Cakes made during the war were made without rationed items like eggs, milk, and butter. In a medium or large saucepan, add 1 cup shortening, 2 cups water, 1-2 cups raisins (depending on how much you like raisins), 1 tsp. ground cinnamon, 1 tsp. ground nutmeg, 1 tsp. ground allspice, ½ tsp. ground cloves, and 2 cups white sugar. Stir to combine the ingredients over low heat and simmer for 10 minutes. After simmering 10 minutes, remove the pan from the heat, place the lid on the saucepan, set it aside, and cool overnight.

Key Idea: During WWII, eggs, milk, and butter, were rationed and in short supply. So, recipes were made without these items.

Storytime | T/I |

Read the following assigned pages:

★ *Coming In on a Wing and a Prayer* p. 18-25

Get the bookmark that you placed in your book last unit. Choose a new section of the bookmark with **three** options at the bottom. At the top of this section of the bookmark, write the book title and the page numbers you read today. Select **one** of the three options at the bottom and place a checkmark next to it. In the blank space under today's pages, respond in writing using your checked option.

Key Idea: Relate to the text in various ways.

Worthy Words | T |

The text of today's speech can be found at http://www.oecd.org/. Then, type "Marshall Plan Harvard speech" in the "Search". Read, analyze, and evaluate Marshall's speech. After reading the speech, answer the following questions on an index card: *In the opening of the speech, how does Marshall describe the world situation after the war? Why was it difficult for people in the U.S. to understand the situation in Europe? What problems were facing the countries in Europe? Explain why farmers were using land for grazing rather than planting needed crops for food to sell. What does Marshall propose? What is your opinion of the Marshall Plan? Why do you think it was or was not needed? What effect do you think it had upon Europe?* Next, meet with a parent to have a Socratic dialogue about the article. Before beginning the dialogue, the parent reads the online speech out loud. Next, discuss the questions using your notes. Use life experiences or text to support your responses.

Key Idea: The Marshall Plan began in 1948.

Independent History Study | I |

Refer to the map on p. 43 of the *United States History Atlas* to see those countries that were under Communist control in Eastern Europe after WWII. Look at the inset map to see the division of Germany.

Key Idea: Germany was divided into East and West Germany, and the Berlin Wall was built in 1961.

Learning the Basics
Focus: Language Arts, Math, Bible, Nature Journal, and Science

Nature Journal [I]

Read and follow the directions in the resource below.

 ★ *Nature Drawing & Journaling: Lesson XXIX* p. 78-79

Note: Do only the assignment described in paragraph **one** on p. 79 today. Wait to complete the second part of the assignment described in paragraph 2 until Unit 22 – Day 3.

Key Idea: Practice shading grass and meadows.

Language Arts [S]

Help students complete one lesson from the following reading program:

★ *Drawn into the Heart of Reading*

Help students complete **one** English option.

★ *Progressing With Courage:* Lesson 82

★ *Progressing With Courage:* Lesson 107 (last half only)

★ Your own grammar program

Work with the students to complete **one** of the writing options listed below:

★ *Write with the Best: Vol. 2* Unit 5 – Day 13 p. 53-54

★ Your own writing program

Key Idea: Practice language arts skills.

Bible Quiet Time [I]

Bible Study: Read and complete the assigned pages in the following resource:

★ *Faith at Work: Lesson 18 – Day Four* p. 135-136

Prayer Focus: Refer to **adoration** on "Preparing Your Heart for Prayer". Then, pray a prayer of adoration to worship and honor God. After your prayer, write 'adoration' at the bottom of today's lesson in *Faith at Work* above *Day Five*. Next to 'adoration', either list key phrases or write a sentence to summarize your prayer. Keep "Preparing Your Heart for Prayer" inside your Bible.

Scripture Memory: Read aloud James 4:4 three times from your Bible.

Music: Read p. 61-62 in *Hymns for a Kid's Heart*. Refer to p. 64 as you sing with Track 8 *"We're Marching to Zion"* (verse 1).

Key Idea: Read and study Romans 14.

Math Exploration [S]

Choose **one** of the math options listed below (see Appendix for details).

★ *Singapore Primary Mathematics 6A/6B, Discovering Mathematics 7A/7B, 8A/8B, No-Nonsense Algebra* or *Videotext Algebra*

★ Your own math program

Key Idea: Use a step-by-step math program.

Science Exploration [I]

★ Read *Atoms in the Family* p. 212-225. After today's reading, on a new sheet of paper, list the characteristics that you learned about Niels Bohr from today's reading.

Key Idea: Niels Bohr was a Nobel Prize-winning atomic physicist. He came from Copenhagen, Denmark, during WWII and eventually ended up at Los Alamos, New Mexico, under the secret cover name Mr. Baker.

Learning Through History

Focus: The Marshall Plan, the Berlin Wall, South African Apartheid, and Chairman Mao

Unit 22 - Day 2

Reading about History | I

Read about history in the following resource:

★ *The Story of the World: Vol. 4* p. 350 – top of p. 355

Open your *Student Notebook* to Unit 22 – Box 5 that contains a poster against apartheid in South Africa. Use a dictionary to look up the meaning of "apartheid". Based on the meaning of apartheid, what do you think this poster is saying?

<u>Key Idea</u>: After WWII, the National Party gained power in South Africa. This political party believed in apartheid, or "apartness" for the races in South Africa. It imposed laws that oppressed the nonwhites. The nonwhites formed the African National Congress and used nonviolent resistance to fight back.

History Project | S

To finish making your war cake, grease a 9" x 13" baking pan. Then, preheat your oven to 350 degrees. Remove the lid from the saucepan containing your cooled raisin mixture from Day 1. If there is some hardened shortening on top of the raisin mixture, spoon it off. Then, stir into the raisin mixture, 3 cups white flour, 1 tsp. baking soda, and a pinch of salt. Stir until just combined. Do not over stir! Pour the cake batter into your 9" x 13" pan. Bake your cake at 350 degrees for 45 minutes. This cake actually gets better when it is a day old. Try some of the cake today with whipped topping. Then, on Day 3, have the remaining cake with tea. You may wish to add one of the frostings mentioned on Day 3 to give the cake a different taste.

<u>Key Idea</u>: South Africa has a lot of poverty.

President Study | I

★ Read p. 54-55 in *Our Presidents...* Then, open your *President Notebook* to Warren G. Harding. Use today's reading to help you complete the information about Harding.

<u>Key Idea</u>: Research Warren G. Harding.

Storytime | T/I

Read the following assigned pages:

★ *Coming In on a Wing and a Prayer* p. 26-39

Get the bookmark that you placed in your book. Locate the same section of the bookmark that you used on Day 1. Beneath Day 1's entry, write the book title and the page numbers you read today. Select one of the **two** remaining response options at the bottom of the bookmark, and place a checkmark next to it. In the blank space under today's pages, respond in writing using your checked option.

<u>Key Idea</u>: Relate to the text in various ways.

Geography | I

For today's activities, use the map listed below.

★ *Student Notebook* Unit 22 – Box 8

Refer to the map on p. 350 of *The Story of the World* to help you label the map of Africa in Box 8 of your *Student Notebook*. In the "key" at the bottom of Box 8 use colored pencils to color a different color next to each of the countries in the key.

Next, refer to the map on p. 118 of *The Story of the World* to help you color the map in Box 8 to show the European countries that controlled the various parts of Africa in 1884. Make sure to also refer to the key in Box 8 to guide you as you color your map. Only Liberia and Ethiopia were not under foreign control at that time. As you look at Box 8, are you surprised that South Africa ended up under the control of the National Party, or the white race?

<u>Key Idea</u>: South Africa became more divided.

Independent History Study | I

Read the timeline entries from 1938-1948 on p. 484-485 of *The Story of the World*. Notice the major events that occurred in this decade!

<u>Key Idea</u>: Boundaries, political parties, and world economies changed much in 10 years.

Biblical Self-Image [T]

Our plans intend for the listed pages in *Who Am I? And What Am I Doing Here?* to be read either silently by both you and your child, or read aloud to the child by you. With this in mind, read and discuss the following pages listed below.

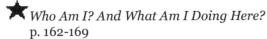 *Who Am I? And What Am I Doing Here?* p. 162-169

Key Idea: Hindus believe in many different gods and goddesses. They also believe in the cycle of rebirth and reincarnation. According to Hindu tradition, parents in India often choose a husband or wife for their child.

Language Arts [S]

Have students complete one studied dictation exercise (see Appendix for passages).

Help students complete one lesson from the following reading program:

★ *Drawn into the Heart of Reading*

Help students complete **one** English option.

★ *Progressing With Courage:* Lesson 83

★ *Progressing With Courage:* Lesson 108 (first half only)

★ Your own grammar program

Key Idea: Practice language arts skills.

Bible Quiet Time [I]

Bible Study: Read and complete the assigned pages in the following resource:

★ *Faith at Work: Lesson 18 – Day Five* and *Notes* p. 136-140

Prayer Focus: Refer to **confession** on "Preparing Your Heart for Prayer". Then, pray a prayer of confession to admit or acknowledge your sins to God. After your prayer, write 'confession' at the bottom of today's lesson on p. 136 in *Faith at Work*. Next to 'confession', either list key phrases or write a sentence to summarize your prayer. Keep "Preparing Your Heart for Prayer" inside your Bible.

Scripture Memory: Memorize James 4:4 from your Bible and recite it.

Music: Refer to p. 64 as you sing with Track 8 *"We're Marching to Zion"* (verse 1).

Key Idea: Read and study Romans 14.

Math Exploration [S]

Choose **one** of the math options listed below (see Appendix for details).

★ *Singapore Primary Mathematics 6A/6B, Discovering Mathematics 7A/7B, 8A/8B, No-Nonsense Algebra* or *Videotext Algebra*

★ Your own math program

Key Idea: Use a step-by-step math program.

Science Exploration [I]

★ Read *Atoms in the Family* p. 226-236. Note: p. 233 contains a graphic description of the results of radiation exposure. Give a summary oral narration to an adult about p. 226-236. The oral narration should be no longer than 6-8 sentences and should summarize the reading. As you narrate, hold up one finger for each sentence shared. The focus of the narration should be on the big ideas, rather than on the details. See *Narration Tips* in the Appendix.

Key Idea: Often those working at Los Alamos were exposed to low levels of radiation through tube alloy, or uranium, and plutonium. In 1945, a critical assembly nuclear reactor passed its critical size, and a noncontrolled chain reaction began exposing a man to enormous amounts of radiation.

Learning Through History

Focus: The Marshall Plan, the Berlin Wall, South African Apartheid, and Chairman Mao

Unit 22 - Day 3

Reading about History | I |

Read about history in the following resource:

★ *The Story of the World: Vol. 4* p. 355-360
After today's reading, open your *Student Notebook* to Unit 22 - Box 6, which shows a Communist Party propaganda poster from 1952 in China. The top caption reads, "The happy life that Chairman Mao has given us." Notice the image of Chairman Mao on the wall. Based on what you read today, do you think that Chairman Mao truly gave families a happy life?

<u>Key Idea</u>: In 1949, the Chinese Communist Party overthrew the Kuomintang government.

History Project | S |

Hopefully, you still have some war cake left. If so, you may wish to top it with one of the following icings. Then, have cake with tea.

Recipe 1: Cream Cheese Icing
In a large bowl, mix 4 oz. of softened cream cheese, ¼ cup softened margarine, 1½ cups powdered sugar, ½ Tbsp. milk, and 1 tsp. vanilla extract. Beat ingredients with mixer until creamy. Then, drizzle over cake.

Recipe 2: Cinnamon Frosting
Mix ½ cup softened butter on low speed until creamy. Add 1 cup powdered sugar and beat on low. Then, add 1 more cup of powdered sugar and beat on low. Mix in 3 Tbsp. milk, 1 tsp. vanilla extract, and 1 tsp. ground cinnamon. If the frosting is too thick, add a tiny splash of milk. If the frosting is too runny, add one Tbsp. of powdered sugar. Frost cake.

<u>Key Idea</u>: Rationing took place all over the world during WWII. So, many families had to get used to cooking without usual ingredients.

State Study | T |

★ This is an **optional** part of the plans. If you have chosen to study your state using *State History from a Christian Perspective*, do Lesson 19 from the *Master Lesson Plan Book*.

<u>Key Idea</u>: Study your individual state.

Storytime | T/I |

Read the following assigned pages:

★ *Coming In on a Wing...* p. 40-55
After today's reading, orally narrate or retell the portion of the story that was read today. See *Narration Tips* in the Appendix as needed.

<u>Key Idea</u>: Practice narrating part of a story.

Timeline | I |

Add to the timeline in your *Student Notebook* today. In Unit 22 – Box 1, draw and color rows of corn or wheat growing in a field. Label it, *Marshall Plan (April 1948-1952 A.D.)*.

In Box 2, draw and color a red star to signify the Communist Party of China. Label it, *Mao Zedong Controls China (1949-1976 A.D.)*.

In Box 3, draw and color a concrete wall. Label it, *Berlin Wall Is Built (August 30, 1961 A.D.)*.

<u>Key Idea</u>: As the Marshall Plan went into effect to aid countries in Europe, Mao Zedong was seizing power in China. Meanwhile, Germany was divided and people were defecting from East Germany into West Germany. Eventually, the Berlin Wall was built to prevent defections.

Independent History Study | I |

Either with your parent, **or** after your parent has previewed "The Wall" at one of the sites below, watch the 9-minute 1962 documentary about the Berlin Wall. This will help you better understand how communism affected the lives of those who lived under this type of rule. Be warned that "The Wall" includes footage of the shooting death of Peter Fechte, an eighteen year old boy trying to escape East Berlin.
http://archive.org/details/the_wall_1962

http://sharky-fourbees.blogspot.com/2012/04/wall-1962-documentary-about-berlin-wall.html (Then, click the play arrow.)

Or, in a search engine, type "The Wall (1962) documentary".

<u>Key Idea</u>: Communism spread to many places.

Learning the Basics
Focus: Language Arts, Math, Bible, Nature Journal, Poetry, and Science

Nature Journal & Poetry | S

The poetry of Longfellow, Wordsworth, and Whitman is scheduled to complement the journaling sessions. Read aloud and discuss today's poem *"Splendour in the Grass"* (see Appendix) with a parent. Then, follow the directions below.

★ *Nature Drawing & Journaling: Lesson XXIX* p. 79

Note: Do only the assignment described in paragraph **two** on p. 79 today.

Key Idea: Practice drawing and shading grass.

Language Arts | S

Have students complete one studied dictation exercise (see Appendix for passages).

Help students complete **one** English option.

★ *Progressing With Courage:* Lesson 84

★ *Progressing With Courage:* Lesson 108 (last half only)

★ Your own grammar program

Work with the students to complete **one** of the writing options listed below:

★ *Write with the Best: Vol. 2* Unit 5 – Day 14 p. 54

★ Your own writing program

Key Idea: Practice language arts skills.

Bible Quiet Time | I

Bible Study: Read and complete the assigned pages in the following resource:

★ *Faith at Work: Lesson 19 – Day One* p. 141 (Note: Refer to p. 137-140 to complete the lesson.)

Prayer Focus: Refer to **thanksgiving** on "Preparing Your Heart for Prayer". Then, pray a prayer of thanksgiving to express gratitude to God for His divine goodness. After your prayer, write 'thanksgiving' at the bottom of today's lesson in *Faith at Work* above *Day Two*. Next to 'thanksgiving', either list key phrases or write a sentence to summarize your prayer. Keep "Preparing Your Heart for Prayer" inside your Bible.

Scripture Memory: Copy James 4:4 in your Common Place Book.

Music: Refer to p. 64 as you sing with Track 8 *"We're Marching to Zion"* (verse 1).

Key Idea: Read and study Romans 14.

Math Exploration | S

Choose **one** of the math options listed below (see Appendix for details).

★ *Singapore Primary Mathematics 6A/6B, Discovering Mathematics 7A/7B, 8A/8B, No-Nonsense Algebra* or *Videotext Algebra*

★ Your own math program

Key Idea: Use a step-by-step math program.

Science Exploration | I

★ Read *Atoms in the Family* p. 237-249. Then, write a written narration about p. 237-249. Refer to *Written Narration Tips* in the Appendix for help as needed. Read your written narration out loud after you have finished writing. Refer to *Written Narration Skills* for help in editing.

Key Idea: On July 16, in southern New Mexico at Alamogordo, the first atomic bomb was exploded. The bomb exploded with an intensely bright light, followed by a blast of air and a sustained mighty roar. In August 6, 1945, an atomic bomb was dropped on Hiroshima. When Japan refused to surrender, a second atomic bomb was dropped on Nagasaki on August 9. Japan surrendered on August 14.

Reading about History | I |

Read about history in the following resource:

 The Story of the World: Vol. 4 p. 362-367

You will be writing a narration about the chapter *Ho Chi Minh and the Viet Minh*. To prepare for writing your narration, look back over p. 362-367 in *The Story of the World: Vol. 4*. Think about the main idea and the most important moments in this part of the reading.

After you have thought about what you will write and how you will begin your narration, turn to Unit 22 in your *Student Notebook*. For more guidance on writing a narration, see *Written Narration Tips* in the Appendix.

In Box 4, write a 12-16 sentence narration about the reading. When you have finished writing, read your sentences out loud to catch any mistakes. Check for the following things: *Did you include **who** or **what topic** the reading was mainly about? Did you include **descriptors** of the important thing(s) that happened? Did you include a **closing sentence**? If not, add those things.* Use the *Written Narration Skills* in the Appendix as a guide for editing the narration.

Key Idea: During WWII, French Indochina fell under Japanese control. Nguyen Ai Quoc, or Ho Chi Minh, led the Vietnamese people and the Indochinese Communist Party against French and Japanese rule in Indochina. His forces were called the Viet Minh. The Viet Minh also worked as spies for Allied forces against the Japanese. When Japan surrendered to the Allied forces in August 1945, they gave up control of Vietnam. In 1946, the French Indochina War began between the Vietnamese and the French.

President Study | I |

 On *The Presidents* DVD Volume 2, select the Chapter "Wilson to Franklin D. Roosevelt" and watch **only** Program 2: Warren G. Harding. Then, open your *President Notebook* to Warren G. Harding. Use today's viewing to add further information about Harding.

Key Idea: Research Warren G. Harding.

Storytime | T/I |

Read the following assigned pages:

 I Am David p. 1-22

Get the bookmark that you placed in your book on Day 2. Locate the same section of the bookmark that you used on Day 2. Beneath Day 2's entry, write the book title and the page numbers you read today. Select the one remaining response option at the bottom of the bookmark, and place a checkmark next to it. In the blank space under today's pages, respond in writing using your checked option.

Key Idea: Relate to the text in various ways.

Economics | I |

Read about economics in the resource below.

 Common Sense Business for Kids p. 17-20

After the reading, open your *Student Notebook* to the "Economic Principles" section at the front of your notebook. Under "Economic Principle", write a one or two sentence summary for the economic principle you learned from today's reading.

Key Idea: Market potential takes into account your potential customer base and the number of people that might buy your product. Two stores aren't always better than one profitable store if there aren't enough customers.

Independent History Study | I |

On the map on p. 362 of *The Story of the World*, find Cochin China, which was ruled by the French. Then, find the city of Hanoi, which was the capital of Vietnam. Last, find the line dividing North Vietnam and South Vietnam.

Key Idea: After the French Indochina War ended, Vietnam was divided in half. Ho Chi Minh and the Communist Party ruled North Vietnam. South Vietnam was to be its own country with elections of its own and its own president.

Learning the Basics
Focus: Language Arts, Math, Bible, Nature Journal, and Science

Biblical Self-Image | T |

Read and discuss with the students the following pages in the resource below.

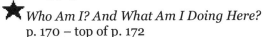 *Who Am I? And What Am I Doing Here?* p. 170 – top of p. 172

Key Idea: Paul compared the Christian life to a race. In preparation for the race, we need daily prayer, Bible study, and worship. This helps us avoid activities that distract us from God's call. Then, we can focus on the race.

Language Arts | S |

Have students complete one studied dictation exercise (see Appendix for passages).

Help students complete one lesson from the following reading program:

★ *Drawn into the Heart of Reading*

Help students complete **one** English option.

★ *Progressing With Courage:* Lesson 85

★ *Progressing With Courage:* Lesson 109 (first half only)

★ Your own grammar program

Key Idea: Practice language arts skills.

Bible Quiet Time | I |

Bible Study: Complete the assignment below.

★ *Faith at Work: Lesson 19 – Day Two* p. 141-142

Prayer Focus: Refer to **supplication** on "Preparing Your Heart for Prayer". Then, pray a prayer of supplication to make a humble and earnest request of God. Write 'supplication' at the bottom of today's lesson in *Faith at Work* above *Day Three*. Next to it, either list several key phrases or write a sentence to summarize your prayer. Keep "Preparing Your Heart for Prayer" inside your Bible.

Scripture Memory: Recite James 4:1-4.

Music: Refer to p. 64 as you sing with Track 8 *"We're Marching to Zion"* (verse 1).

Key Idea: Read and study Romans 15.

Math Exploration | S |

Choose **one** of the math options listed below.

★ *Singapore Primary Mathematics 6A/6B, Discovering Mathematics 7A/7B, 8A/8B, No-Nonsense Algebra* or *Videotext Algebra*

★ Your own math program

Key Idea: Use a step-by-step math program.

Science Exploration | I |

★ Copy the Science Lab Form from the Appendix of this guide. Put on your safety glasses, smooth gloves, and smock as recommended on p. 6 of the *Chemistry C500 Experiment Manual*. Then, follow the directions to perform "Experiment 22" from p. 39 of the Experiment Manual. To clean up, refer to "How to Dispose of Waste" on p. 7 and the Basic Rules on p. 6. After completing Experiment 22, in the top box of the Science Lab Form write: *What will happen when an iron nail is placed in a potassium hexacyanoferrate(II) solution?* In the second box of the form, write your hypothesis. Follow the directions for "Experiment 23" on p. 40 of the Experiment Manual and complete the box "Perform an Experiment" on your lab form. Then, follow the arrows to complete the rest of the Science Lab Form. After that, read p. 41. To clean up, refer to "How to Dispose of Waste" on p. 7 and the Basic Rules on p. 6.

Key Idea: Potassium hexacyanoferrate(II) is an indicator, or reagent, for iron. Yet, it only reacts to iron that is dissolved, so it did not react to the iron nail.

Learning Through History

Focus: Brother Andrew, the Berlin Blockade, and the Vietnam War

Reading about History | I

Read about history in the following resource:

 ★ *All American History: Vol. II* p. 369 – top of p. 374

After today's reading, orally narrate or retell to an adult the portion of text that you read today from *All American History*. Some possible key words to include in your narration might be *Eastern Europe, communist control, iron curtain, Soviet Union, Western Europe, Truman Doctrine, Marshall Plan, economic recovery, Harry S. Truman, "The Buck Stops Here", National Security Act, whistle-stop campaign, Fair Deal, Dwight D. Eisenhower, "I Like Ike", war hero, NATO, Berlin blockade and airlift,* and *Warsaw Pact.*

Key Idea: After the war, much of Eastern Europe fell under Soviet Communist control. After the death of Franklin Delano Roosevelt, Truman became the next U.S. President. The Truman Doctrine and the Marshall Plan gave military and economic aid to European countries that resisted communism. In 1952, Dwight D. Eisenhower was elected president.

History Project | S

Print "The Cold War" **Teacher's Answer Map** from p. 78 of the *Map Trek* CD. To signify "Warsaw Pact" countries, color those countries labeled with a 'W' red. To signify "NATO Countries", color those countries labeled with an 'N' blue. To signify "Neutral Countries", color those countries not labeled with any letter yellow. Then, refer to the *United States History Atlas* p. 43 to see the division of NATO and Warsaw Pact countries.

Key Idea: The world was divided after WWII.

President Study | I

★ Read p. 56-57 in *Our Presidents...* Then, open your *President Notebook* to Calvin Coolidge. Use today's reading to help you complete the information about Coolidge.
Key Idea: Research Calvin Coolidge.

Storytime | T/I

Read the following assigned pages:

★ *I Am David* p. 23-44

Get the bookmark that you placed in your book. Choose a new section of the bookmark with **three** options at the bottom. At the top of this section of the bookmark, write the book title and the page numbers you read today. Select **one** of the three options at the bottom and place a checkmark next to it. In the blank space under today's pages, respond in writing using your checked option.

Key Idea: Relate to the text in various ways.

Timeline | I

You will be adding to the timeline in your *Student Notebook* today. In Unit 23 – Box 1, draw a cargo plane. Label it, *Berlin Blockade and Airlift (June 28, 1948 – May 12, 1949 A.D.).*

In Box 2, draw the outline of Korea. Refer to the map on p. 44 of the *United States History Atlas* to guide you as you draw. Label the box, *Korean War (1950-1953 A.D.).*

In Box 3, outline and color a Bible. Label it, *Brother Andrew – Iron Curtain Bible Smuggler (1957-1967 A.D.).*

Key Idea: Soon after the war ended, the Soviet Union formed a blockade in East Germany. Less than a year later, communist controlled North Koreans marched into South Vietnam.

Independent History Study | I

Richard Nixon was Dwight D. Eisenhower's vice presidential nominee. Six weeks before the presidential election, Nixon was accused of taking campaign funds for his personal use. Read Nixon's speech on p. 190-191 from the *Book of Great American Speeches for Young People* to see his reply.

Key Idea: Nixon and Eisenhower won the 1952 election in a landslide.

Learning the Basics
Focus: Language Arts, Math, Bible, Nature Journal, and Science

Nature Journal | I

Read and follow the directions in the resource below.

 ★ *Nature Drawing & Journaling: Lesson XXX* p. 80-81

Note: Do only the assignment described in paragraph **one** on p. 81 today. Wait to complete the second part of the assignment described in paragraph 2 until Unit 23 – Day 3.

Key Idea: Practice shading skies.

Language Arts | S

Help students complete one lesson from the following reading program:

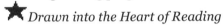 ★ *Drawn into the Heart of Reading*

Help students complete **one** English option.

★ *Progressing With Courage:* Lesson 86

★ *Progressing With Courage:* Lesson 109 (last half only)

★ Your own grammar program

Work with the students to complete **one** of the writing options listed below:

★ *Write with the Best: Vol. 2* Unit 5 – Day 15 p. 54-55

★ Your own writing program

Key Idea: Practice language arts skills.

Bible Quiet Time | I

Bible Study: Read and complete the assigned pages in the following resource:

★ *Faith at Work: Lesson 19 – Day Three* and *Day Four* p. 142

Prayer Focus: Refer to **adoration** on "Preparing Your Heart for Prayer". Then, pray a prayer of adoration to worship and honor God. After your prayer, write 'adoration' at the bottom of today's lesson in *Faith at Work* above *Day Five*. Next to 'adoration', either list key phrases or write a sentence to summarize your prayer. Keep "Preparing Your Heart for Prayer" inside your Bible.

Scripture Memory: Read aloud James 4:5 three times from your Bible.

Music: Read p. 63 in *Hymns for a Kid's Heart*. Refer to p. 64-65 as you sing with Track 8 *"We're Marching to Zion"* (vs. 1-2).

Key Idea: Read and study Romans 15.

Math Exploration | S

Choose **one** of the math options listed below (see Appendix for details).

★ *Singapore Primary Mathematics 6A/6B, Discovering Mathematics 7A/7B, 8A/8B, No-Nonsense Algebra* or *Videotext Algebra*

★ Your own math program

Key Idea: Use a step-by-step math program.

Science Exploration | I

★ Read *Atoms in the Family* p. 250-265. After today's reading, on a new sheet of paper, make a list of facts that you read about Bruno Pontecorvo in today's reading on p. 250-257.

Key Idea: Bruno Pontecorvo was one of the five scientists, along with Fermi, who discovered the slow-neutron process in 1934. Pontecorvo began studying with Joliot-Curie in Paris in 1936 where he married a Swedish girl. When the Nazis reached Paris during WWII, he fled France into Spain and then into Portugal. He sailed for the U.S. in 1940. In 1949, he joined the British atomic project at Harwell. As a nuclear physicist and a Communist, his defection to Russia on August 31, 1950, was alarming.

Reading about History | I

Read about history in the following resource:

★ *Hero Tales: Vol. III* p. 33-43
After today's reading, open your *Student Notebook* to Unit 23. Look at the 1948 film poster in Box 5 titled "The Iron Curtain". The film was about Igor Gouzenko, a clerk at the Soviet Embassy in Canada, who defected in 1945 with documents detailing Soviet spy activities in the West. Why do you think the film was titled "The Iron Curtain"? Reread the first paragraph on p. 369 of *All American History* to understand the term "iron curtain".

Key Idea: Andrew van der Bijl joined the Dutch army to fight in the East Indies after Holland was liberated from the Germans in 1944. He later became known as "Brother Andrew" when he began smuggling Bibles behind the Iron Curtain in 1955.

Storytime | T/I

Read the following assigned pages:

★ *I Am David* p. 45-69
Get the bookmark that you placed in your book. Locate the same section of the bookmark that you used on Day 1. Beneath Day 1's entry, write the book title and the page numbers you read today. Select one of the **two** remaining response options at the bottom of the bookmark, and place a checkmark next to it. In the blank space under today's pages, respond in writing using your checked option.

Key Idea: Relate to the text in various ways.

History Project | S

Today, read an interview with Brother Andrew from his ministry's website "Open Doors": http://www.opendoorsuk.org/resources/berlin wall/interviews.php
Then, pray Psalm 46:1 for the persecuted church that God may be their "refuge and strength", and "an ever-present help in times of trouble". Last, you may wish to consider writing a letter to encourage a persecuted believer through "Open Doors" at http://www.opendoorsuk.org/resources/letter/
Note: The address to send letters is in the U.K. Be sure to read the "simple guidelines".

Key Idea: Believers are still persecuted today.

Geography | I

For today's activities, use the map listed below.

★ *Map Trek CD: Missions to Modern Marvels* p. 70
Print the "Growth of Communism" **Teacher's Answer Map** found on p. 70 of the *Map Trek* CD. Refer to the *United States History Atlas* p. 43 to help you label the Pacific Ocean, the Arctic Ocean, and the Atlantic Ocean on your map. Next, on your Teacher's Answer Map, lightly shade in orange each country that is shown in **dark** orange on p. 43 of the *United States History Atlas*. These countries made up the Eastern Bloc. Then, use the inset box on p. 43 of the *United States History Atlas* to help you label each of the orange countries with the year that they came under Communist control. Make sure to include the note on Yugoslavia. File the map in your *Student Notebook*.

Key Idea: The borders of the Eastern Bloc countries formed the "iron curtain".

President Study | I

★ On *The Presidents* DVD Volume 2, select the Chapter "Wilson to Franklin D. Roosevelt" and watch **only** Program 3: Calvin Coolidge. Then, open your *President Notebook* to Calvin Coolidge and add further information.

Key Idea: Research Calvin Coolidge.

Independent History Study | I

Listen to *What in the World? Vol. 3* Disc 4, Track 7: "Brother Andrew & the Berlin Airlift".

Key Idea: Behind the "iron curtain", communism was a one-party system that denied freedom of religion, of speech, and of the press.

Learning the Basics
Focus: Language Arts, Math, Bible, Nature Journal, and Science

Biblical Self-Image   [T]

Read and discuss with the students the following pages in the resource below.

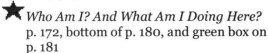 *Who Am I? And What Am I Doing Here?* p. 172, bottom of p. 180, and green box on p. 181

Note: Wait to read the story on p. 173-180 until Unit 23 – Day 4.

Key Idea: Bows and arrows were used by warriors for thousands of years. The Bible compares a man's children to arrows in a warrior's hands. How are the two similar?

Language Arts   [S]

Have students complete one studied dictation exercise (see Appendix for directions and passages).

Help students complete one lesson from the following reading program:

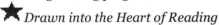 *Drawn into the Heart of Reading*

Help students complete **one** English option.

★ *Progressing With Courage:* Lesson 87

★ *Progressing With Courage:* Lesson 110 (first half only)

★ Your own grammar program

Key Idea: Practice language arts skills.

Bible Quiet Time   [I]

Bible Study: Read and complete the assigned pages in the following resource:

★ *Faith at Work: Lesson 19 – Day Five* and *Notes* p. 142-146

Prayer Focus: Refer to **confession** on "Preparing Your Heart for Prayer". Then, pray a prayer of confession to admit or acknowledge your sins to God. After your prayer, write 'confession' at the bottom of today's lesson on p. 142 in *Faith at Work*. Next to 'confession', either list key phrases or write a sentence to summarize your prayer. Keep "Preparing Your Heart for Prayer" inside your Bible.

Scripture Memory: Memorize James 4:5 from your Bible and recite it.

Music: Refer to p. 64-65 as you sing with Track 8 *"We're Marching to Zion"* (vs. 1-2).

Key Idea: Read and study Romans 15.

Math Exploration   [S]

Choose **one** of the math options listed below (see Appendix for details).

★ *Singapore Primary Mathematics 6A/6B, Discovering Mathematics 7A/7B, 8A/8B, No-Nonsense Algebra* or *Videotext Algebra*

★ Your own math program

Key Idea: Use a step-by-step math program.

Science Exploration   [I]

★ Read *Albert Einstein and the Theory of Relativity* p. 1-23. Note: p. 21-22 includes a beer drinking contest that is portrayed in a negative light. After reading the chapters, read the definition for *alternating current* and *direct current* on p. 174. Then, read the definition for *dynamo* and *electron* on p. 175. Next, either discuss question 1, 3, and 5 on p. 178 with a parent, or write answers to the questions on paper.

Key Idea: When Albert Einstein was a young child in Germany, electric lights were a new invention. Scientists continued to make discoveries about electrons, electric charge, and electric current.

Learning Through History

Focus: Brother Andrew, the Berlin Blockade, and the Vietnam War

Reading about History [I]

Read about history in the following resources:

⭐ *All American History: Vol. II* p. 374-383

After today's reading, open your *Student Notebook* to Unit 23. Box 7 shows a picture of General MacArthur during WWII as American forces swept into the Philippines. In Box 8, make a bulleted list of facts about MacArthur from your reading. To help you, refer to p. 343 of *All American History,* which mentions MacArthur's role in WWII. Then, refer to p. 374, which refers to his role as commander of the Allied occupation of Japan. Last, refer to p. 375-377 for his role in the Korean War.

Key Idea: After WWII, Japan was occupied by Allied forces, and Korea was divided into two occupation zones. In Korea, the northern zone was occupied by Soviet troops, and the southern zone was occupied by American troops. This resulted in North Korea becoming Communist and South Korea becoming Democratic. In 1950, Communist troops from North Korea invaded South Korea leading to the Korean "Conflict". An armistice was signed on July 27, 1953.

History Project [S]

Print "The Korean War" Student Map from p. 81 of the *Map Trek* CD. To help you label your Student Map, refer to or print the *Map Trek* Teacher's Answer Map p. 80. Then, refer to p. 44 of the *United States History Atlas* for a chronological view of the Korean War. Use your finger to trace the paths of the U.N. and the North Korean forces in order by date. Last, view Unit 23 – Box 9 in the *Student Notebook*.

Key Idea: The Korean War lasted three years.

State Study [T]

⭐ This is an **optional** part of the plans. If you have chosen to study your state using *State History from a Christian Perspective,* do Lesson 20 from the *Master Lesson Plan Book*.

Key Idea: Study your individual state.

Storytime [T/I]

Read the following assigned pages:

⭐ *I Am David* p. 70-95

After today's reading, orally narrate or retell the portion of the story that was read today. See *Narration Tips* in the Appendix as needed.

Key Idea: Practice orally narrating, or retelling, a portion of a story.

Worthy Words [T]

Read, analyze, and evaluate the speech below.

⭐ *Book of Great American Speeches for Young People* p. 204-205

After reading the speech, answer the following questions on an index card: *The motto at West Point Military Academy is "Duty, Honor, Country". Look up and write down the definition for each of these three words. Why do you think these words were chosen for the motto at West Point Military Academy? What does MacArthur emphasize as the mission of those graduating from West Point? How does this mission contrast with being a "warmonger"? What is the meaning of the quote of Plato's used by MacArthur in this speech? Do you agree with this quote? From the end of his speech, what do you think MacArthur is remembering as he nears life's end? What wisdom do you desire to pass on before your life is over?* Next, meet with a parent to have a Socratic dialogue about the speech. Before beginning the dialogue, the parent reads the speech out loud. Next, discuss the questions using your notes. All participants should use life experiences or text to support responses.

Key Idea: General Douglas MacArthur was the commander of the Allied occupation of Japan.

Independent History Study [I]

Listen to *What in the World? Vol. 3* Disc 4, Track 8: "Communist China & Korean War".

Key Idea: The Korean War began in 1950.

Learning the Basics

Focus: Language Arts, Math, Bible, Nature Journal, Poetry, and Science

Nature Journal & Poetry [S]

The poetry of Longfellow, Wordsworth, and Whitman is scheduled to complement the journaling sessions. Read aloud and discuss today's poem *"I Wandered Lonely As a Cloud"* (see Appendix) with a parent. Then, follow the directions below.

★ *Nature Drawing & Journaling: Lesson XXX* p. 81

Note: Do only the assignment described in paragraph **two** on p. 81 today.

<u>Key Idea</u>: Practice drawing and shading clouds.

Language Arts [S]

Have students complete one studied dictation exercise (see Appendix for passages).

Help students complete **one** English option.

★ *Progressing With Courage:* Lesson 88 (first half only)

★ *Progressing With Courage:* Lesson 110 (last half only)

★ Your own grammar program

Work with the students to complete **one** of the writing options listed below:

★ *Write with the Best: Vol. 2* Unit 5 – Day 16 p. 55

★ Your own writing program

<u>Key Idea</u>: Practice language arts skills.

Bible Quiet Time [I]

Bible Study: Read and complete the assigned pages in the following resource:

★ *Faith at Work: Lesson 20 – Day One* p. 147 (Note: Refer to p. 143-146 to complete the lesson.)

Prayer Focus: Refer to **thanksgiving** on "Preparing Your Heart for Prayer". Then, pray a prayer of thanksgiving to express gratitude to God for His divine goodness. After your prayer, write 'thanksgiving' at the bottom of today's lesson in *Faith at Work* above *Day Two*. Next to 'thanksgiving', either list key phrases or write a sentence to summarize your prayer. Keep "Preparing Your Heart for Prayer" inside your Bible.

Scripture Memory: Copy James 4:5 in your Common Place Book.

Music: Refer to p. 64-65 as you sing with Track 8 *"We're Marching to Zion"* (vs. 1-2).

<u>Key Idea</u>: Read and study Romans 15.

Math Exploration [S]

Choose **one** of the math options listed below (see Appendix for details).

★ *Singapore Primary Mathematics 6A/6B, Discovering Mathematics 7A/7B, 8A/8B, No-Nonsense Algebra* or *Videotext Algebra*

★ Your own math program

<u>Key Idea</u>: Use a step-by-step math program.

Science Exploration [I]

★ Read *Albert Einstein and the Theory of Relativity* p. 24-45. Next, read the definition for *ammeter* and *amperes* on p. 174 and *physics* on p. 176. Then, write a written narration about p. 24-45. Refer to *Written Narration Tips* in the Appendix for help as needed. Read your written narration out loud after you have finished writing. Refer to *Written Narration Skills* for help in editing.

<u>Key Idea</u>: As Albert grew older, his parents moved to Italy. Albert was left in Germany to finish his schooling. Albert ended up getting expelled from the school and was relieved to rejoin his family.

Reading about History | I

Read about history in the following resource:

★ *The Story of the World: Vol. 4* p. 372-377

You will be writing a narration about the chapter *Argentina's President and His Wife*. To prepare for writing your narration, look back over p. 372-377 in *The Story of the World: Vol. 4*. Think about the main idea and the most important moments in this part of the reading.

After you have thought about what you will write and how you will begin your narration, turn to Unit 23 in your *Student Notebook*. For more guidance on writing a narration, see *Written Narration Tips* in the Appendix.

In Box 4, write a 12-16 sentence narration about the reading. When you have finished writing, read your sentences out loud to catch any mistakes. Check for the following things: *Did you include **who** or **what topic** the reading was mainly about? Did you include **descriptors** of the important thing(s) that happened? Did you include a **closing sentence**? If not, add those things.* Use the *Written Narration Skills* in the Appendix as a guide for editing the narration.

Key Idea: Argentina was divided as to whether to join the Axis or Allied forces in WWII, so it remained "neutral" but friendly toward Germany and Italy. In 1943, Juan Peron overthrew Argentinean President Ramon Castillo. Peron set up a *"junta"*, or military government, to rule the country. Peron's reforms made him popular with the poor working people, but his own government arrested him in 1945 for supporting the Fascists. The working poor demanded Peron's release. After his release, Peron ruled like a dictator. He was overthrown in 1955.

President Study | I

★ Read p. 58-59 in *Our Presidents...* Then, open your *President Notebook* to Herbert Hoover. Use today's reading to help you complete the information about Hoover.

Key Idea: Research Herbert Hoover.

Storytime | T/I

Read the following assigned pages:

★ *I Am David* p. 96 – half of p. 120
Note: p. 120 includes hate, taunting, and name-calling.

Get the bookmark that you placed in your book on Day 2. Locate the same section of the bookmark that you used on Day 2. Beneath Day 2's entry, write the book title and the page numbers you read today. Select the one remaining response option at the bottom of the bookmark, and place a checkmark next to it. In the blank space under today's pages, respond in writing using your checked option.

Key Idea: Relate to the text in various ways.

Economics | I

Read about economics in the resource below.

★ *Common Sense Business for Kids* p. 21-24

After the reading, open your *Student Notebook* to the "Economic Principles" section at the front of your notebook. Under "Economic Principle", write a one or two sentence summary for the economic principle you learned from today's reading.

Key Idea: When setting up a business, it is important to take notice of what a customer really wants and then find a product to fit the market. Observing will help you know more about your market.

Independent History Study | I

Open your *Student Notebook* to Unit 23 – Box 6 to view an image of Eva Peron. Label the image, "Evita" Peron: May 7, 1919 – July 26, 1952.

Key Idea: Maria Eva Duarte, or Evita, was Juan Peron's wife. She was beloved by the people of Argentina. Eva died in 1952 at age 33 and was mourned by thousands.

Biblical Self-Image [T]

Our plans intend for the listed pages in *Who Am I? And What Am I Doing Here?* to be read either silently by both you and your child, or read aloud to the child by you. With this in mind, read and discuss the following pages listed below.

 Who Am I? And What Am I Doing Here? p. 173-180 and top of p. 181

Key Idea: God's Word guides and protects us.

Language Arts [S]

Have students complete one studied dictation exercise (see Appendix for passages).

Help students complete one lesson from the following reading program:

 Drawn into the Heart of Reading

Help students complete **one** English option.

 Progressing With Courage: Lesson 88 (last half only)

 Progressing With Courage: Lesson 111 (first half only)

 Your own grammar program

Key Idea: Practice language arts skills.

Bible Quiet Time [I]

Bible Study: Complete the assignment below.

 Faith at Work: Lesson 20 – Day Two p. 147-148

Prayer Focus: Refer to **supplication** on "Preparing Your Heart for Prayer". Then, pray a prayer of supplication to make a humble and earnest request of God. Write 'supplication' at the bottom of today's lesson in *Faith at Work* above *Day Three*. Next to it, either list several key phrases or write a sentence to summarize your prayer. Keep "Preparing Your Heart for Prayer" inside your Bible.

Scripture Memory: Recite James 4:1-5.

Music: Refer to p. 64-65 as you sing with Track 8 *"We're Marching to Zion"* (vs. 1-2).

Key Idea: Read and study Romans 16.

Math Exploration [S]

Choose **one** of the math options listed below.

 Singapore Primary Mathematics 6A/6B, Discovering Mathematics 7A/7B, 8A/8B, No-Nonsense Algebra or *Videotext Algebra*

 Your own math program

Key Idea: Use a step-by-step math program.

Science Exploration [I]

 Copy the Science Lab Form from the Appendix of this guide. Put on your safety glasses, smooth gloves, and smock as recommended on p. 6 of the *Chemistry C500 Experiment Manual*. Then, read p. 42 and follow the directions to perform "Experiment 24" from p. 43 of the Experiment Manual. **Be careful not to let the black wire's metal tip touch the metal spoon.** After completing Experiment 24, in the top box of the Science Lab Form write: *What reaction does a stainless steel spoon and an electric current produce in a saltwater solution?* In the second box of the form, write your hypothesis. Follow the directions for "Experiment 25" on p. 44 of the Experiment Manual and complete the box "Perform an Experiment" on your lab form. Then, follow the arrows to complete the rest of the Science Lab Form.

Key Idea: The measuring spoon in the saltwater solution is made of stainless steel, whose main component is iron. Potassium hexacyanoferrate(II) does not react to metallic iron, so the Prussian blue color indicates iron must have been dissolved by the electric current instead.

Learning Through History

Focus: Aucas of Ecuador, Republic of Congo, and Missionary Aviation Fellowship

Unit 24 - Day 1

Reading about History | S

Read about history in the following resource:

★ *Hero Tales: Vol. II* p. 45-55

After today's reading, orally narrate or retell to an adult about "Operation Auca" on p. 50-52 and "We've Made Contact" on p. 53-55 of *Hero Tales: Vol. II.* As you retell, the adult will write or type your narration. Some possible key words to include in your narration might be *Auca Indians, savage killers, Dayuma, share Gospel, Operation Auca, Pete Fleming, Nate Saint, Ed McCully, Jim Elliot, Roger Youderian, plane, "Terminal City", gifts, meeting, beach, landing strip, "George", contact, radio, killed by Auca lances.* When the narration is complete, tri-fold the typed or written narration to fit in Unit 24 – Box 7 of the *Student Notebook.* Glue the folded narration in Box 7, so it can be opened and read.

Key Idea: Five missionaries were willing to die, so the Aucas could know Jesus.

History Project | S

In order to eventually share the Gospel with the Auca Indians, Nate Saint first dropped gift items to show the Aucas in Ecuador that the missionaries meant no harm. On one trip, the Aucas gave a gift of feathers and a parrot in return. Open your *Student Notebook* to Unit 24 – Box 9. Follow the directions from p. 51-52 of *Draw and Write Through History* to draw and color a Scarlet Macaw in Box 9. Macaws are members of the parrot family.

Key Idea: The eastern part of Ecuador includes part of the Amazon rainforest. The scarlet macaw lives in the Amazon rainforest.

Storytime | T/I

Read the following assigned pages:

★ *I Am David* half of p. 120 – half of p. 144

Get the bookmark that you placed in your book last unit. Choose a new section of the bookmark with **three** options at the bottom. At the top of this section of the bookmark, write the book title and the page numbers you read today. Select **one** of the three options at the bottom and place a checkmark next to it. In the blank space under today's pages, respond in writing using your checked option.

Key Idea: Relate to the text in various ways.

Timeline | I

You will be adding to the timeline in your *Student Notebook* today. In Unit 24 – Box 1, draw and color a wooden lance. Label the box, *Operation Auca – 5 Missionaries Killed (January 8, 1956 A.D.).*

In Box 2, draw and color a leopard head and a lance. These are on the coat of arms of the Democratic Republic of the Congo. Label it, *Belgian Congo Gains Independence (1960 A.D.).*

In Box 3, draw and color a crate on an airstrip that says 'MAF'. Label it, *Betty Greene – Missionary Aviation Fellowship (1946-1997 A.D.).*

Key Idea: Betty Greene founded the Missionary Aviation Fellowship. Nate Saint was an MAF pilot who was later killed by Auca natives while in Ecuador. Around this same time, the Congo was struggling for its freedom.

Independent History Study | I

★ Open your *Student Notebook* to Unit 24. In Box 6, copy the text from p. 53 of *Draw and Write Through History.*

Key Idea: After the killing of the five missionaries in Ecuador, Nate Saint's sister, Rachel, and Jim Elliot's widow, Elisabeth, eventually lived among the Waorani tribe. Their goal was to show love and forgiveness.

Learning the Basics
Focus: Language Arts, Math, Bible, Nature Journal, and Science

Nature Journal | I |

Read and follow the directions in the resource below.

 ★ *Nature Drawing & Journaling: Lesson XXXI* p. 82-83

Note: Draw the two figure boxes described on p. 83. Then, practice sketching the sunrise and sunset **shown on p. 83** in your figure boxes. After that draw two new blank boxes on a new page in your journal. Label one 'Sunrise' and one 'Sunset'. The next time that you observe a sunrise or sunset, draw it in your journal in the appropriately labeled box.

Key Idea: Sketch sunrises and sunsets.

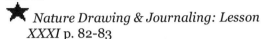

Language Arts | S |

Help students complete one lesson from the following reading program:

★ *Drawn into the Heart of Reading*

Help students complete **one** English option.

★ *Progressing With Courage:* Lesson 89

★ *Progressing With Courage:* Lesson 111 (last half only)

★ Your own grammar program

Work with the students to complete **one** of the writing options listed below:

★ *Write with the Best: Vol. 2* Unit 5 – Day 17 p. 55-56

★ Your own writing program

Key Idea: Practice language arts skills.

Bible Quiet Time | I |

Bible Study: Read and complete the assigned pages in the following resource:

★ *Faith at Work: Lesson 20 – Day Three* p. 148

Prayer Focus: Refer to **adoration** on "Preparing Your Heart for Prayer". Then, pray a prayer of adoration to worship and honor God. After your prayer, write 'adoration' at the bottom of today's lesson in *Faith at Work* above *Day Four*. Next to 'adoration', either list key phrases or write a sentence to summarize your prayer. Keep "Preparing Your Heart for Prayer" inside your Bible.

Scripture Memory: Read aloud James 4:6 three times from your Bible.

Music: Read the verse and pray the prayer from p. 65 in *Hymns for a Kid's Heart*. Refer to p. 64-65 as you sing with Track 8 *"We're Marching to Zion"* (vs. 1-4).

Key Idea: Read and study Romans 16.

Math Exploration | S |

Choose **one** of the math options listed below (see Appendix for details).

★ *Singapore Primary Mathematics 6A/6B, Discovering Mathematics 7A/7B, 8A/8B, No-Nonsense Algebra* or *Videotext Algebra*

★ Your own math program

Key Idea: Use a step-by-step math program.

Science Exploration | I |

★ Read *Albert Einstein and the Theory of Relativity* p. 46-70. After reading the chapters, read the definition for *constant* on p. 174 and *electromagnetism, ether, gravity,* and *mass* on p. 175. Then, read the definition for *matter* and *motion* on p. 176 and *speed of light* on p. 177. Next, either discuss question 7 on p. 178 with a parent, or write the answer to the question on paper.

Key Idea: Albert Einstein enjoyed reading about experiments by Galileo, Newton, Faraday, and Maxwell.

Learning Through History
Focus: Aucas of Ecuador, Republic of Congo, and Missionary Aviation Fellowship

Unit 24 - Day 2

Reading about History | I

Read about history in the following resource:

 The Story of the World: Vol. 4 p. 378-383

After today's reading, open your *Student Notebook* to Unit 24. Box 5 shows a 1961 stamp from the USSR commemorating the life of Patrice Lumumba. Lumumba was the first prime minister of the Republic of the Congo to be legally elected. He was captured and killed by Katanga rebels on January 16, 1961. Why would the USSR issue a stamp to commemorate his life?

Key Idea: After King Leopold II of Belgium was forced to give up his throne, Patrice Lumumba petitioned for the Congo to have more freedom. He formed the Mouvement National Congolais, or MNC, to lead riots and demonstrations for independence. When the French colony of Congo-Brazzaville was allowed by France to declare its freedom, the MNC redoubled its efforts. So, the Belgian government gave the Congo its independence.

History Project | S

Open your *Student Notebook* to Unit 24 – Box 10. Follow the directions from *Draw and Write Through History* p. 49-50 (steps 1-3 only) to draw a jaguar. You will color your drawing on Day 3.

Key Idea: The Republic of Congo is located in central Africa. Leopards are found in central and southern Africa. Leopards belong to the Felidae family along with tigers, lions, and jaguars. The leopard's appearance is similar to that of a jaguar's appearance.

President Study | I

 On *The Presidents* DVD Volume 2, select the Chapter "Wilson to Franklin D. Roosevelt" and watch **only** Program 4: Herbert Hoover. Then, open your *President Notebook* to Herbert Hoover and add further information.

Key Idea: Research Herbert Hoover.

Storytime | T/I

Read the following assigned pages:

 I Am David half of p. 144-165

Get the bookmark that you placed in your book. Locate the same section of the bookmark that you used on Day 1. Beneath Day 1's entry, write the book title and the page numbers you read today. Select one of the **two** remaining response options and respond in writing using your checked option.

Key Idea: Relate to the text in various ways.

Worthy Words | T

Open your *Student Notebook* to Unit 24 – Box 8. Read, analyze, and evaluate the speech. After reading the speech, answer the following questions on an index card: *Why does Lumumba make sure to mention Belgium as "a friendly country with whom we deal as equal to equal"? What contrasts in the treatment of blacks and whites does Lumumba list? What words does Lumumba use to describe the "government"? Why might the people of the Congo region not want a strong central government? What are your thoughts about the speech?* Next, meet with a parent to have a Socratic dialogue. Before beginning the dialogue, the parent reads Box 8 out loud. Next, discuss the questions using your notes.

Key Idea: Patrice Lumumba was elected as the first prime minister of the independent Congo.

Independent History Study | I

In his speech in Box 8, Lumumba says, *"I ask all of you to forget your tribal quarrels. They exhaust us. They risk making us despised abroad."* Only six days after this speech, the eastern Congo, or Katanga, declared itself independent from the Republic of Congo. What did this have to do with the quote above?

Key Idea: Lumumba desired one united Republic of Congo. Other Africans wanted independent states governed by native tribes instead. Katanga rebels murdered Lumumba.

Biblical Self-Image [T]

Read and discuss the following pages listed below.

⭐ *Who Am I? And What Am I Doing Here?* p. 181 – top of p. 184

For "Make a Note of It" on p. 184, make a list with the students on a markerboard or a sheet of paper of ways that you can behave, speak, and dress in a way that reflects Jesus to others.

Key Idea: As you go throughout your day, it is important to remember that as a Christian you are a reflection of Jesus to others.

Language Arts [S]

Have students complete one studied dictation exercise (see Appendix for passages).

Help students complete one lesson from the following reading program:

⭐ *Drawn into the Heart of Reading*

Help students complete **one** English option.

⭐ *Progressing With Courage:* Lesson 90

⭐ *Progressing With Courage:* Lesson 112 (first half only)

⭐ Your own grammar program

Key Idea: Practice language arts skills.

Bible Quiet Time [I]

Bible Study: Read and complete the assigned pages in the following resource:

⭐ *Faith at Work: Lesson 20 – Day Four* p. 148

Prayer Focus: Refer to **confession** on "Preparing Your Heart for Prayer". Then, pray a prayer of confession to admit or acknowledge your sins to God. After your prayer, write 'confession' at the bottom of today's lesson on p. 148 in *Faith at Work*. Next to 'confession', either list key phrases or write a sentence to summarize your prayer. Keep "Preparing Your Heart for Prayer" inside your Bible.

Scripture Memory: Memorize James 4:6 from your Bible and recite it.

Music: Refer to p. 64-65 as you sing with Track 8 *"We're Marching to Zion"* (vs. 1-4).

Key Idea: Read and study Romans 16.

Math Exploration [S]

Choose **one** of the math options listed below (see Appendix for details).

⭐ *Singapore Primary Mathematics 6A/6B, Discovering Mathematics 7A/7B, 8A/8B, No-Nonsense Algebra* or *Videotext Algebra*

⭐ Your own math program

Key Idea: Use a step-by-step math program.

Science Exploration [I]

⭐ Read *Albert Einstein and the Theory of Relativity* p. 71-90. After reading the chapters, read the definition for *atom* on p. 174, *energy* on p. 175, and the definitions for both theories of *relativity* on p. 177. Then, either discuss questions 4, 8, 10, 11, and 13 on p. 178-179 with a parent, or write the answers to the question on paper. Refer to p. 77-88 as needed to aid in the discussion of the questions.

Key Idea: Einstein theorized that nothing travels as fast as light. As an electron takes on enormous energy to move very fast to approach the speed of light, its mass increases which makes its resistance to motion greater. So, it never reaches the speed of light. Einstein also theorized about the relation between mass and energy in that energy equals mass times the speed of light squared. He explained that all motion is relative to the frame of reference from which it is viewed, and time is relative to the motion of the observer.

Reading about History | I |

Read about history in the following resource:

 Hero Tales: Vol. III p. 81-91

Choose **one** of the sets of questions from the sections of *Hero Tales* that you read today to answer orally with an adult. The questions are found on p. 85, 88, and 91.

Key Idea: Betty Greene was a pioneer missionary pilot who combined her love of flying with her desire to do missionary work. She gained experience flying while serving as a WASP during World War II. After the war, she started The Christian Airmen's Missionary Fellowship, which later became Missionary Aviation Fellowship (or MAF). Betty was the first pilot for MAF. She brought medical supplies and food, flew those who were sick to hospitals, and provided safe passage to missionaries and their children.

History Project | S |

Betty Greene served as a pilot for Missionary Aviation Fellowship in Mexico, Peru, Africa, and Indonesia. She saved missionaries and Bible translators much travel time, as she could fly in and out of camps in the jungles and remote areas. Open your *Student Notebook* to Unit 24 – Box 10. Follow the directions from *Draw and Write Through History* p. 50 (step 4 only) to color your jaguar.

Key Idea: Jaguars are only found in the Americas. They have been sighted in the southern U.S., Mexico, Central America, and South America.

State Study | T |

⭐ This is an **optional** part of the plans. If you have chosen to study your state using *State History from a Christian Perspective*, do **part** of Lesson 21 (step 1: Test 1 only) from the *Master Lesson Plan Book*.

Key Idea: Study your individual state.

Storytime | T/I |

Read the following assigned pages:

 *I Am David* p. 166-191

After today's reading, orally narrate or retell the portion of the story that was read today. See *Narration Tips* in the Appendix as needed.

Key Idea: Practice orally narrating, or retelling, a portion of a story.

Geography | I |

For today's activities, use a globe or a world map. Find the locations of the countries to which Betty Greene flew as part of her work with the Missionary Aviation Fellowship. These countries include Mexico, Peru, Africa, and Indonesia. Mexico is in the southern part of North America, Peru is in the western part of South America, and Africa is its own continent. Indonesia contains over 17,000 islands and is located in the southeast part of the continent of Asia. What do you notice about the location of each of these countries in relation to the equator? What type of climate would these countries have? Why would countries with warm tropical climates, jungles, and deserts benefit from missionary pilots?

Key Idea: Betty Greene eventually flew in 12 countries and landed in as many as 20 more.

Independent History Study | I |

Read more about Betty Greene at the MAF site: http://www.maf.org/about/history/betty-greene

Nate Saint was also a Missionary Aviation Fellowship pilot. You can read about him at http://www.maf.org/about/history/nate-saint

Last, you may consider choosing from a variety of small gift donations to help the fellowship at https://www.maf.org/page.aspx?pid=706

Key Idea: Missionary Aviation Fellowship continues its ministry today.

Learning the Basics

Focus: Language Arts, Math, Bible, Nature Journal, Poetry, and Science

Nature Journal & Poetry `S`

The poetry of Longfellow, Wordsworth, and Whitman is scheduled to complement the journaling sessions. Read aloud and discuss today's poem *"A Prairie Sunset"* (see Appendix) with a parent. Then, follow the directions below.

★ *Nature Drawing & Journaling: Lesson XXXII* p. 84-85

Note: For today's assignment, draw the ocean sunset from p. 84. The text on p. 85 refers to a mountain sunrise, but instead use the ocean sunset from p. 84.

<u>Key Idea</u>: Practice drawing a sunset.

Language Arts `S`

Have students complete one studied dictation exercise (see Appendix for passages).

Help students complete **one** English option.

★ *Progressing With Courage:* Lesson 91

★ *Progressing With Courage:* Lesson 112 (last half only)

★ Your own grammar program

Work with the students to complete **one** of the writing options listed below:

★ *Write with the Best: Vol. 2* Unit 5 – Day 18 p. 56

★ Your own writing program

<u>Key Idea</u>: Practice language arts skills.

Bible Quiet Time `I`

Bible Study: Read and complete the assigned pages in the following resource:

★ *Faith at Work: Lesson 20 – Day Five* and *Notes* p. 149-154

Prayer Focus: Refer to **thanksgiving** on "Preparing Your Heart for Prayer". Then, pray a prayer of thanksgiving to express gratitude to God for His divine goodness. After your prayer, write 'thanksgiving' at the bottom of today's lesson on p. 149 in *Faith at Work*. Next to 'thanksgiving', either list key phrases or write a sentence to summarize your prayer. Keep "Preparing Your Heart for Prayer" inside your Bible.

Scripture Memory: Copy James 4:6 in your Common Place Book.

Music: Refer to p. 64-65 as you sing with Track 8 *"We're Marching to Zion"* (vs. 1-4).

<u>Key Idea</u>: Read and study Romans 16.

Math Exploration `S`

Choose **one** of the math options listed below (see Appendix for details).

★ *Singapore Primary Mathematics 6A/6B, Discovering Mathematics 7A/7B, 8A/8B, No-Nonsense Algebra* or *Videotext Algebra*

★ Your own math program

<u>Key Idea</u>: Use a step-by-step math program.

Science Exploration `I`

★ Read *Albert Einstein and the Theory of Relativity* p. 91-115. Next, either discuss question 2 on p. 178 and question 9 on p. 179 with a parent, or write the answers on paper. Refer to p. 112-115 for help with the questions.

<u>Key Idea</u>: Einstein showed that accelerated motion was relative to the observer's frame of reference. He also thought gravity should be explained "as a curvature in the geometry of space".

Reading about History | I

Read about history in the following resource:

⭐ *All American History: Vol. II* p. 385 – middle of p. 389

You will be writing a narration about the pages that you read today. To prepare for writing your narration, look back over p. 385-389 in *All American History: Vol. II*. Think about the main idea and the most important moments in this part of the reading. Plan to write 2-3 sentences for each bolded section in the reading.

After you have thought about what you will write and how you will begin your narration, turn to Unit 24 in your *Student Notebook*. For more guidance on writing a narration, see *Written Narration Tips* in the Appendix.

In Box 4, write a 12-16 sentence narration about the reading. When you have finished writing, read your sentences out loud to catch any mistakes. Check for the following things: *Did you include* **who** *or* **what topic** *the reading was mainly about? Did you include* **descriptors** *of the important thing(s) that happened? Did you include a* **closing sentence***? If not, add those things.* Use the *Written Narration Skills* in the Appendix as a guide for editing the narration.

Key Idea: In the 1950s, business was booming in the U.S. Millions of veterans from WWII returned home, got married, and started families. Children born during this era became known as the "baby boomers". Under the GI Bill, veterans attended college and received home loans. 40,000 miles of new interstate highways led to motels, shopping centers, drive-ins, and movie houses across the U.S. Television replaced radio, as the space race got underway.

President Study | I

⭐ Read p. 60-61 in *Our Presidents...* Then, open your *President Notebook* to Franklin Delano Roosevelt. Use today's reading to help you complete the information about FDR.

Key Idea: Research Franklin Delano Roosevelt.

Storytime | T/I

Read the following assigned pages:

⭐ *I Am David* p. 192-218
Note: p. 202 refers to ill treatment and death. Get the bookmark that you placed in your book on Day 2. Locate the same section of the bookmark that you used on Day 2. Beneath Day 2's entry, write the book title and the page numbers you read today. Select the one remaining response option at the bottom of the bookmark, and place a checkmark next to it. In the blank space under today's pages, respond in writing using your checked option.

Key Idea: Relate to the text in various ways.

Economics | I

Read about economics in the resource below.

⭐ *Common Sense Business for Kids* p. 25-30

After the reading, open your *Student Notebook* to the "Economic Principles" section at the front of your notebook. Under "Economic Principle", write a one or two sentence summary for the economic principle you learned from today's reading.

Key Idea: It is important to know your market, resources, capabilities, and potential profit before starting a business. Do research so you know who your customers will be, what people will want to buy, how much your business will cost, and whether or not it will be profitable.

Independent History Study | I

Read *Great Events in American History* p. 107-110. Then, read Luke 2:13-14. Why do you think President Eisenhower recorded the message included on p. 110?

Key Idea: After the Soviets launched *Sputnik* in 1957, the space race between the United States and the Soviet Union began. The "race" would last until the U.S. landed Apollo 11 on the moon on July 20, 1969.

Learning the Basics
Focus: Language Arts, Math, Bible, Nature Journal, and Science

Biblical Self-Image [T]

Read and discuss with the students the following pages in the resource below.

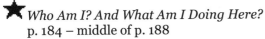 *Who Am I? And What Am I Doing Here?* p. 184 – middle of p. 188

Discuss "Make a Note of It" on p. 188 with the students rather than having them write their responses on paper.

Key Idea: God keeps His promises to us.

Language Arts [S]

Have students complete one studied dictation exercise (see Appendix for passages).

Help students complete one lesson from the following reading program:

★ *Drawn into the Heart of Reading*

Help students complete **one** English option.

★ *Progressing With Courage:* Lesson 92

★ *Progressing With Courage:* Lesson 113 (first half only)

★ Your own grammar program

Key Idea: Practice language arts skills.

Bible Quiet Time [I]

Bible Study: Complete the assignment below.

★ *Faith at Work: Lesson 21 – Day One* p. 155-156 (Note: Refer to p. 150-154 to complete the lesson.)

Prayer Focus: Refer to **supplication** on "Preparing Your Heart for Prayer". Then, pray a prayer of supplication to make a humble and earnest request of God. Write 'supplication' at the bottom of today's lesson in *Faith at Work* above *Day Two*. Next to it, either list several key phrases or write a sentence to summarize your prayer.

Scripture Memory: Recite James 4:1-6.

Music: Refer to p. 64-65 as you sing with Track 8 *"We're Marching to Zion"* (vs. 1-4).

Key Idea: Read and study Romans 16.

Math Exploration [S]

Choose **one** of the math options listed below.

★ *Singapore Primary Mathematics 6A/6B, Discovering Mathematics 7A/7B, 8A/8B, No-Nonsense Algebra* or *Videotext Algebra*

★ Your own math program

Key Idea: Use a step-by-step math program.

Science Exploration [I]

★ Copy the Science Lab Form from the Appendix of this guide. Put on your safety glasses, smooth gloves, and smock as recommended on p. 6 of the *Chemistry C500 Experiment Manual*. Then, follow the directions to perform "Experiment 26" from p. 45 of the Experiment Manual. To clean up, refer to "How to Dispose of Waste" on p. 7 and the Basic Rules on p. 6. After completing Experiment 26, in the top box of the Science Lab Form write: *What will happen when current flows through a penny placed on blotting paper soaked with potassium hexacyanoferrate – table salt solution?* In the second box of the form, write your hypothesis. Follow the directions for "Experiment 27" on p. 46 of the Experiment Manual and complete the box "Perform an Experiment" on your lab form. **Be sure to wear gloves when touching the soaked blotting paper.** Then, follow the arrows to complete the rest of the Science Lab Form. To clean up, refer to "How to Dispose of Waste" on p. 7 and the Basic Rules on p. 6.

Key Idea: As electric current flows through a "copper" penny placed upon wet blotting paper, some of the copper coating dissolves in the salt solution, and when combined with potassium hexacyanoferrate(II) it forms brown copper ferrocyanide on the blotting paper.

Reading about History | I

Read about history in the following resources:

★ *All American History: Vol. II* bottom of p. 389-394

★ *Great Events in American History* p. 99-102

After today's reading, orally narrate or retell to an adult the portion of text that you read today from *All American History*. Some possible key words to include in your narration might be *Supreme Court, Brown v. Board of Education, desegregation, Little Rock High School, Why Johnny Can't Read, Cold War,* "duck and cover", *French fashions, poodle skirts, blue jeans, penicillin, polio vaccine, kitchen appliances, TV dinners, casserole decade,* and *McDonalds.*

Key Idea: The U.S. had a booming economy in the 1950s, with low unemployment and high consumer spending.

History Project | S

During the 1950s, gardening became less popular, and frozen and canned vegetables and fruits became more popular. Convenience foods like TV dinners became available. Canned soups made the 1950s the casserole decade. Green bean casserole, tuna casserole, and hamburger casserole were favorites. Ask your parent(s) what favorite casserole he/she remembers from his/her youth. Then, plan to make that casserole for your family this week.

Key Idea: Cooking habits changed after WWII.

President Study | I

★ On *The Presidents* DVD Volume 2, select the Chapter "Wilson to Franklin D. Roosevelt" and watch **only** Program 5: Franklin Delano Roosevelt. Then, open your *President Notebook* to Franklin Delano Roosevelt and use today's viewing to add further information about Roosevelt.

Key Idea: Research Franklin Delano Roosevelt.

Storytime | T/I

Read the following assigned pages:

★ *I Am David* p. 219-239

After today's reading, photocopy the **two** "Bookmark" pages from the Appendix. Place the copied pages back-to-back and staple them together at the 4 corners. Then, tri-fold the stapled page into thirds to make a bookmark. Save the bookmark in your book until Day 2.

Key Idea: Relate to the text in various ways.

Geography | T

For today's activities, use the map listed below.

★ *United States History Atlas* p. 45

In 1954, the Supreme Court ruled in *Brown v. Board of Education* that school segregation was unconstitutional. Look at the map on p. 45 of the *United States History Atlas* to see each state's segregation policy at the time of the 1954 ruling. In what area of the country was segregation required by law? In what areas of the country was segregation prohibited by law? In which areas of the country was there no legislation about segregation?

Compare the map on p. 45 to the map on p. 25 of the *United States History Atlas*. What similarities do you notice? Why would there be similarities?

Key Idea: President Eisenhower had to send U.S. paratroopers to Little Rock, Arkansas, to enforce desegregation at the local high school.

Independent History Study | I

Read p. 197-199 of the *Book of Great American Speeches for Young People*. Why does Wilkins mention the Cold War and *Sputnik?*

Key Idea: In the years following the Supreme Court ruling in *Brown v. Board of Education*, desegregation often had to be enforced.

Learning the Basics
Focus: Language Arts, Math, Bible, Nature Journal, and Science

Nature Journal [I]

Read and follow the directions in the resource below.

 Nature Drawing & Journaling: Lesson XXXIII p. 86-87

Note: Do only the assignment described in paragraphs **one** and **two** on p. 87 today. Wait to complete the assignment described in paragraph three until Unit 25 – Day 3.

Key Idea: Practice drawing fair weather clouds and clouds at sunset.

Language Arts [S]

Help students complete one lesson from the following reading program:

 Drawn into the Heart of Reading

Help students complete **one** English option.

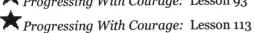 *Progressing With Courage:* Lesson 93

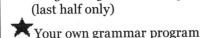 *Progressing With Courage:* Lesson 113 (last half only)

★ Your own grammar program

Work with the students to complete **one** of the writing options listed below:

★ *Write with the Best: Vol. 2* Unit 5 – Day 19 p. 56

★ Your own writing program

Key Idea: Practice language arts skills.

Bible Quiet Time [I]

Bible Study: Read and complete the assigned pages in the following resource:

★ *Faith at Work: Lesson 21 – Day Two* p. 156-157 (Note: Use Galatians 1:3-4 for questions 6 and 7.)

Prayer Focus: Refer to **adoration** on "Preparing Your Heart for Prayer". Then, pray a prayer of adoration to worship and honor God. After your prayer, write 'adoration' at the bottom of today's lesson in *Faith at Work* above *Day Three*. Next to 'adoration', either list key phrases or write a sentence to summarize your prayer. Keep "Preparing Your Heart for Prayer" inside your Bible.

Scripture Memory: Read aloud James 4:7 three times from your Bible.

Music: Read p. 67-68 in *Hymns for a Kid's Heart*. Refer to p. 70 as you sing with Track 9 *"Like a River Glorious"* (verse 1).

Key Idea: Read and study Galatians 1.

Math Exploration [S]

Choose **one** of the math options listed below (see Appendix for details).

★ *Singapore Primary Mathematics 6A/6B, Discovering Mathematics 7A/7B, 8A/8B, No-Nonsense Algebra* or *Videotext Algebra*

★ Your own math program

Key Idea: Use a step-by-step math program.

Science Exploration [I]

★ Read *Albert Einstein and the Theory of Relativity* p. 116-135. After reading the chapters, read the definition for *molecule* on p. 176 and *Quantum Theory* on p. 177.

Key Idea: Einstein expanded Planck's quantum theory to show that light behaved as a particle and a wave. He moved back to Germany to investigate his theories further, yet he retained his Swiss citizenship and his Jewish identity. As Hitler rose to power in Germany, Einstein eventually accepted a position in the U.S.

Learning Through History
Focus: Desegregation, Civil Rights, and Modern Church Movements

Reading about History | I |

Read about history in the following resources:

⭐ *All American History: Vol. II* p. 397-402

⭐ *Great Events in American History* p. 103-106

After today's reading, open your *Student Notebook* to Unit 25. Box 5 shows a picture of Rosa Parks from 1955, which is the year that she refused to give up her seat on a Montgomery Bus. Notice Martin Luther King Jr. standing in the background of the photograph.

Key Idea: After Rosa Parks was arrested for failing to give up her seat on a Montgomery bus to a white passenger, the African-American community in Montgomery declared a strike against the bus company. The strike lasted over a year.

History Project | S |

Open your *Student Notebook* to Unit 25 – Box 8. Read the poem *"The Negro's Complaint"* by William Cowper. Cowper was inspired to write this poem at the request of his friend and abolitionist William Wilberforce. As a member of British Parliament, Wilberforce led the movement to abolish the slave trade in the British Empire. Martin Luther King Jr. quoted the 5th line from the second stanza of Cowper's poem in his 1955 speech "There Comes a Time When People Get Tired". You will read this speech as part of the "Worthy Words" box of plans today. Why do you think King chose to quote from Cowper's poem? Read this poem aloud and think about each stanza.

Key Idea: Slavery was followed by segregation.

President Study | I |

⭐ Read p. 62-63 in *Our Presidents...* Then, open your *President Notebook* to Harry S. Truman. Use today's reading to help you complete the information about Truman.

Key Idea: Research Harry S. Truman.

Storytime | T/I |

Read the following assigned pages:

⭐ *Freedom Walkers* p. xi-13

Get the bookmark you made on Day 1. Find the section of the bookmark that has only **two** options at the bottom. At the top of this section of the bookmark, write the book title and the page numbers you read today. Select **one** of the two options at the bottom of the bookmark and respond to that option in writing in the blank space under today's pages.

Key Idea: Relate to the text in various ways.

Worthy Words | T |

Read, analyze, and evaluate the speech below.

⭐ *Book of Great American Speeches for Young People* p. 192-193

After reading the speech, answer the following questions on an index card: *What things did King list that "people get tired of"? What are some of the descriptive words used in this part of the speech? Why did King not advocate violence? What basis does King give for knowing he is not wrong? Was King right when he mentioned what history books would write in the future? How did the Montgomery Bus Boycott change America? Does any form of segregation still occur where you live?* Next, meet with a parent to have a Socratic dialogue about the speech. Before beginning the dialogue, the parent reads the speech out loud. Next, discuss the questions using your notes. All participants should use life experiences or text to support their responses.

Key Idea: This was King's first civil rights speech.

Independent History Study | I |

Read Pearl Buck's speech on p. 184-186 of the *Book of Great American Speeches for Young People*. Copy an important part of the speech in Unit 25 – Box 6 of your *Student Notebook*.

Key Idea: The Red Scare was a fearful reaction to communism.

Learning the Basics
Focus: Language Arts, Math, Bible, Nature Journal, and Science

Biblical Self-Image [T]

Our plans intend for the listed pages in *Who Am I? And What Am I Doing Here?* to be read either silently by both you and your child, or read aloud to the child by you. With this in mind, read and discuss the following pages listed below.

 Who Am I? And What Am I Doing Here? middle of p. 188-191

Key Idea: It is important to exercise our spiritual discipline. Some of the ways to do this include prayer, Bible study, biblical meditation, worship, and fasting. It is also important that we learn from our mistakes.

Language Arts [S]

Have students complete one studied dictation exercise (see Appendix for passages).

Help students complete one lesson from the following reading program:

 Drawn into the Heart of Reading

Help students complete **one** English option.

★ *Progressing With Courage:* Lesson 94

★ *Progressing With Courage:* Lesson 114 (first half only)

★ Your own grammar program

Key Idea: Practice language arts skills.

Bible Quiet Time [I]

Bible Study: Read and complete the assigned pages in the following resource:

★ *Faith at Work: Lesson 21 – Day Three* p. 157

Prayer Focus: Refer to **confession** on "Preparing Your Heart for Prayer". Then, pray a prayer of confession to admit or acknowledge your sins to God. After your prayer, write 'confession' at the bottom of today's lesson on p. 157 in *Faith at Work*. Next to 'confession', either list key phrases or write a sentence to summarize your prayer. Keep "Preparing Your Heart for Prayer" inside your Bible.

Scripture Memory: Memorize James 4:7 from your Bible and recite it.

Music: Refer to p. 70 as you sing with Track 9 *"Like a River Glorious"* (verse 1).

Key Idea: Read and study Galatians 1.

Math Exploration [S]

Choose **one** of the math options listed below (see Appendix for details).

★ *Singapore Primary Mathematics 6A/6B, Discovering Mathematics 7A/7B, 8A/8B, No-Nonsense Algebra* or *Videotext Algebra*

★ Your own math program

Key Idea: Use a step-by-step math program.

Science Exploration [I]

★ Read *Albert Einstein and the Theory of Relativity* p. 136-157. After reading the chapters, read the definition for *neutron* and *Nobel Prize* on p. 176. Next, either discuss question 14 on p. 179 with a parent, or write the answer to the question on paper. Hint: Refer to p. 140-141 for help with question 14.

Key Idea: Einstein's expanded theory of relativity said that motion that changes speeds, or accelerates, is equivalent to gravity. This means that acceleration is relative motion, and it needs a frame of reference to tell if acceleration or gravity is at work.

Learning Through History
Focus: Desegregation, Civil Rights, and Modern Church Movements

Unit 25 - Day 3

Reading about History | I

Read about history in the following resource:

★ *Hero Tales: Vol. II* p. 129-139

After today's reading, open your *Student Notebook* to Unit 25. In Box 7, you will outline p. 129-130 to tell about John Perkins. Each Roman numeral in Box 7 stands for one paragraph. So, 'I' means the first paragraph on p. 129. Next to 'I' in Box 7, write one sentence to tell who or what the first paragraph was about and the main thing that person did. This is not a summary, but rather just the main topic. Next to 'II' in Box 7, write the main topic of the second paragraph on p. 129. Continue this pattern for the 5 paragraphs on p. 129-130.

<u>Key Idea</u>: After John Perkins accepted Jesus as his Savior, he returned to the South to bring spiritual hope and preach the Gospel to others.

History Project | S

Open your *Student Notebook* to Unit 25 – Box 9. Read the poem *"Question"* by Langston Hughes. Hughes was an African American novelist and poet. He became known as the "Poet Laureate of Harlem". A 'poet laureate' refers to the office of a poet who is attached to either a royal household or government of a country. Harlem is a mainly African-American area of Manhattan in New York City. Why might Hughes be referred to as the "Poet Laureate of Harlem"? What question is Hughes asking in his poem? What point do you think he is trying to make? How would you answer him?

<u>Key Idea</u>: Hughes' poems make the reader think about how it felt to be black in the 1950s.

State Study | T

★ This is an **optional** part of the plans. If you have chosen to study your state using *State History from a Christian Perspective,* do **part** of Lesson 21 (step 2 only) from the *Master Lesson Plan Book.*

<u>Key Idea</u>: Study your individual state.

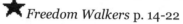

Storytime | T/I

Read the following assigned pages:

★ *Freedom Walkers* p. 14-22

After today's reading, orally narrate or retell the portion of the story that was read today. See *Narration Tips* in the Appendix as needed.

<u>Key Idea</u>: Practice narrating part of a story.

Timeline | I

Add to the timeline in your *Student Notebook* today. In Unit 25 – Box 1, color a red patch. Label it, *The Second Red Scare (1947-1957 A.D.).*

In Box 2, draw and color a yellow bus. Label it, *Montgomery Bus Boycott (Dec. 1, 1955 - Dec. 20, 1956 A.D.).*

In Box 3, draw and color a heart that is half black and half white. Label it, *John Perkins – Reconciliation in the South (1962-1982 and 1998-present A.D.).*

<u>Key Idea</u>: While fears of communism and McCarthyism were sweeping the U.S., Martin Luther King, Jr. was leading the Montgomery Bus Boycott in Alabama. Several years later, in the 1960s, civil rights activist John Perkins returned to the South to preach reconciliation.

Independent History Study | I

Read p. 194-196 of the *Book of Great American Speeches for Young People.* How does Langston Hughes' speech and his poem on p. 196 help you better understand racial discrimination and segregation? Notice the references in Hughes' speech on p. 195 to Rev. Martin Luther King, whom you read about on Day 2 in *All American History,* and Emmet Till, whom you will read about in *Freedom Walkers.*

<u>Key Idea</u>: When slavery ended after the Civil War, segregation and discrimination took its place in America.

Learning the Basics

Focus: Language Arts, Math, Bible, Nature Journal, Poetry, and Science

Nature Journal & Poetry [S]

The poetry of Longfellow, Wordsworth, and Whitman is scheduled to complement the journaling sessions. Read aloud and discuss today's poem *"It Is a Beauteous Evening"* (see Appendix) with a parent. Then, follow the directions below.

★ *Nature Drawing & Journaling: Lesson XXXIII* p. 87

Note: Do only the assignment described in paragraph **three** on p. 87 today.

Key Idea: Practice drawing a variety of clouds.

Language Arts [S]

Have students complete one studied dictation exercise (see Appendix for passages).

Help students complete **one** English option.

★ *Progressing With Courage:* Lesson 95

★ *Progressing With Courage:* Lesson 114 (last half only)

★ Your own grammar program

Work with the students to complete **one** of the writing options listed below:

★ *Write with the Best: Vol. 2* Unit 5 – Day 20 p. 56

★ Your own writing program

Key Idea: Practice language arts skills.

Bible Quiet Time [I]

Bible Study: Read and complete the assigned pages in the following resource:

★ *Faith at Work: Lesson 21 – Day Four* p. 158

Prayer Focus: Refer to **thanksgiving** on "Preparing Your Heart for Prayer". Then, pray a prayer of thanksgiving to express gratitude to God for His divine goodness. After your prayer, write 'thanksgiving' at the bottom of today's lesson in *Faith at Work* above *Day Five*. Next to 'thanksgiving', either list key phrases or write a sentence to summarize your prayer. Keep "Preparing Your Heart for Prayer" inside your Bible.

Scripture Memory: Copy James 4:7 in your Common Place Book.

Music: Refer to p. 70 as you sing with Track 9 *"Like a River Glorious"* (verse 1).

Key Idea: Read and study Galatians 1.

Math Exploration [S]

Choose **one** of the math options listed below (see Appendix for details).

★ *Singapore Primary Mathematics 6A/6B, Discovering Mathematics 7A/7B, 8A/8B, No-Nonsense Algebra* or *Videotext Algebra*

★ Your own math program

Key Idea: Use a step-by-step math program.

Science Exploration [I]

★ Read *Albert Einstein and the Theory of Relativity* p. 158-173. After reading the chapters, read the definition for *nucleus* on p. 176 and *radiation* and *radioactivity* on p. 177. Then, write a written narration about p. 158-173. Refer to *Written Narration Tips* in the Appendix for help as needed. Read your written narration out loud after you have finished writing. Refer to *Written Narration Skills* for help in editing.

Key Idea: As WWII began, Albert Einstein was living in the U.S., and Enrico Fermi was experimenting with uranium fission and the potential chain reaction of splitting atoms. This experimentation gave Einstein's formula about energy equaling mass times the speed of light squared an ominous significance as it predicted the enormous explosive force to be unleashed if the power inside an atom were set free.

Reading about History [I]

Read about history in the following resource:

 Rescue and Redeem p. 193-198

You will be writing a narration about the chapter "Big Moments in Modern Christianity" that you read today. To prepare for writing your narration, look back over p. 193-198 in *Rescue and Redeem*. Think about the main idea and the most important moments in this part. **Note:** Plan to write 3-4 sentences for each of the four sections in this chapter.

After you have thought about what you will write and how you will begin your narration, turn to Unit 25 in your *Student Notebook*. For more guidance on writing a narration, see *Written Narration Tips* in the Appendix.

In Box 4, write a 12-16 sentence narration about the reading. When you have finished writing, read your sentences out loud to catch any mistakes. Check for the following things: *Did you include* **who** *or* **what topic** *the reading was mainly about? Did you include* **descriptors** *of the important thing(s) that happened? Did you include a* **closing sentence**? *If not, add those things.* Use the *Written Narration Skills* in the Appendix as a guide for editing the narration.

Key Idea: The 1906 Azusa Street Revival led to the spread of the Pentecostal movement throughout the world. The rise of modernism, and its focus on science and education rather than Scriptural teaching, led to Fundamentalism, which holds to Christianity's fundamental truths. These truths include the Bible's miracles, the virgin birth, the resurrection, and Christ's second coming. Evangelicals emphasize Christ as the center of their teaching and are active in evangelism. The First and Second Vatican Councils also addressed modernism.

President Study [I]

 On *The Presidents* DVD Volume 3, select the Chapter "Truman to Ford" and watch **only** Program 1: Harry S. Truman. Then, open your *President Notebook* to Harry S. Truman. Use today's viewing to add further information.

Key Idea: Research Harry S. Truman.

Storytime [T/I]

Read the following assigned pages:

 Freedom Walkers p. 23-35
Note: p. 31-32 mention a brutal murder.

Get the bookmark that you placed in your book on Day 2. Locate the same section of the bookmark that you used on Day 2. Beneath Day 2's entry, write the book title and the page numbers you read today. Select the one remaining response option at the bottom of the bookmark, and place a checkmark next to it. In the blank space under today's pages, respond in writing using your checked option.

Key Idea: Relate to the text in various ways.

Economics [I]

Read about economics in the resource below.

 Common Sense Business for Kids p. 31-34

After the reading, open your *Student Notebook* to the "Economic Principles" section at the front of your notebook. Under "Economic Principle", write a one or two sentence summary for the economic principle you learned from today's reading.

Key Idea: When setting a price for your product, first determine how much it will cost you to make the product. Second, calculate how much it will cost your customer to buy it. Third, figure out how much profit you need.

Independent History Study [I]

Read through the entries from 1947-1962 on the "Modern Church Timeline" found on p. 9 of *Rescue and Redeem*. What new discoveries and scientific advancements do you notice? What events are surprising to you?

Key Idea: Some of the main movements and moments in modern Christianity include the Pentecostal movement, the controversy between Fundamentalists and Modernists, the rise of new Evangelicals, and the Vatican Councils.

Learning the Basics

Focus: Language Arts, Math, Bible, Nature Journal, and Science

Biblical Self-Image [T]

Read and discuss with the students the following pages in the resource below.

 Who Am I? And What Am I Doing Here? p. 192-193

Key Idea: The path to eternal life is narrow, so it is important to stay on the narrow path by following God's Word and listening to the Holy Spirit. It is also important to exercise self-control to keep from doing what is wrong.

Language Arts [S]

Have students complete one studied dictation exercise (see Appendix for passages).

Help students complete one lesson from the following reading program:

 Drawn into the Heart of Reading

Help students complete **one** English option.

 Progressing With Courage: Lesson 96

 Progressing With Courage: Lesson 115 (first half only)

★ Your own grammar program

Key Idea: Practice language arts skills.

Bible Quiet Time [I]

Bible Study: Complete the assignment below.

★ *Faith at Work: Lesson 21 – Day Five* and *Notes* p. 158-162

Prayer Focus: Refer to **supplication** on "Preparing Your Heart for Prayer". Then, pray a prayer of supplication to make a humble and earnest request of God. Write 'supplication' at the bottom of today's lesson on p. 158 in *Faith at Work*. Next to it, either list several key phrases or write a sentence to summarize your prayer.

Scripture Memory: Recite James 4:1-7.

Music: Refer to p. 70 as you sing with Track 9 *"Like a River Glorious"* (verse 1).

Key Idea: Read and study Galatians 1.

Math Exploration [S]

Choose **one** of the math options listed below.

★ *Singapore Primary Mathematics 6A/6B, Discovering Mathematics 7A/7B, 8A/8B, No-Nonsense Algebra* or *Videotext Algebra*

★ Your own math program

Key Idea: Use a step-by-step math program.

Science Exploration [I]

★ In the top box of the Science Lab Form write: *What reaction occurs at the negative pole of a battery's copper wire when an electric current is passed through a stainless steel spoon in a saltwater solution?* In the second box of the form, write your hypothesis. Follow the directions for "Experiment 28" on p. 47 of the Experiment Manual and complete the box "Perform an Experiment" on your lab form. Then, follow the arrows to complete the rest of the Science Lab Form. After that, read p. 48. Note: Currently, p. 48 contains an error in the "Crystals Break Down" box as the charges in the pictures of the atoms are correct but are reversed in the writing under the pictures and in the box's explanation. To clean up, refer to p. 6-7.

Key Idea: In sodium chloride, or table salt, sodium atoms have a positive charge, and chlorine atoms have a negative charge. In water, the salt crystals decompose into positively and negatively charged atoms. When two poles of a direct current source, like a battery, are submerged in the solution, the positively-charged atoms migrate to the negative pole, and the negatively-charged atoms migrate to the positive pole. At the negative pole, where the sodium ions migrate, a decomposition of water occurs, and sodium hydroxide is formed. This causes a brief blue color in the red litmus solution.

Learning Through History
Focus: Modern Evangelists, Literature, Music, Art, and Architecture in the 1950s

Reading about History | S

Read about history in the following resource:

 Hero Tales: Vol. III p. 69-79

After today's reading, orally narrate or retell to an adult one section of the text from *Hero Tales*. As you retell, the adult will write or type your narration. Some possible key words to include in your narration of "The Modesto Manifesto" might be *manifesto, list of rules, reputation, wrong behaviors, guard against, greed, faithful to spouse, support local churches, truthful advertising*. Some possible key words for "Billy's Hour of Decision" might be *trustworthiness of Bible, Chuck Templeton, Noah, Jonah, enlightened Christianity, doubts, Paul, God-breathed, accept by faith*. Some possible key words for "The Ends Don't Justify the Means" might be *evil, racial division, President Clinton, Arkansas blacks and whites together, Dr. Martin Luther King Jr., South Africa, apartheid doomed*. When the narration is complete, tri-fold the typed or written narration to fit in Unit 26 – Box 9 of the *Student Notebook*. Glue the folded narration in Box 9, so it can be opened.

Key Idea: Billy Graham led crusades, or evangelistic meetings, where he preached the Gospel of Christ in many cities and countries.

History Project | S

Listen to Billy Graham preach by selecting a sermon to play at the following link: http://www.billygraham.org/videoarchive.asp Click on "Sermons" and scroll through the sermons underneath the video screen to select one to watch. One possibility is "Choices" San Jose, 1981 (32 min.). You may additionally watch "Easter in Birmingham" (3 min.).

Key Idea: Billy Graham spent his life preaching the Gospel.

Storytime | T/I

Read the following assigned pages:

Freedom Walkers p. 36-48

Get the bookmark that you placed in your book last unit. Choose a new section of the bookmark with **three** options at the bottom. At the top of this section of the bookmark, write the book title and the page numbers you read today. Select **one** of the three options at the bottom and place a checkmark next to it. In the blank space under today's pages, respond in writing using your checked option.

Key Idea: Relate to the text in various ways.

Geography | I

For today's activities, use the map listed below.

Student Notebook Unit 26 – Box 8

Open your *Student Notebook* to Unit 26. The map in Box 8 shows the locations of Billy Graham's crusades during his 58 years of ministry around the world. Label the box underneath the map with "Billy Graham's Crusades and Tours During 58 Years of Ministry". Billy Graham has preached on 5 different continents and done over 400 crusades and tours during his lifetime. He was born in North Carolina and attended college in Tennessee, Florida, and later Illinois. With this in mind, where do you notice the greatest concentration of crusades on the map in Box 8? Why do you think there were more crusades closer to the area of the country in which he lived and worked? Later, his ministry would carry him to countries around the world. What can you learn from Billy Graham's example about doing God's work right where you are?

Key Idea: Billy Graham's son, Franklin Graham, carries on the Billy Graham ministry.

Independent History Study | I

Choose **one** of the sets of questions from the sections of *Hero Tales: Vol. III* that you read today to answer orally with an adult. The questions are found on p. 73, 76, and 79.

Key Idea: Billy Graham refused to hold crusades that allowed racial separation or discrimination.

Learning the Basics
Focus: Language Arts, Math, Bible, Nature Journal, and Science

Nature Journal [I]

Read and follow the directions in the resource below.

 Nature Drawing & Journaling: Lesson XXXIV p. 88-89

Note: Draw your night scene either outdoors or from a window indoors.

Key Idea: Practice drawing a night scene.

Language Arts [S]

Help students complete one lesson from the following reading program:

 Drawn into the Heart of Reading

Help students complete **one** English option.

 Progressing With Courage: Lesson 97

 Progressing With Courage: Lesson 115 (last half only)

 Your own grammar program

Work with the students to complete **one** of the writing options listed below:

 Write with the Best: Vol. 2 Unit 6 – Day 1 p. 57-59 (Note: Do not try to find **all** of the nouns, verbs, adjectives, and adverbs, or the assignment will be tedious. Instead, plan to find **some** of each part of speech.)

 Your own writing program

Key Idea: Practice language arts skills.

Bible Quiet Time [I]

Bible Study: Read and complete the assigned pages in the following resource:

 Faith at Work: Lesson 22 – Day One p. 163 (Note: Refer to p. 159-162 to complete the lesson.)

Prayer Focus: Refer to **adoration** on "Preparing Your Heart for Prayer". **T**hen, pray a prayer of adoration to worship and honor God. After your prayer, write 'adoration' at the bottom of today's lesson in *Faith at Work* above *Day Two*. Next to 'adoration', either list key phrases or write a sentence to summarize your prayer. Keep "Preparing Your Heart for Prayer" inside your Bible.

Scripture Memory: Read aloud James 4:8 three times from your Bible.

Music: Read p. 69 in *Hymns for a Kid's Heart*. Refer to p. 70-71 as you sing with Track 9 *"Like a River Glorious"* (vs. 1-2).

Key Idea: Read and study Galatians 1.

Math Exploration [S]

Choose **one** of the math options listed below (see Appendix for details).

 Singapore Primary Mathematics 6A/6B, Discovering Mathematics 7A/7B, 8A/8B, No-Nonsense Algebra or *Videotext Algebra*

 Your own math program

Key Idea: Use a step-by-step math program.

Science Exploration [S]

 Discuss with a parent the questions for Chapter 1 on p. 14 of *Evolution: The Grand Experiment* Teacher's Manual. Next, on the *Evolution: The Grand Experiment* DVD, select "Menu" and then select "Bonus Material". After that select "Chapter Index" and then select "1 – Two Opposing Views". Watch "Two Opposing Views", stopping at 4:05 on the counter. The bottom left corner of the DVD screen flashes a green title bar when a new chapter begins. **Be careful not to go on to the next chapter.** Next, read p. 1-10 in *Evolution: The Grand Experiment* Student Text. Last, complete "Test A" on p. 17 of the Teacher's Manual. You may refer to your Student Text p. 1-10 to help you complete the test.

Key Idea: Americans are divided on their beliefs about the origin of life, and even scientists do not agree.

Reading about History | I |

Read about history in the following resource:

 Hero Tales: Vol. III p. 129-139

Open your *Student Notebook* to Unit 26. Box 7 shows a picture of Luis Palau preaching. On the right side of Box 7, based on today's reading in *Hero Tales*, write a headline to go along with the picture. Then, underneath your headline, write 2-3 opening sentences that could lead-in to an article about Luis Palau.

Key Idea: Luis Palau grew up in Argentina. A missionary led his mother and father to Christ, and Luis gave his life to Christ at a summer camp. As a child, he went to a British-run boarding school near Buenos Aires. Eventually, he began studying for the ministry. After attending graduate school in Oregon, and marrying his wife Pat, he did some brief training with the Billy Graham crusade.

History Project | S |

Today, you will begin work on a bookmark that you can keep in your Bible and use as an evangelistic tool to tell others about Christ. Out of a blank index card or cardstock, cut a bookmark measuring 1½" x 5". Lay the bookmark vertically in front of you. Then, divide your bookmark into 5 equal sections, using a pencil to lightly draw a dividing line between each section. From top to bottom on your bookmark, write the following Scripture references (one per section): John 3:16, Romans 3:23, Romans 6:23, John 1:12, and 2 Peter 3:18. Save your bookmark.

Key Idea: Palau ministers around the world through evangelistic crusades, radio, and TV.

President Study | I |

 Read p. 64-65 in *Our Presidents...* Then, open your *President Notebook* to Dwight D. Eisenhower. Use today's reading to help you complete the information about Eisenhower.

Key Idea: Research Dwight D. Eisenhower.

Storytime | T/I |

Read the following assigned pages:

 Freedom Walkers p. 49-58

Get the bookmark that you placed in your book. Locate the same section of the bookmark that you used on Day 1. Beneath Day 1's entry, write the book title and the page numbers you read today. Select one of the **two** remaining response options at the bottom of the bookmark, and place a checkmark next to it. In the blank space under today's pages, respond in writing using your checked option.

Key Idea: Relate to the text in various ways.

Timeline | I |

You will be adding to the timeline in your *Student Notebook* today. In Unit 26 – Box 1, draw a large white tent. Label it, *Billy Graham Begins His Crusades (1947 A.D.)*.

In Box 2, draw and color a television. Label it, *The Ed Sullivan Show Runs in the U.S. (1948-1971 A.D.)*.

In Box 3, draw and color a radio. Label it, *Luis Palau Begins His First Crusades (1980s A.D.)*.

Key Idea: *The Ed Sullivan Show* was a popular American TV variety show that ran for almost 30 years. During that same time, Billy Graham was speaking and evangelizing. Later, Luis Palau spent time watching and learning from Billy Graham. Palau began his own crusades in the 1980s, reaching out to many young people across the world.

Independent History Study | I |

Choose **one** of the sets of questions from the sections of *Hero Tales: Vol. III* that you read today to answer orally with an adult. The questions are found on p. 133, 136, and 139.

Key Idea: After hearing Billy Graham on a radio station, Luis Palau prayed for God to use him like that to reach others for Christ.

Learning the Basics
Focus: Language Arts, Math, Bible, Nature Journal, and Science

Biblical Self-Image [T]

Our plans intend for the listed pages in *Who Am I? And What Am I Doing Here?* to be read either silently by both you and your child, or read aloud to the child by you. With this in mind, read and discuss the following pages listed below.

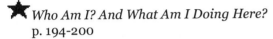 *Who Am I? And What Am I Doing Here?* p. 194-200

Key Idea: Many beliefs and religions borrow portions from Scripture or from Christianity as part of their faith. It is important to be watchful for faiths that add to or detract from God's Word or change what God tells us about Himself, His Son, and the Holy Spirit.

Language Arts [S]

Have students complete one studied dictation exercise (see Appendix for passages).

Help students complete one lesson from the following reading program:

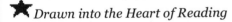 *Drawn into the Heart of Reading*

Help students complete **one** English option.

★ *Progressing With Courage:* Lesson 98

★ *Progressing With Courage:* Lesson 116 (first half only)

★ Your own grammar program

Key Idea: Practice language arts skills.

Bible Quiet Time [I]

Bible Study: Read and complete the assigned pages in the following resource:

★ *Faith at Work: Lesson 22 – Day Two* p. 163-164

Prayer Focus: Refer to **confession** on "Preparing Your Heart for Prayer". Then, pray a prayer of confession to admit or acknowledge your sins to God. After your prayer, write 'confession' at the bottom of today's lesson in *Faith at Work* above *Day Three*. Next to 'confession', either list key phrases or write a sentence to summarize your prayer. Keep "Preparing Your Heart for Prayer" inside your Bible.

Scripture Memory: Memorize James 4:8 from your Bible and recite it.

Music: Refer to p. 70-71 as you sing with Track 9 *"Like a River Glorious"* (vs. 1-2).

Key Idea: Read and study Galatians 2.

Math Exploration [S]

Choose **one** of the math options listed below (see Appendix for details).

★ *Singapore Primary Mathematics 6A/6B, Discovering Mathematics 7A/7B, 8A/8B, No-Nonsense Algebra* or *Videotext Algebra*

★ Your own math program

Key Idea: Use a step-by-step math program.

Science Exploration [S]

★ Discuss with a parent the questions for Chapter 2 on p. 25 of *Evolution: The Grand Experiment* Teacher's Manual. Next, on *Evolution: The Grand Experiment* DVD, select "Menu" and then "Bonus Material". After that select "Chapter Index" and then select "2 – Spontaneous Generation". Watch the DVD from 4:05-8:33 on the counter. The bottom left corner of the screen flashes a green title bar when a new chapter begins. Next, read p. 11-22 in the Student Text. Last, complete "Test A" on p. 29 of the Teacher's Manual. You may refer to the Student Text p. 11-22 to help you complete the test.

Key Idea: The theory of spontaneous generation dates back to around the time of Aristotle and was not disproved until 1859 by Louis Pasteur.

Reading about History | I

Read about history in the following resource:

 *All American History: Vol. II* p. 403-409

After today's reading, open your *Student Notebook* to Unit 26. The image in Box 5 shows Brooklyn Dodgers' baseball player Jackie Robinson as a rookie. Robinson was the first black man to play Major League Baseball since the 1880s. He joined the Brooklyn Dodgers in 1947.

Key Idea: Televisions allowed Americans to watch a wide variety of sports like basketball, baseball, football, boxing, and golf.

History Project | S

Get the bookmark that you began making on Day 2. Today you will color the bookmark. Place your bookmark vertically in front of you. Working from top to bottom on your bookmark, color **around** the Scripture references that you wrote on Day 2, using the following colors in their listed order (one per section): gold, black, red, white, and green. **Gold** is for God, our perfect Creator who wants us to be in heaven with Him one day. **Black** is for the darkness of sin that separates us from God. **Red** is for the blood that Jesus shed to take the punishment for your sin and mine. **White** is for the washing away of our sin when we admit to God that we have sinned, that we believe Jesus is God's Son, and that we choose to follow Him. **Green** reminds us to grow in Christ. Save your bookmark for Unit 27-Day 1.

Key Idea: It is important to share the Good News of Jesus with others.

State Study | T

 This is an **optional** part of the plans. If you have chosen to study your state using *State History from a Christian Perspective*, do Lesson 22 from the *Master Lesson Plan Book*.

Key Idea: Study your individual state.

Storytime | T/I

Read the following assigned pages:

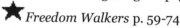 *Freedom Walkers* p. 59-74

After today's reading, orally narrate or retell the portion of the story that was read today. See *Narration Tips* in the Appendix as needed.

Key Idea: Practice orally narrating, or retelling, a portion of a story.

Economics | I

Read about economics in the resource below.

 Common Sense Business for Kids p. 35-36

After the reading, open your *Student Notebook* to the "Economic Principles" section at the front of your notebook. Under "Economic Principle", write a one or two sentence summary for the economic principle you learned from today's reading.

Key Idea: In business, it is important not to become too dependent on any one source for a big percentage of your income.

Independent History Study | I

With your parent's permission, listen and watch short clips of performances by famous singers from the 1950s on *The Ed Sullivan Show*.
Bill Haley & His Comets:
http://www.edsullivan.com/artists/bill-haley-his-comets
Nat King Cole:
http://www.edsullivan.com/artists/nat-king-cole
Elvis Presley:
http://www.edsullivan.com/artists/elvis-presley/

Key Idea: Nat King Cole was a 1940s-1950s jazz and pop artist. In 1953, Bill Haley & His Comets pioneered rock 'n' roll. Elvis Presley became known as the king of rock 'n' roll.

Learning the Basics
Focus: Language Arts, Math, Bible, Nature Journal, Poetry, and Science

Nature Journal & Poetry · S

The poetry of Longfellow, Wordsworth, and Whitman is scheduled to complement the journaling sessions. Read aloud and discuss today's poem *"The Tide Rises, the Tide Falls"* (see Appendix) with a parent. Then, follow the directions below.

★ *Nature Drawing & Journaling: Lesson XXXV* p. 90-91

Note: Use the images on p. 90 as a guide for the drawings inside your two figure boxes. Follow the image on p. 91 as you color the sky.

Key Idea: Practice sketching water.

Language Arts · S

Have students complete one studied dictation exercise (see Appendix for passages).

Help students complete **one** English option.

★ *Progressing With Courage:* Lesson 99 (first half only)

★ *Progressing With Courage:* Lesson 116 (last half only)

Work with the students to complete **one** of the writing options listed below:

★ *Write with the Best: Vol. 2* Unit 6 – Day 2 p. 60

★ Your own writing program

Key Idea: Practice language arts skills.

Bible Quiet Time · I

Bible Study: Read and complete the assigned pages in the following resource:

★ *Faith at Work: Lesson 22 – Day Three* p. 164 (Note: Refer to Acts 15 for questions 1-3.)

Prayer Focus: Refer to **thanksgiving** on "Preparing Your Heart for Prayer". Then, pray a prayer of thanksgiving to express gratitude to God for His divine goodness. After your prayer, write 'thanksgiving' at the bottom of today's lesson in *Faith at Work* above *Day Four*. Next to 'thanksgiving', either list phrases or write a sentence to summarize your prayer.

Scripture Memory: Copy James 4:8 in your Common Place Book.

Music: Refer to p. 70-71 as you sing with Track 9 *"Like a River Glorious"* (vs. 1-2).

Key Idea: Read and study Galatians 2.

Math Exploration · S

Choose **one** of the math options listed below (see Appendix for details).

★ *Singapore Primary Mathematics 6A/6B, Discovering Mathematics 7A/7B, 8A/8B, No-Nonsense Algebra* or *Videotext Algebra*

★ Your own math program

Key Idea: Use a step-by-step math program.

Science Exploration · S

★ Discuss with a parent the questions for Chapter 3 on p. 37 of *Evolution: The Grand Experiment* Teacher's Manual. Next, on *Evolution: The Grand Experiment* DVD, select "Menu" and then "Bonus Material". After that select "Chapter Index" and then select "3 – Acquired Characteristics". Watch the DVD from 8:33-13:28 on the counter. The bottom left corner of the screen flashes a green title bar when a new chapter begins. Next, read p. 23-30 in the Student Text. Last, complete "Test A" on p. 41 of the Teacher's Manual. You may refer to Student Text p. 23-30 to help you complete the test. **Optional:** Extension students may take "Test B" on p. 19, 31, and 43 of the Teacher's Manual as a sectional exam.

Key Idea: During his lifetime, Darwin believed that acquired characteristics were partly responsible for evolution. After Darwin's death, Weisman's tail cutting experiment disproved the concept of disuse.

Reading about History | I |

Read about history in the following resource:

 All American History: Vol. II p. 409-414

You will be writing a narration about **part** of the pages that you read today. To prepare for writing your narration, look back over p. 409-411 in *All American History: Vol. II*. Think about the main idea and the most important moments in this part of the reading. Plan to write 4-5 sentences for each bolded section in the reading (i.e. Literature, Art, Architecture).

After you have thought about what you will write and how you will begin your narration, turn to Unit 26 in your *Student Notebook*. For more guidance on writing a narration, see *Written Narration Tips* in the Appendix.

In Box 4, write a 12-16 sentence narration about the reading. When you have finished writing, read your sentences out loud to catch any mistakes. Check for the following things: *Did you include* **who** *or* **what topic** *the reading was mainly about? Did you include* **descriptors** *of the important thing(s) that happened? Did you include a* **closing sentence**? *If not, add those things.* Use the *Written Narration Skills* in the Appendix as a guide for editing the narration.

Key Idea: During the 1950s, American literature reflected Cold War tensions and questioned conformity. The Revised Standard Version of the Bible topped bestseller lists. German artists who immigrated out of Hitler's Germany impacted art in the United States. Abstract paintings and paintings of everyday objects became popular. Architecture used mostly glass and steel and leaned toward functionality. Look-alike suburb houses were built quickly to meet housing demands.

President Study | I |

 On *The Presidents* DVD Volume 3, select the Chapter "Truman to Ford" and watch **only** Program 2: Dwight D. Eisenhower. Then, open your *President Notebook* to Dwight D. Eisenhower. Use today's viewing to add further information about Eisenhower.

Key Idea: Research Dwight D. Eisenhower.

Storytime | T/I |

Read the following assigned pages:

 Freedom Walkers p. 75-88

Get the bookmark that you placed in your book. Locate the same section of the bookmark that you used on Day 2. Select the one remaining response option at the bottom of the bookmark, and respond beneath Day 2's entry.

Key Idea: Relate to the text in various ways.

Worthy Words | T |

Read, analyze, and evaluate the speech below.

 Book of Great American Speeches for Young People p. 182-183

After reading the speech, answer the following questions on an index card: *How does Faulkner describe his "life's work" in the opening paragraph of his speech? What tragedy does Faulkner say has caused writers to forget about the "problems of the human heart?" Faulkner says, "the basest of all things is to be afraid." What does that mean? From what "truths of the heart" does Faulkner say good writing comes? What differences might be seen when writing from the "glands" versus writing from the "heart?" Why is man immortal according to Genesis 2:7 and 1 Corinthians 15:39-50? Does Faulkner agree? What is our purpose for being on the earth? Read and discuss 1 Corinthians 10:31. How can writing be used to fulfill that purpose?* Next, meet with a parent to have a Socratic dialogue about the speech.

Key Idea: Faulkner wrote at a time when the atomic bomb made people fear nuclear war.

Independent History Study | I |

Open your *Student Notebook* to Unit 26. Copy an important part of p. 182-183 from the *Book of Great American Speeches...* in Box 6. Write "William Faulkner" at the bottom of Box 6.

Key Idea: William Faulkner won the Nobel Prize for Literature in 1950.

Learning the Basics
Focus: Language Arts, Math, Bible, Nature Journal, and Science

Biblical Self-Image [T]

Read and discuss with the students the following pages in the resource below.

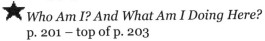 *Who Am I? And What Am I Doing Here?* p. 201 – top of p. 203

Key Idea: The parable of the sower in Mark 4, in Luke, and in Matthew, shows different ways that people will respond to the message of salvation. God wants us to grow as a Christian, mature in our faith, and live our lives for Him.

Language Arts [S]

Have students complete one studied dictation exercise (see Appendix for passages).

Help students complete one lesson from the following reading program:

★ *Drawn into the Heart of Reading*

Help students complete **one** English option.

★ *Progressing With Courage:* Lesson 99 (last half only)

★ *Progressing With Courage:* Lesson 117 (first half only)

★ Your own grammar program

Key Idea: Practice language arts skills.

Bible Quiet Time [I]

Bible Study: Complete the assignment below.

★ *Faith at Work: Lesson 22 – Day Four* p. 165

Prayer Focus: Refer to **supplication** on "Preparing Your Heart for Prayer". Then, pray a prayer of supplication to make a humble and earnest request of God. Write 'supplication' at the bottom of today's lesson in *Faith at Work* above *Day Five*. Next to it, either list several key phrases or write a sentence to summarize your prayer.

Scripture Memory: Recite James 4:1-8.

Music: Refer to p. 70-71 as you sing with Track 9 *"Like a River Glorious"* (vs. 1-2).

Key Idea: Read and study Galatians 2.

Math Exploration [S]

Choose **one** of the math options listed below.

★ *Singapore Primary Mathematics 6A/6B, Discovering Mathematics 7A/7B, 8A/8B, No-Nonsense Algebra* or *Videotext Algebra*

★ Your own math program

Key Idea: Use a step-by-step math program.

Science Exploration [I]

★ Read *Genetics & DNA Experiment Manual* p. 1-2 and p. 4-6. The first 4 experiments in this Experiment Kit need to be done during one longer experiment session. So today, you will read over "Experiment 1" on p. 7, "Experiment 2" on p. 8, "Experiment 3" on p. 9, and "Experiment 4" on the top of p. 10 in your Experiment Manual. Then, you will plan to complete these experiments in one long session next unit. You will need a tomato and two large empty yogurt containers for Unit 27 - Day 4. You will also need to **ask a parent** to fill the brown bottle in this kit with denatured alcohol, or you may be able to use the bottle of denatured alcohol from the *Chemistry C500 Experiment Kit* if some remains. The guide will instruct you to place your bottle of denatured alcohol in the freezer on the day prior to the experiment. Do not place it in the freezer now!

Key Idea: In the next unit, you will isolate genetic material from a tomato, which contains the "code" for the tomato. The tomato is a living organism.

Learning Through History

Focus: The Cuban Missile Crisis, the Space Race, and Kennedy's Assassination

Unit 27 - Day 1

Reading about History | I

Read about history in the following resource:

⭐ *Rescue and Redeem* p. 199-216
After today's reading, orally narrate to an adult p. 199-216 from *Rescue and Redeem.* Some possible key words to include might be *C.S. Lewis, hospital, Joy Gresham, The Last Battle, marriage, Till We Have Faces, Psyche's invisible palace, bone cancer, The Kilns, church wedding, cancer treatments, Reverend Bide, Shadowlands, prayer, losing calcium, take pain, love,* and *Aslan's world.*

Key Idea: C.S. Lewis was born in Belfast, Ireland. After moving to England, he became an author and a scholar of Medieval and Renaissance literature at Cambridge. He secretly married Joy Gresham to allow her and her two sons to remain in England. Yet, over time he fell in love with Joy and cared for her when she was stricken with bone cancer. Joy died in 1960, and Lewis died in 1963. Both were former atheists who became Christians.

History Project | S

Get the bookmark that you created in Unit 26. Practice using your bookmark with a brother, a sister, or a parent. Begin by reading the Scripture from your Bible that is listed in the gold section of the bookmark. Then, refer to the "History Project Box" on Unit 26 – Day 3 to read the meaning of the **gold** color. Next, read the Scripture noted in the black section of the bookmark. Then, read the meaning of the **black** color from the "History Project Box". Continue this pattern until you have gone through the entire bookmark.

Key Idea: Lewis became a Christian in 1931.

President Study | I

⭐ Read p. 66-67 in *Our Presidents...* Then, open your *President Notebook* to John F. Kennedy. Use today's reading to help you complete the information about Kennedy.
Key Idea: Research John F. Kennedy.

Storytime | T/I

Read the following assigned pages:

⭐ *Freedom Walkers* p. 89-99
Note: p. 89-93 include descriptions of violence.
Choose a new section of the bookmark with **three** options at the bottom. At the top of this section of the bookmark, write the book title and the page numbers you read today. Select **one** of the three options at the bottom and place a checkmark next to it. In the blank space under today's pages, respond in writing using your checked option.

Key Idea: Relate to the text in various ways.

Timeline | I

You will be adding to the timeline in your *Student Notebook* today. In Unit 27 – Box 1, draw and color a missile ready to fire. Label the box, *Cuban Missile Crisis (October 1962 A.D.).*

In Box 2, draw and color an American flag at half-mast. Label it, *President Kennedy Is Assassinated (November 22, 1963 A.D.).*

In Box 3, draw and color the moon's surface with an American flag on it. Label it, *Apollo 11 Mission Lands on Moon (July 20, 1969 A.D.).*

Key Idea: President Kennedy took office in 1961 and was killed in 1963. C.S. Lewis died on the same day that Kennedy was assassinated.

Independent History Study | I

During WWII, C.S. Lewis gave a series of radio addresses for the BBC to encourage the nation. This series of talks eventually became Lewis' book *Mere Christianity.* Most of the audio reels of these talks were recycled due to the war effort. Listen to a rare audio of one of C.S. Lewis' talks **in his own voice** (9 min.) here: http://www.youtube.com/watch?v=JHxs3gdtV8A

Key Idea: C.S. Lewis credited both his friend J.R.R. Tolkien and writer George MacDonald with influencing his return to Christianity.

Nature Journal | I |

Read and follow the directions in the resource below.

 Nature Drawing & Journaling: Lesson XXXVI p. 92-93

Note: If weather permits, go outside to sketch rocks. Or, if weather does not permit, either gather a few rocks to take indoors to sketch, or sketch any rocks you may have collected over the years. If none of these options will work, then sketch the rocks shown on p. 93 instead.

Key Idea: Practice drawing a variety of rocks.

Language Arts | S |

Help students complete one lesson from the following reading program:

 Drawn into the Heart of Reading

Help students complete **one** English option.

 Progressing With Courage: Lesson 100

 Progressing With Courage: Lesson 117 (last half only)

Work with the students to complete **one** of the writing options listed below:

 Write with the Best: Vol. 2 Unit 6 – Day 3 p. 60

 Your own writing program

Key Idea: Practice language arts skills.

Bible Quiet Time | I |

Bible Study: Read and complete the assigned pages in the following resource:

 Faith at Work: Lesson 22 – Day Five and *Notes* p. 165-170

Prayer Focus: Refer to **adoration** on "Preparing Your Heart for Prayer". Then, pray a prayer of adoration to worship and honor God. After your prayer, write 'adoration' at the bottom of today's lesson on p. 165 in *Faith at Work*. Next to 'adoration', either list key phrases or write a sentence to summarize your prayer. Keep "Preparing Your Heart for Prayer" inside your Bible.

Scripture Memory: Read aloud James 4:9 three times from your Bible.

Music: Read the verse and pray the prayer from p. 71 in *Hymns for a Kid's Heart*. Refer to p. 70-71 as you sing with Track 9 *"Like a River Glorious"* (vs. 1-3).

Key Idea: Read and study Galatians 2.

Math Exploration | S |

Choose **one** of the math options listed below (see Appendix for details).

 Singapore Primary Mathematics 6A/6B, Discovering Mathematics 7A/7B, 8A/8B, No-Nonsense Algebra or *Videotext Algebra*

 Your own math program

Key Idea: Use a step-by-step math program.

Science Exploration | S |

 Discuss with a parent the questions for Chapter 4 on p. 50 of *Evolution: The Grand Experiment* Teacher's Manual. Next, read p. 31-37 in the Student Text.

Key Idea: Darwin's major basis for how evolution occurs was natural selection, or survival of the fittest. However, natural selection selects from traits that are already present within a species and which function within "limits of variability". So, the modern theory of evolution says that new traits instead come from accidental mutations. This would mean that to form a new body system thousands of letters of DNA would have to be added or changed, be placed in the correct sequence, and be placed in the correct location.

Learning Through History
Focus: The Cuban Missile Crisis, the Space Race, and Kennedy's Assassination

Unit 27 - Day 2

Reading about History | I |

Read about history in the following resource:

 The Story of the World: Vol. 4 p. 385-389

After today's reading, open your *Student Notebook* to Unit 27 – Box 5. The image in Box 5 shows an actual cover of a crewman's Lunar Excursion Module (or LEM) manual for the *Apollo 11* mission. This mission planned for the "first manned lunar landing" just like the manual cover says. U.S. astronauts Neil Armstrong and Buzz Aldrin stepped out of the LEM, named the *Eagle,* onto the moon's surface on July 21, 1969.

Key Idea: On October 4, 1957, the Soviet Union launched the satellite *Sputnik* into space. They followed that launch by launching *Sputnik II* a month later. This ignited a "Space Race" between the Soviet Union and the United States to see who could land on the moon first.

History Project | S |

Open your *Student Notebook* to Unit 27 – Box 8. Follow the directions from *Draw and Write Through History* p. 58-59 (steps 1-3 only) to draw and begin coloring *Apollo 11.* You will finish coloring your drawing on Day 3.

Key Idea: The Space Race took place during the Cold War years, when tensions were high between the Soviet Union and the United States. It went beyond the first moon landing and continued until approximately 1975.

President Study | I |

On *The Presidents* DVD Volume 3, select the Chapter "Truman to Ford" and watch **only** Program 3: John F. Kennedy. Then, open your *President Notebook* to John F. Kennedy. Use today's viewing to add further information about Kennedy.

Key Idea: Research John F. Kennedy.

Storytime | T/I |

Read the following assigned pages:

 Team Moon p. 4-15

Get the bookmark that you placed in your book. Locate the same section of the bookmark that you used on Day 1. Beneath Day 1's entry, write the book title and the page numbers you read today. Select one of the **two** remaining response options at the bottom of the bookmark, and place a checkmark next to it. In the blank space under today's pages, respond in writing using your checked option. Place your bookmark in your book until Day 4.

Key Idea: Relate to the text in various ways.

Economics | I |

Read about economics in the resource below.

 Whatever Happened to Penny Candy? p. 37-39

After the reading, open your *Student Notebook* to the "Economic Principles" section at the front of your notebook. Under "Economic Principle", write a one line or one sentence summary for each of the **two** economic principles you learned from today's reading.

Key Idea: It is important to be willing to adapt your product, your advertising, and the way you do business, if you want your business to endure through the years.

Independent History Study | I |

Read the timeline entries from 1949-1961 on p. 485-486 of *The Story of the World.* Can you remember what most of these entries mean? You have read about almost all of them!

Key Idea: In 1961, Russian cosmonaut Yuri Gagarin was the first man to orbit the earth. It would be 8 more years before American *Apollo 11* astronauts set foot on the moon.

Biblical Self-Image [T]

Read and discuss the following pages listed below.

 Who Am I? And What Am I Doing Here? bottom of p. 203, all of p. 211, and the green box on p. 212

<u>Key Idea:</u> During the Middle Ages, chivalry was the code of conduct by which a knight lived. This meant that developing character through gallantry, honor, and courtesy was as important as developing fighting skills. God desires for us to develop Godly character and to live our life by His standards.

Language Arts [S]

Have students complete one studied dictation exercise (see Appendix for passages).

Help students complete one lesson from the following reading program:

 Drawn into the Heart of Reading

Help students complete **one** English option.

 Progressing With Courage: Lesson 101

 Progressing With Courage: Lesson 118 (first half only)

 Your own grammar program

<u>Key Idea:</u> Practice language arts skills.

Bible Quiet Time [I]

Bible Study: Read and complete the assigned pages in the following resource:

 Faith at Work: Lesson 23 – Day One p. 171 (Note: Refer to p. 166-170 to complete the lesson.)

Prayer Focus: Refer to **confession** on "Preparing Your Heart for Prayer". Then, pray a prayer of confession to admit or acknowledge your sins to God. After your prayer, write 'confession' at the bottom of today's lesson on p. 171 in *Faith at Work*. Next to 'confession', either list key phrases or write a sentence to summarize your prayer.

Scripture Memory: Memorize James 4:9 from your Bible and recite it.

Music: Refer to p. 70-71 as you sing with Track 9 *"Like a River Glorious"* (vs. 1-3).

<u>Key Idea:</u> Read and study Galatians 2.

Math Exploration [S]

Choose **one** of the math options listed below (see Appendix for details).

 Singapore Primary Mathematics 6A/6B, Discovering Mathematics 7A/7B, 8A/8B, No-Nonsense Algebra or *Videotext Algebra*

 Your own math program

<u>Key Idea:</u> Use a step-by-step math program.

Science Exploration [I]

 On the *Evolution: The Grand Experiment* DVD, select "Menu" and then "Bonus Material". After that select "Chapter Index" and then select "4 – Natural Selection". Watch the DVD from 13:29-17:49 on the counter. The bottom left corner of the screen flashes a green title bar when a new chapter begins. Next, read p. 38-42 in the Student Text.

<u>Key Idea:</u> Darwin believed adaptation was one of the ways by which evolution occurred. Today, the term "adaptation" means different things to different people, resulting in confusion over its scientific meaning. Darwin also thought it possible that whales evolved from bears through acquired characteristics and natural selection. Modern evolution scientists instead theorize whales evolved through chance mutations.

Learning Through History

Focus: The Cuban Missile Crisis, the Space Race, and Kennedy's Assassination

Reading about History | I

Read about history in the following resources:

★ *The Story of the World: Vol. 4* p. 389-395

★ *Great Events in American History* p. 111-113

★ *All American History: Vol. II* middle of p. 426 – middle of p. 427

After today's reading, open your *Student Notebook* to Unit 27. Look at the map in Box 7 from the meetings on the Cuban Missile Crisis showing the range of nuclear missiles being brought into Cuba by the Soviets in 1962. Why do you think the U.S. was so concerned?

<u>Key Idea</u>: After WWII, free elections were held in Cuba, and a president was elected. But, in 1952 Fulgencio Batista militarily overthrew the president and his government. Fidel Castro led an armed attack against Batista and was convicted of treason. Batista set Castro free two years later, and Castro went to Mexico to plot to overthrow Batista's government. Che Guevara trained Castro and his men in guerilla warfare, and Castro returned and seized power from Batista. Then, he took money from the Soviet Union and began to make Cuba Marxist.

History Project | S

Open your *Student Notebook* to Unit 27 – Box 8. Follow the directions from *Draw and Write Through History* p. 59 (steps 4-5) to finish coloring *Apollo 11*.

<u>Key Idea</u>: The Space Race was just one part of the Cold War. The Cuban Missile Crisis was another part that lasted 13 days in Oct. 1962.

State Study | T

★ This is an **optional** part of the plans. If you have chosen to study your state using *State History from a Christian Perspective*, do Lesson 23 from the *Master Lesson Plan Book*.

<u>Key Idea</u>: Study your individual state.

Storytime | T/I

Read the following assigned pages:

★ *Team Moon* p. 16-29
Note: p. 29 uses 'God' in a less than worshipful way.
After today's reading, orally narrate or retell the portion of the story that was read today. See *Narration Tips* in the Appendix as needed.

<u>Key Idea</u>: Practice orally narrating, or retelling, a portion of a story.

Geography | I

For today's activities, use the map listed below.

★ *Map Trek CD: Missions to Modern Marvels* p. 90-91

Print the "Cuba" Student Map found on p. 91 of the *Map Trek* CD. Refer to or print the *Map Trek* Teacher's Answer Map on p. 90 to guide you as you label your Student Map to match the Teacher's Answer Map. Notice the Bay of Pigs where Cuban rebels landed in April 1961 to try to overthrow Castro's government. Then, find Guantanamo Bay where a U.S. naval base remains today. View the map on p. 34 of the *United States History Atlas* to see how close Cuba is to the United States. File the map.

<u>Key Idea</u>: The U.S. occupied Cuba in various forms off and on from 1898 to 1934. The U.S. began leasing a naval base at Guantanamo Bay, Cuba, in 1903.

Independent History Study | I

Read p. 206-207 of the *Book of Great American Speeches for Young People*. Why was Berlin a place where a person could easily see the contrast between communism and the free world? You may listen to the speech at http://millercenter.org/president/speeches/detail/3376 (click play arrow under video)

<u>Key Idea</u>: On June 26, 1963, President John F. Kennedy spoke in Berlin, West Germany. The Berlin Wall remained as a constant reminder of the division of communism and the free world.

Nature Journal & Poetry | S |

The poetry of Longfellow, Wordsworth, and Whitman is scheduled to complement the journaling sessions. Read aloud and discuss today's poem *"Written in March"* (see Appendix) with a parent. Students may recognize this poem from a previous guide. Then, follow the directions below.

⭐ *Nature Drawing & Journaling: Lesson XXXVII* p. 96-98

Note: Sketch and color only **one** farm animal today, either based on the sketches on p. 98-99 or based on an illustration in a book.

Key Idea: Practice sketching a farm animal.

Language Arts | S |

Have students complete one studied dictation exercise (see Appendix for passages).

Help students complete **one** English option.

⭐ *Progressing With Courage:* Lesson 102

⭐ *Progressing With Courage:* Lesson 118 (last half only)

⭐ Your own grammar program

Work with the students to complete **one** of the writing options listed below:

⭐ *Write with the Best: Vol. 2* Unit 6 – Day 4 p. 60-61

⭐ Your own writing program

Key Idea: Practice language arts skills.

Bible Quiet Time | I |

Bible Study: Read and complete the assigned pages in the following resource:

⭐ *Faith at Work: Lesson 23 – Day Two* p. 172

Prayer Focus: Refer to **thanksgiving** on "Preparing Your Heart for Prayer". Then, pray a prayer of thanksgiving to express gratitude to God for His divine goodness. After your prayer, write 'thanksgiving' at the bottom of today's lesson in *Faith at Work* above *Day Three*. Next to 'thanksgiving', either list key phrases or write a sentence to summarize your prayer. Keep "Preparing Your Heart for Prayer" inside your Bible.

Scripture Memory: Copy James 4:9 in your Common Place Book.

Music: Refer to p. 70-71 as you sing with Track 9 *"Like a River Glorious"* (vs. 1-3).

Key Idea: Read and study Galatians 3.

Math Exploration | S |

Choose **one** of the math options listed below (see Appendix for details).

⭐ *Singapore Primary Mathematics 6A/6B, Discovering Mathematics 7A/7B, 8A/8B, No-Nonsense Algebra* or *Videotext Algebra*

⭐ Your own math program

Key Idea: Use a step-by-step math program.

Science Exploration | I |

⭐ Read p. 43-54 in the *Evolution: The Grand Experiment* Student Text. Then, complete "Test A" on p. 55 of the *Evolution: The Grand Experiment* Teacher's Manual. You may refer to the Student Text p. 31-54 to help you complete the test. **Note:** Place the **bottle of denatured alcohol** in the freezer for Day 4.

Key Idea: Scientists can estimate the number of chance mutations that would have to take place for one animal to change into another animal, by listing anatomical differences between the two animals and estimating the number of new proteins needed for the changes. Scientists can then use that number to tentatively calculate the odds of one animal changing into another animal by chance mutations.

Reading about History | I |

Read about history in the following resources:

 *All American History: Vol. II* p. 417-419

Great Events in American History p. 115-117

You will be writing a narration about **part** of the pages that you read today. To prepare for writing your narration, look back over p. 417-419 in *All American History: Vol. II*. Think about the main idea and the most important moments in this part of the reading.

After you have thought about what you will write and how you will begin your narration, turn to Unit 27 in your *Student Notebook*. For more guidance on writing a narration, see *Written Narration Tips* in the Appendix.

In Box 4, write a 12-16 sentence narration about the reading. When you have finished writing, read your sentences out loud to catch any mistakes. Check for the following things: *Did you include* **who** *or* **what topic** *the reading was mainly about? Did you include* **descriptors** *of the important thing(s) that happened? Did you include a* **closing sentence**? *If not, add those things.* Use the *Written Narration Skills* in the Appendix as a guide for editing the narration.

Key Idea: During the 1960s, the Cold War continued with key areas of tension in Cuba, Berlin, and Vietnam. During this time, John F. Kennedy became America's youngest president when he took office in 1961. He was also the nation's first Roman Catholic president. Kennedy challenged the American space program to put a man on the moon by the decade's end. America would do just that. On November 22, 1963, President Kennedy was assassinated in Dallas, Texas. Vice-President Lyndon B. Johnson took over as president.

Storytime | T/I |

Read the following assigned pages:

Team Moon p. 30-38

Get the bookmark that you placed in your book. Locate the same section of the bookmark that you used on Day 2. Select the one remaining response option at the bottom of the bookmark, and respond beneath Day 2's entry.

Key Idea: Relate to the text in various ways.

Worthy Words | T |

Read, analyze, and evaluate the speech below.

Book of Great American Speeches for Young People p. 200-203

After reading the speech, answer the following questions on an index card: *What does Kennedy mean when he says, "The world is very different now"? From whom does Kennedy say that the rights of man come? Explain the meaning of Kennedy's reference to being "disciplined by a hard and bitter peace". List the groups to whom Kennedy makes his pledge. What phrasing does Kennedy use to refer to nuclear weapons when speaking to "those nations who would make themselves our adversary"? Read Romans 12:9-12. Which part of the speech is an echo of verse 12? What is the meaning of "Ask not what America will do for you, but what together we can do for the freedom of man"? Is this still a good question to ask today? Could this be carried too far? What line in the speech is your favorite?* Next, meet with a parent to have a Socratic dialogue about the speech.

Key Idea: Kennedy was president during a crucial time in America's history.

President Study | I |

Read p. 68-69 in *Our Presidents...* Then, open your *President Notebook* to Lyndon B. Johnson. Use today's reading to help you complete the information about Johnson.

Key Idea: Research Lyndon B. Johnson.

Independent History Study | I |

Open your *Student Notebook* to Unit 27. Copy an important part of p. 200-203 from the *Book of Great American Speeches...* in Box 6. Write "John F. Kennedy" at the bottom of Box 6.

Key Idea: John F. Kennedy died at age 46.

Learning the Basics
Focus: Language Arts, Math, Bible, Nature Journal, and Science

Biblical Self-Image | T |

Read and discuss with the students the following pages in the resource below.

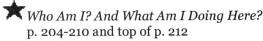 ★ *Who Am I? And What Am I Doing Here?* p. 204-210 and top of p. 212

Key Idea: The Holy Spirit, or Holy Ghost, is God living inside us. As followers of Christ, we are to listen to the promptings of the Holy Spirit and to stand firmly upon the truth of God's Word.

Language Arts | S |

Have students complete one studied dictation exercise (see Appendix for passages).

Help students complete one lesson from the following reading program:

★ *Drawn into the Heart of Reading*

Help students complete **one** English option.

★ *Progressing With Courage:* Lesson 103

★ *Progressing With Courage:* Lesson 119 (first half only)

★ Your own grammar program

Key Idea: Practice language arts skills.

Bible Quiet Time | I |

Bible Study: Complete the assignment below.

★ *Faith at Work: Lesson 23 – Day Three* p. 172-173

Prayer Focus: Refer to **supplication** on "Preparing Your Heart for Prayer". Then, pray a prayer of supplication to make a humble and earnest request of God. Write 'supplication' at the bottom of today's lesson in *Faith at Work* above *Day Four*. Next to it, either list several key phrases or write a sentence to summarize your prayer.

Scripture Memory: Recite James 4:1-9.

Music: Refer to p. 70-71 as you sing with Track 9 *"Like a River Glorious"* (vs. 1-3).

Key Idea: Read and study Galatians 3.

Math Exploration | S |

Choose **one** of the math options listed below.

★ *Singapore Primary Mathematics 6A/6B, Discovering Mathematics 7A/7B, 8A/8B, No-Nonsense Algebra* or *Videotext Algebra*

★ Your own math program

Key Idea: Use a step-by-step math program.

Science Exploration | I |

★ Copy the Science Lab Form from the Appendix of this guide. Put on your safety glasses, smooth gloves, and smock as recommended on p. 4 of the *Genetics & DNA Experiment Manual*. Then, follow the directions to perform "Experiment 1" from p. 7 of the Experiment Manual. **Have an adult help you with the blender.** After completing Experiment 1, in the top box of the Science Lab Form write: *How do you isolate genetic material, or DNA, from a tomato?* In the second box of the form, write your hypothesis. Follow the directions for "Experiment 2" and "Experiment 3" on p. 8-9 of the Experiment Manual and complete the box "Perform an Experiment" on your lab form. Then, follow the arrows to complete the rest of the Science Lab Form. After that complete "Experiment 4" from the top of p. 10 and read p. 11. To clean up, solid substances can be disposed of in the trash, and liquids can be poured down the drain with plenty of water. Review Basic Rules 4, 5, 6, 7, 9, 10, and 11 on p. 4 prior to cleaning up.

Key Idea: Genetic material, or DNA, is finely dissolved and evenly distributed in the watery tomato solution, making it invisible to our eyes. But when that material is surrounded by cold alcohol, it separates and balls up like curdled milk in hot coffee. DNA stands for "deoxyribonucleic acid".

Learning Through History
Focus: The Vietnam War, the Spread of Communism, and Nixon's Resignation

Unit 28 - Day 1

Reading about History | S

Read about history in the following resource:

 The Story of the World: Vol. 4 p. 396 – middle of p. 402

After today's reading, orally narrate or retell to an adult the text from *The Story of the World* that you read today. As you retell, the adult will write or type your narration. Some possible key words to include in your narration might be *John F. Kennedy, Jacqueline Bouvier Kennedy, war hero, Pulitzer Prize, November 1963, Dallas, Texas, Governor John Connally, Secret Service agents, Texas School Book Depository, shots, Parkland Hospital, pink suit, Lyndon Baines Johnson, Air Force One, Camelot, Lee Harvey Oswald, communism, John D. Tippitt, Jack Ruby, died, tombstone.* When the narration is complete, tri-fold the typed or written narration to fit in Unit 28 – Box 10 of the *Student Notebook.* Glue the folded narration in Box 10, so it can be opened and read.

<u>Key Idea</u>: President Kennedy was 43 when he was elected to be President of the U.S. His death has been surrounded with controversy.

History Project | S

On p. 214-215 of the *Book of Great American Speeches for Young People,* read the eulogy given by Supreme Court chief justice Earl Warren at President Kennedy's funeral. With a parent's supervision, you may also choose to listen to newsman Dan Rather's reporting of the shooting at this site: www.timetape.com (Type "JFK" in the "Search" and then click on "Dan Rather's Account from November 25".)

<u>Key Idea</u>: President Kennedy was shot and killed before the end of his first term in office.

Storytime | T/I

Read the following assigned pages:

 Team Moon p. 39-52

Get the bookmark that you placed in your book last unit. Choose a new section of the bookmark with **three** options at the bottom. At the top of this section of the bookmark, write the book title and the page numbers you read today. Select **one** of the three options at the bottom and place a checkmark next to it. In the blank space under today's pages, respond in writing using your checked option.

<u>Key Idea</u>: Relate to the text in various ways.

Timeline | I

You will be adding to the timeline in your *Student Notebook* today. In Unit 28 – Box 1, draw and color dense jungle palm trees and ferns. Label the box, *U.S. Troops - Vietnam War (1965-1973 A.D.).*

In Box 2, draw and color a red star to signify communism. Label it, *Laos and Vietnam Fall Under Communist Rule (1975 A.D.) Cambodia (1978 A.D.)*

In Box 3, draw and color a building labeled "Watergate". Label it, *Richard Nixon Resigns the Presidency (August 9, 1974 A.D.).*

<u>Key Idea</u>: The Paris Peace Accords were signed on January 2, 1973, and President Nixon agreed to remove U.S. troops from Vietnam. Two years later, a North Vietnamese offensive led to all of Vietnam and Laos falling to communist rule. Cambodia followed not long after this. In 1974, President Nixon resigned the presidency to avoid impeachment.

Independent History Study | I

 Open your *Student Notebook* to Unit 28. In Box 6, copy the text written on Kennedy's tombstone from p. 402 of *The Story of the World*. At the bottom of the box write "John F. Kennedy's tombstone".

<u>Key Idea</u>: President Kennedy was buried in Arlington National Cemetery in Washington D.C.

Learning the Basics

Focus: Language Arts, Math, Bible, Nature Journal, and Science

Nature Journal [I]

Read and follow the directions in the resource below.

 Nature Drawing & Journaling: Lesson XXXVIII p. 99-101

Note: Sketch and color **only** a rooster today, based on the sketch on p. 101.

Key Idea: Practice drawing a rooster.

Language Arts [S]

Help students complete one lesson from the following reading program:

 Drawn into the Heart of Reading

Help students complete **one** English option.

 Progressing With Courage: Lesson 104

 Progressing With Courage: Lesson 119 (last half only)

 Your own grammar program

Work with the students to complete **one** of the writing options listed below:

 Write with the Best: Vol. 2 Unit 6 – Day 5 p. 61

 Your own writing program

Key Idea: Practice language arts skills.

Bible Quiet Time [I]

Bible Study: Read and complete the assigned pages in the following resource:

 Faith at Work: Lesson 23 – Day Four p. 173

Prayer Focus: Refer to **adoration** on "Preparing Your Heart for Prayer". Then, pray a prayer of adoration to worship and honor God. After your prayer, write 'adoration' at the bottom of today's lesson in *Faith at Work* above *Day Five*. Next to 'adoration', either list key phrases or write a sentence to summarize your prayer. Keep "Preparing Your Heart for Prayer" inside your Bible.

Scripture Memory: Read aloud James 4:10 three times from your Bible.

Music: Read p. 75-76 in *Hymns for a Kid's Heart*. Refer to p. 78 as you sing with Track 10 *"God of Our Fathers"* (verse 1).

Key Idea: Read and study Galatians 3.

Math Exploration [S]

Choose **one** of the math options listed below (see Appendix for details).

 Singapore Primary Mathematics 6A/6B, Discovering Mathematics 7A/7B, 8A/8B, No-Nonsense Algebra or *Videotext Algebra*

 Your own math program

Key Idea: Use a step-by-step math program.

Science Exploration [S]

 Discuss with a parent the questions for Chapter 5 on p. 63 of *Evolution: The Grand Experiment* Teacher's Manual. Next, on *Evolution: The Grand Experiment* DVD, select "Menu" and then "Bonus Material". After that select "Chapter Index" and then select "5 – Similarities". Watch the DVD from 17:49-19:28 on the counter. The bottom left corner of the screen flashes a green title bar when a new chapter begins. Next, read p. 55-61 in the Student Text.

Key Idea: Since the time of Darwin, scientists have debated the meaning of similarities among animals. Often, scientists see animal similarities as evidence of evolution. Yet, scientists have been proven incorrect through DNA testing in the past when using similarities among certain animals as evidence for evolution.

Reading about History | I |

Read about history in the following resources:

★ *The Story of the World: Vol. 4* p. 410 – middle of p. 415

★ *Great Events in American History* p. 119-121

After today's reading, open your *Student Notebook* to Unit 28. Box 5 shows a British anti-Vietnam war demonstration poster from 1967. The poster refers to the "Washington Mobilisation Against the Vietnam War" which was taking place in the U.S. on October 21.

Key Idea: In 1965, President Johnson ordered U.S. Marines into South Vietnam. U.S. troops fought the Viet Cong in the South.

History Project | S |

Print "The Vietnam War" **Teacher's Answer Map** from p. 82 of the *Map Trek CD*. Then, refer to p. 46 of the *United States History Atlas* to help you label your **Teacher's Answer Map**. Begin, by drawing a red line and labeling it to show the 17th Parallel. Then, label the Demilitarized Zone. Next, draw purple arrows to show the North Vietnamese supply routes, and label the Ho Chi Minh Trail. After that draw green arrows to show the U.S./South Vietnamese movements. Last label the major battles to match those shown on p. 46 of the *United States History Atlas*.

Key Idea: In 1959, Ho Chi Minh and the Viet Minh started a guerilla war against South Vietnam. South Vietnamese forces fought back against communist takeover by North Vietnam.

President Study | I |

★ On *The Presidents* DVD Volume 3, select the Chapter "Truman to Ford" and watch **only** Program 4: Lyndon B. Johnson. Then, open your *President Notebook* to Lyndon B. Johnson. Use today's viewing to add further information about Johnson.

Key Idea: Research Lyndon B. Johnson.

Storytime | T/I |

Read the following assigned pages:

★ *Team Moon* p. 53-69 and p. 77-78
Note: p. 56 uses "God" in an exclamatory way. Get the bookmark that you placed in your book. Locate the same section of the bookmark that you used on Day 1. Beneath Day 1's entry, write the book title and the page numbers you read today. Select one of the **two** remaining response options and respond in writing.

Key Idea: Relate to the text in various ways.

Worthy Words | T |

Read, analyze, and evaluate the speech below.

★ *Book of Great American Speeches for Young People* p. 236-238
Then, answer the following questions on an index card: *In the opening of the speech, what disagreements does Fulbright mention? Discuss these disagreements and share your thoughts. Do any of these disagreements seem similar to the more recent disagreements over the War in Iraq? What reasons does Fulbright give when he states that "America's light burns dim around the world"? What signs of rebellion does Fulbright list? Looking at the questions asked at the end of the speech, what do you notice about how the Vietnam War was viewed in contrast to how WWII was viewed? Why might this be?* Next, meet with a parent to have a Socratic dialogue. Before beginning the dialogue, the parent reads Box 8 out loud. Next, discuss the questions.

Key Idea: For the U.S., the Vietnam War lasted from 1965-1973. After U.S. troops were removed, communist armies invaded South Vietnam and captured it in 1975.

Independent History Study | I |

Read the speech on p. 231-233 of the *Book of Great American Speeches for Young People*. What was Coffin encouraging those opposed to the war and draft to do? Why was he jailed?

Key Idea: Protests were held against the war.

Learning the Basics
Focus: Language Arts, Math, Bible, Nature Journal, and Science

Biblical Self-Image   T

Read and discuss the following pages listed below.

 Who Am I? And What Am I Doing Here? bottom of p. 212 – top of p. 216

Note: Wait to do "Make a Note of It" on p. 216 until Unit 28 – Day 3.

Key Idea: As committed followers of Jesus, we have the Holy Spirit as our guide, teaching us to do what is right. The Holy Spirit helps us become more like Christ. The spiritual fruit that we bear in our lives shows whether we are becoming more like Jesus.

Language Arts   S

Have students complete one studied dictation exercise (see Appendix for passages).

Help students complete one lesson from the following reading program:

 Drawn into the Heart of Reading

Help students complete **one** English option.

 *Progressing With Courage:* Lesson 105

 *Progressing With Courage:* Lesson 120 (first half only)

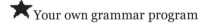 Your own grammar program

Key Idea: Practice language arts skills.

Bible Quiet Time   I

Bible Study: Read and complete the assigned pages in the following resource:

 Faith at Work: Lesson 23 – Day Five and *Notes* p. 173-178

Prayer Focus: Refer to **confession** on "Preparing Your Heart for Prayer". Then, pray a prayer of confession to admit or acknowledge your sins to God. After your prayer, write 'confession' at the bottom of today's lesson on p. 173 in *Faith at Work*. Next to 'confession', either list key phrases or write a sentence to summarize your prayer. Keep "Preparing Your Heart for Prayer" inside your Bible.

Scripture Memory: Memorize James 4:10 from your Bible and recite it.

Music: Refer to p. 78 as you sing with Track 10 *"God of Our Fathers"* (verse 1).

Key Idea: Read and study Galatians 3.

Math Exploration   S

Choose **one** of the math options listed below (see Appendix for details).

 Singapore Primary Mathematics 6A/6B, Discovering Mathematics 7A/7B, 8A/8B, No-Nonsense Algebra or *Videotext Algebra*

★ Your own math program

Key Idea: Use a step-by-step math program.

Science Exploration   I

★ Read p. 62-72 in the *Evolution: The Grand Experiment* Student Text. Then, complete "Test A" on p. 67 of the *Evolution: The Grand Experiment* Teacher's Manual. You may refer to the Student Text p. 55-72 to help you complete the test.

Key Idea: Unrelated animals can have similarities too, just like related animals. This leads to disagreements among scientists who are proponents of evolution as to which similarities could be evidence of evolution and which are not. Scientists who oppose evolution propose that similarities among animals are the result of intentional design or are coincidental.

Learning Through History
Focus: The Vietnam War, the Spread of Communism, and Nixon's Resignation

Unit 28 - Day 3

Reading about History | I

Read about history in the following resources:

★ *All American History: Vol. II* bottom of p. 427 – top of p. 431

★ *Great Events in American History* p. 133-136

After today's reading, open your *Student Notebook* to Unit 28. Box 7 shows the front of the Asbury College Chapel where a revival occurred on the college campus in 1970. To explain more about the revival, choose a paragraph to copy from p. 134-135 of *Great Events in American History* in Box 8.

Key Idea: The 1970 revival at Asbury College occurred during the time of the Vietnam War.

History Project | S

Look at "The Wars in Asia" **Teacher's Answer Map** on p. 84 of the *Map Trek* CD. Then, compare the Teacher's Answer Map to p. 42 of the *United States History Atlas,* which shows this same area during World War II. What was the area shown as North Korea and South Korea called doing WWII? Under whose control was Manchukuo (or Manchuria) during WWII? What was the area shown as North Vietnam and South Vietnam called during WWII? Under whose control was French Indochina during WWII? After the war, why do you think that these areas of Japanese control were split between the main Allied powers? How did this lead to communist type governments in the North and democratic type governments in the South?

Key Idea: Japan controlled Manchukuo and French Indochina during WWII.

State Study | T

★ This is an **optional** part of the plans. If you have chosen to study your state using *State History from a Christian Perspective,* do Lesson 24 from the *Master Lesson Plan Book.*

Key Idea: Study your individual state.

Storytime | T/I

Read the following assigned pages:

★ *Children of the Storm* p. ix-6

After today's reading, orally narrate or retell the portion of the story that was read today. See *Narration Tips* in the Appendix as needed.

Key Idea: Practice orally narrating, or retelling, a portion of a story.

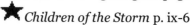

Geography | I

For today's activities, use the map listed below.

★ *Map Trek CD: Missions to Modern Marvels* p. 86 87

Print the "Indonesia" Student Map found on p. 87 of the *Map Trek* CD. Refer to or print the *Map Trek* Teacher's Answer Map on p. 86 to guide you as you label your Student Map to match the Teacher's Answer Map. Notice that Indonesia is mainly south and east of Cambodia.

Indonesia was formerly the Dutch East Indies as shown on p. 42 of the *United States History Atlas.* Cambodia, Laos, and Vietnam were formerly a part of French Indochina as shown on the map on p. 42. Cambodia, Laos, and Vietnam all fell under communist rule in 1975.

Key Idea: Indonesia is comprised of many islands.

Independent History Study | I

Read the speech on p. 245-247 of the *Book of Great American Speeches for Young People.* What did Chisholm mean in her closing sentence when she said, "...the business of America is war, and it is time for a change"? Open your *Student Notebook* to Unit 28. Choose a key portion of the speech from p. 245-247 to copy in Box 9. Write, "Shirley Chisholm" at the bottom of Box 9.

Key Idea: Chisholm spoke against the war.

Learning the Basics

Focus: Language Arts, Math, Bible, Nature Journal, Poetry, and Science

Nature Journal & Poetry [S]

The poetry of Longfellow, Wordsworth, and Whitman is scheduled to complement the journaling sessions. Read aloud and discuss today's poem *"Mad River"* (see Appendix) with a parent. Then, follow the directions below.

⭐ *Nature Drawing & Journaling: Lesson XXXVIII* p. 99-101

Note: Sketch and color **either** a cow **or** a duck, based on the sketches on p. 99 or p. 101.

<u>Key Idea</u>: Practice drawing a farm animal.

Language Arts [S]

Have students complete one studied dictation exercise (see Appendix for passages).

Help students complete **one** English option.

⭐ *Progressing With Courage:* Lesson 106

⭐ *Progressing With Courage:* Lesson 120 (last half only)

Work with the students to complete **one** of the writing options listed below:

⭐ *Write with the Best: Vol. 2* Unit 6 – Day 6 p. 61-62

⭐ Your own writing program

<u>Key Idea</u>: Practice language arts skills.

Bible Quiet Time [I]

Bible Study: Read and complete the assigned pages in the following resource:

⭐ *Faith at Work: Lesson 24 – Day One* p. 179 (Note: Refer to p. 174-178 to complete the lesson.)

Prayer Focus: Refer to **thanksgiving** on "Preparing Your Heart for Prayer". Then, pray a prayer of thanksgiving to express gratitude to God for His divine goodness. After your prayer, write 'thanksgiving' at the bottom of today's lesson on p. 179 in *Faith at Work*. Next to 'thanksgiving', either list phrases or write a sentence to summarize your prayer.

Scripture Memory: Copy James 4:10 in your Common Place Book.

Music: Refer to p. 78 as you sing with Track 10 *"God of Our Fathers"* (verse 1).

<u>Key Idea</u>: Read and study Galatians 3.

Math Exploration [S]

Choose **one** of the math options listed below (see Appendix for details).

⭐ *Singapore Primary Mathematics 6A/6B, Discovering Mathematics 7A/7B, 8A/8B, No-Nonsense Algebra* or *Videotext Algebra*

⭐ Your own math program

<u>Key Idea</u>: Use a step-by-step math program.

Science Exploration [S]

⭐ Discuss with a parent the questions for Chapter 6 on p. 75-76 of *Evolution: The Grand Experiment* Teacher's Manual. Next, on *Evolution: The Grand Experiment* DVD, select "Menu" and then "Bonus Material". After that select "Chapter Index", and then select "6 – The Fossil Record". Watch the DVD from 19:30-22:46 on the counter. The bottom left corner of the screen flashes a green title bar when a new chapter begins. Next, read p. 73-86 in the Student Text. Last, complete "Test A" on p. 79 of the Teacher's Manual. You may refer to the Student Text p. 73-86 to help you complete the test.

<u>Key Idea</u>: Darwin predicted that over time the fossil record would demonstrate his theory of evolution. If evolution is true, the fossil record should reflect dissimilar animals in various intermediary stages slowly changing into other animals over time. Even though the fossil record is not complete, over 200,000,000 fossils have been collected in museums so far.

Reading about History [I]

Read about history in the following resources:

 All American History: Vol. II p. 420 – top of p. 426

⭐ *Great Events in American History* p. 141-144

You will be writing a narration about **part** of the pages that you read today. To prepare for writing your narration, look back over p. 420-426 in *All American History: Vol. II*. Choose to write your narration about only **one** of the four U.S. presidents featured in today's reading. Think about the most important moments in the life of the president that you selected for your narration.

After you have thought about what you will write and how you will begin your narration, turn to Unit 28 in your *Student Notebook*. For more guidance on writing a narration, see *Written Narration Tips* in the Appendix.

In Box 4, write a 12-16 sentence narration about the reading. When you have finished writing, read your sentences out loud to catch any mistakes. Check for the following things: *Did you include **who** or **what topic** the reading was mainly about? Did you include **descriptors** of the important thing(s) that happened? Did you include a **closing sentence**? If not, add those things.* Use the *Written Narration Skills* in the Appendix as a guide for editing the narration.

Key Idea: In 1963, Lyndon B. Johnson became president after John F. Kennedy was assassinated. In 1964, Johnson was elected in a landslide victory. After that Richard Nixon was elected to two terms in office. He was forced to resign in 1974 to avoid impeachment. Gerald Ford became president upon Nixon's resignation. Jimmy Carter was elected in 1977.

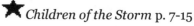

Storytime [T/I]

Read the following assigned pages:

⭐ *Children of the Storm* p. 7-15

Get the bookmark that you placed in your book on Day 2. Locate the same section of the bookmark that you used on Day 2. Beneath Day 2's entry, write the book title and the page numbers you read today. Select the one remaining response option at the bottom of the bookmark, and place a checkmark next to it. In the blank space under today's pages, respond in writing using your checked option. Then, place your bookmark inside your book.

Key Idea: Relate to the text in various ways.

Economics [I]

Read about economics in the resource below.

⭐ *Common Sense Business for Kids* p. 40-41

After the reading, open your *Student Notebook* to the "Economic Principles" section at the front of your notebook. Under "Economic Principle", write a one or two sentence summary for the economic principle you learned from today's reading.

Key Idea: "Needs" are those things that are needed or necessary to live. Food, water, shelter, and clothing are needs. "Wants" are those things that are not necessary for survival but are wanted to make life better. During a recession or a depression, people will purchase needs rather than wants. This makes it a good idea to produce a product that is needed.

President Study [I]

⭐ Read p. 70-71 in *Our Presidents...* Then, open your *President Notebook* to Richard M. Nixon. Use today's reading to help you complete the information about Nixon.

Key Idea: Research Richard M. Nixon.

Independent History Study [I]

Read **either** the speech on p. 253-255 **or** the speech on p. 256-257 of the *Book of Great American Speeches for Young People*.

Key Idea: Nixon announced his resignation after the House Judiciary Committee voted to impeach him.

Learning the Basics
Focus: Language Arts, Math, Bible, Nature Journal, and Science

Unit 28 - Day 4

Biblical Self-Image | T |

Read and discuss with the students the following pages in the resource below.

★ *Who Am I? And What Am I Doing Here?* p. 216 "Make A Note of It" box only

Key Idea: In the story of the Good Samaritan, the Jewish priest and the Levite both passed by the hurting Jewish man. Yet, the Samaritan showed love and kindness to the man, even though Samaritans and Jews were enemies. Love and kindness are spiritual fruits.

Language Arts | S |

Have students complete one studied dictation exercise (see Appendix for passages).

Help students complete one lesson from the following reading program:

★ *Drawn into the Heart of Reading*

Help students complete **one** English option.

★ *Progressing With Courage:* Lesson 107

★ *Progressing With Courage:* Lesson 121 (first half only)

★ Your own grammar program

Key Idea: Practice language arts skills.

Bible Quiet Time | I |

Bible Study: Complete the assignment below.

★ *Faith at Work: Lesson 24 – Day Two* p. 180

Prayer Focus: Refer to **supplication** on "Preparing Your Heart for Prayer". Then, pray a prayer of supplication to make a humble and earnest request of God. Write 'supplication' at the bottom of today's lesson in *Faith at Work* above *Day Three*. Next to it, either list several key phrases or write a sentence to summarize your prayer.

Scripture Memory: Recite James 4:1-10.

Music: Refer to p. 78 as you sing with Track 10 *"God of Our Fathers"* (verse 1).

Key Idea: Read and study Galatians 4:1-5:15.

Math Exploration | S |

Choose **one** of the math options listed below.

★ *Singapore Primary Mathematics 6A/6B, Discovering Mathematics 7A/7B, 8A/8B, No-Nonsense Algebra* or *Videotext Algebra*

★ Your own math program

Key Idea: Use a step-by-step math program.

Science Exploration | I |

★ Copy the Science Lab Form from the Appendix of this guide. We will be omitting Experiment 5 on the bottom of p. 10. Then, read p. 12 in the *Genetics & DNA Experiment Manual*. Next, follow the directions to perform "Experiment 6" from p. 13 of the Experiment Manual. After completing Experiment 6, in the top box of the Science Lab Form write: *How does heredity work?* In the second box of the form, write your hypothesis. Follow the directions for "Experiment 7" on p. 14-15 of the Experiment Manual and complete the box "Perform an Experiment" on your lab form. Then, follow the arrows to complete the rest of the Science Lab Form. After that clean up for today.

Key Idea: Mendel showed that programs for characteristics such as flower color are inherited from the egg and the sperm cells of the mother and father plants. So, "parents" pass instructions for each feature to their offspring, providing two copies of programs for each feature. When both programs for a feature are the same, it is obvious what the feature will be. When programs differ, one program may equally complement the other, or one program may dominate the other. Both produce differing outcomes.

Learning Through History
Focus: The Six-Day War, the OPEC Oil Embargo, and the Civil Rights Act

Unit 29 - Day 1

Reading about History | I

Read about history in the following resource:

★ *The Story of the World: Vol. 4* p. 415-420

After today's reading, orally narrate or retell to an adult the portion of text that you read today from *The Story of the World*. Some possible key words to include in your narration might be *Six-Day War, Israel, Syria, Egypt, Jordan, air force, Gaza Strip, Sinai Peninsula, West Bank, Golan Heights, governed as Jewish state, unhappy Arabs, Yom Kippur War, U.S. sends aid, Soviet Union sends weapons, cease fire, OPEC oil embargo, rationed gas, Jimmy Carter, Anwar el-Sadat, Menachem Begin, Camp David Accords, Egyptian Islamic Jihad, killed Sadat, Hosni Mubarak honored treaty.*

<u>Key Idea</u>: Several wars have been fought over the land around Israel.

History Project | S

The land occupied by Israel is part of the original land of Canaan occupied by the twelve tribes of Israel. Open your *Student Notebook* to Unit 29 – Box 8 to view the land that originally belonged to the twelve tribes. Then, look at Box 9 to see the state of Israel in 1949. Israel managed to keep its independence in spite of being attacked by the 5 surrounding Arab nations shortly after announcing its independence. Next, look at Box 10 to see the land gained by Israel during the Six-Day War. Last, in Box 11 write a brief summary of key points you notice upon comparing the 3 maps.

<u>Key Idea</u>: Israel's land has changed over time.

President Study | I

★ On *The Presidents* DVD Volume 3, select the Chapter "Truman to Ford" and watch **only** Program 5: Richard M. Nixon. Then, open your *President Notebook* to Richard M. Nixon. Use today's viewing to add further information about Nixon.

<u>Key Idea</u>: Research Richard M. Nixon.

Storytime | T/I

Read the following assigned pages:

★ *Children of the Storm* p. 16-24

Get the bookmark that you placed in your book last unit. Choose a new section of the bookmark with **three** options at the bottom. At the top of this section of the bookmark, write the book title and the page numbers you read today. Select **one** of the three options at the bottom and place a checkmark next to it. In the blank space under today's pages, respond in writing using your checked option.

<u>Key Idea</u>: Relate to the text in various ways.

Geography | T

For today's activities, use the map listed below.

★ *Map Trek CD: Missions to Modern Marvels* p. 76

Print "The Nation of Israel" **Teacher's Answer Map** found on p. 76 of the *Map Trek* CD. Next, refer to the map on p. 416 of *The Story of the World* to guide you as you color your **Teacher's Answer Map** to show the territory gained by Israel after the Six-Day War. Label the Gaza Strip, the West Bank, and Golan Heights. Then, make a key on your **Teacher's Answer Map** to show that the colored areas represent the territory gained by Israel after the Six-Day War in 1967. Then, file the map in your *Student Notebook*.

<u>Key Idea</u>: During the Six-Day War, Israel was attacked by the Arab states of Syria, Jordan, and Egypt. Israel defeated these three Arab states, taking the Gaza Strip, the West Bank, the Sinai Peninsula, and Golan Heights.

Independent History Study | I

Read the timeline entries from 1961-1967 on p. 486 of *The Story of the World*. What entries do you recognize? Which ones are new?

<u>Key Idea</u>: The Six-Day War was a decisive victory for Israel.

Learning the Basics
Focus: Language Arts, Math, Bible, Nature Journal, and Science

Nature Journal | I |

Read and follow the directions in the resource below.

 Nature Drawing & Journaling: Lesson XXXIX p. 102-103

Note: Do only the assignment described in the **first** and **second** paragraphs on p. 103 today. Wait to draw birds from life until Unit 29 – Day 3.

Key Idea: Practice drawing a still life bird.

Language Arts | S |

Help students complete one lesson from the following reading program:

 Drawn into the Heart of Reading

Help students complete **one** English option.

 Progressing With Courage: Lesson 108

 Progressing With Courage: Lesson 121 (last half only)

Work with the students to complete **one** of the writing options listed below:

 Write with the Best: Vol. 2 Unit 6 – Day 7 p. 62

 Your own writing program

Key Idea: Practice language arts skills.

Bible Quiet Time | I |

Bible Study: Read and complete the assigned pages in the following resource:

 Faith at Work: Lesson 24 – Day Three p. 180

Prayer Focus: Refer to **adoration** on "Preparing Your Heart for Prayer". Then, pray a prayer of adoration to worship and honor God. After your prayer, write 'adoration' at the bottom of today's lesson on p. 180 in *Faith at Work*. Next to 'adoration', either list key phrases or write a sentence to summarize your prayer. Keep "Preparing Your Heart for Prayer" inside your Bible.

Scripture Memory: Read aloud James 4:11 three times from your Bible.

Music: Read p. 77 in *Hymns for a Kid's Heart*. Refer to p. 78-79 as you sing with Track 10 *"God of Our Fathers"* (vs. 1-2).

Key Idea: Read and study Galatians 4:1-5:15.

Math Exploration | S |

Choose **one** of the math options listed below (see Appendix for details).

 Singapore Primary Mathematics 6A/6B, Discovering Mathematics 7A/7B, 8A/8B, No-Nonsense Algebra or *Videotext Algebra*

 Your own math program

Key Idea: Use a step-by-step math program.

Science Exploration | S |

 Discuss with a parent the questions for Chapter 7 on p. 87-88 of *Evolution: The Grand Experiment* Teacher's Manual. There is no DVD segment to watch for Chapter 7. Next, read p. 87-94 in the Student Text. Last, complete "Test A" on p. 91 of the Teacher's Manual. You may refer to the Student Text p. 87-94 to help you complete the test.

Key Idea: Trilobites are diverse and complex animals without backbones that appear suddenly in the fossil layer without any ancestors. This problem of suddenly appearing vertebrates also occurs for soft-bodied animals. Darwin thought the ancestors of these animals would eventually be found, but so far no direct ancestors have clearly appeared.

Learning Through History

Focus: The Six-Day War, the OPEC Oil Embargo, and the Civil Rights Act

Unit 29 - Day 2

Reading about History   I

Read about history in the following resources:

 All American History: Vol. II p. 437-440

★ *Great Events in American History* p. 129-131

Open your *Student Notebook* to Unit 29. Box 7 shows a picture of a 1973 Lincoln City, Oregon, sign from a gas station during the OPEC oil embargo. Can you imagine what it would be like not to be able to fill your car with gas when needed? Based on what you read today on p. 437 of *All American History*, explain the meaning of the sign pictured in Box 7.

Key Idea: After the 1973 war between Israel and the Arab nations, OPEC stopping shipping oil to Israel's allies. This resulted in an oil shortage in the U.S. The energy crisis also led to a scarcity of consumer products and rising prices. To compensate, the federal government printed more money, which led to inflation. Coupled with high unemployment, this became known as "stagflation."

History Project   S

Reread p. 437 – top of p. 438 in *All American History*. Then, open your *Student Notebook* to the "Economic Principles" section at the front of your notebook. Read through the economic principles that you have listed so far and place a star by any of the principles that reflect what you read about the economy of the 1970s. What created the "stagflation" of the late 1970s? With this in mind, why didn't Jimmy Carter's plan to control inflation by increasing government spending work?

Key Idea: High inflation combined with high unemployment became known as stagflation.

President Study   I

★ Read p. 72-73 in *Our Presidents...* Then, open your *President Notebook* to Gerald R. Ford. Use today's reading to help you complete the information about Ford.

Key Idea: Research Gerald R. Ford.

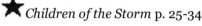

Storytime   T/I

Read the following assigned pages:

★ *Children of the Storm* p. 25-34

Get the bookmark that you placed in your book. Locate the same section of the bookmark that you used on Day 1. Beneath Day 1's entry, write the book title and the page numbers you read today. Select one of the **two** remaining response options at the bottom of the bookmark, and place a checkmark next to it. In the blank space under today's pages, respond in writing using your checked option.

Key Idea: Relate to the text in various ways.

Timeline   I

You will be adding to the timeline in your *Student Notebook* today. In Unit 29 – Box 1, draw and color a sign that says "VOTE". Label it, *The Civil Rights Act (1964 A.D.) The Voting Rights Act (1965 A.D.)*.

In Box 2, draw a blue star for the nation of Israel. Label it, *The Six-Day War (1967 A.D.)*.

In Box 3, draw and color a sign that says "No Gas Today". Label it, *OPEC Oil Embargo (Oct. 1973-March 1974 A.D.)*.

Key Idea: President Johnson signed the Civil Rights Act in 1964 and the Voting Rights Act in 1965. Both of these acts addressed discrimination against African-Americans in the U.S. In Israel, both the Six-Day War and the Yom Kippur War were fought against Arab states.

Independent History Study   I

Read the speech on p. 234-235 of the *Book of Great American Speeches for Young People*. Open your *Student Notebook* to Unit 29. Choose a key portion of the speech from p. 234-235 to copy in Box 6. Write, "Caesar Chavez" at the bottom of Box 6.

Key Idea: Caesar Chavez was a migrant farm worker who founded the United Farm Workers. This nonviolent union desired better working conditions and higher wages for farm workers.

Learning the Basics
Focus: Language Arts, Math, Bible, Nature Journal, and Science

Biblical Self-Image | T |

Read and discuss the following pages listed below.

 Who Am I? And What Am I Doing Here? middle of p. 216 – bottom of p. 218

Key Idea: After Adam's first sin, all men were born in sin and are sinful by nature. This is why it is hard for us to do the right thing, even when we know it is right. Only Christ can free us from the power of our sin. When we follow Christ, the Holy Spirit works in us giving us the desire and power to do what is right and good.

Language Arts | S |

Have students complete one studied dictation exercise (see Appendix for passages).

Help students complete one lesson from the following reading program:

 Drawn into the Heart of Reading

Help students complete **one** English option.

 Progressing With Courage: Lesson 109

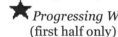 *Progressing With Courage:* Lesson 122 (first half only)

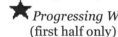 Your own grammar program

Key Idea: Practice language arts skills.

Bible Quiet Time | I |

Bible Study: Read and complete the assigned pages in the following resource:

 Faith at Work: Lesson 24 – Day Four p. 181

Prayer Focus: Refer to **confession** on "Preparing Your Heart for Prayer". Then, pray a prayer of confession to admit or acknowledge your sins to God. After your prayer, write 'confession' at the bottom of today's lesson in *Faith at Work* above *Day Five*. Next to 'confession', either list key phrases or write a sentence to summarize your prayer.

Scripture Memory: Memorize James 4:11 from your Bible and recite it.

Music: Refer to p. 78-79 as you sing with Track 10 *"God of Our Fathers"* (vs. 1-2).

Key Idea: Read and study Galatians 4:1-5:15.

Math Exploration | S |

Choose **one** of the math options listed below (see Appendix for details).

 Singapore Primary Mathematics 6A/6B, Discovering Mathematics 7A/7B, 8A/8B, No-Nonsense Algebra or *Videotext Algebra*

 Your own math program

Key Idea: Use a step-by-step math program.

Science Exploration | S |

 Discuss with a parent the questions for Chapter 8 on p. 98-99 of *Evolution: The Grand Experiment* Teacher's Manual. Next, on *Evolution: The Grand Experiment* DVD, select "Menu" and then "Bonus Material". After that select "Chapter Index" and then select "8 – Fish". Watch the DVD from 22:47-25:42 on the counter. The bottom left corner of the screen flashes a green title bar when a new chapter begins. Next, read p. 95-98 in the Student Text. Last, complete "Test A" on p. 103 of the Teacher's Manual. You may refer to the Student Text p. 95-98 to help you complete the test.

Key Idea: The fossil record for fish is quite extensive, yet transitional forms have not been found between invertebrates and vertebrates. A common ancestor of fish has also not been found in the fossil record.

Learning Through History

Focus: The Six-Day War, the OPEC Oil Embargo, and the Civil Rights Act

Unit 29 - Day 3

Reading about History | I

Read about history in the following resource:

 All American History: Vol. II p. 441-447
After today's reading, open your *Student Notebook* to Unit 29. The image in Box 5 shows a political cartoon related to "stagflation". The 1970s stagflation was a combination of high inflation, high unemployment, and slow economic growth over an extended period of time. Deficit spending, a flood of new "baby boom" aged workers, inflated wages, and inflated prices on goods and services all affected the stagflation.

Key Idea: After a post-WWII economic boom, economic conditions started changing in the early 1970s. The printing of more money in the U.S. led to inflation and eventually stagflation.

History Project | S

Domino's Pizza was founded in 1960. It is a pizza delivering company that made pizza a household meal. To commemorate the founding of the Domino's pizza chain, choose to have pizza for dinner one evening this week. You can either purchase a ready-made pizza, order a pizza delivery, or make your own pizza. If you choose to make your own pizza, it can be as easy as using ready-made pizza dough, prepared pizza sauce, shredded mozzarella cheese, and pepperoni. Or, if your family loves to cook and has a more extensive homemade pizza recipe, you can plan to make that instead!

Key Idea: In the 1960s and 1970s, some new foods were Pop-Tarts, Gatorade, Doritos, and Tang. Domino's Pizza, Taco Bell, and Starbucks all opened during this time too.

State Study | T

This is an **optional** part of the plans. If you have chosen to study your state using *State History from a Christian Perspective*, do Lesson 25 from the *Master Lesson Plan Book*.

Key Idea: Study your individual state.

Storytime | T/I

Read the following assigned pages:

 Children of the Storm p. 51-61

After today's reading, orally narrate or retell the portion of the story that was read today. See *Narration Tips* in the Appendix as needed.

Key Idea: Practice orally narrating, or retelling, a portion of a story.

Economics | I

Read about economics in the resource below.

Common Sense Business for Kids p. 42-43

After the reading, open your *Student Notebook* to the "Economic Principles" section at the front of your notebook. Under "Economic Principle", write a one or two sentence summary for the economic principle you learned from today's reading.

Key Idea: It is important to be "hands-on" when running your own business and to be sure to oversee the whole operation. Use your own common sense when making decisions about your business.

Independent History Study | I

Read the short speech on p. 260 of the *Book of Great American Speeches for Young People* given by Dr. Seuss to graduating seniors at Lake Forest College in Illinois. Note: p. 260 does include the word "darned". What advice about the world is Dr. Seuss giving in this speech?

Key Idea: Antiwar movements were popular on college campuses during the 1970s. Forced integration of schools took place during this time, even if it meant bussing students out of their neighborhoods to achieve it. Racial tension and violence were problems in the schools.

Learning the Basics
Focus: Language Arts, Math, Bible, Nature Journal, Poetry, and Science

Nature Journal & Poetry [S]

The poetry of Longfellow, Wordsworth, and Whitman is scheduled to complement the journaling sessions. Read aloud and discuss today's poem *"Birds of Passage"* (see Appendix) with a parent. Then, follow the directions below.

⭐ *Nature Drawing & Journaling: Lesson XXXIX* p. 103

Note: Follow the directions beginning with the **third** paragraph on p. 103. Try to do 3-6 quick sketches instead of 10 sketches.

<u>Key Idea:</u> Practice sketching birds from life.

Language Arts [S]

Have students complete one studied dictation exercise (see Appendix for passages).

Help students complete **one** English option.

⭐ *Progressing With Courage:* Lesson 110

⭐ *Progressing With Courage:* Lesson 122 (last half only)

⭐ Your own grammar program

Work with the students to complete **one** of the writing options listed below:

⭐ *Write with the Best: Vol. 2* Unit 6 – Day 8 p. 62-63

⭐ Your own writing program

<u>Key Idea:</u> Practice language arts skills.

Bible Quiet Time [I]

Bible Study: Read and complete the assigned pages in the following resource:

⭐ *Faith at Work: Lesson 24 – Day Five* and *Notes* p. 181-185

Prayer Focus: Refer to **thanksgiving** on "Preparing Your Heart for Prayer". Then, pray a prayer of thanksgiving to express gratitude to God for His divine goodness. After your prayer, write 'thanksgiving' at the bottom of today's lesson on p. 181 in *Faith at Work*. Next to 'thanksgiving', either list key phrases or write a sentence to summarize your prayer. Keep "Preparing Your Heart for Prayer" inside your Bible.

Scripture Memory: Copy James 4:11 in your Common Place Book.

Music: Refer to p. 78-79 as you sing with Track 10 *"God of Our Fathers"* (vs. 1-2).

<u>Key Idea:</u> Read and study Galatians 4:1-5:15.

Math Exploration [S]

Choose **one** of the math options listed below (see Appendix for details).

⭐ *Singapore Primary Mathematics 6A/6B, Discovering Mathematics 7A/7B, 8A/8B, No-Nonsense Algebra* or *Videotext Algebra*

⭐ Your own math program

<u>Key Idea:</u> Use a step-by-step math program.

Science Exploration [S]

⭐ Discuss with a parent the questions for Chapter 9 on p. 111-112 of *Evolution: The Grand Experiment* Teacher's Manual. Next, on *Evolution: The Grand Experiment* DVD, select "Menu" and then "Bonus Material". After that select "Chapter Index" and then select "9 – Bats". Watch the DVD from 25:42-28:30 on the counter. The bottom left corner of the screen flashes a green title bar when a new chapter begins. Next, read p. 99-104 in the Student Text. Last, complete "Test A" on p. 115 of the Teacher's Manual. You may refer to the Student Text p. 99-104 to help you complete the test. **Optional:** Extension students may take "Test B" on p. 69-70, 81, 93, 105, and 117 of the Teacher's Manual as a sectional exam.

<u>Key Idea:</u> All fossilized bats discovered so far show fully formed bats. No bat ancestors have been found.

Learning Through History

Focus: The Six-Day War, the OPEC Oil Embargo, and the Civil Rights Act

Unit 29 - Day 4

Reading about History `I`

Read about history in the following resource:

 ★ *The Story of the World: Vol. 4* p. 402-408
You will be writing a narration about the chapter *Civil Rights*. To prepare for writing your narration, look back over p. 402-408 in *The Story of the World: Vol. 4*. Think about the main idea and the most important moments in this part of the reading.

After you have thought about what you will write and how you will begin your narration, turn to Unit 29 in your *Student Notebook*. For more guidance on writing a narration, see *Written Narration Tips* in the Appendix.

In Box 4, write a 12-16 sentence narration about the reading. When you have finished writing, read your sentences out loud to catch any mistakes. Check for the following things: *Did you include **who** or **what topic** the reading was mainly about? Did you include **descriptors** of the important thing(s) that happened? Did you include a **closing sentence**? If not, add those things.* Use the *Written Narration Skills* in the Appendix as a guide for editing the narration.

Key Idea: After slavery ended in the U.S., many segregation laws were passed in the South to limit freedom for black people. The Civil Rights Movement was a way for African-Americans to protest these unfair laws. The Supreme Court ruled in 1954 that racially segregated schools violated the Constitution. In 1955, the Montgomery Bus Boycott led to integrated seating on buses. This boycott brought Martin Luther King Jr. into the forefront as an advocate for civil rights. In 1957, the U.S. President had to use federal troops in Arkansas to enforce integration.

President Study `I`

★ On *The Presidents* DVD Volume 3, select the Chapter "Truman to Ford" and watch **only** Program 6: Gerald R. Ford. Then, open your *President Notebook* to Gerald R. Ford. Use today's viewing to add further information about Ford.

Key Idea: Research Gerald R. Ford.

Storytime `T/I`

Read the following assigned pages:

★ *Children of the Storm* p. 62-68
Get the bookmark that you placed in your book. Locate the same section of the bookmark that you used on Day 2. Select the one remaining response option at the bottom of the bookmark, and respond beneath Day 2's entry.

Key Idea: Relate to the text in various ways.

Worthy Words `T`

Read, analyze, and evaluate the speech below.

★ *Book of Great American Speeches for Young People* p. 225-228
After reading the speech, answer the following questions on an index card: *What was the purpose of Johnson's speech? Which locations that were turning points in history does Johnson mention? Remember Lexington and Concord were the locations of the first battles of the Revolutionary War. Appomattox was the location of the last battle of the Civil War. What happened in Selma, Alabama? Read Luke 9:25. Then, read the paragraph in the speech where Johnson quotes Luke 9:25. What is the meaning in that context? Describe the American problem to which Johnson refers? What barriers needed to be overcome? In looking at America today, do you think there is still prejudice and barriers to overcome? What progress has been made?* Meet with a parent to have a Socratic dialogue. Before beginning the dialogue, the parent reads the speech aloud. Next, discuss the questions.

Key Idea: The Voting Rights Act passed in 1965 outlawed discriminatory voting practices.

Independent History Study `I`

Read the speech on p. 211-213 of the *Book of Great American Speeches for Young People*. Choose a portion of the speech to read aloud to a parent.

Key Idea: Four little girls were killed in the 16th Street Baptist Church bombing in Birmingham.

Learning the Basics

Focus: Language Arts, Math, Bible, Nature Journal, and Science

Biblical Self-Image | T |

Read and discuss with the students the following pages in the resource below.

 Who Am I? And What Am I Doing Here? p. 219 – bottom of p. 220

Discuss "Make a Note of It" on p. 220, rather than having students write their responses.

Key Idea: Gentleness can reflect quiet strength.

Language Arts | S |

Have students complete one studied dictation exercise (see Appendix for passages).

Help students complete one lesson from the following reading program:

 *Drawn into the Heart of Reading*

Help students complete **one** English option.

★ *Progressing With Courage:* Lesson 111

★ *Progressing With Courage:* Lesson 123 (first half only)

★ Your own grammar program

Key Idea: Practice language arts skills.

Bible Quiet Time | I |

Bible Study: Complete the assignment below.

★ *Faith at Work: Lesson 25 – Day One* p. 186 (Note: Refer to p. 182-185 to complete the lesson.)

Prayer Focus: Refer to **supplication** on "Preparing Your Heart for Prayer". Then, pray a prayer of supplication to make a humble and earnest request of God. Write 'supplication' at the bottom of today's lesson in *Faith at Work* above *Day Two*. Next to it, either list several key phrases or write a sentence to summarize your prayer.

Scripture Memory: Recite James 4:1-11.

Music: Refer to p. 78-79 as you sing with Track 10 *"God of Our Fathers"* (vs. 1-2).

Key Idea: Read and study Galatians 4:1-5:15.

Math Exploration | S |

Choose **one** of the math options listed below.

★ *Singapore Primary Mathematics 6A/6B, Discovering Mathematics 7A/7B, 8A/8B, No-Nonsense Algebra* or *Videotext Algebra*

★ Your own math program

Key Idea: Use a step-by-step math program.

Science Exploration | I |

★ Copy the Science Lab Form from the Appendix of this guide. Next, follow the directions to perform "Experiment 8" from p. 16-17 of the *Genetics & DNA Experiment Manual*. After completing Experiment 8, in the top box of the Science Lab Form write: *If human eye color was controlled by a single program, what would be the possibilities of having a blue-eyed child if one or both of the parents had brown eyes (and the only other eye color a parent could have was blue)?* In the second box of the form, write your hypothesis. To perform "Experiment 9", you will need the "Inheritance" worksheet from your *Genetics & DNA Kit* and a red felt-tip pen. Then, follow the directions for "Experiment 9" on p. 18 of the Experiment Manual and complete the box "Perform an Experiment" on your lab form. Then, follow the arrows to complete the rest of the Science Lab Form.

Key Idea: Mendel discovered that each parent passes only one of two possible copies of each program to his/her offspring. So, the offspring only ends up with two copies for each program, one from each parent. A "hidden" feature can only appear if a pair of the "hidden" features is present together in one offspring. Otherwise, the "hidden" feature will remain hidden because the dominant program suppresses it.

Learning Through History
Focus: The Assassinations of Martin Luther King Jr. and Robert F. Kennedy

Unit 30 - Day 1

Reading about History | S |

Read about history in the following resources:

★ *All American History: Vol. II* p.449 – top of p. 452

★ *Great Events in American History* p. 123-128

After today's reading, orally narrate or retell to an adult the text from *All American History* that you read today. As you retell, the adult will write or type your narration. Some possible key words to include in your narration might be *hippies, attack traditional values, Woodstock Festival, civil rights movement, sit-ins, Martin Luther King Jr., "I Have a Dream" speech, desegregation, Black Panthers, Black Muslims, Malcolm X, violent revolution, Watts riot, assassination.* When the narration is complete, tri-fold the typed or written narration to fit in Unit 30 – Box 7 of the *Student Notebook.* Glue the folded narration in Box 7, so it can be opened and read.

Key Idea: At the time of the civil rights movement, a hippie counterculture was also developing. This culture rebelled against the Vietnam War and traditional American values.

History Project | S |

Listen to the 17 minute audio of Martin Luther King Jr. giving his famous "I Have a Dream" speech at one of the following websites:
http://archive.org/details/MLKDream

http://www.americanrhetoric.com/speeches/mlkihaveadream.htm

If preferred, **with parental help**, you may instead search to watch the speech online.

Key Idea: This is King's most famous speech.

Storytime | T/I |

Read the following assigned pages:

★ *Children of the Storm* p. 69-75
Choose a new section of the bookmark with **three** options at the bottom. At the top of this section of the bookmark, write the book title and the page numbers you read today. Select **one** of the three options at the bottom and place a checkmark next to it. In the blank space under today's pages, respond in writing using your checked option.

Key Idea: Relate to the text in various ways.

Worthy Words | T |

Read, analyze, and evaluate the speech below.

★ *Book of Great American Speeches for Young People* p. 208-210
After reading the speech, answer the following questions on an index card: *What was the occasion for which King gave this speech? Why is the last half of the speech especially remarkable, according to the comments prior to the speech? What line does King quote from the Declaration of Independence? Why is this such a key line? Read Isaiah 40:4-5. Why do you think King quotes this passage from Isaiah? While p. 208-210 is only an excerpt, in King's fuller speech he also quotes Amos 5:24. Why might King quote this verse? What reaction do you have to King's speech? Why?* You will listen to King's entire speech for your History Project. Next, meet with a parent to have a Socratic dialogue about the speech. Before beginning the dialogue, the parent reads the speech aloud. Next, discuss the questions. Use text/experiences to support your answers.

Key Idea: King gave this speech in 1963.

Independent History Study | I |

Read the speech on p. 216-219 of the *Book of Great American Speeches for Young People.* How does this speaker, Malcolm X, differ from Martin Luther King Jr. in his approach to racism?

Key Idea: Malcolm X was a Nation of Islam minister who spoke for black separatism and black nationalism.

Learning the Basics
Focus: Language Arts, Math, Bible, Nature Journal, and Science

Nature Journal　　| I |

Read and follow the directions in the resource below.

 Nature Drawing & Journaling: Lesson XL p. 106-107

Note: Sketch and color **only one** feather based on the sketches on p. 106-107.

Key Idea: Practice drawing a feather.

Language Arts　　| S |

Help students complete one lesson from the following reading program:

 Drawn into the Heart of Reading

Help students complete **one** English option.

 Progressing With Courage: Lesson 112

 Progressing With Courage: Lesson 123 (last half only)

 Your own grammar program

Work with the students to complete **one** of the writing options listed below:

 Write with the Best: Vol. 2 Unit 6 – Day 9 p. 63

 Your own writing program

Key Idea: Practice language arts skills.

Bible Quiet Time　　| I |

Bible Study: Read and complete the assigned pages in the following resource:

 Faith at Work: Lesson 25 – Day Two p. 186-187

Prayer Focus: Refer to **adoration** on "Preparing Your Heart for Prayer". Then, pray a prayer of adoration to worship and honor God. After your prayer, write 'adoration' at the bottom of today's lesson in *Faith at Work* above *Day Three*. Next to 'adoration', either list key phrases or write a sentence to summarize your prayer. Keep "Preparing Your Heart for Prayer" inside your Bible.

Scripture Memory: Read aloud James 4:12 three times from your Bible.

Music: Read the verse and pray the prayer from p. 79 in *Hymns for a Kid's Heart*. Refer to p. 78-79 as you sing with Track 10 *"God of Our Fathers"* (vs. 1-4).

Key Idea: Read and study Galatians 5:16-6:18.

Math Exploration　　| S |

Choose **one** of the math options listed below (see Appendix for details).

 Singapore Primary Mathematics 6A/6B, Discovering Mathematics 7A/7B, 8A/8B, No-Nonsense Algebra or *Videotext Algebra*

 Your own math program

Key Idea: Use a step-by-step math program.

Science Exploration　　| S |

 Discuss with a parent the questions for Chapter 10 on p. 124-125 of *Evolution: The Grand Experiment* Teacher's Manual. Next, on *Evolution: The Grand Experiment* DVD, select "Menu" and then "Bonus Material". After that select "Chapter Index" and then select "10 – Seals & Sea Lions". Watch the DVD from 28:30-30:15 on the counter. The bottom left corner of the screen flashes a green title bar when a new chapter begins. Next, read p. 105-112 in the Student Text. Last, complete "Test A" on p. 129 of the Teacher's Manual. You may refer to the Student Text p. 105-112 to help you complete the test.

Key Idea: Sea lions have external ears that distinguish them from seals. Scientists who are advocates of evolution have proposed a variety of possible ancestors for the sea lion, which have not yet been found.

Learning Through History

Focus: The Assassinations of Martin Luther King Jr. and Robert F. Kennedy

Unit 30 - Day 2

Reading about History | I

Read about history in the following resource:

★ *Book of Great American Speeches for Young People* p. 242-244
Open your *Student Notebook* to Unit 30. Box 8 shows a picture of Martin Luther King Jr. and Robert F. Kennedy. Both were known as civil rights activists, and both were assassinated in 1968 within less than two months of one another. Robert F. Kennedy was the brother of President John F. Kennedy, who was assassinated in 1963. Choose a one-sentence quote to copy in Box 9 from Robert Kennedy's speech on p. 242-244. Write "Robert F. Kennedy" under the quote. Then, choose a one-sentence quote to copy in Box 10 from Martin Luther King's speech on p. 239-241 of *Book of Great American Speeches for Young People*. Write "Martin Luther King Jr." under the quote. You will read King's speech for the "Independent History Study" box.

<u>Key Idea:</u> Robert F. Kennedy served as an advisor to his brother President John F. Kennedy. He also served as the U.S. Attorney General and later as a New York Senator. Robert Kennedy was 42 when he was killed by an assassin's bullet.

History Project | S

Open your *Student Notebook* to Unit 30 – Box 11. Follow the directions from *Draw and Write Through History* p. 55-56 (steps 1-4 only) to draw Martin Luther King Jr. You will color your drawing on Day 3.

<u>Key Idea:</u> King spoke outside the Lincoln Memorial near the Washington Monument during the March on Washington in 1963.

President Study | I

★ Read p. 74-75 in *Our Presidents...* Then, open your *President Notebook* to Jimmy Carter. Use today's reading to help you complete the information about Carter.

<u>Key Idea:</u> Research Jimmy Carter.

Storytime | T/I

Read the following assigned pages:

★ *Children of the Storm* p. 76-86
Get the bookmark that you placed in your book. Locate the same section of the bookmark that you used on Day 1. Beneath Day 1's entry, write the book title and the page numbers you read today. Select one of the **two** remaining response options at the bottom of the bookmark, and place a checkmark next to it. In the blank space under today's pages, respond in writing using your checked option.

<u>Key Idea:</u> Relate to the text in various ways.

Timeline | I

You will be adding to the timeline in your *Student Notebook* today. In Unit 30 – Box 1, draw and color the Washington Monument as shown in the background on p. 57 of *Draw and Write Through History*. Label it, *Martin Luther King Jr. Is Assassinated (April 4, 1968 A.D.)*.

In Box 2, draw a newspaper with the headlines *Robert F. Kennedy Is Assassinated (June 6, 1968 A.D.)*.

In Box 3, draw and color a flag divided into 6 horizontal stripes. Color the stripes from top to bottom black, yellow, red, black, yellow, red. Label the box, *Festo Kivengere – Bishop in Uganda (1919-1988 A.D.)*.

<u>Key Idea:</u> Festo Kivengere fled Uganda in 1973 not many years after the assassinations of Martin Luther King Jr. and Robert Kennedy.

Independent History Study | I

Read the speech on p. 239-241 of the *Book of Great American Speeches for Young People*. Martin Luther King Jr. gave this speech the day before he was killed.

<u>Key Idea:</u> Martin Luther King Jr. was a Baptist minister and a leader of the civil rights movement in America. He advocated using nonviolent methods of protesting racism. He was 39 years old when he was killed.

Learning the Basics

Focus: Language Arts, Math, Bible, Nature Journal, and Science

Biblical Self-Image | T |

Read and discuss the following pages listed below.

 ★ *Who Am I? And What Am I Doing Here?* p. 221-224

Note: Discuss "Make a Note of It" on p. 224 with each student individually. Then, pray the prayer on p. 224 together with the students.

Key Idea: To cultivate a strong relationship with the Lord, it is important to spend time with Him daily talking to Him and reading and meditating upon His Word. Submitting to God's pruning and getting rid of distracting "weeds" is another part of spiritual growth.

Language Arts | S |

Have students complete one studied dictation exercise (see Appendix for passages).

Help students complete one lesson from the following reading program:

 ★ *Drawn into the Heart of Reading*

Help students complete **one** English option.

★ *Progressing With Courage:* Lesson 113

★ *Progressing With Courage:* Lesson 124 (Class Practice 'A' – 'D' only)

★ Your own grammar program

Key Idea: Practice language arts skills.

Bible Quiet Time | I |

Bible Study: Read and complete the assigned pages in the following resource:

★ *Faith at Work: Lesson 25 – Day Three* p. 187

Prayer Focus: Refer to **confession** on "Preparing Your Heart for Prayer". Then, pray a prayer of confession to admit or acknowledge your sins to God. After your prayer, write 'confession' at the bottom of today's lesson on p. 187 in *Faith at Work*. Next to 'confession', either list key phrases or write a sentence to summarize your prayer. Keep "Preparing Your Heart for Prayer" inside your Bible.

Scripture Memory: Memorize James 4:12 from your Bible and recite it.

Music: Refer to p. 78-79 as you sing with Track 10 *"God of Our Fathers"* (vs. 1-4).

Key Idea: Read and study Galatians 5:16-6:18.

Math Exploration | S |

Choose **one** of the math options listed below (see Appendix for details).

★ *Singapore Primary Mathematics 6A/6B, Discovering Mathematics 7A/7B, 8A/8B, No-Nonsense Algebra* or *Videotext Algebra*

★ Your own math program

Key Idea: Use a step-by-step math program.

Science Exploration | S |

★ Discuss with a parent the questions for Chapter 11 on p. 137-138 of *Evolution: The Grand Experiment* Teacher's Manual. Next, on *Evolution: The Grand Experiment* DVD, select "Menu" and then "Bonus Material". After that **do not select** "Chapter Index" but instead select **"Pterosaurs"**. Watch the DVD from 0:00-2:00 on the counter. Next, read p. 113-116 in the Student Text. Then, complete "Test A" on p. 141 of the Teacher's Manual. You may refer to the Student Text p. 113-116 to help you complete the test.

Key Idea: Nearly 1,000 fossils of Pterosaurs have been collected. The fossils of these flying reptiles have been found on every continent, including Antarctica! Yet, no evolutionary ancestors of the Pterosaurs have been found. Proponents of evolution believe the reason for this is that the fossil record is incomplete.

Learning Through History
Focus: The Assassinations of Martin Luther King Jr. and Robert F. Kennedy

Unit 30 - Day 3

Reading about History · I

Read about history in the following resource:

★ *All American History: Vol. II* p. 452-461

After today's reading, open your *Student Notebook* to Unit 30. The image in Box 5 shows a poster promoting the 1963 March on Washington where Martin Luther King Jr. gave his famous "I Have a Dream Speech". The poster reads, *"America faces a crisis... Millions of Negroes are denied freedom... Millions of citizens, black and white are unemployed... We demand: Meaningful Civil Rights Laws Massive Federal Works Programs Full and Fair Employment Decent Housing The Right to Vote Adequate Integrated Education"* What problems do you see listed on the poster?

Key Idea: During the 1960s and 1970s, civil rights, school prayer, and abortion were all issues facing America. A controversial new religious movement known as the "Jesus Freaks" also sprung up during this time. Other young people began turning toward mystic Eastern religions like Zen Buddhism.

History Project · S

Open your *Student Notebook* to Unit 30 – Box 11. Follow the directions from *Draw and Write Through History* p. 56-57 (steps 5-6) to color Martin Luther King Jr.

Key Idea: Martin Luther King Jr. spoke to between 200,000 and 300,000 people during the March on Washington.

State Study · T

★ This is an **optional** part of the plans. If you have chosen to study your state using *State History from a Christian Perspective*, do Lesson 26 from the *Master Lesson Plan Book*.

Key Idea: Study your individual state.

Storytime · T/I

Read the following assigned pages:

★ *Children of the Storm* p. 87-94
After today's reading, orally narrate or retell the portion of the story that was read today. See *Narration Tips* in the Appendix as needed.

Key Idea: Practice orally narrating, or retelling, a portion of a story.

Economics · I

Read about economics in the resource below.

★ *Common Sense Business for Kids* p. 44-45
After the reading, open your *Student Notebook* to the "Economic Principles" section at the front of your notebook. Under "Economic Principle", write a one or two sentence summary for the economic principle you learned from today's reading.

Key Idea: Inventory management is an important consideration in a product-driven business. Having enough inventory, without having too much, is the key to good management.

Independent History Study · I

Read the speech on p. 248-250 of the *Book of Great American Speeches for Young People*. Then, open your *Student Notebook* to Unit 30. Choose an important portion from the speech on p. 248-251 to copy in Box 6 of the *Student Notebook*. At the bottom of Box 6, write "Frank James, Wampanoag Native American". What is your opinion of the thoughts shared in the speech?

Key Idea: Upon the 350th anniversary of Plymouth Rock, a descendent of the Wampanoag Native American tribe was asked to speak. His speech gives a different perspective of the Plymouth celebration. During the 1960s and 1970s, Native Americans began to protest and bring lawsuits against the federal government.

Learning the Basics

Focus: Language Arts, Math, Bible, Nature Journal, Poetry, and Science

Nature Journal & Poetry [S]

The poetry of Longfellow, Wordsworth, and Whitman is scheduled to complement the journaling sessions. Read aloud and discuss today's poem *"A Psalm of Life"* (see Appendix) with a parent. Then, follow the directions below.

★ *Nature Drawing & Journaling* p. 104-105 and p. 108-109

Note: There is no drawing today, only reading.

<u>Key Idea:</u> Think of the cycle of life and death.

Language Arts [S]

Have students complete one studied dictation exercise (see Appendix for passages).

Help students complete **one** English option.

★ *Progressing With Courage:* Lesson 114 (first half only)

★ *Progressing With Courage:* Lesson 124 (Written Practice 'A' – 'C' only)

Work with the students to complete **one** of the writing options listed below:

★ *Write with the Best: Vol. 2* Unit 6 – Day 10 p. 63

★ Your own writing program

<u>Key Idea:</u> Practice language arts skills.

Bible Quiet Time [I]

Bible Study: Read and complete the assigned pages in the following resource:

★ *Faith at Work: Lesson 25 – Day Four* p. 188

Prayer Focus: Refer to **thanksgiving** on "Preparing Your Heart for Prayer". Then, pray a prayer of thanksgiving to express gratitude to God for His divine goodness. After your prayer, write 'thanksgiving' at the bottom of today's lesson in *Faith at Work* above *Day Five*. Next to 'thanksgiving', either list phrases or write a sentence to summarize your prayer.

Scripture Memory: Copy James 4:12 in your Common Place Book.

Music: Refer to p. 78-79 as you sing with Track 10 *"God of Our Fathers"* (vs. 1-4).

<u>Key Idea:</u> Read and study Galatians 5:16-6:18.

Math Exploration [S]

Choose **one** of the math options listed below (see Appendix for details).

★ *Singapore Primary Mathematics 6A/6B, Discovering Mathematics 7A/7B, 8A/8B, No-Nonsense Algebra* or *Videotext Algebra*

★ Your own math program

<u>Key Idea:</u> Use a step-by-step math program.

Science Exploration [S]

★ Discuss with a parent the questions for Chapter 12 on p. 149-150 of *Evolution: The Grand Experiment* Teacher's Manual. Next, on *Evolution: The Grand Experiment* DVD, select "Menu" and then "Bonus Material". After that select "Chapter Index" and then select "12 – Dinosaurs". Watch the DVD from 30:17-32:42 on the counter. The bottom left corner of the screen flashes a green title bar when a new chapter begins. Next, read p. 117-128 in the Student Text. Last, complete "Test A" on p. 155 of the Teacher's Manual. You may refer to the Student Text p. 117-128 to help you complete the test.

<u>Key Idea:</u> No direct ancestors for any of the 700 known species of dinosaurs have been discovered yet in the fossil record, including *Tyrannosaurus rex, Triceratops,* and *Apatosaurus.* This contradicts Darwin's prediction that the fossil record over time would confirm his theory of evolution by producing these missing links.

Learning Through History
Focus: The Assassinations of Martin Luther King Jr. and Robert F. Kennedy

Unit 30 - Day 4

Reading about History — I

Read about history in the following resource:

★ *Hero Tales: Vol. II* p. 69-79

You will be writing a narration about the section "Africa's Apostle of Love" that you read today on p. 69-70 of *Hero Tales: Vol. II*. To prepare for writing your narration, look back over p. 69-70 and think about the main idea and the most important moments in this part.

After you have thought about what you will write and how you will begin your narration, turn to Unit 30 in your *Student Notebook*. For more guidance on writing a narration, see *Written Narration Tips* in the Appendix.

In Box 4, write a 12-16 sentence narration about the reading. When you have finished writing, read your sentences out loud to catch any mistakes. Check for the following things: *Did you include **who** or **what topic** the reading was mainly about? Did you include **descriptors** of the important thing(s) that happened? Did you include a **closing sentence**? If not, add those things.* Use the *Written Narration Skills* in the Appendix as a guide for editing the narration.

Key Idea: Festo Kevingere was born in southwest Uganda. He was the grandson of the last king of the Bahororo tribe. Kivengere became a Christian during a revival that started in East Africa. Later, he became the Anglican Bishop of Kigezie. He helped the church stay strong during the reign of Idi Amin. Idi Amin was a military dictator during the 1970s that tried to stamp out Christianity in Uganda. After Amin was deposed, Kivengere worked until his death to heal the country's wounds.

Storytime — T/I

Read the following assigned pages:

★ *Children of the Storm* p. 95-105
Get the bookmark that you placed in your book on Day 2. Locate the same section of the bookmark that you used on Day 2. Beneath Day 2's entry, write the book title and the page numbers you read today. Select the one remaining response option at the bottom of the bookmark, and place a checkmark next to it. In the blank space under today's pages, respond in writing using your checked option.

Key Idea: Relate to the text in various ways.

Geography — I

For today's activities, use the map listed below.

★ *United States History Atlas* p. 54

Find Uganda on the map of Africa on p. 54 of the *United States History Atlas*. Notice that Uganda is bordered by South Sudan to the north, Kenya to the east, Tanzania to the south, Rwanda to the southwest, and the Democratic Republic of the Congo to the west. Next, refer to the map of Africa in Unit 22 – Box 8 of your *Student Notebook*. Find the location of Uganda on the map in Box 8 and label it. Uganda was placed under the charter of the British East Africa Company and ruled by Great Britain as a protectorate in 1894. Uganda gained independence from Britain in 1962.

Key Idea: Idi Amin seized power from Milton Obote in 1971. Amin ruled as a brutal dictator.

President Study — I

★ On *The Presidents* DVD Volume 3, select the Chapter "Carter to George W. Bush" and watch **only** Program 1: Jimmy Carter. Then, open your *President Notebook* to Jimmy Carter. Use today's viewing to add further information about Carter.

Key Idea: Research Jimmy Carter.

Independent History Study — I

Choose **one** of the sets of questions from the sections of *Hero Tales: Vol. II* that you read today to answer orally with an adult. The questions are found on p. 73, 76, and 79.

Key Idea: After escaping from Idi Amin's men, Festo wrote a book about forgiving your enemies. The book was titled, *I Love Idi Amin*.

Learning the Basics
Focus: Language Arts, Math, Bible, Nature Journal, and Science

Unit 30 - Day 4

Biblical Self-Image [T]

Read and discuss with the students the following pages in the resource below.

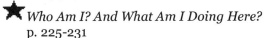 *Who Am I? And What Am I Doing Here?* p. 225-231

Key Idea: Communist countries often promote atheism and enforce restrictive control over religious activities. Communism means that the state controls and provides everything needed by the people. An obedient, productive citizen is the goal.

Language Arts [S]

Have students complete one studied dictation exercise (see Appendix for passages).

Help students complete one lesson from the following reading program:

 *Drawn into the Heart of Reading*

Help students complete **one** English option.

Progressing With Courage: Lesson 114 (last half only)

Progressing With Courage: Lesson 124 (Written Practice 'D' – 'E' only)

Your own grammar program

Key Idea: Practice language arts skills.

Bible Quiet Time [I]

Bible Study: Complete the assignment below.

Faith at Work: Lesson 25 – Day Five and *Notes* p. 188-194

Prayer Focus: Refer to **supplication** on "Preparing Your Heart for Prayer". Then, pray a prayer of supplication to make a humble and earnest request of God. Write 'supplication' at the bottom of today's lesson on p. 188 in *Faith at Work*. Next to it, either list several key phrases or write a sentence to summarize your prayer.

Scripture Memory: Recite James 4:1-12.

Music: Refer to p. 78-79 as you sing with Track 10 *"God of Our Fathers"* (vs. 1-4).

Key Idea: Read and study Galatians 5:16-6:18.

Math Exploration [S]

Choose **one** of the math options listed below.

Singapore Primary Mathematics 6A/6B, Discovering Mathematics 7A/7B, 8A/8B, No-Nonsense Algebra or *Videotext Algebra*

Your own math program

Key Idea: Use a step-by-step math program.

Science Exploration [I]

Today's lesson is an activity, instead of an experiment, so you will not complete a science lab form for it. Begin by reading p. 19 in the *Genetics & DNA Experiment Manual*. Next, follow the directions to read over "Experiment 10" from p. 20 of the Experiment Manual. After completing the reading for "Experiment 10", plan to make a model of the inside of the cell as shown on the cell poster in your *Genetics & DNA Experiment Kit* and on p. 20 of the Experiment Manual. You may choose to make your cell model using various foods, or colored clay or playdough, or art supplies like paper and yarn, or a combination of supplies. When your model is complete, share it with another person by pointing to each part of the model in the numbered order shown on the cell chart and by telling about each part. Last, read p. 21-22 in the Experiment Manual.

Key Idea: DNA is located in the nucleus of a cell. As a cell divides, its individual components are divided.

Reading about History | I |

Read about history in the following resource:

Rescue and Redeem p. 217-234
Note: p. 221 and p. 230-231 contain disturbing violent images and scenes. Parents, be prepared to discuss the content with your child.

After today's reading, orally narrate or retell to an adult *"Janani Luwum: God's Hand Is in This"* that you read today. Some possible key words to include in your narration might be *Archbishop Janani Luwum, Idi Amin, search house, weapons, meeting House of Bishops, letter, official summons, State House, allegiance to Jesus Christ, confessions, traitor, "God's hand is in this", beating, shot, newspaper article, Mary Luwum, Festo Kivengere.*

Key Idea: In 1977, Archbishop Janani Luwum was martyred for his faith because he stood against injustice under Idi Amin's rule in Uganda.

History Project | S |

After reading about Uganda and Janani Luwum's sacrifice, spend some time in prayer for Uganda. **With parental supervision and screening,** visit Operation World's website to read about Uganda's prayer needs. http://operationworld.24-7prayer.com/ Then, click on "Africa" and after that "Uganda".

To encourage you in your prayers for Africa, you may wish to read the following article: http://www.epm.org/resources/2010/Feb/16/uganda-bet-and-prayer/

Key Idea: Prayer is communication with God.

President Study | I |

Read p. 76-77 in *Our Presidents...* Then, open your *President Notebook* to Ronald Reagan. Use today's reading to help you complete the information about Reagan.

Key Idea: Research Ronald Reagan.

Storytime | T/I |

Read the following assigned pages:

Children of the Storm p. 106-116
After today's reading, photocopy the **two** "Bookmark" pages from the Appendix. Place the copied pages back-to-back and staple them together at the 4 corners. Then, tri-fold the stapled page into thirds to make a bookmark. Save the bookmark in your book until Day 2.

Key Idea: Relate to the text in various ways.

Worthy Words | T |

Today's speech can be found at http://www.archbishopofyork.org/index.php. In the "Search" type "If Good Men Do Nothing, Evil Will Prevail". This is a 2012 article of a lecture given by the Archbishop of York to the Royal National Geographic Society. You will read, analyze, and evaluate the lecture. After reading, answer the following questions on an index card: *What was the main topic of the lecture? How does the Archbishop of York describe Janani Luwum? Why do you think Idi Amin killed Luwum? What effect did Luwum's martyrdom have on John Sentamu (now the Archbishop of York)? How does Shelley's poem "Ozymandias" illustrate what happens to dictators? Blinded by vanity and misuse of power, what do dictators forget? How do Pastor Niemoller's words show Christians the need to speak out against injustice? What can you guess about Mugabe and Zimbabwe from reading this lecture?*
Meet with a parent to have a Socratic dialogue. Before beginning the dialogue, the parent reads the lecture aloud. Next, discuss the questions.

Key Idea: Janani Luwum gave his life for his beliefs. He stood firm in his faith.

Independent History Study | I |

Open your *Student Notebook* to Unit 31. Choose one part of the online lecture studied in "Worthy Words" to copy in Box 6. Write "Archbishop of York" at the bottom of Box 6.

Key Idea: Janani Luwum was an inspiration.

Learning the Basics

Focus: Language Arts, Math, Bible, Nature Journal, and Science

Nature Journal | I

Read and follow the directions in the resource below.

 Nature Drawing & Journaling: Lesson XLI p. 110-112

Note: Sketch and color only **one** or **two** insects today.

Key Idea: Practice drawing insects.

Language Arts | S

Help students complete one lesson from the following reading program:

 Drawn into the Heart of Reading

Help students complete **one** English option.

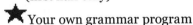 *Progressing With Courage:* Lesson 115

★ *Progressing With Courage:* Lesson 125 (first half only)

★ Your own grammar program

Work with the students to complete **one** of the writing options listed below:

★ *Write with the Best: Vol. 2* Unit 7 – Day 1 p. 64-67

★ Your own writing program

Key Idea: Practice language arts skills.

Bible Quiet Time | I

Bible Study: Read and complete the assigned pages in the following resource:

★ *Faith at Work: Lesson 26 – Day One* p. 195 (Note: Refer to p. 189-194 to complete the lesson.)

Prayer Focus: Refer to **adoration** on "Preparing Your Heart for Prayer". Then, pray a prayer of adoration to worship and honor God. After your prayer, write 'adoration' at the bottom of today's lesson on p. 195 in *Faith at Work*. Next to 'adoration', either list key phrases or write a sentence to summarize your prayer. Keep "Preparing Your Heart for Prayer" inside your Bible.

Scripture Memory: Read aloud James 4:13 three times from your Bible.

Music: Read p. 81-82 in *Hymns for a Kid's Heart*. Refer to p. 84 as you sing with Track 11 *"Come, Ye Thankful People, Come"* (verse 1).

Key Idea: Read and study James 1:1.

Math Exploration | S

Choose **one** of the math options listed below (see Appendix for details).

★ *Singapore Primary Mathematics 6A/6B, Discovering Mathematics 7A/7B, 8A/8B, No-Nonsense Algebra* or *Videotext Algebra*

★ Your own math program

Key Idea: Use a step-by-step math program.

Science Exploration | S

★ Discuss with a parent the questions for Chapter 13 on p. 163 of *Evolution: The Grand Experiment* Teacher's Manual. Next, read p. 129-135 in the Student Text.

Key Idea: Whales are classified as mammals because they are warm-blooded, give birth to and suckle live young, and have some body hair on their "faces". Evolution theorizes that land mammals first evolved from reptiles, and then one species of land mammal went back into the water and evolved into a whale. Evolutionists believe that the evidence for the evolution of whales is very clear. Scientists who oppose evolution believe the opposite is true.

Reading about History | I

Read about history in the following resource:

 *The Story of the World: Vol. 4* p. 422-426

After today's reading, open your *Student Notebook* to Unit 31. Box 7 shows a row of famous Russian leaders as nesting dolls, or "matryoshka". A matryoshka is a symbol of Russian culture. At the bottom of Box 7, list the following names of the Russian leaders in order from left to right: Yeltsin, Gorbachev, Brezhnev, Khrushchev, Stalin, Lenin, Nicholas II, Catherine the Great, Peter the Great, and Ivan the Terrible. According to Box 7, which Russian leaders came after Brezhnev?

Key Idea: In 1964, Brezhnev forced Khrushchev out of power as premier of the USSR.

History Project | S

Today, you will make Czechoslovakian cookies. Cream together 2 sticks of softened butter and 1 cup sugar until light and fluffy. Stir in 2 egg **yolks** and ½ tsp. almond extract. Gradually add 2 cups of all-purpose flour, mixing thoroughly. If desired, stir in 1 cup chopped walnuts. Spoon half of the batter into a greased 8" square pan and spread evenly. Then, spread ½ cup fruit jam (or preserves) over the batter leaving the outer ¼" edge of batter with no jam. Drop the remaining batter by spoonfuls on top of the jam and spread gently to cover the jam. Bake in a preheated oven at 325 degrees for 50 min. or until golden. Turn onto a rack to cool 5 min. and then cut into small squares. Dust with powdered sugar.

Key Idea: The USSR invaded Czechoslovakia.

President Study | I

Storytime | T/I

Read the following assigned pages:

 Children of the Storm p. 117-128

Get the bookmark you made on Day 1. Find the section of the bookmark that has only **two** options at the bottom. At the top of this section of the bookmark, write the book title and the page numbers you read today. Select **one** of the two options at the bottom and place a checkmark next to it. In the blank space under today's pages, respond in writing using your checked option. Keep the bookmark in your book.

Key Idea: Relate to the text in various ways.

Geography | I

For today's activities, use the map listed below.

 *United States History Atlas* p. 43 and 54

On p. 43 of the *United States History Atlas,* view the map inset to see the countries along the western border of the Soviet Union that became a part of the Soviet Empire. The Soviet Union annexed part of Czechoslovakia into the USSR shortly after WWII. It also seized power over the rest of Czechoslovakia after that. The Soviet Union entered Czechoslovakia in 1968 to preserve its communistic hold over Czechoslovakia. Afghanistan was invaded by the Soviet Union in 1979. Find Afghanistan on the map on p. 54 of the *United States History Atlas.*

Key Idea: After WWII, the Soviet Union worked to spread communism by increasing its territory.

Independent History Study | I

 On *The Presidents* DVD Volume 3, select the Chapter "Carter to George W. Bush" and watch **only** Program 2: Ronald Reagan. Then, open your *President Notebook* to Ronald Reagan. Use today's viewing to add further information about Reagan.

Key Idea: Research Ronald Reagan.

Read the timeline entries between 1968-1979 on p. 486-487 of *The Story of the World*. What interesting facts do you notice?

Key Idea: The spread of communism led to alarm in many countries, including the U.S.

Learning the Basics
Focus: Language Arts, Math, Bible, Nature Journal, and Science

Biblical Self-Image [T]

Read and discuss the following pages listed below.

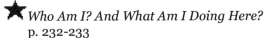 *Who Am I? And What Am I Doing Here?* p. 232-233

Note: Have the students look up the Scriptures that are noted throughout the lesson and read them aloud from their Bibles.

Key Idea: As a child of God, you can approach God's throne with your requests in Jesus' name and trust that the Lord will do what is best for you. You can rest in the knowledge that you can do all things through Christ Jesus.

Language Arts [S]

Have students complete one studied dictation exercise (see Appendix for passages).

Help students complete one lesson from the following reading program:

 *Drawn into the Heart of Reading*

Help students complete **one** English option.

Progressing With Courage: Lesson 116

Progressing With Courage: Lesson 125 (last half only)

Your own grammar program

Key Idea: Practice language arts skills.

Bible Quiet Time [I]

Bible Study: Read and complete the assigned pages in the following resource:

Faith at Work: Lesson 26 – Day Two p. 196

Prayer Focus: Refer to **confession** on "Preparing Your Heart for Prayer". Then, pray a prayer of confession to admit or acknowledge your sins to God. After your prayer, write 'confession' at the bottom of today's lesson in *Faith at Work* above *Day Three*. Next to 'confession', either list key phrases or write a sentence to summarize your prayer.

Scripture Memory: Memorize James 4:13 from your Bible and recite it.

Music: Refer to p. 84 as you sing with Track 11 *"Come, Ye Thankful People, Come"* (verse 1).

Key Idea: Read and study James 1:1-2:13.

Math Exploration [S]

Choose **one** of the math options listed below (see Appendix for details).

Singapore Primary Mathematics 6A/6B, Discovering Mathematics 7A/7B, 8A/8B, No-Nonsense Algebra or *Videotext Algebra*

Your own math program

Key Idea: Use a step-by-step math program.

Science Exploration [I]

Read p. 136-143 in the *Evolution: The Grand Experiment* Student Text. Next, on *Evolution: The Grand Experiment* DVD, select "Menu" and then "Bonus Material". After that select "Chapter Index" and then select "13 – Whales". Watch the DVD from 32:42-39:54 on the counter. The bottom left corner of the screen flashes a green title bar when a new chapter begins.

Key Idea: Proponents of evolution suggest that the predecessor to the whale was either a meat-eating hyena-like mammal, or a cat-like mammal, or a plant-eating hippopotamus. Each theory has its contradictions and its problems. In the proposed second step of whale evolution, *Ambulocetus* was surprisingly classified as a walking whale. This step was followed by the guess that *Rodhocetus* came next with speculated flippers and a fluked tail. The scientist who discovered *Rodhocetus* now says this speculation is mistaken based on further discoveries of its forelimbs, hands, and front arms.

Reading about History | I

Read about history in the following resource:

★ *The Story of the World: Vol. 4* p. 426-431
After today's reading, open your *Student Notebook* to Unit 31. In Box 5, you will see a picture of Libyan ruler Muammar Gaddafi. Gaddafi ruled the Libyan state from 1969-2011 and was known to have used Libya's oil money to help finance the terrorist groups Black September, the Irish Republican Army (or IRA), and the Palestinian Liberation Organization (or PLO). All three of these are terrorist groups that you read about today. Gaddafi was also a supporter of Ugandan President Idi Amin, who was responsible for the death of Archbishop Janani Luwum. What does Gaddafi's use of money for terrorist organizations and his support of Idi Amin tell you about him as a ruler? Where is Libya?

Key Idea: Terrorist groups carry out random violent acts against civilians to create "terror", gain publicity, and force governments to do what they demand.

History Project | S

Open your *Student Notebook* to Unit 31. In Box 8, you can see the outline of a stamp to commemorate the 1972 Summer Olympics. Use colored pencils to design an image for the center of the stamp that shows an event related to the Summer Olympics. Some of the events include track and field, swimming, gymnastics, basketball, canoeing, archery, wrestling, cycling, boxing, volleyball, fencing, field hockey, weightlifting, shooting, and riding.

Key Idea: At the 1972 Olympics in Munich, Germany, the terrorist group Black September was responsible for the Munich massacre.

State Study | T

★ This is an **optional** part of the plans. If you have chosen to study your state using *State History from a Christian Perspective*, do Lesson 27 from the *Master Lesson Plan Book*.
Key Idea: Study your individual state.

Storytime | T/I

Read the following assigned pages:

★ *Children of the Storm* p. 129-135 and p. 35-50
After today's reading, orally narrate or retell the portion of the story that was read today. See *Narration Tips* in the Appendix as needed.

Key Idea: Practice narrating part of a story.

Timeline | I

Add to the timeline in your *Student Notebook* today. In Unit 31 – Box 1, draw and color a golden cross. Label it, *Archbishop Janani Luwum – Martyred in Uganda (1922-1977 A.D.)*.

In Box 2, draw and color the five interlocking Olympic rings as shown on the stamp in Box 8. Label it, *Munich Massacre – 1972 Olympics (September 5, 1972 A.D.)*.

In Box 3, draw the outline of India by referring to the map on p. 432 of *The Story of the World*. Label it, *Indira Gandhi - Prime Minister of India (1966-1977, 1980-1984 A.D.)*.

Key Idea: As Idi Amin was ruling as a military dictator in Uganda, the Munich Massacre took place in Munich, and Indira Gandhi was the prime minister in India.

Independent History Study | I

Find the city of Munich in West Germany on the map on p. 428 of *The Story of the World*. This was the site of the 1972 Summer Olympics. The last time that the Summer Olympics had been held in Germany was under Hitler's Nazi regime during the 1936 Olympic Games in Berlin. Hoping to show the world a changed, more democratic Germany, the 1972 Games motto was "the Happy Games". Instead, a terrorist hostage situation resulting in the deaths of 11 members of the Israeli athletic team overshadowed the games.

Key Idea: Terrorists, like Black September, were a new form of a revolutionary group.

Nature Journal & Poetry S

The poetry of Longfellow, Wordsworth, and Whitman is scheduled to complement the journaling sessions. Read aloud and discuss today's poem *"To a Butterfly"* (see Appendix) with a parent. Then, follow the directions below.

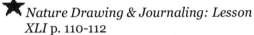*Nature Drawing & Journaling: Lesson XLI* p. 110-112

Note: Sketch and color only **one** insect today. Then, on your journal page, either copy a stanza of today's poem or write about your day.

Key Idea: Practice drawing an insect.

Language Arts S

Have students complete one studied dictation exercise (see Appendix for passages).

Help students complete **one** English option.

★ *Progressing With Courage:* Lesson 117

★ *Progressing With Courage:* Lesson 126 (first half only)

Work with the students to complete **one** of the writing options listed below:

★ *Write with the Best: Vol. 2* Unit 7 – Day 2 p. 68

★ Your own writing program

Key Idea: Practice language arts skills.

Bible Quiet Time I

Bible Study: Read and complete the assigned pages in the following resource:

★ *Faith at Work: Lesson 26 – Day Three* p. 196-197

Prayer Focus: Refer to **thanksgiving** on "Preparing Your Heart for Prayer". Then, pray a prayer of thanksgiving to express gratitude to God for His divine goodness. After your prayer, write 'thanksgiving' at the bottom of today's lesson in *Faith at Work* above *Day Four*. Next to 'thanksgiving', either list phrases or write a sentence to summarize your prayer.

Scripture Memory: Copy James 4:13 in your Common Place Book.

Music: Refer to p. 84 as you sing with Track 11 *"Come, Ye Thankful People, Come"* (verse 1).

Key Idea: Read and study James 1:1-2:13.

Math Exploration S

Choose **one** of the math options listed below (see Appendix for details).

★ *Singapore Primary Mathematics 6A/6B, Discovering Mathematics 7A/7B, 8A/8B, No-Nonsense Algebra* or *Videotext Algebra*

★ Your own math program

Key Idea: Use a step-by-step math program.

Science Exploration I

★ Read p. 144-146 in the *Evolution: The Grand Experiment* Student Text. Then, complete "Test A" on p. 169 of the *Evolution: The Grand Experiment* Teacher's Manual. You may refer to the Student Text p. 129-146 to help you complete the test.

Key Idea: *Basilosaurus* is proposed by some whale evolution experts as the final missing link or last step in whale evolution. *Basilosaurus* was an extremely long whale with tiny back legs. However, not all experts agree that *Basilosaurus* is the missing link, as *Basilosaurus* is known to have existed at the same time as baleen whales and also lived at a time when toothed whales are presumed to have existed. The overall fossil evidence for whale evolution has its share of contradictions.

Reading about History | I |

Read about history in the following resource:

★ *The Story of the World: Vol. 4* p. 432-437

You will be writing a narration about the chapter "India After Partition" that you read today. To prepare for writing your narration, look back over p. 432-437 in *The Story of the World*. Think about the main idea and the most important moments in this part.

After you have thought about what you will write and how you will begin your narration, turn to Unit 31 in your *Student Notebook*. For more guidance on writing a narration, see *Written Narration Tips* in the Appendix.

In Box 4, write a 12-16 sentence narration about the reading. When you have finished writing, read your sentences out loud to catch any mistakes. Check for the following things: *Did you include* **who** *or* **what topic** *the reading was mainly about? Did you include* **descriptors** *of the important thing(s) that happened? Did you include a* **closing sentence**? *If not, add those things.* Use the *Written Narration Skills* in the Appendix as a guide for editing the narration.

<u>Key Idea</u>: After India gained its independence, Jawaharlal Nehru became its first prime minister. He served for 13 years. Then, his daughter Indira Gandhi became prime minister. In 1970, India was caught in the middle of a war between East and West Pakistan. After West Pakistan bombed airports in India, Indian troops allied with East Pakistan to help them gain their independence. East Pakistan became Bangladesh, and West Pakistan became Pakistan. In 1984, after the Golden Temple invasion, Indira Gandhi was assassinated by her Sikh bodyguards.

President Study | I |

★ Read p. 78-79 in *Our Presidents...* Then, open your *President Notebook* to George H.W. Bush. Use today's reading to help you complete the information about George H.W. Bush.

<u>Key Idea</u>: Research George H.W. Bush.

Storytime | T/I |

Read the following assigned pages:

★ *Teresa of Calcutta* p. 1-12

Get the bookmark that you placed in your book on Day 2. Locate the same section of the bookmark that you used on Day 2. Beneath Day 2's entry, write the book title and the page numbers you read today. Select the one remaining response option at the bottom of the bookmark, and place a checkmark next to it. In the blank space under today's pages, respond in writing using your checked option.

<u>Key Idea</u>: Relate to the text in various ways.

Economics | I |

Read about economics in the resource below.

★ *Common Sense Business for Kids* p. 46-50
After the reading, open your *Student Notebook* to the "Economic Principles" section at the front of your notebook. Since today's reading does not really demonstrate a specific economic principle, under "Economic Principle", write a one or two sentence summary for the overall principle you learned from today's reading instead.

<u>Key Idea</u>: If you are a business owner, it is important to think about your employees as individuals and to learn their personalities. It is also important to be genuine and honest and to have integrity in your business dealings.

Independent History Study | I |

Open your *Student Notebook* to Unit 31. Read the quotes in Box 9 by Indira Gandhi, prime minister of India. Decide which quote is your favorite and circle it.

<u>Key Idea</u>: After gaining independence, India had difficult times. People were without work, and many were hungry. Indira Gandhi encouraged the U.S. to help India with money and grain exports for the starving, while she worked to improve India's farming production.

Learning the Basics
Focus: Language Arts, Math, Bible, Nature Journal, and Science

Biblical Self-Image · T

Our plans intend for the listed pages in *Who Am I? And What Am I Doing Here?* to be read either silently by both you and your child, or read aloud to the child by you. With this in mind, read and discuss the following pages listed below.

★ *Who Am I? And What Am I Doing Here?* p. 235-243 and the top of p. 245

Key Idea: You are a child of the King of kings.

Language Arts · S

Have students complete one studied dictation exercise (see Appendix for passages).

Help students complete one lesson from the following reading program:

★ *Drawn into the Heart of Reading*

Help students complete **one** English option.

★ *Progressing With Courage:* Lesson 118

★ *Progressing With Courage:* Lesson 126 (last half only)

★ Your own grammar program

Key Idea: Practice language arts skills.

Bible Quiet Time · I

Bible Study: Complete the assignment below.

★ *Faith at Work: Lesson 26 – Day Four* p. 197

Prayer Focus: Refer to **supplication** on "Preparing Your Heart for Prayer". Then, pray a prayer of supplication to make a humble and earnest request of God. Write 'supplication' at the bottom of today's lesson in *Faith at Work* above *Day Five*. Next to it, either list several key phrases or write a sentence to summarize your prayer.

Scripture Memory: Recite James 4:1-13.

Music: Refer to p. 84 as you sing with Track 11 *"Come, Ye Thankful People, Come"* (verse 1).

Key Idea: Read and study James 1:1-2:13.

Math Exploration · S

Choose **one** of the math options listed below.

★ *Singapore Primary Mathematics 6A/6B, Discovering Mathematics 7A/7B, 8A/8B, No-Nonsense Algebra* or *Videotext Algebra*

★ Your own math program

Key Idea: Use a step-by-step math program.

Science Exploration · I

★ Copy the Science Lab Form from the Appendix of this guide. Next, follow the directions to perform "Experiment 11" from p. 23 of the *Genetics & DNA Experiment Manual*. After completing Experiment 11, in the top box of the Science Lab Form write: *What happens if a child has one additional 21st chromosome?* In the second box of the form, write your hypothesis. Follow the directions for "Experiment 12" on p. 24 of the Experiment Manual and complete the box "Perform an Experiment" on your lab form. Then, follow the arrows to complete the rest of the Science Lab Form. After that read p. 25 of the Experiment Manual, and then clean up for today.

Key Idea: Chromosomes are threads of hereditary material found within a cell's nucleus. Each body cell always has the exact same number of chromosomes. The chromosomes in a cell are organized into 22 matched pairs. There are also two extra individual chromosomes called 'X' and 'Y' chromosomes. Boys have one 'X' and one 'Y 'chromosome, while girls have two 'X' chromosomes. Having three copies of the 21st chromosome is a sign of the genetic disorder Trisomy 21, or Down Syndrome.

Learning Through History
Focus: Calcutta, Carter, Khomeini, and Chernobyl

Unit 32 - Day 1

Reading about History | S |

Read about history in the following resource:

 Hero Tales: Vol. III p. 165-175

Note: p. 168 and p. 174 include disturbing descriptions. You should screen today's reading and be prepared to discuss it with your child.

After today's reading, orally narrate or retell to an adult "Friend of the Poor" on p. 165-166 of *Hero Tales: Vol. III*. As you retell, the adult will write or type your narration. Some possible key words to include in your narration of "Friend of the Poor" might be *Agnes Bojaxhiu, Macedonia, serve Christ, Loreto Nuns, India, Calcutta slums, sari, serving the poorest of the poor, Mother Teresa, Missionaries of Charity*. When the narration is complete, fold the typed or written narration in quarters to fit in Unit 32 – Box 9 of the *Student Notebook*. Glue the folded narration in Box 9, so it can be opened.

Key Idea: Agnes Bojaxhiu became a Catholic nun known as "Mother Teresa". She spent much of her life ministering to the poorest of the poor in Calcutta, India.

History Project | S |

Choose **one** of the sets of questions from the sections of *Hero Tales: Vol. III* that you read today to discuss orally with an adult. The questions are found on p. 169, 172, and 175. Please note that there is some disturbing content on p. 168 and 174 and that the story on p. 173-175 talks about abortion.

Key Idea: Mother Teresa won the Nobel Prize in 1979 for her humanitarian efforts. She also founded more Missionaries of Charity Centers around the world.

Storytime | T/I |

Read the following assigned pages:

 Teresa of Calcutta p. 13-22

Get the bookmark that you placed in your book last unit. Choose a new section of the bookmark with **three** options at the bottom. At the top of this section of the bookmark, write the book title and the page numbers you read today. Select **one** of the three options at the bottom and place a checkmark next to it. In the blank space under today's pages, respond in writing using your checked option.

Key Idea: Relate to the text in various ways.

Timeline | I |

You will be adding to the timeline in your *Student Notebook* today. In Unit 32 – Box 1, draw and color a hand giving a cup of cold water in Jesus' name. Label the box, *Mother Teresa (1910-1997 A.D.)*.

In Box 2, draw and color two rectangular flags to represent Iran and Iraq. Draw Iran's flag with horizontal stripes colored green, white, and red from top to bottom. Draw Iraq's flag with horizontal stripes colored red, white, and black from top to bottom. Label the box, *Iran-Iraq War (1980-1988 A.D.)*.

In Box 3, outline a calendar-like sign that says 444 days. Label it, *Iranian Hostage Crisis (November 4, 1979-January 20, 1981 A.D.)*.

Key Idea: During Mother Teresa's lifetime of work in Calcutta, Iran and Iraq fought a war over the Shatt Al-Arab River, and Iran held 52 Americans hostage for 444 days.

Independent History Study | I |

Open your *Student Notebook* to Unit 32. In Box 6, copy the last paragraph from p. 171 of *Hero Tales: Vol. III* that you read today. Write "Mother Teresa" under the quote in Box 6.

Key Idea: Mother Teresa chose to work and live among the poorest of the poor in Calcutta, India. She devoted her life to comforting the sick and dying. In each person she helped, she saw the face of Jesus.

Nature Journal | I |

Read and follow the directions in the resource below.

 Nature Drawing & Journaling: Lesson XLII p. 113-114

Note: For today's lesson, sketch from www.enature.com. In the "Search" bar, type "catfish". Then, click on either "Black Bullhead Catfish" or "Brown Bullhead Catfish" and sketch it. Or, if you prefer to sketch a gecko, type "gecko" in the "Search" bar instead. If you click on a picture a second time it will enlarge.

Key Idea: Draw a catfish or a gecko.

Language Arts | S |

Help students complete one lesson from the following reading program:

 Drawn into the Heart of Reading

Help students complete **one** English option.

★ *Progressing With Courage:* Lesson 119

★ *Progressing With Courage:* Lesson 127 (first half only)

★ Your own grammar program

Work with the students to complete **one** of the writing options listed below:

★ *Write with the Best: Vol. 2* Unit 7 – Day 3 p. 68

★ Your own writing program

Key Idea: Practice language arts skills.

Bible Quiet Time | I |

Bible Study: Read and complete the assigned pages in the following resource:

★ *Faith at Work: Lesson 26 – Day Five* and *Notes* p. 197-204

Prayer Focus: Refer to **adoration** on "Preparing Your Heart for Prayer". Then, pray a prayer of adoration to worship and honor God. After your prayer, write 'adoration' at the bottom of today's lesson on p. 197 in *Faith at Work*. Next to 'adoration', either list key phrases or write a sentence to summarize your prayer. Keep "Preparing Your Heart for Prayer" inside your Bible.

Scripture Memory: Read aloud James 4:14 three times from your Bible.

Music: Read p. 83 in *Hymns for a Kid's Heart*. Refer to p. 84-85 as you sing with Track 11 *"Come, Ye Thankful People, Come"* (vs. 1-2).

Key Idea: Read and study James 1:1-2:13.

Math Exploration | S |

Choose **one** of the math options listed below (see Appendix for details).

★ *Singapore Primary Mathematics 6A/6B, Discovering Mathematics 7A/7B, 8A/8B, No-Nonsense Algebra* or *Videotext Algebra*

★ Your own math program

Key Idea: Use a step-by-step math program.

Science Exploration | S |

★ Discuss with a parent the questions for Chapter 14 on p. 177-178 of *Evolution: The Grand Experiment* Teacher's Manual. Next, read p. 147-153 in the Student Text.

Key Idea: Since *Archaeopteryx* was thought to possess traits of a dinosaur and of a bird, many scientists saw *Archaeopteryx* as a missing link showing the evolution of birds from dinosaurs. There is much debate today over what *Archaeopteryx* really looked like, leading to controversy over whether *Archaeopteryx* truly is a missing link.

Learning Through History
Focus: Calcutta, Carter, Khomeini, and Chernobyl

Unit 32 - Day 2

Reading about History │ I │

Read about history in the following resources:

★ *All American History: Vol. II* p. 431-435

★ *Great Events in American History* p. 137-139

After today's reading, open your *Student Notebook* to Unit 32. Box 5 shows a poster referring to the 1980 boycott of the Olympics in Moscow. What do you notice about the chains binding the wrists of the hands on the poster? What is the meaning of the poster?

Key Idea: Nixon reopened trade with China and visited Russia in 1972.

History Project │ S │

Open your *Student Notebook* to Unit 32- Box 7 which shows a map of some of the countries that boycotted the Olympics in 1976, 1980, and 1984. Look up the word 'boycott' in the dictionary. What does it mean? In 1976, many African nations boycotted the Olympic games over the handling of a New Zealand rugby tour in South Africa. South Africa had been banned from the Olympics due to apartheid since 1964. In 1980, the United States chose to boycott the Olympic Games in Moscow to protest the Soviet war in Afghanistan. In response to the 1980 U.S. boycott, the Soviet Union chose to boycott the 1984 Summer Olympic Games in Los Angeles, CA. Other countries joined the boycotts in 1980 and 1984. From looking at the map in Box 7, what can you learn about the world's issues at the time of each boycott?

Key Idea: The Olympic boycotts provide a glimpse into world politics.

President Study │ I │

★ On *The Presidents* DVD Volume 3, select the Chapter "Carter to George W. Bush" and watch **only** Program 3: George H.W. Bush. Then, open your *President Notebook* to George H.W. Bush. Use today's viewing to add further information about George H.W. Bush.

Key Idea: Research George H.W. Bush.

Storytime │ T/I │

Read the following assigned pages:

★ *Teresa of Calcutta* p. 23-34
Note: p. 34 includes disturbing descriptions. Locate the same section of the bookmark that you used on Day 1. Beneath Day 1's entry, write the book title and the page numbers you read today. Select one of the **two** remaining response options and respond in writing.

Key Idea: Relate to the text in various ways.

Worthy Words │ T │

Today's speech is at http://www.irib.ir/world service/imam/speech/16.htm. Or, search for "Khomeini's speech 16" and click on "**cached**". Read, analyze, and evaluate Ayatollah Khomeini's speech. After reading, answer these questions: *List some of the key things about which the Ayatollah is upset. Which countries does he list in his speech? What emotion does he display toward these countries? Why? What thoughts does the Ayatollah express about the Shah and the Parliament? In what context does the Ayatollah speak about God? What religion or religious book does he mention each time he speaks of God? With this in mind, when the Ayatollah speaks of the religious leaders, what type of religion do they represent? Is it surprising that the Ayatollah was a Muslim religious leader who overthrew the government of the Shah of Iran in 1979? Explain. What can you learn about Islam from this speech?* Meet with a parent to have a Socratic dialogue. Before beginning the dialogue, the parent reads the speech aloud. Next, discuss the questions.

Key Idea: Khomeini seized power in 1979.

Independent History Study │ I │

Listen to a 1½ min. audio clip about the Olympic Boycott at http://www.history.com. In the "Search" type "U.S. Boycotts 1980 Moscow Olympics". Then, click on the speech and audio that comes up.

Key Idea: Carter advocated the 1980 boycott.

Learning the Basics
Focus: Language Arts, Math, Bible, Nature Journal, and Science

Biblical Self-Image `T`

Read and discuss the following pages listed below.

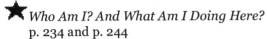 ★ *Who Am I? And What Am I Doing Here?* p. 234 and p. 244

Note: Discuss what the pages that you read today have to do with the story that you read on p. 235-243 in Unit 31.

Key Idea: Wolves made formidable opponents during the Middle Ages. They often roamed the countryside in packs, and travelers learned to be wary of them. During this same time, Edward the III of England led the English armies against France in what would become the Hundred Years' War.

Language Arts `S`

Have students complete one studied dictation exercise (see Appendix for passages).

Help students complete one lesson from the following reading program:

★ *Drawn into the Heart of Reading*

Help students complete **one** English option.

★ *Progressing With Courage:* Lesson 120

★ *Progressing With Courage:* Lesson 127 (last half only)

★ Your own grammar program

Key Idea: Practice language arts skills.

Bible Quiet Time `I`

Bible Study: Read and complete the assigned pages in the following resource:

★ *Faith at Work: Lesson 27 – Day One* p. 205 (Note: Refer to p. 198-204 to complete the lesson.)

Prayer Focus: Refer to **confession** on "Preparing Your Heart for Prayer". Then, pray a prayer of confession to admit or acknowledge your sins to God. After your prayer, write 'confession' at the bottom of today's lesson on p. 205 in *Faith at Work*. Next to 'confession', either list key phrases or write a sentence to summarize your prayer. Keep "Preparing Your Heart for Prayer" inside your Bible.

Scripture Memory: Memorize James 4:14 from your Bible and recite it.

Music: Refer to p. 84-85 as you sing with Track 11 *"Come, Ye Thankful People, Come"* (vs. 1-2).

Key Idea: Read and study James 1:1-2:13.

Math Exploration `S`

Choose **one** of the math options listed below (see Appendix for details).

★ *Singapore Primary Mathematics 6A/6B, Discovering Mathematics 7A/7B, 8A/8B, No-Nonsense Algebra* or *Videotext Algebra*

★ Your own math program

Key Idea: Use a step-by-step math program.

Science Exploration `I`

★ Read p. 153-159 in the *Evolution: The Grand Experiment* Student Text. Next, on *Evolution: The Grand Experiment* DVD, select "Menu" and then "Bonus Material". After that select "Chapter Index" and then select "14 – Birds: Archaeopteryx". Watch the DVD from 39:54-46:07 on the counter. The bottom left corner of the screen flashes a green title bar when a new chapter begins.

Key Idea: The wing claws, long tail, and teeth of *Archaeopteryx* have led many evolution scientists to suggest that it was a descendent of a dinosaur. Opponents of evolution feel that *Archaeopteryx* was just a bird.

Learning Through History
Focus: Calcutta, Carter, Khomeini, and Chernobyl

Unit 32 - Day 3

Reading about History | I

Read about history in the following resources:

★ *The Story of the World: Vol. 4* p. 438-443

★ *Great Events in American History* p. 145-148

After ending the war with Iraq, Khomeini said in addressing his people, "You dear ones know better than anyone that, for me, this decision is like a lethal poison. But I am content with the satisfaction of the sublime God, and if I have any prestige, I will expend it to preserve His religion and to safeguard the Islamic Republic." What does this show you about Khomeini?

Key Idea: Khomeini ruled Iran for 10 years.

History Project | S

Open your *Student Notebook* to Unit 32 – Box 8. Look at the map of the war between Iran and Iraq. The red squares with black missiles show areas of missile attacks. The yellow circles with the gas masks designate areas of chemical attack. The white circles with the airplanes show aerial bombing sites. Print the **Teacher's Answer Map** from p. 74 of the *Map Trek* CD. Then, on the Teacher's Answer Map, use a fine-tipped marker to make a red dot at each missile attack site as shown in Box 8 of your *Student Notebook*. Next, use a yellow marker to make a yellow dot at each chemical attack site. Last, use either white out or a black marker to mark each aerial bombing site on your Teacher's Answer Map in white or black. In which country did most of the attacks occur? Where were the attacks concentrated?

Key Idea: Iraq attacked Iran in Sept. 1980.

State Study | T

★ This is an **optional** part of the plans. If you have chosen to study your state using *State History from a Christian Perspective*, do **part** of Lesson 28 (steps 1-2 only) from the *Master Lesson Plan Book*.

Key Idea: Study your individual state.

Storytime | T/I

Read the following assigned pages:

★ *Teresa of Calcutta* p. 35-45

After today's reading, orally narrate or retell the portion of the story that was read today. See *Narration Tips* in the Appendix as needed.

Key Idea: Practice orally narrating, or retelling, a portion of a story.

Geography | I

For today's activities, use the map listed below.

★ *Map Trek CD: Missions to Modern Marvels* p. 74-75

Refer to "The Middle East" Student Map that you completed on Unit 21 – Day 3 from the *Map Trek* CD. Or, you may refer to the *Map Trek* Teacher's Answer Map on p. 74 of the *Map Trek* CD instead. Trace with your finger the Tigris and Euphrates Rivers to the place where they meet. This area is the Shatt Al-Arab, or the "Stream of the Arabs". It empties into the Persian Gulf and was controlled by Iran. Iraq invaded Iran soon after the Ayatollah seized power, hoping to reclaim the Shatt Al-Arab. This resulted in a war that lasted 8 years. Why did the U.S. and many other countries help arm Saddam Hussein and his Iraqi forces against Iran?

Key Idea: Iran and Iraq fought a war over control of the Shatt Al-Arab. The war lasted 8 years.

Independent History Study | I

Read the timeline entries from 1980-1986 on p. 487 of *The Story of the World*. What events were happening while Iran and Iraq were at war?

Key Idea: Both Iran and Iraq are predominantly Islamic countries. Iran is mainly Shi'a Muslim. Even though Iraq also has a Shi'a majority, this religion was suppressed by Sunni Muslims like al-Qaeda and the Islamic Army.

Learning the Basics
Focus: Language Arts, Math, Bible, Nature Journal, Poetry, and Science

Nature Journal & Poetry [S]

The poetry of Longfellow, Wordsworth, and Whitman is scheduled to complement the journaling sessions. Read aloud and discuss today's poem *"The Windmill"* (see Appendix) with a parent. Then, follow the directions below.

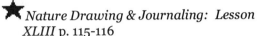 *Nature Drawing & Journaling: Lesson XLIII* p. 115-116

Note: It is not necessary to go far away to find "treasures" in nature to draw. It is likely that you will need adult transportation and permission to find a drawing spot along the "periphery of nature". So, for today, instead choose to draw something nearer to home.

Key Idea: Draw outdoor treasures.

Language Arts [S]

Have students complete one studied dictation exercise (see Appendix for passages).

Help students complete **one** English option.

★ *Progressing With Courage:* Lesson 121

★ *Progressing With Courage:* Lesson 128 (first half only)

Work with the students to complete **one** of the writing options listed below:

★ *Write with the Best: Vol. 2* Unit 7 – Day 4 p. 68

★ Your own writing program

Key Idea: Practice language arts skills.

Bible Quiet Time [I]

Bible Study: Read and complete the assigned pages in the following resource:

★ *Faith at Work: Lesson 27 – Day Two* p. 206

Prayer Focus: Refer to **thanksgiving** on "Preparing Your Heart for Prayer". Then, pray a prayer of thanksgiving to express gratitude to God for His divine goodness. After your prayer, write 'thanksgiving' at the bottom of today's lesson in *Faith at Work* above *Day Three*. Next to 'thanksgiving', either list phrases or write a sentence to summarize your prayer.

Scripture Memory: Copy James 4:14 in your Common Place Book.

Music: Refer to p. 84-85 as you sing with Track 11 *"Come, Ye Thankful People, Come"* (vs. 1-2).

Key Idea: Read and study James 2:14-3:18.

Math Exploration [S]

Choose **one** of the math options listed below (see Appendix for details).

★ *Singapore Primary Mathematics 6A/6B, Discovering Mathematics 7A/7B, 8A/8B, No-Nonsense Algebra* or *Videotext Algebra*

★ Your own math program

Key Idea: Use a step-by-step math program.

Science Exploration [I]

★ Read p. 160-164 in the *Evolution: The Grand Experiment* Student Text. Then, complete "Test A" on p. 183 of the *Evolution: The Grand Experiment* Teacher's Manual. You may refer to the Student Text p. 147-164 to help you complete the test.

Key Idea: Scientists who are proponents of evolution do not agree from which type of animal *Archaeopteryx* could have evolved. Some believe it is from a dinosaur, and others believe it is from a reptile.

Learning Through History
Focus: Calcutta, Carter, Khomeini, and Chernobyl

Reading about History | I |

Read about history in the following resource:

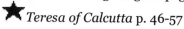 *The Story of the World: Vol. 4* p. 444-449
Note: p. 449 includes a graphic description.

You will be writing a narration about the chapter "Chernobyl and Nuclear Power" that you read today. To prepare for writing your narration, look back over p. 444-449 in *The Story of the World.* Think about the main idea and the most important moments in today's reading.

After you have thought about what you will write and how you will begin your narration, turn to Unit 32 in your *Student Notebook.* For more guidance on writing a narration, see *Written Narration Tips* in the Appendix.

In Box 4, write a 12-16 sentence narration about the reading. When you have finished writing, read your sentences out loud to catch any mistakes. Check for the following things: *Did you include **who** or **what topic** the reading was mainly about? Did you include **descriptors** of the important thing(s) that happened? Did you include a **closing sentence**? If not, add those things.* Use the *Written Narration Skills* in the Appendix as a guide for editing the narration.

Key Idea: In the 1940s, research on atomic fission led to the production of nuclear missiles and atomic bombs. Later, nuclear power was discovered as a source of electricity too, and nuclear power plants were built to produce electricity for cities. In 1979, an accident at a Pennsylvania nuclear power plant Three Mile Island led to fears of exposure to radioactivity. In 1986, a nuclear reactor explosion at a Russian nuclear power plant in Chernobyl led to exposure and severe side effects from radioactivity.

President Study | I |

 Read p. 80-81 in *Our Presidents...* Then, open your *President Notebook* to William J. Clinton. Use today's reading to help you complete the information about Clinton.

Key Idea: Research William J. Clinton.

Storytime | T/I |

Read the following assigned pages:

 Teresa of Calcutta p. 46-57

Get the bookmark that you placed in your book on Day 2. Locate the same section of the bookmark that you used on Day 2. Beneath Day 2's entry, write the book title and the page numbers you read today. Select the one remaining response option at the bottom of the bookmark, and place a checkmark next to it. In the blank space under today's pages, respond in writing using your checked option. Then, place your bookmark inside your book.

Key Idea: Relate to the text in various ways.

Economics | I |

Read about economics in the resource below.

 Common Sense Business for Kids p. 51-52
After the reading, open your *Student Notebook* to the "Economic Principles" section at the front of your notebook. Since today's reading does not demonstrate a specific economic principle, under "Economic Principle", write a one or two sentence summary for the overall principle you learned from the reading instead.

Key Idea: It is important to be honest and to believe in the product/service that you sell.

Independent History Study | I |

On the map on p. 444 of *The Story of the World,* find the location of Chernobyl in the USSR. What other cities are near Chernobyl? Moscow was the capital city of the USSR. It remains the capital city of Russia today and is its largest city as well. According to what you read today in *The Story of the World,* why was the nuclear accident at Chernobyl so much worse than the one at Three Mile Island in Pennsylvania?

Key Idea: Radioactivity from nuclear power is a far-reaching concern.

Biblical Self-Image [T]

Read and discuss with the students the following pages in the resource below.

⭐ *Who Am I? And What Am I Doing Here?* middle of p. 245 – middle of p. 246

Key Idea: When Adam and Eve disobeyed God, their relationship with God changed. Fear, anxiety, and shame entered the world along with sin. This is why it is important for us to spend time in God's Word each day to combat the thinking that rises from a sinful world.

Language Arts [S]

Have students complete one studied dictation exercise (see Appendix for passages).

Help students complete one lesson from the following reading program:

⭐ *Drawn into the Heart of Reading*

Help students complete **one** English option.

⭐ *Progressing With Courage:* Lesson 122

⭐ *Progressing With Courage:* Lesson 128 (last half only)

⭐ Your own grammar program

Key Idea: Practice language arts skills.

Bible Quiet Time [I]

Bible Study: Complete the assignment below.

⭐ *Faith at Work: Lesson 27 – Day Three* p. 206

Prayer Focus: Refer to **supplication** on "Preparing Your Heart for Prayer". Then, pray a prayer of supplication to make a humble and earnest request of God. Write 'supplication' at the bottom of today's lesson on p. 206 in *Faith at Work*. Next to it, either list several key phrases or write a sentence to summarize your prayer.

Scripture Memory: Recite James 4:1-14.

Music: Refer to p. 84-85 as you sing with Track 11 *"Come, Ye Thankful People, Come"* (vs. 1-2).

Key Idea: Read and study James 2:14-3:18.

Math Exploration [S]

Choose **one** of the math options listed below.

⭐ *Singapore Primary Mathematics 6A/6B, Discovering Mathematics 7A/7B, 8A/8B, No-Nonsense Algebra* or *Videotext Algebra*

⭐ Your own math program

Key Idea: Use a step-by-step math program.

Science Exploration [I]

⭐ Copy the Science Lab Form from the Appendix of this guide. Next, follow the directions to perform "Experiment 13" from p. 27 of the *Genetics & DNA Experiment Manual*. After completing Experiment 13, in the top box of the Science Lab Form write: *What is the structure of a DNA molecule?* In the second box of the form, write your hypothesis. Follow the directions for "Experiment 14" on p. 28-29 of the Experiment Manual and complete the box "Perform an Experiment" on your lab form. Then, follow the arrows to complete the rest of the Science Lab Form. After that read p. 30 of the Experiment Manual.

Key Idea: DNA in chromosomes contains the program that shapes our bodies' construction. DNA is a molecule, or a chemical building block of a cell, that is two millionths of a millimeter wide. It contains two sugar-phosphoric acid chains that turn on their own axis. The chains are joined by base pairs of adenine and thymine, and guanine and cytosine, which are connected by hydrogen bridges to form a double helix.

Learning Through History

Focus: The End of the Cold War, the *Challenger* Disaster, and the Fall of Communism

Unit 33 - Day 1

Reading about History | I

Read about history in the following resources:

⭐ *The Story of the World: Vol. 4* p. 449-452

⭐ *Great Events in American History* p. 153-159

After today's reading, orally narrate or retell to an adult the portion of text that you read today from *The Story of the World*. Some possible key words to include in your narration might be *Cold War, thawing, USSR, United States, Ronald Reagan, Mikhail Gorbachev, perestroika, glasnost, nuclear weapons, "Peace Through Strength", INF Treaty, short-range missiles,* and *hatred turned to friendship.*

Key Idea: After 40 years of the Cold War, Gorbachev and Reagan worked to thaw relations between the USSR and the U.S.

History Project | S

View the fall of communism by visiting **one** or more of the online addresses below. This is a changing map showing the fall of communism: http://news.bbc.co.uk/2/hi/europe/7972232.stm (Click "NEXT" under the map.)

This is another map of the fall of communism: http://users.erols.com/mwhite28/communis.htm

Here is a look at the key events in the fall: http://news.bbc.co.uk/2/hi/europe/7961732.stm

Key Idea: The fall of communism moved quickly once communism began to unravel.

President Study | I

⭐ On *The Presidents* DVD Volume 3, select the Chapter "Carter to George W. Bush" and watch **only** Program 4: William J. Clinton. Then, open your *President Notebook* to William J. Clinton. Use today's viewing to add further information about William J. Clinton.

Key Idea: Research William J. Clinton.

Storytime | T/I

Read the following assigned pages:

⭐ *Teresa of Calcutta* p. 58-67
Note: p. 58 and 64 contain graphic, disturbing content. A parent must check before reading.

Get the bookmark that you placed in your book last unit. Choose a new section of the bookmark with **three** options at the bottom. At the top of this section of the bookmark, write the book title and the page numbers you read today. Select **one** of the three options at the bottom and place a checkmark next to it. In the blank space under today's pages, respond in writing using your checked option.

Key Idea: Relate to the text in various ways.

Geography | T

For today's activities, use the map listed below.

⭐ *United States History Atlas* p. 47

Refer to the map on p. 47 of the *United States History Atlas* to view the state of Europe, the Middle East, and Africa after the Cold War between 1990-1995. Name the countries that had ethnic conflicts between two or more people groups or religious groups. Name the countries that had terrorist bases. Name the countries that had major wars during those years. Name the countries that were occupied by U.N. (or United Nations) troops.

Key Idea: Even after the threat of the Cold War was minimized, other countries still had ongoing ethnic conflicts and new wars that occurred. The threat of nuclear weapons remained a factor in these conflicts.

Independent History Study | I

Read the timeline entries from 1987-1989 on p. 487 of *The Story of the World*. What entries do you recognize? Which ones are new?

Key Idea: The end of the Cold War was celebrated in Russia and America.

Learning the Basics
Focus: Language Arts, Math, Bible, Nature Journal, and Science

Nature Journal   I

Read and follow the directions in the resource below.

 Nature Drawing & Journaling: Lesson XLIV p. 118-119

Note: Do **only** the sketching of the barn or shanty today. Wait until Unit 33 – Day 3 to go over the drawing in black pen and color it.

<u>Key Idea</u>: Practice drawing a barn or shanty.

Language Arts   S

Help students complete one lesson from the following reading program:

 Drawn into the Heart of Reading

Help students complete **one** English option.

 Progressing With Courage: Lesson 123

 Progressing With Courage: Lesson 129 (first half only)

 Your own grammar program

Work with the students to complete **one** of the writing options listed below:

 Write with the Best: Vol. 2 Unit 7 – Day 5 p. 68-69

 Your own writing program

<u>Key Idea</u>: Practice language arts skills.

Bible Quiet Time   I

Bible Study: Read and complete the assigned pages in the following resource:

 Faith at Work: Lesson 27 – Day Four p. 204

Prayer Focus: Refer to **adoration** on "Preparing Your Heart for Prayer". Then, pray a prayer of adoration to worship and honor God. After your prayer, write 'adoration' at the bottom of today's lesson in *Faith at Work* above *Day Five*. Next to 'adoration', either list key phrases or write a sentence to summarize your prayer. Keep "Preparing Your Heart for Prayer" inside your Bible.

Scripture Memory: Read aloud James 4:15 three times from your Bible.

Music: Read the verse and pray the prayer from p. 85 in *Hymns for a Kid's Heart*. Refer to p. 84-85 as you sing with Track 11 *"Come, Ye Thankful People, Come"* (vs. 1-4).

<u>Key Idea</u>: Read and study James 2:14-3:18.

Math Exploration   S

Choose **one** of the math options listed below (see Appendix for details).

 Singapore Primary Mathematics 6A/6B, Discovering Mathematics 7A/7B, 8A/8B, No-Nonsense Algebra or *Videotext Algebra*

 Your own math program

<u>Key Idea</u>: Use a step-by-step math program.

Science Exploration   S

 Discuss with a parent the questions for Chapter 15 on p. 191 of *Evolution: The Grand Experiment* Teacher's Manual. Next, read p. 165-173 in the Student Text.

<u>Key Idea</u>: In the mid 1990s, fossils labeled as "feathered dinosaurs" were found in the Liaoning Province of China. Today, evolution scientists are divided over whether these fossils actually show a type of flightless bird or a type of dinosaur with feathers. Problems with the feathers, the age, and the authenticity of the fossils are raising further questions among scientists.

Learning Through History

Focus: The End of the Cold War, the *Challenger* Disaster, and the Fall of Communism

Unit 33 - Day 2

Reading about History | I |

Read about history in the following resource:

★ *All American History: Vol. II* p. 463-471

After today's reading, open your *Student Notebook* to Unit 33. Look at the image in Box 7 of Reagan and Gorbachev signing the nuclear arms treaty. In Box 8, list bulleted facts from p. 471 of *All American History* about the meetings leading up to the signing of the treaty.

Key Idea: Reagan and Gorbachev signed the Intermediate-Range Nuclear Forces Treaty in December 1987. The treaty led to reduction and elimination of various nuclear weapons.

Storytime | T/I |

Read the following assigned pages:

★ *Teresa of Calcutta* p. 68-77
Note: p. 70 and 73 contain vivid, graphic descriptions. Parental supervision is needed. Get the bookmark that you placed in your book. Locate the same section of the bookmark that you used on Day 1. Beneath Day 1's entry, write the book title and the page numbers you read today. Select one of the **two** remaining response options and respond in writing.

Key Idea: Relate to the text in various ways.

History Project | S |

View the following online videos of President Reagan. The first is a video clip from Reagan's 1987 speech in Berlin. It contains the famous line, "Mr. Gorbachev, Tear Down This Wall". http://www.awesomestories.com/assets/reagan-wall

The second video is an excerpt from an interview that President Reagan did with Larry King in which Reagan tells about the day that he was shot. http://www.awesomestories.com/assets/ronald-reagan-describes-attempted-assassination-1

If the links above do not work, instead go to http://www.awesomestories.com/. Then, near the top click on "Videos" and type "Ronald Reagan" in the "Search" bar. In the listings that come up, select "Tear Down This Wall". After watching the video, then select "Describes Attempted Assassination".

Key Idea: An assassination attempt was made on President Reagan's life in 1981.

Worthy Words | T |

Read, analyze, and evaluate the speech below.

★ *Book of Great American Speeches for Young People* p. 271-273
Then, answer the following questions on an index card: *What reason does Reagan give for American presidents coming to speak in Berlin? How does Reagan describe the wall? What contrasts does he point out between the free world of the West and the Communist world? List the changes that have come from the "new policy of reform and openness" in Moscow. How would Gorbachev's tearing down the wall signify unmistakable change to the world? Explain the paragraph that contains, "East and West do not mistrust each other because...". The Berlin Wall fell 2½ years after this speech. What did this signify? How do you think the world changed?* Next, meet with a parent to have a Socratic dialogue. Before beginning the dialogue, the parent reads p. 271-273 out loud. Discuss the questions.

Key Idea: Communism began to fall in 1989.

President Study | I |

★ Read p. 82-83 in *Our Presidents...* Then, open your *President Notebook* to George W. Bush. Use today's reading to help you add information about George W. Bush.

Key Idea: Research George W. Bush.

Independent History Study | I |

Open your *Student Notebook* to Unit 33. Copy an important part of p. 271-273 from the *Book of Great American Speeches...* in Box 6. Write "Ronald Reagan" at the bottom of Box 6.

Key Idea: The Berlin Wall divided Germany.

Learning the Basics
Focus: Language Arts, Math, Bible, Nature Journal, and Science

Biblical Self-Image · T

Read and discuss the following pages listed below.

 Who Am I? And What Am I Doing Here? middle of p. 246-248

<u>Key Idea</u>: As a follower of Jesus Christ, we need to strive to think and live differently. We are new creations, or new people in Christ. In order to overcome Satan and to overcome the world, we need to see ourselves as children of the Most High King and realize we are justified through faith in Christ Jesus.

Language Arts · S

Have students complete one studied dictation exercise (see Appendix for passages).

Help students complete one lesson from the following reading program:

⭐ *Drawn into the Heart of Reading*

Help students complete **one** English option.

⭐ *Progressing With Courage:* Lesson 124 (first half only)

⭐ *Progressing With Courage:* Lesson 129 (last half only)

⭐ Your own grammar program

<u>Key Idea</u>: Practice language arts skills.

Bible Quiet Time · I

Bible Study: Read and complete the assigned pages in the following resource:

⭐ *Faith at Work: Lesson 27 – Day Five* and *Notes* p. 207-212

Prayer Focus: Refer to **confession** on "Preparing Your Heart for Prayer". Then, pray a prayer of confession to admit or acknowledge your sins to God. After your prayer, write 'confession' at the bottom of today's lesson on p. 208 in *Faith at Work*. Next to 'confession', either list key phrases or write a sentence to summarize your prayer. Keep "Preparing Your Heart for Prayer" inside your Bible.

Scripture Memory: Memorize James 4:15 from your Bible and recite it.

Music: Refer to p. 84-85 as you sing with Track 11 *"Come, Ye Thankful People, Come"* (vs. 1-4).

<u>Key Idea</u>: Read and study James 2:14-3:18.

Math Exploration · S

Choose **one** of the math options listed below (see Appendix for details).

⭐ *Singapore Primary Mathematics 6A/6B, Discovering Mathematics 7A/7B, 8A/8B, No-Nonsense Algebra* or *Videotext Algebra*

⭐ Your own math program

<u>Key Idea</u>: Use a step-by-step math program.

Science Exploration · I

⭐ Read p. 174-179 in the *Evolution: The Grand Experiment* Student Text. Next, on *Evolution: The Grand Experiment* DVD, select "Menu" and then "Bonus Material". After that select "Chapter Index" and then select "15 – Feathered Dinosaurs". Watch the DVD from 46:07-54:05 on the counter. The bottom left corner of the screen flashes a green title bar when a new chapter begins.

<u>Key Idea</u>: As Dr. Rowe scanned and analyzed *Confuciusornis* and *Archaeoraptor* from the Chinese collection of "feathered dinosaurs", he discovered that the fossils contained substituted parts not from the original fossils. Within the fossil of *Archaeoraptor* alone, there were 39 rock pieces that did not belong, and 26 fossil bones from four other animals included.

Learning Through History

Focus: The End of the Cold War, the *Challenger* Disaster, and the Fall of Communism

Unit 33 - Day 3

Reading about History | I

Read about history in the following resources:

★ *All American History: Vol. II* p. 483 – top of p. 490

★ *Great Events in American History* p. 149-152

After today's reading, open your *Student Notebook* to Unit 33. In Box 5, you will see a part of the Space Shuttle *Challenger* Memorial from the Arlington National Cemetery. It reads as follows:

IN GRATEFUL
AND LOVING TRIBUTE
TO THE BRAVE CREW
OF THE UNITED STATES
SPACE SHUTTLE CHALLENGER
28 JANUARY 1986

Key Idea: In January 1986, the space shuttle *Challenger* exploded 73 seconds after liftoff, killing all seven astronauts onboard the shuttle.

History Project | S

Open your *Student Notebook* to Unit 33 – Box 9. Follow the directions from p. 60-62 of *Draw and Write Through History* to draw and color the space shuttle *Challenger* in Box 9. Leave room either near the top, or the bottom, or the side of your drawing to copy the quote noted in the Independent History Study box.

Key Idea: The first launch of NASA's Space Shuttle program was the launch of the *Columbia* in 1981. The *Challenger* followed in 1983.

State Study | T

★ This is an **optional** part of the plans. If you have chosen to study your state using *State History from a Christian Perspective*, do part of Lesson 28 (steps 3-5 only) from the *Master Lesson Plan Book*.

Key Idea: Study your individual state.

Storytime | T/I

Read the following assigned pages:

★ *Teresa of Calcutta* p. 78-87

After today's reading, orally narrate or retell the portion of the story that was read today. See *Narration Tips* in the Appendix as needed.

Key Idea: Practice narrating part of a story.

Timeline | I

You will add to the timeline in your *Student Notebook* today. In Unit 33 – Box 1, draw and color a bullet flying through the air. Label it, *Assassination Attempt of President Reagan (March 30, 1981 A.D.)*.

In Box 2, draw and color a red, yellow, and orange cloud of fiery smoke. Label it, *Challenger Disaster (January 28, 1986 A.D.)*.

In Box 3, draw and color a concrete wall with chunks chipped off. Label it, *The Fall of the Berlin Wall (November 9, 1989-October 3, 1990 A.D.)*

Key Idea: As William Hinckley Jr. attempted to assassinate President Reagan, the space shuttle *Columbia* was preparing for its upcoming flight on April 12. During Reagan's second term in office, the *Challenger* exploded shortly after liftoff.

Independent History Study | I

Read the speech on p. 266-267 of the *Book of Great American Speeches for Young People*. Then, open your *Student Notebook* to Unit 33. In Box 9, either along the top, the side, or the bottom of your sketch of the *Challenger*, copy the last paragraph of the speech from p. 267.

Key Idea: On the evening of the explosion of the space shuttle *Challenger*, President Reagan addressed the nation. The president had been scheduled to deliver his State of the Union address instead.

Nature Journal & Poetry | S |

The poetry of Longfellow, Wordsworth, and Whitman is scheduled to complement the journaling sessions. Read aloud and discuss today's excerpt from the poem *"Song of Myself"* (see Appendix) with a parent. Then, follow the directions below.

★ *Nature Drawing & Journaling: Lesson XLIV* p. 119

Note: Follow the directions in the **second** paragraph on p. 119 to complete your sketch.

<u>Key Idea</u>: Outline and color a barn or a shanty.

Language Arts | S |

Have students complete one studied dictation exercise (see Appendix for passages).

Help students complete **one** English option.

★ *Progressing With Courage:* Lesson 124 (last half only)

★ *Progressing With Courage:* Lesson 130 (first half only)

Work with the students to complete **one** of the writing options listed below:

★ *Write with the Best: Vol. 2* Unit 7 – Day 6 p. 69

★ Your own writing program

<u>Key Idea</u>: Practice language arts skills.

Bible Quiet Time | I |

Bible Study: Read and complete the assigned pages in the following resource:

★ *Faith at Work: Lesson 28 – Day One* p. 213 (Note: Refer to p. 209-212 to complete the lesson.)

Prayer Focus: Refer to **thanksgiving** on "Preparing Your Heart for Prayer". Then, pray a prayer of thanksgiving to express gratitude to God for His divine goodness. After your prayer, write 'thanksgiving' at the bottom of today's lesson in *Faith at Work* above *Day Two*. Next to 'thanksgiving', either list phrases or write a sentence to summarize your prayer.

Scripture Memory: Copy James 4:15 in your Common Place Book.

Music: Refer to p. 84-85 as you sing with Track 11 *"Come, Ye Thankful People, Come"* (vs. 1-4).

<u>Key Idea</u>: Read and study James 2:14-3:18.

Math Exploration | S |

Choose **one** of the math options listed below (see Appendix for details).

★ *Singapore Primary Mathematics 6A/6B, Discovering Mathematics 7A/7B, 8A/8B, No-Nonsense Algebra* or *Videotext Algebra*

★ Your own math program

<u>Key Idea</u>: Use a step-by-step math program.

Science Exploration | I |

★ Read p. 180-184 in the *Evolution: The Grand Experiment* Student Text. Then, complete "Test A" on p. 195 of the *Evolution: The Grand Experiment* Teacher's Manual. You may refer to the Student Text p. 165-184 to help you complete the test. **Optional:** Extension students may take "Test B" on p. 131, 143, 157, 171, 185, and 197 of the Teacher's Manual as a sectional exam.

<u>Key Idea</u>: Interpretations of museum fossils can often be misleading, as artist renderings can lead viewers to believe things about evolution that are not supported by scientific evidence.

Reading about History | I |

Read about history in the following resource:

⭐ *All American History: Vol. II* p. 490-498

You will be writing a narration about **part** of the pages that you read today. To prepare for writing your narration, look back over p. 491-494 in *All American History: Vol. II*. Choose to write about **either** the section titled "Religion During the 1980s and 1990s" **or** the section titled "Recreation and the Arts During the 1980s and 1990s". Think about the main idea and the most important moments in your chosen part of the reading.

After you have thought about what you will write and how you will begin your narration, turn to Unit 33 in your *Student Notebook*. For more guidance on writing a narration, see *Written Narration Tips* in the Appendix.

In Box 4, write a 12-16 sentence narration about the reading. When you have finished writing, read your sentences out loud to catch any mistakes. Check for the following things: *Did you include* **who** *or* **what topic** *the reading was mainly about? Did you include* **descriptors** *of the important thing(s) that happened? Did you include a* **closing sentence**? *If not, add those things.* Use the *Written Narration Skills* in the Appendix as a guide for editing the narration.

Key Idea: During the 1980s-1990s, religious organizations began to influence politics, and the numbers of megachurches with over 2000 members continued to grow. In entertainment, large movie complexes, VCRs, and cable television led the media industry. *Thriller* became the best-selling record album, and CDs replaced cassettes. Mega bookstores replaced small bookshops. Art became more abstract.

President Study | I |

⭐ On *The Presidents* DVD Volume 3, select the Chapter "Carter to George W. Bush" and watch **only** Program 5: George W. Bush. Then, open your *President Notebook* to George W. Bush. Use today's viewing to add further information about George W. Bush.

Key Idea: Research George W. Bush.

Storytime | T/I |

Read the following assigned pages:

⭐ *Teresa of Calcutta* p. 88-97

Get the bookmark that you placed in your book on Day 2. Locate the same section of the bookmark that you used on Day 2. Beneath Day 2's entry, write the book title and the page numbers you read today. Select the one remaining response option at the bottom of the bookmark, and place a checkmark next to it. In the blank space under today's pages, respond in writing using your checked option.

Key Idea: Relate to the text in various ways.

Economics | I |

Read about economics in the resource below.

⭐ *Common Sense Business for Kids* p. 53-57

After the reading, open your *Student Notebook* to the "Economic Principles" section at the front of your notebook Under "Economic Principle", write a one or two sentence summary for the economic principle you learned from today's reading.

Key Idea: As far as small businesses go, you often have a better chance of success as a service-related business than as a product-related business. Either way, don't base your business strategy only on competitive pricing.

Independent History Study | I |

Read the speech on p. 279-280 of the *Book of Great American Speeches for Young People*. What is your favorite line of the speech?

Key Idea: On September 6, 1995, Cal Ripken Jr. played his 2,131st game, surpassing Lou Gehrig's record for the most consecutive games played. Ripken's speech to the Oriole fans was given at a postgame ceremony.

Learning the Basics

Focus: Language Arts, Math, Bible, Nature Journal, and Science

Biblical Self-Image | T

Read and discuss with the students the following pages in the resource below.

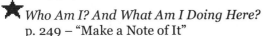 *Who Am I? And What Am I Doing Here?* p. 249 – "Make a Note of It"

For "Make a Note of It", look up each Scripture and insert your name in the verse as you read it aloud. Copying the verses on paper is **optional.**

Key Idea: A saint is a person who is justified through faith in Jesus.

Language Arts | S

Have students complete one studied dictation exercise (see Appendix for passages).

Help students complete one lesson from the following reading program:

★ *Drawn into the Heart of Reading*

Help students complete **one** English option.

★ *Progressing With Courage:* Lesson 125

★ *Progressing With Courage:* Lesson 130 (last half only)

★ Your own grammar program

Key Idea: Practice language arts skills.

Bible Quiet Time | I

Bible Study: Complete the assignment below.

★ *Faith at Work: Lesson 28 – Day Two* p. 213-214

Prayer Focus: Refer to **supplication** on "Preparing Your Heart for Prayer". Then, pray a prayer of supplication to make a humble and earnest request of God. Write 'supplication' at the bottom of today's lesson in *Faith at Work* above *Day Three*. Next to it, either list several key phrases or write a sentence to summarize your prayer.

Scripture Memory: Recite James 4:1-15.

Music: Refer to p. 84-85 as you sing with Track 11 *"Come, Ye Thankful People, Come"* (vs. 1-4).

Key Idea: Read and study James 4:1-5:6.

Math Exploration | S

Choose **one** of the math options listed below.

★ *Singapore Primary Mathematics 6A/6B, Discovering Mathematics 7A/7B, 8A/8B, No-Nonsense Algebra* or *Videotext Algebra*

★ Your own math program

Key Idea: Use a step-by-step math program.

Science Exploration | I

★ Copy the Science Lab Form from the Appendix of this guide. Follow the directions to perform "Experiment 15" from p. 31 of the *Genetics & DNA Experiment Manual*. In step 2 on p. 31, after dividing the two strands, break one of the strands into pieces that represent "nucleotides" as shown at the bottom of p. 31. After completing Experiment 15, in the top box of the Science Lab Form write: *What happens to the number of chromosomes when an egg and sperm cell fuse?* In the second box of the form, write your hypothesis. Next, follow the directions for "Experiment 16" on p. 32 of the Experiment Manual and complete the box "Perform an Experiment" on your lab form. Then, follow the arrows to complete the rest of the Science Lab Form. On p. 31-32 it is also important to note that God governs the design and function of cells and molecules rather than "nature".

Key Idea: When an egg and a sperm cell fuse, they from a zygote that has 46 chromosomes. A zygote contains DNA from both parents, providing all needed genetic information to form a new person.

Learning Through History
Focus: The Cultural Revolution, the Fall of Communism, and the Persian Gulf War
Unit 34 - Day 1

Reading about History | S |

Read about history in the following resource:

★ *Hero Tales: Vol. III* p. 105-115
After today's reading, orally narrate to an adult p. 105-106 of *Hero Tales: Vol. III*. As you narrate, the adult will write or type your narration. Some possible key words to include might be *Gordon McLean, Canada, ministry, open doors, wisdom, Youth for Christ, Vancouver, British Columbia, Frank, murder charge, jail, life in prison, witness for Christ, return to the streets, ministry grows, move to U.S., Metro Chicago Youth for Christ, gang kids*. When the narration is complete, tri-fold it to fit in Unit 34 – Box 9 of the *Student Notebook*. Glue the folded narration in Box 9.

Key Idea: Mr. McLean ministers to gang kids.

History Project | S |

It can be difficult to know what to do when you have a disagreement with someone. Yet, it is important to remember the words of Proverbs 18:19 about a brother that is offended. What is the meaning of this verse? The Bible offers wise counsel as to the process to pursue when we have a disagreement with a brother. What does Matthew 18:15 tell you to do first? Why is it important to go to your brother alone? According to Ephesians 4:31-32, what should you do if your brother is sorry? If your brother is not sorry, what does Matthew 18:16 say to do next? As you approach your brother, it is important to keep in mind Matthew 7:1-5. If your brother still is not sorry, what does Matthew 18:17 say to do? Before going to the church, since you are still under the authority of your parents at home, go first to a parent. Remember 1 John 1:8-9 through this process.

Key Idea: God helps us repent and reconcile.

Storytime | T/I |

Read the following assigned pages:

★ *Teresa of Calcutta* p. 98-109
Note: p. 105 contains a description of leprosy. Choose a new section of the bookmark with **three** options at the bottom. At the top of this section of the bookmark, write the book title and the page numbers you read today. Select **one** of the three options at the bottom and place a checkmark next to it. In the blank space under today's pages, respond in writing using your checked option.

Key Idea: Relate to the text in various ways.

Worthy Words | T |

Read, analyze, and evaluate the speech below.

★ *Book of Great American Speeches for Young People* p. 274-275
After reading the speech, answer the following questions on an index card: *Why wasn't Jackson "supposed to make it"? What does Jackson mean when he says, "I had a shovel programmed for my hand"? What are your thoughts about his mother? Discuss the paragraph that begins, "I was born in the slum, but the slum..." What line does Jackson repeat 4 times near the end of his speech? Keeping in mind that Jackson was a civil rights activist, a Baptist minister, and a presidential hopeful, what meaning could "Keep hope alive" have? Who was Jackson addressing in this speech? How would that affect the speech? What is the theme of the speech?* Next, meet with a parent to have a Socratic dialogue about the speech. Before beginning the dialogue, the parent reads the speech aloud. Next, discuss the questions. Use text/experiences to support your answers.

Key Idea: Jackson gave this speech in 1988.

Independent History Study | I |

Open your *Student Notebook* to Unit 34. Choose one part from p. 274-275 of the *Book of Great American Speeches for Young People* to copy in Box 6. Write "Jesse Jackson" at the bottom of Box 6.

Key Idea: Jackson was born to a teenage mother and grew up in the slums, yet he ran for president.

Learning the Basics

Focus: Language Arts, Math, Bible, Nature Journal, and Science

Nature Journal | I |

Read and follow the directions in the resource below.

 Nature Drawing & Journaling: Lesson XLV p. 120-121

Note: Do **only** the sketching of the window today. Wait until Unit 34 – Day 3 to go over the drawing in black pen and color it.

<u>Key Idea:</u> Practice drawing a rustic window.

Language Arts | S |

Help students complete one lesson from the following reading program:

 Drawn into the Heart of Reading

Help students complete **one** English option.

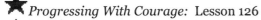 *Progressing With Courage:* Lesson 126

 Progressing With Courage: Lesson 131 (Class Practice 'A' – 'F' only)

 Your own grammar program

Work with the students to complete **one** of the writing options listed below:

 Write with the Best: Vol. 2 Unit 7 – Day 7 p. 69

 Your own writing program

<u>Key Idea:</u> Practice language arts skills.

Bible Quiet Time | I |

Bible Study: Read and complete the assigned pages in the following resource:

 Faith at Work: Lesson 28 – Day Three p. 214-215

Prayer Focus: Refer to **adoration** on "Preparing Your Heart for Prayer". Then, pray a prayer of adoration to worship and honor God. After your prayer, write 'adoration' at the bottom of today's lesson in *Faith at Work* above *Day Four*. Next to 'adoration', either list key phrases or write a sentence to summarize your prayer. Keep "Preparing Your Heart for Prayer" inside your Bible.

Scripture Memory: Read aloud James 4:16 three times from your Bible.

Music: Read p. 87-88 in *Hymns for a Kid's Heart*. Refer to p. 90-91 as you sing with Track 12 *"My Country, 'Tis of Thee"* (vs. 1-2).

<u>Key Idea:</u> Read and study James 4:1-5:6.

Math Exploration | S |

Choose **one** of the math options listed below (see Appendix for details).

 Singapore Primary Mathematics 6A/6B, Discovering Mathematics 7A/7B, 8A/8B, No-Nonsense Algebra or *Videotext Algebra*

 Your own math program

<u>Key Idea:</u> Use a step-by-step math program.

Science Exploration | S |

 Discuss with a parent the questions for Chapter 16 on p. 204 of *Evolution: The Grand Experiment* Teacher's Manual. Next, read p. 185-190 in the Student Text. Then, complete "Test A" on p. 207 of the *Evolution: The Grand Experiment* Teacher's Manual. You may refer to the Student Text p. 185-190 to help you complete the test.

<u>Key Idea:</u> Even though a plethora of fossil flowering plants have been discovered, the origin of the flowering plant remains a mystery from an evolutionary perspective.

Learning Through History
Focus: The Cultural Revolution, the Fall of Communism, and the Persian Gulf War

Unit 34 - Day 2

Reading about History   I

Read about history in the following resource:

 The Story of the World: Vol. 4 p. 454-458
Open your *Student Notebook* to Unit 34. Box 7 shows a picture of Mao Zedong. In Box 8, you will outline p. 455-456 from *The Story of the World* to tell about Mao Zedong. Each Roman numeral in Box 8 stands for one paragraph. So, 'I' means the first paragraph on p. 455. Next to 'I' in Box 8, write one sentence to tell who or what the first paragraph was about and the main thing that person did. This is not a summary, but rather just the main topic. Next to 'II' in Box 8, write the main topic of the second paragraph on p. 455. Continue this pattern for the 8 paragraphs on p. 455-456.

Key Idea: Mao Zedong desired to make China large and powerful under communist rule. He created collective farms similar to those in the Soviet Union. He forced many peasants who had been farmers to work in steel mills instead. This led to a famine causing 30 million deaths.

History Project   S

Today, on a white sheet of paper, you will make a propaganda poster to try to persuade a parent to allow you do something that you want to do. Some ideas for topics might be to stay up later than usual, to eat more dessert, to gain more computer time, to have fewer chores, to have a shorter school day, etc. In your reasoning on your poster, you should inflate, stretch, or exaggerate the reasons why you should be allowed to do your chosen thing. Share your poster with your intended audience.

Key Idea: Mao used propaganda to persuade Chinese citizens to support him.

President Study   I

 Read p. 84-85 in *Our Presidents...* Then, open your *President Notebook* to Barack H. Obama. Use today's reading to help you complete the information about Obama.

Key Idea: Research Barack H. Obama.

Storytime   T/I

Read the following assigned pages:

 Teresa of Calcutta p. 110-118
Get the bookmark that you placed in your book. Locate the same section of the bookmark that you used on Day 1. Beneath Day 1's entry, write the book title and the page numbers you read today. Select one of the **two** remaining response options at the bottom of the bookmark, and place a checkmark next to it. In the blank space under today's pages, respond in writing using your checked option.

Key Idea: Relate to the text in various ways.

Timeline   I

You will be adding to the timeline in your *Student Notebook* today. In Unit 34 – Box 1, draw and color a little red book to symbolize Chairman Mao's red book of statements and quotes. Label it, *Mao's Cultural Revolution in China (1966-1976 A.D.)*.

In Box 2, draw and color a rectangular Russian flag with 3 horizontal stripes. Color the stripes white, blue, and red from top to bottom. Label the flag, *Soviet Union Dissolved – Gorbachev Resigns (December 25-26, 1991 A.D.)*.

In Box 3, draw and color an oil well burning in the desert. Label the box, *Persian Gulf War (August 2, 1990-February 28, 1991 A.D.)*.

Key Idea: Deng Xiaoping was head of the Communist Party of China when Gorbachev resigned and communism was outlawed in Russia.

Independent History Study   I

On a globe, find the following countries where the Communist Party remains dominant today: China, Laos, North Korea, Vietnam, and Cuba.

Key Idea: Deng Xiaoping and the Communist Party leaders sought to replace Mao. So, Mao brought part of the Chinese army to Beijing for protection. After Mao's death, Xiaoping became General Secretary of the Communist Party.

Learning the Basics

Focus: Language Arts, Math, Bible, Nature Journal, and Science

Biblical Self-Image   T

Our plans intend for the listed pages in *Who Am I? And What Am I Doing Here?* to be read either silently by both you and your child, or read aloud to the child by you. With this in mind, read and discuss the following pages listed below.

 Who Am I? And What Am I Doing Here? bottom of p. 249-252

Key Idea: As a follower of Jesus Christ, your name is written in the Book of Life, and your citizenship is in heaven.

Language Arts   S

Have students complete one studied dictation exercise (see Appendix for passages).

Help students complete one lesson from the following reading program:

 Drawn into the Heart of Reading

Help students complete **one** English option.

 *Progressing With Courage:* Lesson 127

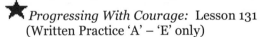 *Progressing With Courage:* Lesson 131 (Written Practice 'A' – 'E' only)

 Your own grammar program

Key Idea: Practice language arts skills.

Bible Quiet Time   I

Bible Study: Read and complete the assigned pages in the following resource:

★ *Faith at Work: Lesson 28 – Day Four* p. 215

Prayer Focus: Refer to **confession** on "Preparing Your Heart for Prayer". Then, pray a prayer of confession to admit or acknowledge your sins to God. After your prayer, write 'confession' at the bottom of today's lesson in *Faith at Work* above *Day Five*. Next to 'confession', either list key phrases or write a sentence to summarize your prayer. Keep "Preparing Your Heart for Prayer" inside your Bible.

Scripture Memory: Memorize James 4:16 from your Bible and recite it.

Music: Refer to p. 90-91 as you sing with Track 12 *"My Country, 'Tis of Thee"* (vs. 1-2).

Key Idea: Read and study James 4:1-5:6.

Math Exploration   S

Choose **one** of the math options listed below (see Appendix for details).

★ *Singapore Primary Mathematics 6A/6B, Discovering Mathematics 7A/7B, 8A/8B, No-Nonsense Algebra* or *Videotext Algebra*

★ Your own math program

Key Idea: Use a step-by-step math program.

Science Exploration   S

★ Discuss with a parent the questions for Chapter 17 on p. 214 of *Evolution: The Grand Experiment* Teacher's Manual. Next, read p. 191-194 in the Student Text.

Key Idea: Deoxyribonucleic acid, or DNA, is a necessary component for life. Organisms cannot reproduce, function, or survive without DNA. All living organisms contain DNA as their genetic blueprint. Scientists who are proponents of evolution have difficulty explaining how DNA could occur through random chemical interaction because DNA is needed to make proteins, yet many proteins are involved in copying and translating DNA information into proteins.

Reading about History | I

Read about history in the following resource:

 The Story of the World: Vol. 4 p. 459-462
After today's reading, open your *Student Notebook* to Unit 34. The image in Box 5 shows a poster warning against the spread of communism.

Key Idea: Gorbachev was the premier, or leader, of the USSR. As he worked to change the USSR, a group of communist leaders tried to take over the government and make Gorbachev resign. Yeltsin joined with Gorbachev to help overthrow communism.

History Project | S

Visit **one** or more of the websites below to better understand what the fall of the Berlin Wall meant to the world. First, read an article about reactions when the Berlin Wall was built. http://graphics8.nytimes.com/images/blogs/learning/pdf/2009/archival/19610825BerlinWall.pdf (You must scroll down to view the article.)

Then, at the following site, scroll down to read various memories of the fall of the Berlin Wall: http://news.bbc.co.uk/2/hi/europe/8350397.stm

Watch actual video footage of the Berlin Wall being torn down here: http://archive.org/details/TheFallOfTheBerlinWall1989

Click on the square boxes at the site below to view images from the fall of the Berlin Wall. http://www.cnn.com/SPECIALS/2009/autumn.of.change/berlin.wall/

Key Idea: The fall of the Berlin Wall signaled the fall of communism to the world.

State Study | T

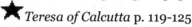 This is an **optional** part of the plans. If you have chosen to study your state using *State History from a Christian Perspective,* do Lesson 29 from the *Master Lesson Plan Book.*

Key Idea: Study your individual state.

Storytime | T/I

Read the following assigned pages:

 Teresa of Calcutta p. 119-125

After today's reading, orally narrate or retell the portion of the story that was read today. See *Narration Tips* in the Appendix as needed.

Key Idea: Practice orally narrating, or retelling, a portion of a story.

Economics | I

Read about economics in the resource below.

 Common Sense Business for Kids p. 58-60

After the reading, open your *Student Notebook* to the "Economic Principles" section at the front of your notebook. Under "Economic Principle", write a one or two sentence summary for the main principle you learned from today's reading.

Key Idea: To succeed in business, it is important to acquire skills in mathematics, accounting, and business law. These skills are learned through study rather than observation. Accurate and complete records are necessary for a successful business.

Independent History Study | I

Read the timeline entries for 1990-1991 on p. 487 of *The Story of the World.* As we are getting closer to studying the present, you may wish to ask your parent(s) if they remember the events on the timeline that you read about today. You may also wish to watch a short video online about Yeltsin rising to power in Russia at: http://www.history.com/
In the "Search" type "Boris Yeltsin". Then, click on "Boris Yeltsin: The People's Choice".

Key Idea: Yeltsin was elected as the first president of the Russian Federation in 1991. Gorbachev resigned in 1991 after the dissolution of the USSR.

Nature Journal & Poetry [S]

The poetry of Longfellow, Wordsworth, and Whitman is scheduled to complement the journaling sessions. Read aloud and discuss today's excerpt from the poem *"Admonition"* (see Appendix) with a parent. Then, follow the directions below.

⭐ *Nature Drawing & Journaling: Lesson XLV* p. 121

Note: Follow the directions in the **second** paragraph on p. 121 to go over your pencil sketch in black pen. Color it if you wish.

Key Idea: Outline and color a rustic window.

Language Arts [S]

Have students complete one studied dictation exercise (see Appendix for passages).

Help students complete **one** English option.

⭐ *Progressing With Courage:* Lesson 128

⭐ *Progressing With Courage:* Lesson 131 (Written Practice 'F' – 'I' only)

Work with the students to complete **one** of the writing options listed below:

⭐ *Write with the Best: Vol. 2* Unit 7 – Day 8 p. 69-70

⭐ Your own writing program

Key Idea: Practice language arts skills.

Bible Quiet Time [I]

Bible Study: Read and complete the assigned pages in the following resource:

⭐ *Faith at Work: Lesson 28 – Day Five* and *Notes* p. 215-218

Prayer Focus: Refer to **thanksgiving** on "Preparing Your Heart for Prayer". Then, pray a prayer of thanksgiving to express gratitude to God for His divine goodness. After your prayer, write 'thanksgiving' at the bottom of today's lesson on p. 215 in *Faith at Work*. Next to 'thanksgiving', either list phrases or write a sentence to summarize your prayer.

Scripture Memory: Copy James 4:16 in your Common Place Book.

Music: Refer to p. 90-91 as you sing with Track 12 *"My Country, 'Tis of Thee"* (vs. 1-2).

Key Idea: Read and study James 4:1-5:6.

Math Exploration [S]

Choose **one** of the math options listed below (see Appendix for details).

⭐ *Singapore Primary Mathematics 6A/6B, Discovering Mathematics 7A/7B, 8A/8B, No-Nonsense Algebra* or *Videotext Algebra*

⭐ Your own math program

Key Idea: Use a step-by-step math program.

Science Exploration [I]

⭐ Read p. 195-198 in the *Evolution: The Grand Experiment* Student Text. Then, complete "Test A" on p. 217 of the *Evolution: The Grand Experiment* Teacher's Manual. You may refer to the Student Text p. 191-198 to help you complete the test.

Key Idea: DNA strands up to 20 letters long have been observed forming naturally in a laboratory, however after that the DNA starts to break apart. The chemical properties of DNA prevent long strands of DNA from forming naturally. The DNA formed in laboratories also has deformed strands that are non-spiraled. To start life, the letters of DNA must be in a certain order and cannot be random. This is another barrier to naturally formed DNA.

Reading about History | I |

Read about history in the following resources:

★ *All American History: Vol. II* p. 472-473

★ *The Story of the World: Vol. 4* p. 464-468

You will be writing a narration about the pages that you read today in *The Story of the World*. To prepare for writing your narration, look back over p. 464-468 in *The Story of the World*. Think about the main idea and the most important moments in your chosen part of the reading.

After you have thought about what you will write and how you will begin your narration, turn to Unit 34 in your *Student Notebook*. For more guidance on writing a narration, see *Written Narration Tips* in the Appendix.

In Box 4, write a 12-16 sentence narration about the reading. When you have finished writing, read your sentences out loud to catch any mistakes. Check for the following things: *Did you include **who** or **what topic** the reading was mainly about? Did you include **descriptors** of the important thing(s) that happened? Did you include a **closing sentence**? If not, add those things.* Use the *Written Narration Skills* in the Appendix as a guide for editing the narration.

Key Idea: Saddam Hussein invaded Kuwait in August 1990. The U.N. forced Hussein out of Kuwait in the First Persian Gulf War in 1991.

President Study | I |

Since there is no program for Barack H. Obama on *The Presidents* DVD, an additional resource is needed for information about Obama. An online encyclopedia article or a brief book about Obama would be options. Two possible online article options might be as follows: http://www.whitehouse.gov/about/presidents (Scroll down and click on "Barack Obama").

http://www.bbc.co.uk/news/world-us-canada-13434315 (an article from the United Kingdom) After reading, open your *President Notebook* to Barack H. Obama. Use today's research to add further information about Obama.

Key Idea: Research Barack H. Obama.

Storytime | T/I |

Read the following assigned pages:

★ *Teresa of Calcutta* p. 126-131
Get the bookmark that you placed in your book on Day 2. Locate the same section of the bookmark that you used on Day 2. Beneath Day 2's entry, write the book title and the page numbers you read today. Select the one remaining response option at the bottom of the bookmark, and place a checkmark next to it. In the blank space under today's pages, respond in writing using your checked option.

Key Idea: Relate to the text in various ways.

Geography | I |

For today's activities, use the map listed below.

★ *Map Trek CD: Missions to Modern Marvels* p. 92

Print "The Gulf War" **Teacher's Answer Map** found on p. 92 of the *Map Trek* CD. Then, you will mark your **Teacher's Answer Map** to match the *United States History Atlas* p. 51. First, draw green dotted lines on your map to show the pipelines. Next, make a black 't' on your map at the location of each oil field. Then, draw a brown oval to mark each coalition land base. After that draw a blue anchor to mark the locations of the coalition naval bases. Last, use gray lines to mark the U.S. battleship locations. Add an additional key to your map to explain your color coding and symbols.

Key Idea: The Persian Gulf War was also called "Operation Desert Storm".

Independent History Study | I |

Read p. 161-163 in *Great Events in American History*. Why do you think the Persian Gulf War resulted in many American soldiers and people at home turning toward Christ and the Christian faith?

Key Idea: The Persian Gulf War ended quickly.

Learning the Basics
Focus: Language Arts, Math, Bible, Nature Journal, and Science

Biblical Self-Image   [T]

Read and discuss with the students the following pages in the resource below.

★ *Who Am I? And What Am I Doing Here?* p. 253-254

For "Make a Note of It" on p. 254, work together with your students to make the list. Then, pray the prayer on p. 254 together with your students.

Key Idea: Jesus has overcome the world, so our trials and difficulties are only temporary.

Language Arts   [S]

Have students complete one studied dictation exercise (see Appendix for passages).

Help students complete one lesson from the following reading program:

★ *Drawn into the Heart of Reading*

Help students complete **one** English option.

★ *Progressing With Courage:* Lesson 129

★ *Progressing With Courage:* Lesson 132 (Class Practice 'A' – 'E' only)

★ Your own grammar program

Key Idea: Practice language arts skills.

Bible Quiet Time   [I]

Bible Study: Complete the assignment below.

★ *Faith at Work: Lesson 29 – Day One* p. 219-220 (Note: Refer to p. 216-218 to complete the lesson.)

Prayer Focus: Refer to **supplication** on "Preparing Your Heart for Prayer". Then, pray a prayer of supplication to make a humble and earnest request of God. Write 'supplication' at the bottom of today's lesson in *Faith at Work* above *Day Two*. Next to it, either list several key phrases or write a sentence to summarize your prayer.

Scripture Memory: Recite James 4:1-16.

Music: Refer to p. 90-91 as you sing with Track 12 *"My Country, 'Tis of Thee"* (vs. 1-2).

Key Idea: Read and study James 4:1-5:6.

Math Exploration   [S]

Choose **one** of the math options listed below.

★ *Singapore Primary Mathematics 6A/6B, Discovering Mathematics 7A/7B, 8A/8B, No-Nonsense Algebra* or *Videotext Algebra*

★ Your own math program

Key Idea: Use a step-by-step math program.

Science Exploration   [I]

★ Copy the Science Lab Form from the Appendix of this guide. Read p. 33 of the *Genetics & DNA Experiment Manual*. Follow the directions to perform "Experiment 17" from p. 34-35 of the Experiment Manual. In step 1, the four bases are **A**denine, **T**hymine, **G**uanine, and **C**ytosine. So, for step 2, make four columns on paper, and label the columns 'A', 'T', 'G', 'C' from left to right. In each column, list all possible combinations that **begin** with that column's letter. It is not necessary to spend long amounts of time finding every codon. Set your timer for 15 min. and see how many you find. Then, in the top box of the Science Lab Form write: *How can DNA be used to help solve a crime?* In the second box of the form, write your hypothesis. Next, read p. 36-38. Then, follow the directions for "Experiment 18" on p. 39 of the Experiment Manual and complete the box "Perform an Experiment" on your lab form. **Be warned that the answer is included on p. 39, so you may wish to have an adult cover it before you read p. 39.** Then, follow the arrows to complete the rest of the Science Lab Form. Last, read p. 40.

Key Idea: Each person's DNA has a unique genetic "fingerprint" that results in a visible pattern.

Reading about History | I

Read about history in the following resource:

★ *The Story of the World: Vol. 4* p. 469-474

After today's reading, orally narrate to an adult p. 469-474 from *The Story of the World.* Some possible key words to include might be *African nations, freed from colonial rule, Ruanda-Urundi, independence from Belgium, Batutsi or "Tutsi", Bahutu or "Hutu", Hutus attacked Tutsis, divide country, Rwanda ruled by Hutus, and Burundi ruled by Tutsis, Rwandan Patriotic Front, plane crash, refugee camps, genocide, South Africa, apartheid, Unjust Laws, African National Congress, nonviolent resistance, bombs and threats, Nelson Mandela, prison, UN embargo on weapons, boycott, P.W. Botha, state of emergency, outcry, Desmond Tutu, evils of apartheid, F.W. de Klerk, repealed laws of apartheid, Nelson Mandela released, open election.*

Key Idea: The nations of Africa were freed from colonial rule between 1960-1971.

History Project | S

Nelson Mandela was released from prison after serving 27 consecutive years of his lifetime prison sentence. After the first free elections, he became South Africa's first black president. Watch his release at **one** of the sites below.
http://www.biography.com/people/nelson-mandela-9397017
Or, with parental screening for ads, view http://abcnews.go.com/Archives/video/feb-11-1990-nelson-mandela-freed-prison-9395738

Key Idea: Nelson Mandela's release from prison gained worldwide attention.

President Study | I

★ If a 45th president of the United States has been elected, then choose a print resource to research the 45th president. Complete the page in your *President Student Notebook* about the 45th president.

Key Idea: Research the 45th president.

Storytime | T/I

Read the following assigned pages:

★ *Teresa of Calcutta* p. 132-142
Choose a new section of the bookmark with **three** options at the bottom. At the top of this section of the bookmark, write the book title and the page numbers you read today. Select **one** of the three options at the bottom and place a checkmark next to it. In the blank space under today's pages, respond in writing using your checked option.

Key Idea: Relate to the text in various ways.

Timeline | I

You will be adding to the timeline in your *Student Notebook* today. In Unit 35 – Box 1, draw and color a heart that is half white and half black. Label it, *Apartheid Laws Repealed – South Africa (1991 A.D.).*

In Box 2, draw and color two silver twin skyscraper towers side-by-side. Label the box, *9-11 Terrorist Attack on U.S. (September 11, 2001 A.D.).*

In Box 3, draw and color a camouflage army helmet. Label it, *War in Iraq (March 20, 2003-December 15, 2011 A.D.).*

Key Idea: Nelson Mandela served as president of South Africa from 1994-1999. Mandela retired in 1999 and was succeeded by Thabo Mbeki. During Mbeki's term as president of South Africa, terrorists attacked the U.S. World Trade Center and the Pentagon. The wars in Afghanistan and Iraq followed.

Independent History Study | I

Read the timeline entries from 1994-2001 on p. 487 of *The Story of the World.* How close were these events to the year that you were born? View all of the different African nations on p. 54 of the *United States History Atlas.*

Key Idea: Africa consists of many different nations. It is a very diverse continent.

Learning the Basics
Focus: Language Arts, Math, Bible, Nature Journal, and Science

Nature Journal   I

Read and follow the directions in the resource below.

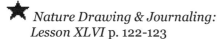 *Nature Drawing & Journaling: Lesson XLVI p. 122-123*

Note: Do **only one** window study in your journal today. Choose to either draw with black pen or with colored pencils.

<u>Key Idea</u>: Practice drawing either a view from a window or a view of a window.

Language Arts   S

Help students complete one lesson from the following reading program:

 *Drawn into the Heart of Reading*

Help students complete **one** English option.

⭐ *Progressing With Courage:* Lesson 130

⭐ *Progressing With Courage:* Lesson 132 (Class Practice 'F' – 'G' only)

⭐ Your own grammar program

Work with the students to complete **one** of the writing options listed below:

⭐ *Write with the Best: Vol. 2* Unit 7 – Day 9 p. 70

⭐ Your own writing program

<u>Key Idea</u>: Practice language arts skills.

Bible Quiet Time   I

Bible Study: Read and complete the assigned pages in the following resource:

⭐ *Faith at Work: Lesson 29 – Day Two* p. 220-221

Prayer Focus: Refer to **adoration** on "Preparing Your Heart for Prayer". Then, pray a prayer of adoration to worship and honor God. After your prayer, write 'adoration' at the bottom of today's lesson in *Faith at Work* above *Day Three*. Next to 'adoration', either list key phrases or write a sentence to summarize your prayer. Keep "Preparing Your Heart for Prayer" inside your Bible.

Scripture Memory: Read aloud James 4:17 three times from your Bible.

Music: Read p. 89 in *Hymns for a Kid's Heart*. Refer to p. 90-91 as you sing with Track 12 *"My Country, 'Tis of Thee"* (vs. 1-4).

<u>Key Idea</u>: Read and study James 5:7-20.

Math Exploration   S

Choose **one** of the math options listed below (see Appendix for details).

⭐ *Singapore Primary Mathematics 6A/6B, Discovering Mathematics 7A/7B, 8A/8B, No-Nonsense Algebra* or *Videotext Algebra*

⭐ Your own math program

<u>Key Idea</u>: Use a step-by-step math program.

Science Exploration   S

⭐ Discuss with a parent the questions for Chapter 18 on p. 225 of *Evolution: The Grand Experiment* Teacher's Manual. Next, read p. 199-204 in the Student Text. Then, complete "Test A" on p. 229 of the *Evolution: The Grand Experiment* Teacher's Manual. You may refer to the Student Text p. 199-204 to help you complete the test.

<u>Key Idea</u>: Proteins are necessary for life to begin. Scientists who support evolution suggest that proteinoids eventually converted into proteins. However, proteinoids have never been shown to convert into proteins, proteins have never been observed forming naturally, and proteinoids cannot copy DNA.

Reading about History | I |

Read about history in the following resources:

★ *All American History: Vol. II* p. 474-475

★ *Great Events in American History* p. 169-175

After today's reading, open your *Student Notebook* to Unit 35. Box 5 shows an aerial view of part of "Ground Zero" in New York City, where the World Trade Center towers collapsed after being attacked by terrorists. Buildings surrounding the twin towers of the World Trade Center were heavily damaged by the impact and debris of the falling towers.

Key Idea: On September 11, 2001, al-Qaeda terrorists hijacked four U.S. commercial airliners with the intent of using the airplanes as bombs that explode on impact. Two planes crashed into the World Trade Center towers, a third plane crashed into the Pentagon, and a fourth plane crashed in a field in Pennsylvania.

History Project | S |

One way to better understand the sequence of events that happened on 9-11 is to watch news clips of the events in the order that they took place on that morning. **With a parent,** watch clips automatically play at the site below by clicking on the large play "arrow" on the tower: http://archive.org/details/911#videosummary If the address above does not work, instead go to http://archive.org/details/911. Then, click on "Watch a video summary of key events" under the picture of "News Live Coverage: World Trade Center".

Key Idea: 3000 people died in the 9-11 attacks.

President Study | I |

★ If a 45ᵗʰ president of the United States has been elected, choose a second resource to research the 45ᵗʰ president. Then, add further information to the page in your *President Student Notebook* about the 45ᵗʰ president.

Key Idea: Research the 45ᵗʰ president.

Storytime | T/I |

Read the following assigned pages:

★ *Teresa of Calcutta* p. 143-155

Get the bookmark you made on Day 1. Find the section of the bookmark that has only **two** options at the bottom. At the top of this section of the bookmark, write the book title and the page numbers you read today. Select **one** of the two options at the bottom and place a checkmark next to it. In the blank space under today's pages, respond in writing using your checked option. Keep the bookmark in your book.

Key Idea: Relate to the text in various ways.

Geography | I |

For today's activities, use the map listed below.

★ *Map Trek CD: Missions to Modern Marvels* p. 94-95

Print the "Attack on the United States" Student Map found on p. 95 of the *Map Trek* CD. Refer to or print the *Map Trek* Teacher's Answer Map on p. 94 to guide you as you label your Student Map to match the Teacher's Answer Map. Notice that all four of the attacks occurred within the span of 1 hour and 7 min.

Key Idea: The U.S. was attacked on Sept. 11.

Independent History Study | I |

Refer to the map of "The Conflict in Afghanistan, 2001" on p. 52 of the *United States History Atlas*. Trace the red arrows that show the major refugee movements to see the countries where these refugees went. Name these countries. Look on p. 54 of the *United States History Atlas* to find Afghanistan and its surrounding countries.

Key Idea: After the terrorist attacks in the U.S. on September 11, the U.S. and Great Britain invaded Afghanistan as part of the war on terrorism. Afghanistan harbored al-Qaeda and was ruled by the Islamic militant Taliban.

Learning the Basics
Focus: Language Arts, Math, Bible, Nature Journal, and Science

Biblical Self-Image [T]

Our plans intend for the listed pages in *Who Am I? And What Am I Doing Here?* to be read either silently by both you and your child, or read aloud to the child by you. With this in mind, read and discuss the following pages listed below.

 Who Am I? And What Am I Doing Here? p. 255-261

<u>Key Idea</u>: China is a communist country where Christianity is considered dangerous. The government persecutes those who follow Jesus.

Language Arts [S]

Have students complete one studied dictation exercise (see Appendix for passages).

Help students complete one lesson from the following reading program:

 Drawn into the Heart of Reading

Help students complete **one** English option.

 Progressing With Courage: Lesson 131

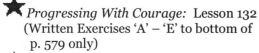 *Progressing With Courage:* Lesson 132 (Written Exercises 'A' – 'E' to bottom of p. 579 only)

 Your own grammar program

<u>Key Idea</u>: Practice language arts skills.

Bible Quiet Time [I]

Bible Study: Read and complete the assigned pages in the following resource:

 Faith at Work: Lesson 29 – Day Three p. 221

Prayer Focus: Refer to **confession** on "Preparing Your Heart for Prayer". Then, pray a prayer of confession to admit or acknowledge your sins to God. After your prayer, write 'confession' at the bottom of today's lesson in *Faith at Work* above *Day Four*. Next to 'confession', either list key phrases or write a sentence to summarize your prayer. Keep "Preparing Your Heart for Prayer" inside your Bible.

Scripture Memory: Memorize James 4:17 from your Bible and recite it.

Music: Refer to p. 90-91 as you sing with Track 12 *"My Country, 'Tis of Thee"* (vs. 1-4).

<u>Key Idea</u>: Read and study James 5:7-20.

Math Exploration [S]

Choose **one** of the math options listed below (see Appendix for details).

 Singapore Primary Mathematics 6A/6B, Discovering Mathematics 7A/7B, 8A/8B, No-Nonsense Algebra or *Videotext Algebra*

 Your own math program

<u>Key Idea</u>: Use a step-by-step math program.

Science Exploration [S]

 Discuss with a parent the questions for Chapter 19 on p. 237 of *Evolution: The Grand Experiment* Teacher's Manual. Next, read p. 205-210 in the Student Text. Then, complete "Test A" on p. 241 of the *Evolution: The Grand Experiment* Teacher's Manual. You may refer to the Student Text p. 205-210 to help you complete the test. **Optional:** Extension students may take "Test B" on p. 209, 219, 231, and 243 of the Teacher's Manual as a sectional exam.

<u>Key Idea</u>: Amino acids are necessary for life to begin because they make up the links of the protein chain. In 1953, Stanley Miller produced amino acids in the laboratory, leading some scientists to theorize that amino acids could have begun spontaneously in a similar way. This theory has never been proven.

Learning Through History
Focus: Nelson Mandela, September 11, and Wars in Afghanistan and Iraq
Unit 35 - Day 3

Reading about History [I]

Read about history in the following resource:

★ *All American History: Vol. II* p. 476-480 and p. 501-504
After today's reading, open your *Student Notebook* to Unit 35. Box 7 shows a picture of a statue of Saddam Hussein being toppled in Baghdad on April 9, 2003, after the U.S. invasion of Iraq. Saddam Hussein was captured on Dec. 13, 2003, and tried and hung for crimes against humanity by an Iraqi Special Tribunal. In Box 8, list bulleted notes from p. 476-477 of *All American History*.

Key Idea: The War in Iraq lasted over 8 years.

History Project [S]

Print the "Conflict in Iraq" Student Map from p. 97 of the *Map Trek* CD. To help you label your Student Map, refer to or print the *Map Trek* Teacher's Answer Map p. 96. Say the names of the cities in Iraq where the red stars note the largest battles. Notice the Tigris and Euphrates Rivers that run through Iraq. These rivers are mentioned in Genesis 2:8-15, before the Flood, as being part of the location of the Garden of Eden. Mount Ararat, the Biblical resting place of Noah's Ark, is located in Turkey on the border of Iran not far from Iraq. Remember that Iraq was formerly a part of the Persian Empire, whose capital was Babylon. Present-day Baghdad is near the site of Babylon. Saddam Hussein thought of himself as a modern-day Nebuchadnezzar and built a palace over part of the ruins of Babylon. He also began rebuilding the city of Babylon before the Conflict in Iraq began.

Key Idea: The Conflict in Iraq began in 2003.

State Study [T]

★ This is an **optional** part of the plans. If you have chosen to study your state using *State History from a Christian Perspective*, do Lesson 30 from the *Master Lesson Plan Book*.
Key Idea: Study your individual state.

Storytime [T/I]

Read the following assigned pages:

★ *Teresa of Calcutta* p. 156-161
After today's reading, orally narrate or retell the portion of the story that was read today. See *Narration Tips* in the Appendix as needed.

Key Idea: Practice orally narrating, or retelling, a portion of a story.

Worthy Words [T]

Read, analyze, and evaluate the speech below.

★ *Book of Great American Speeches for Young People* p. 281-283
After reading the speech, answer the following questions on an index card: *What issue does Robb address in this speech? According to the Marine Corps Colonel quoted in this speech, what should be the "object of our protection"? What did he mean when he said that "we have but one Constitution..."? How is a flag to be properly disposed of when it is tattered or damaged? Why then is the burning of an American flag in protest so upsetting? What does the flag represent? Why does Robb oppose the proposed amendment to the Constitution to punish flag burners? What is your opinion about this proposed amendment?* Next, meet with a parent to have a Socratic dialogue about the speech. Before beginning the dialogue, the parent reads the speech out loud. Next, discuss the questions using your notes. All participants should use life experiences or text to support responses.

Key Idea: The American flag stands for freedom and represents the country's values.

Independent History Study [I]

Open your *Student Notebook* to Unit 35. Choose one part from p. 281-283 of the *Book of Great American Speeches for Young People* to copy in Box 6. Write "Charles S. Robb" at the bottom of Box 6.

Key Idea: Protestors sometimes burned flags.

Learning the Basics
Focus: Language Arts, Math, Bible, Nature Journal, Poetry, and Science

Nature Journal & Poetry | S

The poetry of Longfellow, Wordsworth, and Whitman is scheduled to complement the journaling sessions. Read aloud and discuss today's excerpt from the poem *"The Labourer's Noon-Day Hymn"* (see Appendix) with a parent. Then, follow the directions below.

★ *Nature Drawing & Journaling: Lesson XLVII* p. 125

<u>Key Idea</u>: Look back over your journal pages and reflect upon your progress.

Language Arts | S

Have students complete one studied dictation exercise (see Appendix for passages).

Help students complete **one** English option.

★ *Progressing With Courage:* Lesson 132 (first half only)

★ *Progressing With Courage:* Lesson 132 (Written Exercises 'E' from the top of p. 580 – 'F' only)

Work with the students to complete **one** of the writing options listed below:

★ *Write with the Best: Vol. 2* Unit 7 – Day 10 p. 70-71 (Note: Unit 8 will be omitted.)

★ Your own writing program

<u>Key Idea</u>: Practice language arts skills.

Bible Quiet Time | I

Bible Study: Read and complete the assigned pages in the following resource:

★ *Faith at Work: Lesson 29 – Day Four* p. 221-222

Prayer Focus: Refer to **thanksgiving** on "Preparing Your Heart for Prayer". Then, pray a prayer of thanksgiving to express gratitude to God for His divine goodness. After your prayer, write 'thanksgiving' at the bottom of today's lesson in *Faith at Work* above *Day Five*. Next to 'thanksgiving', either list phrases or write a sentence to summarize your prayer.

Scripture Memory: Copy James 4:17 in your Common Place Book.

Music: Refer to p. 90-91 as you sing with Track 12 *"My Country, 'Tis of Thee"* (vs. 1-4).

<u>Key Idea</u>: Read and study James 5:7-20.

Math Exploration | S

Choose **one** of the math options listed below (see Appendix for details).

★ *Singapore Primary Mathematics 6A/6B, Discovering Mathematics 7A/7B, 8A/8B, No-Nonsense Algebra* or *Videotext Algebra*

★ Your own math program

<u>Key Idea</u>: Use a step-by-step math program.

Science Exploration | S

★ On *Evolution: The Grand Experiment* DVD, select "Menu" and then "Bonus Material". After that select "Chapter Index" and then select "20 – Conclusion". Watch the DVD from 54:05-end of the segment on the counter. The bottom left corner of the screen flashes a green title bar when a new chapter begins. Read p. 211-222 in the *Evolution: The Grand Experiment* Student Text. **Optional Reading:** You may enjoy reading some of the Appendix on p. 223-234 in your free time. **Optional Final Exam:** Extension students may take a Comprehensive Final Exam by completing "Test C" from Chapters 1-19 as described on p. 245 in the Teacher's Manual. This is **not** a required part of the course for extension students.

<u>Key Idea</u>: What do you think? Could life have formed spontaneously, or does the origin of life rest with a magnificent Creator?

Reading about History | I |

Read about history in the following resource:

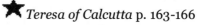 *Rescue and Redeem* p. 235-244

You will be writing a narration about part of the pages that you read today. To prepare for writing your narration, look back over p. 235-244 in *Rescue and Redeem*.

Choose **four** people included in p. 235-244 about which to write your narration. Plan to write 3-4 sentences about each person. Think about the main idea and the most important moments for each person that you chose.

After you have thought about what you will write and how you will begin your narration, turn to Unit 35 in your *Student Notebook*. For more guidance on writing a narration, see *Written Narration Tips* in the Appendix.

In Box 4, write a 12-16 sentence narration about the reading. When you have finished writing, read your sentences out loud to catch any mistakes. Check for the following things: *Did you include **who** or **what topic** the reading was mainly about? Did you include **descriptors** of the important thing(s) that happened? Did you include a **closing sentence**? If not, add those things.*

Use the *Written Narration Skills* in the Appendix as a guide for editing the narration.

<u>Key Idea</u>: The modern era has many significant Christians. The book *Rescue and Redeem* has included some key Christian figures through stories in its narrative chapters and has included summaries of other key figures in its closing chapter.

President Study | I |

 When the 46th president of the United States is elected, refer to two different resources to research the 46th president. Then, add an additional page to your *President Student Notebook* about the 46th president.

<u>Key Idea</u>: Research the 46th president.

Storytime | T/I |

Read the following assigned pages:

 Teresa of Calcutta p. 163-166

Get the bookmark that you placed in your book on Day 2. Locate the same section of the bookmark that you used on Day 2. Beneath Day 2's entry, write the book title and the page numbers you read today. Select the one remaining response option at the bottom of the bookmark, and place a checkmark next to it. In the blank space under today's pages, respond in writing using your checked option.

<u>Key Idea</u>: Relate to the text in various ways.

Economics | I |

Read about economics in the resource below.

 Common Sense Business for Kids p. 61-62

After the reading, open your *Student Notebook* to the "Economic Principles" section at the front of your notebook. Read through the Economic Principles that you have listed this school year. Think how much you have learned about economics and business that you did not know when you first started this guide!

<u>Key Idea</u>: Even though each business is different, common sense, observation, and learning from experience are invaluable for success in any business.

Independent History Study | I |

Open your *Student Notebook* to Unit 35 – Box 9. Listen to Billy Graham's sermon given one month after the September 11 attacks on the U.S. As you listen, take notes on the sermon in Box 9. The sermon is located at http://www.billygraham.org/ videoarchive.asp Click on "Sermons" and scroll through the sermons at the bottom until you reach the 21st image "Billy Graham Recalls 9/11". Click on the picture to play Graham's 15 min. sermon.

<u>Key Idea</u>: God is always in control and on the throne. He is not surprised by human events.

Learning the Basics
Focus: Language Arts, Math, Bible, Nature Journal, and Science

Biblical Self-Image `T`

Read and discuss with the students the following pages in the resource below.

⭐ *Who Am I? And What Am I Doing Here?* p. 262

Note: Read and discuss the meaning of each part of the wall in the House of Truth.

Key Idea: God expects us to live in a way that reflects our saving relationship with Him through Christ Jesus.

Language Arts `S`

Have students complete one studied dictation exercise (see Appendix for passages).

Help students complete one lesson from the following reading program:

⭐ *Drawn into the Heart of Reading*

Help students complete **one** English option.

⭐ *Progressing With Courage:* Lesson 132 (last half only)

⭐ *Progressing With Courage:* Lesson 132 (Written Exercises 'G' – 'J' only)

⭐ Your own grammar program

Key Idea: Practice language arts skills.

Bible Quiet Time `I`

Bible Study: Complete the assignment below.

⭐ *Faith at Work: Lesson 29 – Day Five* and *Notes* p. 222-226 (Note: We will omit *Lesson 30.*)

Prayer Focus: Refer to **supplication** on "Preparing Your Heart for Prayer". Then, pray a prayer of supplication to make a humble and earnest request of God. Write 'supplication' at the bottom of today's lesson on p. 222 in *Faith at Work*. Next to it, either list several key phrases or write a sentence to summarize your prayer.

Scripture Memory: Recite James 4:1-17.

Music: Refer to p. 90-91 as you sing with Track 12 *"My Country, 'Tis of Thee"* (vs. 1-4).

Key Idea: Read and study James 5:7-20.

Math Exploration `S`

Choose **one** of the math options listed below.

⭐ *Singapore Primary Mathematics 6A/6B, Discovering Mathematics 7A/7B, 8A/8B, No-Nonsense Algebra* or *Videotext Algebra*

⭐ Your own math program

Key Idea: Use a step-by-step math program.

Science Exploration `I`

⭐ Copy the Science Lab Form from the Appendix of this guide. Read p. 41-42 and follow the directions to perform "Experiment 19" from p. 43 of the *Genetics & DNA Experiment Manual*. You **must** have a **parent's help and supervision** to complete Experiment 19. After completing Experiment 19, in the top box of the Science Lab Form write: *How can you prove the presence and growth of bacteria?* In the second box of the form, write your hypothesis. Let the medium from Experiment 19 **cool for at least 30 min. before proceeding.** Next, follow the directions for "Experiment 20" on p. 44 of the Experiment Manual and complete the box "Perform an Experiment" on your lab form. Then, follow the arrows to complete the rest of the Science Lab Form. Then, read p. 45-46. Since today is the last day of this guide, you will need to check the dishes daily for a week or more on your own. **After a week of observing, do not open the lids of the dishes!** Instead, leave them sealed and throw the dishes into the garbage.

Key Idea: Bacteria multiply quickly, even from only a few individual bacteria. Some medicines today are produced from bacteria.

Appendix

Bibliography: Storytime Titles

This list includes 14 narrative resources that provide meaningful text connections with the history theme in *Hearts for Him Through Time: Missions to Modern Marvels*. Each book was very carefully chosen as an excellent Storytime read-aloud selection for this listening level. If you are already doing a read-aloud package with a different Heart of Dakota program, then you may choose to have your seventh or eighth grade students read these books on their own instead. A daily schedule is provided within the guide. In order to read these selections on their own, students should be strong independent readers that are not overly sensitive. Otherwise, reading aloud is the preferred method for using this package. This package is highly recommended, unless you need to economize. For your convenience, these resources may be purchased from Heart of Dakota either as an entire set called the *Hearts for Him Through Time: Missions to Modern Marvels* **Basic Package,** or as individual titles. View packages on the website www.heartofdakota.com. Book descriptions are taken from the book or the publisher listing.

Basic Package:

Units 1-2: *Under the Hawthorn Tree* by Marita Conlon-McKenna, 2009 Sourcebooks Jabberwocky
Ireland in the 1840s is in the grip of a terrible famine. The three O'Driscoll children are left to fend for themselves when their father and mother go missing in a desperate search for food. The children's only hope for survival is to find the great aunts they have only heard about in their mother's stories. Prepare to join Eily, Michael, and Peggy on their incredible journey as they overcome tragedy, famine, and poverty to make their way in a dangerous new world. Winner of many awards and accolades, you are sure to find this all-time classic historical fiction book to be deeply moving, historically true, and fictionally vivid!

Units 2-4: *God's Adventurer* by Phyllis Thompson, 2004 O M F International
Hudson Taylor was only a teenager when God told him to go to China. Though he was completely alone, flat broke, and critically ill, he hung on to that goal and to the God who he knew in his heart was sending him. Danger and adventure abound in this inspiring true story of a man who dared to risk everything he had and place his trust in God for a purpose that would change the world.

Units 4-6: *Factory Girl* by Barbara Greenwood, 2007 Kids Can Press
The year is 1912, and Emily Watson's dreams of completing her 8th grade education and entering one of the newly opened occupations for women such as a clerk, nurse, or teacher, come to an abrupt end. Mysteriously her father's letters stop arriving, and her family is thrown into poverty. Twelve year old Emily is soon forced to seek employment in a sweatshop, snipping garment threads for four dollars a week. At the dingy, overcrowded Acme Garment Factory, Emily stands for 11 hours a day clipping threads from blouses. When a reporter arrives to expose the terrible working conditions, Emily finds herself caught between her desperation for a job and her hope for change. What will Emily do?

Units 6-8: *Mama's Bank Account* by Kathryn Forbes and Kathryn N. Anderson McLeann, Mariner Books
Meet Mama and see life in a brand new way! This true story, set as a series of reminiscences, is about a Norwegian immigrant family living in San Francisco in the early 1900s. Mama's shrewd, yet completely selfless, personality determines to see the good in everyone, while still being stubborn enough to know how to get things done in spite of insurmountable odds. Look through Mama's eyes as you meet some interesting characters, and be encouraged by how this remarkable woman sees life's possibilities in unique ways that warm the heart!

Bibliography: Storytime Titles
(continued)

Units 9-12: *Angel on the Square* by Gloria Whelan, 2003 HarperCollins
 The fall of 1914 finds Katya Ivanova safe behind palace walls living in the seemingly
 magical setting of St. Petersburg. As the daughter of a lady-in-waiting to Empress
 Alexandra, Katya spends all her time with the Grand Duchesses, which makes Russian Tsar
 Nikolai II and his royal family feel like her own. However, just outside the palace, a terrible
 war is sweeping through Europe, and Russia is beginning to crumble under the weight of a
 growing revolution. As Katya's once certain future begins to dissolve, she must seek to
 understand what is happening to her beloved country and, for the first time in her life, take
 charge of her own destiny.

Units 12-14: *War Horse* by Michael Morpurgo, 2011 Scholastic Press
 In 1914, Joey, a beautiful bay-red foal with a distinctive cross on his nose, is sold to the
 army and thrust into the midst of the war on the Western Front. With his officer, he
 charges toward the enemy, witnessing the horror of the battles in France. But even in the
 desolation of the trenches, Joey's courage touches the soldiers around him, and he is able
 to find warmth and hope. But his heart aches for Albert, the farmer's son he left behind.
 Will he ever see his true master again?

Units 14-18: *Gladys Aylward* by Janet and Geoff Benge, 1998 YWAM Publishing
 Gladys Aylward felt called by God to be a missionary in China, but at the age of twenty-
 seven, she was dismissed from missionary training school for failing her Bible class.
 Without formal education or a missionary organization to back her, Gladys raised her own
 finances for the overland trip that would bring her to the country and people that God had
 etched so deeply on her heart... China! What follows is an amazing adventure of faith and
 determination. Gladys Aylward, a housemaid from England, dared to trust God in the face
 of dire and seemingly hopeless circumstances. Her life is one of the truly great missionary
 stories of our era.

Unit 18-21: *Shadow of His Hand: A Story Based on the Life of Holocaust Survivor Anita
 Dittman* by Wendy Lawton, 2004 Moody Publishers
 Politics don't matter to 5 year old Anita Dittman. She only knows that her Aryan father is
 abandoning her, her Jewish mother, and her sister. Young Anita Dittman's world crumbles
 as Hitler rises to power in Germany, but because she's a Christian and only half-Jewish,
 Anita feels sure she and her family are safe from the final solution. She couldn't have been
 more wrong. Amid Hitler's persecution, they're forced to leave everything they cherish –
 including each other. Follow Anita's struggle against Nazi persecution and watch her grow
 in her relationship with God through the worst of times. Based on a true story of shattered
 dreams, the nightmare of Nazi Germany, and God's faithfulness, this young adult historical
 fiction book is one you're sure to remember long after the final page.

Units 21-22: *Coming in on a Wing and a Prayer* by Kelly J. Brown, 2005 Vision Forum, Inc.
 Bill Brown was only 5 years old when a local barnstormer offered to take him for a flight in
 a biplane in exchange for one of his mother's homecooked meals. That day birthed a
 lifelong fascination with aviation. By twenty-one, Brown had earned his own wings and
 found himself flying as a P-51 Mustang fighter, performing daring raids on battlefields like
 Iwo Jima. Ultimately, he was shot down during a combat mission over Japan but would
 live to become a dynamic servant of the Cross. Prompted by a family trip back to Iwo Jima,
 Kelly shares her grandfather's WWII memories in a series of letters she imagines she's
 writing. Family and vintage photographs are included throughout this engaging true story.

Bibliography: Storytime Titles
(continued)

Units 22-25: *I Am David* by Anne Holm, 2004 Sandpiper
David's entire life of twelve years has been spent behind barbed wire in prison camp in Eastern Europe. He knows nothing of the outside world, yet when he is given the unlikely chance to escape, he seizes it. With his vengeful enemies hot on his heels, David struggles to cope in this strange new world, where his only resources are a compass, a few crusts of bread, his two aching feet, and some vague advice to seek refuge in Denmark. Will this be enough to survive? David's extraordinary odyssey is dramatically chronicled in this classic story about the meaning of true freedom and the life changing power of hope.

Units 25-27: *Freedom Walkers: The Story of the Montgomery Bus Boycott* by Russell Freedman, 2009 Holiday House
Join together with legendary heroes like Rosa Parks and Martin Luther King, important activists like Jo Ann Robinson and teenager Claudette Colvin, and numerous lawyers and politicians, to resist segregated bussing. This 381-day triumphant historical event will have you cheering on all those brave souls who stood together to spearhead the civil rights movement. Numerous personal memoirs, important articles, and beautifully reproduced black and white photos make this well researched work an inspiration to read!

Units 27-28: *Team Moon: How 400,000 People Landed Apollo 11 on the Moon* by Catherine Thimmesh, 2006 Houghton Mifflin Company
This behind-the-scenes look at the first Apollo moon landing gives names and voices to the army that got Neil Armstrong and company to the moon and back. From the seamstresses who put together 22 layers of fabric for each space suit, to the engineers who created a special heat shield to protect the capsule during its fiery reentry; from the flight directors to the telescope crew; from the software experts to the suit testers, this dramatic account will mesmerize even readers already familiar with this event! Be prepared to be awed by the level of care and dedication it took to surmount the many daunting challenges 'Team Moon' faced, and get ready for the exciting finale of taking that 'one giant leap'... together!

Units 28-31: *Children of the Storm: The Autobiography of Natasha Vins* by Natasha Vins, 2002 JourneyForth
Natasha Vins finds herself caught in a country determined to bully her into denying the existence of God and embracing the State as her head. As a young school-aged girl, she receives pressure from teachers to give unquestioning allegiance to the Soviet State. Since Natasha's father is a leader in the underground church, anti-Christian sentiments dog her family's life as well. When Natasha's father is forced to spend time in hiding and in prison, Natasha looks to her beloved grandmother for spiritual guidance, but in her teens, Natasha reaches a spiritual crossroads. In a homeland that demands that she embrace communist ideals and deny God, will she follow Christ into a life of poverty and hardship, or will she renounce her parents' Christ for the open doors which higher education has to offer?

Units 31-35: *Teresa of Calcutta: Serving the Poorest of the Poor* by Jeanene D. Watson, 1984 Mott Media
As a child, Agnes eagerly read letters by missionaries, and her favorites were those from Calcutta, India. This fascination led Agnes to Calcutta where she taught young, well-to-do girls who came to know her as Sister Teresa. Unsatisfied, Teresa searched for her calling in life and after much prayer, decided to work with "the poorest of the poor." Despite many hardships and heartrending decisions, she stayed with the work, for she knew in her heart that God had sent her to care for these people who simply had no one else to love them.

Bibliography: Self-Study Extension Package for Older Students

When to use this Extension Package Schedule: Adding this package to the Economy Package extends the study of history for students in grades 9 - 10. The books in this package are not intended to fulfill your student's high school literature credit, as students need to be reading separate higher-level literature to fulfill that need. Instead, the books in this package were chosen to help students experience various historical time periods, bringing the past to life through the pages of these books. Due to some mature content and themes contained in this time period (i.e. famine, war, disease, martyrdom, mentions of suicide, persecution, revolution, discrimination, segregation, terrorism, poverty, communism, etc.), students younger than grades 9-10 should use the Basic Package instead.

Note: As students are entering their high school years and are reading higher-level literature, there can be more language and mature content to be aware of within the readings. For this reason, it will be very important to carefully read the warnings provided in the Extension Schedule.

Books for the Extension Package Schedule:
Note: The books listed below are required in order to use the Extension Package Schedule. For ease of use, Heart of Dakota Publishing sells the books listed below as a set called Self-Study **Extension Package** for Older Students on the website www.heartofdakota.com. Book descriptions are from the publisher or book reviewer.

Units 1-4: *Esty's Gold* by Mary Arrigan, 2010 Frances Lincoln Children's Books
This is the story of one family that is forever changed by The Great Irish Famine of 1845-1851. Esty's childhood world is shattered when her father is killed defending starving Irish peasants. Suddenly forced to leave home and work as a maid, it is only the dream of gold and a better life in Australia that keeps her going. With stubborn determination, she gets her family to the goldfields of Ballarat. There, harsh conditions, deceit, and rebellion threaten to ruin them, but Esty will let nothing destroy her dream. This gripping adventure story written by an award-winning Irish author tells a timeless tale of hope and courage.

Units 4-7: *The Cereal Tycoon: Henry Parsons Crowell: Founder of the Quaker Oats Co.* by Jo Musser, 2002 Moody Publishers
Born into a wealthy family and endowed with a large inheritance after the death of his father, Henry Parsons Crowell had many opportunities to try his hand at business, a passion that suited him well. His shrewd business sense eventually brought him to the top of the oatmeal business, and to the potential of even greater wealth, if he would compromise his values. But Crowell was a man of integrity and compassion, who above all sought to share Christ with those around him. Read this compelling story of a man who struggled through a debilitating illness in his youth, survived the loss of two wives, faced opposition in almost every venture he tried, and who through it all, did big things for God!

Units 8-10: *Silent in an Evil Time: The Brave War of Edith Cavell* by L.M. Jack Batten, 2007 Tundra Books
Dutiful nurse, hospital matron, courageous resistance fighter - Edith Cavell was all of these. Dedicated to the methods of Florence Nightingale, Edith didn't hesitate when she was asked to help assist British and French soldiers trapped behind German lines. Edith sheltered escaping soldiers in her hospital, using skill and planning to keep the suspicious Germans from discovering them. Arranging a secret route to neutral Holland and back to England, she enabled soldiers of all ranks to slip through German lines. In this riveting account, Jack Batten brings an incredibly brave woman and her turbulent times to life.

Units 10-13: *Hattie Big Sky* by Kirby Larson, 2008 Yearling
Hattie has been moved from family member to family member so often she calls herself "Hattie Here-and-There." So when a land claim is passed to her from her uncle, she jumps at the chance to have a home where she belongs. Living under the big sky for a year, Hattie struggles to complete the terms of her claim – adding 480 rods of fence and cultivating 40 acres. Her German "neighbors" lend a hand and provide companionship, but as WWII rages on, loyalties are questioned, and holding onto her claim becomes harder and harder!

Units 13-15: *Eric Liddell: Something Greater Than Gold* by Janet and Geoff Benge, 1998 YWAM Publishing
Scottish missionary and runner Eric Liddell stunned the world by refusing to run in the Olympic 100 meter race on Sunday. His incredible victory in the 400 meter race further strengthened his belief in God's promise, "He who honors Me, I will honor." Years later, Eric would be tested far beyond mere physical ability as a missionary to China. His character, perseverance, and endurance are a challenge for all who would obey the call to bring the gospel to the nations.

Units 16-17: *Six Days in October: The Stock Market Crash of 1929: A Wall Street Journal Book for Children* by Karen Blumenthal, Focus on the Family Radio Theatre, 2002 Atheneum Books for Young Readers
Over six desperate days in October 1929, the fabulous fortune that Americans had built in stocks plunged with a fervor never seen before. At first, the drop seemed like a mere glitch in the system, but as the decline gathered steam, so did the destruction. Over 25 billion dollars in individual wealth was lost... vanished. Here "Wall Street Journal" bureau chief Blumenthal chronicles the six-day period that brought the country to its knees. Fascinating tales of stock market players, like Michael J. Meehan, an immigrant who started his career hustling cigars and helped convince thousands to gamble their hard-earned money, to riveting accounts of the power struggles between Wall Street and Washington, to poignant stories from those who lost their savings line the pages of this book. For readers living in an era of stock market fascination, this engrossing account explains stock market fundamentals while bringing to life the darkest days of the crash of 1929.

Units 17-19: *Friedrich* by Hans Peter Ricther, 1987 Puffin
A young German boy recounts the fate of his best friend, a Jew, during the Nazi regime in this tragic story of a Jewish boy in Germany during the 1930s. His best friend thought Friedrich was lucky. His family had a good home and enough money, and in Germany in the early 1930s, many were unemployed. But when Hitler came to power, things began to change. Friedrich was expelled from school, and then his mother died, and his father was deported... for Friedrich was Jewish. This book is one that shows in compelling fashion how sentiments in Germany gradually shifted toward hatred and persecution of the Jewish people. It demonstrates that the changes did not all occur at once, showing why many Germans turned a blind-eye to the happenings around them and why the Jews were lulled into a sense that things couldn't possibly get any worse... until it was too late.

Units 19-22: *Gunner's Run: A World War II Novel* by Rick Barry, 2007 JourneyForth
The call of duty takes Jim Yoder far away from his home, his nation, and his attractive friend Margo, thrusting him into mortal peril in Nazi Europe. Hailing from the Hoosier State and a Mennonite-pacifist background, he's determined that despite the loss of human life, the European countries are worth defending with his own life. At the young

age of nineteen years old, Jim becomes part of the 44th division stationed in England during World War II. When Jim's plane is shot down over enemy lines, to survive he must learn to trust the God that he used to disbelieve. Rife with historical detail and adventure, *Gunner's Run* brings both history and faith alive.

Units 22-24: *Revolution Is Not a Dinner Party* by Ying Chang Compestine, 2009 Square Fish
Nine year old Ling has a very happy life. Her parents are both dedicated surgeons at the best hospital in Wuhan, and her father teaches her English as they listen to the *Voice of America* every evening on the radio. But when one of Mao's political officers moves into a room in their apartment, Ling begins to witness the gradual disintegration of her world. In an atmosphere of increasing mistrust and hatred, Ling fears for the safety of her neighbors, and soon, for herself and her family. For the next four years, Ling will suffer more struggles than many people face in a lifetime. Will she be able to grow and blossom under the oppressive rule of Chairman Mao? Or will fighting to survive destroy her spirit – and her life? Drawing from her own childhood experience, author Ying Yang Compestine brings hope and humor to this fascinating story of a younger girl growing up and fighting to survive during the Cultural Revolution in China.

Units 25-27: *Miles to Go for Freedom: Segregation and Civil Rights in the Jim Crow Years* by Linda Barrett Osborne, 2012 Abrams Books for Young Readers
Told through unforgettable first person accounts, photographs, and other primary sources, and published in association with the Library of Congress, this book is an overview of racial segregation and early civil rights efforts in the United States from the 1890s to 1954, a period known as the Jim Crow years. Multiple perspectives are examined as the book looks at the impact of legal segregation and discrimination in the day-to-day life of black and white Americans across the country. Osborne expertly guides readers through this turbulent time and enables them to better understand the struggles, the triumphs, and the courage it took to set things right. Readers will come away moved, saddened, and troubled by this stain on their country's past, but they will also be filled with an enduring and abiding respect for those who fought… and overcame.

Units 27-28: *Escape from Saigon: How a Vietnam Orphan Became an American Boy* by Andrea Warren, 2008 Square Fish
This is an unforgettable true story of an orphan caught in the midst of war. Over a million South Vietnamese children were orphaned by the Vietnam War. This affecting true account tells the story of Long, who like more than 40,000 orphans, is Amerasian – a mixed race child – with little future in Vietnam. Experience Long's struggle to survive in war-torn Vietnam, his dramatic escape to America as part of "Operation Babylift" during the last chaotic days before the fall of Saigon, and his life in the United States as "Matt," part of a loving Ohio family. Finally, join Long as a young doctor when he journeys back to Vietnam to reconcile his Vietnamese past with his American present. This compelling account provides a fascinating introduction to the war and the plight of children caught in the middle of it.

Units 29-32: *The Dressmaker of Khair Khana: Five Sisters, One Remarkable Family, and the Woman Who Risked Everything to Keep Them Safe* by Gayle Tzemach Lemmon, 2011 Harper
The life Kamila Sidiqi had known changed overnight when the Taliban seized control of Kabul. After receiving a teaching degree during the civil war, a rare achievement for any Afghan woman, Kamila was banned from school and confined to her home. When her

father and brother were forced to flee the city, Kamila became the sole breadwinner for her five siblings. Armed only with grit and determination, she picked up a needle and thread and created a thriving business of her own. This is a story of war, but it is also a story of sisterhood and resilience in the face of despair. These women are not victims; they are the glue that holds families together and the backbone and heart of their nation.

Units 33-35: *Careful Enough* by Gayle Dillon Forbes, 2008 JourneyForth
Missionaries are illegal in China; yet God is calling Daniel's parents to move there and establish a house church. Daniel has a choice. He can either stay in America for his last year of high school, or he can spend ten months in a country where he can only say the word "Christian" to trusted friends. Though Daniel makes the courageous choice to go to China, once he arrives, he discovers there is a fine line between being cautious and being ashamed of his faith, between disobeying man's law and upholding God's commands. As the strain of constant caution increases, Daniel wonders if being a missionary in China is really worth the risk.

All Throughout the Units: *The American Testimony – DVD Set 2: United States History from 1877 to 2006* by EduMedia
Academically-rich and well-suited for students at the high school /college level, history enthusiasts, and patriotic citizens, these 5 U.S. History DVD's bring America's story into perspective. These are NOT boring classroom lecture videos! They are visually rich documentaries that use newsreel video, motion picture footage, archival photographs, illustrations of antiquity, and filmed reenactments to bring history to life. More than just a classroom or homeschool audiovisual tool, this series is also an excellent American History refresher course for those who have long been out of school. Corresponding DVD segments are scheduled within the Appendix of *Missions to Modern Marvels* in coordination with the history readings in the guide to provide more in-depth coverage for older students. Using these DVD's along with the rest of the Extension Package in conjunction with the other required books for *Missions to Modern Marvels* raises the level of the history study to make it worthy of high school credit.

Note: History readings are broken down into manageable daily assignments that coordinate with the various time periods in *Hearts for Him Through Time: Missions to Modern Marvels*. The reading assignments are meant for your older students to read independently. Depending on your goals for your older students' independent readings, you may want to assess their reading comprehension in some way. Some suggestions for assessment include:
- Give a detailed oral narration – suggested once during each unit:
  After the reading, students will retell what they've read using a detailed oral narration. The parent reads the opening paragraph from the chapter out loud to the students. This will be the starting point for the narration. Set a timer for 9 minutes. When the timer rings, the narration is over, even if it isn't complete. A detailed, descriptive narration is the goal. The "Narration Tips" found in the Appendix may be used for help as needed.
- Give a summary oral narration – suggested once during each unit:
  After the reading, students will retell what they've read using a summary oral narration. The oral narration must be no longer than 9 sentences and should summarize the reading. As students narrate, have them hold up one finger for each sentence until all 9 sentences are shared. Remind students that the focus should be on the big ideas, rather than on the details.
- Write a summary of the reading – suggested once during each unit:
  After the reading, students will write a summary of the reading that is at least 3-5

paragraphs long. The "Written Narration Skills" found in the Appendix should be used for help in editing. Have the students hand in their narration, and when you are ready to correct it, have them read their narration out loud to you. This is to help students catch as many of their own mistakes as possible, so if students find an error while reading aloud, they may fix the error and then continue reading.

- Write a written narration ending with an opinion – suggested once during each unit: The written narration could be detailed, summary, or a combination of both. The final paragraph of the narration should be an opinion paragraph, where the students state their opinion about something from the reading and support their opinion with examples from personal experiences, Scripture references, details from the reading, or examples from other literature they have read. The opinion paragraph should also have something to do with the rest of the content of the written narration. The "Written Narration Skills" found in the Appendix should be used for help in editing. Have the students hand in their narration, and when you are ready to correct it, have them read their narration out loud to you. This is to help students catch as many of their own mistakes as possible, so if students find an error while reading aloud, they may fix the error and then continue reading. Expressing opinions with adequate support is a difficult skill, which takes time to learn, so be sure to give students quite a bit of leeway as they grow into this important skill.

The assessments suggested above are meant to relieve parents of the need to preread the extension books and take the pressure off the parent to be all-knowing about the book. These assessments let the students do the work of thinking about a book instead, causing it to be more firmly placed in their minds. For example, on the oral narration days, the student would hand the parent the extension package book open to the starting page of the reading. As the student narrates, the parent skims through the pages in order and listens to see how well the student is narrating (which is easy to do with the book in hand). At the end of the oral narration, the parent might mention a missed part by saying, "Could you tell me a bit more about..." Then, the parent would give a lead for the student to narrate the missed part. This puts the focus on the student interacting with the text, rather than on the parent coming up with great discussion questions (which is an area already thoroughly covered in *Drawn into the Heart of Reading*).

On the written narration days, the student would hand in the extension package book marked to the opening page of the reading, along with the written narration. When the parent has a free moment, the parent would call the student to read the narration out loud, which helps the student catch any mistakes and fix them. Meanwhile, the parent is looking through the pages as the student reads the written narration to see if the high points of the story are mentioned. In written narrations, the parent can always expect a less thorough narration and shouldn't make the student go back and add more. Instead, after complimenting the student on what was done well, the parent may mention one thing to work on, like, "On your next written narration, try to add a few more details... or cover more of the story... or mention more of the characters' names...". The parent would then watch for that skill when going over the next narration, and if it isn't there, help the student add it. Again, the focus is on the student's interaction with the text, and not on the parent's ability to come up with questions. The "Written Narration Skills" section in the Appendix should also be used to help with editing.

Self-Study History Extension Package Schedule

Unit 1: Note: *The American Testimony DVD's* are keyed to match the "Reading About History" box in the daily plans. Also, as students read higher-level literature, there is more language to be aware of, and *Esty's Gold* uses God's name several times in a less than worshipful way. Should you wish to use white out in these instances, you will need to do so on p. 115, 127, 187, and 196.

    <u>Day 1</u>: *Esty's Gold* Ch. 1-2, p. 8-21
    <u>Day 2</u>: *Esty's Gold* Ch. 3-5, p. 22-36
    <u>Day 3</u>: *Esty's Gold* Ch. 6-7, p. 37-49
    <u>Day 4</u>: *Esty's Gold* Ch. 8-10, p. 50-68

Unit 2:
    <u>Day 1</u>: *Esty's Gold* Ch. 11-12, p. 69-82
    <u>Day 2</u>: *Esty's Gold* Ch. 13-15, p. 84-102
    <u>Day 3</u>: *Esty's Gold* Ch. 16-18, p. 103-122 (Note: p. 120 includes a violent threat meant to be humorous.)
    <u>Day 4</u>: *Esty's Gold* Ch. 19-21, p. 123-142 (Note: p. 139 includes a brief inappropriate comment.)

Unit 3:
    <u>Day 1</u>: *Esty's Gold* Ch. 22-23, p. 143-157
    <u>Day 2</u>: *Esty's Gold* Ch. 24-26, p. 158-171
    <u>Day 3</u>: *Esty's Gold* Ch. 27-28, p. 172-187
    <u>Day 4</u>: *Esty's Gold* Ch. 29-30, p. 188-195

Unit 4:
    <u>Day 1</u>: *Esty's Gold* Ch. 31-32, p. 196-208; *The American Testimony DVD Set 2* Disc 6, Track 5: "A Splendid Little War"
    <u>Day 2</u>: *Esty's Gold* Epilogue-Historical Note, p. 209-221 (Note: p. 213 includes a view of teaching religion with which you may or may not agree.)
    <u>Day 3</u>: *The Cereal Tycoon* p. 7-16; *The American Testimony DVD Set 2* Disc 6, Track 1: "Twilight of the Frontier Era"
    <u>Day 4</u>: *The Cereal Tycoon* p. 17-middle of p. 31

Unit 5:
    <u>Day 1</u>: *The Cereal Tycoon* middle of p. 31-39; *The American Testimony DVD Set 2* Disc 6, Track 3: "Progress and Pain"
    <u>Day 2</u>: *The Cereal Tycoon* p. 40-51
    <u>Day 3</u>: *The Cereal Tycoon* p. 52-middle of p. 62; *The American Testimony DVD Set 2* Disc 6, Track 4: "Course Corrections"
    <u>Day 4</u>: *The Cereal Tycoon* middle of p. 62—top of p. 71; *The American Testimony DVD Set 2* Disc 6, Track 6: "The Tumultuous Turn of the Century"

Unit 6:
    <u>Day 1</u>: *The Cereal Tycoon* p. 71-87; *The American Testimony DVD Set 2* Disc 6, Track 7: "Winds of Change"
    <u>Day 2</u>: *The Cereal Tycoon* p. 88-middle of p. 97; *The American Testimony DVD Set 2* Disc 7, Track 1: "Mr. Wilson and 'Colonel' House"
    <u>Day 3</u>: *The Cereal Tycoon* middle of p. 97-middle of p. 106
    <u>Day 4</u>: *The Cereal Tycoon* middle of p. 106-117

Unit 7:
    <u>Day 1</u>: *The Cereal Tycoon* p. 118-top of p. 126
    <u>Day 2</u>: *The Cereal Tycoon* top of p. 126-top of p. 136 (Note: p. 126-127 mention prostitution and the red light district in describing crime in Chicago.)
    <u>Day 3</u>: *The Cereal Tycoon* top of p. 136-top of p. 147
    <u>Day 4</u>: *The Cereal Tycoon* top of p. 147-160; *The American Testimony DVD Set 2* Disc 6, Track 2: "The New Religions"

Unit 8:

Day 1: *Silent in an Evil Time* p. 1-middle of p. 12

Day 2: *Silent in an Evil Time* middle of p. 12-23

Day 3: *Silent in an Evil Time* p. 24-middle of p. 35

Day 4: *Silent in an Evil Time* middle of p. 35-top of p. 46

Unit 9:

Day 1: *Silent in an Evil Time* top of p. 46-top of p. 58

Day 2: *Silent in an Evil Time* top of p. 58-top of p. 70

Day 3: *Silent in an Evil Time* top of p. 70-middle of p. 81

Day 4: *Silent in an Evil Time* middle of p. 81-bottom of p. 93

Unit 10:

Day 1: *Silent in an Evil Time* bottom of p. 93-104

Day 2: *Silent in an Evil Time* p. 105-117 (Note: p. 111 includes a hanging, and p. 116 includes death by a firing squad.)

Day 3: *Silent in an Evil Time* p. 118-126

Note: As students read higher-level literature, there is more language to be aware of, and *Hattie Big Sky* uses "darn", "darned", and "danged" throughout in keeping with the time period of homesteading in the "Wild West". Should you wish to use white out in these instances, you will need to do so on p. 20, 28, 42, 50, 60, 168, 202, 210, 227, and 258.

Day 4: *Hattie Big Sky* p. 1-23

Unit 11:

Day 1: *Hattie Big Sky* p. 24-48; *The American Testimony DVD Set 2* Disc 7, Track 2: "The Growing International Crisis"

Day 2: *Hattie Big Sky* p. 49-75

Day 3: *Hattie Big Sky* p. 76- top of p. 99; *The American Testimony DVD Set 2* Disc 7, Track 3: "Unrestrained Authority"

Day 4: *Hattie Big Sky* top of p. 99-123

Unit 12:

Day 1: *Hattie Big Sky* p. 124-146; *The American Testimony DVD Set 2* Disc 7, Track 4: "The 'Great War' and Its Aftermath"

Day 2: *Hattie Big Sky* p. 147-178

Day 3: *Hattie Big Sky* p. 179-203

Day 4: *Hattie Big Sky* p. 204-232; *The American Testimony DVD Set 2* Disc 7, Track 5: "Return to Normalcy"

Unit 13:

Day 1: *Hattie Big Sky* p. 233-253

Day 2: *Hattie Big Sky* p. 254-279

Day 3: *Hattie Big Sky* p. 280-288

Day 4: *Something Greater Than Gold* Ch. 1-2, p. 11-26

Unit 14:

Day 1: *Something Greater Than Gold* Ch. 3-4, p. 27-52

Day 2: *Something Greater Than Gold* Ch. 5-6, p. 53-74

Day 3: *Something Greater Than Gold* Ch. 7-8, p. 75-99

Day 4: *Something Greater Than Gold* Ch. 9-10, p. 101-122

Unit 15:

Day 1: *Something Greater Than Gold* Ch. 11, p. 123-135

Day 2: *Something Greater Than Gold* Ch. 12-13, p. 137-156

Day 3: *Something Greater Than Gold* Ch. 14-15, p. 157-180

Day 4: *Something Greater Than Gold* Ch. 16-17, p. 181-199; *The American Testimony DVD Set 2* Disc 8, Track 1: "Herbert Hoover's Crisis"

Unit 16:

Note: As part of the Stock Market Crash and the Depression Era, suicide is mentioned on p. 112 and 129 of *Six Days in October.*

Day 1: *Six Days in October* p. 2-top of p. 26; *The American Testimony DVD Set 2* Disc 8, Track 2: "FDR"

Day 2: *Six Days in October* top of p. 26-48

Day 3: *Six Days in October* p. 49-74

Day 4: *Six Days in October* p. 75-105

Unit 17:

Day 1: *Six Days in October* p. 107-122; *The American Testimony DVD Set 2* Disc 8, Track 3: "Prolonging the Depression"

Day 2: *Six Days in October* p. 123-146

Note: *Friedrich* is a book that gives a perspective of the growing persecution of Jews in Germany over 9 years. It is a book that should only be read in combination with the plans in *Missions to Modern Marvels* to gain a fuller perspective of this time period. This book is for a mature audience.

Day 3: *Friedrich* p. 1-middle of p. 19; *The American Testimony DVD Set 2* Disc 8, Track 4: "The Age of the Aggressors"

Day 4: *Friedrich* middle of p. 19-middle of p. 38 (Note: p. 36-37 includes a graphic description of a cow being slaughtered for a Jewish sacrifice.); *The American Testimony DVD Set 2* Disc 8, Track 5: "The Dawn of World War 2"

Unit 18:

Day 1: *Friedrich* middle of p. 38-top of p. 59; *The American Testimony DVD Set 2* Disc 8, Track 6: "America Enters the War"

Day 2: *Friedrich* top of p. 59-bottom of p. 78 (Note: p. 67 uses God's name in a way that is less than worshipful.)

Day 3: *Friedrich* bottom of p. 78-middle of p. 95

Day 4: *Friedrich* middle of p. 95-113 (Note: p. 98-100 describes a death in a disturbing way, and p. 113 mentions a brief kiss.)

Unit 19:

Day 1: *Friedrich* p. 114-top of p. 133 (Note: p. 122-123 includes a violent story of an attack upon an ancient Jewish city and its inhabitants.)

Day 2: *Friedrich* top of p. 133-149 (Note: p. 135-138 includes a heart-rending scene.)

Day 3: *Gunner's Run* p. 1-18

Day 4: *Gunner's Run* p. 19-38

Unit 20:

Day 1: *Gunner's Run* p. 39-58; *The American Testimony DVD Set 2* Disc 8, Track 7: "The Road to Victory"

Day 2: *Gunner's Run* p. 59-74

Day 3: *Gunner's Run* p. 75-93

Day 4: *Gunner's Run* p. 94-114

Unit 21:

Day 1: *Gunner's Run* p. 115-135

Day 2: *Gunner's Run* p. 136-153

Day 3: *Gunner's Run* p. 154-176 (Note: p. 166 describes war wounds and death.)

Day 4: *Gunner's Run* p. 177-194

Unit 22:

Day 1: *Gunner's Run* p. 195-215 (Note: p. 202 mentions a corpse.)

Note: *Revolution Is Not a Dinner Party* is a book that begins when the character is very young and progresses as she grows older, so it begins very simply and becomes much more mature as you read. Each simple event in the first half of the book has new meaning in the last half of the book. Due to its content, this book is **only** for a mature audience.

Day 2: *Revolution Is Not a Dinner Party* p. 5-26

Day 3: *Revolution Is Not a Dinner Party* p. 27-51; *The American Testimony DVD Set 2* Disc 9, Track 1: "War's Aftermath"

Day 4: *Revolution Is Not a Dinner Party* p. 52-75

Unit 23:

Day 1: *Revolution Is Not a Dinner Party* p. 76-100; *The American Testimony DVD Set 2* Disc 9, Track 2: "Global Communism"

Day 2: *Revolution Is Not a Dinner Party* p. 101-124

Day 3: *Revolution Is Not a Dinner Party* p. 125-150 (Note: p. 129-130 mentions an attempted suicide.); *The American Testimony DVD Set 2* Disc 9, Track 3: "China, Korea, and the Loss of American Resolve"

Day 4: *Revolution Is Not a Dinner Party* p. 151-172 (Note: p. 157 includes a suicide, and p. 158 includes a violent beating.)

Unit 24:

Day 1: *Revolution Is Not a Dinner Party* p. 173-194 (Note: p. 190-191 includes a violent fight.)

Day 2: *Revolution Is Not a Dinner Party* p. 195-219 (Note: p. 196 and p. 201 include brief graphic descriptions.)

Day 3: *Revolution Is Not a Dinner Party* p. 220-229

Day 4: *Revolution Is Not a Dinner Party* p. 230-248 (Note: p. 234 and p. 238-239 include beatings and descriptions of violence.)

Unit 25:

Day 1: *Miles to Go for Freedom* p. 1-11; *The American Testimony DVD Set 2* Disc 9, Track 4: "The Eisenhower Years"

Day 2: *Miles to Go for Freedom* p. 12-23

Day 3: *Miles to Go for Freedom* p. 24-35

Day 4: *Miles to Go for Freedom* p. 36-49

Unit 26:

Day 1: *Miles to Go for Freedom* p. 50-61

Day 2: *Miles to Go for Freedom* p. 62-73

Day 3: *Miles to Go for Freedom* p. 74-85

Day 4: *Miles to Go for Freedom* p. 86-97

Unit 27:

Day 1: *Miles to Go for Freedom* p. 98-107

Note: *Escape from Saigon* mentions the death by possible suicide of the mother of the main character several times throughout the book. Suicide is also mentioned in conjunction with the coming of the Communist troops. Should you wish to discuss these instances, they occur briefly on p. 10, 42, and 65.

Day 2: *Escape from Saigon* Introduction, Prologue, and p. 3-11; *The American Testimony DVD Set 2* Disc 9, Track 5: "Coexistence"

Day 3: *Escape from Saigon* p. 12-middle of p. 27 (Note: p. 16 mentions butchering animals and stealing.)

Day 4: *Escape from Saigon* middle of p. 27-bottom of p. 43

Unit 28:

Day 1: *Escape from Saigon* bottom of p. 43-59; *The American Testimony DVD Set 2* Disc 9, Track 6: "Kennedy and Johnson"

Day 2: *Escape from Saigon* p. 60-72; *The American Testimony DVD Set 2* Disc 10, Track 1: "Nixon's Challenge"

Day 3: *Escape from Saigon* p. 73-87 (Note: p. 80 includes derogatory name-calling.)

Day 4: *Escape from Saigon* p. 88-98; *The American Testimony DVD Set 2* Disc 10, Track 2: "Losing Public Confidence"

Unit 29:

Day 1: *The Dressmaker of Khair Khana* p. xi-xxvi

Day 2: *The Dressmaker of Khair Khana* p. 1-15 (Note: p. 14 includes a beating.)

Day 3: *The Dressmaker of Khair Khana* p. 16-middle of p. 30

Day 4: *The Dressmaker of Khair Khana* p. 30-49 (Note: p. 48 mentions prostitution.)

Unit 30:

Day 1: *The Dressmaker of Khair Khana* p. 50-63

Day 2: *The Dressmaker of Khair Khana* p. 64-top of p. 80

Day 3: *The Dressmaker of Khair Khana* top of p. 80-91

Day 4: *The Dressmaker of Khair Khana* p. 92-bottom of p. 108

Unit 31:

Day 1: *The Dressmaker of Khair Khana* bottom of p. 108-middle of p. 125

Day 2: *The Dressmaker of Khair Khana* middle of p. 125-140

Day 3: *The Dressmaker of Khair Khana* p. 141-top of p. 157

Day 4: *The Dressmaker of Khair Khana* top of p. 157-middle of p. 172

Unit 32:

Day 1: *The Dressmaker of Khair Khana* middle of p. 172-middle of p. 188

Day 2: *The Dressmaker of Khair Khana* middle of p. 188-top of p. 203; *The American Testimony DVD Set 2* Disc 10, Track 3: "The Carter Crisis and Reagan Revolution"

Day 3: *The Dressmaker of Khair Khana* top of p. 203-216

Day 4: *The Dressmaker of Khair Khana* p. 217-235

Unit 33:

Day 1: *Careful Enough* p. 1-18

Day 2: *Careful Enough* p. 19-40

Day 3: *Careful Enough* p. 41-56 (Note: p. 45 mentions abortion.); *The American Testimony DVD Set 2* Disc 10, Track 4: "Triumph Over Tyranny"

Day 4: *Careful Enough* p. 57-71

Unit 34:

Day 1: *Careful Enough* p. 72-84

Day 2: *Careful Enough* p. 85-103

Day 3: *Careful Enough* p. 104-119

Day 4: *Careful Enough* p. 120-132 (Note: p. 130 describes an upsetting meal, and p. 131 mentions flirtation.); *The American Testimony DVD Set 2* Disc 10, Track 5: "Political Gridlock"

Unit 35:

Day 1: *Careful Enough* p. 133-147 (Note: p. 142-143 mention a discussion about evolution and creationism.)

Day 2: *Careful Enough* p. 148-163 (Note: p. 154 includes a discussion of drinking alcohol.); *The American Testimony DVD Set 2* Disc 10, Track 6: "The War on Terror"

Day 3: *Careful Enough* p. 164-175

Day 4: *Careful Enough* p. 176-193

NARRATION TIPS: TEACHER'S LIST

Notes: When children narrate, they tell back in their own words what they have just read or heard. It allows them to share their own version of the passage with accuracy, individual personality, spirit, and originality.

Narrating is an essential skill in life. To be able to give an opinion of a book, relay a telephone message, summarize a letter, give driving directions, write an article, or share a doctor's instructions – are all examples of practical applications of narration skills. Narrating is an important skill to learn. You can begin to teach your children to narrate by following the steps listed below. Just be patient, and have fun with it! Narration is a way of life.

BEFORE NARRATING:

1. **Choose a living book.** Living books are alive with ideas and have a story aspect to them. The books read in this curriculum are living books.

2. **Skim the section your child will use for narration.** Children's narrations usually show how well they understand the book, but sometimes a child gives a confident, articulate narration that is eloquently wrong.

3. **Children should briefly remind themselves of what they read last time.** If children will be narrating on a book they've read a portion of already, it is helpful for them to take a moment to recall what happened during the last reading session.

4. **Children should have forewarning they will be narrating after the reading.** When children know they will narrate, they attend the reading with sharper attention. The plans in this curriculum let children know when they will be expected to narrate.

5. **Children should read the selected passage once.** Children should do their own reading by age 9, as this will help improve narrations. Since the target age range for this guide is ages 12-14, children should be doing their own reading at this level. If you have more than one child, only one child should narrate at a time.

DURING NARRATING:

1. **Have children tell you all they remember about the reading.** Say, *Tell me all you can about what you just read.* They should not be looking at the book. Do not interrupt a narration. It distracts the train of thought. Do not correct children while they are narrating.

2. **The teacher is a listener; not a lecturer.** Let the child's mind do the sorting, rejecting, and classifying of what should be shared.

3. **Children may use exact phrasing from the book.** They may pick up phrasing and vocabulary that strikes them. This allows children to make the language of good living books their own.

4. **Children may share connections made.** Children may compare what was read to another book, situation, or memory of their own. However, the connection should not take over the narration.

5. **The length of the narration is not the point.** If children can retell the most pertinent information in a few sentences, that may be enough. The purpose of narration is the process of ordering and selecting what to tell. Every narration doesn't need to be in full detail.

6. **There is not one "right" narration.** A dozen children could read the same section and give a dozen different good narrations. A teacher should not listen for a long list of words to be shared from the text.

AFTER NARRATING:

1. **Share comments or details.** You can ask questions, correct misinformation, and ask for clarification at this point. However, avoid being overly critical. Limit what you say to a few important points.

2. **Do not grade narrations.** Grading a narration gives the impression that there is only one right way to do it. Children are left searching for the elusive "one right narration", rather than using their own originality.

OTHER HELPFUL NARRATING TIPS:

1. **Be patient with your child.** If your child is frustrated or seems to be missing the meaning of the reading, shorten the sections he narrates on or take a turn narrating yourself. Try to be as encouraging as possible; make sure not to be overly critical or to give too lengthy advice.

2. **Help your children develop the habit of attention to reading.** If your children have been used to "gobbling up" books instead of giving focused attention to their reading, shorten the sections used for narration and focus on what they know – not on what they don't know.

3. **Children begin written narrations at age 10.** Instructions for written narrations are included in this guide's plans as well. When children begin written narrations, oral narrations are still continued. Each kind of narration is carefully noted in this guide's plans, to maintain an excellent balance of oral and written narrations. For this reason, written narrations should not be substituted for oral narrations in the plans, or vice versa, as these 2 types of narrations require very different types of skills, both necessary for children to learn to possess.

HOW TO NARRATE: STUDENT'S LIST

1. If you are in the middle of a book, briefly remind yourself what was read last time.

2. During the reading, think carefully about what you are reading. Pay attention to names, places, events, and things that grab your attention.

3. Be ready to tell all you can remember when the reading is done.

4. Retell what was read with as much detail as you can. There is not one right way to do this.

5. It's fine to repeat words or phrases that sound just like the book. It's fine to share connections you made with what was read.

6. Do not make things up or begin everything you say with, "And then...".

7. Listen to what your teacher says after you narrate. Try to do these things the next time you narrate.

WRITTEN NARRATION TIPS: TEACHER'S LIST

When children narrate, they tell back in their own words what they have just read or heard. Narration allows them to share their own version of the passage with accuracy, individual personality, spirit, and originality. Oral narration is considered the earliest form of composition, and the words "narration" and "composition" may be used interchangeably. Children under age 9 take care of their composition instruction by orally narrating, and by intertwining these narrations with history, science, reading, and the like.

By age 10, children's oral composition skills should be developed enough to begin written compositions. According to Charlotte Mason, composition in the form of written narration is "as natural as running and jumping to children who have been allowed to read lots of books". If they orally narrate first of all, they will compose sooner or later, but they should not be taught "composition" as a separate body of information to be learned. Instead, it is important that the child and the author be trusted to be left alone together, without a middle-man such as a teacher telling the child what the book said, or about what to think. According to Charlotte Mason, our business as teachers is to "provide children the material for their lessons, while leaving the handling of that material to themselves". In short, we are not to hamper them by too many instructions.

Children who have gotten into the habit of reading good literature absorb what they will from it themselves, in their own way, whether it's a lot or a little. Reading living books and narrating from them helps children to begin to form their own literary style. Because they have been in the company of great minds, their style will not be an exact copy of any one in particular, but will instead be shaped as an individual style from the wealth of materials they possess to create a natural style of their own. Narration done properly develops the power of self-expression and invites a child's personality to become part of the learning process. A child should choose vocabulary he finds appealing, make it his own, and then give it forth again with that own unique touch that comes from his own mind. This is why no two narrations should be exactly alike, and it is also why teachers should not expect their children to give the same narration they would have given.

Narrating requires a higher level of thinking. Consider the skill it takes to fill in blanks or choose from multiple-choice answers. Now, consider the skills it takes to retell a story you have just heard or read! Clearly the latter proves to require higher-level thinking. In order to demonstrate the complex skill of narrating, try your hand at it yourself. Now that you've read most of this page, turn it over and get a sheet of paper to write all that you can remember, or would you find it easier if you were given multiple-choice questions instead?

Narration provides far more information about children's comprehension because they must answer without the support clues provided by questions. The quiz, test, chapter review, and book report have all been replaced by something far more effective. What children take time to put in their own words is retained because it has become their own. With narration, you've just found the key to really knowing what your children know, which is why even after children have become skilled at writing narrations, oral narrations are still continued. Maintaining oral narrations keeps improving both a child's composing ability and his public speaking skills. There is simply not a better way to "test" a child's comprehension and retention than oral and written narration!

BEFORE BEGINNING WRITTEN NARRATIONS:

1. **Children should be experienced in giving oral narrations.** At about age 10, children can usually begin to do written narrations. However, children who have not learned to orally narrate need to first spend time working on that skill.

2. **Children should only narrate on living books.** Living books are alive with ideas and have a story aspect to them. Living books are used in this curriculum.

3. **Small portions of living books should initially be used for narrations.** The passage length may be longer as children get older. Appropriate lengths of passages for this age are narrated upon in this curriculum.

4. **Children should know they are going to be asked to write a narration.** This helps children attend the reading with sharper attention. This curriculum lets children know prior to their reading when they'll be expected to write a narration.

5. **Children should independently be reading the books for their written narrations.** This will help improve their narrations. Children should not be asked to independently write a narration for a book that is read to them.

6. **Teachers should skim the section the children will use for narration.** Children's narrations usually show how well they understand the book, but sometimes a child gives a confident, articulate narration that is eloquently wrong.

DURING THE WRITTEN NARRATION:

1. **Children should write all they remember about the reading directly after they have read.** The book may be used as a reference and for assistance in spelling. Teachers should not interrupt or correct a narration while children are writing, as it distracts their train of thought.

2. **Children may use exact phrasing from the book.** They may pick up phrasing and vocabulary that strikes them. This allows children to make the language of good living books their own.

3. **Children may share connections made.** Children may compare what was read with another book, situation, or memory of their own. However, the connection should not take over the narration.

4. **There is not one "right" narration.** A dozen children could read the same section and give a dozen different good written narrations.

AFTER WRITING A WRITTEN NARRATION:

1. **Children should read their written narration out loud to their teacher.** This will help them begin to edit their narration. Charlotte Masons says the teacher's role is to listen actively, alertly, and enthusiastically without interrupting.

2. **The teacher should first respond with encouragement.** Take time to share several specific things the children did well. Perhaps the beginning sentence caught your attention, the order was logical, or a certain phrase used vivid words. Taking on the role of an encourager with children sets a positive tone for working together.

3. **The teacher and children should work together to edit the narration.** Teachers should first read the "Written Narration Skills: Teacher's List" on their own. That list, along with the "Written Narration Skills: Student's List", should be used to help children learn to edit. <u>Note:</u> Older children that are experienced with written narrations may do this step on their own, and then meet with the teacher.

4. **Be careful not to expect a summary instead of a narration.** A teacher should not listen for a long list of things to be shared from the text. The children narrating should be allowed to choose the emphasis, and even the omissions.

5. **Do not grade narrations.** Grading a narration gives the impression that there is only one right way to do it, and children do not learn to use their own originality.

A Few Notes on the Transition to Written Narrations

The transition from oral narrations to written narrations will be a gradual one. It may take several years for children's written narrations to "catch up" to their oral narrations. Moving to written narrations often means moving to shorter narrations initially. Though it is hard to give up that detail we are used to in oral narrations, the length of the written narration is of less importance than the thinking that goes into it. Children progress at their own pace with narrating, and we should not expect every narration to be a finely crafted presentation. Narration that begins as a somewhat strained effort will, with practice, become longer, more detailed, and full of personality. It is worth the wait!

OTHER HELPFUL NARRATING TIPS:

1. **Be patient with your child.** If your child is frustrated or seems to be missing the meaning of the reading, shorten the sections he narrates. Continue to work on oral narration skills as well, as this will continue to improve written narrations too.

2. **Help your children develop the habits of listening and attention.** If your children have been used to "gobbling up" books instead of giving focused attention to reading, shorten the sections used for narration and focus on what they know.

3. **If a child is having difficulty writing, have him write part and dictate to you to write the rest.** This should be done only in special circumstances.

4. **If a child is struggling, you can make a list of important names, dates, and places on a marker board before the reading.** The child may then use the list as a reference for any words he decides he'd like to use in his narration.

5. **Obstinate attitudes are not allowed.** Simply do not tolerate any balking. Cheerfully show yourself ready to listen and then wait for your children to comply.

WRITTEN NARRATION SKILLS: TEACHER'S LIST

Notes: When children do written narrations, they use their writing to tell back in their own words what they have just read or heard. Written narrations allow children to use their writing to share their own version of the passage they have just read or heard with accuracy, individual personality, spirit, and originality.

You can begin to help your children with their written narrations by following the steps listed below. If you are new to Heart of Dakota and have not yet worked through the copywork, oral narration, and dictation in the guides, then you should plan to spend longer moving through the list of skills below. This is quite normal, so don't be surprised if you do not get through all of the skills in the list this year.

The skills listed below range from beginning writing skills to more difficult writing skills that require knowing higher levels of grammar, usage, and punctuation. Skills are based on a continuum of increasing difficulty, so related skills may be spread out to be placed where they each fall best on the overall continuum. For example, the third skill on the list is beginning and ending sentences correctly, as well as correcting sentence fragments. But, fixing run-on sentences, which is a related skill, is not addressed until the seventh skill. For this reason, it is best to read the list over in its entirety, so you can see the overall flow of the continuum. Focusing on teaching <u>one</u> new numbered skill at time <u>in the order it is listed</u> will help you to avoid overwhelming your child with too many skills at once, and will give your child a manageable plan for successfully learning to do written narrations.

For new or struggling writers, you should start with the skill listed first on the list below. Once that skill is <u>mastered</u>, move on to the next skill. The skills should be cumulative, meaning <u>each time a new skill is added, the old skills are still required</u>. You may either make <u>gentle</u> comments as students are writing each sentence of their narration, or wait until the narration is complete to make your <u>gentle</u> comments then.

If your child already routinely does the beginning skills on the list, you should jump to the first skill on the list that your child has not mastered. Before editing, always have your children read the narration aloud to you so they can catch any of their own mistakes first.

The skills list below is for the teacher's use. There is also a list for students' use that can be used for their reference; however, it should not be used in place of the teacher's list since written narration is a new skill being taught.

WRITTEN NARRATION SKILLS LIST:

1. **Indent each paragraph.** Leave a space about the size of one thumb tip at the beginning of the first sentence in each paragraph.

2. **Make sure the first sentence is on the right topic.** Reword it if necessary.

3. **Begin each sentence with a capital letter, and end each sentence with the correct punctuation mark (. ! ?).** To do this you will also need to correct any sentence fragments to make complete sentences.

4.   **Begin working on writing with correct spelling by using a combination of the following options.** Note: <u>Option 1</u> is a better habit for students to acquire than <u>Option 2</u>, and <u>Option 2</u> is a better habit for students to acquire than <u>Option 3</u>, and so on. <u>Option 4</u> should only be used for very poor spellers, as it is not the same as having students write something in their own words.

   <u>Option 1:</u> Have students look back in the book to copy the correct spelling of key words.
   <u>Option 2:</u> Write words that <u>students ask you to spell for them</u> on a markerboard or paper while they are writing. Then, they can copy the word(s) as they write.
   <u>Option 3:</u> Spell orally any words the students ask you to spell for them while they are writing.
   <u>Option 4:</u> Allow students to dictate the narration to you for you to write, and have them copy it at the end.

   Spelling will also be addressed more fully later on in the skills list, so when students have become good at using these spelling options, move on to number 5.

5.   **Make sure that sentences do not all start with the same word or words.** Vary the first word of the sentences within each paragraph as much as possible.

6.   **Use correct capitalization within each sentence.** Check to be sure all proper nouns, titles, etc. are capitalized.

7.   **Fix any sentences that are run-ons by providing a gentle reminder while students are writing.** For example, "That's the start of a new sentence now."

8.   **Write a good closing sentence.** This sentence should wrap up the paragraph in an interesting way, and make the reader feel like your writing is coming to a close. Ideas for a strong closing sentence include the following:
   * restating the introduction using different words
   * using a quote
   * asking a question
   * stating the main theme or idea
   * giving your personal opinion

9.   **Use correct spelling within your writing.** Edit the student's narration for spelling by underlining incorrect spelling in pencil and writing the correct spelling of the word in the margin of their paper or on a markerboard.

10.   **Use correct punctuation within the sentences.** Check to be sure students have properly used commas in a series, commas between two sentences, apostrophes, etc.

11.   **Divide a longer narration into proper paragraphs.** Each paragraph should tell about only one topic. Ideas not related to the topic sentence should be left out or put into a different paragraph.

WRITTEN NARRATION SKILLS: STUDENT'S LIST

1. Indent each paragraph by leaving a space at the beginning.

2. Make sure the first sentence is on the right topic.

3. Begin each sentence with a capital letter, and end each sentence with the correct punctuation mark: . ? !

4. Begin working on writing with correct spelling by using the different options your teacher suggests.

5. Make sure that sentences do not all start with the same word or words.

6. Use correct capitalization within each sentence, like for special names or places.

7. Fix any sentences that are run-ons.

8. Write a good closing sentence.

9. Use correct spelling within your writing.

10. Use correct punctuation within the sentences.

11. Divide a longer narration into proper paragraphs.

Dictation Passages – Level 6

Special instructions for the dictation passages: Each student needs a notebook for dictation. A wide-lined notebook is best. On each dictation day, your student will study the dictation passage. It is helpful to write any difficult words on markerboard or paper for the students to focus on. New words are in bold. Also, call attention to any capital letters and punctuation marks in the passage. Discuss them briefly as needed.

When students feel ready, remove the dictation passage from the students' sight. Call out the passage one phrase at a time. Pause after each phrase for students to repeat it back to you and write it. Continue until the entire passage has been dictated.

Give students a moment to look over their passage for mistakes. Then, have them compare their sentences with the key. Students should circle any mistakes they made on the key and correct the mistakes in their own notebook. If the passage was correct, place a checkmark next to the passage in the key. All items in the sentence must be correct, including punctuation marks, before going on to the next passage. If students made any mistakes, they'll repeat the same passage as many days as it takes to get it right.

Always begin the next session where the student left off. If your child is repeatedly stuck on passages, he or she may need to move to an easier level of dictation passages. Three different levels of passages are provided in this guide.
*Dictation passages are taken from *Dictation Day by Day: Book Two* by Kate Van Wagenen. (MacMillan Company 1916, 1923).

Level 6 – Dictation Passages

1

Abraham Lincoln is one of the **marvels** of history. No land but America has produced his like. His goodness of heart, his sense of duty, his **unselfishness**, his **simplicity** were never **disturbed** either by power or by **opposition**.

- Goldwyn Smith

2

O **blackbird**! Sing me something well. While all the neighbors shoot thee round, I keep **smooth** plats of **fruitful** ground, Where thou may'st **warble**, eat, and dwell.

- Tennyson

3

Last Saturday my brother took me to see the game between **Harvard** and **Yale**. "Be sure," said mother, that you do not lose either your **gloves** or your **handkerchief** in that great crowd, for I cannot **provide** you with new ones."

4

Helen Keller, whose **marvelous** life **resembles** that of Laura Bridgman, was born in 1880 in a small Southern town. When she was a baby, a **serious illness** closed forever the two **gateways** of knowledge – sight and hearing.

5

Her mother read of the means **employed** to teach Laura Bridgman; so she **applied** to Perkins' Institute and there **procured** a teacher. At that time Helen was seven years old and a very **sensitive** and **retiring** child.

6

The teacher who was **engaged** to instruct Helen **commenced** the training by giving her a doll. Then the word "doll" was **frequently** spelled into Helen's hand, until it **occurred** to the child that this was the name of the object.

7

She had great **difficulty** in learning "mug" and "water". She constantly **confused** them, though her teacher with the **utmost patience endeavored** to explain which was which.

8

One day Helen's teacher **guided** her to a well, and, as the stream **struck against** one of the child's **palms** the teacher spelled "water" into the other. At once the **mystery** of language seemed to dawn upon the child.

9

She needed no **further urging** to learn. Her teacher was often **compelled** to scold her for working too much. During her first sea bath she **inquired**, "Who put salt into the water?"

10

When she was ten years old, she was taught to speak. She was **continually practicing** sounds of all kinds, and when her **earnest** efforts met with **success** she said, "Now I feel as though I were let out of **prison**."

11

When Helen was twenty, she passed her **examination** for college, using a **typewriter** to do the work. Then she spoke and read French and **German**. Does not the story of her success **create** a feeling of **admiration** for her sublime courage?

12

Many of the **artists** whose works are on **exhibition** in our **museums acquired** their **reputations** in the countries of Europe. Most of them believe, therefore, that one must study art in the Old World.

13

In 1813 **Commodore** Perry, under most **fearful** difficulties, won a great **naval** victory on Lake Erie. Before the **actual contest** began, he raised a flag bearing these words: "Don't Give Up the Ship."

14

When we consider the **superior** training of the British, the result of the **expedition** seems like a **miracle**. Perry **announced** his **conquest** in the following words: "We have met the enemy and they are ours."

15

Mother goes to the dry goods stores every Friday, because that is **bargain** day. I shall leave here at two o'clock today and go with her to **choose** a **flannel waistcoat** and a **raincoat** to wear to school.

16

A **sacred** burden is this life ye bear;
Look on it, lift it, bear it **solemnly**;
Stand up and walk beneath it **steadfastly**.
Fail not for sorrow, **falter** not for sin,
But onward, upward, till the **goal** ye win.
- Frances A. Kemble

17

Last week we bought several small articles, such as **scissors** and **buttons**, which we took home. Finally we bought nineteen yards of **calico**. "If I send this **parcel**," said the **salesman**, "you may not receive it until Monday."

18

Some of your hurts you have cured,
And the sharpest you still have **survived**,
But what **torments** of **grief** you **endured**
From **evils** which never arrived!
- Ralph Waldo Emerson

19

For many years our **national government** has been controlled either by the **Republican** or the **Democratic** party. There are several other **political** parties in the United States. Can you **mention** some of them?

20

The teacher wrote a **declarative** sentence on the **blackboard**, and then called Alice to the front of the room. "Underline the **adjective**," said she, "and use the colored **chalk** to do it."

21

There are so many different ways of forming the **plurals** of **nouns** that I sometimes confuse them. During the next grammar lesson I **intend** to make an **attempt** to understand the **explanation** of the rules.

22

The **inventor**, Thomas A. Edison, was born in Ohio; while at school, he showed no signs of the **genius** for which he is **remarkable**. Before he was nine years old, however, he read with his mother's **assistance** many books on **electricity**.

23

When he was eleven, he began to earn his living by selling **newspapers** on a **railway** train. His business grew so **rapidly** that he soon employed a helper. Then he spent his time making **experiments** in the **baggage** car.

24

He always took a great interest in the work of the **telegraph operators** at the **various stations** and longed for a **favorable** opportunity to learn the business.

25

One day while waiting for a train, Edison looked in the **direction** of the track and saw the operator's child playing in the path of an approaching **locomotive**. **Luckily** he **rescued** her, and in return the operator taught him **telegraphy**.

26

In less than the **ordinary** length of time he became an **expert** telegraph operator. He later went to New York, where, **weary** and **lonesome** and with scarcely a **penny** in his pocket, he walked the streets until he was **attracted** by a crowd of workmen in a large office.

27

One of the **instruments** used in this office was out of **repair**, and the men had spent hours trying to **locate** the trouble. In a **flash** Edison saw what was the **matter** and, to the **amazement** of everybody, he corrected it at once.

28

One of the **members** of the firm immediately offered Edison a **salary** of three hundred dollars a month. He then began to **prosper**, as he had **sufficient** money to perfect those wonderful **schemes** which were forever passing through his mind.

29

Edison perfected the Bell **telephone** and the **electric** light. He also invented the **phonograph** and many instruments used in telegraphy. "Every **invention** with which my name is connected," said Edison to a friend, "has been the **result** of months of patient toil."

30

A lady while **entertaining** Turner, a **celebrated** English **painter**, **implored** him to tell her what his **secret** was. "I have no secret, **Madam**," he replied, "but hard work."

31

There are no fairy **folk** that ride
About the world at night,
Who give you rings and other things
To pay for doing right.
But if you do to others what
You'd have them do to you,
You'll be as **blest** as if the best
Of story books were true.

      - Alice Cary

32

The first **scenes** of the Revolution took place in the **neighborhood** of Boston, the capital of Massachusetts. The **unjust measures** of the **British** had **stirred** the Americans to very great activity.

33

During the years of 1773 and 1774 there was a **popular belief** among the **colonists** that the unjust **taxation** of the English **Parliament** would finally bring on a **struggle**.

34

In 1773 and 1774 many hundreds of colonists obtained **muskets** and **bayonets** and drilled without **ceasing**. They promised that, in the **event** of war, they would be ready to **assemble** at a minute's notice.

35

In the spring of 1775 Paul Revere, one of the most **courageous** of the minute men, discovered General Gage's plan. It was the general's **intention** to send a **regiment** to Concord to destroy the American stores which were **hidden** throughout that **district**.

36

Paul Revere **resolved** to warn the patriots of the approach of the British. He went to the **opposite** side of the river and there, a lonely **horseman**, **awaited** the **signal** that was to tell him which way the English were going.

37

As soon as he could **distinguish** the **gleam** of the **lanterns**, he gave **rein** to his horse and rode through Lexington to Concord. His **midnight** ride aroused the entire country.

38

When General Gage reached Lexington, he **beheld** a **throng** of sixty minute men, who **defied** his **authority**. "**Disperse**, ye **rebels**!" cried the English officer, "lay down your arms and disperse!"

39

As the Americans did not **surrender**, the soldiers fired, and seven patriots fell. Here then at Lexington was the first battle of the **Revolutionary** War. In this war against Great **Britain** the colonists were forced to **defend** themselves in many hard-fought battles.

40

The anniversary of the Battle of Lexington is a **legal** holiday in Massachusetts. In 1908 the school children of Boston took a **prominent** part in **unveiling** a **marble tablet** to the memory of Paul Revere in Faneuil Hall.

41

Study his story closely, boys and girls. It grows greater with each retelling; for, as time goes on, Abraham Lincoln will rise above his fellows as the greatest, **noblest** man of the wonderful **nineteenth century**.

- Phillips Brooks

42

Do you remember why Columbus **undertook** his voyages of discovery? He was **striving** to find shorter trade routes. From that time until today, men have **sought** by every possible means to **conquer** distance.

43

With the **completion** of the Suez Canal the sea trip from western Europe to India was greatly **lessened**. After that **engineers** became interested in the question of a similar **canal** at Panama.

44

The French Panama Canal Company was the first to **undertake** the build a canal at the **Zone**. Ferdinand de Lesseps was made president of this company. The French people believed that his **experience** at Suez would **doubtless** enable him to manage this **affair** successfully.

45

Ten years after the **commencement** of the work, the French Company was unable to **proceed** through lack of money. Many millions had been spent in **connection** with the work, and a **multitude** had died of **fatal** fevers.

46

In 1904 Congress purchased from the French Company and from the Republic of Panama all rights in this **territory**. Have you ever read of any of the **dreadful** difficulties which our engineers overcame in this **tropical** country?

47

The **climate** of Panama is tropical, and there is also an **enormous percentage** of **moisture** in the air. The land is very **fertile**.

48

In the rainy season the rivers become raging **torrents**. Hence a canal in this **region** must **render ample** protection against all such **perils**, as its route follows the course of the most violent stream on the isthmus.

49

In many places the laborers were forced to cut their way through **treacherous swamps**, where it was difficult to find a solid **foundation** on which to build. Here the workmen also fought **malaria** and other **diseases**.

50

The **principal** cut on the isthmus is at Culebra. The cutting of nine miles of solid rock and the **removal** of such vast **quantities** of material formed one of the greatest **problems** of the work.

51

Congress **discussed** for some months the **advantages** of both a sea-**level** canal and a lock canal. Before reaching a **decision** much expert **testimony** was taken. Finally the plans for a lock canal were **adopted**.

52

Many millions were spent on the canal, but it is a great benefit to **commerce generally**, and a great advantage to several **sections** of our country. Now it is a **common** thing for goods to be **transported** entirely by water from **California** to New York.

53

Nothing can supply the place of books. They are cheering or **soothing** companions in **solitude**, illness, **affliction**. The wealth of both continents would not **compensate** for the good they **impart**.

- William E. Channing

54

Summer or winter, day or night,
The woods are ever a new **delight**;
They give us peace, and they make us strong
Such wonderful **balms** to them belong;
So living or dying, I'll take my ease
Under the trees, under the trees.

- Richard Henry Stoddard

55

One of the most beautiful marches ever written is the **wedding hymn** from the **opera** of Lohengrin. Whenever the opera is **performed**, the **orchestra** plays this hymn at the **marriage** of Lohengrin and Elsa of Brabant.

56

The story on which this **particular** opera is founded **relates** that Godfrey, Duke of Brabant, has **vanished**. Elsa, his sister, is **accused** of **spiriting** him away.

57

The one who accuses Elsa is Count **Frederick**, whose chief desire is to gain **possession** of Elsa's **property** and to be made ruler of the duchy. Elsa is **summoned** before King Henry and there declares that she is **innocent**.

58

Count Frederick says he will fight any one who **volunteers** to defend Elsa. Elsa, in **extreme distress**, says she will become the bride of the **knight** who defends her.

59

Before the assembled **courtiers** the **heralds** blow the summons, but no defender appears for the **solitary** Elsa. Suddenly, at the **supreme** moment, a small skiff approaches drawn by a beautiful white swan with a gold chain **suspended** from its neck.

60

There, in the **wondrous** swan boat, stands a knight in **dazzling armor**. His **gracious countenance** inspires **confidence**, and, as he steps upon the shore, he is welcomed by the knights and ladies of the court.

61

As Lohengrin **kneels** before Elsa, he says he will defend her if she will **swear** never to inquire his name. Elsa is in such **desperate** straits that she **consents**. The knight then seizes a **weapon** and defeats Frederick.

62

At the **appointed** hour Elsa and the knight are **married**. After the **banquet** Elsa, unmindful of her promise, begs him to **reveal** his name. She is so **persistent** that at last he exclaims, with a look of despair: "Lohengrin is my name."

63

Lohengrin says that, having revealed his name, he has **forfeited** his right to remain and must now go into **exile**. As he **arises** and turns from the **terrified** Elsa, the **group** of people exclaim: "The swan! The swan!"

64

Yes, there is the swan with the golden chain **attached** to its neck. Just above the skiff **flutters** a lovely white dove, and, as it **steadily** approaches, the **spectacle** becomes **visible** to all.

65

As soon as Lohengrin **loosens** the chain from the neck of the **faithful** swan, it **gradually** sinks. Then Lohengrin, leaving the **miserable** Elsa, springs into the skiff. The dove seizes the chain, and, to the **horror** of all, Lohengrin vanishes as strangely as he came.

66

Saw the **rainbow** in the heaven,
Whispered, "What is that, Nokomis?"
And the good Nokomis **answered**:
All the wild flowers of the forest,
All the lilies of the **prairie**,
When on earth they fade and **perish**,
Blossom in that heaven above us."

- Henry Wadsworth Longfellow

67

As Emily knew how to **manage** the gas **range**, she cooked some **steak** for supper. I am sure she **spoiled** the **salad** dressing, however, by using too much **vinegar**.

68

Little Margaret, whose parents were both **buried** in a **cemetery** near her home, always spoke of them as sleeping in "God's **Acre**". Each week she went to the cemetery and placed a fresh **bouquet** of **choicest** flowers upon their graves.

69

As Mrs. Morris walked down Tremont Street, she noticed a little child with a **shawl** over her head, gazing **timidly** into a **florist's** window. When she **pressed** a lovely scarlet **geranium** into the girl's hand, the child was overcome with joy.

70

One pleasant autumn day **Katharine** sat in the **orchard** watching the brook, as it flowed **peacefully** over the pebbles. "Where are you going, little brook?" said she, but the brook only answered as it **sparkled** on, "**Goodbye**! Goodbye! Goodbye!"

71

Such a **toothache** as Tommy had! He cried and he cried. Then his mother put some **camphor** on the tooth, and, drawing the sofa toward the **radiator, wrapped** Tommy up and made him very **comfortable**.

72

Small **service** is true service while it lasts;
Of **humblest** friends, dear children, **scorn**
      not one.
The daisy, by the shadow that it casts,
Protects the **lingering dewdrop** from
      the sun.

                - Wordsworth

73

Aunt Katharine gave a **picnic** for some children; she treated them to **sandwiches**, cake, **lemonade**, nuts, and **raisins**. When they were tired of play, they visited the greenhouses and saw the tall **banana** trees.

74

An immense audience gathered to **applaud** the famous singer. Not a seat was **vacant**, and even the **aisles** were crowded. At the **conclusion** of the performance the artist sang, "Home, Sweet Home" in the most **delightful** manner.

75

Some of the **domestic** evils of **drunkenness** are houses without windows, gardens without **fences**, barns without roofs, and children without clothing, **principles**, morals, or manners.

                - Benjamin Franklin

76

The **immigrant**, who desired his son **Michael** to attend school, was surprised to learn that no child could be **accepted** without a **certificate** of **vaccination**.

77

Josephine bought some handkerchiefs on which to **embroider** her mother's **initials**. When she opened the **package** containing silks and **worsteds**, she found the marking to be too **indistinct** to be of use.

78

A Persian **philosopher**, being asked by what **method** he had acquired so much knowledge, answered, "By not being **prevented** by **shame** from asking questions where I was **ignorant**."

79

Have you ever seen a **funeral** in any foreign country? As the carriages move **onward** to the place of **burial**, men on the streets and even in the cars remove their hats and pause for a moment until the **procession** passes.

80

Every afternoon at five o'clock **Theodore** helped **Dorothy** with her lessons. "Now, Dorothy," I heard him say, "I shall be very much **disappointed** if you cannot point out the **predicates** in all these **imperative** sentences."

81

If **solid** happiness we **prize**,
Within our **breast** this jewel lies,
And they are fools who **roam**.
The world has nothing to bestow;
From our own **selves** our joy must flow.
- Nathaniel Cotton

82

Helen's **decimal** work was so poor that she **dreaded** the arithmetic lesson. However, when the grammar hour came, she was **positive** the teacher would not complain of the work she **presented**, which was often shown as a **model**.

83

Instead of going to the **theater** on Saturday, Theodore and his friends obtained **permission** to go to Bronx Park. They remained several hours **viewing** the lovely gardens. For **luncheon** they had sandwiches, fruit, and some **delicious** cake.

84

Grown people do not always like to see the snow **whirling** about. They know it means more coal for the furnace. Boys cannot use their **bicycles** and must often **shovel** snow, and yet most of them **prefer** this season.

85

In the age of **chivalry** there lived in England a youth named **Arthur**. He had a fair **complexion** and golden hair and at an early age gave **evidence** of the lovable **disposition** which distinguished him through life.

86

Arthur lived with the mighty **warrior**, Sir Hector, whom he called father. Sir Hector used to **encourage** Arthur to go in search of **adventure**. He wished to **strengthen** the youth and so **assist** him to fight his own battles in life.

87

In the woods Arthur frequently **encountered** a **gorgeous** company of knights and ladies on horseback. Their saddles were studded with rubies and **emeralds**. The knights wore **glittering helmets**, and their coats of mail were made of tiny links of steel.

88

When Arthur was twenty-one, a quaint and beautiful **ceremony** made him a knight. At this time there was no king in England. Some time had **elapsed** since the **decease** of the former powerful **monarch**, and several strong lords were **ambitious** to be king.

89

Merlin, a wise **magician**, asked the **archbishop** to summon all the great lords to **London** to choose a king. They assembled in a church, and after **psalms** of praise had been sung, they implored **Providence** to make right and justice **triumph**.

90

After these religious ceremonies the brilliant **pageant** filed into the churchyard, where **spectators** saw a huge **circular** stone. This stone **supported** an **anvil** of steel, and fixed therein a sword on which was written: "Whosoever pulls this sword out of this anvil is the rightful king of England."

91

The great lords tried to remove the sword, but so **securely** was it fixed that none could **boast** of moving it. Finally the spectators were **admitted** and allowed to try. Arthur **clutched** the sword and with a **steady** hand drew if from the anvil.

92

Then Sir Hector **confessed** that Arthur was the son of the **former** king. He said that the great lords of the **realm** had been **jealous** of Arthur; so he had **concluded** to hide him for a time.

93

At the sound of a **trumpet** Arthur was then declared king, and all the people swore **allegiance** to him. He made haste to **relieve** those who had **previously** been **oppressed**. He was soon known throughout the kingdom as "Good King Arthur".

94

Arthur and Merlin once saw on the **border** of a lake three fair women crowned with **wreaths** of lovely flowers. Arthur thought the **unusual** sight a **delusion**, but Merlin **pronounced** them three queens who would aid him if he were ever in distress.

95

Looking out on the lake, they saw an uplifted arm holding a richly **decorated** sword. **Overcoming** his fear, Arthur **cautiously** rowed out and seized the **exposed** sword, and instantly the arm became **invisible**.

96

Merlin said: "Use this sword so that **persecution** shall cease, and right and **justice** shall **prevail**." After many **quarrels** had been settled throughout the kingdom, peace restored, and the **guilty punished**, Arthur established at his court the Order of the Round Table.

97

This order **consisted** of one hundred fifty knights who had proved themselves without **exception** worthy **disciples** of "Good King Arthur". Before entering this **league** or order, they **pledged** themselves to the service of God and mankind.

98

These knights looked upon **falsehoods** as a most **cowardly** vice. They **despised** everything mean, cruel, or **dishonest**; and by their unselfish lives they did much to **purify** their native land.

99

The knight whom Arthur **favored** more than any other, and the **leader beloved** by all throughout the **empire**, was Sir Launcelot. The knight whose character seemed nearest to **perfection**, who was purer than all others, was Sir Galahad.

100

After many years of peace and **prosperity** throughout Arthur's **broad** kingdom, there arose a **rebellion** so serious that the king himself was obliged to take the field. He was **betrayed** and mortally wounded by one of his own knights who proved to be a **traitor.**

101

Though almost **insensible**, King Arthur **entreated** Sir Bedivere to carry him to the shore of the lake. Overcome with grief, Sir Bedivere **complied** and there beheld a **ghostly** barge heavily draped in black.

102

An air of mystery prevailed, and among the **unearthly** figures that moved to and fro were the three queens. When they saw the **exhausted condition** of the king, they uttered a **mournful** cry, and, placing him on his **shield**, tenderly lifted Arthur into the barge.

103

One queen gently put her hand **underneath** Arthur's head and took off his broken helmet. "Like a **shattered column** lay the king," while Sir Bedivere cried: "Ah, my lord, **whither** shall I go? Now the whole Round Table is **dissolved**."

104

Sir Bedivere was so **intent** on this **pathetic** scene that the king's last words were scarcely **audible**: "Old **customs** pass away, yielding place to new. The Round Table did its work and now has disappeared. Pray for me. More things are wrought by prayer than the world dreams of. Farewell!"

Dictation Passages – Level 7

<u>Special instructions for the dictation passages</u>: Each student needs a notebook for dictation. A wide-lined notebook is best. On each dictation day, your student will study the dictation passage. It is helpful to write any difficult words on markerboard or paper for the students to focus on. New words are in bold. Also, call attention to any capital letters and punctuation marks in the passage. Discuss them briefly as needed.

When students feel ready, remove the dictation passage from the students' sight. Call out the passage one phrase at a time. Pause after each phrase for students to repeat it back to you and write it. Continue until the entire passage has been dictated.

Give students a moment to look over their passage for mistakes. Then, have them compare their sentences with the key. Students should circle any mistakes they made on the key and correct the mistakes in their own notebook. If the passage was correct, place a checkmark next to the passage in the key. All items in the sentence must be correct, including punctuation marks, before going on to the next passage. If students made any mistakes, they'll repeat the same passage as many days as it takes to get it right.

Always begin the next session where the student left off. If your child is repeatedly stuck on passages, he or she may need to move to an easier level of dictation passages. Three different levels of passages are provided in this guide.

*Dictation passages are taken from *The Modern Speller: Book Two* by Kate Van Wagenen. (MacMillan Company 1923).

Level 7 – Dictation Passages Key

1

Let **reverence** for the laws be taught in all schools and colleges; let it be written in **primers**, in spelling books, and in **almanacs**; let it be preached from the **pulpit**, proclaimed in **legislative** halls, and **enforced** in courts of justice.

- Abraham Lincoln

2

'Mid pleasures and **palaces** though we may
    roam,
Be it ever so **humble**, there's no place like home.
A charm from the skies seems to hallow us there,
Which, seek through the world, is ne'er met with
    elsewhere.

- John **Howard** Payne

3

You find yourself **refreshed** by the presence of cheerful people. Why not make an **effort** to **confer** that pleasure on others? You will find half the battle is gained if you never **allow** yourself to say anything gloomy.

- Mrs. L. M. Child

4

When Washington **declined** a **military escort** on the **occasion** of his **inauguration**, he said, "I desire none. I require no guard but the affections of the people."

5

Abraham Lincoln always displayed the most tender, **sympathetic** interest in all those who **grieved** or suffered. An **instance** that occurred during the Rebellion will serve to **illustrate** Lincoln's **Christian** spirit toward his fellowmen.

6

During the **Civil** War Lincoln devoted hours to the army hospitals. As soon as his **arrival** became known, every **wretched** soldier there was **desirous** of hearing **genuine** words of sympathy, and every man who was able, saluted as the Chief **Executive** passed by.

7

Lincoln was once **accompanied** by a youthful house **physician**. As they approached the ward where the Southern **prisoners** lay, the young **surgeon** drew the President **aside** and with a **frown** said, "Oh, Mr. President, you don't want to go in there. They don't **deserve** it. They are only rebels."

8

At this **remark** the **melancholy features** of the President lighted for a moment with a smile. **Indicating** the Southern ward, he said, without the slightest **reproach**, "You mean that they are our **Confederate brethren**. I want to see them."

9

As Lincoln passed through the aisles, he spoke as kindly and as **courteously** to these men as to those who belonged to the **Union** army. **Revenge** or **hatred** of an enemy had no place in his **generous character**.

10

Money never yet made a man happy. There is nothing in its nature to produce **happiness**. That was a true **proverb** of the wise man; **rely** upon it: "Better is little with the fear of the Lord than great treasure and trouble **therewith**."

- **Benjamin** Franklin

11

Doctors all **advise** that those who wish to overcome the **plague** of **civilization** – **consumption** – must **ventilate** their rooms thoroughly and sleep in the fresh air. Those who live as directed often recover their **energy**.

12

A very rich woman founded an **orphan asylum** as a **memorial** to a beloved daughter who died in **infancy**. Many of the **destitute** children who gained **admission** were adopted and removed far from the scenes of their early life.

13

Last Tuesday or Wednesday I **witnessed** in one of our parks the **destruction** of some lovely **chrysanthemum** plants. The boy who uprooted them **possibly** was not **conscious** that he was destroying a **portion** of his own property.

14

This **occurrence** reminds me of a **student** who says: "My father doesn't pay taxes; he only pays rent." The **average** boy, **unfortunately**, has no **notion** where the money comes from to **maintain** and improve parks, hospitals, schools, and streets.

15

The money used for the **development** of our town or city is raised chiefly by a tax on real estate. Since landlords are **responsible** for the **payment** of this money, they must collect if from their **tenants**. **Additional** taxes, therefore, mean **increased** rents.

16

On Tuesday our class had a long grammar lesson in which we **reviewed** the various kinds of **phrases**. "**Josephine**," said the teacher at last, "write a sentence which shall contain both an **adverbial** and an **attribute phrase**."

17

Consider the lilies of the field, how they grow; they **toil** not, **neither** do they spin. Yet even **Solomon** in all his glory was not **arrayed** like one of these.

18

Benjamin Franklin, the **author** of the following **selection**, is **esteemed** as one of our wise men. He says: "The way to **wealth** is as plain as the way to market. It depends **chiefly** on two words – **industry** and frugality; that is, waste neither time nor money, but make the best use of both."

19

Paul met **Ralph** on the street and said to his friend, "Will you be sure to come to my house at four o'clock to help me **solve** some of my problems in arithmetic? **Maybe** they are correct, but I fear the **fifth** and **seventh** are **wrong**."

20

Live for **something**. Write your name in **kindness**, love, and **mercy** on the hearts of thousands you come in **contact** with year by year, and you will never be **forgotten**.
- Chalmers

21

One by one **thy** duties **wait** thee,
Let thy **whole strength** go to each,
Let no future dreams elate thee,
Learn thou first what these can teach.
- Adelaide A. Procter

22

A mint is a place where under legislative authority gold, silver, copper, and nickel are **converted** into **currency**. The use of money is not a **modern** invention. From earliest times gold and silver **coins** have been used in buying, selling, and paying **debts**.

23

Originally one article was exchanged for another, but this **process** was **exceedingly** troublesome. To **remedy** the difficulty, it was necessary to **alter** the **system** itself. Gold and silver pieces were used. They were not of one **pattern** but were in the form of lumps or buttons.

24

With the **growth** of business, it was necessary to have a more **convenient** method of **exchange**. **Accordingly** coins of the same value were made to **correspond** in **quality** and weight.

25

In **rural communities** where the buildings are low, danger from fire is greatly **diminished**. In large cities a fire is a most **thrilling** sight. There **anyone** attracted by **mere curiosity** is often apt to **neglect** even his business in order to watch the scene.

26

Recently there was a **terrific** fire in a building **occupied** by a firm engaged in making furniture. The fumes of the **turpentine** nearly **suffocated** several members of the **local** fire company.

27

The fire was caused by crossed wires. Every modern **apparatus** was used to **quench** the flames, but it was feared that several firemen would be caught in the back **draft**, before the **furious** flames could be **extinguished**.

28

As usual, the **plucky** firemen made a **series** of thrilling rescues from the **swaying** building. Many **mechanics** were trapped on the top floor, but after a brief **interval** they were taken by **scaling** ladders to the roof of a neighboring tenement.

29

Remember that what you **possess** in the world will be found at the day of your **death** to **belong** to someone else; but what you are, will be yours forever.

- Henry Van Dyke

30

I like books. I was born and **bred** among them and have the easy **feeling**, when I get in their **presence**, that a **stable**-boy has among horses.

- **Oliver** Wendell Holmes

31

Washington! A fitting name for a beautiful city! **Situated** in the District of Columbia on the eastern bank of the **Potomac**, Washington, the capital of the United States, stands as an **imposing tribute** to our **illustrious** President. The selection of this splendid location is a **credit** to Washington and his **advisers.**

32

Congress had **formerly** held **sessions** in New York, Philadelphia, and **Baltimore**. In 1800 the capital was **permanently** established at Washington, which has since been the seat of the legislative, executive, and **judicial departments** of the United States Government.

33

The original city was **totally** destroyed during the War of 1812. In 1814 the work of **restoration** was begun, and Washington stands today a great city, **nobly** planned. **Ambassador** Bryce truly said, "Washington is the expression of the majesty and the **stateliness** of the whole nation."

34

The arrangement of the streets is unlike that of most cities. **Diverging** from different centers are avenues of unusual **width**. **Pennsylvania** Avenue is especially fine. Others of importance are **Connecticut**, **Massachusetts**, and **New Hampshire** Avenues.

35

Washington abounds in places of interest. Among these are: the **Capitol**; the White House; the Washington Monument, a magnificent **shaft** of white marble; and the **Congressional** Library, where anybody may **consult** a great **collection** of books, **including pamphlets** of all sorts.

36

In **ancient** times "All roads led to Rome". In Washington all roads lead to the Capitol. Erected at a **splendid** height, commanding **views** of the principal streets and avenues, the Capitol is the growth of a century. Its beautiful dome **ornamented** by a **bronze** statue, the Goddess of Freedom, is an **appropriate** crown to the stately building.

37

The **residence** of the President, **officially** termed the Executive Mansion but **familiarly** called the White House, is on Pennsylvania Avenue. Though modern **improvements** have been added, it is **practically** the same as the original. The executive offices are **detached**, and thus the President is enabled to enjoy some measure of **privacy**.

38

The **suburbs** of Washington are worthy of mention. To the south is the Arlington National Cemetery. Mount Vernon is a short **journey** from the city. This was the home of Washington. The house is **preserved** as he left it, and here, on a **sloping** hillside, is his **final** resting place.

39

When the weather becomes **changeable** and the **thermometer** suddenly falls, then the **germs** of **whopping-cough** and **pneumonia** are active until the return of the pleasant days of spring.

40

What does the poor man's son **inherit**?
  Stout muscles and a **sinewy** heart,
A hardy frame, a **hardier** spirit;
  King of two hands, he does his part
  In every useful toil and art;
A **heritage**, it seems to me,
A king might wish to hold in fee.

      - James Russell Lowell

41

Philip's mother gave him very careful instruction in **hygiene**, because she wished him to avoid all sickness. Though his **appetite** was very good, he was not **foolish** enough to eat **pickles** and other **indigestible** things.

42

Mr. J. B. Foster was very successful in the **commercial** world. He said his motto was: "Quick sales and small **profits**." Besides that, he never kept a **creditor** waiting. He instructed his **cashier** to take special pains to meet all just claims **punctually**.

43

There are some Eastern countries where many **unhappy missionaries** have been **attacked** by soldiers who resented the **introduction** of Western ideas. Those who escaped death were often separated from their friends, **kidnapped**, and conducted across the frontier. There they received **instructions** never to return.

44

My mother's influence in **molding** my character was **conspicuous**. She forced me to learn daily long **chapters** of the Bible by heart. To that **discipline** and patient, accurate resolve, I owe not only much of my general power of taking pains but the best part of my taste for **literature**.

45

The Song of Hiawatha, **published** in 1855, was quickly **recognized** as a **delicate** and delightful piece of verse. The poet pictures many of the **traditions** of Native American life. He shows a thorough knowledge of his subject, which could have been gained only by **association** with the Indian.

46

And a hundred suns seemed looking
At the **combat** of the **wrestlers**.
Suddenly upon the **greensward**
All alone stood Hiawatha,
Panting with his wild **exertion**,
Palpitating with the struggle;
And before him, breathless, lifeless,
Lay the youth, with hair **disheveled**.
Plumage torn, and garments **tattered**,
Dead he lay there in the sunset.

      - Longfellow

47

A **representative** of the committee on **vocational** schools addressed our class. **Referring** to letters received, he said, "Here is an **application** for a position; here a letter of complaint; another, enclosing a statement of **expenses**: all are of faulty **construction**."

48

"The **relations** of the writer to the one addressed," he continued, "determine the form of the **complimentary** close. In letters of friendship we use 'Yours **affectionately**,' or 'Yours **sincerely**'. Sometimes '**Cordially** yours' is used in a friendly letter. In business letters 'Yours **respectfully**' and 'Yours truly' are proper forms."

49

After the Revolution the South was not very **prosperous**. Her **plantations** were **mortgaged**; her **population** was **decreasing**, and employment was scarce. Then, in 1793, came the invention of the cotton-gin by Eli Whitney. This single invention was the **source** of the **future** prosperity of the South.

50

The cotton-gin or engine is a machine for separating the seeds from the cotton fiber. With the cotton-gin a slave could separate, without **tedious** labor, fifty times as much cotton as he could by hand. Through this **circumstance** cotton became a leading **agricultural production** of the South.

51

With the growth of the cotton industry there appeared **everywhere** an increased **demand** for slaves. One writer has said, "Whitney was, through his invention, probably one of the greatest **agencies** for the **extension** of slavery." **Undoubtedly** the cotton-gin **contributed** largely to the bitter struggle which ended in the Civil War.

52

Formerly an **expensive** article, cotton now became cheap; and the demand for cotton wearing **apparel** increased. In the North the manufacture of cotton goods increased in **proportion**. As these goods came into **competition** with cotton goods from Europe, where factory labor was cheap, the manufacturers declared a **tariff** or **protective** tax was **desirable**.

53

The South, having few manufactures to protect, insisted upon free trade. Her leaders declared that a protective tariff was not **constitutional**. The **perplexing** question began to **assume** serious proportions and has since caused much **discussion**. Shall we have tariff for **revenue** only or a high protective tariff with frequent **revision** of **schedules**?

54

The flag has an **etiquette** of its own, which should always be observed. Some rules **issued** by the Sons of the Revolution are as follows:

The flag should not be **hoisted** before sunrise or allowed to remain up after sunset.

When the national colors are passing in **parade**, the spectator should, if walking, halt; if sitting, arise and uncover.

This life is too short and precious to **waste** it in bearing that **heaviest** of all **burdens** – a **grudge**. **Forgive** and forget if you can; but forgive anyway.

- Henry Van Dyke

It is not work that kills men; it is **worry**. Work is **natural**. You can hardly put more upon a man than he can bear. Worry is rust upon the blade. It is not the revolution that destroys the **machinery**, but **friction**.

- Henry Ward Beecher

Dictation Passages – Level 8

<u>Special instructions for the dictation passages</u>: Each student needs a notebook for dictation. A wide-lined notebook is best. On each dictation day, your student will study the dictation passage. It is helpful to write any difficult words on markerboard or paper for the students to focus on. New words are in bold. Also, call attention to any capital letters and punctuation marks in the passage. Discuss them briefly as needed.

When students feel ready, remove the dictation passage from the students' sight. Call out the passage one phrase at a time. Pause after each phrase for students to repeat it back to you and write it. Continue until the entire passage has been dictated.

Give students a moment to look over their passage for mistakes. Then, have them compare their sentences with the key. Students should circle any mistakes they made on the key and correct the mistakes in their own notebook. If the passage was correct, place a checkmark next to the passage in the key. All items in the sentence must be correct, including punctuation marks, before going on to the next passage. If students made any mistakes, they'll repeat the same passage as many days as it takes to get it right.

Always begin the next session where the student left off. If your child is repeatedly stuck on passages, he or she may need to move to an easier level of dictation passages. Three different levels of passages are provided in this guide.
*Dictation passages are taken from *The Modern Speller: Book Two* by Kate Van Wagenen. (MacMillan Company 1923).

Level 8 – Dictation Passages Key

1

The heavens declare the glory of God;

the skies proclaim the work of His hands.

Day after day they pour forth speech;

night after night they display knowledge.

There is no speech or language

where their voice is not heard.

Their voice goes out into all the earth,

their words to the ends of the world.

2

I care not, **Fortune**, what you me **deny**;

You cannot rob me of free Nature's grace,

You cannot shut the windows of the sky

Through which Aurora shows her

   brightening face.

— James Thomson

3

A traveler said that he could not attempt a **description** of the services in the great **cathedral** at Rome. He closed with these words: "That which made the deepest **impression** upon me was the **reverent attitude** of an **audience** of sixty thousand souls."

4

To avoid **confusion** in **reckoning** time, a **uniform calendar** is **indispensable**.

A natural or **solar** year is the time required by the earth to make one revolution around the sun. The calendar year is arranged to correspond with the solar year.

5

Julius Caesar, with the help of a Greek **astronomer**, altered and corrected the **irregular** Roman calendar. They planned to have the year consist of three hundred sixty-five and a quarter days and, in order to **dispense** with the fraction, **proposed** that every fourth year should be a leap year. This was, however, eleven minutes in excess of the true year.

6

These minutes **accumulated** until in 1582 they amounted to ten days. To remedy this **defect** Pope **Gregory** XIII ordered that ten days be **omitted**. He also **originated** the **Gregorian** calendar, which **decreed** that years which may be evenly divided by one hundred – but not by four hundred – are not leap years.

7

Thus, while 1600 was a leap year, 1700 was not. This method of reckoning makes the calendar year **vary slightly** from the solar year.

To have the **majority** of countries using **exactly** the same calendar is very convenient. Russia did not **acknowledge** the authority of Pope Gregory and still **adheres** to the old calendar.

8

Hail, Columbia! Happy land!
Hail, ye **heroes**, heav'n-born band!
Who fought and bled in Freedom's cause,
And, when the storm of war was gone,
Enjoyed the peace your **valor** won.
Let independence be our boast,
Ever mindful what it cost.

- Joseph Hopkinson

9

Relative to the habit of **cigarette** smoking, Edison says: "The **substance** formed from the burning paper wrapper has a violent action on the nerve centers, **producing injury** to the minute cells of the brain. Unlike the effect of many **narcotics**, this evil effect seems permanent."

10

From the earliest times nations have settled their **disputes** by an **appeal** to arms. Yet war has always been regarded as a **calamity**, and all thoughtful people have **realized** that by this means **society** could never **progress**.

11

Wise men have **perceived** that the **employment** of force in the settlement of disputes is totally wrong. As war always **breeds** future **conflicts**, its **injurious** effects are often felt for **generations**.

12

The **Czar** of Russia called a **conference** at The Hague on May 18, 1899. He hoped to **advance** plans to settle all disputes between nations by **arbitration**. At this **universal** Peace Conference twenty-six nations were **represented**.

13

Of entrance to a quarrel; but being in,
Bear't that the **opposed** may **beware** of thee.
Give every man thy ear, but few thy voice;
Take each man's **censure** but **reserve** thy
    judgment.

                                    - Shakespeare

14

Science has greatly **advanced** the **medical** profession; it has **lengthened** life; it has increased the **fertility** of the soil; it has lighted up the night with the **splendor** of the day; it has extended the range of human **vision**, and it has made distant places seem near.

15

   The Yellowstone National Park is a tract of land originally **comprising** 3575 square miles in northwestern **Wyoming**. It was a **wilderness** of **virgin** forest, set apart by the **Federal** Government to preserve from destruction the most remarkable **phenomena** known within the **boundaries** of the United States.

16

   The park contains wonderful **geysers** from which water and steam gush **upward** in fountainlike columns. The **locality** also abounds in hot springs in which are found mineral **deposits**. Mountains, **evidently** of **volcanic** origin, rise upon a vast **plateau**.

17

   Of the geysers **Excelsior** is the greatest in size. Old Faithful is **entitled** to its name because of its **regularity**. Frequent **observations** have proved the wonderful fact that at each **eruption**, which occurs every sixty-four minutes, Old Faithful **discharges** one and a half million gallons of water.

18

   The falls and **canyons** of the Yellowstone are most wonderful. In many places in the park the very earth is **scarred** and **wrinkled**, from a constant rise and fall of the earth's crust. This is due to the high **temperature** just below the surface. Wild animals may be approached near enough to be **photographed**.

19

   In this famous **resort** everything is **carefully** **controlled**. Regulations **prescribe** that visitors shall not remove **specimens** or post **advertisements**. Visitors are also **prohibited** from injuring any living thing except in **self-defense**.

20

My **crown** is in my heart, not on my head,
Not **decked** with diamonds and Indian **stones**,
Nor to be seen. My crown is called content:
A crown it is that **seldom** kings enjoy.

                                    - Shakespeare

21

Small kindnesses, small courtesies, small **considerations**, **habitually** practiced, give a greater charm to the character than the **display** of great talents and **accomplishments**.

- Kelly

22

"The **avaricious** man is like the barren sandy ground of the **desert**, which sucks in all the rain and dews with **greediness** but **yields** no fruitful herbs or plants for the benefit of others."

23

"An ounce of **prevention** is worth a pound of cure." How many **disastrous** fires could be prevented if we realized the truth of this and exercised proper care in handling **inflammable** fluids like **alcohol**, **kerosene**, **gasoline**, and turpentine."

24

Numerous are the **appliances** used in a city fire department: axes, ladders, **chemical** engines, water towers, door openers for opening a door without **damaging** it, and many other **ingenious contrivances**. When **perpendicular**, the water tower can direct a vast volume of water into a building.

25

The soldier is **animated** by the noblest **sentiment** in the heart of man – the defense of his country. The fireman has not this incentive; yet it is an **undeniable** fact that, in **fulfilling** his duty, he often exhibits a bravery unsurpassed in the **annals** of war.

26

Do not think of knocking out another **person's** brains, because he **differs** in **opinion** from you. It would be quite as **intelligent** to knock yourself on the head, because you differ from yourself ten years ago.

- Horace Mann

27

To procure practical instruction in the course in business methods, it has been **suggested** that the classes be supplied with printed forms. These forms should include a **variety** of **material**: **receipts**, **absence** blanks, **investigation** slips, and **invoices**.

28

To procure practical instruction in the course in business methods, it has been **suggested** that the classes be supplied with printed forms. These forms should include a **variety** of **material**: **receipts**, **absence** blanks, **investigation** slips, and **invoices**.

29

In a business school pupils are often required to put their **signatures** to the tickets attached to the various blanks and file them with the **secretary**. "In **commending** this work," once said an **instructor**, "I chose the specimens that were neat, **legible**, and accurate."

30

Don't **flatter** yourself that friendship **authorizes** you to say **disagreeable** things to your **intimates**. On the **contrary**, the nearer you come into relation with a person, the more necessary do tact and courtesy become. Except in cases of **necessity** leave your friend to learn unpleasant truths from his enemies.

- Oliver Wendell Holmes

31

A little consideration of what takes place around us would show us that a higher law than that of our will **regulates** events; that our **painful** labors are often **unnecessary** and **fruitless**; that only in our easy, simple, **spontaneous** action are we strong, and by contenting **ourselves** with **obedience** we become divine.

- Ralph Waldo Emerson

32

The purest treasure **mortal** times afford
Is **spotless** reputation; that away,
Men are but **gilded** loam or painted clay.
Mine **honor** is my life; both grow in one.
Take honor from me and my life is done.

- Shakespeare

33

In the fifteenth century the **interior** of France was laid waste by years of **warfare** over the **succession** to the throne. It was **claimed** by the Dauphin, or eldest son of the French king, and Henry V of England. The **latter** had contracted an **alliance** with a French princess and insisted on the **recognition** of their son.

34

In **accordance** with an old custom, the **hereditary** kings of France were always crowned and their **standards** raised in the cathedral at Rheims. Charles, the Dauphin, felt **confident** that, if he could be crowned as the rightful **sovereign**, his claim would then be **absolute** and unquestioned.

35

The ceremony was impossible, however, because Rheims was occupied by a **formidable garrison** of English soldiers. Charles did not seem **capable** of capturing the city, because he **lacked** the necessary **heroism**. He lived a life of **luxury**; in his **castles** south of Orleans he devoted himself to pleasure.

36

Orleans was the most strongly defended city of France, and the **inhabitants** sincerely **sympathized** with their king. The **program** of the English was to capture the city despite its **stubborn resistance**. "The Story of Joan of Arc," by Andrew Lang, tells very simply how a lovely **peasant** girl saved the city as by a miracle.

37

John of Arc was born in Domremy in 1412 of **devout** parents, whose great **anxiety** was to rear their family in the fear of God. Her early years, filled with humble daily duties, gave no hint of the final **tragedy** of her life. On account of **poverty** she had scant **leisure** and was **grateful** for simple pleasures.

38

When she was thirteen, Joan reached a **crisis** in her life. Her manner changed entirely, and she declared that heavenly voices, which she could scarcely **comprehend**, were **perpetually** telling her that she was **destined** to deliver France from the English. Even those who thought the voices unreal said, "She seems **altogether** happy, lifting her eyes to Heaven."

39

When Joan was sixteen, she said there was a constant **repetition** of these **celestial** voices, **counseling** her to **forsake** her home and save the empire. She felt that, despite all **consequences**, she must seek the Dauphin. She declared that she heard: "Daughter of God, go on! I shall be with you."

40

As nothing seemed to **discourage** Joan, her father finally said she could depart. When she reached the castle, she did not appear **frightened** or **embarrassed** by the strange manners **connected** with court etiquette. She gazed calmly at the **assembly** and begged the **privilege** of being taken into the **royal** presence.

41

When the Dauphin received the Maid, he wore a **costume** of **severe** simplicity in order to **deceive** her, but she went directly to him and knelt at his feet. He thought this convincing evidence of her **divine** power, and at her earnest request he promised to **terminate** the **gayeties** at court and advance against the English, who were **besieging** Orleans.

42

The surrender of the English caused southern France to **rally** to the **support** of the Dauphin. The Maid **counseled** him to proceed at once to Rheims, and he felt that the time was favorable for **continuing** his **campaign**. He entered Rheims accompanied by the Maid and was crowned as the rightful **heir** in the great cathedral.

43

The French were **indebted** to Joan for many victories, but, when she was taken **captive**, no one attempted to rescue her. The English, **clamorous** for her life, tried her for being a witch. She was finally **condemned** to be burned. There was no one to **intercede** for her; so she paid for her **loyalty** with her life.

44

An **eminent** French artist, Bastien-Lepage, has painted an **exquisite** picture called "Joan of Arc Listening to the Voices". It is a **representation** of Joan of Arc wearing a troubled expression and gazing into the depths of the forest. The **phantom** figure at her right represents the **guardian** spirit on whose counsel she was **dependent**.

45

Do not keep **alabaster** boxes of your love and **tenderness sealed** up until your friends are dead. Bring them out now and open them, that they may be refreshed and cheered by the **perfumes** of **sympathy** and **affection.**

- Margaret Sangster

46

When my eyes shall be turned to behold for the last time the sun in heaven, may I not see him shining on the broken and **dishonored fragments** of a once glorious Union; on states **dissevered**, discordant, **belligerent**; on a land rent with civil **feuds**, or **drenched**, it may be, in **fraternal** blood!

- Daniel Webster

47

Religion is something which a man cannot **invent** for himself or keep to himself. If it does not show in his conduct, it does not **exist** in his heart. Good **citizens**, honest workmen, cheerful comrades – that is what the **product** of religion should be.

- Henry Van Dyke

48

Banks are most necessary for business. They offer an easy means of **borrowing** money and of **transferring** it safely from place to place. They provide for the payment of **merchandise** by check, and they forward **remittances** to **correspondents** in a **prompt** and accurate manner.

49

In early times banks were simply benches in the market place for **exchanging** money. When a man became a **debtor** to the extent of being **insolvent**, his bench was broken; hence the word **bankrupt**, meaning "broken bench". The greatest **financial institution** in the world is generally **conceded** to the Bank of England, which is in London.

50

Formerly banks were used almost **exclusively** by wealthy people and businessmen. Today, many of their patrons are those in **moderate** circumstances, who find the **settlement** of bills by check or draft to be most convenient. Before opening an account these **patrons** must furnish **satisfactory references**.

51

"Read not," says Lord Bacon in a famous **essay**, "to **contradict** and **confute**; nor to believe and take for granted; nor to find talk and **discourse**; but to weigh and consider. Some books are to be tasted, others to be swallowed, and some few to be chewed and **digested**.

52

We hold these truths to be **self-evident**: that all men are created equal; that they are **endowed** by their **Creator** with certain **inalienable** rights; that among these are life, liberty, and the **pursuit** of happiness.

- Declaration of Independence

53

Do you believe in fairies? Though you don't take them **seriously**, read Barrie's **renowned** tale, "Peter and Wendy". Follow the **career** of that **curious** being, Peter Pan – the boy who refused to grow up.

While Wendy and her brothers are asleep, the **slender** figure of Peter enters like **magic** through the open window. He is accompanied by a **shifting**, **jingling** spot of light.

54

The children were guarded by Nana, a wonderful nurse dog. Peter thought he had entered with the greatest **secrecy**, but Nana's **instinct** told her of some **disturbance** in the **nursery**; so she ran into the room as the unearthly Peter escaped through the window. This **amazing** dog shut down the window on Peter's shadow. Peter **shrieked**, but his shadow was left behind.

55

One night when no one **anticipated** his visit, the **mysterious** Peter Pan, who had been **loitering** in the treetops, **descended** upon the nursery in quest of his shadow. The children were overjoyed to see him, but, as they watched Peter, they felt **envious** of him. He **volunteered** to teach them to fly, and they soon learned to **imitate** him. In the delight of flying, they flew out of the window and were off to Neverland on the wings of the wind.

56

Peter Pan, Captain of the Lost boys, concealed the children in the underground **refuge** of his band. You must, however, read the book for a **detailed** account of their adventures with both fairies and **pirates**. All boys will love the part where the **immortal** Captain Hook was **consigned** to **oblivion** by a clever trick of the daring, **saucy** Peter.

57

J.M. Barrie was born in a small town in Scotland, and his books portray with **surpassing delicacy** the **humor** and sadness of village life. "**Sentimental** Tommy" and "The Little **Minister**" are even better known than "Peter Pan".

In spite of his **literary** ability, Barrie is shy and reserved and hates to be **interviewed**. King George honored Barrie by making him a knight.

58

'Tis common **proof**,
That **lowliness** is young **ambition's** ladder,
Whereto the **climber**-upward turns his face;
But when he once **attains** the upmost round,
He then unto the ladder turns his back,
Looks in the clouds, **scorning** the base **degrees**
By which he did **ascend**.

        - Shakespeare

Math Schedule: *Singapore Primary Mathematics 6A & 6B* (U.S. Edition)
(Marshall Cavendish Education, 2008)

NOTE: This schedule is written to coincide with the **four** day a week plan used in *Hearts for Him Through Time: Resurrection to Reformation*. If you find you need to use the fifth day for math, you can easily do so by spreading out this schedule. When using this plan, remember that the "Textbook" pages should be used as a <u>teaching tool</u> with your child. We highly recommend that, as much as possible, the Textbook portion be done together with your child on a markerboard with markers. This will help your child understand that each math lesson has 2 parts; the Textbook portion completed with your teaching and assistance, and the Workbook portion completed independently. On days that there is only a Textbook portion assigned, part of it can be done on markerboard and part of it can be done on notebook paper. If you wish to spread out the end-of-the-year review lessons more, you may use the extra Week 36 to do so.

Unit 1:
<u>Day 1:</u> *Textbook 6A* p. 6-8; *Workbook 6A* p. 5-6
<u>Day 2:</u> *Textbook 6A* p. 9; *Workbook 6A* p. 7
<u>Day 3:</u> *Textbook 6A* p. 10-11; *Workbook 6A* p. 8-9
<u>Day 4:</u> *Textbook 6A* p. 12-13; *Workbook 6A* p. 10-11

Unit 2:
<u>Day 1:</u> *Textbook 6A* p. 14
<u>Day 2:</u> *Textbook 6A* p. 15-16; *Workbook 6A* p. 12-13
<u>Day 3:</u> *Textbook 6A* p. 17-18; *Workbook 6A* p. 14-15
<u>Day 4:</u> *Textbook 6A* p. 19; *Workbook 6A* p. 16-18

Unit 3:
<u>Day 1:</u> *Textbook 6A* p. 20; *Workbook 6A* p. 19-21
<u>Day 2:</u> *Textbook 6A* p. 21-23; *Workbook 6A* p. 22-23
<u>Day 3:</u> *Textbook 6A* p. 24-26; *Workbook 6A* p. 24-25
<u>Day 4:</u> *Textbook 6A* p. 27; *Workbook 6A* p. 26-27

Unit 4:
<u>Day 1:</u> *Textbook 6A* p. 28; *Workbook 6A* p. 28-29
<u>Day 2:</u> *Textbook 6A* p. 29
<u>Day 3:</u> *Textbook 6A* p. 30-32; *Workbook 6A* p. 30-31
<u>Day 4:</u> *Textbook 6A* p. 33

Unit 5:
<u>Day 1:</u> *Textbook 6A* p. 34-35; *Workbook 6A* p. 32-33
<u>Day 2:</u> *Textbook 6A* p. 36-37; *Workbook 6A* p. 34-36
<u>Day 3:</u> *Textbook 6A* p. 38
<u>Day 4:</u> *Textbook 6A* p. 39-40

Unit 6:
<u>Day 1:</u> *Textbook 6A* p. 41-42
<u>Day 2:</u> *Workbook 6A* p. 37-39
<u>Day 3:</u> *Workbook 6A* p. 40-42
<u>Day 4:</u> *Textbook 6A* p. 43-44

Math Schedule: *Singapore Primary Mathematics 6A & 6B* (U.S. Edition)

Unit 7:
Day 1: *Textbook 6A* p. 45-46
Day 2: *Textbook 6A* p. 47 – number 6 on p. 50; *Workbook 6A* p. 43-45
Day 3: *Textbook 6A* numbers 7 through 11 on p. 50; *Workbook 6A* p. 46-47
Day 4: *Textbook 6A* p. 51; *Workbook 6A* p. 48-49

Unit 8:
Day 1: *Workbook 6A* p. 50-51
Day 2: *Textbook 6A* p. 52; *Workbook 6A* p. 52-53
Day 3: *Textbook 6A* p. 53
Day 4: *Textbook 6A* p. 54

Unit 9:
Day 1: *Textbook 6A* p. 55 – number 3 on p. 57; *Workbook 6A* p. 54-55
Day 2: *Textbook 6A* number 4 on p. 57 – number 6 on p. 58; *Workbook 6A* p. 56-57
Day 3: *Textbook 6A* number 7 on p. 58-59; *Workbook 6A* p. 58-59
Day 4: *Workbook 6A* p. 60-61

Unit 10:
Day 1: *Textbook 6A* p. 60
Day 2: *Textbook 6A* p. 61-62; *Workbook 6A* p. 62-63
Day 3: *Textbook 6A* p. 63-64; *Workbook 6A* p. 64-65
Day 4: *Textbook 6A* p. 65-66; *Workbook 6A* p. 66-69

Unit 11:
Day 1: *Textbook 6A* p. 67
Day 2: *Textbook 6A* p. 68
Day 3: *Workbook 6A* p. 70-71
Day 4: *Workbook 6A* p. 72-73

Unit 12:
Day 1: *Textbook 6A* p. 69-70
Day 2: *Textbook 6A* p. 71-73
Day 3: *Textbook 6A* p. 74 – number 5 on p. 76; *Workbook 6A* p. 74
Day 4: *Textbook 6A* numbers 6 and 7 on p. 76 – number 9 on p. 77; *Workbook 6A* p. 75-76

Unit 13:
Day 1: *Textbook 6A* number 10 on p. 77 – p. 78; *Workbook 6A* p. 77-78
Day 2: *Textbook 6A* p. 79; *Workbook 6A* p. 79-82
Day 3: *Textbook 6A* p. 80; *Workbook 6A* p. 83-84
Day 4: *Textbook 6A* p. 81

Unit 14:
Day 1: *Textbook 6A* p. 82
Day 2: *Workbook 6A* p. 85-86
Day 3: *Workbook 6A* p. 87-89
Day 4: *Textbook 6A* p. 83-84

Math Schedule: *Singapore Primary Mathematics 6A & 6B* (U.S. Edition)

Unit 15:
>   Day 1: *Textbook 6A* p. 85-86
>   Day 2: *Workbook 6A* p. 90-91, 94
>   Day 3: *Workbook 6A* p. 92-93, 95-96
>   Day 4: *Textbook 6A* p. 87-88, 91

Unit 16:
>   Day 1: *Textbook 6A* p. 89-90, 92
>   Day 2: *Textbook 6A* p. 93-94
>   Day 3: *Textbook 6A* p. 95-96
>   Day 4: *Textbook 6B* p. 6 – number 3 on p. 7; *Workbook 6B* p. 5-6

Unit 17:
>   Day 1: *Textbook 6B* number 4 on p. 7 – number 6 on p. 8; *Workbook 6B* p. 7
>   Day 2: *Textbook 6B* numbers 7 through 9 on p. 8 – p. 9; *Workbook 6B* p. 8
>   Day 3: *Textbook 6B* p. 10
>   Day 4: *Textbook 6B* p. 11 – number 7 on p. 13; *Workbook 6B* p. 9

Unit 18:
>   Day 1: *Textbook 6B* numbers 8 through 10 on p. 13 – number 13 on p. 14; *Workbook 6B* p. 10-11
>   Day 2: *Textbook 6B* numbers 14 and 15 on p. 14; *Workbook 6B* p. 12-13
>   Day 3: *Textbook 6B* p. 15
>   Day 4: *Textbook 6B* p. 16-17; *Workbook 6B* p. 14-15

Unit 19:
>   Day 1: *Textbook 6B* p. 18-19; *Workbook 6B* p. 16-17
>   Day 2: *Textbook 6B* p. 20
>   Day 3: *Textbook 6B* p. 21
>   Day 4: *Textbook 6B* p. 22-25; *Workbook 6B* p. 18-20

Unit 20:
>   Day 1: *Textbook 6B* p. 26 – number 8 on p. 29; *Workbook 6B* p. 21-23
>   Day 2: *Textbook 6B* numbers 9 through 11 on p. 29; *Workbook 6B* p. 24-25
>   Day 3: *Textbook 6B* p. 30
>   Day 4: *Textbook 6B* p. 31 – number 7 on p. 34; *Workbook 6B* p. 26-27

Unit 21:
>   Day 1: *Textbook 6B* numbers 8 and 9 on p. 34; *Workbook 6B* p. 28-29
>   Day 2: *Textbook 6B* number 10 on p. 35; *Workbook 6B* p. 30-32
>   Day 3: *Textbook 6B* numbers 11 and 12 on p. 35; *Workbook 6B* p. 33-35
>   Day 4: *Workbook 6B* p. 36-37

Unit 22:
>   Day 1: *Textbook 6B* p. 36
>   Day 2: *Textbook 6B* p. 37
>   Day 3: *Textbook 6B* p. 38-39; *Workbook 6B* p. 38-41
>   Day 4: *Textbook 6B* p. 40; *Workbook 6B* p. 42-45

Math Schedule: *Singapore Primary Mathematics 6A & 6B* (U.S. Edition)

Unit 23:
Day 1: *Textbook 6B* p. 41; *Workbook 6B* p. 46-49
Day 2: *Textbook 6B* p. 42-43
Day 3: *Textbook 6B* p. 44-45
Day 4: *Textbook 6B* p. 46-47

Unit 24:
Day 1: *Workbook 6B* p. 50-51, 54
Day 2: *Workbook 6B* p. 52-53, 55
Day 3: *Textbook 6B* p. 48-49, 51
Day 4: *Textbook 6B* p. 50, 52-53

Unit 25:
Day 1: *Workbook 6B* p. 56-57, 60
Day 2: *Workbook 6B* p. 58-59, 61-62
Day 3: *Textbook 6B* p. 54-55; *Workbook 6B* p. 63-64
Day 4: *Textbook 6B* p. 56; *Workbook 6B* p. 65-67

Unit 26:
Day 1: *Textbook 6B* p. 57; *Workbook 6B* p. 68-71
Day 2: *Textbook 6B* p. 58; *Workbook 6B* p. 72-75
Day 3: *Textbook 6B* p. 59
Day 3: *Textbook 6B* p. 60

Unit 27:
Day 1: *Textbook 6B* p. 61
Day 2: *Workbook 6B* p. 76-77
Day 3: *Workbook 6B* p. 78-80
Day 4: *Workbook 6B* p. 81-82

Unit 28:
Day 1: *Workbook 6B* p. 83-84
Day 2: *Textbook 6B* p. 62-63; *Workbook 6B* p. 85-88
Day 3: *Textbook 6B* p. 64-65; *Workbook 6B* p. 89-92
Day 4: *Textbook 6B* p. 66

Unit 29:
Day 1: *Textbook 6B* p. 67
Day 2: *Textbook 6B* p. 68-69
Day 3: *Textbook 6B* p. 70-72
Day 4: *Textbook 6B* p. 73-74

Unit 30:
Day 1: *Textbook 6B* p. 75-77
Day 2: *Workbook 6B* p. 93-94, 97
Day 3: *Workbook 6B* p. 95-96, 98
Day 4: *Textbook 6B* p. 78-79

Math Schedule: *Singapore Primary Mathematics 6A & 6B* (U.S. Edition)

Unit 31:
> Day 1: *Textbook 6B* p. 80-82
> Day 2: *Textbook 6B* p. 83-87
> Day 3: *Textbook 6B* p. 88-92
> Day 4: *Textbook 6B* p. 93

Unit 32:
> Day 1: *Workbook 6B* p. 99-100
> Day 2: *Workbook 6B* p. 101-104
> Day 3: *Textbook 6B* p. 94-96
> Day 4: *Textbook 6B* p. 97

Unit 33:
> Day 1: *Textbook 6B* p. 98
> Day 2: *Textbook 6B* p. 99-101
> Day 3: *Textbook 6B* p. 102-105
> Day 4: *Textbook 6B* p. 106-107

Unit 34:
> Day 1: *Textbook 6B* p. 108-110
> Day 2: *Workbook 6B* p. 105-106, 111
> Day 3: *Workbook 6B* p. 107-110, 112
> Day 4: *Textbook 6B* p. 111-112

Unit 35:
> Day 1: *Textbook 6B* p. 113-114
> Day 2: *Textbook 6B* p. 115-116
> Day 3: *Textbook 6B* p. 117-118
> Day 4: *Textbook 6B* p. 119-120

Index of Poetry

Becalmed

Becalmed upon the sea of Thought,

Still unattained the land it sought,

My mind, with loosely-hanging sails,

Lies waiting the auspicious gales.

On either side, behind, before,

The ocean stretches like a floor,--

A level floor of amethyst,

Crowned by a golden dome of mist.

Blow, breath of inspiration, blow!

Shake and uplift this golden glow!

And fill the canvas of the mind

With wafts of thy celestial wind.

Blow, breath of song! until I feel

The straining sail, the lifting keel,

The life of the awakening sea,

Its motion and its mystery!

Henry Wadsworth Longfellow

The Tables Turned
(An Evening Scene on the Same Subject)

Up! up! my Friend, and quit your books;
Or surely you'll grow double:
Up! up! my Friend, and clear your looks;
Why all this toil and trouble?

The sun, above the mountain's head,
A freshening lustre mellow
Through all the long green fields has spread,
His first sweet evening yellow.

Books! 'tis a dull and endless strife:
Come, hear the woodland linnet,
How sweet his music! on my life,
There's more of wisdom in it.

And hark! how blithe the throstle sings!
He, too, is no mean preacher:
Come forth into the light of things,
Let Nature be your teacher.

She has a world of ready wealth,
Our minds and hearts to bless -
Spontaneous wisdom breathed by health,
Truth breathed by cheerfulness.

One impulse from a vernal wood
May teach you more of man,
Of moral evil and of good,
Than all the sages can.

Sweet is the lore which Nature brings;
Our meddling intellect
Mis-shapes the beauteous forms of things:-
We murder to dissect.

Enough of Science and of Art;
Close up those barren leaves;
Come forth, and bring with you a heart
That watches and receives.

William Wordsworth

A Day of Sunshine
(Birds of Passage. Flight the Second)

O gift of God! O perfect day:
Whereon shall no man work, but play;
Whereon it is enough for me,
Not to be doing, but to be!

Through every fibre of my brain,
Through every nerve, through every vein,
I feel the electric thrill, the touch
Of life, that seems almost too much.

I hear the wind among the trees
Playing celestial symphonies;
I see the branches downward bent,
Like keys of some great instrument.

And over me unrolls on high
The splendid scenery of the sky,
Where through a sapphire sea the sun
Sails like a golden galleon,

Towards yonder cloud-land in the West,
Towards yonder Islands of the Blest,
Whose steep sierra far uplifts
Its craggy summits white with drifts.

Blow, winds! and waft through all the rooms
The snow-flakes of the cherry-blooms!
Blow, winds! and bend within my reach
The fiery blossoms of the peach!

O Life and Love! O happy throng
Of thoughts, whose only speech is song!
O heart of man! canst thou not be
Blithe as the air is, and as free?

Henry Wadsworth Longfellow

Lines Written in Early Spring

I heard a thousand blended notes,

While in a grove I sate reclined,

In that sweet mood when pleasant thoughts

Bring sad thoughts to the mind.

To her fair works did Nature link

The human soul that through me ran;

And much it grieved my heart to think

What man has made of man.

Through primrose tufts, in that green bower,

The periwinkle trailed its wreaths;

And 'tis my faith that every flower

Enjoys the air it breathes.

The birds around me hopped and played,

Their thoughts I cannot measure:—

But the least motion which they made,

It seemed a thrill of pleasure.

The budding twigs spread out their fan,

To catch the breezy air;

And I must think, do all I can,

That there was pleasure there.

If this belief from heaven be sent,

If such be Nature's holy plan,

Have I not reason to lament

What man has made of man?

William Wordsworth

A Sonnet: Eliot's Oak

Thou ancient oak! whose myriad leaves are loud

With sounds of unintelligible speech,

Sounds as of surges on a shingly beach,

Or multitudinous murmurs of a crowd;

With some mysterious gift of tongues endowed,

Thou speakest a different dialect to each;

To me a language that no man can teach,

Of a lost race, long vanished like a cloud.

For underneath thy shade, in days remote,

Seated like Abraham at eventide

Beneath the oaks of Mamre, the unknown

Apostle of the Indians, Eliot, wrote

His Bible in a language that hath died

And is forgotten, save by thee alone.

Henry Wadsworth Longfellow

Petals

Life is a stream

On which we strew

Petal by petal the flower of our heart;

The end lost in dream,

They float past our view,

We only watch their glad, early start.

Freighted with hope,

Crimsoned with joy,

We scatter the leaves of our opening rose;

Their widening scope,

Their distant employ,

We never shall know. And the stream as it flows

Sweeps them away,

Each one is gone

Ever beyond into infinite ways.

We alone stay

While years hurry on,

The flower fared forth, though its fragrance still stays.

Henry Wadsworth Longfellow

Poetry: Unit 7
The Day Is Done

The day is done, and the darkness
Falls from the wings of Night,
As a feather is wafted downward
From an eagle in his flight.

I see the lights of the village
Gleam through the rain and the mist,
And a feeling of sadness comes o'er me
That my soul cannot resist:

A feeling of sadness and longing,
That is not akin to pain,
And resembles sorrow only
As the mist resembles the rain.

Come, read to me some poem,
Some simple and heartfelt lay,
That shall soothe this restless feeling,
And banish the thoughts of day.

Not from the grand old masters,
Not from the bards sublime,
Whose distant footsteps echo
Through the corridors of Time,

For, like strains of martial music,
Their mighty thoughts suggest
Life's endless toil and endeavor;
And tonight I long for rest.

Read from some humbler poet,
Whose songs gushed from his heart,
As showers from the clouds of summer,
Or tears from the eyelids start;

Who, through long days of labor,
And nights devoid of ease,
Still heard in his soul the music
Of wonderful melodies.

Such songs have a power to quiet
The restless pulse of care,
And come like the benediction
That follows after prayer.

Then read from the treasured volume
The poem of thy choice,
And lend to the rhyme of the poet
The beauty of thy voice.

And the night shall be filled with music,
And the cares, that infest the day,
Shall fold their tents, like the Arabs,
And as silently steal away.

Henry Wadsworth Longfellow

A Whirl-Blast from behind the hill

Rushed o'er the wood with startling sound;

Then - all at once the air was still,

And showers of hailstones pattered round.

Where leafless oaks towered high above,

I sat within an undergrove

Of tallest hollies, tall and green;

A fairer bower was never seen.

From year to year the spacious floor

With withered leaves is covered o'er,

And all the year the bower is green.

But see! where'er the hailstones drop

The withered leaves all skip and hop;

There's not a breeze--no breath of air--

Yet here, and there, and everywhere

Along the floor, beneath the shade

By those embowering hollies made,

The leaves in myriads jump and spring,

As if with pipes and music rare

Some Robin Good-fellow were there,

And all those leaves, in festive glee,

Were dancing to the minstrelsy.

William Wordsworth

"Give me of your bark, O Birch-Tree!
Of your yellow bark, O Birch-Tree!
Growing by the rushing river,
Tall and stately in the valley!
I a light canoe will build me,
Build a swift Cheemaun for sailing,
That shall float upon the river,
Like a yellow leaf in Autumn,
Like a yellow water-lily!

"Lay aside your cloak, O Birch-Tree!
Lay aside your white-skin wrapper,
For the Summer-time is coming,
And the sun is warm in heaven,
And you need no white-skin wrapper!"

Thus aloud cried Hiawatha
In the solitary forest,
By the rushing Taquamenaw,
When the birds were singing gayly,
In the Moon of Leaves were singing,
And the sun, from sleep awaking,
Started up and said, "Behold me!
Gheezis, the great Sun, behold me!"

And the tree with all its branches
Rustled in the breeze of morning,
Saying, with a sigh of patience,
"Take my cloak, O Hiawatha!"

With his knife the tree he girdled;
Just beneath its lowest branches,
Just above the roots, he cut it,
Till the sap came oozing outward:
Down the trunk, from top to bottom,
Sheer he cleft the bark asunder,
With a wooden wedge he raised it,
Stripped it from the trunk unbroken.

"Give me of your boughs, O Cedar!
Of your strong and pliant branches,
My canoe to make more steady,
Make more strong and firm beneath me!"

Through the summit of the Cedar
Went a sound, a cry of horror,
Went a murmur of resistance;
But it whispered, bending downward,
"Take my boughs, O Hiawatha!"

Down he hewed the boughs of cedar,
Shaped them straightway to a framework,
Like two bows he formed and shaped them,
Like two bended bows together.

"Give me of your roots, O Tamarack!
Of your fibrous roots, O Larch-Tree!
My canoe to bind together.
So to bind the ends together,
That the water may not enter,
That the river may not wet me!"

And the Larch, with all its fibres,
Shivered in the air of morning,
Touched his forehead with its tassels,
Said, with one long sigh of sorrow,
"Take them all, O Hiawatha!"

From the earth he tore the fibres,
Tore the tough roots of the Larch-Tree,
Closely sewed the bark together,
Bound it closely to the framework.

"Give me of your balm, O Fir-Tree!
Of your balsam and your resin,
So to close the seams together
That the water may not enter,
That the river may not wet me!"

And the Fir-Tree, tall and sombre,
Sobbed through all its robes of darkness,
Rattled like a shore with pebbles,
Answered wailing, answered weeping,
"Take my balm, O Hiawatha!"

And he took the tears of balsam,
Took the resin of the Fir-Tree,
Smeared therewith each seam and fissure,
Made each crevice safe from water.

"Give me of your quills, O Hedgehog!
All your quills, O Kagh, the Hedgehog!
I will make a necklace of them,
Make a girdle for my beauty,
And two stars to deck her bosom!"

From a hollow tree the Hedgehog
With his sleepy eyes looked at him,
Shot his shining quills, like arrows,
Saying, with a drowsy murmur,
Through the tangle of his whiskers,
"Take my quills, O Hiawatha!"

From the ground the quills he gathered,
All the little shining arrows,
Stained them red and blue and yellow,
With the juice of roots and berries;
Into his canoe he wrought them,
Round its waist a shining girdle,

Round its bow a gleaming necklace,
On its breast two stars resplendent.

Thus the Birch Canoe was builded
In the valley, by the river,
In the bosom of the forest;
And the forest's life was in it,
All its mystery and its magic,
All the lightness of the birch-tree,
All the toughness of the cedar,
All the larch's supple sinews;
And it floated on the river
Like a yellow leaf in Autumn,
Like a yellow water-lily.

Paddles none had Hiawatha,
Paddles none he had or needed,
For his thoughts as paddles served him,
And his wishes served to guide him;
Swift or slow at will he glided,
Veered to right or left at pleasure.

Then he called aloud to Kwasind,
To his friend, the strong man, Kwasind,
Saying, "Help me clear this river
Of its sunken logs and sand-bars."

Straight into the river Kwasind
Plunged as if he were an otter,
Dived as if he were a beaver,
Stood up to his waist in water,
To his arm-pits in the river,
Swam and shouted in the river,
Tugged at sunken logs and branches,
With his hands he scooped the sand-bars,
With his feet the ooze and tangle.

And thus sailed my Hiawatha
Down the rushing Taquamenaw,
Sailed through all its bends and windings,
Sailed through all its deeps and shallows,
While his friend, the strong man, Kwasind,
Swam the deeps, the shallows waded.

Up and down the river went they,
In and out among its islands,
Cleared its bed of root and sand-bar,
Dragged the dead trees from its channel,
Made its passage safe and certain
Made a pathway for the people,
From its springs among the mountains,
To the water of Pauwating,
To the bay of Taquamenaw.

Henry Wadsworth Longfellow

To the Small Celandine

Pansies, Lilies, Kingcups, Daisies,
Let them live upon their praises;
Long as there's a sun that sets
Primroses will have their glory;
Long as there are Violets,
They will have a place in story:
There's a flower that shall be mine,
'Tis the little Celandine.

Eyes of some men travel far
For the finding of a star;
Up and down the heavens they go,
Men that keep a mighty rout!
I'm as great as they, I trow,
Since the day I found thee out,
Little flower! - I'll make a stir
Like a great Astronomer.

Modest, yet withal an Elf
Bold, and lavish of thyself,
Since we needs must first have met,
I have seen thee, high and low,
Thirty years or more, and yet
'Twas a face I did not know;
Thou hast now, go where I may,
Fifty greetings in a day.

Ere a leaf is on a bush,
In the time before the Thrush
Has a thought about its nest,
Thou wilt come with half a call,
Spreading out thy glossy breast
Like a careless Prodigal;
Telling tales about the sun,
When we've little warmth, or none.

Poets, vain men in their mood!
Travel with the multitude;
Never heed them: I aver
That they all are wanton Wooers;
But the thrifty Cottager,
Who stirs little out of doors,
Joys to spy thee near her home,
Spring is coming, Thou art come!

Comfort have thou of thy merit,
Kindly, unassuming Spirit!
Careless of thy neighbourhood,
Thou dost shew thy pleasant face
On the moor, and in the wood,
In the lane - there's not a place,
Howsoever mean it be,
But 'tis good enough for thee.

Ill befall the yellow Flowers,
Children of the flaring hours!
Buttercups, that will be seen,
Whether we will see or no;
Others, too, of lofty mien;
They have done as worldlings do,
Taken praise that should be thine,
Little, humble Celandine!

Prophet of delight and mirth,
Scorned and slighted upon earth!
Herald of a mighty band,
Of a joyous train ensuing,
Singing at my heart's command,
In the lanes my thoughts pursuing,
I will sing, as doth behove,
Hymns in praise of what I love!

William Wordsworth

Flowers

Spake full well, in language quaint and olden,
One who dwelleth by the castled Rhine,
When he called the flowers, so blue and golden,
Stars, that in earth's firmament do shine.

Stars they are, wherein we read our history,
As astrologers and seers of eld;
Yet not wrapped about with awful mystery,
Like the burning stars, which they beheld.

Wondrous truths, and manifold as wondrous,
God hath written in those stars above;
But not less in the bright flowerets under us
Stands the revelation of his love.

Bright and glorious is that revelation,
Written all over this great world of ours;
Making evident our own creation,
In these stars of earth, these golden flowers.

And the Poet, faithful and far-seeing,
Sees, alike in stars and flowers, a part
Of the self-same, universal being,
Which is throbbing in his brain and heart.

Gorgeous flowerets in the sunlight shining,
Blossoms flaunting in the eye of day,
Tremulous leaves, with soft and silver lining,
Buds that open only to decay;

Brilliant hopes, all woven in gorgeous tissues,
Flaunting gayly in the golden light;
Large desires, with most uncertain issues,
Tender wishes, blossoming at night!

These in flowers and men are more than seeming;
Workings are they of the self-same powers,

Which the Poet, in no idle dreaming,
Seeth in himself and in the flowers.

Everywhere about us are they glowing,
Some like stars, to tell us Spring is born;
Others, their blue eyes with tears o'er-flowing,
Stand like Ruth amid the golden corn;

Not alone in Spring's armorial bearing,
And in Summer's green-emblazoned field,
But in arms of brave old Autumn's wearing,
In the centre of his brazen shield;

Not alone in meadows and green alleys,
On the mountain-top, and by the brink
Of sequestered pools in woodland valleys,
Where the slaves of nature stoop to drink;

Not alone in her vast dome of glory,
Not on graves of bird and beast alone,
But in old cathedrals, high and hoary,
On the tombs of heroes, carved in stone;

In the cottage of the rudest peasant,
In ancestral homes, whose crumbling towers,
Speaking of the Past unto the Present,
Tell us of the ancient Games of Flowers;

In all places, then, and in all seasons,
Flowers expand their light and soul-like wings,
Teaching us, by most persuasive reasons,
How akin they are to human things.

And with childlike, credulous affection
We behold their tender buds expand;
Emblems of our own great resurrection,
Emblems of the bright and better land.

Henry Wadsworth Longfellow

Sonnet: The Harvest Moon

It is the Harvest Moon! On gilded vanes

And roofs of villages, on woodland crests

And their aerial neighborhoods of nests

Deserted, on the curtained window-panes

Of rooms where children sleep, on country lanes

And harvest-fields, its mystic splendor rests!

Gone are the birds that were our summer guests,

With the last sheaves return the laboring wains!

All things are symbols: the external shows

Of Nature have their image in the mind,

As flowers and fruits and falling of the leaves;

The song-birds leave us at the summer's close,

Only the empty nests are left behind,

And pipings of the quail among the sheaves.

Henry Wadsworth Longfellow

The day is cold, and dark, and dreary;

It rains, and the wind is never weary;

The vine still clings to the mouldering wall,

But at every gust the dead leaves fall,

    And the day is dark and dreary.

My life is cold, and dark, and dreary;

It rains, and the wind is never weary;

My thoughts still cling to the mouldering past,

But the hopes of youth fall thick in the blast,

    And the days are dark and dreary.

Be still, sad heart, and cease repining;

Behind the clouds is the sun still shining;

Thy fate is the common fate of all,

Into each life some rain must fall,

    Some days must be dark and dreary.

Henry Wadsworth Longfellow

There is a Reaper whose name is Death,
And, with his sickle keen,
He reaps the bearded grain at a breath,
And the flowers that grow between.

"Shall I have nought that is fair?" saith he;
"Have nought but the bearded grain?
Though the breath of these flowers is sweet to me,
I will give them all back again."

He gazed at the flowers with tearful eyes,
He kissed their drooping leaves;
It was for the Lord of Paradise
He bound them in his sheaves.

"My Lord has need of these flowerets gay,"
The Reaper said, and smiled;
"Dear tokens of the earth are they,
Where he was once a child.

"They shall all bloom in fields of light,
Transplanted by my care,
And saints, upon their garments white,
These sacred blossoms wear."

And the mother gave, in tears and pain,
The flowers she most did love;
She knew she should find them all again
In the fields of light above.

O, not in cruelty, not in wrath,
The Reaper came that day;
'Twas an angel visited the green earth,
And took the flowers away.

Henry Wadsworth Longfellow

September 1815

WHILE not a leaf seems faded; while the fields,

With ripening harvest prodigally fair,

In brightest sunshine bask; this nipping air,

Sent from some distant clime where Winter wields

His icy scimitar, a foretaste yields

Of bitter change, and bids the flowers beware;

And whispers to the silent birds, "Prepare

Against the threatening foe your trustiest shields."

For me, who under kindlier laws belong

To Nature's tuneful quire, this rustling dry

Through leaves yet green, and yon crystalline sky,

Announce a season potent to renew,

'Mid frost and snow, the instinctive joys of song,

And nobler cares than listless summer knew.

William Wordsworth

One summer-day I chanced to see
This old Man doing all he could
To unearth the root of an old tree,
A stump of rotten wood.
The mattock tottered in his hand;
So vain was his endeavour,
That at the root of the old tree
He might have worked for ever.

"You're overtasked, good Simon Lee,
Give me your tool," to him I said;
And at the word right gladly he
Received my proffered aid.
I struck, and with a single blow
The tangled root I severed,
At which the poor old Man so long
And vainly had endeavoured.

The tears into his eyes were brought,
And thanks and praises seemed to run
So fast out of his heart, I thought
They never would have done.
—I've heard of hearts unkind, kind deeds
With coldness still returning;
Alas! the gratitude of men
Hath oftener left me mourning.

William Wordsworth

Poetry: Unit 17
Changed

FROM the outskirts of the town,

Where of old the mile-stone stood,

Now a stranger, looking down

I behold the shadowy crown

Of the dark and haunted wood.

Is it changed, or am I changed?

Ah! the oaks are fresh and green,

But the friends with whom I ranged

Through their thickets are estranged

By the years that intervene.

Bright as ever flows the sea,

Bright as ever shines the sun,

But alas! they seem to me

Not the sun that used to be,

Not the tides that used to run.

Henry Wadsworth Longfellow

I stood upon the hills, when heaven's wide arch
Was glorious with the sun's returning march,
And woods were brightened, and soft gales
Went forth to kiss the sun-clad vales.
The clouds were far beneath me; bathed in light,
They gathered mid-way round the wooded height,
And, in their fading glory, shone
Like hosts in battle overthrown.
As many a pinnacle, with shifting glance.
Through the gray mist thrust up its shattered lance,
And rocking on the cliff was left
The dark pine blasted, bare, and cleft.
The veil of cloud was lifted, and below
Glowed the rich valley, and the river's flow
Was darkened by the forest's shade,
Or glistened in the white cascade;
Where upward, in the mellow blush of day,
The noisy bittern wheeled his spiral way.

I heard the distant waters dash,
I saw the current whirl and flash,
And richly, by the blue lake's silver beach,
The woods were bending with a silent reach.
Then o'er the vale, with gentle swell,
The music of the village bell
Came sweetly to the echo-giving hills;
And the wild horn, whose voice the woodland fills,
Was ringing to the merry shout,
That faint and far the glen sent out,
Where, answering to the sudden shot, thin smoke,
Through thick-leaved branches, from the dingle broke.

If thou art worn and hard beset
With sorrows, that thou wouldst forget,
If thou wouldst read a lesson, that will keep
Thy heart from fainting and thy soul from sleep,
Go to the woods and hills! No tears
Dim the sweet look that Nature wears.

Henry Wadsworth Longfellow

As a fond mother, when the day is o'er,

   Leads by the hand her little child to bed,

   Half willing, half reluctant to be led,

   And leave his broken playthings on the floor,

Still gazing at them through the open door,

   Nor wholly reassured and comforted

   By promises of others in their stead,

   Which, though more splendid, may not please him more;

So Nature deals with us, and takes away

   Our playthings one by one, and by the hand

   Leads us to rest so gently, that we go

Scarce knowing if we wish to go or stay,

   Being too full of sleep to understand

   How far the unknown transcends the what we know.

Henry Wadsworth Longfellow

Sundown

THE summer sun is sinking low;

Only the tree-tops redden and glow:

Only the weathercock on the spire

Of the neighboring church is a flame of fire;

All is in shadow below.

O beautiful, awful summer day,

What hast thou given, what taken away?

Life and death, and love and hate,

Homes made happy or desolate,

Hearts made sad or gay!

On the road of life one mile-stone more!

In the book of life one leaf turned o'er!

Like a red seal is the setting sun

On the good and the evil men have done, -

Naught can to-day restore!

Henry Wadsworth Longfellow

The Sun Has Long Been Set

THE sun has long been set,

The stars are out by twos and threes,

The little birds are piping yet

Among the bushes and trees;

There's a cuckoo, and one or two thrushes,

And a far-off wind that rushes,

And a sound of water that gushes,

And the cuckoo's sovereign cry

Fills all the hollow of the sky.

Who would "go parading"

In London, "and masquerading,"

On such a night of June

With that beautiful soft half-moon,

And all these innocent blisses?

On such a night as this is!

William Wordsworth

Poetry: Unit 22
Splendour in the Grass

What though the radiance

which was once so bright

Be now for ever taken from my sight,

Though nothing can bring back the hour

Of splendour in the grass,

of glory in the flower,

We will grieve not, rather find

Strength in what remains behind;

In the primal sympathy

Which having been must ever be;

In the soothing thoughts that spring

Out of human suffering;

In the faith that looks through death,

In years that bring the philosophic mind.

William Wordsworth

I wandered lonely as a cloud

That floats on high o'er vales and hills,

When all at once I saw a crowd,

A host, of golden daffodils;

Beside the lake, beneath the trees,

Fluttering and dancing in the breeze.

Continuous as the stars that shine

And twinkle on the Milky Way,

They stretched in never-ending line

Along the margin of a bay:

Ten thousand saw I at a glance,

Tossing their heads in sprightly dance.

The waves beside them danced, but they

Out-did the sparkling waves in glee:

A poet could not but be gay,

In such a jocund company:

I gazed -and gazed -but little thought

What wealth the show to me had brought.

For oft, when on my couch I lie

In vacant or in pensive mood,

They flash upon that inward eye

Which is the bliss of solitude;

And then my heart with pleasure fills,

And dances with the daffodils.

William Wordsworth

Poetry: Unit 24
A Prairie Sunset

Shot gold, maroon and violet, dazzling silver,

    emerald, fawn,

The earth's whole amplitude and Nature's

    multiform power consign'd for once

    to colors;

The light, the very air possess'd by them—

    colors till now unknown

No limit, confine—not the western sky alone—

    the high meridian—north, south, all,

Pure luminous color fighting the silent shadows

    to the last.

Walt Whitman

IT is a beauteous evening, calm and free,

The holy time is quiet as a nun

Breathless with adoration; the broad sun

Is sinking down in its tranquility;

The gentleness of heaven broods o'er the sea:

Listen! the mighty Being is awake,

And doth with his eternal motion make

A sound like thunder - everlastingly.

Dear Child! dear Girl! that walkest with me here,

If thou appear untouched by solemn thought,

Thy nature is not therefore less divine:

Thou liest in Abraham's bosom all the year,

And worship'st at the Temple's inner shrine,

God being with thee when we know it not.

William Wordsworth

The tide rises, the tide falls,

The twilight darkens, the curlew calls;

Along the sea-sands damp and brown

The traveller hastens toward the town,

And the tide rises, the tide falls.

Darkness settles on roofs and walls,

But the sea, the sea in the darkness calls;

The little waves, with their soft, white hands,

Efface the footprints in the sands,

And the tide rises, the tide falls.

The morning breaks; the steeds in their stalls

Stamp and neigh, as the hostler calls;

The day returns, but nevermore

Returns the traveller to the shore,

And the tide rises, the tide falls.

Henry Wadsworth Longfellow

Written In March

The cock is crowing,

The stream is flowing,

The small birds twitter,

The lake doth glitter

    The green field sleeps in the sun;

The oldest and youngest

Are at work with the strongest;

The cattle are grazing,

Their heads never raising;

    There are forty feeding like one!

Like an army defeated

The snow hath retreated,

And now doth fare ill

On the top of the bare hill;

    The plowboy is whooping-anon-anon:

There's joy in the mountains;

There's life in the fountains;

Small clouds are sailing,

Blue sky prevailing;

    The rain is over and gone!

William Wordsworth

TRAVELLER
Why dost thou wildly rush and roar,
   Mad River, O Mad River?
Wilt thou not pause and cease to pour
Thy hurrying, headlong waters o'er
   This rocky shelf forever?

What secret trouble stirs thy breast?
   Why all this fret and flurry?
Dost thou not know that what is best
In this too restless world is rest
   From over-work and worry?

THE RIVER
What wouldst thou in these mountains seek,
   O stranger from the city?
Is it perhaps some foolish freak
Of thine, to put the words I speak
   Into a plaintive ditty?

TRAVELLER
Yes; I would learn of thee thy song,
   With all its flowing number;
And in a voice as fresh and strong
As thine is, sing it all day long,
   And hear it in my slumbers.

THE RIVER
A brooklet nameless and unknown
   Was I at first, resembling
A little child, that all alone
Comes venturing down the stairs of stone,
   Irresolute and trembling.

Later, by wayward fancies led,
   For the wide world I panted;
Out of the forest dark and dread
Across the open fields I fled,
   Like one pursued and haunted.

I tossed my arms, I sang aloud,
   My voice exultant blending
With thunder from the passing cloud,
The wind, the forest bent and bowed,
   The rush of rain descending.

I heard the distant ocean call,
   Imploring and entreating;
Drawn onward, o'er this rocky wall
I plunged, and the loud waterfall
   Made answer to the greeting.

And now, beset with many ills,
   A toilsome life I follow;
Compelled to carry from the hills
These logs to the impatient mills
   Below there in the hollow.

Yet something ever cheers and charms
   The rudeness of my labors;
Daily I water with these arms
The cattle of a hundred farms,
   And have the birds for neighbors.

Men call me Mad, and well they may,
   When, full of rage and trouble,
I burst my banks of sand and clay,
And sweep their wooden bridge away,
   Like withered reeds or stubble.

Now go and write thy little rhyme,
   As of thine own creating.
Thou seest the day is past its prime;
I can no longer waste my time;
   The mills are tired of waiting.

Henry Wadsworth Longfellow

Black shadows fall
From the lindens tall,
That lift aloft their massive wall
Against the southern sky;

And from the realms
Of the shadowy elms
A tide-like darkness overwhelms
The fields that round us lie.

But the night is fair,
And everywhere
A warm, soft vapor fills the air,
And distant sounds seem near;

And above, in the light
Of the star-lit night,
Swift birds of passage wing their flight
Through the dewy atmosphere.

I hear the beat
Of their pinions fleet,
As from the land of snow and sleet
They seek a southern lea.

I hear the cry
Of their voices high
Falling dreamily through the sky,
But their forms I cannot see.

Oh, say not so!
Those sounds that flow
In murmurs of delight and woe
Come not from wings of birds.

They are the throngs
Of the poet's songs,
Murmurs of pleasures, and pains, and wrongs,
The sound of winged words.

This is the cry
Of souls, that high
On toiling, beating pinions, fly,
Seeking a warmer clime.

From their distant flight
Through realms of light
It falls into our world of night,
With the murmuring sound of rhyme.

Henry Wadsworth Longfellow

Poetry: Unit 30
A Psalm of Life
What the heart of the young man said to the psalmist

TELL me not, in mournful numbers,
Life is but an empty dream!--
For the soul is dead that slumbers,
And things are not what they seem.

Life is real! Life is earnest!
And the grave is not its goal;
Dust thou art, to dust returnest,
Was not spoken of the soul.

Not enjoyment, and not sorrow,
Is our destined end or way;
But to act, that each to-morrow
Find us farther than to-day.

Art is long, and Time is fleeting,
And our hearts, though stout and brave,
Still, like muffled drums, are beating
Funeral marches to the grave.

In the world's broad field of battle,
In the bivouac of Life,
Be not like dumb, driven cattle!
Be a hero in the strife!

Trust no future, howe'er pleasant!
Let the dead Past bury its dead!
Act,-act in the living present!
Heart within, and God o'erhead!

Lives of great men all remind us
We can make our lives sublime,
And departing, leave behind us
Footprints on the sands of time;

Footprints, that perhaps another,
Sailing o'er life's solemn main,
A forlorn and shipwrecked brother,
Seeing, shall take heart again.

Let us, then, be up and doing,
With a heart for any fate;
Still achieving, still pursuing,
Learn to labor and to wait.

Henry Wadsworth Longfellow

To a Butterfly

I've watched you now a full half-hour;
Self-poised upon that yellow flower
And, little Butterfly! indeed
I know not if you sleep or feed.
How motionless!--not frozen seas
More motionless! and then
What joy awaits you, when the breeze
Hath found you out among the trees,
And calls you forth again!

This plot of orchard-ground is ours;
My trees they are, my Sister's flowers;
Here rest your wings when they are weary;
Here lodge as in a sanctuary!
Come often to us, fear no wrong;
Sit near us on the bough!
We'll talk of sunshine and of song,
And summer days, when we were young;
Sweet childish days, that were as long
As twenty days are now.

Stay near me-do not take thy flight!
A little longer stay in sight!
Much converse do I find in thee,
Historian of my infancy!
Float near me; do not yet depart!
Dead times revive in thee:
Thou bring'st, gay creature as thou art!
A solemn image to my heart,
My father's family!

Oh! pleasant, pleasant were the days,
The time, when, in our childish plays,
My sister Emmeline and I
Together chased the butterfly!
A very hunter did I rush
Upon the prey:-with leaps and springs
I followed on from brake to bush;
But she, God love her, feared to brush
The dust from off its wings.

William Wordsworth

Behold! a giant am I!
Aloft here in my tower,
With my granite jaws I devour
The maize, and the wheat, and the rye,
And grind them into flour.

I look down over the farms;
In the fields of grain I see
The harvest that is to be,
And I fling to the air my arms,
For I know it is all for me.
I hear the sound of flails
Far off, from the threshing-floors
In barns, with their open doors,
And the wind, the wind in my sails,
Louder and louder roars.

I stand here in my place,
With my foot on the rock below,
And whichever way it may blow,
I meet it face to face,
As a brave man meets his foe.

And while we wrestle and strive,
My master, the miller, stands
And feeds me with his hands;
For he knows who makes him thrive,
Who makes him lord of lands.

On Sundays I take my rest;
Church-going bells begin
Their low, melodious din;
I cross my arms on my breast,
And all is peace within.

Henry Wadsworth Longfellow

The big doors of the country barn stand open and ready,

The dried grass of the harvest time loads the slow-drawn wagon,

The clear light plays on the brown gray and green intertinged,

The armfuls are packed to the sagging mow.

I am there, I help, I came stretched atop of the load,

I felt its soft jolts, one leg reclined on the other,

I jump from the crossbeams and seize the clover and timothy,

And roll head over heels and tangle my hair full of wisps.

Walt Whitman

Admonition

Well may'st thou halt-and gaze with brightening eye!

The lovely Cottage in the guardian nook

Hath stirred thee deeply; with its own dear brook,

Its own small pasture, almost its own sky!

But covet not the Abode;-forbear to sigh,

As many do, repining while they look;

Intruders-who would tear from Nature's book

This precious leaf, with harsh impiety.

Think what the home must be if it were thine,

Even thine, though few thy wants!-Roof, window, door,

The very flowers are sacred to the Poor,

The roses to the porch which they entwine:

Yea, all, that now enchants thee, from the day

On which it should be touched, would melt away.

William Wordsworth

The Labourer's Noon-Day Hymn

Up to the throne of God is borne
The voice of praise at early morn,
And he accepts the punctual hymn
Sung as the light of day grows dim:

Nor will he turn his ear aside
From holy offerings at noontide:
Then here reposing let us raise
A song of gratitude and praise.

What though our burden be not light,
We need not toil from morn to night;
The respite of the mid-day hour
Is in the thankful Creature's power.

Blest are the moments, doubly blest,
That, drawn from this one hour of rest,
Are with a ready heart bestowed
Upon the service of our God!

Each field is then a hallowed spot,
An altar is in each man's cot,
A church in every grove that spreads
Its living roof above our heads.

Look up to Heaven! the industrious Sun
Already half his race hath run;
'He' cannot halt nor go astray,
But our immortal Spirits may.

Lord! since his rising in the East,
If we have faltered or transgressed,
Guide, from thy love's abundant source,
What yet remains of this day's course:

Help with thy grace, through life's short day,
Our upward and our downward way;
And glorify for us the west,
When we shall sink to final rest.

William Wordsworth

Preparing Your Heart for Prayer

Choose **one** question from the part of prayer mentioned in your guide today to reflect upon as you prepare to pray.
As you turn to the Lord in prayer, think of this as your own special time to talk with and meet with the Lord.

Adoration: to worship and honor God	Confession: to admit or acknowledge your sins to God
* Have you had beautiful weather lately? If so, praise God for it! * Has the Lord just healed your body in some way, or has He simply blessed you with good health? Praise Him for His healing power! * Do you know that God has always been, and always will be? Honor Him as the one true God. * How has God's Word spoken to you lately? Give glory to God for His words and teachings! * Have you seen a beautiful sunrise, a rainbow, some stars, or any marvel of creation lately? Praise God as Maker of heaven and earth! * How has Jesus' death on the cross changed your life? Worship Him for finishing God's work of salvation and paying for your sins! * Have you seen Christians give God the glory while going through a hardship? Praise God for revealing Himself to you through them! * Do you understand how holy the Lord is, yet He cares for you? Kneel before Him and worship Him with reverence. * How has God provided for your family? Knowing not all children are blessed with the same provision, worship God for His care! * What things happening in the world today are a concern to you? Praise God for being in control and knowing what the future holds! * How has God given you the opportunity to know Him? Praise God for the opportunity to know Him and be saved! * Do you realize that you are made in God's image? Praise God for making you in such a special way! * How has God amazed you? Through His Word? His Son? His miracles? His love? His forgiveness? His Creation? Praise Him today!	* Have you felt angry about something or toward someone lately? Ask God to forgive you for your anger and help you do what is right. * Have you struggled with complaining lately? Ask the Lord to forgive you for complaining about… and to help you be more joyful. * What sinful thoughts or motives have you struggled with lately? Pray for God to help you have a more pleasing heart. * Do you sometimes let your mind wander during church, at prayer, or during Bible devotions? Pray for God to help you focus on Him. * What are some things you are afraid of? Pray for God to help you not to be afraid and to place your trust in Him. * Do you worry about what others think about you? Pray to be more focused on the Lord and less worried about what others think. * Have you blamed others for your sins or made excuses for your sins? Pray for God to forgive your sinful nature when you… * What Christians in your life have you had trouble listening to lately? Your parents? Your pastor? Pray to be able develop the habit of attention, so you may listen better. * What struggles do you have in life right now? Have you asked God for help? Instead of failing on your own, ask God to help you… * Do you compare yourself to others and often find yourself thinking you are "better"? Remember to be humble and exalt God instead. * Have you been feeling sorry for yourself lately? Choose to sing and to pray instead, knowing others will then see Christ living in you. * Do you know in your heart what is right, but continue sinful habits? Pray for help to listen to the Holy Spirit and make a life change!
Thanksgiving: to express gratitude for God's divine goodness	Supplication: to make a humble and earnest request of God
* Who has the Lord provided as spiritual leaders for you? Praise Him for their Christian guidance and love! * What blessings has God given you? Good health? A family? A free country to live in? A church to attend? Thank God for these today! * What prayers have you prayed that God has already answered? Be sure to thank Him for always listening to your prayers! * Who have you prayed for that you have seen God help? Thank Him for His goodness and mercy. * What sins have you struggled with and been able to overcome? Thank the Holy Spirit for being your wise Counselor and helper! * How has the Lord helped you in a time of need? Thank Him for always being with you and taking care of you! * What choices have you made more definitively because you know what God would want you to do? Thank God for making His will clear! * What growth have you seen in your church? Pray for your church to be strengthened, to grow in numbers, and to be encouraged! * Have you confessed a sin and felt the peace of God's forgiveness wash over you? Thank the Lord for coming to save you! *Do you have a Bible? A church to attend? Christians in your life? People who pray for you? Thank God for giving you this support! * Have you struggled with something and looked back to see the good that came from it? Thank God for having a plan for your life! * Where can you see God at work? In changing someone's heart? In winning a spiritual battle? In comforting someone? Thank God! * What life challenges has the Lord helped you through recently? Thank Him for being Lord of all!	* Who are the people you love? What needs do they have right now? Bring them to the Lord in prayer. * Who are some people in your church for whom you could pray? Check your church bulletin for prayer concerns. * Has God given you the chance to share the gospel with someone? Ask God to give you the words to share His message of salvation. * What are some temptations you are facing in your life right now? Bring them to the Lord in prayer. * Do you think about the person you may marry someday? Ask God to help you marry a person who loves Him and is pleasing to Him. * Who are some missionaries around the world that could use your prayer? Pray for the spread of the gospel. * Do you desire to please God with your life? Pray to find favor in God's eyes and to have success for Him in… * Are you setting an example to others that is pleasing to the Lord? Ask Him to help you avoid sin, and instead, be fully devoted to Him. * How do you feel about God's Word? Ask Him to put a love for His Word in your heart. * How often do you think of the Lord during the day? Ask Him to draw you nearer to Him each day. * Are you ready for Christ's return? Ask God to help you have a deep faith in Christ's resurrection and the gift of eternal life. * How often do you talk to the Lord during the day? Ask Him to fill you with the desire to pray earnestly and often, trusting He'll answer. * Do you know in your heart that Jesus is God's Son and the only way to heaven? Ask God to fill you with His Spirit, so you can believe!

Science Lab Form

Identify the Problem
What do you want to know or explain? Copy the question from the Science Exploration box of the guide.

Form a Hypothesis
A hypothesis is an educated guess based on observations and your knowledge of the topic. What do you think will happen? Predict the answer to your question or the outcome of the experiment.

Perform an Experiment
List the steps in the procedure to perform your experiment. Record information and observations!

Analyze the Data
Data is information gathered during an experiment. Do your observations from the experiment support your hypothesis? Circle **YES** or **NO** below and follow the corresponding arrow.

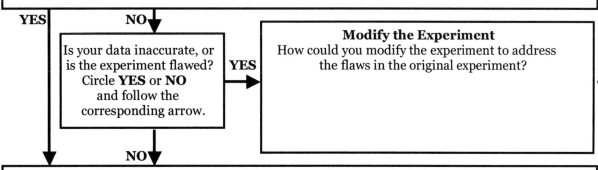

YES

NO

Is your data inaccurate, or is the experiment flawed? Circle **YES** or **NO** and follow the corresponding arrow.

YES

Modify the Experiment
How could you modify the experiment to address the flaws in the original experiment?

NO

Communicate the Results
Write a conclusion based upon your experiment's results. Refer to the key idea in your guide for help.

BOOKMARK

Note: Whenever you begin a new book, write the title above the pages.

Book: _____

Pages: _____ - _____

BOOKMARK

Note: Whenever you begin a new book, write the title above the pages.

Book: _____

Pages: _____ - _____

BOOKMARK

Note: Whenever you begin a new book, write the title above the pages.

Book: _____

Pages: _____ - _____

Pages: _____ - _____

Pages: _____ - _____

Pages: _____ - _____

F
O
L
D

F
O
L
D

Pages: _____ - _____

Pages: _____ - _____

Pages: _____ - _____

☐ Copy one or more lines you enjoyed from today's reading and comment on them.

☐ Finish this question about today's reading: I wonder why...?

☐ Copy one important or significant quote.

☐ Write a question you would like to ask the character.

☐ Connect this book to something in your own life. Explain in writing.

☐ Use a quick sketch or doodle to give a visual commentary about today's reading.

☐ Write one or more clarifying or probing question(s) about the reading.

☐ Connect this book to something in the world. Explain in writing.

BOOKMARK

Note: Whenever you begin a new book, write the title above the pages.

Book: _____

Pages: _____ - _____

BOOKMARK

Note: Whenever you begin a new book, write the title above the pages.

Book: _____

Pages: _____ - _____

BOOKMARK

Note: Whenever you begin a new book, write the title above the pages.

Book: _____

Pages: _____ - _____

Pages: _____ - _____

Pages: _____ - _____

Pages: _____ - _____

F
O
L
D

F
O
L
D

Pages: _____ - _____

Pages: _____ - _____

Pages: _____ - _____

☐ What questions did this book bring to mind that you would like answered?

☐ What was the author saying about life and living through this book? Explain.

☐ Connect this book to another book you've read. Explain the connection.

☐ Copy several sentences of dialogue that show a character's personality.

☐ What do you know now that you didn't know before? Explain.

☐ What character can you relate to, and why?

☐ Draw a symbol with a caption to represent the theme of today's reading.

☐ What is something this book has made you thankful for in your own life? Explain why.

☐ What is something this book has made you stop and think about?

Books by This Author:

Little Hands to Heaven
A preschool program for ages 2-5

Little Hearts for His Glory
An early learning program for ages 5-7

Beyond Little Hearts for His Glory
An early learning program for ages 6-8

Bigger Hearts for His Glory
A learning program for ages 7-9
With extensions for ages 10-11

Preparing Hearts for His Glory
A learning program for ages 8-10
With extensions for ages 11-12

Hearts for Him Through Time: Creation to Christ
A learning program for ages 9-11
With extensions for ages 12-13

Hearts for Him Through Time: Resurrection to Reformation
A learning program for ages 10-12
With extensions for ages 13-14

Hearts for Him Through Time: Revival to Revolution
A learning program for ages 11-13
With extensions for ages 14-15

Hearts for Him Through Time: Missions to Modern Marvels
A learning program for ages 12-14
With extensions for ages 15-16

Drawn into the Heart of Reading
A literature program for ages 7-15 that
Works with any books you choose

These books are published by
Heart of Dakota Publishing, Inc.

See the website: www.heartofdakota.com
For placement information, product details, or to order a catalog

For ordering questions, email: carmikeaustin@msn.com
Or, call: 605-428-4068